Food Preparat

General Editor

Dr Edwin Kerr
Chief Officer, Council for National Academic Awards

Subject Editor

D. Ashen
Head of Department of Hotel and Catering Science,
Plymouth College of Further Education

Food Preparation

CLIVE F. FINCH
MHCIMA, DMS
Senior Lecturer in Food Studies,
School of Hotel Catering and Administration,
Middlesex Business School,
Middlesex Polytechnic

Pitman

PITMAN PUBLISHING
128 Long Acre, London WC2E 9AN

First published in Great Britain 1984
Reprinted 1987, 1988

British Library Cataloguing in Publication Data

Finch, Clive F.
Food preparation
1. Cookery
I. Title
641.5 TX651

ISBN 0273 02772 7

Origination by Gil Jackson Typesetting, Playmouth

Produced by Longman Singapore Publishers Pte Ltd
Printed in Singapore

Foreword

The need for a suitable textbook giving a modern approach to professional cookery for students on BTEC and HCIMA courses has prompted the author to write this text.

The book has the added advantage that it can be used in conjunction with any conventional recipe book — whether in haute cuisine or in simple basic cookery. It guides the student carefully through the recipes, explaining what is being done and why so that possible disasters are avoided and common pitfalls anticipated.

Another distinguishing feature of this book is the range of advice and helpful hints which is given over and above essential information, and the insight which it gives on up-to-date trade practices in leading hotel and restaurant kitchens.

In all, a work to be highly commended.

Anton Mosimann
Executive Chef
The Dorchester Hotel
London

Preface

The text of this book has been designed for students of catering at all levels from the preliminary to the advanced stages, whether craft, supervisory or management in orientation. The contents cover the practical aspects of food preparation for BTEC courses at all levels, and is ideal for the City and Guilds series of courses 706, Cooking for the Catering Industry. For those studying at degree level this book will be helpful for the initial stages of dish planning and in the analysis of various aspects of food production and service. Other students of supervision and management should find this text beneficial in the development of an analytical and problem-solving approach to their work from the pre-planning to the operational stages, as well as helping to establish both qualitative and quantitative standards for dishes, implementing a system of control and assessing where faults have occurred. The text will also be of value to students taking the Hotel, Catering and Institutional Management Association's courses, Parts "A" and "B", as a basis for food and beverage management.

One of the primary objectives of the book is to isolate, examine and comment upon technical problems associated with the preparation, cooking and serving of food. This fault-finding element has been based on the author's own experience of teaching students at all levels, from preliminary to advanced professional cookery as well as in management and supervision. The faults highlighted are, as a result, simply those most frequently encountered by the student and are not intended to be exhaustive — rather it is hoped the reasons put forward will stimulate the student towards a further detailed study of the subject.

Secondly, an insight is also given into the practices of the nouvelle cuisine style of cooking to demonstrate the modern approach to the subject rapidly gaining momentum, and to illustrate in addition how the skills and knowledge of classical French cookery may be adapted to suit other styles.

Whilst it is fully appreciated that equipment technology is continually developing, in most instances established principles and practices remain unaltered. In order not to confuse the student with too much technical detail reference to such development has been minimised. However, during the formulation of this book the catering students at Middlesex Polytechnic have been engaged in experimental work, a significant aspect of which has been in measuring and recording cooking temperatures for meat and poultry and assessing the amount of salt required when cooking potatoes and vegetables. The results of these experiments have been used to present the readers of this text with guidelines to follow in this very important area of cookery.

Colleagues in the field of catering education have long expressed their need for a text along these lines. This attempt to provide such a text will hopefully go some way in improving the understanding and performance of catering students everywhere.

Acknowledgments

I greatly acknowledge my personal debt to many friends and colleagues for their helpful contributions by way of ideas and suggestions in getting this project off the ground.

In particular I would like to thank my colleagues at Middlesex Polytechnic — Dave Evans, George Fraser, Bill Francis, Paul Lock, Virginia Maclean, Sam Nash, Ken Saunders, Dr Eva Wittenberg and Professor Don Harper, Dean of Middlesex Business School. I would also like to thank Terry Garrison, Brenda Gibbon, Mike Hollingsworth, Graham Leedom and, in particular, David Wilks for helping me develop the concept of the book. I am also grateful to the staff of Gidleigh Park, Chagford, Devon, for their help with the nouvelle cuisine sections of the book, to Alan Heulin for authenticating the chapter on pastry and sweets, and to Peter Williams for his professionalism, involvement and guidance in helping me to bring this book to fruition.

The responsibility for any errors or omissions is, of course, totally mine.

1984

C.F.F.

Contents

List of Tables

Dedicated to Esther, Adrienne and Michael for their patience, understanding and encouragement during the writing of this book

CHAPTER ONE

Introduction

Before proceeding to the main body of the text the student is well advised to study this introductory chapter carefully to gain useful background knowledge of various aspects of food preparation and how best to use this book.

It should first be appreciated that recipe formulae and cookery manuals in professional use are by no means infallible. They can never be more than guides and should always be used as such. Moreover, just as important as the recipe itself for any dish is the consideration of those criteria against which the completed item may be assessed. These include such aspects as the size of portion, colour, texture, flavour, crispness and so on. The student needs to know exactly what he is attempting to achieve and must be able to check the quality of the item he has produced against pre-established measurements.

In the preparation and cooking of any dish there are a number of definite stages and critical points leading towards completion. The quality of each completed dish is dependent on each of these stages being carried out correctly before continuing to the next, just as in any production process, and the ability to spot faults and correct them before the situation becomes irretrievable is of vital importance. This text sets out to enable the student to achieve just that ability.

It is also necessary to bear in mind the management aspect: the purchasing of food and the organisation of the kitchen, especially of the people who work in it. The human factor is perhaps the most complex variable within the area of food preparation and certainly the most unpredictable. The skill and commitment of those responsible for and involved in the preparation and cooking of food have a profound effect on the success or failure of any particular dish. Factors such as these, however, are outside the scope of this present text but their importance should not be underestimated.

OUTLINE OF THE TEXT

Before proceeding with any recipe students should read it through *thoroughly*, familiarising themselves not only with the basic principles involved, but also any special points to be taken into consideration, the assessment of the finished dish if given and *in particular* any areas which need special attention to avoid problems at a later stage.

Recipes

The recipes which appear in this text fall into two main categories:

(a) basic recipes that need to be thoroughly mastered as they form the foundation for a number of other dishes made in the same way;

(b) extension dishes to the basic recipes which most frequently appear on menus.

The basic cooking principles involved are first clearly explained together with any technical knowledge considered critical to the successful completion of the dish. Where appropriate reference is made to current trade practices for the student's guidance.

The name of the dish is given in both French and English where there are appropriate translations. Where the dish is a regional speciality, e.g. Lancashire hot pot, no attempt at translation is made.

Each recipe is individually numbered for ease and economy of cross reference. Where dishes are all prepared in the same way, the only difference being the main commodity used, then recipes are not repeated. Variations appear in the text as appropriate. A little imagination in the combination of main items, sauces and garnishes will extend the student's repertoire far beyond the suggestions for recipes contained in this text.

Quantities and ingredients

These are given for all basic dishes and in the majority of cases are based on multiples of ten portions. Extension dishes based on particular recipes with additional garnishes or small variations follow on from these basic guides, quantities being given where appropriate.

Portion yield, cooking times and temperatures

At the beginning of each recipe basic portion yields and cooking times have been provided with oven temperatures and so on where appropriate. These may be used as guides for planning production. Portion yields in particular are given only as general guides and are in no way put forward as accurate.

The cooking time refers to the approximate time it takes for the main item under review to cook; it does not take into consideration the total preparation time for the complete dish nor the cooking time for each component part, e.g. a dish may need a sauce or a garnish which will also have to be prepared. The allocation of sufficient time for the various parts of a dish is, of course, important from the point of view of drawing up work plans, but this has been left up to the individual to work out according to his specific requirements.

To test when cooked

The ability to judge when an item of food is cooked to perfection remains one of individual skill, experience and knowledge. Although cooking times and, where appropriate, temperatures are given these may not be totally reliable, especially where modern equipment is not available. Guidance therefore is given under this heading wherever possible, either giving the visual appearance and feel of the cooked item or using the more scientific method of monitoring the internal temperature with a thermo-needle.

Retention and reheating

These sections are intended as a guide in certain recipes where problems may otherwise be encountered. Specific advice on methods of retention and reheating is given where this may differ from more conventional procedures.

Service

In most instances the type of dish on which a certain item should be served is indicated, although it is fully appreciated that the trend today in the industry is to serve food to the customer already arranged on a plate (*see* 6–9).

Assessment of the completed dish

Before setting out to produce any dish it is essential to know what the result should be — how it should look, what should be its colour, flavour and other characteristics. These important features are listed under this heading in a number of basic dishes and should be thoroughly familiar to the student before preparation of the dish commences.

The qualities listed are based on the following criteria intended as a general guide.

(a) *Presentation*. The right size, type and shape of plate, serving dish, tureen, etc. should be used and consideration given to whether it should be hot, chilled or cold. The plate or dish should always be clean (*see* also below, p. 7). The overall presentation should be pleasing to the eye, with a clean finish and neat appearance. The main commodity should be placed in the centre of the dish and where garnishes are used colours and textures arranged so that they complement rather than dominate the main ingredient. Rims of dishes should be completely free from all traces of grease and food splashes. It should always be remembered that simplicity of presentation is essential and should be a guiding principle at all times.

(b) Assessment of the food. Some of the more important aspects of the food are highlighted — the size of the portion, the smell, colour, texture, consistency, clarity, flavour and seasoning, the degree it should be cooked and, where appropriate, comments on any sauce or garnish that forms part of the dish or is served as an accompaniment. All these factors have a bearing on the quality of the finished dish and are further discussed below.

(c) Size of portion. This indicates the weight, quantity or size and shape of an average portion. This may well vary according to the policies of individual establishments and is included as a general guide.

(d) Smell. This is a very important aspect of any dish — an appetising aroma will enhance the customer's enjoyment of his meal. There is also a connection between the smell of the fresh raw item and its smell when cooked which should not become distorted.

(e) Colour. The final colour of an item is generally determined by the cooking process. It is not always desirable to maintain or even enhance the natural colour of the food, although in general the colour of the completed item should be a pleasant natural hue. Where the dish includes several different commodities their colours should be combined to give the best visual effect.

(f) Texture. The texture of food is related to its organic structure and, where appropriate, the cooking process to which it has been subjected. Terms used to describe this aspect are hard, tough, soft, smooth, chewy, stringy, rough and so on.

(g) Consistency. This term applies to the density of a liquid and is generally used when assessing sauces, soups and stews. Terms used to describe this aspect include thick, thin, smooth and velvety. In this text the consistency of single cream is often used as a guide and refers to a liquid's ability to coat the back of a spoon — its coating capacity.

(h) Clarity. This is a term used in connection with clear soups and jellies which have had any impurities and sediment removed.

(i) Flavour and seasoning. These are highly subjective aspects and judgment of them is very much influenced by an individual's own tastes and experiences as well as age, culture and sex. As a general guide an attempt should be made to bring about a delicate

natural flavour — except of course in highly seasoned dishes such as curries, goulashes and certain hors-d'oeuvre.

The seasoning should bring out the natural flavour of the dish without predominating. An acceptable balance should be aimed for, bearing in mind that what is acceptable will vary from person to person.

(j) Degree cooked. The degree to which foods are cooked may be identified by touch or sight or by more scientific methods using thermoneedles and probes.

The terms rare, underdone, well done and rosé are some of those used to describe the degree to which meats should be cooked. When cooking vegetables the term "nutty" is often used to imply that they are cooked to the correct degree, although the term "al dente" is gaining popularity to describe this aspect on menus. More often the term al dente is used in connection with farinaceous items such as spaghetti, lasagnes and canneloni to indicate that the pasta is just cooked.

Problems, causes and solutions

Many of the basic dishes also have this section which analyses some of the more frequent problems encountered during preparation and cooking. These are aspects that would normally come to light in a practical situation but are here discussed with a view to showing where particular problems do in fact lie and how they may be avoided or, if possible, rectified. This section is perhaps the most important part of each recipe or group of recipes and should be thoroughly grasped before preparation begins. In many instances once the problem has occurred there is very little which can be done to rectify the situation other than to start again — which is both wasteful and time consuming. In these cases areas to which particular attention should be paid in order to achieve perfect results first time are highlighted.

NOTE

It is not the author's intention to list every conceivable reason why a dish has failed to reach a certain standard. The reasons given are the most frequent ones and the stages singled out for special attention are those found to be in the author's own experience where students most frequently encounter difficulty.

Problems may also arise as a result of a number of other factors such as faulty storage or purchasing. Care must therefore be taken in each of the following four stages of preparation.

(a) Purchasing and storage. Only the best quality items should be bought to ensure the highest standard of finished product. Commodities should also be stored correctly to avoid unnecessary wastage. Attention must also be paid to stock levels to ensure adequate supplies when they are required.

(b) Preparation. The correct preparation of items for cooking is of vital importance not only to ensure that the item is cooked correctly but also to give a professional appearance to the finished dish. Particular attention must be paid to the correct jointing of meat and filleting of fish to avoid unnecessary wastage.

(c) Cooking. The principles and practices of cookery given in the text must be followed in detail if mistakes are to be avoided. Remember there are no short cuts to the production of the highest quality of finished item. Where necessary the correct procedures for retention and subsequent reheating must be carried out to prevent costly deterioration of the cooked items before they are served to the customer. Remember once again there can be no short cuts.

(d) Holding period. This is the period between the completion of the dish and its actual service to the customer. Care must be taken at this point not to allow the completed dish to deteriorate and it is at the actual moment of service that the dish should be compared with the assessment section outlined above.

PLATED FOOD

Food is nowadays served to the customer far more frequently directly on a plate than from a silver service. With developments such as the Nouvelle Cuisine style of cooking and its emphasis on simplicity influencing attitudes regarding the presentation of food, plated service is now encountered at every level of catering from the low budget cafeteria type meal to the high-cost labour-intensive haute cuisine restaurant meal more so than ever before. This type of service must therefore be considered in some depth, for the manner in which food is presented to the customer, even the type of dish on which it is placed, is all part of the gastronomic experience.

The caterer has an almost infinite variety of shape, size, colour, thickness and material from which he may choose his plates. Important factors in his decision as to which combination is most suited to his own type of operation include basic aspects such as the choices available to the customer on the menu and the colour, shape and complexity of each individual dish. Equally important are the conditions of service themselves. The range of catering situations is diverse — service may be directly from a hotplate or cold zone; in a staff canteen or self-service operation the customer will actually see his food being dished up; the food may be plated away from the customer in the kitchen of a restaurant; even the lighting and general style of the establishment are factors for consideration.

In the short space available in this text it is not possible to deal in depth with this complex, varied and highly subjective topic. The following guidelines give the basic principles involved in serving food on a plate.

(a) Plates must be perfectly clean and free from all traces of smears or finger marks; where plates have a glazed surface they should be shiny.

(b) Plates should be either hot, cold or chilled according to the type of food to be served.

(c) Plates should never be filled to capacity; for example, soup plates should never be more than two thirds full. Do not overfill a plate with food or pile food onto a plate to give the impression of value for money.

(d) Single items should be placed in the centre of the plate.

(e) Rims of plates should be entirely free from any traces of food.

(f) When serving a combination dish, i.e. a main item with vegetables, potatoes and accompaniments, then the following points apply.

(i) The main item — be it fish, meat or poultry — should be placed in the centre of the plate.

(ii) Vegetables are placed to one side and potatoes on the other.

(iii) Garnishes should be placed in a position that will improve the overall visual impression.

(iv) Sauces that are intended to coat foods should do so, leaving no area of food uncovered. Sauces that are served as an accompaniment should be placed at the side of the plate but not on the rim.

(v) Sauces and gravies should never be added in such quantity that they appear to saturate the product; the amount should be complementary.

(g) All items served on a plate should be visible; some slight degree of overlap may be necessary, with the exception of such items as bread croûtons specially made to stand food upon when served.

(h) Sweets should be served on the appropriate size of plate. When a single item is served it should be in the centre; sauces, whether hot or cold, as a general rule should be served at the side rather than over the sweet.

(i) It is as important to serve what appears to be a well balanced product in terms of size, colour and texture when it is plated as when it is served on a silver dish.

(j) Simplicity of presentation is essential from the point of view of speed of service, thereby reflecting current attitudes to this aspect of the catering operation.

NOUVELLE CUISINE FRANCAISE AND CUISINE MINCEUR

French cookery until comparatively recently meant cooking in the classical style established by the great French chefs of the past such as Escoffier. Classic French cookery is characterised by methods which produce rich and highly flavoured dishes served with elaborate garnishes and sauces. These are achieved by extensive use of marinades in which wine plays an important part; the sauces are mostly flour based and cooked for prolonged periods with reductions and glazes and enriched with eggs, butter and cream.

Whilst there is still considerable demand for this traditionally rich style of cookery a new style is now gaining in popularity, stemming from the modern awareness of the relationship between health and diet and the desire to return to more simple methods of presenting food, whilst still using the same basic principles and skills on which traditional cooking is based.

La Nouvelle Cuisine Française

This style of cooking was developed by Paul Bocuse who researched the subject thoroughly both in theory and practice before introducing it to the catering world. Through his work Bocuse has reminded us of the fundamental principles of cookery and the full potential of the commodities and foods used. The aim is to serve food with its natural taste undisguised by either the cooking process or accompanying sauces or garnishes. Food should always be fresh, the daily menu being composed of dishes made of commodities purchased on the same day rather than the menu dictating what should be bought. One result of this approach is that many establishments now offer customers a "menu surprise" composed of foods in season and at the height of their perfection. These dishes, often prepared in an original way, may not appear on the printed menu since their availability may be unpredictable.

Under this approach, food is very lightly cooked so that as little as possible of the nutritional value is allowed to leach out. The guideline is just to cook or, in some instances, undercook foods so that their individual flavours, textures and characteristics may be enjoyed to the fullest.

Cuisine Minceur

Recently developed by Michael Guerard this style of cooking has brought commonsense into the art of traditional cookery by eliminating much of its richness and reducing the high calorific value of some of the dishes. No butter or flour is used and the number of eggs and amount of oil reduced. Sauces and gravies are made from the juices produced from the cooking of the main item using, for example, plain yoghurt or cottage cheese as thickening agents.

Though these two styles of cooking were developed separately, they complement each other and some establishments have adopted and used them both together without distinguishing one from the other. There is no reason why they should not be combined to fulfil the needs of the discerning customer.

General principles of nouvelle cuisine

There is currently some debate as to what is actually meant by nouvelle cuisine. It has been referred to as "Classique Nouveau" implying that it is not new but a development of the classical French style. It is not the author's intention to enter into such debate but to present the current trends and developments to the student so that he may seek out further information and make up his own mind as to what the concept implies.

The underlying principles associated with nouvelle cuisine may be identified as follows. It must, however, be remembered that there are many interpretations of this style and that the repertoire is continually developing.

(a) With the exception of basic stocks most other foods are cooked to the customer's order.

(b) The basic sauces béchamel, velouté and demi-glace play no part in any dish. Dishes based on or featuring these, or indeed any roux based thickened sauces, gravies, soups, stews or braised items, are completely avoided.

(c) Convenience foods are also avoided. All fish, meats, poultry, game, vegetables and so on should be purchased fresh each day.

(d) The foods, their texture and accompanying sauces should be

extremely light and free from any trace of grease, with a natural blend of colours, textures and flavours.

(e) Vegetables are only lightly cooked — they should be crisp, nutty and full of natural flavour.

(f) Presentation is more important than display when serving. The chef himself should arrange the food on the plate just as he wishes the customer to view it rather than a waiter serve it from a silver dish. The plate itself is considered part of the dish so care should be taken to select those of good quality with suitable shapes and patterns that will complement the food being served (*see* pp. 6–8). The actual arrangement of the food should give full regard to the shape of the plate and the contrasting shapes, colours and textures of the items of food to be placed on it to achieve maximum visual appeal.

(g) The sizes of individual portions are smaller than is usual with more traditional styles of cooking. Since every morsel of food should be cooked to perfection it is hoped there should be no waste.

CONVENIENCE FOODS

Strictly speaking there is nothing recent or new about "convenience foods"; after all, mankind has through the ages had the ability and expertise to salt, pickle or smoke dry various types of food in order to preserve them as a safeguard against times of shortage or simply to give variety to his diet. However, within the context of today's advanced technology a precise definition of the term is impossible as products may be purchased in such a diverse number of forms. A generally accepted loose definition, however, is that the term refers to items purchased at some stage of preparation still requiring some finishing — however limited — by the caterer before service to the customer.

It is not the author's intention to discuss the merits or demerits of such products — especially in view of their avoidance in the sphere of nouvelle cuisine — but where possible to show what is available and how, in a general way, they may be handled to advantage in modern catering situations. One obvious gain, of course, is that in many instances the size of portions can be more strictly controlled thereby reducing waste and cutting costs. The elimination of a number of stages of production also cuts down on the time involved in preparation as well as avoiding stages where the dish may go wrong.

In short convenience products, as the term implies, are easy and quick to handle. However, it should be remembered that their use should not mean a drop in the quality of the dish being produced. Above all, care should be taken not to mislead the customer intentionally into believing he is receiving fresh products cooked in traditional ways.

CHAPTER TWO

Hors-d'Oeuvre and Salads

HORS-D'OEUVRE

The term hors-d'oeuvre generally refers to those items served as the opening course of a meal and covers a whole range of consumable commodities.

Most hors-d'oeuvre are made from items of cooked foods such as vegetables, potatoes and fish. Methods of preparing these items are given elsewhere in this text and the student is advised to study them in detail before attempting the hors-d'oeuvre given in this chapter.

There are two main categories of hors-d'oeuvre — variés and single.

HORS-D'OEUVRE VARIES

Under this heading — perhaps more than in any other on the menu — creativity and artistic flair may be practised, but it must be emphasised that the preparation of hors-d'oeuvre requires not only skill but also an understanding of how well the commodities used blend together in order to complement their flavour, texture and appearance.

The main principles to be followed are given below.

(a) Visual appearance. The hors-d'oeuvre should be presented as attractively as possible. They are generally served in raviers (hors-d'oeuvre dishes), and should be lightly decorated to take full advantage of the natural colour — and in certain instances the shape — of the food itself.

(b) Texture. A selection of hors-d'oeuvre should endeavour to incorporate the full range of textures available from soft and tender to firm and crunchy.

(c) Flavour and seasoning. Maximum advantage may be taken of skilful blending and combination of the numerous and varied natural flavours available. The extent to which this may be carried out is almost without limit.

There are five main types of standard dish:

(a) vegetables and salads with mayonnaise or featuring mayonnaise;

(b) vegetables prepared à la Portugaise;

(*c*) vegetables prepared à la Grecque;
(*d*) vegetables and salads simply seasoned with a vinaigrette dressing; and
(*e*) vegetables and fruits with acidulated cream.

From these basic dishes a large number of others may be derived.

In addition there are several items which may be purchased specifically for serving as hors-d'oeuvre variés and require only a simple garnish for presentation. These include anchovies, roll-mops, sardines, tunny fish, gherkins, sweetcorn and olives.

Hors-d'oeuvre with a mayonnaise dressing

The flavour of this type of hors-d'oeuvre varié is very much influenced by the kind of oil and vinegar used in making the mayonnaise, e.g. olive oil or corn oil, malt or white wine vinegar.

2.1 COLESLAW SALAD

Quantity	*Ingredient*
250 g	shredded white cabbage
75 g	julienne of carrots
30 g	chopped onion
½ dl	French Dressing (2.47)
2 dl	Mayonnaise (3.13)
	seasoning of salt and pepper

Method

(1) Lightly marinate the prepared vegetables in french dressing.
(2) Cohere with mayonnaise.
(3) Season to taste.

2.2 CELERIAC SALAD — SALADE DE CELERI-RAVE

Quantity	*Ingredient*
250 g	Prepared Celeriac (8.10)
1	juice from lemon
4 dl	Mayonnaise (3.13)
	seasoning of salt and pepper

Method

(1) Cut the celeriac into very fine julienne strips. Place immediately into a basin of cold water to which lemon juice has been added to prevent discoloration.

(2) Drain the celeriac, season with salt and pepper to taste and cohere with mayonnaise.

2.3 *EGG MAYONNAISE — OEUF MAYONNAISE*

Quantity	*Ingredient*
5	hard boiled eggs
¼	finely shredded lettuce
2 dl	Mayonnaise (3.13)
5	fillets of anchovy
10	capers
5	stoned olives
5	cucumber slices
1	tomato, either sliced or in wedges

Method

(1) Cut eggs into halves or quarters and place round side upwards on a bed of shredded lettuce.

(2) Lightly coat with mayonnaise and decorate with fillets of anchovy trellis fashion, capers, olives, cucumber slices and small pieces of tomato.

2.4 *FISH SALAD — SALADE DE POISSON*

Quantity	*Ingredient*
250 g	fish
¼	finely shredded lettuce
2 dl	Mayonnaise (3.13)
5	fillets of anchovy
10	capers
5	stoned olives
5	cucumber slices
1	tomato, either sliced or in wedges

Method

(1) Poach fish (*see* Chapter 6, pp. 159–78) and flake free from skin and bone.

(2) Place the prepared fish dome shape on a bed of shredded lettuce.

(3) Lightly coat with mayonnaise and decorate with fillets of anchovy trellis fashion, capers, olives, cucumber slices and small pieces of tomato.

2.5 *POTATO SALAD — SALADE DE POMMES DE TERRE*

Quantity	*Ingredient*
250 g	very small potatoes
15 g	chopped onion or chives
	chopped parsley
¼ dl	French Dressing (2.47)
1 dl	Mayonnaise (3.13)
	seasoning of salt and pepper

Method

(1) Boil in skins, cool and then peel (*see* 9.5).
(2) Dice or slice to a thickness of about 1 cm.
(3) Lightly marinate the cooked potato, onion and parsley in french dressing whilst the potatoes are still warm.
(4) When cold cohere with mayonnaise and season to taste.

Notes

(1) It is general trade practice to slice new potatoes.
(2) Other varieties of potato than new are suitable for making potato salad.

2.6 VEGETABLE SALAD (also known as RUSSIAN SALAD) — SALADE RUSSE

Quantity	*Ingredient*
150 g	carrots } cut into
75 g	turnips } 5 mm dice
75 g	french beans, cut into small diamonds
75 g	peas
8 dl	Mayonnaise (3.13)
	seasoning of salt and pepper

Method

(1) Cook all vegetables separately in boiling salted water until nutty and firm yet cooked (*see* p. 393).
(2) Drain immediately and allow to cool completely.
(3) Cohere with mayonnaise and season to taste.

Service

Present in the shape of a dome along the length of a ravier.

Assessment of the completed dish

(1) The consistency of the mayonnaise should be just right to bind lightly the main ingredients.
(2) The decoration should be in direct proportion to the anticipated number of servings and the size of the dish; the shape of the salad should enhance the overall presentation.
(3) There should be a balanced ratio of vegetables. All the vegetables should be neatly and evenly cut to size. They should be lightly impregnated with flavour from the mayonnaise to a degree that enhances the full flavour of every item included in the dish.

2.7 WALDORF SALAD — SALADE WALDORF

Quantity	*Ingredient*
100 g	Prepared Celery (8.11).
100 g	eating apples
50 g	walnuts
4 dl	Mayonnaise (3.13)
	seasoning of salt and pepper

Method

(1) Cut the celery into julienne; slice the apples and chop the walnuts.

(2) Cohere with the mayonnaise and season to taste.

Vegetables Portuguese style — à la Portugaise

The term à la Portugaise implies that the vegetables have been cooked in a particular liquid (*see* 2.8). The following vegetables may be prepared in this way:

(a) artichoke bottoms cut into quarters;
(b) button onions;
(c) cauliflower florets;
(d) celery — the white part cut into batons approximately 3 cm × 1 cm;
(e) leeks — the white part only cut into the required shape after cooking;
(f) mushrooms — the white button variety with stalks removed;
(g) fennel trimmed and cut into quarters.

Once prepared and washed all vegetables are blanched for about five minutes and immediately refreshed in cold water. They may then be cooked à la Portugaise.

2.8 VEGETABLES PORTUGUESE STYLE — A LA PORTUGAISE

Quantity	*Ingredient*
250 g	prepared and blanched vegetables
100 g	finely chopped onion
1 dl	oil
1 clove	crushed garlic
250 g	diced, peeled and pipped tomato
3 dl	dry white wine
10 g	tomato purée
1 small sprig	thyme
1	bayleaf
	chopped parsley
	seasoning of salt and pepper

Method

(1) Lightly cook the onion and garlic in oil without colour.
(2) Add the tomato, wine, tomato purée, thyme, bayleaf and seasoning. Gently simmer for a few minutes.
(3) Add the prepared vegetables to the mixture, then gently cook either on top of the stove or in an oven at a setting of approximately 120 °C covered with buttered greaseproof paper and a lid.

Service

Present the vegetables in a ravier and barely cover with the cooking liquid. Place a bayleaf and a sprig of thyme in the centre on top of the vegetables.

Assessment of the completed dish

(1) The vegetables where appropriate should be neatly and evenly cut to size.
(2) They should be firm yet cooked and impregnated with the full flavour of the à la Portugaise mixture.

Vegetables à la Grecque

As with vegetables à la Portugaise, the term à la Grecque implies that the vegetables have been cooked in a particular liquid (*see* 2.9). The same vegetables may be used as for the à la Portugaise method, and should be prepared in the same way prior to cooking à la Grecque.

2.9 VEGETABLES A LA GRECQUE

Quantity	*Ingredient*
250 g	prepared and blanched vegetables
½ l	water
1 dl	oil
1	juice of lemon
1 small sprig	thyme
1	bayleaf
10	coriander seeds
10	peppercorns
10 g	salt

Method

(1) Simmer all the ingredients together for about five minutes before adding the vegetables, which should be cooked completely submerged in the liquid.
(2) Once cooked allow to cool completely in the liquid before serving.

Service

Present the vegetables in a ravier and barely cover with the cooking liquid. Place a bayleaf and a sprig of thyme in the centre on top of the vegetables.

Assessment of the completed dish

(1) The vegetables should be neatly and evenly cut to size and white in colour.

(2) They should be firm yet cooked and impregnated with the full flavour of the à la Grecque mixture.

Hors-d'oeuvre with a vinaigrette dressing

A vinaigrette or french dressing may be added to a number of commodities either cooked or raw to form a wide range of hors-d'oeuvre variés.

2.10 BEETROOT SALAD — SALADE DE BETTERAVES

Cut previously cooked beetroot into batons approximately 2 cm × ½ cm. Season with salt and pepper and moisten with French Dressing (2.47). Dress in a ravier and garnish with onion rings and chopped parsley.

2.11 BEEF SALAD — SALADE DE BOEUF

Cut previously cooked beef into small dice and add to diced cooked potato, diced peeled tomatoes and chopped onion. Season with salt and pepper to taste and moisten with French Dressing (2.47). Dress in a ravier and sprinkle with chopped parsley.

2.12 CAULIFLOWER SALAD — SALADE DE CHOU-FLEUR

Season previously cooked fleurets of cauliflower with salt and pepper to taste and moisten with French Dressing (2.47). Dress in a ravier and sprinkle with chopped parsley.

2.13 CUCUMBER SALAD — SALADE DE CONCOMBRES

Peel and thinly slice cucumber and dress on a ravier slightly overlapping. Season with salt and pepper to taste and lightly coat with French Dressing (2.47).

2.14 NICOISE SALAD — SALADE NICOISE

Cut cooked French beans into diamond shapes (if the beans are small they may be left whole). Add to quarters of peeled tomatoes and small diced potatoes, season with salt and pepper to taste and mix with French Dressing (2.47). Dress in a ravier and decorate with anchovy fillets, capers and stoned olives.

2.15 RICE SALAD — SALADE DE RIZ

Mix Boiled Rice (5.53) or Rice Pilaff (5.54) with peeled, pipped and diced tomatoes and cooked peas. Season with salt and pepper to taste and a little crushed garlic and moisten with French Dressing (2.47). Dress in a ravier slightly dome shape.

2.16 TOMATO SALAD — SALADE DE TOMATES

Dress peeled sliced tomatoes neatly in a ravier and season with salt and pepper to taste. Garnish with finely chopped onion and parsley and lightly mask with French Dressing (2.47).

Hors-d'oeuvre with acidulated cream dressing

An acidulated cream dressing may be used on such items as sardines, shredded celeriac, sliced and peeled cucumber and a number of salads.

2.17 FLORIDA SALAD — SALADE FLORIDA

Bind segments of grapefruit, diced pineapple, sliced apple and diced celery with Acidulated Cream (2.46). Dress in a ravier slightly dome shape and decorate with small lettuce leaves.

2.18 SALADE JAPONAISE

Bind diced, peeled and pipped tomatoes, diced pineapple and segments of orange with Acidulated Cream (2.46). Dress in a ravier slightly dome shape and decorate with small lettuce leaves.

2.19 SALADE MIMOSA

Bind segments of orange, pipped grapes and slices of banana with Acidulated Cream (2.46). Dress in a ravier slightly dome shape and decorate with small lettuce leaves.

SINGLE HORS-D'OEUVRE

As this title implies each dish within this category may be looked on as complete in itself. Generally these items are à la carte and priced individually according to the amount served as a portion.

In terms of appearance, flavour and texture single hors-d'oeuvre are highly individual. Although some may be cooked, in many instances very little preparation is involved as much of the work will have been carried out by the manufacturer (as with smoked salmon and pâté de foie gras), whilst many others may be served in their natural state apart from simple decoration (as with melon portions and avocado pears). There are of course many other possible single hors-d'oeuvre such as seafood cocktail, Parma ham, salami, dressed crab and escargots which make this course such an interesting and varied one.

2.20 *ASPARAGUS TIPS WITH FRENCH DRESSING — POINTES D'ASPERGES VINAIGRETTE*

See 8.2 and 8.41 for the preparation and cooking of asparagus. Allow approximately 6–8 tips per portion.

Service

Arrange the asparagus on a folded napkin and garnish with sprigs of parsley. Serve the french dressing separately.

2.21 *AVOCADO PEARS WITH FRENCH DRESSING — AVOCATS VINAIGRETTE*

Prepare the avocado pears as in 2.39. Garnish with lettuce leaves, a slice of peeled cucumber, a quarter or segment of tomato and a quarter or segment of lemon. Accompany with French Dressing (2.47).

2.22 *AVOCADO PEARS WITH PRAWNS — AVOCATS AUX CREVETTES*

Prepare the avocado pears as in 2.39. Fill with peeled prawns bound with Cocktail Sauce (3.42) and garnish with lettuce leaves, a slice of peeled cucumber and segments of tomato and lemon.

Note

Peeled shrimps may be used in place of prawns.

2.23 *CAVIAR*

Caviar is the salted roe of various kinds of sturgeon. It is generally served in the container in which it is purchased, set in crushed ice and presented in a special dish called a timbale. Serve accompanied with quarters of lemon, sieved white and yolk of hard boiled egg, chopped onion and hot buttered toast or blinis (10.9).

2.24 *CHARENTAIS MELON WITH PORT WINE*

Small melon for a single portion: Cut a small slice from the top to form a lid and remove the seeds. Add a quantity of port, replace the lid, chill and serve as required.

Larger melon for two portions: Cut into separate halves across the centre, remove the seeds, add port, chill and serve as required.

2.25 CRAB COCKTAIL — COCKTAIL DE CRABE

Makes: 10 portions.

Quantity	*Ingredient*
500 g	prepared crabmeat (*see* 6.63)
1 × 200 g	shredded lettuce
½ l	Cocktail Sauce (3.42)
3	quartered lemons
3	quartered tomatoes
10 g	chopped parsley

Method

Prepare as outlined in 2.41.

2.26 FLORIDA COCKTAIL

Makes: 10 portions.
Prepare approximately 5 whole grapefruit and 5 whole oranges as in 2.40. Serve lightly chilled and arranged neatly in a coupe or glass goblet. Barely cover with juice from the fruit. A maraschino cherry may also be placed in the centre as decoration.

2.27 GRAPEFRUIT COCKTAIL

Makes: 10 portions.
Prepare approximately 10 whole grapefruit as in 2.40. Serve as for Florida Cocktail (2.26).

2.28 GLOBE ARTICHOKES WITH FRENCH DRESSING — ARTICHAUTS VINAIGRETTE

See 8.18 and 8.78 for the preparation and cooking of artichokes.

Service

Arrange the whole artichoke on a folded napkin and garnish with sprigs of parsley. Serve the french dressing separately.

2.29 LOBSTER COCKTAIL — COCKTAIL DE HOMARD

Makes: 10 portions.

Quantity	*Ingredient*
500 g	cooked lobster meat, diced or sliced
1 × 200 g	shredded lettuce
½ l	Cocktail Sauce (3.42)

Quantity	Ingredient
3	quartered lemons
3	quartered tomatoes
10 g	chopped parsley

Method

Prepare as outlined in 2.41. Serve garnished with a shelled lobster claw per portion.

2.30 MELON

Cut the melon in half and remove the seeds, then cut into portions. Serve chilled or on crushed ice. Sliced oranges and cocktail cherries may be used as decoration. Ground ginger and castor sugar may also be served separately as accompaniments.

2.31 MELON COCKTAIL — COCKTAIL DE MELON

Makes: 10 portions.
Cut the melon in half and remove the inner seeds. Scoop the flesh out with a parisienne cutter and retain the balls in a bowl until required with any juice to keep them moist. Place the balls in a coupe or glass goblet with a maraschino cherry on top and serve slightly chilled. Allow approximately 2 melons for 10 portions.

2.32 MIAMI COCKTAIL — COUPE MIAMI

Makes: 10 portions.
Prepare approximately 4 grapefruit and 4 oranges as in 2.40. Add approximately 150 g small wedges of pineapple and serve as for Florida Cocktail (2.26).

2.33 ORANGE COCKTAIL

Makes: 10 portions.
Prepare approximately 10 whole oranges as in 2.40. Serve as for Florida Cocktail (2.26).

2.34 OYSTERS

Open the oysters and release the flesh where it is joined to the bottom rounded shell. Serve on crushed ice accompanied with brown bread and butter and segments of lemon. Shallot sauce which consists of chopped shallots, vinegar, pepper from the mill and tabasco is also sometimes served as accompaniment.

2.35 PATE DE FOIE GRAS

See 2.36 for Pâté Maison.

Service

This may be served on a dish with a little lettuce and tomato and chopped aspic or port wine jelly. Hot toast is also served as an accompaniment.

2.36 PATE MAISON

Oven temperature: 125 °C. Cooking time: 2 hours approx.

Quantity	*Ingredient*
½ dl	oil
250 g	diced lean pork
50 g	bacon fat
100 g	chopped onion
pinch	powdered thyme
1	bayleaf
1 clove	crushed garlic
500 g	chicken livers, hearts and kidneys, the gall removed
1½ dl	double cream
¼ dl	brandy
250 g	lean bacon with rind removed, or salt pork fat
	seasoning of salt and pepper

Method

(1) Heat the oil in a frying pan and quickly fry the lean pork and bacon fat. Add the chopped onion, thyme, bayleaf and crushed garlic.

(2) Add the chicken livers, hearts and kidneys and continue to fry very quickly until they are sealed; on no account should the livers become cooked through. Season with salt and pepper to taste.

(3) Allow to cool, then pass through a fine mincer several times or finely chop in a bowl chopper.

(4) Add the cream and brandy and correct the seasoning.

(5) Line a mould with the lean bacon allowing for overlapping once the mould has been filled with the mixture.

(6) Fill the lined mould with the mixture, then fold over the bacon slices.

(7) Place the mould in a bain-marie; cover with either greaseproof paper or a lid and cook in oven.

(8) When cooked remove mould from the bain-marie. Remove the lid or greaseproof paper. Place a flat dish on top of the pâté together with a weight to push the pâté down. Allow the pâté to

become cold so that the fat sets, preferably for about eight hours in a refrigerator.

Notes

(1) To obtain a very fine and smooth pâté pass through a sieve or a food processor.

(2) To judge when cooked the juice and fat should be clear and free of all traces of blood.

Service

Serve slices garnished with lettuce, tomato and slices of cucumber. Hot toast is also served as an accompaniment.

Assessment of the completed dish

(1) The texture should be fine and smooth.
(2) It should not crumble when portioned.
(3) It should be moist with a blend of flavours.

Possible problem	*Possible cause and solution*
(1) Pâté is bitter in flavour	— too high a proportion of livers; care must be taken during preparation to measure the ingredients exactly as once cooked this cannot be rectified.
	— livers not properly cleaned of gall stains; care must be taken over this aspect during preparation as once cooked this cannot be rectified.
(2) Pâté is dry and crumbles when cooked	— insufficient fat used; care must be taken during preparation as once cooked this cannot be rectified.
	— mixture is too coarse; care must be taken during preparation to mince the ingredients finely as once cooked this cannot be rectified.
	— pâté is overcooked; this cannot be rectified.
	— not enough cream used in the pâté; care must be taken during preparation to measure the ingredients exactly as once cooked this cannot be rectified.

2.37 POTTED SHRIMPS

Serve in a dish dressed with a leaf of lettuce and a segment of lemon, accompanied by brown bread and butter.

2.38 PRAWN COCKTAIL — COCKTAIL DE CREVETTES

Makes: 10 portions.

Quantity	*Ingredient*
500 g	prepared prawns
1 × 200 g	shredded lettuce
½ l	Cocktail Sauce (3.42)
3	quartered lemons
3	quartered tomatoes
10 g	chopped parsley

Method

Prepare as outlined in 2.41.

2.39 PREPARATION OF AVOCADO PEARS

Cut the pear lengthways around the middle and towards the centre stone. Divide the fruit into two halves and discard the stone. Allow half a pear per portion.

Note

Do not prepare in advance as the flesh may turn blackish in colour once cut into two.

2.40 PREPARATION OF FRUIT FOR FRUIT COCKTAILS

Cut off both ends of the fruit and place it on a chopping board. Cut downwards following the shape of the fruit to remove all traces of the peel and pith. Remove each segment of fruit by cutting towards the centre of the fruit as close to the dividing membrane as possible. Retain the segments in a basin with the juice from the fruit.

2.41 PREPARATION OF SHELLFISH/SEAFOOD COCKTAILS

Method

(1) Lightly chill the shellfish.

(2) Three-quarters fill the cocktail glass with shredded lettuce (approximately 20 g).

(3) Place approximately 50 g of shellfish on top of the lettuce and coat with cocktail sauce.

(4) Garnish with quarters of tomato, quarters of lemon and a little chopped parsley.

Note

Shellfish cocktails are also known as seafood cocktails and may consist of a single item of shellfish or a combination of two or more, e.g. crab and mussel or shrimp and lobster.

Assessment of the completed cocktail

(1) The lettuce should be neatly shredded.

(2) The shellfish should be lightly chilled, moist and tender without any traces of watery liquid from either the shellfish itself or the lettuce.

(3) The cocktail sauce should be pink in colour and lightly and evenly coat all the shellfish. The sauce should not seep through the shellfish leaving it uncoated — this is an indication that the cocktail has been prepared too far in advance.

(4) The segments of lemon should have all the pith and pips removed; the tomatoes should be neatly quartered and have the hard centre core removed; the parsley should be finely chopped.

2.42 SEAFOOD COCKTAIL — COCKTAIL DE FRUITS DE MER

Makes: 10 portions.

Quantity	*Ingredient*
200 g	prepared mussels (6.70)
200 g	prepared prawns
50 g	prepared crabmeat
50 g	sliced scallops
1 × 200 g	shredded lettuce
½ l	Cocktail Sauce (3.42)
3	quartered lemons
3	quartered tomatoes
10 g	chopped parsley

Method

Prepare as outlined in 2.41.

2.43 SMOKED EEL

If the fish is large or whole rather than a fillet serve carved very thinly. Garnish with lettuce leaves, tomato, cucumber, segments of lemon and picked parsley. Brown bread and butter and horseradish sauce are served separately as accompaniments.

2.44 SMOKED SALMON

Trim the side of the salmon using a thin bladed carving knife, removing all surface skin and small bones with the minimum of wastage. Carve on a slant commencing at the tail end cutting into very thin slices.

Serve either on a dish or on a plate and garnish with mustard, cress and segments of lemon. Brown bread and butter are served separately as accompaniments.

2.45 *SMOKED TROUT*

Serve whole with the skin removed but the head may be left on. To remove the skin pierce with the point of a small knife at the tail end along the back bone. Cut down the length of the trout without cutting into the fish to the point where the head commences. Gently fold back and remove the skin from gills to tail. Repeat for the other side of the fish.

Present garnished with lettuce leaves, tomato, cucumber, segments of lemon and picked parsley. Brown bread and butter and horseradish sauce are served separately as accompaniments.

SALADS

Salads play an important part in most menus. Their popularity stems from a number of factors — they are considered as a health food; they lend themselves particularly to cold buffets; they blend with and thus complement many types of hot dish; traditionally they are served with main courses such as grills of meat and poultry or with roasts of meat, poultry and game, usually in place of a second vegetable. Many salads can also be served as an hors-d'oeuvre or side-salad.

There are two main kinds of salad — the simple ones consisting of several raw salad vegetables or a single commodity such as cucumber served accompanied by the appropriate dressing, and the combination salads made with several ingredients, bound with the dressing and served in a complete form. Crudités are also a form of salad as they are cuts of crisp salad items for dipping in various cold sauces whilst awaiting the arrival of the first course.

Salads may also be made with cooked vegetables flavoured with the appropriate sauce either when cold or when still warm, as in the case of carrots, turnips, peas and french beans.

Various types of lettuce, e.g. chinese leaves, Webb's Wonder, iceberg and cos lettuce, may be included and, if desired, combinations of curly and Belgium endive, celery and watercress. Dandelions, nettles and many different herbs may also be added.

There is no end to the extent of the repertoire of the salad. A number of the most commonly found salads have already been described earlier in this chapter, but it should always be remembered that the recipes are given as a guide only. In many instances the ingredients are interchangeable and as with hors-d'oeuvre a little imagination can yield outstanding results.

Service

Salads may be served in glass or wooden bowls, on side plates or crescent shaped side dishes.

Possible problem	*Possible cause and solution*
(1) Salad looks limp	— salad stuffs not fresh; unless finished with a dressing place in a salad bowl with a little vinegar water to freshen the lettuce (this is not possible if already finished with a dressing).
	— dressing added too soon before salad is required; dress the salad at the last possible moment as this cannot be rectified.
	— salad overmixed; care must be taken during preparation as this cannot be rectified.
	— salad not kept chilled; this cannot be rectified.
(2) Mayonnaise overpowers the salad	— too much mayonnaise used; care must be taken when preparing and adding the dressing.
	— mayonnaise is too thick; dilute the mayonnaise with a little cream or water.

Salad dressings

There are quite a number of different salad dressings in use, the most popular being mayonnaise and french dressing (also known as vinaigrette). Salad cream is a less expensive form of mayonnaise but is really only suitable for binding combination salads. Other dressings — some of which are really only variations of mayonnaise and french dressing — include acidulated cream, mustard, roquefort and thousand island. Some salads are first treated with french dressing and then bound with mayonnaise.

2.46 ACIDULATED CREAM DRESSING

Mix one part lemon juice into five parts lightly whipped cream seasoned with salt and pepper.

2.47 FRENCH DRESSING — VINAIGRETTE

Makes: 1 litre.

Quantity	*Ingredient*
3 dl	vinegar
10 g	salt
	pepper from the mill
5 g	French mustard (optional)
7 dl	oil
5 g	chopped herbs { parsley, tarragon, chervil, chives }

Method

(1) Put the vinegar, oil, salt and pepper (and mustard if used) into a basin. Gently mix with a whisk until it forms an emulsion.

(2) Add the chopped herbs.

2.48 FRENCH DRESSING FOR CALF'S HEAD OR FEET AND POULTRY SALADS

Prepare French Dressing as in 2.47 adding 10 g finely chopped onions or shallots, 10 g finely diced capers and 8 g finely diced anchovy fillets.

MAYONNAISE

See 3.13.

2.49 MUSTARD DRESSING

Makes: 1 litre.

Quantity	*Ingredient*
20 g	English mustard
5 dl	French Dressing (2.47)
3 dl	Mayonnaise (3.13)
2 dl	cream

Method

Mix all the ingredients together well until smooth.

2.50 ROQUEFORT DRESSING

Mash 100 g roquefort cheese with a fork in a basin. Gradually add 3 dl French Dressing (2.47), mixing continuously until all the cheese is incorporated into the dressing.

2.51 THOUSAND ISLAND DRESSING

Makes: 1 litre.

Quantity	*Ingredient*
a few drops	tabasco
10 g	salt
	pepper from the mill
2 dl	vinegar
8 dl	oil
100 g	red pimento, peeled and chopped
100 g	green pimento, peeled and chopped
25 g	chopped parsley
3	sieved hard-boiled eggs

Method

(1) Put the tabasco, salt, pepper and vinegar into a basin and whisk.

(2) Add the oil and continue to whisk while adding the remaining ingredients.

NOUVELLE CUISINE

The recipes for hors-d'oeuvre and salads given in this chapter are also in accord with the principles and practices of nouvelle cuisine as outlined in Chapter 1. Emphasis should be placed on the lightness of the product and full regard should be paid to the natural flavours and textures of the various foodstuffs used in the preparation. The full range of fresh, smoked and pickled commodities available may be used including fish, poultry, game, oysters, caviar and pâtés.

2.52 FOIE GRAS DE CANARD SAUCE HOLLANDAISE

Makes: 10 portions. Cooking time: 3 minutes.

Quantity	*Ingredient*
10 ×30 g	slices of Foie Gras (2.35)
2 dl	Hollandaise Sauce (3.12)
10	slices of black truffle

Method

(1) Place the slices of foie gras into lightly buttered individual cocotte moulds. Heat in an oven for a few minutes.

(2) Coat with the Hollandaise sauce and place under a salamander grill to glaze.

(3) Serve on small plates lined with a dish paper. Garnish the top of each with a slice of truffle.

CONVENIENCE PRODUCTS

Hors-d'oeuvre variés may be produced from a wide range of convenience products that have been tinned, pickled, salted, frozen or otherwise pre-prepared. Many fresh items may also be purchased in a ready prepared form, e.g. pre-packed, washed and shredded lettuce, and there is a comprehensive range of cold sauces and many mayonnaise and vinaigrette based products available.

However, this does not imply that those principles and practices associated with traditionally made products are rendered completely redundant. In fact the skills outlined in this chapter may be applied to augment or complement both fresh made items and convenience ones. By contrasting flavours, textures, seasonings and colours and by utilising the convenience product as a base an almost unlimited range of items may be prepared. Integrating freshly made products with convenience ones and exercising the imagination in the decoration and presentation of the completed dish will ensure a never ending variety of hors-d'oeuvre to attract the eye and stimulate the appetite.

CHAPTER THREE

Stocks and Sauces

STOCKS

A stock may be defined as the liquid formed by the extraction during cooking of flavour, nutrients and salts from bones, vegetables and aromatic herbs. Indeed, since stocks form the foundation for many kitchen preparations — soups, sauces, stews, fish dishes and rice dishes — their importance cannot be underestimated, particularly in traditional cookery.

The two main types of stock are white and brown stock. The name of the stock is determined by the type of bone used in its making, e.g. brown beef stock is made from beef bones that have been coloured in the oven.

The following list indicates the different types of stock and the appropriate cooking time for each one according to the type of bone used. All the stocks listed with the exception of fish stock may be made either white or brown, the main difference lying in the preparation in the early stages of production.

White or brown stock:	
Chicken and game stock	2 hours
Veal stock	2–3 hours
Beef stock	3–4 hours
Mutton and lamb stock	1 hour
Fish stock	20 mins

There is little point in cooking stock for a longer period than that prescribed with the intention of extracting extra flavour. In fact cooking a stock beyond the time recommended may be detrimental to the finished result — and indeed to the dish for which it forms the basis, especially in the case of fish stock which becomes bitter and dark in colour.

White and brown stocks

The ingredients for all meat, poultry and game stocks, whether brown or white, are the same. It is only the type of bone that differs according to the stock being prepared.

3.1 WHITE AND BROWN STOCKS

Makes: 10 litres. Cooking time: See above.

Quantity	*Ingredient*	
3½ kg	bones for the required type of stock, chopped into small pieces with the fat removed	
250 g	carrots	prewashed, peeled and roughly cut
250 g	onions	
250 g	leek	
250 g	celery	
100 g	mushrooms (use trimmings if available)	
1 sprig	thyme	herbs
2	bayleaves	
	parsley stalks	
10	peppercorns	
10 l	water	

Note

Herbs may be added in the form of a bouquet garni consisting of thyme, bayleaf and parsley stalks tied in a bundle together with celery and leek, but this is not really necessary as stocks are always strained after cooking.

Method: White stock

(1) Blanch the bones by covering them with cold water. Bring to the boil and simmer for a few minutes, then run off the water and wash the bones under hot water to remove all traces of fat and scum. Rinse under cold water until all the impurities have been washed away.

Method: Brown stock

(1) Brown the bones in fat in an oven at 220 °C then strain off all surplus fat. Brown the vegetables in fat in a frying pan on top of the stove or in a hot oven then strain off all surplus fat.

Method: White and brown stock

(2) Place the bones in a stock pot, cover with cold water and bring gently to the boil.

(3) Remove any scum that rises to the surface.

(4) Add the vegetables and herbs.

(5) Gently simmer for the required time continuously removing all traces of scum and grease.

(6) When cooked strain through a conical strainer into a clean saucepan, reboil and use as required or cool as rapidly as possible and place in a refrigerator at 7–8 °C until required.

(7) To cool stock rapidly place the pot on a pot stand in a sink of cold water. Allow cold water to run in and surplus to drain out of the sink, or leave the pot to stand in a cool place raised on a pot stand until cool.

Notes

In order to prepare a quality stock the following points need to be considered.

(1) *(a)* The bones must be fresh, free from fat and chopped into manageable pieces.

(b) The vegetables should be of sound quality. The following vegetables should not be used in stocks as they tend to render it either cloudy or their strong flavour distorts the natural flavour of the meat, poultry or game used: swedes, turnips, parsnips, cabbage, cauliflower, potatoes.

(2) Do not season basic stocks with salt. If the stock is to be reduced to a glaze or added to a delicately flavoured dish, the addition of salt to the basic stock may have an adverse effect which would be difficult to rectify.

(3) The colour and clarity of white stock is influenced very largely at the blanching stage. Brown stock derives its colouring from the colouring of the bones and vegetables during the initial stages.

(4) During the cooking process:

(a) always cover the bones with cold water;

(b) simmer the stock gently throughout;

(c) skim off fat and other impurities both at the initial stage, then before adding vegetables and herbs and at intervals during cooking;

(d) do not cover stocks with a lid during cooking;

(e) keep the inner sides of the pot free from fat and scum by periodically wiping around with a clean damp cloth;

(f) do not stir stocks or disturb them during cooking.

(5) When straining stocks do not disturb the cooked bones and vegetables. A stockpot with a tap and strainer is therefore ideal.

(6) Stocks that have been strained should be reboiled.

(7) If stocks are not for immediate use they should be cooled as quickly as possible and stored in a refrigerator.

Assessment of the completed stock

(1) The stock, whether white or brown, should be clear.

(2) The body of the stock, derived from the gelatine in the bones and other soluble products, may be identified by taste and can be seen in the viscous nature of the product.

(3) The stock should have a delicate flavour of the bones from which it has been made. Veal stock, however, is rather bland in flavour and so lends itself to a wide range of uses as its characteristic flavour will not predominate.

(4) The stock should be free from all traces of fat and grease.
(5) Brown stock should be light amber in colour.

Possible problem	*Possible cause and solution*
(1) Stock is cloudy	— in a white stock the bones were not blanched correctly; care must be taken during the initial preparation as this cannot later be rectified.
	— excess fat not removed from the bones; care must be taken during the preparation as this cause cannot later be rectified.
	— bones were covered with hot water; care must be taken to follow the correct procedure during cooking as this cannot later be rectified.
	— impurities such as fat and scum not removed during cooking; care must be taken to follow the correct procedure during cooking as this cannot later be rectified.
	— a lid was put on during cooking; care must be taken to follow the correct procedure during cooking as this cannot later be rectified.
	— liquid was stirred or agitated during cooking; care must be taken to follow the correct procedure during cooking as this cannot later be rectified.
	— stock was rapidly boiled; care must be taken to follow the correct procedure during cooking as this cannot later be rectified.
	— overcooked; stock should only be cooked for the prescribed time as once cooked this cannot later be rectified.
	— potato or cabbage used in the stock; only the correct ingredients should be used as this cannot later be rectified.
	— stock incorrectly strained; care must be taken to follow the correct straining procedure as this cannot later be rectified.

Note

Although cloudy stock may be clarified it is both time consuming and expensive unless the stock is required for consommé.

Possible problem	*Possible cause and solution*
(2) Stock lacks flavour	— poor quality ingredients; use only the best quality ingredients as this cannot later be rectified.
	— stock undercooked not allowing the bones and vegetables to give out their flavour; taste before straining and continue to cook as necessary.
	— incorrect ratio of bones and vegetables to water (i.e. not enough bones and vegetables or not enough water); if sufficient time reduce the stock after straining by boiling to concentrate the flavour.
	— strong or sweet flavoured vegetables (e.g. turnips, swedes, parsnips) used; use only the correct root vegetables as this cannot later be rectified.
	— in a brown stock the bones were not sufficiently coloured before being used for the stock; care must be taken during the preparation of the ingredients as this cause cannot later be rectified.

3.2 FISH STOCK

Makes: 5 litres. Cooking time: 20 minutes.

Quantity	*Ingredient*
50 g	butter
2 kg	fish bones, previously washed under cold water
200 g	sliced onions
1	juice of lemon
1	bayleaf
1 small sprig	thyme
	parsley stalks
5	peppercorns
5 l	water

Note

The fish bones should preferably be one or more of the following: halibut, sole, turbot, whiting.

Method

(1) Melt the butter in a deep sided saucepan.

(2) Add the remainder of the ingredients with the exception of the water.

(3) Cover with greaseproof paper and a lid and sweat for a few minutes without coloration in order to extract the juices from the bones.

(4) Cover the ingredients with cold water, bring to the boil and skim away all impurities that rise to the surface.

(5) Simmer for the prescribed time.

(6) Strain off the stock into a clean pan, reboil and use as required.

Assessment of the completed stock

(1) The stock should be clear in appearance.

(2) The strength of the stock may be identified by touch — a gelatinous liquid should immediately be apparent.

(3) The stock should have a delicate flavour of fish.

(4) The colour should be white; it should not be of a milky appearance nor have too much sediment in it.

Possible problem	*Possible cause and solution*
(1) Stock lacks flavour	— incorrect type of fish bones used; use only the bones of the fish suggested as this cannot later be rectified. — bones not sweated sufficiently in the initial stages to extract their flavour; care must be taken at this stage in the preparation as this cannot later be rectified. — too high a ratio of water to fish bones; after straining reduce the stock by boiling. — stock undercooked; continue to cook for the prescribed time.
(2) Stock has a strong or bitter flavour and is dark in colour	— incorrect type of fish bones used; use only the bones of the fish suggested as this cannot later be rectified. — stock overcooked; cook for the correct length of time as this cannot later be rectified. — ingredients have been oversweated and allowed to colour; care must be taken in the initial stages as this cannot later be rectified. — bones have been left in the stock for too long once the stock is cooked; care must be taken to follow the correct procedure during cooking as this cannot later be rectified.

Possible problem	*Possible cause and solution*
(3) Stock is cloudy and dirty	— incorrect type of bones used; use only the bones of the fish suggested as this cannot later be rectified.
	— stock not skimmed enough during cooking; care must be taken to follow the correct procedure during cooking as this cannot later be rectified.
	— stock undercooked; continue to cook for the prescribed time.
	— bones have been left in the stock too long once the stock is cooked; care must be taken to follow the correct procedure during cooking as this cannot later be rectified.

Glazes

A glaze is a reduction of a stock by continuous boiling until it becomes a gluey, tacky substance which is highly concentrated in flavour. As it reduces in quantity the stock should be transferred to smaller sized pans. Once reduced the glaze should be cooled and stored in a refrigerator at 7 °C in plastic or porcelain containers.

Glazes are used for enhancing the flavour of sauces, stews and other dishes, e.g. Pommes Parisienne (9.34), Fillets of Sole Aiglon (6.9).

SAUCES

Sauces are thickened liquids which may be savoury or sweet and hot, warm or cold according to type and purpose. They may be served with or as an accompaniment to a wide variety of dishes with the intention of contrasting or complementing the flavour and texture of the items with which they are served, aiding the digestion of the main dish or enhancing its appearance. The range of flavours is considerable, from the most delicate to the very rich and distinctive, and can vary in cost from the inexpensive to the almost prohibitive. Whatever their function, the importance attached to sauces should never be underestimated.

As sauces play such an important and significant part in cookery the caterer must fully understand the basic principles involved in preparing a quality sauce, and be able to rectify any of the many faults which frequently occur in their preparation. He must also be familiar with their many uses and be able to evaluate them in an objective and professional manner.

Thickening agents

The principal thickening agent used in a wide range of sauces is a cooked mixture of flour and fat known as a *roux* (*see* 3.3 below). There are three types of roux:

(*a*) white roux (roux blanc), also known as a first stage roux;
(*b*) fawn roux (roux blond), also known as a second stage roux;
(*c*) brown roux (roux brun), also known as a third stage roux.

The degree to which a roux is cooked determines its colour which in turn affects the colour and flavour of the sauce that is made from it.

Other thickening agents (also known as liaisons) used in the preparation of sauces include the following:

(*a*) cornflour;
(*b*) arrowroot;
(*c*) potato flour or other starch;
(*d*) flour;
(*e*) a mixture of flour and fat;
(*f*) cream;
(*g*) egg yolks;
(*h*) butter;
(*i*) mixture of egg yolks and cream;
(*j*) oil;
(*k*) blood (as in jugged jare).

3.3 PREPARATION OF ROUX

Makes: 5 litres.

Quantity	*Ingredient*	
450 g	butter	white and fawn roux
450 g	flour	
300 g	dripping or other cooking fat	brown roux
350 g	flour	

Method

(1) Melt the fat in a deep saucepan.
(2) Stir in the flour with a wooden spatula.
(3) Cook over a gentle heat to the required stage.

Notes

(1) Margarine may be used in place of butter when making white or fawn roux as appropriate.

(2) The colour of the roux depends on the length of time it is cooked and, of course, the degree of heat applied.

(3) All roux may be cooked either on top of the cooker or in an

oven, the latter being preferred because of the all round even temperature.

(4) Whichever cooking method is applied, roux need to be stirred from time to time, especially when preparing a third stage roux which, because of the colour required, takes longer to cook.

Assessment of the completed roux

(1) First stage (white) roux — when cooked should be a light sandy texture without coloration.

(2) Second stage (fawn) roux — when cooked should be fawn in colour as the name suggests, and sandy in texture.

(3) Third stage (brown) roux — becomes thinner as it cooks to the required colour of brown.

Correcting the consistency

It is important at this stage to rectify the consistency if necessary. A roux that is too soft could result in less than the desired amount of sauce, or excess fat could rise to the surface whilst cooking. Extra flour may be added to compensate.

A roux that is too hard either as a result of too little fat or too much flour will result in a lumpy sauce. In this case more fat may be added.

Overcooking the roux or subjecting it to a long slow heat will have the effect of drying out the roux without necessarily colouring it. The roux will become difficult to incorporate into a liquid and usually results in a lumpy sauce.

Liquids

The following liquids are frequently used to form the basis for a range of sauces:

(a) milk;
(b) cream;
(c) oil;
(d) butter (clarified);
(e) stocks such as fish, meat, poultry, game and vegetables.

With the various roux these liquids may be used as follows:

(a) first stage roux — use milk;

(b) second stage roux — use a white stock of fish, meat or poultry;

(c) third stage roux — use a brown stock of meat, poultry or game.

Foundation sauces

Table 1 gives the basic sauces which are used in the production of many other sauces and extensions. Unless used as sauces in their own right these foundation sauces are not seasoned as the extraction of salts from other ingredients such as bones could result in an over-salty product.

TABLE I. FOUNDATION SAUCES

Sauce	*Liquid*	*Thickening agent*	*Cooking time*
Béchamel	milk	first stage roux	20 mins
Velouté	white stock	second stage roux	1 hour
Espagnole	brown stock	third stage roux	6–8 hours
Jus lié*	brown stock	cornflour or arrowroot	2 hours
Demi-glace	brown stock	third stage roux	1 hour
Tomato sauce	white stock	second stage roux	1 hour
Butter (emulsified) sauces:			
Béarnaise	melted butter	egg yolks	30 mins
Hollandaise	melted butter	egg yolks	30 mins
Mayonnaise	oil	egg yolks	20 mins

*Jus lié is used extensively in place of sauce demi-glace.

A large number of sauces can be produced from these foundation sauces, but in order to achieve a good quality derivative a great deal of attention needs to be given to the making of the basic item.

WHITE SAUCE

Basic white sauce — generally simply referred to by its French name béchamel — consists of hot milk thickened with equal quantities of butter and flour to form a first stage roux and is flavoured with onion, bayleaf and clove. This sauce forms the basis for a number of other sauces; it is also used when making cream soups and other dishes made from eggs, farinaceous products and vegetables.

Provided the roux is of the correct texture this sauce can be rectified at any stage in its production. Generally, attention needs to be paid to the consistency of the sauce whilst cooking — it should be that of double cream. If the sauce is too thick there is a tendency for it to burn, and in addition a considerable loss of volume is found during straining, especially if small amounts are involved.

3.4 WHITE SAUCE — SAUCE BECHAMEL

Makes: 5 litres. Cooking time: 20 minutes.

Quantity	*Ingredient*	
450 g	butter	
450 g	flour	
5 l	milk	
1	small onion	studded onion — oignon clouté
½	bayleaf	
1	clove	

Method

(1) Make a first stage roux with the butter and flour as in 3.3. Allow to cool.

(2) Infuse the milk and studded onion by bringing the milk to boil with the studded onion. Allow to stand over the heat without boiling for 5–8 minutes.

(3) Remove the studded onion and discard.

(4) Gradually add the milk to the roux, stirring with a wooden spatule until the milk has been completely absorbed and beating out any lumps that may appear.

(5) Gently simmer for 20 minutes, occasionally stirring with the wooden spatule.

(6) At this point adjust the thickness of the sauce if necessary. If the sauce is obviously too thick to pass through a conical strainer thin it with a little hot milk. If the sauce is too thin, whisk into the boiling sauce a mixture of equal quantities of flour and butter made into Beurre Manié (3.53), adding a little at a time until the required consistency is achieved.

(7) When the sauce is properly cooked, strain through a conical strainer into a clean receptacle. Place a small quantity of melted butter and, if desired, greaseproof paper on top to prevent a skin from forming.

(8) Retain until required in a bain-marie of hot water.

Notes

(1) Béchamel is a foundation sauce and should not be seasoned.

(2) In order to produce a wide range of derivative sauces cream is in most instances added.

Assessment of the completed sauce

(1) The sauce should be white in colour.

(2) The sauce should be rather thick in consistency as it is a foundation sauce, like double cream.

(3) The flavour of the sauce should be a slight blend of bayleaf, onion and clove.

(4) The texture should be smooth and even.

Possible problem	*Possible cause and solution*
(1) Sauce lacks flavour	— sauce undercooked; continue to cook for the prescribed time.
(2) Sauce is too dark	— roux overcoloured; care must be taken to avoid overcolouring when preparing the roux as this cannot later be rectified.
	— milk allowed to boil for too long before adding to the roux; care must be taken in the initial stages as this cannot later be rectified.
	— sauce allowed to boil for too long; care must be taken to follow the correct procedure during cooking as this cannot later be rectified.
	— aluminium utensils have been used (i.e. spoon, whisk, saucepan); aluminium utensils must be avoided as this cannot later be rectified.
	— completed sauce retained in a bain-marie for too long; ensure that the sauce is made close to the time it is required as this cannot later be rectified.
(3) Sauce is pinky in colour or curdled	— sauce overcooked, especially in an aluminium pan; avoid using aluminium utensils as this cannot later be rectified.
	— completed sauce retained in a bain-marie for too long; ensure that the sauce is made close to the time it is required as this cannot later be rectified.
(4) Sauce is starchy or gluey in texture and floury in flavour	— sauce undercooked; continue to cook for the prescribed time.
	— sauce too thick; dilute with more milk and continue to cook.
(5) Sauce is lumpy	— roux too hard (i.e. too much flour in proportion to the butter); pass the sauce through a conical strainer.
	— roux has dried out; pass the sauce through a conical strainer.
	— milk not incorporated into the roux correctly; pass the sauce through a conical strainer.

Possible problem	*Possible cause and solution*
	— roux around the edges of the pan not incorporated into the milk; pass the sauce through a conical strainer.
	— milk added to the roux too fast; pass the sauce through a conical strainer.
(6) Excess fat on the surface of the sauce either during cooking or when holding in a bain-marie	— roux too soft (i.e. too much fat in proportion to the flour); excess fat may be skimmed off before use.

VELOUTE SAUCES

Velouté sauces are white stocks of meat, poultry, game or fish thickened with a mixture of equal quantities of butter and flour cooked to a second stage roux.

These sauces form the basis of a number of preparations for meat and poultry entrées, soups, white stews, fish and vegetable dishes, in cold and hot savoury soufflés, in mousses and cold sauces, and also in the preparation of cold meat, poultry and fish dishes as a basis for cold buffet decoration.

The name of the sauce is determined by the type of white stock from which it is made, e.g. fish velouté is made from fish stock, chicken velouté from chicken stock, and veal velouté from white stock made from veal. Whatever the type of velouté, the ratio of ingredients and method of preparation is the same in all instances.

3.5 VELOUTE SAUCE

Makes: 5 litres. Cooking time: 1 hour.

Quantity	*Ingredient*
450 g	butter
450 g	flour
5 l	white stock used hot

Method

(1) Prepare a second stage roux with the butter and flour as in 3.3. Allow to cool.

(2) Add the hot stock to the cold roux a little at a time, mixing with a wooden spatule until all the stock has been absorbed.

(3) Simmer the sauce gently for one hour.

(4) Strain the sauce into a bain-marie pot.

(5) Place melted butter and, if desired, greaseproof paper on top to prevent a skin forming.

(6) Retain until required in a bain-marie of hot water.

Note

This sauce may also be cooked in an oven at 170 °C for one hour.

Assessment of the completed sauce

(1) The sauce should be ivory in colour.

(2) It should be rather thick in consistency like double cream — it should be borne in mind that this is a basic sauce that will be adjusted with other ingredients.

(3) It should have a delicate flavour of the commodities from which the foundation stock was made.

(4) It is very important that this sauce has a smooth velvety texture.

Possible problem	*Possible cause and solution*
(1) Sauce lacks flavour NOTE: this may be intentional if the sauce is to be used for a specific dish.	— poor quality stock used; care must be taken when preparing the stock as this cannot later be rectified. — undercooked; continue to cook for the prescribed time.
(2) Sauce is too dark	— poor quality or dark coloured stock used; care must be taken when preparing the stock as this cannot later be rectified. — roux overcoloured; care must be taken during the preparation of the roux as this cannot be rectified. — sauce overcooked; cook for the correct length of time as this cannot be remedied. — a reduction of mushroom trimmings has been added to the stock making it dark in colour; care must be taken when preparing the stock as this cannot later be rectified.
(3) Sauce is starchy and gluey in texture and has a floury flavour	— sauce undercooked; continue to cook for the prescribed time. — too thick; dilute with more stock and continue to cook.

Possible problem	*Possible cause and solution*
(4) Sauce is lumpy	— roux too hard (i.e. too much flour in proportion to the fat); if necessary pass the sauce through a conical strainer.
	— roux has dried out; if necessary pass the sauce through a conical strainer.
	— roux not cooled sufficiently before adding the hot liquid; if necessary pass the sauce through a conical strainer.
	— stock not incorporated into the roux with a spatule; if necessary pass the sauce through a conical strainer.
	— roux around the edges of the pan not incorporated into the stock; if necessary pass the sauce through a conical strainer.
	— stock added to the roux too fast; if necessary pass the sauce through a conical strainer.

BASIC BROWN SAUCES

Brown sauce

Although a foundation sauce, brown sauce is not a sauce in its own right. Only the sauces made from it will appear on menus.

Brown sauce may be described as:

(a) brown meat stock thickened with a mixture of dripping and flour made into a third stage roux, with the addition of coloured fried vegetables, herbs and tomato purée, all cooked together for 6–8 hours;

(b) brown meat stock thickened with flour that has previously been dried and coloured brown in a hotplate or in a hot cupboard at a very low temperature, with the addition of coloured fried vegetables and tomato purée, all cooked together for 6–8 hours.

Jus Lié (3.8) is frequently used as the modern alternative to both brown sauce and sauce demi-glace.

3.6 BROWN SAUCE — SAUCE ESPAGNOLE

Makes: 5 litres. Cooking time: 6–8 hours.

Quantity	*Ingredient*
300 g	dripping
350 g	flour

Quantity	*Ingredient*	
100 g	tomato purée	
8 l	brown stock	
400 g	carrots	roughly cut (*see Note* below)
400 g	onions	
200 g	leek	
200 g	celery	
200 g	bacon trimmings	
400 g	tomatoes	if available
400 g	mushroom trimmings	
	parsley stalks	
1	bayleaf	
1 sprig	thyme	

Method

(1) Melt the dripping in a deep sided saucepan, add the flour and cook to a third stage roux. Allow to cool.

(2) Add the tomato purée, then add the brown stock, stirring with a wooden spatule.

(3) Bring to the boil.

(4) Lightly fry the vegetables and the bacon trimmings to a light brown colour, drain off all the excess fat and add to the sauce.

(5) Add the herbs, tomatoes and mushroom trimmings.

(6) Cook for 6–8 hours by gently simmering, skimming as and when necessary.

(7) Strain the sauce into a saucepan, reboil and retain for the next stage (usually the making of sauce demi-glace).

Note

Trimmings from shaping vegetables, ends of leeks and celery and so on are sufficient in all stock and sauce recipes.

Assessment of the completed sauce

See Assessment for Sauce Demi-glace, p. 48.

Sauce demi-glace

This is fifty per cent brown meat stock and fifty per cent brown sauce reduced by half.

3.7 SAUCE DEMI-GLACE

Makes: 1 litre. Cooking time: 1 hour.

Quantity	*Ingredient*
1 l	brown stock
1 l	Brown Sauce (3.6)

Method

(1) Place the brown stock and brown sauce together in a saucepan.

(2) Bring to the boil and continue to boil and reduce until half its original quantity, skimming continuously.

(3) Strain into a clean saucepan.

(4) Place melted butter on top to prevent a skin from forming.

(5) Retain until required standing in a bain-marie.

Note

To make sauce demi-glace mellow in flavour knobs of butter may be added at the last moment.

Assessment of the completed sauce

This description also applies to Brown Sauce (3.6) which forms the basis for this sauce.

(1) The sauce should be a rich reddish brown in colour with a definite sheen or gloss.

(2) The consistency should be that of single cream — a light coating consistency sufficient to mask lightly the back of a spoon.

(3) The sauce should be smooth in texture but not gluey in appearance, and be free from all particles.

(4) There should be no bitterness in the flavour.

Possible problem	*Possible cause and solution*
(1) Sauce lacks flavour	— basic brown stock lacks flavour; care must be taken when preparing the stock as this cannot later be rectified.
	— sauce undercooked; continue to cook for the prescribed time.
	— roux or coloured flour undercooked; care must be taken when preparing the roux or colouring the flour as this cannot be rectified.
	— sauce too thick; dilute with a little more stock and continue to cook.
(2) Sauce is too pale	— roux or coloured flour undercooked; care must be taken when preparing the roux or colouring the flour although the colour of the sauce may be adjusted with a little gravy browning.
	— brown stock lacks colour; care must be taken when preparing the stock although

Possible problem	*Possible cause and solution*
	the colour of the sauce may be adjusted with a little gravy browning.
	— sauce undercooked; continue to cook for the prescribed time.
(3) Sauce is bitter	— roux or coloured flour overcooked; care must be taken when preparing the roux or colouring the flour as this cannot be rectified.
	— overcooked stock used; care must be taken when preparing the stock as this cannot be rectified.
	— sauce undercooked; continue to cook for the prescribed time.
(4) Sauce is too dark	— brown stock too dark; care must be taken when preparing the basic brown stock as this cannot be rectified.
	— roux or coloured flour overcooked or overcoloured; care must be taken when preparing the roux or colouring the flour as this cannot be rectified.
	— vegetables in the brown sauce overcoloured; care must be taken when preparing the brown sauce as this cannot be rectified.
(5) Excess fat or grease in the sauce	— roux too soft (i.e. too much fat in proportion to the flour); skim off excess fat.
	— insufficient skimming during the cooking process; skim off excess fat continuously whilst cooking.

Jus lié

Jus lié — frequently used as the modern alternative to brown sauce and sauce demi-glace — is brown meat or poultry stock (or a combination of the two) thickened with diluted cornflour or arrowroot with the addition of fried coloured vegetables, herbs and tomato purée, all cooked together for 1–3 hours.

To suggest that jus lié is a thickened *gravy* within the general use of the term is misleading. However, a thickened gravy is used extensively when pot roasting certain white meats such as veal and turkey, when the liquid may be completed as a jus lié of the meat in question.

It would appear that jus lié has taken the place of demi-glace as a basis for all brown sauces in most catering units, its subtle flavour being more acceptable to today's tastes.

Several different ways of producing jus lié are employed, but broadly speaking they follow the two methods outlined below.

3.8 JUS LIE (Method 1)

Makes: 5 litres. Cooking time: 2 hours.

Quantity	*Ingredient*
200 g	dripping
400 g	carrots (roughly cut (*see Note* to 3.6))
400 g	onions (roughly cut (*see Note* to 3.6))
200 g	leek (roughly cut (*see Note* to 3.6))
200 g	celery (roughly cut (*see Note* to 3.6))
5 l	brown stock (generally a combination of veal, chicken and beef)
120 g	cornflour or arrowroot diluted with cold water
400 g	squashed tomatoes
400 g	mushroom trimmings
100 g	tomato purée
1 small sprig	thyme
2	bayleaves
1 clove	garlic

Method

(1) Lightly fry the vegetables to a light brown colour, drain off all the excess fat and retain for other use.

(2) Boil the brown stock, skim off all traces of fat and scum.

(3) Lightly thicken with the diluted arrowroot or cornflour.

(4) Add the drained lightly fried vegetables, tomato purée, squashed tomatoes and mushroom trimmings and herbs.

(5) Allow to simmer, skimming throughout the cooking process.

3.9 JUS LIE (Method 2)

Makes: 5 litres. Cooking time: 2 hours.

Quantity	*Ingredient*
200 g	dripping
2 kg	bones, beef, chicken or veal, cut or chopped very small and free from excess fat
400 g	carrots (roughly cut (*see Note* to 3.6))
400 g	onions (roughly cut (*see Note* to 3.6))
200 g	leek (roughly cut (*see Note* to 3.6))
200 g	celery (roughly cut (*see Note* to 3.6))
1 small sprig	thyme
3	bayleaves
1 clove	garlic

Quantity	*Ingredient*
6 l	stock
120 g	cornflour or arrowroot diluted with cold water
400 g	squashed tomatoes
400 g	mushroom trimmings
100 g	tomato purée

Method

(1) Place the dripping, vegetables, bones and herbs into a roasting tray; place in a hot oven and lightly brown. Drain off all excess fat.

(2) Place the lightly browned bones and vegetables in a deep sided saucepan, cover with cold stock and bring to the boil.

(3) Skim off all traces of fat and scum.

(4) Lightly thicken with the diluted arrowroot or cornflour.

(5) Add the squashed tomatoes, mushroom trimmings and tomato purée.

(6) Allow to simmer, skimming continuously throughout the cooking process.

(7) When cooked strain the sauce, reboil and use as required.

Assessment of the completed sauce

(1) The sauce should be a rich tomato brown in colour but translucent with a definite sheen.

(2) It should be very light in consistency and should easily coat items of food.

(3) It should be seasoned to bring out the meaty characteristics of the stock from which it has been produced.

(4) The sauce should not appear gluey in texture but smooth and free from all particles of food.

Possible problem	*Possible cause and solution*
(1) Sauce lacks flavour	— basic stock lacks flavour; care must be taken when preparing the stock as this cannot be later rectified.
	— sauce undercooked; continue to cook for the prescribed time.
(2) Sauce is too pale	— basic stock lacks colour; care must be taken when preparing the stock although the colour may be adjusted with a little gravy browning.
	— insufficient tomato purée; add a little more purée and cook for a further half hour.

Possible problem	*Possible cause and solution*
(3) Sauce is bitter	— overcooked stock used; care must be taken when preparing the stock as this cannot later be rectified.
	— vegetables overcoloured or burnt; care must be taken in the initial stages as this cannot be rectified.
(4) Completed sauce is starchy and gluey in texture	— sauce not sufficiently cooked once thickening agent has been added; continue to cook until the required consistency is achieved.
	— too much thickening used; dilute with a little more stock.

TOMATO SAUCE

This is a tomato flavoured and coloured sauce based on a second stage roux, vegetables, herbs, bacon trimmings and white stock to which a reduction of vinegar and sugar is added at the last stage of cooking. It is a sauce in its own right.

3.10 TOMATO SAUCE — SAUCE TOMATE

Makes: 5 litres. Cooking time: 1 hour.

Quantity	*Ingredient*	
350 g	butter	
400 g	carrots	roughly cut (*see Note* to 3.6)
400 g	onions	
200 g	celery	
1 small sprig	thyme	
1	bayleaf	
1 clove	crushed garlic	
200 g	bacon trimmings	
400 g	flour	
500 g	tomato purée	
5 l	White Stock (3.1)	
	seasoning of salt and pepper	
1 dl	vinegar	
30 g	sugar	

Method

(1) Melt the butter in a thick bottomed saucepan.

(2) Add the vegetables, herbs and bacon trimmings and fry until a light golden colour.

(3) Add the flour, stir with a wooden spatule and cook until it takes a second stage roux texture and colour.

(4) Add the tomato purée; cool slightly and add the boiling white stock.

(5) Gently simmer for an hour, skimming as and when necessary.

(6) Add the reduction of vinegar and sugar in order to adjust the degree of tartness.

(7) Pass the sauce through a conical strainer, reboil, season to taste and use as necessary.

Assessment of the completed sauce

(1) The sauce should be a natural tomato red in colour with a slight sheen.

(2) It should be light in consistency and sufficiently runny to just coat the back of a spoon. (When served separately in a sauceboat the consistency should be marginally thicker.)

(3) It should be slightly sweet in flavour, tasting of herb and bacon.

(4) It should be smooth in texture and not appear gluey. It should also be free from any particles from the cooking process.

Possible problem	*Possible cause and solution*
(1) Sauce burns during cooking	— sauce too thick, i.e. too much flour or too little stock; care must be taken when measuring the ingredients as a burnt sauce cannot be rectified.
(2) Sauce is rather acid in flavour	— too much tomato purée added; add a reduction of sugar and vinegar.
(3) Sauce is gluey in texture	— sauce undercooked; continue to cook for the prescribed time.
(4) Sauce is rather pale	— insufficient tomato purée; add a little more purée and cook for a further half hour.

3.11 CURRY SAUCE — SAUCE CURRIE

Makes: 1 litre. Cooking time: 1 hour.

Quantity	*Ingredient*
100 g	butter
100 g	finely chopped onions
1 clove	garlic
30 g	curry powder
30 g	flour
50 g	tomato purée
1 l	White Stock (3.1)

Quantity	*Ingredient*
30 g	finely chopped chutney
50 g	finely diced apple
30 g	Tomato Concassée (8.169)
10 g	desiccated coconut
½ dl	cream (optional)

Method

(1) Melt the butter in a deep saucepan. Add the chopped onions and garlic and lightly colour.

(2) Add the flour and curry powder and make a second stage roux. Add the tomato purée and allow to cool slightly.

(3) Add the stock and allow to boil. Skim, then add the remaining ingredients. Allow to simmer gently for approximately 45 minutes, skimming as necessary.

(4) Season to taste and correct the consistency.

(5) Complete, if desired, with the cream at the last moment.

Note

If desired this sauce may be puréed, in which case it should be reboiled and may be completed with cream.

BUTTER SAUCES

Butter sauces consist of egg yolks cooked to a temperature not exceeding 60 °C with the addition of butter. The flavour of these sauces is to a large extent influenced by the various reductions which may be added consisting of herbs and vinegar. They are generally served as accompaniments but may also be presented as coating sauces for certain vegetables.

Sauces in this category may be used to complement a wide variety of dishes:

Fish — boiled, grilled, poached or shallow fried;

Meats — usually small individual items such as steaks, chops and cutlets that are either grilled or shallow fried;

Vegetables — individual vegetables as in the case of asparagus and globe artichokes; or
— vegetables forming part of a composite garnish such as garnish Renaissance in which a number of vegetables are used including cauliflower coated with a butter sauce.

The two most commonly used sauces in this category are Sauce Hollandaise and Sauce Béarnaise, the former being used primarily for fish and vegetables and the latter for meat and fish. There are two possible methods for preparing these sauces in the initial stages, as can be seen in 3.12 below, though both sauces can be made in the same way.

3.12 SAUCE HOLLANDAISE and SAUCE BEARNAISE

Makes: ½ litre. Cooking time: 30 minutes.

Quantity	*Ingredient*		
5	egg yolks		Sauce Hollandaise
500 g	clarified butter		Sauce Hollandaise
½ dl	vinegar	reduction	Sauce Hollandaise
10	crushed peppercorns	reduction	Sauce Hollandaise
1	juice of lemon	completion	Sauce Hollandaise
	seasoning of salt and cayenne pepper	completion	Sauce Hollandaise
½ dl	vinegar	reduction	Sauce Béarnaise
10	crushed peppercorns	reduction	Sauce Béarnaise
a few	tarragon and chervil stalks	reduction	Sauce Béarnaise
5 g	parsley stalks	reduction	Sauce Béarnaise
10 g	chopped tarragon	completion	Sauce Béarnaise
5 g	chopped chervil	completion	Sauce Béarnaise
5 g	chopped parsley	completion	Sauce Béarnaise
	seasoning of salt and cayenne pepper	completion	Sauce Béarnaise

Method 1

(1) Make the reduction and allow it to cool using a tin-lined or stainless steel sloping sided saucepan.

(2) Add the egg yolks and a little cold water.

(3) Cook the egg yolks whilst whisking continuously (either by standing the pan on a warm part of the cooker or standing the saucepan in a bain-marie of hot water) until the mixture has the consistency of double cream and reaches the ribbon stage (i.e. light, creamy and thick). Do not allow the mixture to reach a temperature above 60 °C.

(4) Remove the pan from the cooker and add the butter gradually, whisking all the time.

(5) Strain the sauce by passing it through a muslin cloth or a very fine strainer.

(6) Add any garnish of herbs or additional flavourings required at this stage.

(7) Season to taste, correct the flavour and consistency, and serve.

Method 2

(1) Make the reduction and allow it to cool, using a tin-lined or stainless steel sloping sided saucepan.

(2) Add the egg yolks, all the butter in unclarified form and a little cold water.

(3) Stand the preparation in a bain-marie of hot water and whisk occasionally to prevent the egg yolks from scrambling. Cook to the ribbon stage whilst at the same time emulsifying the butter and cooked egg yolks.

(4) When cooked continue from stage (4) in *Method 1* above.

Assessment of the completed Sauce Hollandaise

(1) The sauce should be an egg yolk yellow in colour similar to mayonnaise.

(2) It should be similar to double cream in consistency and rather thick.

(3) It should have a rich flavour of butter with a delicate blend of lemon and the reduction of vinegar and peppercorns. There should be no identifiable taste of cooked egg, and it should be seasoned to bring out the flavour of all the ingredients without the seasoning being apparent.

(4) It should be smooth in texture with absolutely no traces of coagulated egg yolk or of curdling.

(5) This should be a warm sauce when served, with a temperature above blood heat but below 65 °C.

Possible problem	*Possible cause and solution*
(1) Sauce lacks flavour	— insufficient reduction added; add a little more reduction to improve the flavour.
	— insufficient seasoning; add a little more seasoning to improve the flavour.
(2) Sauce is too dark	— too much reduction added; add more cooked egg yolks and butter to lighten the colour.
(3) Sauce has a greyish tint	— sauce was cooked in an aluminium saucepan; avoid using any utensils made of aluminium as this cannot be rectified.
(4) Sauce has the flavour and texture of scrambled eggs	— egg yolks allowed to reach too high a temperature; care must be taken during the preparation of the sauce as this cannot later be rectified.

(5) Sauce has curdled
— egg yolks not sufficiently cooked; care must be taken during the preparation of the sauce as this cannot be later rectified.
— clarified butter too hot when added to the cooked yolks; either *(a)* whisk the sauce slowly onto a little cold water, or *(b)* whisk the sauce onto some uncurdled sauce.
— sauce allowed to stand in a hot environment when completed; either: *(a)* whisk the sauce slowly onto a little cold water, *(b)* whisk the sauce onto a raw egg yolk, or *(c)* whisk the sauce onto some uncurdled sauce.
— sauce has been reheated after being allowed to cool; either: *(a)* whisk the sauce slowly onto a little hot water, *(b)* whisk the sauce onto some cooked egg yolks, or *(c)* whisk the sauce onto some uncurdled sauce.

MAYONNAISE SAUCE

Mayonnaise may be defined as a cold sauce. It may be served either as sauce in its own right or form the basis of other sauces. It is an emulsification of egg yolks and oil with additional flavour derived from vinegar and mustard. The type of oil used, e.g. olive oil or corn oil, and the type of vinegar — usually malt but may occasionally be one of the wine variety — very largely determines the flavour.

Mayonnaise sauce is served exclusively with cold foods — salads, meat, poultry, game and fish, offals and cold made-up dishes such as pies. However, sauces derived from mayonnaise may be used as an accompaniment to hot fish dishes, e.g. Tartare Sauce (3.45) may be served with fried fish in breadcrumbs.

3.13 MAYONNAISE SAUCE

Makes: 1 litre. Preparation time: by hand — 15 minutes, by machine — 5 minutes.

Quantity	*Ingredient*
¼ dl	vinegar
1 teaspoon	dry English mustard
5–6	egg yolks
1 l	oil
	seasoning of salt and pepper

Method

(1) Place the vinegar, mustard and egg yolks into a basin or the bowl of a mixing machine and begin whisking.

(2) Slowly incorporate the oil until it has all been added.

(3) If whisked by machine, remove. Season to taste.

Note

(1) To make a light coloured sauce lemon juice should be used instead of vinegar.

(2) A little hot water may be added to thin the sauce.

Assessment of the completed sauce

(1) The sauce should be yellow in colour.

(2) Its consistency depends upon its use, ranging from a thick sauce that will pipe through a star tube and hold its shape to a light coating consistency.

(3) The flavour depends upon the type of oil and vinegar used.

(4) It should be well seasoned to bring out the flavours of the ingredients.

(5) It should be smooth and velvety in texture.

(6) It should be kept cold but not chilled.

Possible problem	*Possible cause and solution*
(1) Sauce has curdled	— eggs were stale or too cold; use only fresh ingredients of good quality. — oil added too fast; whisk the sauce slowly onto a little uncurdled mayonnaise or egg yolks. — oil too cold when added; whisk the sauce slowly onto a little warm water or a little uncurdled mayonnaise. — oil too hot when added; whisk the sauce slowly onto a little cold water, a little uncurdled mayonnaise or additional egg yolks. — completed sauce held at the wrong temperature; if held at too low a temperature rectify as for adding cold oil; if held at too high a temperature rectify as for adding hot oil.

EXTENSIONS

Extensions of the basic sauces — béchamel, velouté made from fish, poultry and veal, demi-glace, jus lié, butter sauces and mayonnaise — are prepared by the addition of other ingredients. These can affect the colour and flavour and, in certain instances, the thickness or coating capability.

Béchamel based sauces

Béchamel (3.4) is a very versatile sauce as is shown by the following list of possible extensions.

3.14 ANCHOVY SAUCE — SAUCE ANCHOIS

Prepared by the addition of 15–20 g anchovy essence and completed with 50 g butter and 1 dl cream.

May be served with poached, boiled and grilled fish.

3.15 CHEESE SAUCE — SAUCE MORNAY

Prepared by the addition of 75 g grated Parmesan cheese, 2 egg yolks (sabayon) and 1 dl cream.

May be served with vegetable dishes. (*See* 6.15 for a cheese sauce for fish dishes.)

3.16 CREAM SAUCE — SAUCE CREME

Prepared by the addition of 50 g butter and 1 dl cream.

May be served with boiled fish and vegetables.

3.17 EGG SAUCE — SAUCE AUX OEUFS

Prepared by the addition of 3 diced hard boiled eggs and completed with 50 g butter and 1 dl cream.

May be served with poached or boiled fish.

3.18 MUSTARD SAUCE — SAUCE MOUTARDE

Prepared by the addition of 25 g diluted English mustard and completed with 50 g butter and 1 dl cream.

May be served with grilled fish, herrings in particular.

3.19 ONION SAUCE — SAUCE AUX OIGNONS

Prepared by the addition of 100 g sliced onions cooked in 50 g butter without coloration and completed with 1 dl cream.

May be served with roast mutton.

3.20 PARSLEY SAUCE — SAUCE PERSIL

Prepared by the addition of 15 g chopped and blanched parsley and completed with 1 dl cream.

May be served with boiled fish and vegetables.

3.21 SHRIMP SAUCE — SAUCE AUX CREVETTES

Prepared by the addition of 75 g shrimp butter, garnished with shrimp tails and completed with 1 dl cream.

May be served with boiled fish.

Velouté based sauces

3.22 CAPER SAUCE — SAUCE AUX CAPRES

Prepared by adding 100 g capers to 6 dl mutton velouté and completed with 1 dl cream.

May be served with boiled mutton.

Chicken velouté

The following is the main sauce derived from chicken velouté.

3.23 SAUCE SUPREME

Pass chicken velouté through a fine strainer and complete with 50 g butter and 1 dl cream. The flavour may be enhanced by the addition of a reduction consisting of chicken stock and mushroom trimmings.

May be served with a number of chicken dishes.

Fish velouté

From basic fish velouté two main types of sauce are made — glazed sauces such as Sauce Bonne-Femme (*see* 6.14), and unglazed sauces such as Sauce Dugléré (*see* 6.12).

Demi-glace or jus lié based sauces

3.24 BOLOGNAISE SAUCE — SAUCE BOLOGNAISE

Makes: 10 portions. Cooking time: 1½ hours.

Quantity	*Ingredient*
500 g	minced beef
3 dl	oil
150 g	chopped onion
1 clove	crushed and chopped garlic
50 g	tomato purée
4 dl	Demi-glace (3.7) or Jus Lié (3.8)
	seasoning of salt and pepper

Method

(1) Place the oil in a deep sided saucepan, add the minced meat and allow to fry until it is lightly coloured. Add the chopped onion and garlic and allow to cook until it becomes rather soft, but do not brown.

(2) Drain off any surplus fat, add the tomato purée and brown sauce. Bring to the boil, season and gently simmer until the meat is

cooked. Skim as necessary removing all traces of fat and grease that may surface.

(3) Season to taste, correct the consistency which should allow the sauce to lightly coat the meat.

(4) Retain in a clean saucepan, placing a few knobs of butter on the surface to prevent a skin from forming. Retain until required in a bain-marie of hot water.

Note

May be served with farinaceous dishes, e.g. spaghetti, ravioli.

3.25 BORDELAISE SAUCE — SAUCE BORDELAISE

Prepared by reducing by two-thirds the following: 50 g chopped shallots or onion, 10 crushed peppercorns, 1 bayleaf, small sprig thyme and 2 dl red wine. Add 8 dl basic Sauce Demi-glace (3.7) or Jus Lié (3.8), gently simmer, pass through a conical strainer and complete with 25 g meat glaze (*see* p. 38) and 50 g butter.

May be served with shallow fried and grilled steaks.

3.26 BROWN ONION SAUCE — SAUCE LYONNAISE

Prepared by the addition to 8 dl Sauce Demi-glace (3.7) or Jus Lié (3.8), 500 g sliced onion lightly coloured in 100 g butter, and 1 dl white wine and 1 dl vinegar reduced by two-thirds.

May be served with shallow fried liver and beef bitocks.

3.27 CHASSEUR SAUCE — SAUCE CHASSEUR

Cook 250 g sliced button mushrooms in 50 g butter. Add 150 g chopped shallots or onion, cook for a few moments, then add 250 g diced, peeled and pipped tomatoes and 2 dl dry white wine. Boil and reduce by half. Add 6 dl Sauce Demi-glace (3.7) or Jus Lié (3.8), and 2 g chopped tarragon and gently simmer for a few moments. Complete the sauce with 5 g chopped parsley and 50 g butter.

May be served with grilled meats and shallow fried meats and poultry.

3.28 DEVILLED SAUCE — SAUCE DIABLE

Prepared by the addition of a reduction of 50 g chopped shallots or onion, 20 crushed peppercorns, 1 bayleaf, small sprig of thyme, 1 dl vinegar and 1 dl white wine to 1 l Sauce Demi-glace (3.7). Pass through a strainer and complete with 50 g butter.

May be served with grilled fish, meat or poultry.

3.29 GRATIN SAUCE — SAUCE GRATIN

Cook 100 g chopped shallots in 50 g butter without colouring, then add 450 g chopped mushrooms and continue to cook until the liquid has almost completely reduced. Add 6 dl basic Brown Sauce (3.6) and gently simmer. Complete the sauce with 5 g chopped parsley.

May be served with grilled fish, meat or poultry.

3.30 MADEIRA SAUCE — SAUCE MADERE

Prepared by adding 1 dl madeira to 6 dl Sauce Demi-glace (3.7) or Jus Lié (3.8), and completed with 50 g butter.

May be served with sweetbreads, veal escalopes and ham.

3.31 MARSALA SAUCE — SAUCE MARSALA

Proceed as for Madeira Sauce (3.30) but use 1 dl marsala in place of the madeira.

3.32 ROBERT SAUCE — SAUCE ROBERT

Cook 100 g chopped shallots in 50 g butter without colouring. Add 2 dl dry white wine and reduce by half. Add 6 dl basic Brown Sauce (3.6) and gently simmer. Complete with 5 g diluted English mustard and pass through a strainer.

May be served with grilled meat and poultry dishes and grilled fish.

3.33 REFORM SAUCE — SAUCE REFORME

Prepared by reducing 6 dl Sauce Poivrade (3.35), 2 dl Brown Stock (3.1) and 50 g redcurrant jelly by two-thirds. Pass through a conical strainer and garnish with the following cut into julienne strips: 30 g ham, 30 g tongue, 30 g white of hard boiled egg, 30 g gherkins, and 30 g button mushrooms cooked in lemon juice and water (8.91).

Notes

(1) In classical cookery truffle is also added cut into strips.
(2) May be served with Breaded Lamb Cutlets (7.194).

3.34 SAUCE PIQUANTE

Prepared by adding the following to Devilled Sauce (3.28): 50 g chopped gherkins, 25 g chopped capers, and chopped parsley, chives, tarragon and chervil. Complete with 50 g butter.

May be served with grilled meats.

3.35 *SAUCE POIVRADE*

Makes: 1 litre. Cooking time: 30 minutes.

Quantity	*Ingredient*
75 g	butter or oil
100 g	carrots (chopped finely)
100 g	onion (chopped finely)
75 g	celery (chopped finely)
1	bayleaf
1 sprig	thyme
1 dl	dry red wine
1 dl	vinegar
1 l	Demi-glace (3.7) or Jus Lié (3.8)
20	crushed peppercorns
50 g	butter
	seasoning of salt and pepper

Method

(1) Heat the butter in a shallow sided pan. Add the vegetables and herbs and fry until brown in colour.

(2) Add the red wine and vinegar. Boil and reduce until it forms a slightly sticky glaze.

(3) Add the brown sauce and gently simmer for a few minutes. Add the crushed peppercorns and continue to cook for a further 5 minutes, skimming the surface continuously.

(4) Strain through a conical strainer into a clean pan, reboil, skim and season to taste.

(5) Complete the sauce at the moment of serving with knobs of butter.

Note

May be served with game such as hare and venison.

Sauces based on hollandaise

3.36 *SAUCE CHANTILLY (or SAUCE MOUSSELINE)*

Prepared by the addition of 1 dl lightly whipped cream.

May be served with poached salmon and salmon trout and hot asparagus.

3.37 *SAUCE MALTAISE*

Prepared by the addition of the juice of 1 blood orange plus the grated zest.

May be served with hot asparagus.

3.38 SAUCE NOISETTE

Prepared by the addition of 50 g Nut Brown Butter (6.48) at the moment of serving.

May be served with poached fish, particularly salmon, salmon trout and trout.

Sauces based on béarnaise

The following group of sauces is generally served as accompaniments for grilled and shallow fried meat dishes.

3.39 SAUCE CHORON

Prepared by the addition of 200 g puréed Tomato Concassée (8.169).

3.40 SAUCE FOYOT (or SAUCE VALOIS)

Prepared by the addition of 20 g meat glaze (*see* p. 38).

3.41 SAUCE PALOISE

Prepared by substituting chopped mint stalks for tarragon and chervil with 5 g chopped mint leaves added at the final stage.

Mayonnaise based sauces

3.42 COCKTAIL SAUCE

Prepared by the addition of approximately 1 dl tomato ketchup and 1 dl cream to 8 dl mayonnaise.

3.43 REMOULADE SAUCE—SAUCE REMOULADE

Prepared as for Tartare Sauce (3.45) with the addition of anchovy essence.

May be served with deep fried fish in breadcrumbs.

3.44 SAUCE VERTE

Prepared by adding a mixture of 200 g of a fine purée of picked, washed and blanched spinach, tarragon, chervil, chives and watercress.

May be served with cold trout, salmon and salmon trout.

3.45 TARTARE SAUCE—SAUCE TARTARE

Prepared by the addition of the following chopped items: 50 g capers, 50 g gherkins and chives, tarragon, chervil and parsley.

May be served with deep fried fish in breadcrumbs.

MISCELLANEOUS SAUCES

3.46 *APPLE SAUCE — SAUCE AUX POMMES*

Proceed as for Apple Purée (*see* 10.175).

3.47 *BREAD SAUCE — SAUCE PAIN*

Makes: 10 portions. Cooking time: 10 minutes.

Quantity	*Ingredient*	
½ l	milk	
1	small onion	studded onion — oignon clouté
	bayleaf	
	clove	
150 g	white breadcrumbs	
50 g	butter	
	seasoning	

Method

(1) Infuse the milk and studded onion by bringing the milk to the boil with studded onion. Allow to stand over heat without boiling for 5–8 minutes.

(2) Remove the onion, discard and add the breadcrumbs. Lightly whisk until the bread has absorbed the milk.

(3) Add the butter and season to taste. Correct the consistency which should be rather thick.

Note

If this sauce is too thin it may be thickened by adding additional breadcrumbs; if too thick adjustment is made by adding more hot milk.

3.48 *CRANBERRY SAUCE*

See pp 577–8.

3.49 *MINT SAUCE — SAUCE MENTHE*

Makes: ½ litre.

Quantity	*Ingredient*
120 g	mint leaves
5 g	castor sugar
¼ dl	hot water
3 dl	vinegar

Method

(1) Chop the mint leaves with the sugar and place in a basin. Add the hot water and cool.

(2) Add the vinegar to the mixture.

SAVOURY AND OTHER BUTTERS

Savoury butters

3.50 LOBSTER BUTTER — BEURRE D'HOMARD

Mix together equal quantities of butter and lobster brain removed from the head.

3.51 PARSLEY BUTTER — BEURRE MAITRE D'HOTEL

Mix together 500 g butter, 25 g chopped parsley, juice of 1 lemon and a little cayenne pepper and mould into a cylinder shape approximately 3 cm in diameter. Roll in greaseproof paper and store in a refrigerator until firm.

When required cut into 1 cm slices using a knife dipped into hot water and serve either directly on the item at the last possible moment or present in a sauceboat on some crushed ice.

3.52 SHRIMP BUTTER — BEURRE DE CREVETTES

Mix together equal quantities of fine purée of shrimps and butter. Proceed as in 3.51.

Other butters

3.53 BEURRE FONDU (BEURRE BLANC)

Whisk the butter into a little warm water and lemon juice in order to melt the butter without separating the fat from the non-fat constituents.

May be served with poached salmon and trout.

3.54 BEURRE MANIE

Mix equal parts of soft butter and plain flour to form a smooth soft paste.

3.55 CLARIFIED BUTTER

Melt the butter in a saucepan standing in a bain-marie of hot water. When the surface is clear and sediment and impurities have sunk to the bottom, carefully drain off the clear oiled butter into a clean pan.

Note

In this text it is generally referred to as melted butter.

NOUVELLE CUISINE

Stocks

Great emphasis should always be placed on the careful preparation of all stocks as they form the basis for most sauces, gravies, soups, light stews and braisings. All the stocks found in this chapter together with their methods of preparation may be used in the Nouvelle Cuisine style of cooking.

Once cooked meat and game stocks should be strained and then placed back on the stove to cook gently until the liquid has reduced by almost half its original volume. It should then be strained again, permitted to cool and stored in a refrigerator until required.

Sauces

Roux and roux-based sauces are never used in the Nouvelle Cuisine style of cooking. This of course applies in particular to the three foundation sauces béchamel, velouté and demi-glace. Sauces should always be very light in consistency and smooth in texture and should never be made in advance of requirements. They are usually made in the receptacle in which the main ingredients have been cooked so as to incorporate any sediment and flavour into the sauce.

A wide range of vinegars, wines, liqueurs, herbs and vegetables are at the disposal of the caterer in this style of cooking. The butter-based sauces (3.36–41) and cold sauces such as mayonnaise (3.13) are ideal as starting points to create other sauces by adding vinegars, oils or herbs.

The preparation of most sauces in the Nouvelle Cuisine style of cooking is clearly illustrated in the first two recipes given for White Wine Fish Sauce (6.1–3). The same principle of a reduction of stocks or wines with the addition of butter or butter and cream as an emulsifying agent may be used when preparing sauces for use with meats, poultry and game.

CONVENIENCE STOCKS AND SAUCES

Stocks

Stocks are widely available in concentrated crystal, cube and powder forms. As with traditionally made stocks, these may form the basis of many products, including sauces, soups and stews, and the basic principles outlined in this chapter will still apply. However, convenience type stocks are often very concentrated in nature and should not be used in the belief that they will improve the quality of the final product. In fact the result will inevitably be a distortion of the flavour of the dish to which it has been added. Moreover, such stocks cannot be effectively reduced and so should be avoided when making sauces, soups and stews which involve the process of reduction in their preparation.

The same criteria used to assess fresh stocks may also be used to assess those made from convenience forms, although it should always be remembered that the latter is a quite different product made in a completely different way and so can never be exactly the same.

Sauces

Most, if not all, of the sauces outlined in this chapter are available as convenience products in powder, canned, frozen or boil-in-the-bag form. The foundation sauces in convenience form may be used to make the same wide range of extension sauces as fresh foundation sauces by adding the appropriate reductions of wine or vinegar and by finishing with suitable herbs and garnishes. Cream or yolks of eggs may also be added as a liaison, although it must be remembered that the sauce should not be allowed to boil once it has been added. Knobs of butter may also be added to give a mellow effect to the sauce as with fresh sauces.

The guiding principle that a sauce should complement rather than clash with the food it accompanies applies no matter whether a fresh or convenience sauce is used. The same criteria for assessing flavour, consistency, colour and so on of fresh sauces also apply to convenience products.

CHAPTER FOUR

Soups

INTRODUCTION

"Soup" is an all-embracing word that includes every possible kind whether thick, thin or clear. In French the word for soup is *potage*, but this is usually applied only to the thick soups and is never applied to clear soups.

Although usually served hot as the first course of an everyday meal, many soups can also be served cold, and clear soups in particular can be served in jellied form.

Soups are made from an almost unlimited range of ingredients. It is possible to put both a clear and a thick soup on the menu every day of the year without having to repeat a recipe once.

Classification

It is possible to classify soups under ten main headings as follows.

(a) Consommés: clarified stocks with the flavour of the basic ingredient; may be served plain or garnished, hot or cold.

(b) Bouillons: unclarified but clear stocks served plain or with a garnish; always hot.

(c) Potages: a very good quality white stock thickened with cream and egg yolks and finished with a garnish.

(d) Broths: cut vegetables cooked in a stock, sometimes with meat or poultry, not passed; always served hot.

(e) Purées: smooth, passed soups made from dried pulses or fresh vegetables.

(f) Creams: smooth passed soups made of vegetables, a dried pulse or chicken and always finished with cream; may be served hot or cold.

(g) Veloutés: made with a second stage roux and an appropriate white stock and always finished with egg yolks and cream; may be served hot or cold.

(h) Fawn roux-based: made with a second stage roux and white stock, and may be finished with cream; may be served hot or cold.

(i) Brown roux-based: thick passed meat soups such as oxtail and kidney garnished with meat; always served hot.

(j) Bisques: thick passed shellfish soup finished with cream; may be served hot or cold.

Terminology

The following terms are used in connection with the making of soups.

Boiling: the cooking of ingredients in a liquid at 100 °C. The liquid is visibly moving thus giving rapid cooking.

Clarification: the removal of all impurities from a stock with the object of improving its flavour and clarity as, for example, in consommés.

Gratinated: prepared soup served in an earthenware soup bowl (marmite), the surface of which is layered with dried or toasted slices of bread known as croûtes, sprinkled with Parmesan and Gruyère cheeses and placed under a salamander grill until a golden skin is formed with the cheese (e.g. French Onion Soup (4.45)).

Infusion: the flavouring of some soups by the addition of various herbs and spices in a muslin bag which is immersed in a little of the hot soup and allowed to give off flavour and aroma but without cooking. The infusion is then added to the bulk of the soup so that it permeates throughout with a little more gentle cooking (e.g. Turtle Soup (4.11)).

Poaching: almost the same as simmering — the liquid is brought to the boil, then the heat is reduced to stop it boiling but cooking still takes place but at a slower rate.

Puréeing: the pulping of vegetables after cooking to a smooth paste by either passing through a sieve-type soup machine or by means of an electric liquidiser (e.g. Purée of Split Pea Soup (*see* 4.21)).

Reduction: an essence of meat or fish diluted with a liquid so as to produce a soup. The word cullis indicates a strong concentrated essence which can be used to make a soup. Nowadays a purée of shellfish soup (bisque) is made this way.

Simmering: the cooking of an item in a liquid which is just below boiling point so as to give it a gentle boiling action. The temperature would be about 95 °C. Consommés are cooked at this temperature to keep them crystal clear.

Staggered commodity cookery: the identification of those items used in the production of a soup that take the longest to cook and those that take the least time, the aim being to add them in the correct order so that they all become cooked at the same time (e.g. Petite Marmite (4.12)).

Sweating: the cooking of vegetables in melted butter in a saucepan with a lid on but without coloration, the aim being to extract the flavour from the vegetables and to soften them as in Potage Paysanne (4.14).

Thickenings: there are three ways of using thickenings:

(*a*) using a second or third stage roux with the addition of stock;
(*b*) the addition of diluted arrowroot or cornflour to boiling liquid;
(*c*) the addition of rice;
(*d*) the addition of cream and butter to a completed soup to thicken and enrich it as in a cream type soup (e.g. Cream of Chicken (4.26)) or the addition of a combination of egg yolks, cream and butter to a completed soup as in a velouté type soup (e.g. Velouté Dame Blanche (4.40)). This type of thickening is called a *liaison*.

Adjustment of consistency

Great care needs to be taken when adjusting the consistency of soups. Whatever the reason for the adjustment — whether the soup is too thick or too thin — the flavour must always be considered. Either thinning down or thickening a soup will effect its final flavour whatever the method used.

Purée of vegetable soup may be adjusted, if too thick, by the addition of white stock. Those that are too thin may be adjusted by the addition of a purée of the same type of vegetable from which the soup is made, or if none is available by adding a small quantity of potato powder or granules. Diluted arrowroot or rice flour may also be used as a thickening agent, but the soup in question must be allowed to cook through for a time in order to avoid either a glassy appearance or a slight rawness of taste.

Creams and veloutés may be adjusted, if too thick, by the addition of more of the same white stock used in the recipe. Those that are too thin may be adjusted by the addition of béchamel in the case of cream soups, or velouté in the case of the latter. Extra liaison of cream or egg yolks and cream may be used but only as a last resort because of the costs involved.

Fawn and brown roux-based soups may be adjusted if too thick by the addition of more of the same type of stock used in the recipe. Those that are too thin may be adjusted by adding some extra thick basic sauce — velouté for fawn roux-based soups (in which case some degree of colour adjustment may be necessary), and basic brown sauce for brown roux-based soups. Alternately diluted arrowroot may be used to adjust them but it should be used sparingly and must be allowed to cook through to avoid any other distortion of the soup.

Adjustment of colour

Most soups do not require any artificial colour adjustments. A guiding rule is that where possible allow the natural colours of the vegetables used in the production to determine the final colour of the soup.

There are a few types of soups that may need some colour adjustment, namely consommés, creams, veloutés and those with a brown roux base.

(a) Consommés. Generally the problem is that the consommé is too pale in colour in which case gravy browning may be added very carefully, a little at a time. The addition of too much colouring agent is very difficult to rectify and is not always possible. It is far better to serve a very pale consommé type soup than one that has been ruined by adding too much colour.

(b) Creams and veloutés. Generally the problem is that these soups are too dark in colour but this may be rectified by adding additional liaison. If these soups are too light in colour then additional egg yolks may be added to the velouté type soup and additional basic béchamel to the cream type soups.

(c) Brown roux-based soups. Generally the problem is that these soups are too pale in colour. This can be rectified by the addition of tomato purée and gravy browning. Where the soup is too dark in colour the colour adjustment is most difficult, costly and time consuming as it will need to be added to a lighter coloured base soup.

Accompaniments and garnishes

Diced fried bread croûtons and sliced bread sippets are served as an accompaniment with purées and some fawn roux-based soups.

Vegetable garnishes are added to clear, cream, velouté, brown and some fawn roux-based soups.

Parmesan cheese is served as an accompaniment with some bouillons and with many Italian soups.

Cheese straws are served as accompaniments with turtle soup and potage Germiny.

Slices of poached beef marrow are served as a garnish with some bouillons.

Sliced and dried croûtes are served as an accompaniment with some bouillons and consommés, and in soups served in individual marmites and many of the traditional French country soups.

Pluches (sprigs of chervil blanched to preserve their green colour) are added to consommés and some broth type soups.

Storage of soup

Consommés, bouillons and roux-based soups should be reboiled after passing, cooled as quickly as possible and then stored in a refrigerator at 7–8 °C.

Clear soups such as broths and those made with a stewed vegetable base and stock should be cooled as quickly as possible and stored in plastic, stainless steel or porcelain containers in the refrigerator.

Chilled and jellied soups must be kept in a refrigerator at 4 °C until required. Jellied soup should not be stirred before serving as this will break up the set and may turn the soup cloudy.

Keep all hot soups in a proper bain-marie pot for the minimum period of time. It is important to use containers that will not cause deterioration, especially for soups containing liaisons. Stainless steel containers are the best for this purpose, but even so the quality of the soup kept in them will deteriorate if stored for any length of time as it will continue to evaporate thus causing it to condense and so develop a strong taste.

Veloutés or cream soups should *not* be retained for future use once the liaison has been added (unless it is intended to retain them as chilled soups) as reboiling will cause them to curdle.

Wine and fortified wine in soup

Fortified wines may be used to finish certain soups. They are added at the moment of service.

Dry sherry is added to consommés — particularly those served cold — and to the brown roux-based soups such as mock turtle and clear turtle soup.

White wine, red wine and madeira may be added to soups whilst cooking.

Brandy is generally used in making shellfish soups and is added during the initial stages when it is flambé to concentrate the alcohol. This is done by pouring in the brandy and igniting it by tipping the pan over an open flame. The flame from the brandy will die out of its own accord.

Stock for soups

In the trade foundation stocks for soups are generally made in advance (*see* Chapter 3). In the recipes that follow it is assumed that the stock has already been produced and is strained ready for use.

CONSOMME

Consommé is a clarified meat or poultry stock (or a combination of the two, either brown or white), amber in colour and transparent and crystal clear in appearance. It is completed at the point of service with a garnish that may consist of cuts of vegetables, savoury egg custards, farinaceous or cereal foods, small meat or fish quenelles, shredded savoury pancakes, and many other items. Some consommés are slightly thickened with tapioca or arrowroot; others are served cold or jellied.

4.1 BASIC CONSOMME

Makes: 2 litres. Cooking time: 2 hours.

Quantity	*Ingredient*
2	egg whites
500 g	shin of beef, free from fat and gristle, coarsely minced
100 g	carrots } coarsely cut
100 g	onions } coarsely cut
100 g	leek } coarsely cut
100 g	celery } coarsely cut
10	peppercorns
1	bayleaf
1 sprig	thyme
5 g	salt
3 l	cold beef stock, brown or white
	seasoning of salt and pepper

Method

(1) Whisk the egg whites briskly in the pan in which the consommé is to be cooked.

(2) Add the minced beef, vegetables and herbs, salt and peppercorns.

(3) Add the cold stock and mix well together.

(4) Bring gently to the boil, stirring the soup at intervals with a wooden or metal spatule to prevent it sticking to the bottom of the pan and burning.

(5) Once the consommé comes to the boil allow it to simmer very gently for 1½–2 hours.

(6) Strain the consommé through a fine muslin with the minimum of disturbance of the crust that settles on the surface during cooking.

(7) Reboil, remove all traces of fat from the surface, season to taste and, if necessary, correct the colour, and serve.

Notes

(1) Do not use cabbage, potatoes, turnips, swede or parsnips when making a consommé.

(2) If white stock or light coloured brown stock is used the onions — cut in halves across — may be coloured on top of the stove before being added to the consommé during the initial stages.

(3) Do not adjust seasoning until the consommé is completed.

Service

Serve in a consommé cup, soup bowl or soup plate. It is most usually served in a hot consommé cup placed on a saucer with a small dish paper and an underplate.

Assessment of the completed dish

The quality of the completed dish depends upon the following factors.

(1) The criteria used in judging a foundation stock (*see* Chapter 3, p. 34) should apply.

(2) The correct method should be used in the clarification process (*see* Stages (1)–(6)):

(a) the shin of beef should be free of fat and sinew and be coarsely minced;

(b) good quality vegetables should be used;

(c) stock should be cold when added to the beaten egg whites;

(d) there should be the correct ratio of stock to egg whites, shin of beef and vegetables;

(e) the soup should be stirred occasionally during the initial stages of cooking;

(f) once the soup has boiled it should never be stirred but allowed to simmer gently;

(g) the crust that forms during clarification should never be disturbed;

(h) the pan should never be covered with a lid during cooking;

(i) the soup should never be skimmed during cooking;

(j) the correct straining method (*see* Stage (6)) should be used to avoid disturbance of the crust formed during cooking.

Possible problem	*Possible cause and solution*
(1) Consommé has a burnt and bitter flavour	— saucepan or stockpot used for making the soup has a thin bottom causing the soup to burn; use only a thick bottomed saucepan as once the soup is burnt it cannot be rectified. — the heat was too fierce during the initial stages; care must be taken in the initial stages not to burn the egg whites and minced shin as this cannot be rectified.

Possible problem	*Possible cause and solution*
	— soup was not stirred whilst bringing to the boil; the soup must be stirred at this stage to prevent the ingredients sticking to the bottom of the pan and burning.
	— soup has been overcooked for a long period; take care to cook the soup for the correct length of time as this cannot be rectified later.
(2) Consommé lacks colour	— poor quality brown stock used; add a little gravy browning at the final stage.
	— if using white stock the onions were insufficiently coloured; add a little gravy browning at the final stage.
	— incorrect proportion of beef to stock; add a little gravy browning at the final stage.
	— wrong type of meat used for clarification; add a little gravy browning at the final stage.
(3) Consommé is cloudy	— poor quality stock used
	— stock too hot when added to the other ingredients at the initial stages of clarification
	— soup stirred or agitated whilst simmering
	— incorrect ratio of stock to egg whites and shin of beef
	— beef not minced to the correct degree of coarseness
	— soup covered with a lid during cooking
	— soup skimmed during cooking
	— potato or cabbage added
	— soup not simmered gently

Consommé that has not clarified properly should be cooled as quickly as possible — large amounts may be divided up to quicken the process. To re-clarify whisk the cooled soup onto either additional egg whites and finely chopped vegetables, or repeat the whole process starting with more minced shin of beef.

Possible problem	*Possible cause and solution*
(4) Consommé is too dark	— poor quality stock used; only the best quality ingredients should be used as this cannot be rectified at a later stage. — soup cooked for too long; care must be taken not to overcook the soup as this cannot later be rectified. — once completed the soup has been kept too long in its container in a bain-marie; the soup should be made nearer to the time it is required as this cannot be rectified later.
(5) Consommé lacks body	— poor quality foundation stock used; care should be taken when preparing the foundation stock as this cause cannot be rectified later. — soup undercooked; continue to cook for the prescribed time. — poor quality meat used for the clarification; only the best quality meat should be used as this cannot later be rectified. — insufficient meat used for the clarification; the weak consommé may be used to start again.
(6) Excess fat on the surface of the completed consommé	— finished soup not properly skimmed; take care to skim off all the fat with a ladle or soak it up with kitchen paper. — garnish has been stewed in butter or fatty and soft quenelles have been added too soon before serving; care must be taken to avoid these causes.
(7) Particles of egg white still present after straining	— holes in the muslin through which the soup has been passed; restrain the soup until the particles are removed. — soup not cooked for the prescribed period; reheat and simmer for 15 minutes then restrain.

4.2 CHILLED CONSOMME

This is a single or double consommé that has been cooled to a temperature of 4 °C before serving.

4.3 DOUBLE CONSOMME

This is made with a very strong stock or the reduction of a normal consommé to about half its quantity. It is advisable not to season this type of consommé until the completion stage as there is a tendency for it to be naturally salty as a result of the extraction of the mineral salts from the raw ingredients.

4.4 JELLIED CONSOMME — CONSOMME EN GELEE

This is Basic Consomme (4.1) with the addition of 45 g soaked leaf gelatine at the point where the consommé has been clarified completely and just before passing it through a muslin. It is advisable to test a small quantity of the jellied consommé quickly to see if it will set so that adjustments can be made as necessary.

Double Consommé (4.3) should have a natural capacity to form a light jelly when cold without the addition of gelatine.

Consommé extensions

Extensions to basic consommés are produced by the addition of a range of garnishes. Generally, 100 g of garnish are sufficient for 10 standard portions and should be cooked separately. Some examples follow below.

Additional garnishes may be added at the time of service.

4.5 BORTSCH SOUP — BORTSCH POLONAISE

Note

Bortsch is traditionally an unclarified bouillon, flavoured with vegetables, beef, duck and beetroot and garnished with strips of vegetable including beetroot, that is served accompanied by sour cream, small duck patties and beetroot juice. It is, however, common trade practice for a clarified consommé to be used as the base stock for this soup.

Makes: 2 litres. Cooking time: 2 hours.

Quantity	*Ingredient*	
3 l	white stock, cold	
250 g	thick flank of beef	
1×2 kg	duck	
2 dl	beetroot juice	
100 g	carrots	
100 g	leek	coarsely cut
100 g	celery	
1	bouquet garni	
	Garnished with:	
75 g	carrots	cut into julienne strips approximately 1 mm×4 cm cooked in butter without coloration
75 g	leek	
75 g	raw beetroot	

Quantity	*Ingredient*
	Accompanied by:
2 dl	beetroot juice
2 dl	sour cream
10	very small duck patties
	grated raw beetroot
	seasoning of salt and pepper

Method

(1) Roast the prepared duck in a very hot oven for approximately 20 minutes allowing it to colour well; drain off the surplus fat.

(2) Blanch the beef in cold water and refresh.

(3) Add the cold stock to the duck, beef, vegetables, beetroot juice and bouquet garni.

(4) Bring to the boil, skim and gently simmer, removing the duck and the beef as they become cooked. Cool and cut into small dice for the garnish.

(5) Strain the liquid through a muslin as for a consommé then reboil and skim off all traces of fat.

(6) Add the diced beef and duck plus the julienne strips of cooked vegetables.

(7) Season to taste and, if necessary, correct the colour and serve with accompaniments.

Notes

(1) The quality of the finished soup will depend upon the quality of the foundation stock or consommé.

(2) If the beef is not blanched before adding to the liquid the soup will become cloudy.

(3) A good duck stock or a brown beef stock to which duck bones and giblets have been added may be used in place of whole duck.

(4) If the duck is not roasted until at least half cooked the amount of fat subsequently produced may give the soup a greasiness which will be difficult to remove and will require continuous boiling and skimming.

(5) Continuous skimming is necessary to avoid cloudiness as the impurities may cook back into the liquid.

(6) Once the meat and poultry have been removed after cooking they must be immediately cut into dice and retained in some of the cooking liquid. If this procedure is not followed at once the meat will dry out.

Service

Bortsch may be served in a soup tureen or in soup plates. It should be accompanied by the beetroot juice and sour cream in sauceboats together with the duck patties.

Assessment of the completed dish

(1) The soup should be hot.

(2) The colour should be a reddish amber similar to that of a consommé.

(3) The liquid part of the soup should be clear.

(4) The flavour should be a combination of beef, duck and vegetables — with a slight emphasis on that of duck.

(5) The surface of the soup should be free of fat.

(6) The garnish should be cut evenly to the appropriate size.

(7) The garnish should be in the correct proportion to the liquid — about one-third.

(8) The duck patties should be small in size (about the size of a 2p piece) and baked to a light golden colour.

(9) The beetroot juice should be strained free from sediment.

(10) The soured cream should be slightly thick in consistency and served chilled.

4.6 CONSOMME BRUNOISE

Prepare Basic Consommé (4.1) and add 100 g of cooked brunoise of vegetables (*see* Table 23 on p. 91).

4.7 CONSOMME CELESTINE

Prepare Basic Consommé (4.1) and add 100 g of savoury pancakes (*see Note* on p. 495) cut into strips approximately 4 cm × 1 cm.

4.8 CONSOMME JULIENNE

Prepare Basic Consommé (4.1) and add 100 g of mixed julienne of vegetables (*see* Table 23 on p. 91), approximately 4 cm in length.

Note

If the vegetable garnish (especially the celery) floats on the surface of the consommé then in all probability the vegetables are not cooked.

Assessment of the completed dish

(1) The consommé should be hot.

(2) It should be light amber in colour.

(3) It should have a high degree of clarity, being almost transparent.

(4) It should be *full bodied*, meaning that it has a slight viscosity.

(5) It should be full flavoured with a discreet combination of beef, vegetables and herb flavours.

(6) It should be correctly seasoned to bring out the maximum flavour.

(7) There should be no traces of fat on the surface.

(8) The garnish should be evenly cut into strips small enough to fit into the soup spoon.

(9) The ratio of different vegetables should be well balanced with no one single vegetable predominant.

(10) All the vegetables should be cooked to the correct degree.

4.9 CONSOMME MADRILENE

Prepare Basic Consommé (4.1) and add 300 g celery, 100 g tomato purée, 200 g fresh tomatoes and 100 g pimento at the initial clarification stage.

The finished consommé should be garnished with 50 g cooked vermicelli, 30 g shredded sorrel cooked in a little butter, 30 g peeled and pipped tomatoes cut into strips and 30 g peeled and pipped red pimento cut into small diamonds.

4.10 CONSOMME ROYALE

Prepare Basic Consommé (4.1) and garnish with 110 g of Savoury Egg Custard (*see* 10.117) cut into small diamond shapes.

4.11 TURTLE SOUP—TORTUE CLAIRE

Turtle soup is a slightly thickened consommé flavoured with an infusion of turtle herbs and garnished with small dice of turtle flesh. It is invariably served accompanied with cheese straws.

Makes: 2 litres. Cooking time: 45 minutes.

Quantity	*Ingredient*
2 l	Basic Consommé (4.1)
10 g	diluted arrowroot
1 pkt	turtle herbs
1 dl	dry sherry or madeira
100 g	turtle flesh (canned if necessary)
	seasoning of salt and pepper

Method

(1) Boil the consommé. Slightly thicken with diluted arrowroot and skim.

(2) Infuse the turtle herbs separately in a little consommé, then add to the main bulk.

(3) Pass through a muslin as for consommé.

(4) Complete with the wine. (Some may be retained for adding when the soup is served.)

(5) Add the garnish of canned turtle flesh cut into small squares.

Notes

(1) The quality of the finished soup will depend on the quality of the foundation consommé.

(2) The arrowroot must be diluted in cold water before adding.

(3) The consommé must be boiling when the arrowroot is added or lumps will occur.

(4) The correct degree of thickness is only slightly oily so that it covers the back of a spoon with a thin layer.

(5) The infusion of herbs must not be prolonged or the soup may become bitter and the flavours distorted.

BOUILLONS

A bouillon is an unclarified meat or poultry stock, or a combination of the two. It should be amber in colour and clear in appearance with a range of small shaped pieces of vegetables, beef and chicken served as part of the completed dish and added at different stages in the cooking process. (The principle of staggered commodity cooking referred to on p. 70 is used in the production of this type of soup.)

In classical cookery bouillons were cooked in an earthenware container known as a *marmite*. In modern commercial catering the

TABLE 2. INGREDIENTS FOR BOUILLON-TYPE SOUPS

Ingredient	*Croûte-au-pot*	*Pot-au-feu Petite marmite*
Chicken/beef consommé	Yes	Yes
Carrots	Turned	Paysanne
Turnips	Turned	Paysanne
Cabbage	Paysanne	Paysanne
Celery	Batons	Paysanne/julienne
Leek	Batons	Paysanne
Chicken	None	Dice/winglets
Beef	None	Dice
Bone marrow	Sliced/diced	Sliced/diced
Croûtes (served separately)	Yes	Yes
Parmesan cheese (served separately)	None	Yes

soup is transferred to individual or multi-sized marmites at the point of service.

The definition given above — based on classical cookery — suggests an unclarified stock. However, common trade practice (with very few exceptions) is to use instead a clarified consommé as the foundation.

An analysis of a number of cookery books highlights numerous contradictions regarding the ingredients of bouillon type soups. Those most commonly used are given in line with usual trade practice in Table 2.

4.12 PETITE MARMITE

Makes: 2 litres. Cooking time: 2 hours.

Quantity	*Ingredient*
2½ l	chicken and beef consommé (4.1)
400 g	very lean beef, blanched
150 g	celery (prepared and cut paysanne)
200 g	carrots (prepared and cut paysanne)
75 g	cabbage (prepared and cut paysanne)
100 g	leek (prepared and cut paysanne)
200 g	turnip (prepared and cut paysanne)
10	winglets of chicken, blanched with the bones removed and cut in two
10 slices	beef marrow
30	sliced and dried bread croûtes
50 g	grated Parmesan cheese
	seasoning of salt and pepper

Method

(1) Boil the consommé and add in the following order the beef, celery, carrots, cabbage, leek, winglets and turnips, permitting the soup to simmer and skimming continuously, according to the principles of staggered commodity cooking.

(2) Remove the beef when cooked; cool, then cut into approximately 1 cm dice and return to the soup.

(3) Remove all traces of fat from the surface of the soup, season to taste and correct the ratio of garnish to liquid.

(4) Serve in marmites, adding one slice of beef marrow per portion at the point of service, placing it on the surface of the soup.

Service

Should be served in individual or multi-portion earthenware marmites placed on an underdish. A standard portion should be approximately 2 dl per person. Bread croûtes and grated cheese should be served in separate sauceboats.

Assessment of the completed dish

(1) The soup should be hot.

(2) The colour should be amber and clear.

(3) The flavour should be of double strength consommé with a decisive taste. It should also be a combination of beef, chicken and vegetables in flavour with no one vegetable predominating.

(4) The beef should be cut into small even dice. The size of the vegetable garnish should be even in keeping with the soup, fitting easily into a soup spoon. The chicken winglets should have the point end removed and be cut across in two pieces with the bone removed.

(5) The beef marrow should be evenly sliced across and should not have disintegrated by overcooking; it should be added at the last moment.

(6) The croûtes should be thinly sliced so as to be almost translucent, then evenly coloured till a light golden brown and crisp.

(7) The Parmesan cheese should be finely grated.

Possible problem	*Possible cause and solution*
(1) Bouillon is cloudy	— poor quality consommé used; reclarify as for consommé (4.1). — not skimmed sufficiently; reclarify as for consommé (4.1). — bouillon overcooked; reclarify as for consommé (4.1). — bouillon allowed to boil rapidly; reclarify as for consommé (4.1). — bouillon covered with a lid during cooking; reclarify as for consommé (4.1).
(2) Vegetables overcooked	— to avoid this make sure that the vegetables are added in the order in which they will be cooked.

Note

See also 4.1 for problems associated with consommé which forms the basis for this type of soup.

POTAGES

A potage is a very good quality white stock thickened with a liaison of egg yolks and cream and completed with knobs of butter and the relevant garnish. The most well-known and popular soup in this category is Potage Germiny (frequently featured on menus simply as Germiny).

4.13 POTAGE GERMINY

The most difficult aspect of producing this soup is to thicken it to the consistency of double cream without making it curdle. A further problem is that following the traditional method of production the soup must be served immediately — this obviously does not lend itself readily to many catering situations.

The older word for the soup cook's stock was consommé, which has now come to mean a finished clear soup made by clarifying stock. Consommé can be used for making Potage Germiny and other soups of this kind, but this is strictly incorrect. It is obviously inefficient practice to clarify a soup only to cloud it by mixing in a liaison of egg yolks and cream.

Makes: 2 litres. Cooking time: 30 minutes.

Quantity	*Ingredient*	
1½ l	White Stock (chicken or veal and chicken — 3.1)	
12	egg yolks	liaison
3 dl	cream	liaison
50 g	butter	liaison
200 g	sorrel, shredded and stewed in the butter	garnish
50 g	butter	garnish
	chervil leaves	garnish
20	cheese straws	accompaniment

Method

(1) Boil the white stock, then remove from the heat to prevent any further boiling.

(2) Whisk in the liaison until the soup thickens slightly.

(3) Add small knobs of butter.

(4) Season to taste, correct consistency, add the garnish and serve.

Notes

(1) If the strained white stock is slightly thickened with diluted arrowroot (50 g), permitted to boil for a few minutes then strained

again and slightly cooled, the danger of curdling will be avoided when the liaison is added. The required degree of thickening will then be more easily achieved (which also makes it less expensive to produce and the holding quality of the soup will be greatly enhanced.

(2) Good quality chicken stock made in the usual way (*see* 3.1) is ideal for potages.

Service

May be served in a soup tureen, consommé cup or soup plate. A standard portion should be approximately 2 dl per person.

Assessment of the completed dish

(1) The soup should be as hot as possible without being curdled.
(2) The colour should be a light creamy yellow.
(3) The texture should be smooth, even and velvety — the consistency of double cream.
(4) The flavour should be delicate yet a distinctive combination of chicken and sorrel with a hint of chervil. It should be rather rich.
(5) The garnish should consist of evenly shredded sorrel and small blanched leaves of chervil.
(6) The accompaniment should consist of the correct number of cheese straws per person which should be even in length, a light gold in colour, crisp and with a light cheese flavour.

Possible problem	*Possible cause and solution*
(1) Soup has curdled	— soup allowed to boil once the liaison has been added; care must be taken not to allow the soup to boil as once curdled it cannot be rectified.
	— soup not allowed to cool sufficiently before adding the liaison; care must be taken to allow the soup to cool sufficiently as once curdled it cannot be rectified.
	— soup kept in a bain-marie at too high a temperature; care must be taken to avoid this as once curdled it cannot be rectified.
(2) Soup is dark	— poor quality stock used; care must be taken in the preparation of the stock as this cannot be rectified later.
	— if an aluminium pan has been used the bottom has been scraped with the whisk

Possible problem	*Possible cause and solution*
	when adding the liaison; care must be taken when adding the liaison to avoid this as it cannot be rectified later.
	— garnish has been overcooked — the sorrel has been allowed to colour when being stewed or the butter was too hot when the sorrel was added; care must be taken to avoid this as it cannot be rectified later.
(3) Soup is too thin	— insufficient liaison used for the amount of stock; add more liaison until the soup thickens to the correct consistency.
	— incorrect ratio of egg yolks and cream in the liaison; correct the balance by adding more yolks.
	— single cream used in the liaison; take care to use the correct ingredients as this cannot be rectified later.
	— liaison not allowed to thicken sufficiently; continue to cook until the soup thickens to the required degree

UNPASSED CLEAR VEGETABLE SOUPS

The vegetables for soups of this type are cut into various shapes, usually julienne or paysanne. As these soups are not passed to make into a purée, all the vegetables are cut properly before cooking.

Where potatoes are included in the recipe they are always added after the liquid. Fresh peas, beans and farinaceous ingredients are added at the later stages of the cooking process.

Clear vegetable soups may be served in a soup tureen or soup plate.

4.14 PEASANT SOUP — POTAGE PAYSANNE

Makes: 2 litres. Cooking time: 1 hour.

Quantity	*Ingredient*	
75 g	butter	
75 g	carrots	cut paysanne
75 g	turnips	cut paysanne
75 g	leek	cut paysanne
75 g	celery	cut paysanne
75 g	onion	cut paysanne
2 l	White Stock (3.1)	

Quantity	*Ingredient*
1	bouquet garni
50 g	french beans, cut into diamonds
50 g	peas
	chopped parsley
	seasoning of salt and pepper

Method

(1) Melt the butter in a deep saucepan and sweat the paysanne of vegetables.

(2) Add the stock, bring to the boil and skim.

(3) Add the bouquet garni and seasoning.

(4) Simmer gently until the vegetables are cooked (approximately 20 minutes).

(5) Add the french beans and peas; simmer for a further 15 minutes until they are cooked.

(6) Remove the bouquet garni and skim all traces of fat from the surface.

(7) Season to taste, add the parsley and check the ratio of ingredients to liquid.

Note

To test if cooked remove a selection of the vegetables with a perforated spoon and test for softness by squeezing between the fingers, paying special attention to those ingredients added in the later stages of making the soup.

Assessment of the completed dish

(1) Soup should be served as hot as possible.

(2) Liquid should be clear, white and free from traces of fat on the surface.

(3) Vegetables should be cut evenly to a size that will enable several to fit into the soup spoon.

(4) The flavour should be a combination of all vegetables, not taste predominantly of one.

(5) Seasoning should be such that it brings out the full flavour of all the ingredients.

(6) The correct ratio of vegetables to liquid should be one-third vegetables to two-thirds liquid.

(7) A standard portion should be approximately 2 dl per person.

Possible problem	*Possible cause and solution*
(1) Soup liquid is off-white in colour	— vegetables allowed to colour during sweating; care must be taken to avoid this as it cannot be rectified later.

Possible problem	Possible cause and solution
	— wrong colour stock used; ensure the correct ingredients are used as this cannot be rectified later. — butter allowed to turn brown after melting before adding the vegetables; take care to avoid this as it cannot be rectified later.
(2) Soup lacks flavour or the flavour is distorted	— vegetables not sweated correctly; care must be taken to follow the correct procedure when sweating the vegetables as this cannot be rectified later. — poor quality stock used; care must be taken in the preparation of the stock as this cannot be rectified later. — soup underseasoned; add more seasoning to taste. — incorrect proportions of vegetables giving rise to the dominance of one particular flavour; care must be taken when measuring out the ingredients as this cannot be rectified later.
(3) Soup liquid is cloudy	— poor quality stock used; care must be taken in the preparation of the stock as this cannot be rectified later. — soup has been allowed to boil rapidly causing the vegetables to mash; care must be taken to avoid this as it cannot be rectified later. — soup not skimmed during cooking; care must be taken to follow the correct procedures in the preparation of the soup as this cannot be rectified later.

4.15 MINESTRONE

Makes: 2 litres. Cooking time: 1 hour.

Quantity	*Ingredient*	
50 g	butter	
50 g	carrots	cut paysanne
50 g	turnips	cut paysanne
50 g	leek	cut paysanne
50 g	celery	cut paysanne
50 g	onion	cut paysanne
50 g	cabbage	cut paysanne
2 l	White Stock (3.1)	
25 g	tomato purée	

Quantity	*Ingredient*
50 g	potatoes cut paysanne
1	bouquet garni
50 g	spaghetti broken into 2 cm lengths
50 g	peas
50 g	french beans cut into diamonds
50 g	Tomato Concassée (8.169)
25 g	fat bacon
1 clove	garlic
	chopped parsley
	seasoning of salt and pepper
50 g	grated Parmesan cheese
30	croûtes de flûte

Method

(1) Melt the butter in a deep saucepan and sweat the paysanne of vegetables.

(2) Add the stock, bring to the boil and skim.

(3) Add the tomato purée, potatoes, bouquet garni and seasoning.

(4) Simmer gently for approximately 20 minutes.

(5) Add the french beans, peas, tomato concassée and spaghetti; simmer for a further 15 minutes until they are cooked.

(6) Remove the bouquet garni and skim all traces of fat from the surface.

(7) Make the fat bacon and garlic into a fine paste, add to the simmering soup in small pieces and cook until they have completely disintegrated.

(8) Complete the soup with the chopped parsley.

(9) Season to taste and check the ratio of ingredients to liquid.

(10) Serve grated Parmesan cheese and croûtes de flûte separately as accompaniments.

Note

The correct ratio of ingredients to liquid should be approximately two-thirds vegetables to one-third liquid.

4.16 COCK-A-LEEKIE

Makes: 2 litres. Cooking time: ¾ hour.

Quantity	*Ingredient*	
2 l	White Chicken Stock (3.1)	
75 g	butter	
450 g	white of leek	cut into
100 g	breast of boiled chicken	julienne
10	cooked prunes	strips
	seasoning of salt and pepper	

Method

(1) Melt the butter in a deep saucepan, add the strips of leek and sweat them.

(2) Add the stock, bring to the boil and skim.

(3) Add the strips of chicken and prunes.

(4) Season to taste and correct the ratio of garnish to liquid.

Note

The correct ratio of garnish to liquid should be approximately one-third garnish to two-thirds liquid.

4.17 LEEK AND POTATO SOUP — POTAGE POIREAU ET POMMES

Makes: 2 litres. Cooking time: 1 hour.

Quantity	*Ingredient*
75 g	butter
2½ l	White Chicken Stock (3.1)
450 g	white of leek } cut into paysanne
450 g	potatoes } cut into paysanne
1	bouquet garni
	seasoning of salt and pepper

Method

(1) Melt the butter in a deep saucepan, add the paysanne of leek and sweat them.

(2) Add the stock, bring to the boil and skim.

(3) Add the bouquet garni, paysanne of potatoes and seasoning.

(4) Simmer gently for approximately 15 minutes until the vegetables are cooked.

(5) Remove the bouquet garni and skim all traces of fat from the surface.

(6) Season to taste and check the ratio of ingredients to liquid.

Note

The correct ratio of ingredients to liquid should be approximately one-third vegetables to two-thirds liquid.

BROTH SOUPS

A broth soup is a brunoise of various kinds of vegetables cooked in a clear white mutton, chicken or game stock, with the addition of a cereal and a garnish of diced meat or poultry according to the type of broth. The type of stock used is indicated by the name of the broth being made, e.g. chicken broth is made with white chicken stock and mutton broth is made with white mutton stock. All vegetables for broth soups are cut brunoise, but may sometimes be a little larger. Any additional cereal garnish such as pearl barley or rice may be cooked separately and added to the broth at the completion stage. Some examples of broth soups are:

Chicken Broth	Scotch Broth
Mutton Broth	Game Broth

4.18 CHICKEN BROTH

Makes: 2 litres. Cooking time: 1 hour.

Quantity	*Ingredient*
2½ l	White Chicken Stock (3.1)
75 g	carrots } cut brunoise
75 g	turnips } cut brunoise
75 g	leek } cut brunoise
75 g	celery } cut brunoise
1	bouquet garni
40 g	washed patna rice
150 g	chicken flesh, boiled and diced
	seasoning of salt and pepper
	chopped parsley

Method

(1) Boil the stock, add the brunoise of vegetables, bouquet garni and seasoning.

(2) Gently simmer for about 15 minutes. Add the washed rice and skim as necessary.

(3) When all the vegetables and rice are cooked, remove the bouquet garni.

(4) Season to taste and correct the ratio of vegetables and cereal to stock; remove all traces of fat.

(5) Add the cooked chicken cut into small dice and remove any surface fat.

(6) Finish with the chopped parsley.

Notes

(1) The correct ratio of vegetables to stock should be one part vegetables to two parts liquid.

(2) If cereal is added to cook in the soup it must be blanched first.

Service

Broths may be served in a soup tureen or soup plate.

Assessment of the completed dish

(1) The soup must be hot.

(2) The liquid should be clear.

(3) There should be a light but distinctive flavour of chicken.

(4) There should be the correct ratio of vegetables to liquid.

(5) There should be no trace of surface fat.

(6) The soup should be sufficiently seasoned to bring out the full flavour of the ingredients.

(7) A standard portion should be approximately 2 dl per person.

Possible problem	*Possible cause and solution*
(1) Soup liquid is cloudy	— poor quality stock used; care must be taken in the preparation of the stock as this cannot later be rectified.
	— soup has been allowed to boil rapidly; care must be taken to avoid this as it cannot be rectified later.
	— soup not skimmed during cooking; care must be taken to follow the correct procedures during cooking as this cannot be rectified later.
	— unblanched cereal added; care must be taken to avoid adding unblanched cereal as this cannot be rectified later.
(2) Broth is too thick and therefore cloudy	— soup cooked too quickly causing a reduction in the cooking liquid; care must be taken to avoid this as it cannot be rectified later.
(3) Broth is dark	— poor quality stock used; care must be taken in the preparation of the stock as this cannot be rectified later.
	— soup not skimmed during cooking; care must be taken to follow the correct procedures during cooking as this cannot be rectified later.

PUREE SOUPS

Purée soups are made from a dry pulse or fresh vegetables cooked in a liquid then passed through a sieve, soup machine or liquidiser. Vegetables which contain a high level of starch will thicken by themselves; those with a low level of starch will require an additional thickening agent such as potatoes, potato flour or powder or rice.

Purée soups may be divided into two main categories:

(a) pulse vegetable based;

(b) fresh vegetable based.

Generally soups based on pulse vegetables are slightly coarser in texture than other purée soups.

Purée soups can also form the basis of cream and velouté type soups.

Purée soups are rarely garnished but are served with diced fried bread croûtons or toasted or dried bread sippets as an accompaniment.

4.19 BREAD SIPPETS

Remove the four crusts from the entire length of a loaf of bread. Cut across into very thin triangular shapes of approx. 6 mm across. Arrange them on a baking sheet taking care not to overlap them. Place in a hot cupboard or cool oven to dry out and colour slightly golden on each side.

Bread sippets may also be toasted under a salamander grill but because they are thin they will easily burn. If this method is used constant attention is required

4.20 DICED FRIED BREAD CROUTONS (for soup)

Remove the crusts from slices of bread and slice into 1 mm dice. Shallow fry in melted butter until they are golden. Drain off the fat as soon as the croûtons are coloured as they will continue to cook and colour even when removed from the heat.

Purée soups based on pulse vegetables

Pulse vegetables with an outer shell require soaking in cold water for approximately twelve hours before cooking; they are then washed in cold water in preparation for cooking. Those pulse vegetables such as split green peas and lentils with no outer shell do not require soaking before cooking as it may make them difficult to cook through.

Where the basic soup has a distinctive flavour as in the case of pulse vegetables (and certain fresh vegetables such as carrots and mixed vegetables), water may be used in place of stock. Water is considered by some to be preferable to stock for all vegetable soups as meat and poultry stock may distort the natural flavour of the vegetables.

The name of the soup is determined by the type of pulse vegetable used. In all cases the basic method is the same. For example:

Purée of Yellow Split Peas — Purée Egyptienne
Purée of Green Split Peas — Purée St Germain (or Potage St Germain)

Purée of White Haricot Beans — Purée Soissonaise (or Potage Soissonaise)

4.21 PUREE OF PULSE VEGETABLE SOUP

Makes: 2 litres. Cooking time: 2 hours.

Quantity	*Ingredient*
600 g	pulse vegetable
3 l	white stock or water
1	whole carrot
1	whole onion
150 g	bacon trimmings or ham bone
1	bouquet garni
	seasoning of salt and pepper
100 g	Diced Bread Croûtons (4.20)

Method

(1) Wash the pulse vegetable. (If it is one with an outer shell it should have previously been soaked in cold water.)

(2) Cover with stock or water.

(3) Bring to the boil and skim.

(4) Add the remainder of the ingredients and allow to simmer. The soup may be cooked in an oven with a lid on to ensure even cooking.

(5) When cooked, remove whole vegetables, bouquet garni and ham bone and discard.

(6) Purée the soup, reboil, season to taste and correct the consistency as necessary.

Notes

(1) If the liquid from cooking a ham is used then not more than a quarter of the total liquid content should consist of this; the remainder should be made up with water.

(2) Do not season a pulse soup that contains ham bones or ham liquid until it is nearly cooked.

(3) To test if cooked remove some of the pulse with a perforated spoon and rub between the fingers to a smooth paste. If it is slightly gritty it requires further cooking.

(4) Tomato purée may be added to purées made of lentils.

Service

May be served in a soup tureen or soup plate. Croûtons or sippets are served separately in a sauceboat.

Assessment of completed purée of green split pea soup (Purée St Germain or Potage St Germain)

(1) The soup should be hot.

(2) The colour should be that naturally produced by the peas. This may differ according to the quality of the peas and therefore need not be altered.

(3) The texture should be fine yet not too smooth.

(4) The flavour should be a mixture of peas with a slight hint of ham.

(5) The consistency should be slightly thicker than other types of soups such as creams and veloutés and cover the back of a spoon.

(6) A standard portion should be approximately 2 dl per person.

(7) The croûtons or sippets should be neatly cut and an even golden colour. If fried (as in the case of croûtons) there should be no trace of fat.

Possible problem	*Possible cause and solution*
(1) Soup has a gritty texture	— pulse was puréed before it was properly cooked (a very common fault); return the soup to the saucepan for further cooking. The addition of a small amount of cooking soda will help rectify this problem.
	— pulse with outer shells not soaked prior to cooking; return the soup to the saucepan for further cooking. The addition of a small amount of cooking soda will help rectify this problem.
	— liquid lost during cooking through absorption and evaporation not replaced so that some of the pulse, especially in the corners of the pan, does not cook thoroughly; return the soup to the saucepan for further cooking. The addition of a small amount of cooking soda will help rectify this problem.
(2) Soup lacks flavour	— lack of seasoning; add more seasoning to bring out the flavour of the pulse.
	— poor quality raw pulse; avoid using pulse that has been held in storage for prolonged periods as this cannot later be rectified.
	— ham bone or liquid from cooking a ham not included; care must be taken to include all the ingredients as this cannot be rectified later.

Possible problem	*Possible cause and solution*
	— pulse not sufficiently cooked; return the soup to the saucepan for further cooking. The addition of a small amount of cooking soda will help rectify this problem.
	— too much liquid used; care must be taken to avoid using too much liquid as this cannot be rectified later.
(3) Soup lacks volume	— ingredients have been undercooked; if the residue has not been discarded return it to the pan for further cooking.
	— soup has been poorly puréed; if the residue has not been discarded re-purée the soup.

Purée soups based on fresh vegetables

The name of the soup is determined by the main vegetable used, e.g. carrots, turnips, jerusalem artichokes, celery. For example:

Purée of Carrot Soup — Purée Crécy
Purée of Turnip Soup — Purée Freneuse
Purée of Mixed Vegetable Soup — Purée de Légumes

4.22 PUREE OF FRESH VEGETABLE SOUP

Makes: 2 litres. Cooking time: 1½ hours.

Quantity	*Ingredient*
100 g	butter
1 kg	roughly cut vegetables
2½ l	White Stock (3.1) or water
450 g	potatoes
1	bouquet garni
	seasoning of salt and pepper
100 g	Diced Bread Croûtons (4.20)

Method

(1) Melt the butter in a deep saucepan.
(2) Add all the vegetables and sweat them.
(3) Add the stock or water, bring to the boil and skim.
(4) Add the potatoes at this stage, the bouquet garni and seasoning.
(5) Allow to simmer until all the ingredients are cooked. (If other thickening agents are being used, they should be added at this stage.)
(6) Remove the bouquet garni.
(7) Purée the soup.
(8) Reboil, correct consistency, and season to taste.

Notes

(1) Other possible thickening agents are rice, potato flour and potato powder. Thickening agents, including potatoes if used, must not be added at the initial stewing stage.

(2) To test if cooked remove some of the vegetables with a perforated spoon and test for softness by squeezing between the fingers. If they are cooked they should not resist the pressure but form a pulp.

(3) If sweating the vegetables in order to extract their flavour and cook them is not carried out properly the flavour of the soup will be affected and prolonged cooking may be necessary.

(4) If the vegetables are not thoroughly cooked before puréeing, a very coarse texture and graining will result. It is possible to rectify this to some degree by passing the soup through a very fine strainer, though this will have a direct effect upon the volume reducing it considerably.

(5) When making a white purée soup with cauliflower, jerusalem artichokes, haricot beans, etc., the colour will be affected if it is cooked in an aluminium pan. The soup may become grey in colour and the flavour distorted.

(6) The degree of fineness of the sieve or soup machine will affect the texture of the soup. This can be rectified by passing the soup through a fine conical strainer a second time, but there may be a loss of volume, especially where only a small quantity is being made.

4.23 PUREE OF LEEK AND POTATO SOUP—POTAGE PARMENTIER

Makes: 2 litres. Cooking time: 1½ hours.

Quantity	*Ingredient*
100 g	butter
150 g	white leek } sliced
100 g	onions } sliced
2½ l	White Stock (3.1) or water
750 g	roughly cut potatoes
1	bouquet garni
	seasoning of salt and pepper

Method

Prepare as for Purée of Fresh Vegetable Soup (4.22).

CREAM AND VELOUTE SOUPS

There are four different methods of preparing cream soups, each reflecting traditional cooking methods, but there is one aspect common to them all — the finishing. At the point of service the soup is completed with cream and (optionally) butter.

Most soups described as creams may also be made as veloutés and are generally prepared in the same way, the only difference being the liaison added at the end; for velouté soup this consists of egg yolks mixed lightly with cream and knobs of butter. The only other variation encountered is when adding a béchamel to make a cream soup (*see* 4.24); this should be replaced by a basic velouté sauce when preparing a velouté soup.

NOTE

Garnished cream and velouté soups are by tradition served only at dinner, although this principle now appears to be out of fashion. It is true to say, however, that the more expensive and elaborate soups are more appropriate for dinner than for lunch.

The four methods of making cream soup are as follows.

(a) Under this method the vegetables are first sweated in butter to which flour is then added to form a roux. White stock is added and the soup is cooked, puréed and then completed with cream.

(b) Under this method a purée type soup is prepared with the addition of béchamel and white stock which is then completed with cream.

(c) Under this method a second stage roux is prepared with the addition of white stock to make a velouté which is then completed with cream.

(d) Under this method the basic ingredients are cooked in a prepared velouté, then passed and finished with cream.

First method

4.24 CREAM OF CARROT SOUP — CREME CRECY

Makes: 2 litres. Cooking time: 1½ hours.

Quantity	*Ingredient*
100 g	butter
1 kg	sliced carrots
100 g	sliced onions
100 g	flour
2½ l	White Stock (3.1)
1	bouquet garni
	seasoning of salt and pepper
2 dl	cream
50 g	butter

Method

(1) Melt the butter in a deep pan.
(2) Add and sweat the vegetables.
(3) Add the flour to make a roux.
(4) Add the stock, mixing it into the roux.
(5) Bring to the boil, add seasoning and bouquet garni.
(6) Cook for the prescribed time by gentle simmering.
(7) When the vegetables are cooked, remove the bouquet garni and pass the soup through a sieve, soup machine or liquidiser.
(8) Reboil the soup and correct the consistency, and season to taste; a finer texture may be obtained by passing through a fine strainer with the aid of a ladle.
(9) Finish the soup with the cream and the butter.

Note

This soup may also be served as Velouté Crécy by finishing with the appropriate liaison of egg yolks, cream and butter.

Service

Cream soups may be served in a soup tureen, consommé cup or a soup plate. Cold cream soup is served in a chilled consommé cup. It should be remembered that soup becomes thicker when cold so needs to be of a thin consistency before chilling.

Assessment of the completed dish

(1) The soup is hot or chilled as the case may be.
(2) In colour the soup should in general be close to that of the main vegetable — in this case carrots. This applies to most vegetable cream soups, with the exception of white vegetables such as cauliflower, jerusalem artichoke or turnip.
(3) The smoothness is the main characteristic of this type of soup — it should be creamy.
(4) The flavour should be delicate but easily identifiable as that of carrots.
(5) In consistency the soup should be similar to single cream, just coating the back of a spoon.
(6) The seasoning should be sufficient to enhance the full flavour of the soup.
(7) A standard portion should be approximately 2 dl per person.

Possible problem	*Possible cause and solution*
(1) Soup does not have the correct flavour	— poor quality stock used; care must be taken when preparing the stock as distorted flavour because of poor stock cannot be rectified later.
	— incorrect type of fat used to sweat the vegetables; lard or dripping must not be used as the soup will acquire their characteristic taste and cannot be rectified.
(2) Soup is dark	— dripping used instead of butter to sweat the vegetables; if dripping is used the dark colour cannot be rectified.
	— poor quality stock used; care must be taken when preparing the stock as a dark colour as a result of poor stock cannot be rectified.
	— vegetables oversweated and allowed to colour; care must be taken to avoid this as it cannot be rectified later.
	— roux overcooked; care must be taken in the preparation of the roux as overcooked roux cannot be rectified.
	— too little cream added in proportion to the quantity of soup; add a little more cream to lighten the colour.
	— retained for too long in a bain-marie; prepare the soup nearer to the time it is required as this cannot be rectified.
	— aluminium pan used; avoid aluminium utensils as their effect on the soup cannot be rectified.
(3) Excess fat rises to the surface whilst cooking or storing in a bain-marie	— too much fat used in proportion to the flour; simmer and skim off the fat with a ladle.
	— soup overcooked; skim off the fat with a ladle.
	— butter added too soon at the completion stage; skim off the fat with a ladle or soak it up with kitchen paper.
	— soup allowed to boil once the cream and butter have been added; skim off the fat with a ladle.
(4) Soup is curdled	— unsound cream used; care must be taken to use fresh cream as soup which curdles because of the cream cannot be rectified.

Possible problem	*Possible cause and solution*
	— retained too long in a hot bain-marie or water in bain-marie allowed to boil; care must be taken in this respect as soup which curdles cannot be rectified.
(5) Soup is gritty	— vegetables were not sufficiently sweated and were partially uncooked; care must be taken when sweating the vegetables to ensure that they are cooked as a gritty texture cannot be rectified later.

Second method

All the vegetables referred to in the section on purée soups are suitable as a basis for this method of producing a cream soup.

4.25 CREAM OF VEGETABLE SOUP — CREME DE LEGUMES

Makes: 2 litres. Cooking time: 1¼ hours.

Quantity	*Ingredient*
7 dl	Purée Soup (4.21 or 22)
7 dl	Béchamel (3.4)
7 dl	White Stock (3.1)
2 dl	cream

Method

(1) Produce a purée of vegetable soup. When cooked add the béchamel.

(2) Purée the soup again by passing through a sieve, soup machine or liquidiser.

(3) Return to the pan, reboil and thin as necessary with white stock; season to taste.

(4) Finish the soup with the cream and required garnish.

Note

The béchamel should be added just before passing the soup.

Third method

4.26 CREAM OF CHICKEN SOUP — CREME DE VOLAILLE

Makes: 2 litres. Cooking time: 1½ hours.

Quantity	*Ingredient*
120 g	butter
120 g	flour
2 l	White Chicken Stock (3.1)
2 dl	cream
50 g	butter

Method

(1) Melt the butter in a pan.
(2) Add the flour, cook to a second stage roux and allow to cool.
(3) Add the white stock and simmer gently for 1 hour.
(4) Pass through a conical strainer into a clean saucepan.
(5) Reboil, correct consistency and season to taste and remove from heat.
(6) Finish the soup with the cream and the required garnish.

Fourth method

Some examples of cream soups made using this method are:

Cream of Asparagus Soup	—	Crème d'Asperges (or Crème Argenteuil)
Cream of Cauliflower Soup	—	Crème Dubarry
Cream of Celery Soup	—	Crème de Céleri
Cream of Mushroom Soup	—	Crème de Champignons

4.27 CREAM OF CAULIFLOWER SOUP — CREME DUBARRY

Makes: 2 litres. Cooking time: 1½ hours.

Quantity	*Ingredient*
120 g	butter
120 g	flour
2½ l	White Chicken Stock (3.1)
1 kg	cauliflower
	seasoning of salt and pepper
2 dl	cream
50 g	butter

Method

(1) Melt the butter in a pan.
(2) Add the flour, cook to a second stage roux and allow to cool.
(3) Add the white stock and allow to simmer.
(4) Set aside 100 g of florets of cauliflower for garnishing, blanch the remainder, add to the soup and season.
(5) Cook the florets of cauliflower in salted water, refresh and retain in a basin of cold water until required.
(6) When the soup has cooked for about 1 hour test that the cauliflower is done.
(7) Pass through a fine sieve, soup machine or liquidiser.
(8) Reboil, correct the seasoning, consistency, and season to taste; add the florets of cauliflower.
(9) Finish the soup with the cream and butter.

Note

This soup may also be served as Velouté Dubarry by finishing with the appropriate liaison of egg yolks, cream and butter.

4.28 CREAM OF MUSHROOM SOUP — CREME DE CHAMPIGNONS

When making cream of mushroom soup it is advisable if the mushrooms are rather dark to add a purée of raw mushrooms at a later stage than indicated in the general method outlined above to avoid a soup that is dark in colour.

The garnish consists of mushrooms cut into either slices or julienne, cooked in a liquor made up of water, lemon juice, butter and salt (*see* 8.91).

Note

This soup may be served as Velouté aux Champignons by finishing with the appropriate liaison of egg yolks, cream and butter.

Cream and velouté soup extensions

4.29 CREME AMBASSADEUR

Prepare 2 l cream of pea soup. Garnish with 50 g cooked rice, 50 g shredded lettuce and 50 g shredded sorrel cooked in butter. To serve as Velouté Ambassadeur finish with the appropriate liaison of egg yolks, cream and butter.

4.30 CREAM OF ASPARAGUS — CREME D'ASPERGES (CREME ARGENTEUIL)

Prepare 2 l cream of asparagus soup. Garnish with 100 g sprue cut into 5 mm lengths. To serve as Velouté d'Asperges (Velouté Argenteuil) finish with the appropriate liaison of egg yolks, cream and butter.

4.31 CREME CAMELIA

Prepare 2 l cream of pea soup. Garnish with 75 g julienne breast of chicken and 75 g julienne white of leek cooked in butter. To serve as Velouté Camelia finish with the appropriate liaison of egg yolks, cream and butter.

4.32 CREME CHOISEUL

Prepare 2 l cream of lentil soup. Garnish with 75 g shredded sorrel cooked in butter and 50 g rice. To serve as Velouté Choiseul finish with the appropriate liaison of egg yolks, cream and butter.

4.33 CREME CRESSONIERE

Prepare 2 l Purée of Leek and Potato Soup (4.23) adding the washed stalks of two bunches of watercress at stage 1. Garnish with blanched watercress leaves. To serve as Velouté Cressonière finish with the appropriate liaison of egg yolks, cream and butter.

4.34 CREME FONTANGES

Prepare 2 l cream of green pea soup. Garnish with 75 g shredded sorrel cooked in butter and 25 g pluches of chervil. To serve as Velouté Fontanges finish with the appropriate liaison of egg yolks, cream and butter.

4.35 CREME LAMBALLE

Prepare 2 l cream of pea soup. Garnish with 100 g cooked tapioca. To serve as Velouté Lamballe finish with the appropriate liaison of egg yolks, cream and butter.

4.36 CREME LONGCHAMPS

Prepare 2 l cream of pea soup. Garnish with 75 g cooked broken vermicelli, 50 g shredded sorrel cooked in butter and 25 g pluches of chervil. To serve as Velouté Longchamps finish with the appropriate liaison of egg yolks, cream and butter.

4.37 CREME REINE

Prepare 2 l cream of chicken soup. Garnish with 50 g cooked rice and 75 g breast of chicken cut into small dice. To serve as Velouté Reine finish with the appropriate liaison of egg yolks, cream and butter.

4.38 CREME WASHINGTON

Prepare 2 l cream of maize soup. Garnish with 75 g cooked grains of maize. To serve as Velouté Washington finish with the appropriate liaison of egg yolks, cream and butter.

4.39 VELOUTE AGNES SOREL

Prepare 2 l chicken velouté. Garnish with 75 g cooked julienne of button mushrooms, 50 g julienne of tongue and 50 g julienne breast of chicken. Complete with a liaison of egg yolks, cream and butter.

4.40 *VELOUTE DAME BLANCHE*

Prepare 2 l cream of chicken soup. Garnish with 75 g breast of chicken cut into small dice. Complete with a liaison of egg yolks, cream and butter.

4.41 *VICHYSOISSE*

Prepare 2 l Purée of Leek and Potato Soup (4.23). Garnish with 100 g chopped chives. Complete with a liaison of cream and butter.

Note

This soup may be served hot or chilled.

FAWN AND BROWN ROUX-BASED SOUPS

Some examples of these types of soups are as follows:

Fawn roux-based:	Tomato soup
	Mulligatawny soup
Brown roux-based:	Thick oxtail soup
	Kidney soup
	Mock turtle soup

Fawn roux-based soups

4.42 *TOMATO SOUP — CREME DE TOMATE*

This is a tomato flavoured and coloured passed soup which is based upon a second stage roux, sweated vegetables, herbs, bacon trimmings and white stock, to which a reduction of vinegar and sugar are added. The soup is completed with cream at the point of service.

Variations of tomato soup are Crème Malakoff (4.43) and Crème Portugaise (4.44).

Makes: 2 litres. Cooking time: 1 hour.

Quantity	*Ingredient*
100 g	butter
150 g	carrots } cut roughly
150 g	onions } cut roughly
100 g	celery } cut roughly
100 g	bacon trimmings
1 clove	garlic
1 sprig	thyme
1	bayleaf
130 g	flour
150 g	tomato purée

Quantity	*Ingredient*
2½ l	White Stock (3.1)
	seasoning
2 dl	cream
1 dl	vinegar } reduction
30 g	sugar } reduction

Method

(1) Melt the butter in a thick bottomed saucepan.

(2) Add the vegetables, herbs, bacon trimmings and garlic; gently fry until a light golden colour.

(3) Add the flour and stir with a wooden spatule until a roux is formed. Cook until the texture and colour of a second stage roux.

(4) Add the tomato purée; cool slightly and add the boiling white stock.

(5) Simmer for the prescribed time, skimming as necessary.

(6) When cooked, taste the soup and add the required amount of vinegar and sugar reduction in order to adjust the degree of tartness.

(7) Pass the soup through a conical strainer and reboil.

(8) Correct and adjust the seasoning, colour and consistency.

(9) Complete the soup at the very last moment before serving with cream or cream and knobs of butter.

Assessment of the completed dish

(1) The colour should be a natural shade of tomato.

(2) The consistency should be such that it just coats the back of a spoon, similar to that of single cream.

(3) The flavour should be slightly sweet of tomatoes, herbs and bacon.

(4) The texture should be smooth.

Possible problem	*Possible cause and solution*
(1) Soup burns whilst cooking	— soup is too thick because of excess flour or insufficient stock; care must be taken to measure out the exact amount of flour and stock to avoid making the soup too thick as a burnt soup cannot be rectified.
(2) Soup has an acid flavour	— too much tomato purée added; add more reduction of vinegar and sugar.
(3) Soup is gluey in texture	— soup undercooked; dilute with a little stock and continue to cook for the prescribed time.

Possible problem	*Possible cause and solution*
(4) Soup is rather pale	— insufficient tomato purée added; if cream has already been added this cannot be rectified, but note, however, that the addition of cream will lighten the colour of the soup.

4.43 CREME MALAKOFF

Consists of half final volume of Tomato Soup (4.42) and half final volume of potato soup garnished with shredded spinach or sorrel cooked in butter.

4.44 CREME PORTUGAISE

Consists of cream of Tomato Soup (4.42) garnished with Tomato Concassée (8.169) and plain boiled long grain rice.

4.45 FRENCH ONION SOUP — SOUPE A L'OIGNON GRATINEE

Makes: 2 litres. Cooking time: 1 hour.

Quantity	*Ingredient*
50 g	butter
750 g	sliced onions
30 g	flour
2 l	Brown Stock (3.1)
50	croûtes de flûte
100 g	grated Parmesan and Gruyère cheese

Method

(1) Melt the butter in a deep saucepan. Add the sliced onions and sweat, then allow them to lightly colour golden brown by removing the lid.

(2) Add the flour, cook to a second stage roux and allow to cool.

(3) Add the brown stock and allow to simmer gently for approximately 30 minutes until the onions are cooked. Season to taste.

(4) Ladle the soup into earthenware soup bowls (marmites) and layer the surface of the soup with dried toasted slices of bread (croûtes de flûte). Sprinkle with the grated cheeses and place under a salamander grill until a golden skin is formed.

4.46 MULLIGATAWNY SOUP

Makes: 2 litres. Cooking time: 1½ hours.

Quantity	*Ingredient*	
100 g	butter	
400 g	sliced onions	
50 g	curry powder	
100 g	flour	
30 g	tomato purée	
2½ l	White Stock (3.1)	
1 clove	garlic	
1	bouquet garni	
30 g	finely chopped chutney	
50 g	finely diced apple	
50 g	Patna Rice (5.53)	garnish
2 dl	cream (optional)	

Method

(1) Melt the butter in a deep saucepan, add the sliced onions and lightly colour.

(2) Add the flour and curry powder to make a second stage roux, and then the tomato purée; allow to cool slightly.

(3) Add the stock and allow to boil; skim, then add the remainder of the ingredients. Allow to simmer gently for approximately 45 minutes skimming as and when necessary.

(4) Strain the soup through a conical strainer or sieve, or liquidise to use all the ingredients.

(5) Reboil the soup and correct the consistency; season to taste.

(6) Garnish with previously boiled and drained patna rice.

(7) Complete, if required, at the last moment with cream.

Service

This type of soup may be served in a soup tureen or soup plate.

Assessment of the completed dish

(1) The soup should be hot.

(2) The colour should be a reddish-brown to yellow ochre. If cream is added the colour will be lighter.

(3) The texture depends upon the method used for straining, a sieve or liquidiser generally giving a smooth creamy finish.

(4) The flavour should be of curry with a slight hint of tomato, but not too sweet. A special characteristic of this soup is that the curry flavour touches the back of the throat but does not burn.

(5) The garnish of rice should not be overcooked and should be in the correct proportion to the rest of the soup.

(6) A standard portion should be approximately 2 dl per person.

Brown roux-based soup

The following lists some of the problems and likely causes to be found in association with any brown roux-based soup.

Possible problem	*Possible cause and solution*
(1) Soup lacks flavour	— poor quality stock used; care must be taken in the preparation of the basic stock as lack of flavour due to poor quality stock cannot be rectified, though the addition of a little meat glaze may help.
	— vegetables insufficiently coloured; care must be taken to colour the vegetables sufficiently so that they impart their flavour otherwise the flavour cannot be rectified, though the addition of a little meat glaze may help.
	— insufficient vegetables and herbs; care must be taken to add the correct amounts of vegetables and herbs as lack of flavour on this account cannot be rectified, though the addition of a little meat glaze may help.
	— roux undercooked; care must be taken in the preparation of the roux as lack of flavour on this account cannot be rectified later, though the addition of a little meat glaze may help.
	— soup underseasoned; add a little more seasoning to taste.
	— soup not cooked for long enough; continue to cook for the prescribed time.
(2) Soup is pale	— roux not sufficiently cooked; add a little gravy browning and tomato purée.
	— vegetables not sufficiently coloured; add a little gravy browning and tomato purée.
(3) Soup is bitter or dark	— roux overcooked; care must be taken in the preparation of the roux as a bitter flavour or dark colour on this account cannot be rectified.
	— vegetables were burnt during colouring; care must be taken when colouring the vegetables as a bitter flavour or dark colour on this account cannot be rectified later.

Possible problem	*Possible cause and solution*
	— poor quality basic stock; care must be taken in the preparation of the stock as a bitter flavour or dark colour on this account cannot be rectified later.
(4) Soup is greasy	— incorrect ratio of flour to fat in the roux making it too soft; boil the soup and skim off the fat.
	— soup not skimmed sufficiently; boil the soup and skim off the fat.

4.47 MOCK TURTLE SOUP — POTAGE FAUSSE TORTUE

Makes: 2 litres. Cooking time: 1½ hours.

Quantity	*Ingredient*
100 g	dripping
120 g	flour
30 g	tomato purée
2½ l	Brown Stock (3.1)
200 g	onions } roughly cut
200 g	carrots } roughly cut
100 g	celery } roughly cut
½	boned calf's head
1 pkt	turtle herbs
1 dl	dry sherry

Method

(1) Heat the dripping; add the flour and cook to a third stage roux. Add the tomato purée and allow to cool.

(2) Add the hot brown stock a little at a time, mixing well to prevent lumps forming.

(3) Lightly fry and colour the vegetables, drain and add to the soup; add the boned calf's head and permit the soup to simmer gently for the prescribed time, skimming the soup as necessary.

(4) Infuse the turtle herbs with some of the brown stock.

(5) When the calf's head is cooked, remove from the soup, cool and cut into small dice. Retain in stock until required for garnishing the soup at the point of service.

(6) Pass the soup through a fine strainer with the aid of a ladle; reboil, skim and add the infusion of turtle herbs, sherry and diced calf's head.

(7) Correct the seasoning, colour, flavouring and consistency.

4.48 KIDNEY SOUP — SOUPE AUX ROGNONS

Proceed as for Mock Turtle Soup (4.47) substituting for the turtle herbs and boned calf's head 500 g minced and fried ox kidney. Once the soup has cooked and has been passed garnish with 150 g ox kidney cut into dice, lightly fried and drained. Finish with sherry.

4.49 THICK OXTAIL SOUP — POTAGE QUEUE DE BOEUF LIE

Proceed as for Mock Turtle Soup (4.47) substituting for the turtle herbs and boned calf's head 1½ kg oxtail ends lightly fried in dripping and drained. Allow to simmer for approximately 2 hours. When the soup is cooked remove the oxtail flesh and cut into small squares for garnishing. Pass the soup through a fine strainer, reboil and garnish with 100 g small balls of carrot and turnip (previously cooked in salt water) and the pieces of oxtail flesh. Complete the soup when serving with ½ dl sherry.

SHELLFISH SOUPS

Shellfish soups or bisques are smooth, thickened with a roux or with rice and completed at the point of service with brandy, cream and knobs of butter. They are usually referred to as bisques. The name of the soup is determined by the type of shellfish used, i.e. lobster bisque, shrimp bisque, crab bisque, and so on.

Due to the high cost of shellfish an alternative method to the classical recipe given first below is frequently used (*see* 4.51).

4.50 TRADITIONAL SHELLFISH SOUP RECIPE

Makes: 2 litres. Cooking time: 45 minutes.

Quantity	*Ingredient*
75 g	butter, or
1 dl	oil
750 g	prepared shellfish
100 g	carrots } roughly cut
100 g	onions } roughly cut
50 g	celery } roughly cut
	parsley stalks
1 sprig	thyme
1	bayleaf
½ dl	brandy
2 l	Fish Stock (3.2)
2 dl	white wine
50 g	tomato purée
150 g	ground rice
	seasoning of salt and pepper
50 g	butter
1 dl	cream

Method

(1) Heat the butter or oil in a shallow pan, add the shellfish, vegetables and herbs and allow the shellfish to colour; cover with a lid and allow ingredients to cook in their own juices.

(2) Flambé with the brandy.

(3) Add the fish stock, white wine and tomato purée and allow to simmer for the prescribed time.

(4) Remove the shells from the fish and reserve some of the flesh for garnishing the soup. Crush the shells of the remainder of the fish and return to the cooking liquid; add the rice and cook for a further 15 minutes.

(5) Pass the soup through a coarse strainer, then through a fine strainer into a pan and reboil.

(6) Complete the soup with knobs of butter, cream and brandy and the garnish of diced shellfish.

(7) Correct the colour, seasoning, consistency, degree of smoothness if necessary, and temperature.

Note

During the initial cooking of the shellfish, vegetables and herbs in their own juices some light frying and coloration of the vegetables is acceptable.

4.51 LOBSTER BISQUE — BISQUE DE HOMARD (based on current trade practice)

Makes: 2 litres. Cooking time: 1½ hours.

Quantity	*Ingredient*
1 dl	oil
100 g	carrots } roughly cut
100 g	onions } roughly cut
50 g	celery } roughly cut
	parsley stalks
1 sprig	thyme
1	bayleaf
2 kg	crushed lobster shells
1 l	Fish Stock (3.2)
50 g	tomato purée
1½ l	fish or veal velouté
	seasoning of salt and pepper
50 g	butter
1 dl	cream
½ dl	brandy
100 g	diced cooked lobster to garnish

Method

(1) Heat the oil in a shallow pan; add and lightly colour the

vegetables with the herbs.

(2) Add the crushed lobster shells and lightly cook.

(3) Add the fish stock and tomato purée and allow to simmer for about 1 hour.

(4) Strain the cooking liquid into another saucepan and boil to reduce to about half the quantity.

(5) Whisk in the velouté and continue cooking for a further 5–10 minutes.

(6) Pass the soup through a fine strainer; reboil, remove from the heat and adjust the thickness and seasoning.

(7) Complete the soup with the cream, knobs of butter, brandy and the garnish of diced lobster.

Note

When whisking in the velouté, if it is considered that the soup will be too pale in colour after adding the cream, extra tomato purée may be added.

Service

Bisques may be served in a soup tureen or soup plate.

Assessment of the completed dish

(1) The soup should be hot.

(2) The colour should be a light pale pink to red.

(3) The texture can either be coarse like a purée soup, or very smooth and velvety.

(4) This is a very richly flavoured soup; there should be a blend of the lobster and herbs with an awareness of the brandy.

(5) The consistency should be similar to that of single cream well able to coat the back of a spoon.

(6) The garnish should be neatly cut into dice, moist but not stringy through overcooking.

(7) A standard portion should be approximately 2 dl per person.

Possible problem	*Possible cause and solution*
(1) Soup has a burnt flavour	— vegetables have been burnt when being sweated in the initial stages; care must be taken to avoid this as the burnt flavour may be passed through to the finished soup and cannot be rectified.
	— when being reboiled the soup has stuck to the bottom of the pan and burnt; great care

Possible problem	*Possible cause and solution*
	must be taken at this stage when the soup is in a purée state and most likely to burn as the flavour cannot be rectified.
	— the soup is also likely to burn during the second stage of preparation when the lobster has been crushed and returned with the rice, especially if the soup is particularly thick; great care must also be taken at this stage as the burnt flavour cannot be rectified later.
(2) Soup is too thin	— too much stock added; thicken with some lobster butter, more velouté sauce or a little beurre manié.
	— insufficient thickening agent such as rice used; thicken with some lobster butter, some more velouté sauce or a little beurre manié.
(3) Soup is too thick	— soup has been cooked rapidly causing the liquid to reduce excessively; thin with additional white stock, white wine or a combination of the two.
	— too much thickening agent used; thin with additional white stock, white wine or a combination of the two.

NOUVELLE CUISINE

Many of the recipes, principles and practices outlined in this chapter are in accord with this style of cookery. There are, however, the following exceptions:

(a) creams, veloutés, fawn roux-based and brown roux-based soups may not be used as they are all based upon roux or flour thickenings.

(b) Soups are made to order therefore the traditional method of holding them once cooked in a bain-marie of heated water or steam is no longer necessary.

(c) Soups are made from stocks previously prepared.

Bouillons, consommés, broths, potages and bisques may be used as foundations. Creams and veloutés may be made but without a roux or flour base, generally by the addition of the respective liaison to a purée of either meat, poultry, vegetables or fish.

4.52 MUSSEL AND CREAM SOUP

Makes: 10 portions. Cooking time: 30 minutes.

Quantity	Ingredient
1 kg	live mussels, washed and scraped
15 g	chopped shallot
60 g	roughly chopped onion
6 dl	dry white wine
50 g	butter
5 g	parsley stalks
1	bayleaf
1	sprig thyme
	seasoning of salt, freshly ground black pepper and cayenne pepper
8 dl	double cream
6	egg yolks, lightly beaten

Method

(1) Place the mussels into a deep sided pan with the shallots, onion, dry white wine, butter, parsley stalks, bayleaf, thyme and seasonings.

(2) Cover with a lid and bring to the boil. Simmer gently for 8–10 minutes — when cooked the shells will open.

(3) Strain the liquid through a muslin cloth into a clean pan.

(4) Remove the mussels from their shells and beard and set aside in a little of the strained liquid for use as the garnish. Discard any that fail to open.

(5) Bring the remainder of the strained liquid to the boil. Add the cream, reboil and remove from the heat.

(6) Whisk some of the cream liquid onto the egg yolks and add to the saucepan of mussel and cream liquid.

(7) Reheat but do not boil, allowing the soup to slightly thicken.

(8) Season to taste. Serve garnished with the mussels, allowing them to heat through before serving.

Note

This soup may also be served chilled.

4.53 CHILLED WATERCRESS SOUP WITH WHITE GRAPES

Prepare Crème Cressonière as in 4.33. Serve chilled in soup cups with a circle of unsweetened whipped cream on top. Garnish each portion with 3 peeled, pipped and halved white grapes and 3 blanched watercress leaves.

CONVENIENCE SOUPS

A wide variety of soups are available in convenience form — they may be powdered, canned, frozen, boil-in-the-bag or even purchased freshly made. They may be classified in exactly the same way as fresh soups, though the finished product may well have been produced by a totally different method. Any instructions given by the manufacturer for the production of these items, however, should be followed.

Convenience soups may, of course, be served to the customer just as they are with no further preparation, or they may be combined with fresh soup at the discretion of the caterer. Additional garnishes may be included, such as cooked julienne of vegetables, small dice of cooked chicken or previously cooked cereals such as rice or pearl barley. All these will add variety, texture and colour. Bread sippets and croûtons may also be used to accompany convenience soups in exactly the same way as they would accompany freshly prepared soup.

Any type of convenience soup may be adjusted for consistency, seasoning and colour. Purée and cream type convenience soups may be finished with liaisons of cream or egg yolks and cream just as freshly prepared soups are. Freshly chopped parsley and diced cooked meat or poultry added at the point of service will enhance what might otherwise be an ordinary convenience broth type soup. Thick brown convenience soups may be completed with a freshly cooked garnish of vegetables and herbs, and in some instances a fortified wine such as sherry or madeira may also be added to enhance the flavour. Bisques may be finished at the last moment with brandy, cream and small pieces of freshly cooked shellfish in keeping with the name of the soup to give the impression of care and forethought.

Convenience soups are infinitely more complex in nature and variety than may at first be realised. The experience and expertise of the professional chef, his care, judgment and pride in the dish to be served are just as important whether the soup is made from wholly fresh commodities, comes out of a packet or is a combination of the two.

CHAPTER FIVE

Egg, Farinaceous and Rice Dishes

EGG DISHES

One factor which differentiates the cooking of eggs from cooking most other commodities is the short space of time between the point when the eggs are cooked to the peak of perfection and when they are almost inedible because they have been overcooked. The decision as to whether they are cooked to the required degree must be made in a matter of seconds rather than minutes. The holding time — the period between when the dish is cooked and when it is consumed — must always be taken into consideration. Unlike some other foods, eggs continue to cook when removed from the heat and are very susceptible even to low levels of heat such as a warmed plate.

There are four main ways to cook eggs.

(a) Poaching. This is cooking eggs without their shells in water so as to set the white around the yolk which should remain soft. The term also covers oeufs en cocotte which are eggs cooked in a special earthenware mould with various garnishes.

(b) Boiling. This is cooking eggs in their shells for varying lengths of time: 2–3 minutes for soft boiled served in the shell; 5–7 minutes for soft centred eggs to be shelled for further use; and 10 minutes for hard boiled eggs.

(c) Shallow frying. This is cooking eggs in a small amount of fat. The term also covers the making of omelettes.

(d) Scrambled. This is cooking beaten eggs until almost set with the addition of butter and cream.

The following points should be borne in mind when cooking eggs.

(a) When making any egg dish, it is advisable for a better result to use eggs at room temperature.

(b) Never allow cooked eggs to remain in direct contact with metal dishes or containers for any length of time. Although some methods imply that the eggs are to be cooked in a metal vessel, to leave them in such receptacles once cooked will result in discoloration.

(c) Due consideration needs to be given to poached egg dishes that are completed with a sauce coating, especially lightly

gratinated dishes as the eggs will continue to cook under the direct heat of the salamander grill.

(d) All loose particles of cooked egg white should be removed once the egg is poached.

(e) Garnishes should be hot and served in suitable quantity as if accompaniments.

Retention of cooked eggs

(a) Eggs that have been poached may be kept in a basin of cold water.

(b) Omelettes and scrambled eggs must be served immediately as they become rubbery and hard if kept for any length of time.

(c) Soft and hard boiled eggs may be retained in cold water. However, soft boiled eggs cannot be successfully reheated as this would obviously result in them becoming hard boiled.

(d) Shallow fried eggs must also be served immediately as they become hard and cannot be successfully reheated.

POACHED EGGS AND EGGS EN COCOTTE

Poaching is the gentle simmering of eggs which are completely submerged in water containing salt, vinegar or both. Eggs can also be poached in a special pan, in which case they are cooked by steam and acquire a moulded shape.

Eggs en cocotte are prepared by steaming under a lid with butter and seasoning in an earthenware dish specially designed for single eggs known as a cocotte.

Poached eggs

5.1 POACHED EGG — OEUF POCHE

Method

(1) Bring the pan of water to the boil and gently simmer. Add salt or vinegar as preferred using approximately 1 part vinegar to 20 parts water.

(2) Add the eggs from their shells one at a time, allowing a second for each to begin to set before adding the next.

(3) Whilst cooking, the egg white should fold over and surround the yolk. This action may be helped by the use of a perforated spoon, but care must be taken not to pierce the yolk.

(4) When the egg white appears to have solidified and is firm but not hard, remove from the water for testing if cooked to perfection (*see Note* (5) below).

(5) If undercooked gently replace in the poaching liquid. If cooked to the required degree, transfer the egg to a cloth, held in one hand, which has been folded several times to prevent the possibility of scalding should the eggs not be completely drained of hot water.

(6) When all water has been drained transfer it back onto the spoon and place on the prepared base in the dish or plate in which it will be served.

Notes

(1) Use a shallow sided pan of sufficient size to allow ample room for the eggs to be manipulated whilst cooking.

(2) If poaching is correctly carried out in batches the water may be used several times.

(3) The choice whether to add salt or vinegar to the water before the eggs are poached is a personal one. Vinegar being an acid lowers the temperature at which the egg protein will set. The lower the temperature a protein is set at, the softer is the product, therefore if eggs are poached in water and vinegar the final poached egg is a softer coagulum. On the other hand, salt may cause the white of the egg to fray during poaching.

(4) Poached eggs when served hot are generally presented on a base which may consist of a variety of warmed vegetables, toast, muffins or pastry tartlets with a filling.

(5) To test if cooked remove the egg from the water using a perforated spoon. The white of the egg should appear set and the yolk should be soft. Slight pressure may be applied to the yolk with a finger in order to test its firmness.

(6) If the poached eggs are to be retained, do not drain them on a cloth but place them directly in a basin of cold water. Do not attempt to store too many eggs in one receptacle.

(7) If using a special poached-egg pan use the following *Method.*

Method using a poached-egg pan

(1) Lightly butter the mould, season with salt and pepper and break the egg into the mould. (Alternatively lightly season the mould, place in it a knob of butter and heat gently until melted. Add the egg.)

(2) Cover with the lid and cook until the egg white has set and the egg yolk is still soft.

(3) Remove from the mould and serve.

Notes

(1) Eggs cooked in this way are not suitable for reheating but can be served with the same garnishes and sauces or used to make the same extensions detailed in 5.2 just as poached eggs made in water.

(2) The egg cannot always be successfully turned out of the mould if undercooked.

Extensions of poached eggs

Poached eggs may be served on toast as they are, may be coated with an appropriate sauce or glazed.

5.2 POACHED EGG WITH ASPARAGUS — OEUF POCHE ARGENTEUIL

Place a poached egg in a tartlet case with asparagus tips and Sauce Suprême (3.23).

5.3 POACHED EGG BENEDICTINE — OEUF POCHE BENEDICTINE

Place a poached egg on a toasted muffin or toasted slice of bread with a slice of ox tongue and coat with Sauce Hollandaise (3.12). A slice of truffle is added by tradition.

5.4 POACHED EGG A LA REINE — OEUF POCHE A LA REINE

Place a poached egg on some finely diced breast of chicken lightly bound with Sauce Suprême (3.23) and then coat with the sauce.

5.5 POACHED EGG WASHINGTON — OEUF POCHE WASHINGTON

Place a poached egg on sweetcorn and coat with Cream Sauce (3.16).

Lightly gratinated poached egg dishes

5.6 POACHED EGG MORNAY — OEUF POCHE MORNAY

Place a poached egg on a base of sauce Mornay (3.15) and coat with the sauce; sprinkle with grated Parmesan cheese and melted butter and lightly gratinate under a salamander grill.

5.7 POACHED EGG WITH SPINACH — OEUF POCHE FLORENTINE

Place a poached egg on a bed of leaf spinach lightly heated in butter and seasoned with salt and pepper from the mill. Coat with Sauce Mornay (3.15), sprinkle with grated Parmesan cheese and melted butter and lightly gratinate under a salamander grill.

Service

Serve in a porcelain egg dish the size of an individual portion on an underdish with a dish paper.

Assessment of the completed dish

(1) The eggs should appear evenly glazed on the surface to a light golden colour.

(2) The shape of the egg should be easily discernible under the sauce. The eggs should be evenly and lightly coated with no sign of the spinach forming the base of the dish.

(3) There should be no water around the edges from the spinach.

(4) The eggs should be oval, similar in shape to a tablespoon. All loose pieces of white should be removed. When pierced, the yolk should be runny and the white firm and white.

(5) The spinach should be green, moist and well seasoned.

(6) The sauce mornay should be smooth and of the right consistency to mask the egg.

Eggs en cocotte

5.8 EGG EN COCOTTE — OEUF EN COCOTTE

Method

(1) Butter and season the mould and place in a shallow pan.

(2) Break open the shell and turn the egg into the mould.

(3) Add boiling water to the pan until it comes half way up the moulds, cover with a lid and gently simmer on top of the cooker until cooked.

(4) Take the cocotte out of the pan and clean with a cloth.

Note

When cooked the white of the egg should be firm but the yolk should still be soft.

Service

Place the cocotte on a suitable size of underdish with a dish paper.

Extensions of egg en cocotte

All garnishes should be warm when added. Additional ingredients may be placed at the bottom of the mould before cooking, or placed on top of the cooked item before serving.

5.9 EGGS EN COCOTTE A LA CREME

Add warm cream.

5.10 EGGS EN COCOTTE PORTUGAISE

Add Tomato Concassée (8.169).

5.11 EGGS EN COCOTTE A LA REINE

Add finely diced chicken bound with Sauce Suprême (3.23).

BOILED EGGS

Boiled eggs are a very versatile item. They may be served hot in their shells; hot out of their shells with additional commodities; hard boiled, shelled, covered with an outer coating and deep fried, and served with a range of accompaniments as a hot dish; included in cold pies and served with a range of salad items; or served with a light sauce.

Boiled eggs may be categorised as follows:

			Cooking time
Soft boiled in their shells	—	Oeufs à la Coque	2–4 mins
Soft boiled out of their shells	—	Oeufs Mollets	5 mins
Hard boiled	—	Oeufs Durs	10 mins

(Note that these times are for Size 2 eggs; smaller eggs will not require as long cooking time.)

In order to prepare soft boiled eggs out of their shell, the eggs, when cooked, should be plunged into cold water for a few seconds and the shell carefully removed. They then need to be reheated in hot water for a few seconds to replace the lost heat. They may be served with the same garnishes and sauces as poached eggs, e.g. Oeufs Mollets Florentine. The points of description listed for Oeufs Pochés Florentine also apply to soft boiled eggs with the exception of the shape of the egg. The egg should be whole, and when slight pressure is placed on it, it will easily yield to signify that it is soft boiled.

Hard boiled eggs, once cooked, should also be immediately plunged into cold water and kept under a running cold tap. When cold right through, remove the shell and retain the egg in a basin of cold water until required. If they are to be served hot, plunge them into cold water and quickly remove the shells, then re-dip into hot water to replace the lost heat. Hard boiled eggs served hot are usually presented in a shallow white porcelain dish on an underdish with a dish paper.

5.12 HARD BOILED EGGS WITH CURRY SAUCE AND RICE — OEUFS DURS A L'INDIENNE

Halve or quarter hot hard boiled eggs and serve on a bed of Boiled Rice (5.53). Coat with Curry Sauce (3.11).

5.13 STUFFED HARD BOILED EGGS WITH CHEESE SAUCE— OEUFS DURS CHIMAY

Makes: 10 portions.

Quantity	*Ingredient*
10	hard boiled eggs
100 g	purée of mushrooms; Duxelles (8.167)
½ l	Sauce Mornay (3.15)
50 g	melted butter
50 g	grated Parmesan cheese

Method

(1) Cut the eggs in half lengthways, remove the yolks and pass them through a sieve.

(2) Mix the sieved egg yolks with a quantity of puréed mushrooms and place the mixture back in the empty whites either by piping with a star tube or by using a spoon.

(3) Place into a previously buttered porcelain egg dish.

(4) Coat with sauce mornay and sprinkle the surface with grated Parmesan cheese and melted butter.

(5) Lightly gratinate under a salamander grill.

5.14 SCOTCH EGGS

Makes: 10 portions. Cooking time: 8 minutes. Fat temperature: 175 °C.

Quantity	*Ingredient*
10	hard boiled eggs
800 g	sausage meat
	flour
	eggwash
	breadcrumbs

Method

(1) Divide the sausage meat into even portions.

(2) Completely enclose each egg in the sausage meat, moulding it to the shape of a large egg.

(3) Coat with flour, eggwash and breadcrumbs (*see* 6.42).

(4) Deep fry until cooked (*see Note*).

Note

Provided the outer shell of sausage meat is not too thick it should be cooked when coloured to a golden brown.

Service

Scotch eggs may be served cold with an accompanying salad or hot with an appropriate sauce, e.g. Tomato Sauce (3.10) or Devilled Sauce (3.28). It is usual to cut them in half lengthways. They may be presented on a plate with a sprig of parsley or served on an oval flat dish with a dish paper.

Assessment of the completed dish

(1) The outer coating should be crisp and evenly coloured with the egg set in the centre of the sausage meat.

(2) The egg should look fresh and moist with no dark or black line surrounding the yolk.

(3) The sausage meat should be cooked through.

SHALLOW FRIED EGGS AND OMELETTES

There are three ways to shallow fry eggs:

(a) in fat in a frying pan;

(b) in butter in a shallow porcelain dish (these are known as Oeufs sur le Plat);

(c) as omelettes.

Pan or griddle fried eggs

Butter, bacon fat or oil can be used to fry eggs. There are two basic approaches to frying eggs depending on how the cooked egg is required to look. Follow *Method 1* below if the white is to be bubbly, lightly coloured and crisp on the outer fringe. Use *Method 2* below if the white is to be smooth and perfectly white without any crispness.

5.15 FRIED EGGS — OEUFS FRITS

Method 1

Break the eggs into the fat and shallow fry, basting the egg with some of the fat until cooked to the right degree. Crispness is obtained by control of the heat of the fat.

Method 2

Shallow fry the eggs, preferably one at a time, in an omelette pan, cooking them slowly and basting from time to time until the egg is set.

Note

Eggs fried on a griddle plate are generally cooked in an egg ring which is similar in type but much smaller than a flan ring. They should be griddled on a surface of fat.

Service

When serving fried eggs, remove them from the fat with an egg slice and allow all excess fat to drain back into the pan. It is advisable to serve them directly onto a plate as contact with a metal tray once they are cooked will turn the eggs black or grey. Always serve them as soon as possible as they quickly dry out and deteriorate.

Description of the completed egg

(1) The yolk should be in the centre of the white indicating that the egg is not old.
(2) The white and yolk should be set to the desired degree.

Oeufs sur le plat

These are sometimes put on the menu as Shirred Eggs.

5.16 EGGS COOKED IN BUTTER — OEUFS SUR LE PLAT

Method

(1) Heat a little butter in an egg dish and lightly season it with salt and pepper.
(2) Break in the eggs, allowing one or two per portion.
(3) Allow the egg to cook on the side of the cooker until the white has set then flash finish it under a salamander grill for a few seconds until the yolk is also set.

Note

This method is sometimes referred to as baking in which case the egg, once lightly set, is placed in a moderate oven until set.

Service

Serve in a porcelain dish on an underdish with a dish paper.

Description of the completed dish

(1) The egg should be cooked to the desired degree.
(2) The yolk should be in the centre of the white and the dish.
(3) The garnish should be strategically placed to show off the dish to maximum visual effect.

5.17 OEUFS SUR LE PLAT BERCY

Garnish with Grilled Chipolatas (7.232) and ring with thin Tomato Sauce (3.10).

5.18 OEUFS SUR LE PLAT AU LARD

Garnish with Grilled Rashers of Bacon (7.218).

Omelettes

Omelettes are a versatile dish and may be served as a snack, breakfast dish, starter, or main course dish for lunch, dinner or supper.

There are two types of savoury omelette:

(a) oval in shape or folded;
(b) flat round shape.

A number of points should be borne in mind when preparing any omelette.

(a) Three eggs are necessary to produce a reasonable size omelette, although two eggs may be used. However, producing a two egg omelette in a standard size commercial omelette pan is rarely successful.

(b) Never add water or milk to the eggs with the intention of stretching the ingredients. A small amount of water, however, say ¼ tsp, to each three egg mixture helps to break them up.

(c) Always season the eggs with salt and pepper.

(d) Use a fork to beat the eggs vigorously, as using a whisk may change the characteristics of the omelette by incorporating too much air.

(e) Never use an aluminium basin to beat the egg mixture in as it may affect the colour of the omelette. A plastic or stainless steel bowl is preferable.

(f) Beat the mixture vigorously until the white of the egg is completely integrated into the mixture. The finished omelette should be completely free of egg white streaks.

(g) When making savoury omelettes do not beat or whisk the egg yolks and whites separately, as is sometimes done, with a view to making the mixture go further. The result is a rubbery textured dish.

(h) When making large numbers of individual omelettes a bulk egg mix may be produced, in which case the proportionate amount of water and seasoning is added. It may be whisked either by hand or machine and it is prudent to pass the mixture through a conical strainer before use. A ladle of 180 ml capacity is used to ensure the correct size of omelette is produced (i.e. made with three eggs).

(i) When large numbers are required, one large omelette for up to eight people may be produced, in which case the same principle as in *(h)* applies.

(j) Care of the omelette pan is essential. Washing the omelette pan can make the omelette stick and tear.

(k) Always wipe out an omelette pan with a dry cloth each time an omelette has been made before proceeding to the next.

(l) If the omelette is turned out onto a silver flat dish and left, even for a couple of minutes, the omelette and dish will begin to discolour.

(m) Omelettes should not be kept with the intention of reheating them at a later stage. It is possible, however, to reheat an omelette in a microwave oven or by using a cook–chill system.

Oval shaped or folded omelettes

Fillings for these types of omelette may be added:

(a) to the raw mixture;
(b) when rolling up;
(c) when the omelette has been cooked and turned out by making a slit along the top surface and placing the filling in the slit.

All garnishes need to be warm when the omelette is served.

5.19 PLAIN OMELETTE — OMELETTE NATURE

Quantity	*Ingredient*
3	beaten and seasoned eggs
15 g	butter or oil
	melted butter

Method

(1) Heat the omelette pan.

(2) Add the butter and when hot but before it begins to change colour add the mixture.

(3) Distribute the mixture around the complete base of the pan with the back of a fork — do not use the points as this will scratch the base of the omelette pan. Fold in the mixture as it sets on the sides.

(4) Whilst cooking continue to distribute the mixture with the fork, at the same time shaking the pan backward and forward, keeping the base of it on the cooker.

(5) When it is set remove from the heat, slightly tilt the pan and fold the omelette with the inside of the fork away from the handle to the leading edge of the pan. Bring in the extreme ends with the fork, still using the inside of the fork, to form an oval shape and bring the join to the centre by hitting the handle of the pan with the side of the hand. Return to the heat to set if necessary, adding a little butter to the leading edge of the pan.

(6) Turn out onto a dish by resting the omelette pan on the leading edge and bringing up the handle until the omelette is turned over into the centre of the dish.

(7) Reform the omelette if necessary by covering it with a clean cloth and reshaping with the hands.

(8) Brush the surface with melted butter and serve.

Service

Serve on a warm plate or shallow oval earthenware dish, or on a silver or stainless steel flat dish.

Description of the completed omelette

(1) The omelette should be placed in the centre of the dish, evenly shaped with the surface glistening and light golden in colour.

(2) It should be an even oval or cigar shape with the ends neatly pointed.

(3) The colour of the omelette itself depends on the freshness and quality of the eggs used. The top surface may either be very lightly and evenly coloured over the centre area, or have hardly any colour at all.

(4) It should be soft in texture, referred to as baveuse (meaning "soft textured").

(5) It should be correctly seasoned.

(6) There should be no white streaks to indicate that the mixture has not been thoroughly beaten.

(7) There should be no seepage of liquid egg mixture from the omelette into the dish.

5.20 TOMATO OMELETTE — OMELETTE AUX TOMATES

Make a Plain Omelette as in 5.19. Add a filling of Tomato Concassée (8.169) either at Stage (5) when folding the omelette or after Stage (7) once the omelette has been turned out and reformed, by cutting a slit in the centre of the omelette about 5 cm long and spooning in the warm filling. Place a small amount of filling at each end of the omelette, brush with melted butter and if required pour a small amount of Tomato Sauce (3.10) around the edge of the omelette before serving.

Note

It is preferable to add the filling for a Tomato Omelette either when folding in the pan or once the omelette has been cooked. The acid in the tomatoes would have an adverse effect on the raw egg mixture making it difficult to cook correctly to achieve the desired result.

5.21 CHEESE OMELETTE — OMELETTE AU FROMAGE

Add a filling of grated cheese.

5.22 HAM OMELETTE — OMELETTE AU JAMBON

Add a filling of diced ham with diamonds of ham for decoration.

5.23 HERB OMELETTE — OMELETTE AUX FINES HERBES

Add a filling of chopped parsley, tarragon and chives. (In trade practice sometimes only parsley is used.)

5.24 MUSHROOM OMELETTE — OMELETTE AUX CHAMPIGNONS

Add a filling of sliced and cooked White Button Mushrooms (*see* 8.91).

Flat round omelettes

One factor that determines whether an omelette is made cigar or flat round in shape is the amount of garnish to be added. A flat round omelette will hold much more than a folded one.

When making flat round omelettes the garnish is generally added to the mixture before cooking. Follow the *Method* for Plain Omelette (5.19) up to Stage (4) then continue:

Method

(5) When set and firm enough, toss like a pancake and immediately transfer it to a warm, buttered dish. Alternatively, lightly set the top exposed area under a salamander grill. This takes only a few moments, the length of time being highly critical as even a second or two too long will make the omelette hard, dry and rubbery.

(6) Transfer the cooked omelette to a plate or round buttered flat dish, bottom side uppermost.

(7) Brush the surface with melted butter and complete with the appropriate garnish items.

5.25 SPANISH OMELETTE — OMELETTE ESPAGNOLE

There are many variations for making the garnish. However, the generally accepted garnish consists of peeled, pipped and diced tomato, skinned red pimento cut into thin strips, and onion thinly sliced and cooked until slightly coloured in butter or oil. Complete with about four small even sized pieces of red pimento cut into diamonds.

5.26 OMELETTE FERMIERE

The garnish consists of diced ham and chopped parsley. Complete with four diamond shaped pieces of ham.

5.27 OMELETTE PAYSANNE

The garnish consists of diced ham, small dice of shallow fried potatoes, shredded sorrel previously stewed in butter, a little chopped chervil and chopped parsley.

SCRAMBLED EGGS

When preparing scrambled eggs the following points should be borne in mind.

(a) Scrambled eggs should preferably be cooked to meet immediate demand.

(b) Use two eggs per portion.

(c) Always season the eggs with salt and pepper.

(d) Do not add milk with the intention of increasing the number of portions.

(e) The eggs must be vigorously beaten in order to integrate the whites and yolks.

(f) Never use an aluminium or unlined copper receptacle at any stage in the cooking process as this would cause the eggs to turn grey or green in colour. This is undesirable in appearance quite apart from the health aspect.

(g) When preparing more than three or four portions it is advisable to cook the eggs in a bain-marie. (It is also possible to cook smaller portions in a bain-marie if this gives the student more confidence while learning.)

(h) Do *not* use a metal implement when cooking scrambled eggs and certainly not a whisk or metal spoon.

(i) In contradiction to *(h)*, if it is thought necessary to lighten the coagulated eggs when making a large quantity, do so with a whisk. This should be carried out lightly and the whisk must never be allowed to come into contact with the receptacle in which the eggs are cooking.

(j) Additions to the basic dish are never cooked with the mixture but are added once the cooked egg has been placed in the service dish.

(k) Garnishes must always be warm or hot and fresh looking.

As much attention must be given to them as to the scrambled eggs themselves.

5.28 SCRAMBLED EGGS — OEUFS BROUILLES

Quantity	*Ingredient*
2 per portion	eggs
15 g	butter
	cream

Method 1 (for small amounts)

(1) Gently heat the butter in a shallow saucepan.

(2) Add the seasoned and beaten eggs.

(3) Stir with a wooden spoon gently and continuously, making certain to integrate the mixture that generally begins to coagulate first, particularly in the corners of the pan.

(4) When the mixture is lightly coagulated add a little cream.

(5) Season to taste and serve immediately.

Method 2 (for larger amounts)

(1) Cook gently in the bain-marie. Do not try to rush the scrambling process.

(2) Stir frequently with a wooden spoon.

(3) Egg that coagulates on the side of the receptacle should not where possible be integrated into the main mixture.

(4) Continue as for Stages 4 and 5 in *Method* 1.

Notes

(1) Where possible cook in batches.

(2) A little thin Béchamel (3.4) or cream may be added when the scrambled egg is nearly cooked. This keeps it from becoming too firm.

Service

Serve on a plate or an oval or round white earthenware dish on an underdish with a dish paper.

Assessment of the completed dish

(1) If cream has been added then the natural colour of the eggs will have been lightened considerably — more so than if milk had been added.

(2) The eggs should be seasoned to bring out their flavour.

(3) They should be very light and moist in texture.

Extensions of scrambled eggs

5.29 SCRAMBLED EGGS WITH MUSHROOMS — OEUFS BROUILLES AUX CHAMPIGNONS

Serve on toast with sliced and cooked mushrooms in the centre.

5.30 SCRAMBLED EGGS WITH CHICKEN LIVERS — OEUFS BROUILLES AUX FOIES DE VOLAILLE

Serve on toast with chicken livers that have been shallow fried and bound with a little Madeira Sauce (3.30).

5.31 SCRAMBLED EGGS WITH TOMATOES — OEUFS BROUILLES AUX TOMATES

Serve on toast with cooked Tomato Concassée (8.169) in the centre.

FARINACEOUS DISHES

Italian pastas are manufactured from noodle paste (*see* below) in a wide range of shapes and sizes. The most common shapes in use are as follows:

Alphabets	— letters of the alphabet, used only for garnishing soups
Canneloni	— cylindrical shapes filled with a savoury stuffing
Lasagnes	— 2½ cm wide × 50 cm long
Macaroni	— small cylindrical shapes available as long and short cuts and elbow shaped.
Noodles (Nouilles)	— approx. 3 mm wide × 20 cm long × 1 mm thick
Tagliatelli Fettucine	— Italian names for noodles up to 6 mm wide
Ravioli	— small squares or rounds of pasta in double layers with a savoury stuffing
Spaghetti	— thin solid rods up to 50 cm in length
Vermicelli	— the finest form of pasta in very thin hairs

Noodle paste

This paste is used in the making of a number of farinaceous items such as Canneloni (5.34) and Ravioli (5.33). It is made with strong flour with the addition of seasoning, egg, olive oil and water, and once prepared should be allowed to rest before further use. It is rolled very thinly and should almost be transparent when ready to use.

Unlike other pastes it is poached in boiling water, and because of its rather bland flavour is served with a variety of savoury fillings and sauces.

5.32 NOODLE PASTE — PATE A NOUILLES

Quantity	*Ingredient*	
800 g	strong flour	sieve together
	salt	
	nutmeg	
4	yolks of eggs	mix together
4	eggs	
1 cl	oil (preferably olive oil)	
1½ dl	water	

Method

(1) Sieve the flour, salt and nutmeg into a basin. Make a bay in the centre and add the previously mixed eggs, oil and water.

(2) Mix all the ingredients together to form a firm smooth dough.

(3) Cover with a damp cloth and allow to rest for approximately 45 minutes before using.

(4) The paste may either be rolled mechanically or with a rolling pin to the required thickness and cut to the appropriate shape as detailed above.

Notes

(1) Various other ingredients may also be added to give flavour and colour. The most common are extra egg yolks to give a yellow tint, spinach to give a green tint and tomato powder to give a red tint.

(2) *See* pp. 136–41 for other aspects of making and using pastes which also apply to noodle paste.

5.33 RAVIOLI

Makes: 10 portions.

Quantity	*Ingredient*
1 kg	Noodle Paste (5.32)
500 g	Filling (5.35 or 36)

Method

(1) Roll the paste into an oblong shape approximately 80 cm × 50 cm and no more than 2 mm in thickness.

(2) Cut the paste into two equal parts. Lay one rolled out piece onto the table.

(3) Place the filling into a piping bag with a 1 cm plain tube. Pipe the filling into neat rows approximately 4 cm apart.

(4) Eggwash between each piece of filling and lay the second piece of thinly rolled out paste over the top.

(5) Press down the pieces of paste between the filling with either a small cutter or a serrated pastry wheel.

(6) Spread out the individual ravioli pieces on a tray previously sprinkled with fine semolina and allow to dry out for about 45 minutes.

(7) Proceed to cook as described in 5.38.

5.34 CANNELONI

Makes: 10 portions.

Quantity	*Ingredient*
1 kg	Noodle Paste (5.32)

Method

(1) Roll out the paste very thinly, approximately 2 cm thick. Cut into squares approximately 8 cm×8 cm.

(2) Spread out the individual pieces onto a tray previously sprinkled with fine semolina and allow to dry out for about 45 minutes.

(3) Proceed to cook as described in 5.38.

Fillings for pasta

5.35 FLORENTINE FILLING

Makes: 10 portions.

Quantity	*Ingredient*
75 g	finely chopped onion
75 g	butter
450 g	cooked and chopped spinach (8.105)
1 clove	crushed garlic
1	egg yolk
½ dl	Demi-Glace (3.7) or Jus Lié (3.8)
	seasoning of salt and pepper

Method

(1) Melt the butter in a saucepan, add the chopped onions and cook without colouring.

(2) Combine the remaining ingredients.

5.36 ITALIENNE FILLING

Makes: 10 portions.

Quantity	*Ingredient*
75 g	finely chopped onion
75 g	butter
150 g	minced braised beef (7.126)
100 g	diced cooked calfs' brains (7.245)
200 g	cooked and chopped spinach (8.105)
1 clove	crushed garlic
1	egg yolk
½ dl	Demi-Glace (3.7) or Jus Lié (3.8)
	seasoning of salt and pepper

Method

(1) Melt the butter in a saucepan, add the chopped onions and cook without colouring.

(2) Combine the remaining ingredients.

General rules for cooking pasta

All pastas, even those not specifically mentioned, may be cooked according to the principles outlined in this chapter. Briefly, all pasta is cooked in gently boiling salted water (though the term used is poaching when referring to canneloni and ravioli). Baking or full gratination are terms applied to lasagnes and canneloni when they are barely covered with sauce in a service dish, sprinkled with grated parmesan cheese and melted butter and placed in an oven at a temperature of 170 °C until the cheese melts and forms a light crust or skin. Light gratination is a term applied to those items mixed with Sauce Mornay (3.15), sprinkled with grated Parmesan cheese and melted butter and placed under a salamander grill until an even golden colour on the surface.

The following list indicates a number of general points to be borne in mind when cooking pasta.

(a) Cooking times are: 5–7 minutes for the very fine type (i.e. vermicelli); 9–12 minutes for medium size pastas (i.e. noodles and spaghetti); 12–15 minutes for thick pastas (i.e. macaroni, lasagne and ravioli).

(b) Allow 10 g raw weight per person of pasta when used as a garnish with a soup, e.g. Consommé Vermicelli; 30 g raw weight of pasta when used as a garnish with a main dish, e.g. Escalope de Veau Milanaise; and 50–60 g when served as the basis of a main course, e.g. Spaghetti Bolognaise.

(c) Always cook pasta items in plenty of water (*see* 5.37 and 5.38).

(d) Overcooked pasta items cannot be rectified.

(e) Never overfill the cooking receptacle with pasta.

(f) Stir or agitate the pasta whilst it is cooking, especially at the initial stages, with a wooden spatule.

(g) Canneloni and lasagnes are always refreshed after cooking in order to facilitate further handling, e.g. inserting the filling.

(h) Leave the strands of spaghetti, noodles and vermicelli unbroken both before and during cooking unless they are specifically for soup garnishes.

(i) Whether the pasta is for immediate use or is to be retained for later use, it should be cooked to a degree that is referred to as *al dente*; it should not be overcooked so that it becomes too soft. The Italian term has a very clear meaning and describes a very slightly chewy texture.

(j) In most instances all pasta items are served with an accompanying sauce (but *see* Pasta à l'Italienne (5.40)) and grated Parmesan cheese. The sauce is generally an extension of a basic sauce.

(k) Once butter or a sauce has been added to pasta the dish cannot be reheated using traditional methods.

(l) Change the chaudfont water frequently when reheating pasta.

5.37 PASTAS WITHOUT FILLINGS

Quantity	*Ingredient*
5 l (approx.)	boiling water
60 g	salt
600 g	Pasta (5.32)

Method

(1) Add the pasta to the boiling salted water in a deep sided saucepan without breaking the strands. Spaghetti, noodles and lasagnes should be placed in the saucepan resting on the bottom and side of the pan; as they begin to soften in the hot water they will gently submerge.

(2) At the initial stage of cooking all pasta submerged under the water should be gently stirred with a wooden spatule. When satisfied that all strands are separated, lower the cooking temperature to gentle boiling.

(3) Gently boil the pasta for the prescribed time.

(4) When cooked, refresh under controlled running water until perfectly cold, or use immediately according to recipe.

Notes

(1) When refreshing large amounts, drain off the hot water and

replace it with cold several times. This helps to bring down the temperature of the pasta and prevents further cooking.

(2) If any of the pasta is slightly overcooked then repeat the process of draining off the hot water and replacing it with cold until the pasta is cold and no further cooking is possible.

Possible problem	*Possible cause and solution*
(1) Pasta is dry and hard	— pasta undercooked; the pasta should be cooked for the correct length of time as dry or hard pasta cannot be rectified.
	— stale pasta; the pasta should be reasonably fresh when used as stale pasta from old stock which becomes dry and hard when cooked cannot be rectified.
	— held for too long at a high temperature before service; this should be avoided as it makes the pasta dry and hard and cannot be rectified.
(2) Pasta is too soft	— pasta overcooked; pasta should be cooked for the correct length of time to avoid it going soft — once overcooked and soft it cannot be rectified.
	— temperature of the pasta not reduced quickly enough once cooked; the temperature must be quickly reduced once the pasta is cooked to prevent it cooking further in its own heat — once it has gone soft it cannot be rectified.
	— stored for too long in cold water; this should be avoided as once the pasta has gone soft it cannot be rectified.
	— reheated for too long in boiling water; this has the effect of overcooking the pasta making it soft which cannot be rectified.
	— held for too long on a hotplate once dished up before service; this has the effect of overcooking the pasta making it soft which cannot be rectified.

5.38 PASTAS WITH FILLINGS

Quantity	*Ingredient*
5 l	simmering water
60 g	salt

Quantity	*Ingredient*
1 tablespoon	oil
600 g	pasta — Canneloni (5.34) or Ravioli (5.33)

Method

(1) Add the oil and salt to the water and heat until simmering. Place the pasta items onto the surface where they will float because of the film of oil.

(2) Whilst cooking move the items around very gently as there is the possibility that the stuffing may be forced out of the ravioli, or the canneloni pasta pieces may break.

(3) When cooked, refresh under controlled running water until perfectly cold or use immediately according to the recipe (*see Notes*).

Notes

(1) Using a shallow sided saucepan helps prevent the pastas from breaking when handled.

(2) The addition of oil to the water when cooking helps to prevent the pasta from sticking together during cooking.

Possible problem	*Possible cause and solution*
(1) The ravioli have broken and the filling has come out	— water was boiling rather than gently simmering; care must be taken not to boil the water as this will cause the ravioli to break up which cannot be rectified.
	— rough handling when poaching; take care not to mishandle the ravioli as they are poaching as if they break up the situation cannot be rectified.
	— mishandled when being refreshed; care must be taken at this stage as if the ravioli break up the situation cannot be rectified.
	— held for too long in cold water; this softens the pasta causing the ravioli to fall apart and cannot be rectified.
(2) The canneloni have broken and are difficult to handle	— water was boiling rather than simmering gently; care must be taken not to boil the water as this will cause the canneloni to break up.
	— pasta has stuck together during cooking and tears when separated as it has not cooked through where joined; care must be taken

Possible problem	*Possible cause and solution*
	to prevent the canneloni sticking together during cooking as once torn the problem cannot be rectified.
	— held too long in cold water; this softens the pasta and care must be taken to avoid the prolonged retention as the problem cannot be rectified.
	— pasta has been handled roughly during cooking or when refreshed; care must be taken when handling canneloni as any damage cannot be rectified.

Methods of serving pasta

Pasta may be served directly into a soup plate, in an entrée dish of earthenware, stainless steel or silver or a vegetable dish. Parmesan cheese is generally served separately, but the amount used may be restricted if it is sprinkled over the surface of the completed pasta at the time of service.

Alternatively the pasta may be served as follows:

(a) a standard portion may be served in a dish with the sauce along the centre;

(b) a standard portion may be served with the sauce separately in a sauceboat, to be added in the restaurant;

(c) canneloni and lasagnes may be served in the dish in which they have been baked, in which case they should be perfectly cleaned for presentation purposes.

Storage of cooked pasta

Once cooked, refreshed and cold, pasta may be stored in a refrigerator by one of two methods, either submerged in a basin of cold water or completely drained and placed on a tray, lightly and evenly coated with a small amount of oil and covered with a damp cloth. However, either method can cause problems. Retention in cold water removes some of the starch and the pasta becomes white in appearance and soft. On the other hand, when stored on a tray with a little oil the distribution of the oil must be carried out correctly or else it may dry out in the areas not coated with oil and become dry and even brittle. In any case, retention should be for a limited period only.

Reheating pastas

5.39 REHEATING PASTA

Makes: 10 portions.

Quantity	*Ingredient*
300–600 g	pasta (i.e. lasagnes, macaroni, noodles, ravioli and spaghetti)
100 g	butter
1 clove	garlic (optional)
50 g	grated Parmesan cheese
	seasoning of salt and pepper

Method

(1) Dip the cooked pasta, using a dipper, into boiling salted water for a few moments until heated through to the centre.

(2) Remove the pasta and allow all surplus water to drain away.

(3) Melt the butter in a shallow sided saucepan but do not let it colour. If desired, add the clove of garlic for a few moments in order to flavour the butter, then remove the clove.

(4) Add the drained pasta, stir in gently either with a fork if spaghetti or noodles or a service spoon if ravioli. Season with salt and pepper from the mill.

(5) Arrange the pasta in a pre-heated service dish and serve.

Extensions

Lasagnes, macaroni, noodles, ravioli and spaghetti may be served with all the sauces and garnishes listed in 5.40–46. Canneloni may be served à la Crème, au Gratin, au Jus, Bolognaise or Napolitaine.

5.40 PASTA A L'ITALIENNE

Add butter and Parmesan cheese.

5.41 PASTA A LA CREME

Add cream or cream and yolks of eggs.

5.42 PASTA AU GRATIN

As for à la Crème but also lightly gratinated.

5.43 PASTA AU JUS

Add a brown sauce such as Jus Lié (3.8).

5.44 PASTA BOLOGNAISE

Add either minced beef cooked in Brown Sauce (*see* 3.24) or quick sautéd fillet of beef cut into small dice with chopped shallots and brown sauce.

Assessment of the completed Spaghetti Bolognaise

(1) The spaghetti should be arranged in a slight dome shape. It should be creamy in colour with the sauce arranged in the centre of the pasta along its length. The finely grated Parmesan cheese should be served separately.

(2) The spaghetti should be cooked to the correct degree *al dente*. The strands of spaghetti should be unbroken, lightly coated with butter with a slight garlic flavour and seasoned to the correct degree.

(3) The sauce should be a rich tomato brown in colour. The meat should be free from gristle and fat, firm in texture, yet cooked. It should have a full meaty taste and be well seasoned.

(4) A standard portion should have a ratio of approximately 60 g spaghetti to 1 dl of sauce.

5.45 PASTA MILANAISE

Add julienne of ham, tongue and mushrooms with Tomato Concassée (8.169) and Tomato Sauce (3.10).

5.46 PASTA NAPOLITAINE

Add Tomato Sauce (3.10) and Tomato Concassée (8.169).

5.47 CANNELONI AU JUS

Makes: 10 portions.

Quantity	*Ingredient*
20	pieces cooked Canneloni Pasta (5.34)
200 g	filling (5.35 or 36)
50 g	butter
½ l	Jus Lié (3.8) or Sauce Demi-glace (3.7)
50 g	grated Parmesan cheese
	seasoning of salt and pepper

Method

(1) Lay out a clean and adequately sized cloth on a work surface.

(2) Arrange the cooked cold and drained pieces of pasta in rows along the cloth.

(3) Pipe the filling along the leading widest edge of the pasta strips.

(4) Roll up the pasta enclosing the filling.

(5) Butter the dish in which they are to be cooked and place a little sauce in the bottom.

(6) Place the stuffed canneloni into the dishes with the overlapping part down.

(7) Lightly cover with the hot prepared sauce.
(8) Sprinkle with grated Parmesan cheese and melted butter.
(9) Place the prepared dishes onto baking sheets and bake until fully gratinated.

Note

The cloth used may be dry or damp, or lightly sprinkled with semolina.

5.48 LASAGNES BOLOGNAISE

Makes: 10 portions.

Quantity	*Ingredient*
300–600 g	cooked and refreshed lasagnes
50 g	butter
½ l	Bolognaise Sauce (3.24)
50 g	grated Parmesan cheese
	seasoning of salt and pepper

Method

(1) Butter the bottom of the dish in which the lasagnes are to be served.
(2) Lay in the lasagnes either trellis fashion or in lines so that the bottom of the dish is completely covered.
(3) Place a layer of bolognaise sauce on the lasagnes and repeat the process of alternative layers of lasagnes and sauce all the way up the dish finishing with a layer of sauce.
(4) Sprinkle the surface with the cheese and butter.
(5) Bake to full gratination.

DUMPLINGS — GNOCCHI AND POLENTA

There are four main types of small dumplings:

(a) Gnocchi Romaine produced from semolina, egg yolks and cheese;
(b) Gnocchi Parisienne produced from small pieces of chou paste;
(c) Gnocchi Piemontaise produced from potatoes, flour and egg yolk;
(d) Polenta produced from maize flour and salted water.

Gnocchi Romaine and Piemontaise are generally served as first course dishes on their own, whilst Gnocchi Parisienne are served as a garnish for Goulash (7.159). Polenta is a very popular dish in

Italy and is usually served as a garnish with meat or fish, e.g. Osso Bucco (7.158). They are not usually served on their own.

5.49 GNOCCHI ROMAINE

Makes: 10 portions. Cooking time: 5–8 minutes.

Quantity	*Ingredient*
1 l	milk or white stock
200 g	semolina
	seasoning of salt, nutmeg and pepper
2	egg yolks
75 g	butter
75 g	grated Parmesan cheese

Method

(1) Boil the liquid in a deep sided saucepan.

(2) Sprinkle in the semolina, whisking well whilst adding it.

(3) Season and gently cook on top of the stove but not over a fierce heat or it will burn easily. Stir occasionally with a wooden spoon.

(4) When cooked add the egg yolks and cheese, mixing in with a wooden spoon or spatule.

(5) Season to taste.

(6) Transfer to a previously buttered tray and spread evenly to a depth of about 1 cm. Cover the surface with a little melted butter or buttered greaseproof paper and allow to cool until it is easy to handle; it should be firm and cold.

(7) Remove the paper and either turn out onto a work surface or leave in dish. Cut into crescents or small scone shapes with a 5 cm pastry cutter.

(8) Place the gnocchi into a previously buttered earthenware dish, first putting the trimmings underneath then the shaped pieces on top neatly arranged to follow the shape of the dish.

(9) Sprinkle with grated Parmesan cheese and melted butter and gratinate under a salamander grill to a light even golden colour.

Notes

(1) Check that the mixture is not too soft before adding the egg yolks and cheese.

(2) A little Tomato Sauce (3.10) may be poured around the gnocchi before serving.

Service

Serve on an earthenware or porcelain shallow gratin dish set on an underdish with a dishpaper.

Assessment of the completed dish

(1) The gnocchi should be of an even shape with an even light golden surface coloration.
(2) They should have a firm texture and not be sticky.
(3) There should be a slight flavour of nutmeg.
(4) If sauce is served it should be around the base of the dish and not cover the dumplings.

Possible problem	*Possible cause and solution*
The gnocchi are sticky	— mixture was too soft due to an incorrect ratio of liquid to semolina; add more semolina before the egg yolks and cheese until the mixture becomes firm and does not stick to the hands when moulding.

5.50 GNOCCHI PARISIENNE (GNOCCHI MORNAY)

Makes: 10 portions. Cooking time: 8 minutes.

Quantity	*Ingredient*
1 l	Chou Paste (10.45)
75 g	butter
½ l	Mornay Sauce (3.15)
	seasoning of salt and pepper
50 g	grated Parmesan cheese

Method

(1) Use a shallow sided saucepan three-quarters filled with gently simmering salted water.
(2) Place the prepared chou paste into a piping bag with a 1 cm plain tube. Pipe it into the simmering water in lengths of about 2 cm, resting the tube on the side of the saucepan and cutting off the lengths with a knife as the paste leaves the bag.
(3) Poach the lengths of paste until cooked (*see Note* (2) below).
(4) When cooked, if for immediate use, strain the dumplings by either draining in a colander or removing from the water with a spider.
(5) Melt the butter in a shallow pan.
(6) Add the cooked gnocchi, season and heat gently. Add either cream or Sauce Crème (3.16) which should be of a light consistency. Gently incorporate all the ingredients with a metal spoon or by a tossing and shaking motion.
(7) Transfer the preparation to an earthenware dish.
(8) Sprinkle with grated parmesan cheese and melted butter.
(9) Lightly gratinate under a salamander grill.

Notes

(1) When piping the paste into the simmering water it is necessary to dip the knife into hot water from time to time to prevent sticking.

(2) Whilst cooking the dumplings will swell in size and become light in colour. They are cooked when they become firm to the touch.

(3) Instead of tossing the cooked dumplings in butter they may be placed directly into a buttered earthenware dish and coated with the sauce.

(4) To store, drain the cooked dumplings, transfer them to a basin of cold water and keep in a refrigerator.

Assessment of the completed dish

Gnocchi Parisienne should be very light and firm on the outside but smooth and soft textured on the inside.

5.51 POTATO DUMPLINGS — GNOCCHI PIEMONTAISE

Makes: 10 portions. Cooking time: 1 hour.

Quantity	*Ingredient*
400 g	Purée Jacket Potato (9.43) made very dry
4	egg yolks
100 g	strong flour
	seasoning of salt, nutmeg and pepper
100 g	potato flour or cornflour (for moulding)
50 g	butter
50 g	grated Parmesan cheese

Method

(1) Return the freshly mashed potatoes to the stove in a deep sided saucepan to aid mixing.

(2) Add the egg yolks, flour and seasoning and mix thoroughly with a wooden spatule.

(3) At this point the texture should be rectified if necessary after testing a few small balls of the mixture by gently poaching in simmering salted water (*see Note* (1) below).

(4) Divide the mixture into small walnut-sized pieces with the aid of potato flour or cornflour. Roll them into the shape of either small balls or walnut shapes. If walnut shaped, place on a sieve, lightly press with a fork and roll — the effect will be an apricot shaped dumpling with slight indentation in its side.

(5) Lightly poach in a shallow sided pan in salted water — the water must be simmering when the gnocchi are added.

(6) Drain by gently lifting from the water with a spider and place into a buttered earthenware dish.

(7) Sprinkle with grated Parmesan cheese and melted butter and slightly colour under a salamander grill.

Notes

(1) If when testing the mixture the balls begin to break up it is probably because the mixture is too soft.

(2) The dish may be completed with a little Tomato Sauce (3.10) poured around the dumplings before serving.

Possible problem	*Possible cause and solution*
(1) Mixture is too soft	— insufficient flour; add a little more potato flour, dry mashed potato or potato powder mix until the mixture is the correct consistency.
(2) Mixture is too hard	— insufficient butter; add a little butter until the mixture is the correct consistency.

5.52 MAIZE FLOUR DUMPLINGS — POLENTA

Makes: 10 portions. Cooking time: 25–30 minutes.

Quantity	*Ingredient*
1 l	boiling salted water
200 g	maize flour
2	egg yolks
75 g	grated Parmesan cheese
100 g	melted butter (or oil)

Method

(1) Sprinkle the maize flour into the boiling salted water in a deep sided saucepan. Mix it with a whisk to prevent lumps from forming.

(2) Cook by continuously mixing vigorously with a wooden spatule.

(3) When cooked remove from the heat, add the egg yolks and cheese.

(4) Transfer to a previously buttered tray and spread evenly to a thickness of 1–2 cm. Cover the surface with melted butter or buttered greaseproof paper and allow to cool in a refrigerator until firm and easy to handle.

(5) Remove the paper if used and either turn out the mixture onto a work surface or leave in the dish.

(6) Cut into scone or square shapes.

(7) Shallow fry in hot butter or oil until a light golden colour on both sides.

Notes

(1) Whilst it is cooking the mixture becomes very thick and a crust will form on the bottom and sides of the saucepan. This should not be disturbed when turning out the soft pasta.

(2) If served as a separate garnish with meat do not shallow fry but place in an earthenware dish, sprinkle with grated cheese and Nut Brown Butter (6.48) and place under a salamander grill until evenly gratined.

Assessment of the completed dish

(1) The polenta should be evenly and lightly coloured golden, but as they are naturally yellow in colour this may not be so evident.

(2) They should be firm and slightly grainy in texture but not gritty.

(3) They should be moist but dry enough to hold together without undue pressure.

RICE

There are three basic methods of preparing rice: boiling, braising and stewing.

(a) Boiled rice is used as an accompaniment for curry and as a garnish for soup.

(b) Braised rice — referred to as savoury or pilaff — is cooked in an oven with white stock. It is used as a garnish to a variety of first course dishes and main meal entrées.

(c) Stewed rice — referred to as risotto — is cooked in white stock on top of the stove. It is generally served as the first course of a meal, but also forms the main course fish dish Paella.

Long grain patna rice may be used for any of the three methods of preparation, though for pilaff piedmont (a variety of long grain rice) is also used, and for risotto short grain or carolina rice may be used in place of long grain, provided it is good quality with no broken grains.

Blanched rice in raw form is available for all purposes except rice pudding. It has already been steamed by the manufacturer to remove some of the starch so that it does not stick when cooked.

The following is a guide to how much uncooked rice to allow per standard portion:

Boiled rice	—	30 g as an accompaniment with curried meat
Savoury/pilaff	—	30 g as a garnish 50 g as a main course
Risotto	—	30 g as a first course 50 g as a main dish

Boiled rice

5.53 PLAIN BOILED RICE

Makes: 10 portions. Cooking time: Approximately 20 minutes.

Quantity	*Ingredient*
500 g	rice — long grain patna type
5 l	boiling salted water
60 g	salt

Method

(1) Boil the salted water in a deep pan.

(2) Rain in the rice and stir occasionally with a wooden spoon until it reboils, then continue to boil gently until cooked.

(3) When cooked, refresh under cold running water and, when cold, drain in a colander.

Note

To reheat for service:

(1) Place the rice in a colander under running hot water until it is quite hot, then drain thoroughly.

(2) Line a suitable tray with a cloth and spread the rice over the total surface to a depth of not more than about 5 cm.

(3) Check if it is necessary to season with salt.

(4) Cover with a damp cloth and place the tray on a hotplate or in an oven at about 60 °C until the rice is hot and dry. From time to time redistribute the rice with a fork.

Alternative method

(1) Place the rice into a deep sided saucepan large enough to allow the rice to expand during cooking. Add the salt.

(2) Add water to a depth of approximately 6 cm.

(3) Bring to the boil, cover with a tight fitting lid then either *(a)* cook in a pressure steamer, or *(b)* cook on top of the stove.

Notes

(1) It may be necessary to add a little water during cooking

following the alternative method, but when cooked the rice will be white and fluffy with each grain separate. It is not necessary to refresh the rice under cold running water.

(2) During cooking following either method a crust will form on the bottom and sides of the pan from the starch. It should not be disturbed.

(3) To reheat add a little water, cover with a lid and reheat in a steamer.

Assessment of the completed dish

The rice should be white and fluffy with each grain separate, tender and yet firm, and seasoned with salt.

Storage

Cover a tray with a damp cloth and place on it the boiled refreshed rice. Cover the rice with another damp cloth and store in a refrigerator.

Savoury rice

5.54 *SAVOURY/BRAISED RICE — RIZ PILAFF*

Makes: 10 portions. Cooking time: 15–20 minutes. Oven temperature: 200 °C.

Quantity	*Ingredient*
75 g	butter
75 g	chopped onion
500 g	rice
1 l	white stock (preferably chicken)
1	bayleaf
1 clove	crushed garlic
	seasoning

Method

(1) Melt the butter in a shallow sided saucepan. Add the onion and cook without coloration.

(2) Add the rice, incorporating it into the butter and onion; lightly fry but do not allow the onions to colour.

(3) Add the hot stock, seasoning, bayleaf and garlic.

(4) Bring to the boil, stirring with a wooden spoon, then cover immediately with buttered greaseproof paper and a lid and place in the preheated oven.

(5) Braise the rice for the prescribed time or until cooked (*see Notes* for a test to see if cooked).

(6) Separate the grains of rice with a fork, incorporating at the

same time a few knobs of butter; season to taste and remove the bayleaf.

(7) Transfer to a clean receptacle, cover with a clean piece of greaseproof paper and retain in a warm area.

Notes

(1) Ratio of stock to rice should be approximately two parts stock to one part rice.

(2) To test if cooked test the grains of rice by squeezing between the fingers. When cooked the rice should be firm and nutty but not hard.

(3) Make certain that once the hot stock has been added to the rice it boils and is stirred with a wooden spatule.

(4) For pilaff (and risotto) always use a fork when attending to the rice once it is cooked.

Possible problem	*Possible cause and solution*
(1) Rice looks soggy, lumpy and watery	— incorrect type of rice used; care must be taken to use the correct type of rice — short grain does not give the best results. — incorporate the butter into the rice which helps the grains to remain separate. — rice cooked too slowly; care must be taken to follow the correct method when cooking the rice as this problem cannot be rectified. — too much stock added; care must be taken to use the correct quantities as this cannot be rectified later. — rice and stock not boiling when placed into the oven to braise; care must be taken to follow the correct method when cooking the rice as this cannot be rectified later.
(2) Rice is greyish in colour	— stock was dark in colour; care must be taken when preparing the stock as this problem caused by faulty stock cannot later be rectified. — held in a refrigerator in contact with a metal container; this should be avoided as the problem cannot later be rectified.

Storage

Store in an earthenware container covered with greaseproof paper or cling film.

Reheating

Place in a shallow pan with a little stock and butter. Cover with greaseproof paper and a lid and reheat in the oven.

5.55 SAFFRON RICE

The addition of saffron gives the rice a saffron yellow colour and saffron flavour, as in Risotto Milanaise (5.58).

Once the rice has been fried in butter, add 1 g saffron then the stock. Alternatively, add the saffron to the stock before it is added to the rice.

Stewed rice

5.56 RISOTTO

Makes: 10 portions. Cooking time: 30 minutes.

Quantity	*Ingredient*
75 g	butter
75 g	chopped onion
500 g	rice
1½ l	white stock (preferably chicken)
1	bayleaf
	seasoning

Method

(1) Melt the butter in a deep sided pan. Add the onion and cook without coloration.

(2) Add the rice, incorporating it into the butter and onion for a few moments, but do not allow the onion to colour.

(3) Add the hot stock. Bring to the boil; add seasoning and bayleaf.

(4) Cover with a lid, stew, occasionally stirring with a wooden spoon.

(5) When cooked, remove the bayleaf.

(6) Season to taste, transfer to a clean receptacle and retain in a bain-marie covered with a lid.

Notes

(1) The ratio of stock to rice should be approximately three parts stock to one part rice.

(2) Do not use too large a bayleaf or it may make the risotto smell too strong.

(3) A bouquet garni may be added, but as the stock has already been prepared with one it should not be necessary.

(4) Another method of making risotto is as above, but adding

the boiling stock gradually throughout the cooking process as it is absorbed into the rice.

(5) To test if cooked squeeze between the fingers. Risotto rice should be soft and moist.

(6) Risotto may be completed by adding grated Parmesan cheese and knobs of butter when cooking has been completed (Risotto Italienne (5.59)).

(7) Always use a fork when attending to the rice once it has cooked.

Storage

Risotto may be stored in an earthenware container covered with greaseproof paper.

Reheating

Risotto does not always reheat well, but the same method may be used as for reheating pilaff. Do not attempt to reheat rice to a depth of more than 5 cm.

Extensions of rice dishes

5.57 PILAFF DE FOIES DE VOLAILLE

Add quick sautéed chicken livers to Pilaff Rice (5.54).

5.58 RISOTTO MILANAISE

Add strips of ham, tongue, mushroom and Tomato Concassée (8.169) to Saffron Rice (5.55).

5.59 RISOTTO ITALIENNE

Add grated Parmesan cheese.

NOUVELLE CUISINE

The dishes outlined in this chapter may also be prepared in the Nouvelle Cuisine style of cooking. However, care must be taken when preparing sauces to be used as a coating or as part of the dish or served as an accompaniment as those thickened with a roux or based on flour may not be used. For further guidance on sauces *see* Chapter 3.

CONVENIENCE PRODUCTS

Because of their delicate nature eggs are not widely processed into convenience forms. Generally a better result is achieved using fresh products cooked to order. However, hard boiled eggs are available in convenience form as in ready cooked Scotch eggs, shelled hard boiled eggs, pickled eggs and the long egg as found in commercial veal, ham and egg pie. Frozen whole egg (i.e. without the shell) and powdered egg are also available but are mainly used in confectionery and bakery items. Ready-to-reheat omelettes, scrambled and fried eggs both plain and savoury may also be purchased.

Very few establishments make ravioli and canneloni products themselves. Ravioli in particular may be purchased freshly made uncooked, whilst canneloni paste ready cooked, rolled and stuffed is also available. These may be used as outlined in this chapter. Ready-made canneloni squares, dried and packaged, may also be purchased and prepared as described in this chapter from poaching the paste to stuffing, rolling and completing with various sauces.

Ravioli, canneloni and lasagnes are available as complete frozen dishes, boil-in-the-bag ravioli and tinned canneloni. Spaghetti is available in a variety of convenience forms — boil-in-the-bag, frozen and canned.

Rice dishes, in particular a variety of risottos and pilaffs, are available in boil-in-the-bag form and convenience dried packs, generally in multiples of four portions. The directions of the manufacturers should always be followed.

Finishing touches may be made to all ready prepared convenience products by adding extra garnishes of fresh commodities, seasonings and in most instances sauces.

CHAPTER SIX

Fish

INTRODUCTION

The range of fish available to the caterer is extensive and is in no way limited to those varieties discussed in this chapter. The types of fish selected for discussion are those most commonly used within the catering industry and are aligned with specific principles, methods and dishes — and, it is hoped, good trade practice.

Fish may be classified in a number of different ways, e.g. marine or fresh water, or according to their shape — tapering, arrow-shaped, flat, round. In professional cookery it is generally accepted that fish are categorised under two main headings:

(a) shellfish, further subdivided into crustaceans and molluscs (*see* p. 205);

(b) other fish further subdivided as follows:

(i) oily fish, e.g. mackerel, red mullet, salmon, salmon trout, trout, skate, whitebait;

(ii) white fish, e.g. brill, cod, haddock, halibut, hake, lemon sole, Dover sole, plaice, turbot, whiting.

These categorisations provide a handy guide to specific methods of cooking and styles of serving but should not be treated as hard and fast rules as there are exceptions. Generally those fish listed as oily are not suitable for deep fat frying, but apart from this all fish may be cooked by any of the traditional methods of poaching, boiling, shallow frying and so on. Large fish, whatever their category (but again there are exceptions), are cut into portion sizes before cooking. This provides not only an effective means of controlling the number of portions and the amount of waste but also helps the preparation and avoids problems such as drying out during cooking. For example, whilst it is possible to grill or shallow fry a whole turbot weighing 2 kg, because of its thickness doing so would in all probability make it dry and therefore inedible once cooked.

This chapter falls into two main parts. The first is concerned with many types of fish dishes and the method of cookery is used as the means of categorisation. The second follows the heading shellfish, once again dealing with many of the most popular varieties.

PREPARATION OF FISH FOR COOKING

All fish should be washed in cold water and dried before handling for cooking.

Preparation of whole round fish

Examples of whole round fish to be prepared in the following manner are herring, salmon and trout.

(1) Remove the scales by scraping them with a knife, working from tail to head.

(2) Remove all fins using a pair of scissors.

(3) Make an opening from the vent to the belly and remove all the gut with either the fingers or the handle of a fork.

(4) If the head is to be left on remove the gills gently with a small knife from the opening alongside the gills. Remove the eyes with the pointed end of a peeler. Care should be taken not to break the connective skin joining the underpart of the head to the body.

(5) If the head is to be removed then cut an inverted V-shaped incision each side of the head just below the gills.

(6) Make two very shallow incisions on each side of the fish just penetrating the skin at the thickest part — this is to facilitate cooking.

Preparation of Dover sole

Sole cannot be skinned in the same way as other flat fish. This method should be followed before filleting.

(1) Remove all fins using a pair of scissors.

(2) Remove the skin commencing at the tail end; make a slight incision across the centre of the tail, scrape backwards and forwards until the skin begins to lift, then take the loosened skin between the fingers and separate it from the fish by pulling upwards and away. It may be helpful to hold the skin in a cloth to prevent it slipping.

(3) Remove the head by cutting at an angle following the direction of the natural shape of the head formation.

(4) Remove the gut and roe by pushing with the fingers along the external area, or use a knife.

Preparation of other flat fish

Flat fish other than sole such as turbot, halibut and plaice are prepared in this way.

(1) Remove the fins by cutting through them close to the body of the fish but against the natural formation.

(2) Remove the gills and scales.

(3) Remove the head by cutting along the natural line and following the shape of the head.

(4) Remove the gut and roe by cutting an opening just under the head; scrape clean and remove all traces of blood and gut that may adhere to the bone.

To fillet flat fish

(1) Make an incision down the length of the fish following the natural line of the backbone and working from head to tail.

(2) With a flexible knife cut down against the bone structure allowing the bone formation to direct the flat side of the knife. With a clean sweeping motion cut from the centre of the fish to the fins. Remove the fillet and repeat this action until all four fillets have been removed.

To fillet round fish

(1) Commence by cutting a deep incision along the backbone of the fish.

(2) Continue cutting with the flat of the knife following the natural formation of the rib bones until the fillet comes free. Repeat on the other side.

Removal of skin from fillets

(1) Place the fillets on a work surface skin side down and with the tail end towards you. Gently cut and lift the fish from the extreme tail end then commence cutting downwards and pulling back the skin with the fingers.

(2) Fillets and suprêmes once skinned should be lightly flattened by dipping them in cold water and gently beating them with a butcher's bat.

(3) Two small incisions should be made in the surface of the fish on the skin side before cooking.

CUTS OF FISH

Fillet

The flesh of the fish is completely cut from the bone in its natural form. Flat fish yield four fillets, e.g. sole, plaice, halibut. Round fish yield two fillets, e.g. cod, whiting, salmon, herring. They are suitable for poaching, shallow and deep frying, grilling and baking.

Suprême

This term generally applies to fillets of large fish cut into small pieces or portions on the slant, e.g. suprême of halibut or turbot. They are suitable for poaching, shallow and deep frying, grilling and baking.

Goujons and goujonettes

This term refers to fillets of fish cut on the slant into small strips approximately 6–8 cm × 1 cm. Though generally applying to fillets of small fish, there is no reason why larger fish fillets may not be cut into goujons.

As the name implies goujonettes are a smaller version of goujons and are cut into strips 3–4 cm × 5 mm. Both goujons and goujonettes are suitable for deep frying and shallow frying and are sometimes poached.

Tronçon

This is a slice weighing 180–250 g cut on the bone from a large flat fish such as halibut, turbot or brill. They are suitable for boiling and grilling.

Darne

This is a slice cut from round fish on the bone, each portion weighing the same as a tronçon. The term applies to large round fish such as cod, fresh haddock and salmon. They are suitable for boiling, grilling and shallow frying.

Délice

A variation of fillet of small flat fish, this consists of a quarter of the head end and a quarter of the tail end of the fillet folded under, the skin side being folded inwards. They are suitable for poaching.

Paupiette

Another variation of fillet of small flat fish, for this the fillet is spread with a fish stuffing and rolled skin side innermost. The fish stuffing — referred to as Farce de Poisson — consists of finely minced fish (usually whiting) combined with egg whites and cream (*see* 6.23). They are suitable for poaching.

COOKING METHODS

Poaching

Poaching (sometimes referred to as shallow poaching) is carried out by covering the fish with a liquid made up of cold fish stock and wine according to the recipe using a shallow sided pan or, ideally, a special shallow two-handled oven pan made of tin-lined copper.

The main characteristic of the method is that the liquid in which the fish is poached is never permitted to boil.

Boiling

Sometimes referred to as deep poaching, this is the gentle simmering of the fish either in a court-bouillon (consisting of vegetables, water and herbs) or plenty of water containing lemon juice and salt, depending on the type and cut of fish being cooked, on top of the stove. Ideally a special fish kettle should be used.

Steaming

Fish which is to be shallow or deep poached may instead be steamed. The method for the preparation of the fish and the additional ingredients and cooking liquid are identical.

High pressure steamers have now been introduced to give a new method of "dry" steaming. Darnes of salmon, for example, can be cooked using this method with a variety of herbs or vegetables to give a whole range of dishes for the à la carte trade.

Deep frying

This is the cooking of small cuts of fish totally immersed in clarified fat or oil at a high temperature.

Shallow frying

This is the cooking of small whole fish such as sole or trout or small cuts of fish in shallow fat or oil in a frying pan on top of the stove.

Grilling

This is the cooking of small whole fish such as sole or trout or small cuts of fish under direct heat with the aid of fat or oil to prevent sticking or burning.

SHALLOW POACHED FISH

Small whole fish, fillets of small fish or small cuts of large fish off the bone may be shallow poached using a liquid consisting of water, lemon juice and salt. For white fish such as sole, plaice, halibut and turbot fish stock and white or red wine may be used.

Shallow poaching is carried out by covering the fish with the appropriate liquid in a shallow sided pan. In order to obtain the even cooking temperature necessary for these delicate products, an oven temperature of 175 °C is required and a cooking time of approximately 8 minutes is sufficient.

A considerable number of different dishes may be produced by adding a variety of other ingredients. Two well-known dishes using the principle of shallow poaching are Fillets of Sole Bonne Femme (which has a garnish of chopped shallots and parsley and sliced mushrooms), and Suprême of Turbot Dugléré (which has a garnish of chopped shallots and parsley and diced tomatoes).

Fish dishes prepared by shallow poaching are served in four basic ways:

(a) in a white wine sauce;
(b) in a sauce mornay;
(c) in a red wine sauce;
(d) in a shellfish flavoured sauce.

The main differentiation between dishes in each category is the garnish used. These dishes may be unglazed or glazed, the former is simply coated with the sauce and served whilst the latter is placed under a salamander grill to give the sauce an even coloration.

Fleurons — crescent shaped items of puff pastry — are generally served with unglazed fish dishes. They add colour and crispness to what may otherwise be a completely white and soft textured dish.

Shallow poached fish served with a white wine sauce

The majority of shallow poached fish dishes are served with a white wine sauce. There are several methods for preparing a white wine sauce, but whatever the method used the quality of the sauce basically depends upon the following:

(a) the quality of the fish stock used;
(b) the quality of the fish velouté used;
(c) the reduction of the cooking liquid in which the fish has been poached;
(d) the addition of butter and lightly beaten cream to the sauce;
(e) the addition (optional) of a sabayon of cooked egg yolks.

The three most widely used methods for preparing white wine sauces are given in 6.1–3 below. The first two are recommended for producing sufficient sauce for between one and ten portions of fish and should be cooked and served immediately. The third is the common trade practice recommended for any quantity when there is some delay between completion of the dish and service to the customer.

Recipe 1

6.1 WHITE WINE SAUCE — SAUCE VIN BLANC

Makes: 2 portions. Cooking time: 10 minutes.

Quantity	*Ingredient*
3 dl	strained liquid in which the fish has been previously poached
85 g	butter (preferably unsalted)

Method

(1) Boil the strained cooking liquid in a shallow sided saucepan until it reduces in volume and thickens to a syrupy consistency. Allow to cool for a few minutes.

(2) Briskly whisk nut size pieces of butter one at a time into the reduction which should emulsify together to form a sauce.

(3) Test for seasoning and consistency.

(4) Test how well the sauce will glaze on the back of a dish under a salamander grill before proceeding; it should form a skin, rise and colour.

(5) Arrange the cooked, well drained and trimmed fish in a serving dish on a little of the sauce and dry off any surface moisture under a salamander grill for a few moments.

(6) Coat the fish evenly with the sauce and glaze under a very hot salamander grill.

Notes

(1) Avoid using an aluminium or iron saucepan as these can cause the sauce to discolour.

(2) If the sauce is not required for glazing, Stages 4 and part of 6 do not apply.

Recipe 2

6.2 *WHITE WINE SAUCE — SAUCE VIN BLANC*

Makes: 2 portions. Cooking time: 10 minutes.

Quantity	*Ingredient*
2 dl	strained liquid in which the fish has been previously poached
70 g	butter (preferably unsalted)
1 dl	lightly beaten double cream

Method

(1) Boil the strained cooking liquid in a shallow sided saucepan until it reduces in volume and thickens to a syrupy consistency. Allow to cool for a few minutes.

(2) Briskly whisk nut size pieces of butter one at a time into the reduction which will emulsify together forming a sauce.

(3) Add the lightly beaten cream a little at a time using a whisk.

(4) Test for seasoning and consistency.

(5) Test how well the sauce will glaze on the back of a dish under a salamander grill before proceeding; it should form a skin, rise and colour.

(6) Arrange the cooked, well drained and trimmed fish in a serving dish on a little of the sauce and dry off any surface moisture under a salamander grill for a few moments.

(7) Coat the fish evenly with the sauce and glaze under a very hot salamander grill.

Notes

(1) Avoid using an aluminium or iron saucepan as these can cause the sauce to discolour.

(2) If the sauce is not required for glazing, Stages 5 and 7 do not apply.

Possible problem	*Possible cause and solution*	
(1) Butter will not emulsify with the reduced cooking liquid,.or sauce curdles when glazed	— fish stock in which the fish was poached was weak because it was not cooked out for the correct length of time or the wrong type of bones were used	Whisk the curdled sauce onto a little double cream or fish velouté, but care must be taken to use only the minimum necessary as these ingredients will alter the nature of the sauce and may make it too thick. If this occurs thin the sauce with a little fish stock or the liquid in which the fish was poached, or a combination of the two.
	— fish stock was not reduced sufficiently	
	— insufficient fish stock reduced	
	— reduced cooking liquid not allowed to cool sufficiently before adding the butter	
	— reduced cooking liquid and butter were too hot	
	— reduction at the correct temperature but butter was cold and hard	
(2) Completed sauce is too salty	— basic fish stock in which the fish was poached was overcooked; care must be	

Possible problem	*Possible cause and solution*
	taken when preparing the basic stock as problems caused by poor quality stock cannot be rectified later. — the amount of cooking liquid reduced was too great for the amount of butter added or sauce required; care must be taken to reduce the correct amount of cooking liquid as this cannot be rectified later. — salted butter was used; only unsalted butter should be used as this cannot be rectified later.
(3) Sauce is too thick	— too much butter added to the reduction; thin with a little cooking liquid or dry white wine. — butter was hard; thin with a little cooking liquid or dry white wine.
(4) Sauce is too dark	— poor quality fish stock used; lightly beaten cream may be used to lighten the sauce but it may be less expensive to discard the sauce and begin again. — the amount of cooking liquid reduced was too great for the amount of butter added or sauce required; lightly beaten cream may be used to lighten the sauce but it may be less expensive to discard the sauce and begin again.

Recipe 3

6.3 WHITE WINE SAUCE — SAUCE VIN BLANC

Makes: 10 portions. Cooking time: 15–20 minutes.

Quantity	*Ingredient*
2 dl	reduction of the strained liquid in which the fish has been previously poached
6 dl	fish velouté strained through a fine strainer or muslin
75 g	butter (preferably unsalted)
1 dl	lightly beaten double cream
	sabayon of 2 cooked egg yolks (optional)

Method

(1) Reduce the strained cooking liquid.
(2) Add the reduction to the fish velouté.
(3) Add the butter a little at a time.

(4) Add the lightly beaten cream, using either a whisk or a ladle.

(5) Test for seasoning and consistency.

(6) Test how well the sauce will glaze on the back of a dish under a salamander grill before proceeding; it should form a skin, rise and colour.

(7) Arrange the cooked, well drained and trimmed fish in a serving dish on a little of the sauce and dry off any surface moisture under a salamander grill for a few moments.

(8) Coat the fish evenly with the sauce and glaze under a very hot salamander grill.

Notes

(1) If the sauce is not required for glazing, Stages 6 and part of 8 do not apply.

(2) If a sabayon of cooked egg yolks is used, it is added to the fish velouté before it is passed through a strainer or muslin.

(3) The sauce, once completed with butter and cream (and the sabayon if included), should not be permitted to stand in a hot bain-marie for any length of time. Certainly, the water in the bain-marie should never be allowed to boil. If this is ignored then there is a real danger that the sauce will lose its lightness and may glaze badly, for the simple reason that the sauce continues to cook and forces out air incorporated by the addition of the lightly beaten cream and sabayon.

(4) To prevent a skin from forming on the surface of the sauce it should be spread with knobs of butter and/or a covering of greaseproof paper.

*Possible problem**	*Possible cause and solution*
(1) Glaze on surface of fish is uneven	— velouté undercooked; care must be taken to cook the velouté thoroughly as this cannot later be rectified.
	— too much fat in the roux on which the velouté is based; care must be taken to cook the velouté properly as this cannot later be rectified.
	— completed sauce is too thick; care must be taken to prepare the sauce correctly as this cannot be rectified once the sauce is glazed.
	— completed sauce too thin; care must be taken to prepare the sauce correctly as this cannot be rectified once the sauce is glazed.

*The sauce should be tested on the back of a flat dish and glazed to see if there are any problems that can be rectified before the fish is finished with the sauce and glazed.

*Possible problem**	*Possible cause and solution*
	— insufficient lightly beaten cream added; care must be taken to use the correct quantity of cream as this cannot be rectified once the sauce is glazed. — insufficient cooked egg yolks or sabayon used; care must be taken to use the correct quantity of these as this cannot be rectified once the sauce is glazed. — completed sauce held at too high a temperature; care must be taken at this stage as once the sauce is glazed the problem cannot be rectified. — temperature of salamander grill too low; the grill must be hot enough to glaze the sauce quickly as this cannot be rectified once the fish is glazed. — fish not sufficiently dried before coating with the completed sauce; care must be taken at this stage as the problem cannot be rectified once the sauce is glazed.
(2) Sauce runs off the fish when placed under the grill	— sauce is too thin; care must be taken when preparing the sauce as once it is glazed any problem cannot be rectified. — temperature of the salamander grill too low; care must be taken to heat the grill sufficiently as once the sauce is glazed the problem cannot be rectified. — fish not dried sufficiently before coating with the sauce; care must be taken at this stage as the problem cannot be rectified once the sauce is glazed.
(3) Sauce is too dark	— poor quality fish velouté used; care must be taken when preparing the velouté as problems caused by faulty velouté cannot be rectified later. — poor quality fish stock used to poach the fish; the fish stock used to poach the fish must be of good quality as problems caused by faulty stock cannot later be rectified. — insufficient cream used; care must be taken to add the correct quantity of cream as once the sauce is glazed the problem cannot be rectified.

*Possible problem**	*Possible cause and solution*
(4) Sauce is floury in flavour and gluey in texture	— velouté undercooked; care must be taken when preparing the velouté as problems caused by faulty ingredients cannot later be rectified.
(5) Sauce is too salty	— too high a proportion of reduced cooking liquid to velouté used; care must be taken to get these proportions correct as once the sauce is glazed any problems cannot be rectified.
	— salted butter used; only unsalted butter should be used to avoid this problem as it cannot be rectified once the sauce has been glazed.
	— basic velouté was already seasoned; the basic velouté should not be seasoned to avoid this problem as it cannot be rectified once the sauce has been glazed.

6.4 POACHED FILLET OF SOLE IN A GLAZED WHITE WINE SAUCE — FILET DE SOLE AU VIN BLANC GLACE

Makes: 10 portions. Cooking time: 8 minutes.

Quantity	*Ingredient*
10 × 85 g	fillets of Dover sole
125 g	butter (unsalted)
	seasoning of salt and pepper
50 g	finely chopped shallots or onion

Method

(1) Lightly butter and season a shallow rimmed tray of approximately 3 cm in depth.

(2) Place in the finely chopped shallots or onion.

(3) Lay in the prepared fish in single layer only.

(4) Add the cold fish stock and white wine just to cover the fish.

(5) Place a lightly buttered piece of greaseproof paper on top.

(6) Apply the principle of shallow poaching in an oven at a temperature setting of 175 °C for approximately 8 minutes.

(7) Remove the fillets, retain them in an earthenware dish with a little cooking liquid, cover them and keep warm.

(8) Prepare the sauce following one of the methods outlined in 6.1–3, discarding the garnish.

Note

This dish is glazed under a very hot salamander grill. If served unglazed it is known simply as Filet de Sole au Vin Blanc.

Service

Serve on an oval silver or stainless steel flat, or on an oval earthenware dish on an underdish and dish paper.

Assessment of the completed dish

The fillets should be:

(1) neatly folded;
(2) arranged to follow the shape of the dish;
(3) without distortion to their shape;
(4) white and moist in appearance;
(5) cooked to the correct degree;
(6) in the correct quantity for a standard portion of one large and one small fillet per person, or 1 × 85 g fillet.

Depending on the recipe used in its production, the sauce should have the following general characteristics:

(1) it should have a very light creamy colour;
(2) it should be light and creamy in consistency so that it evenly coats the fillets and completely coats the bottom of the serving dish;
(3) it should be lightly seasoned with a blend of the flavours of wine, fish, cream and butter with none predominant;
(4) it should be smooth and light in texture;
(5) there should be an adequate amount so that each customer receives a balanced portion of both fish and sauce.

Once glazed the sauce should:

(1) have an even colour over the whole surface area;
(2) show no trace of breaking or curdling;
(3) show no trace of liquid seeping out because moisture was not drained away at an earlier stage.

Possible problem	*Possible cause and solution*
(1) Fillets distort during cooking	— skin not removed before poaching; care must be taken to prepare the fish correctly before cooking as this problem cannot later be rectified. — incisions not made in the sinew on the skin side of the fillets before cooking; care must be taken to prepare the fish correctly before

Possible problem	*Possible cause and solution*
	cooking as this cannot be rectified later.
	— raw fillets not lightly beaten before cooking; care must be taken to prepare the fish correctly as this cannot later be rectified.
	— pan in which the fish was poached was filled too full; care must be taken to avoid overfilling the pan as distorted fish cannot be rectified later.
	— fish allowed to boil during poaching; care must be taken not to boil the fish as distortion cannot later be rectified.
	— fish poached for too long; care must be taken to poach the fish for the correct length of time as distortion due to overcooking cannot later be rectified.
	— fish retained too long once dished up in a hot cupboard; the fish should be cooked closer to the time they are required as distortion because of this reason cannot be rectified later.
(2) Fish sticks to tray during cooking	— tray in which the fish was poached was not buttered; care must be taken to prepare the dish correctly as this problem cannot be rectified.
(3) Surface of the cooked fish is dry	— fish not covered with greaseproof paper during cooking; care must be taken to follow the correct method of cooking to avoid this problem which cannot be rectified.
(4) Greaseproof paper sticks to fish during cooking	— paper not buttered before covering the fish; care must be taken to follow the correct procedure when cooking the fish to avoid this problem which cannot be rectified later.
(5) Shape of the fillet is distorted, texture hard, lacks moisture and is dark in colour	— fish poached at too high a temperature; care must be taken not to boil the fish to avoid this problem as it cannot be rectified later.
	— fish has been allowed to boil; care must be taken to avoid boiling the fish as these problems due to boiling cannot later be rectified.
(6) Cooking liquid has seeped	— fish not drained sufficiently on a cloth before arrangement on the service dish;

Possible problem	*Possible cause and solution*
around the edge of the completed dish	care must be taken to drain the fish before service as this cannot later be rectified.
	— surplus moisture not dried off under a salamander grill before coating with the sauce; care must be taken to follow this procedure as the problem cannot later be rectified.

Extensions

Garnishes cooked with the fish are, once cooked, strained out of the liquid, retained and placed back into the sauce once completed.

The following dishes have been selected to illustrate how a number of different types and cuts of fish may be used with a variety of sauces based on white wine sauce to give a wide choice on the menu. The sauces and cuts of fish are interchangeable.

6.5 *DELICE OF FILLET OF SOLE BERCY — DELICE DE SOLE BERCY*

The fish is poached with 100 g finely chopped shallots and 10 g chopped parsley. This dish is glazed.

6.6 *DELICE OF PLAICE PALACE — DELICE DE PLIE PALACE*

The fish is poached with 50 g finely chopped shallots, 250 g sliced button mushrooms, 200 g Tomato Concassée (8.169) and 5 g chopped tarragon. The sauce is completed with ¼ dl brandy. This dish is glazed.

6.7 *DELICE OF SOLE VERONIQUE — DELICE DE SOLE VERONIQUE*

Prepare as for Poached Fillet of Sole in a Glazed White Wine Sauce (6.1–3). Garnish with 250 g white grapes, skin and pips removed. The grapes are served chilled on the dish once it has been glazed.

6.8 *FILLET OF PLAICE DANTIN — FILET DE PLIE DANTIN*

The fish is poached with 50 g finely chopped shallots, 10 g chopped parsley and 500 g Tomato Concassée (8.169). This dish is not glazed. When serving sprinkle surface of dish with 200 g diced fried bread Croûtons (7.105).

6.9 *FILLET OF SOLE AIGLON — FILET DE SOLE AIGLON*

Prepare as for Filet de Sole au Vin Blanc (*see* 6.4, *Note*). Dress the cooked fillets on a base of 250 g Duxelles (8.167). Coat with a

White Wine Sauce (6.1–3) to which has been added a quantity of Onion Sauce (3.19). Finish the dish with a thread of Meat Glaze (p. 38). This dish is not glazed.

6.10 PAUPIETTE OF SOLE BERCY — PAUPIETTE DE SOLE BERCY

Wash the skinned fillets in cold water, dry and lightly flatten. Place the skin side uppermost, season and lightly spread with 250 g Farce de Poisson (6.23). Roll the fillets stuffed side innermost from the thin end and place them upright in a buttered and seasoned shallow saucepan so that they support themselves and do not unroll. Poach with 100 g finely chopped shallots and 10 g chopped parsley. Glaze under a very hot salamander grill.

6.11 SUPREME OF BRILL SUCHET — SUPREME DE BARBUE SUCHET

The fish is poached with blanched julienne of the following vegetables: 75 g carrots, 75 g turnips, 75 g leeks, 75 g celery and 50 g truffle. This dish is not glazed.

6.12 SUPREME OF COD DUGLERE — SUPREME DE CABILLAUD DUGLERE

The fish is poached with 50 g finely chopped shallots, 10 g chopped parsley and 500 g Tomato Concassée (8.169). This dish is not glazed.

6.13 SUPREME OF HALIBUT BREVAL — SUPREME DE FLETIN BREVAL

The fish is poached with 50 g finely chopped shallots, 10 g chopped parsley, 250 g sliced button mushrooms and 200 g Tomato Concassée (8.169). This dish is glazed.

6.14 SUPREME OF TURBOT BONNE FEMME — SUPREME DE TURBOT BONNE FEMME

The fish is poached with 50 g finely chopped shallots, 10 g chopped parsley and 250 g sliced button mushrooms. This dish is glazed.

Shallow poached fish served with a red wine sauce

Fish to be shallow poached and served with a red wine sauce are prepared in exactly the same way as for serving with a white wine sauce. Red wine sauce is made in much the same way as Recipes 1 or 2 (6.1 or 2) for white wine sauce, incorporating a small amount of flour with the butter before it is added to the reduced cooking liquid.

Fish served in a red wine sauce appear on the menu according to the type of red wine used in the sauce, e.g. Filet de Sole Chambertin.

Shallow poached fish served with sauce mornay

There are four important stages or elements in the production of these dishes:

(a) shallow poaching the fish;
(b) producing the sauce mornay;
(c) bringing together the component parts of the dish — the poached fish and the sauce mornay — and considering additional ingredients to produce extensions of the basic dish;
(d) rapid gratination of completed item under a salamander grill.

6.15 CHEESE SAUCE — SAUCE MORNAY (for fish dishes)

Makes: 10 portions. Cooking time: 20 minutes.

Quantity	*Ingredient*
75 g	grated cheese, either: *(a)* cheddar; *(b)* cheddar and gruyère; or *(c)* cheddar and Parmesan.
6 dl	Béchamel (3.4)
2 dl	strained fish stock or the cooking liquid in which the fish has previously been poached reduced by half
75 g	butter
1 dl	lightly beaten cream
2	egg yolks (preferably cooked as a sabayon)
	seasoning

Method

(1) Add the grated cheese to the béchamel and allow the cheese to melt by heating the receptacle in a bain-marie of hot water or on top of the cooker.
(2) Add the reduced strained cooking liquid or stock, bringing the sauce to a coating consistency.
(3) Add the egg yolks or sabayon.
(4) Add the butter and cream.
(5) Test the seasoning and consistency of the sauce.

Note

Once the sauce is completed, it may stand in a bain-marie of hot water for a reasonable length of time before it starts to deteriorate.

It is important that the water in the bain-marie is not allowed to boil. To prevent a skin from forming on the surface area of the sauce it should be spread with knobs of butter and/or a covering of greaseproof paper.

Assessment of the completed dish

*Possible problem**	*Possible cause and solution*
(1) Glaze is uneven on the surface of the fish	— béchamel was undercooked; care must be taken when preparing the basic sauce to avoid this problem as it cannot be rectified.
	— too much fat used in the roux as the basis of the béchamel; care must be taken when preparing the basic sauce to avoid this problem as it cannot later be rectified.
	— completed sauce was too thick; care must be taken to avoid this problem as it cannot be rectified once the sauce is glazed.
	— completed sauce too thin; care must be taken to avoid this problem as it cannot be rectified once the sauce is glazed.
	— cooked egg yolks not added; care must be taken at this stage to thicken the sauce with the egg yolks as the problem cannot be rectified once the sauce is glazed.
	— completed sauce held at too high a temperature or for too long; prolonged retention must be avoided as problems on this account cannot be rectified once the sauce is glazed.
	— temperature of the salamander grill was too low; the grill must be hot enough to glaze the sauce quickly to avoid this problem as it cannot be rectified later.
	— stale cheese used which was difficult to melt; ensure that the ingredients are fresh to avoid this type of problem at a later stage as it cannot be rectified.
	— completed dish was not sprinkled with cheese and melted butter before glazing; care must be taken to follow the correct method for glazing to avoid this problem which cannot be rectified.

*The sauce should be tested on the back of a flat dish and glazed to see if there are any problems that can be rectified before the fish is finished with the sauce and glazed.

*Possible problem**	*Possible cause and solution*
(2) Sauce runs off the fish when under the salamander grill	— sauce was too thin; care must be taken to achieve the correct consistency as this problem cannot be rectified once the sauce is glazed. — temperature of the salamander grill was too low; the temperature of the grill must be hot enough to glaze the sauce quickly as this problem cannot be rectified later. — surface of the fish not dried before coating with the sauce; care must be taken to follow this procedure to avoid this problem as it cannot be rectified once the sauce is glazed.
(3) Cooking liquid seeps around the edges of the completed dish	— fish not drained sufficiently on a cloth before arrangement on the service dish; care must be taken to drain the fish adequately before coating with the sauce and glazing as this problem cannot later be rectified. — surplus moisture not dried off under a salamander grill before coating with the sauce and glazing; care must be taken to dry the fish adequately before coating with the sauce and glazing as this problem cannot later be rectified.
(4) Sauce is too dark	— poor quality béchamel used; care must be taken when preparing the basic sauce as this problem cannot later be rectified. — fish stock used to poach the fish and the subsequent reduction was poor in quality; care must be taken in preparing the stock as problems due to poor quality cannot be rectified later. — completed sauce held for too long in warm or hot conditions; the sauce should be prepared closer to the time it is required to avoid prolonged retention as this problem cannot be rectified later. — aluminium pans used to prepare either the béchamel or the cheese sauce; aluminium should not be used on any account as this problem cannot be rectified later.

*Possible problem**	*Possible cause and solution*
(5) Sauce is floury in flavour and gluey in texture	— béchamel was undercooked; care must be taken when preparing the basic sauce to avoid this problem as it cannot be rectified later.

6.16 POACHED SUPREME OF COD IN CHEESE SAUCE — SUPREME DE CABILLAUD MORNAY

Makes: 10 portions. Cooking time: 10 minutes. Oven temperature: 175 °C.

Quantity	*Ingredient*
10 × 100 g	cod suprêmes
50 g	butter
	seasoning of salt and pepper
50 g	finely chopped shallots or onion
3 dl	fish stock
1 dl	dry white wine
8 dl	Mornay Sauce (6.15)
50 g	grated Parmesan cheese

Method

(1) Lightly butter and season a shallow rimmed tray approximately 3 cm in depth.

(2) Place in the finely chopped shallots or onion.

(3) Lay in the prepared fish in a single layer only.

(4) Add the cold fish stock and white wine just to cover the fish.

(5) Place a lightly buttered piece of greaseproof paper on top.

(6) Shallow poach in the oven at the correct temperature for approximately 10 minutes.

(7) Remove the suprêmes, retain them in an earthenware dish with a little cooking liquid, cover and keep warm.

(8) Make the mornay sauce as outlined in 6.15.

(9) Arrange the well drained and trimmed fish in a service dish on a little of the sauce.

(10) Place the fish under a salamander grill for a few moments to remove any surface moisture.

(11) Coat the fish evenly with the sauce.

(12) Sprinkle the surface of the coated fish with finely grated Parmesan cheese and melted butter.

(13) Lightly gratinate under a salamander grill.

Extensions

The following dishes have been selected to illustrate how a number of different types and cuts of fish may be used with cheese sauce to give a wide choice on the menu.

6.17 DELICE OF PLAICE CUBAT — DELICE DE PLIE CUBAT

This is prepared in the same way as Poached Suprême of Cod in Cheese Sauce (6.16), placing the poached delice onto a base of 250 g Duxelle (8.167).

6.18 FILLET OF SOLE FLORENTINE — FILET DE SOLE FLORENTINE

This is prepared in the same way as Poached Suprême of Cod in Cheese Sauce (6.16), placing the poached fillets onto a base of 250 g buttered leaf Spinach (8.106).

6.19 SUPREME OF HALIBUT WALEWSKA — SUPREME DE FLETIN WALEWSKA

This is prepared in the same way as Poached Suprême of Cod in Cheese Sauce (6.16), placing a slice of cooked lobster on each suprême before coating with the sauce and gratinating.

Shallow poached fish dishes served with a shellfish flavoured sauce

Shellfish flavoured sauces may also be served with plain poached fish dishes. The recipes for lobster sauce given below are good examples of modern culinary practice combining good quality with low cost. They are also very versatile sauces and can be used in other fish dishes either glazed or unglazed (in which case a little slightly whipped cream and sabayon should be added), served with prawn and scampi dishes or over quenelles and mousselines, or served as a sauce accompanying fish soufflé.

6.20 LOBSTER SAUCE (1)

Makes: 10 portions. Cooking time: 1½ hours.

Quantity	*Ingredient*
1½ dl	oil
150 g	roughly cut vegetables — carrots, onion, celery
1	bayleaf
1	sprig of thyme
2 cloves	crushed garlic
2 kg	crushed cooked lobster shells
1 l	Fish Stock (3.2)

Quantity	Ingredient
450 g	squashed tomatoes
100 g	tomato purée
1 l	thick velouté of fish or veal
75 g	butter
2 dl	cream
1 dl	brandy
	seasoning

Method

(1) Heat the oil in a shallow pan. Add the roughly cut vegetables, garlic and herbs and fry until lightly coloured.

(2) Add the crushed lobster shells and lightly cook.

(3) Add the fish stock, tomatoes and tomato purée and allow to boil gently for approximately 1 hour.

(4) Strain the cooking liquid into another saucepan and reduce by about half.

(5) Whisk in the velouté and continue cooking for a further 5–10 minutes. If it is considered that the sauce will be too pale in colour once the cream has been added additional tomato purée may be added.

(6) Pass through a fine strainer and reboil. Remove from the heat and adjust the thickness and test for seasoning.

(7) Complete by shaking or whisking in knobs of butter followed by the cream and brandy. Do not reboil.

6.21 LOBSTER SAUCE (2)

Makes: 10 portions. Cooking time: 1½ hours.

Quantity	Ingredient
1½ dl	oil
150 g	roughly cut vegetables — carrots, onion, celery
1	bayleaf
1	sprig of thyme
2 cloves	crushed garlic
2 kg	crushed cooked lobster shells
1 dl	brandy
¼ l	white wine
1 l	Fish Stock (3.2)
450 g	squashed tomatoes
75 g	tomato purée
200 g	butter
2 dl	cream

Method

(1) Heat the oil in a pan. Add the vegetables, herbs and crushed garlic and lightly colour.

(2) Add the crushed lobster shells and lightly cook. Drain off surplus fat and flambé with the brandy.

(3) Add the white wine, fish stock, fresh tomatoes and tomato purée.

(4) Boil, skim and gently simmer for approximately 1 hour.

(5) Strain off the liquid into a shallow sided saucepan and reduce by about two-thirds.

(6) Finish by thickening with butter — or lobster butter if available. The sauce should not be boiling at this stage and the butter should be added whilst shaking the pan and test for seasoning.

Note

This sauce may also be completed with cream which will lighten the colour considerably, changing it from one that resembles Sauce Americaine (*see* 6.69) — which is a rather rich red in colour — to that of a velouté-based sauce.

6.22 LOBSTER SAUCE (3)

Makes: 10 portions. Cooking time: 1½ hours.

Quantity	*Ingredient*
1½ dl	oil
150 g	roughly cut vegetables — carrots, onion, celery
1	bayleaf
1	sprig of thyme
2 cloves	crushed garlic
2 kg	crushed cooked lobster shells
150 g	flour
75 g	tomato purée
450 g	squashed tomatoes
1 l	Fish Stock (3.2)
¾ l	white wine
1 dl	brandy
2 dl	cream
	seasoning

Method

(1) Heat the oil in a pan. Add the vegetables, herbs and crushed garlic and lightly colour.

(2) Add the crushed lobster shells and lightly cook.

(3) Add the flour to make a roux. Cook for a few minutes then add the tomato purée and fresh tomatoes. Cook for a few moments.

(4) Add the fish stock and white wine to form a sauce. Bring to

the boil, simmer gently for approximately 1 hour continuously skimming and removing all traces of fat.

(5) Strain through a coarse strainer under pressure, followed by passing a second time through a finer strainer without undue pressure. This will help to bring out the full flavour of the fleshy parts attached to the shell.

(6) Reboil, test for seasoning and if necessary the colour. Remove from the heat and finish with the brandy and, if desired, some double cream.

Fish forcemeat, mousses, mousselines and quenelles

These are made in much the same way as for meat forcemeat, mousses, mousselines and quenelles (*see* pp. 368–73), and may be assessed using the same criteria.

6.23 FISH FORCEMEAT — FARCE DE POISSON

Proceed as for a Hot Savoury Mousse mixture (7.255) using raw fillets of whiting in place of chicken.

6.24 COLD FISH MOUSSE

This is a finely minced preparation made as for Cold Savoury Mousse (7.254) using cold pre-poached salmon or boiled lobster.

It is trade practice to use fish stock to make the aspic jelly for coating the mousse. The liquid should be clarified with egg whites only as for a Consommé (*see* 4.1) using 3 egg whites to ½ l liquid. Once clarified the liquid should be passed through a muslin cloth and 50–75 g soaked leaf gelatine added so that it will set when cold.

6.25 FISH MOUSSELINE

Fish mousselines are made using the rather firm types of fish such as salmon and sole in the same way as Mousselines made with meat (*see* 7.257) substituting the raw fish in place of the meat.

Fish mousselines may be served with any of the white wine based fish sauces given in this chapter, for example:

Mousseline de Sole Sauce Bercy

6.26 FISH QUENELLES

These are made from the same mixture as Fish Mousselines (6.25) but are shaped much smaller using teaspoons to mould them.

Fish quenelles may be served with any of the white wine based sauces given in this chapter, for example:

Quenelles of Whiting with Sauce Bonne Femme —
Quenelles de Merlan Sauce Bonne Femme

BOILED FISH

Boiling — or deep poaching — is suitable for a number of types and cuts of fish, as the following table demonstrates:

TABLE 3. TYPES AND CUTS OF FISH FOR BOILING

Type and cut of fish	*Liquid for boiling*
Oily fish:	
Mackerel — fillets Salmon — whole, cross sections, steaks, fillets Salmon trout — whole, fillets Skate — wings Trout — live trout (blue trout)	A court-bouillon consisting of water, vinegar, vegetables and herbs (*see* 6.27, Methods 1 and 2)
White round and flat fish:	
Brill — tronçons, suprêmes Cod — steaks, suprêmes Coley — steaks, suprêmes Haddock — steaks, suprêmes Halibut — tronçons, suprêmes Turbot — tronçons, suprêmes	Water, lemon juice and salt (*see* 6.32)
Smoked fish:	
Haddock Coley	Milk or water or a combination of both (*see* 6.38)
Kippers	Water

Cooking times and procedures vary considerably according to the size of fish being deep poached. A 180 g cod or salmon steak takes approximately 8–10 minutes and is ready to serve immediately, whereas a whole salmon weighing 7–8 kg which is generally served cold should be maintained just at boiling point for 10 minutes, then left in the cooking pan in which it has been poached until cold (preferably for 12 hours and under refrigeration once it has cooled). Ideally a special fish kettle should be used for boiling fish and, as for shallow poached fish, the liquid in which the fish is cooked should gently simmer.

The term boiled fish is seldom used when referring to items of fish cooked in this manner. According to trade practice it is referred to as poached, but for the sake of clarity the term poached will not be used in this section to mean boiled except in recipe headings.

Testing if cooked

Due to its delicate nature cooked fish is difficult to handle and prone to breaking. Moreover, that the fish *appears* cooked on the outside is no guarantee that it is cooked right through at the thickest point.

Fish in a court-bouillon continues to cook as the liquid cools. It is therefore not possible to know if the fish is cooked to the correct degree when it is removed from the cooker without considerable experience. Careful attention to time and procedure are the surest guides and are therefore of great importance.

To test if cooked

(1) Remove the fish from the cooking liquid and place on the fish kettle drainer.

(2) Small whole fish and cuts of large fish should be firm to the touch and show signs of breaking or flaking when slight pressure is applied. If the fish gives a feeling of springiness then it is not cooked.

(3) With fish steaks such as darnes and tronçons the centre bone should detach easily from the fish with no traces of flesh adhering to it. It may be possible to move one of the fillets gently away from the centre bone at its thickest point using the point of a small knife. This has the advantage that you can *see* if the fish is cooked as well as feel, and the fish can easily be reformed for the next stage of the recipe.

Service of boiled fish dishes

With cuts such as darnes and tronçons the dark skin may be removed either at the time the food is dressed up or at the actual point of service.

Place the fish in an earthenware dish, remove the centre bone and the dark skin with the point of a small knife, and add sufficient of the cooking liquid to cover the base of the dish. Garnish with slices of lemon, small turned boiled potatoes and sprigs of picked parsley. Serve the appropriate sauce separately.

Items cooked in a court-bouillon are served with some of the cooking liquid, slices of the carrot and onion, bayleaf and peppercorns, sprigs of picked parsley and small turned boiled potatoes. The appropriate sauce is served separately.

Darnes of salmon are served with an accompaniment of sliced peeled cucumber.

Boiling in a court-bouillon

6.27 FISH BOILED IN A COURT-BOUILLON

Makes: 10 portions. Cooking time: 8–10 minutes.

Quantity	*Ingredient*
5 l	water
½ l	vinegar
10	peppercorns
2	bayleaves
10 g	parsley stalks
150 g	onions cut into rings
150 g	grooved and sliced carrots
5 g	salt

Method 1

(1) Boil the court-bouillon preparation for 20 minutes, then skim.

(2) Place the prepared fish into the hot liquid and gently simmer.

Notes

(1) This method is suitable for cuts of fish such as salmon steaks, wings of skate and trout.

(2) *See* p. 186 for an analysis of boiled fish.

Method 2

(1) Cover the whole fish, the fillets or sections of salmon with a raw court-bouillon (i.e. the ingredients listed before any cooking takes place).

(2) Bring to the boil, skim and allow to simmer gently for:

whole salmon	— 10 mins
sections of salmon	— 10 mins
fillets of salmon	— 5 mins

(3) Remove from the stove and permit the fish to cool completely in the liquid, preferably for 12 hours and in a refrigerator.

Notes

(1) This method is suitable for whole fish such as salmon and fillets or cross-sections of salmon.

(2) *See* p. 186 for an analysis of boiled fish.

Extensions

Some examples of fish dishes in which the main item is boiled in a court-bouillon are given below.

6.28 BLUE TROUT — TRUITE AU BLEU

Makes: 2 portions. Cooking time: 8 minutes.

Quantity	*Ingredient*
3 l	boiling court-bouillon
2	trout (live)
½ dl	vinegar

Method

(1) Remove the trout from the tank.

(2) Stun by hitting the back of the head with the back of a knife.

(3) Make a small incision in the belly of the fish and take out the gut carefully with the fingers.

(4) Place the trout into a shallow tray or dish containing the vinegar and let it soak for a few moments until the surface turns blue. It is necessary to turn the fish during this operation to ensure complete exposure to the vinegar.

(5) Remove the trout from the vinegar and immediately boil in the hot court-bouillon for approximately 8 minutes.

(6) Serve the trout either in the fish kettle in which it has been poached or on a table napkin, and garnish it with sprigs of freshly picked parsley.

Note

The trout should be handled as little as possible, especially during the preparation stages, as there is a risk of removing the natural outer mucus which, when contact is made with the vinegar, turns blue in colour.

Service

This dish is served accompanied by a dish of small barrel-shaped boiled potatoes and a suitable sauce, either Sauce Hollandaise (3.12) or Beurre Fondu (3.53).

6.29 POACHED FILLET OF MACKEREL WITH PARSLEY SAUCE— FILET DE MACQUEREAU AU PERSIL

Makes: 10 portions. Cooking time: 6 minutes.

Quantity	*Ingredient*
10 × 100 g	mackerel fillets
5 l	Court-Bouillon (6.27)
½ l	Parsley Sauce (3.20)
10	Plain Boiled Potatoes (9.1)
	sprigs of parsley

Method

(1) Place the prepared fillets into the simmering court-bouillon and allow to cook.

(2) Remove from the cooking liquid, drain and remove the skin.

(3) Dress on a serving dish with a little of the cooking liquid. Garnish with the plain boiled potatoes.

(4) Serve the Parsley Sauce in a sauceboat separately.

6.30 POACHED SALMON STEAK WITH HOLLANDAISE SAUCE — DARNE DE SAUMON POCHEE SAUCE HOLLANDAISE

Makes: 10 portions. Cooking time: 8 minutes.

Quantity	*Ingredient*
10 × 150 g	salmon steaks
5 l	Court-Bouillon (6.27)
10	Plain Boiled Potatoes (9.1)
½	peeled and thinly sliced cucumber
	sprigs of parsley
2	lemons
½ l	Hollandaise Sauce (3.12)

Method

(1) Place the prepared salmon steaks into the simmering court-bouillon and allow to cook.

(2) Remove from the cooking liquid, drain and remove the skin and the centre bone.

(3) Dress on a serving dish with a little of the cooking liquid. Garnish with slices of lemon, picked parsley and the plain boiled potatoes.

(4) Accompany separately with a dish of the sliced cucumber and the Hollandaise Sauce in a sauceboat.

6.31 SKATE WITH BLACK BUTTER — RAIE AU BEURRE NOIR

Makes: 10 portions. Cooking time: 8 minutes.

Quantity	*Ingredient*
10 × 100 g	skate wing pieces
5 l	Court-Bouillon (6.27)
100 g	capers
150 g	butter
¼ dl	vinegar
5 g	chopped parsley

Method

(1) Place the prepared pieces of skate into the simmering court-bouillon and allow to cook.

(2) Remove from the cooking liquid and drain.

(3) Dress on an earthenware dish, sprinkled with the capers.

(4) Place the butter into a pre-heated omelette pan and cook until light brown in colour. Remove to the side of the stove, add the vinegar and the chopped parsley and pour over the portions of boiled skate immediately.

Boiling in water, lemon juice and salt

6.32 FISH BOILED IN WATER, LEMON JUICE AND SALT

Makes: 10 portions. Cooking time: 8–10 minutes.

Quantity	*Ingredient*
5 l	water
2	juice of lemons
5 g	salt

Method

(1) Boil the water, lemon juice and salt.

(2) Place in the prepared cuts of fish, bring back to boiling point, skim and gently simmer.

Notes

(1) This method is suitable for cuts of fish such as tronçons and suprêmes of brill, cod, haddock, halibut and turbot.

(2) *See* p. 186 for an analysis of boiled fish.

Extensions

Some examples of fish dishes in which the main item is boiled in water, lemon juice and salt are given below.

6.33 POACHED BRILL STEAK WITH MELTED BUTTER— TRONCON DE BARBUE POCHE BEURRE FONDU

Makes: 10 portions. Cooking time: 8–10 minutes.

Quantity	*Ingredient*	
5 l	water	court-bouillon
2	lemons	court-bouillon
5 g	salt	court-bouillon
10 × 180 g	brill steaks	
150 g	Beurre Fondu (3.53)	
3	lemons	
	sprigs of parsley	
10	Plain Boiled Potatoes (9.1)	

Method

(1) Boil the water, lemon juice and salt.

(2) Place in the prepared cuts of fish. Bring back to boiling point, skim and gently simmer until cooked.

(3) Remove from the cooking liquid. Drain and remove the skin and the centre bone.

(4) Dress on a serving dish with a little of the cooking liquid. Garnish with slices of lemon, picked parsley and the plain boiled potatoes.

(5) Serve the beurre fondu separately in a sauceboat.

Service

There are four ways of serving fish prepared in this way:

(a) on an oval silver or stainless steel flat dish;
(b) on a white earthenware dish with underdish and dish paper;
(c) on an oval silver or stainless steel flat dish with special inbuilt strainer;
(d) on a table napkin on an oval flat dish of silver or stainless steel.

Assessment of the completed dish

(1) The fish should be white in appearance.
(2) The flavour should be delicate and fresh.
(3) The fish should be moist and flaky in texture, perfectly formed and not distorted.
(4) The centre bone and dark skin should have been removed without causing the fish to break.
(5) The correct standard portion is approximately 180 g.
(6) The garnish of parsley sprigs should be clean and fresh in appearance and the lemon slices should be evenly and neatly cut.
(7) A little of the cooking liquid should accompany the fish on the dish in which it is served.
(8) There should be two or three white plain boiled barrel-shaped potatoes per portion.
(9) The accompanying sauce should be served separately in a sauceboat.

6.34 POACHED COD STEAK WITH EGG SAUCE — DARNE DE CABILLAUD POCHEE SAUCE AUX OEUFS

Prepare 10 × 180 g cod steaks as in 6.33 and serve accompanied by ½ l Egg Sauce (3.17).

6.35 POACHED SUPREME OF HADDOCK WITH ANCHOVY SAUCE — SUPREME D'AIGLEFIN POCHEE SAUCE ANCHOIS

Prepare 10 × 100 g haddock suprêmes as in 6.33 and serve accompanied by ½ l Anchovy Sauce (3.14).

6.36 POACHED HALIBUT STEAK WITH PARSLEY SAUCE — TRONCON DE FLETIN POCHE SAUCE PERSIL

Prepare 10 × 180 g halibut steaks as in 6.33 and serve accompanied by ½ l Parsley Sauce (3.20).

6.37 POACHED SUPREME OF TURBOT WITH CHANTILLY SAUCE — SUPREME DE TURBOT POCHEE SAUCE CHANTILLY

Prepare 10 × 100 g turbot suprêmes as in 6.33 and serve accompanied by ½ l Sauce Chantilly (3.36).

Smoked fish boiled in milk/water

6.38 POACHED FINNAN HADDOCK

Makes: 10 portions. Cooking time: 5 minutes.

Quantity	*Ingredient*
10 × 200 g	smoked haddock
2 l	milk
2 l	water

Method

(1) Remove fins and tail with scissors.

(2) Place the prepared haddock into a shallow sided saucepan and cover with the milk and water.

(3) Bring to the boil and gently simmer for the prescribed time.

(4) Dress in an earthenware dish and remove the centre bone. Serve with a little of the cooking liquid.

Notes

(1) Smoked coley may be substituted for haddock and cooked in exactly the same way.

(2) Milk may be used on its own instead of a combination of milk and water.

(3) *See* below for an analysis of boiled fish.

Analysis of boiled fish

Possible problem	*Possible cause and solution*
(1) Fish is distorted in shape, dark in colour and hard and dry in texture	— fish has been overcooked; care must be taken to boil the fish by gentle simmering and for the correct length of time as these problems cannot be rectified later.
(2) White fish, when cooked, is	— fish cooked in wrong type of liquid; care must be taken when boiling fish to select the

Possible problem	*Possible cause and solution*
dark in colour	correct type of liquid as these problems cannot be rectified later.
(3) Fish cooked in a court-bouillon takes on an oily smell and flavour	— court-bouillon overused; when cooking smaller cuts of fish for immediate consumption as a hot dish ensure that the court-bouillon is changed frequently as this problem cannot be rectified later.
	— if required cold the fish was not allowed to cool completely in the cooking liquid and the liquid was used to cook several subsequent batches of fish; care must be taken to follow the correct procedure to avoid this problem which cannot be rectified later.

STEAMED FISH

All fish dishes that are prepared by shallow or deep poaching may alternatively be steamed. Exactly the same procedures are followed in preparing the fish, the cooking liquid and any additional ingredients. When using a pressure steamer, however, it is advisable to cover the fish with lightly buttered greaseproof paper to prevent moisture from the steam diluting the cooking liquid and to avoid discoloration of the fish.

Fish dishes that require a sauce may be steamed in the appropriate cooking liquid together with any additional garnish that may be required. The fish should be covered with buttered greaseproof paper and a lid to prevent water from the steam diluting the cooking liquid. The sauce may be produced from the liquid in exactly the same way as for poaching, and possible problems and causes are in most instances exactly the same. It should be stressed, however, that unless the steaming equipment is thoroughly cleaned before cooking fish there is a danger that the flavour may become contaminated.

Some distortion of shape, in particular for those items that are cooked off the bone such as fillets and delice, may be experienced. It is advisable to refer to the guides supplied by the manufacturers of the steaming equipment for the best method of cooking and the length of time for cooking wherever possible.

DEEP FRIED FISH

Deep frying is the cooking of small cuts of fish in clarified fat or oil at a high temperature with the fish totally immersed in the fat. It is the fastest traditional method of cooking fish.

Small whole fish such as Dover sole, lemon sole, whiting and whitebait are suitable for deep frying, as are cuts of fish such as fillets, goujons, goujonettes and suprêmes.

All deep fried fish must have some form of outer coating:

(a) to prevent fat or oil penetrating the fish;
(b) to give the outer coating of the fish crispness;
(c) to enhance the texture, flavour and appearance of the fish in a variety of ways.

There are three different coatings used for deep fried fish:

(a) batters — used for any kind of fish cooked à l'Orly;
(b) breadcrumbs — used in the cooking of fish à l'Anglaise;
(c) flour — used in the cooking of fish à la Française;

Whatever kind of coating is used it is advisable to serve deep fried fish as soon as possible after it is cooked as the coating quickly loses its fresh taste and crisp texture.

Garnishes and accompaniments for deep fried fish are provided according to the kind of cooking:

(a) à l'Orly — a quarter of lemon and picked parsley with hot Tomato Sauce (3.10) served separately;
(b) à l'Anglaise — a quarter of lemon and deep fried picked parsley with Tartare Sauce (3.45) served separately;
(c) à la Française — a quarter of lemon and picked parsley with *no* sauce.

Fish deep fried in batter
The most common batters are:

(a) yeast (*see* 6.40);
(b) convenience batter mixtures.

Before the application of the batter the fish may be marinated in lemon juice, oil and seasoning (6.39). This process is generally associated with haute cuisine and adds fat to the fish, the acid acting as a tenderiser on the flesh.

6.39 MARINADE FOR DEEP FRIED FISH

Method

The prepared fish is placed in a tray, sprinkled with lemon juice, oil and a seasoning of salt and pepper together with a few parsley stalks, and left for approximately 30 minutes.

6.40 *YEAST BATTER*

Makes: 10 portions. Preparation time: 1 hour.

Quantity	*Ingredient*
400 g	strong flour
15 g	yeast
5 dl	milk at 37 °C
5 g	sugar
5 g	salt

Method

(1) Sieve the flour, place into a basin and make a hollow in the centre.
(2) Dissolve the yeast in the milk with the sugar.
(3) Pour the liquid into the hollow and whisk to a smooth batter.
(4) Add the salt and allow the batter to stand in a warm place for about 1 hour to prove before using.

Note

Yeast batter may improve with keeping but do not retain it in a refrigerator below 7 °C if it is required for immediate use.

6.41 *FILLET OF SOLE IN BATTER — FILET DE SOLE A L'ORLY*

Makes: 10 portions. Cooking time: 5 minutes.

Quantity	*Ingredient*	
10 × 85 g	fillets of Dover sole	
250 g	flour	
	Yeast Batter (6.40)	
1	juice of lemon	Marinade (6.39)
5 g	chopped parsley	Marinade (6.39)
1 dl	oil	Marinade (6.39)
3	lemons	
	sprigs of parsley	
½ l	Tomato Sauce (3.10)	

Method

(1) Marinate the fish for approximately 30 minutes.
(2) Pass the fish through seasoned flour shaking off all the surplus flour.
(3) Pass the fish through the batter. Drain off all excess batter by gently pulling through the fingers.
(4) Place the fish into the hot fat away from oneself.
(5) Fry until crisp and golden turning the fillets during cooking to ensure even cooking and coloration (*see Note* (3) below).

(6) Drain the fillets by placing them onto absorbent kitchen paper. Season with salt.

(7) Dress on a dish paper on a flat dish. Garnish with lemon wedges and picked parsley and serve accompanied by a sauceboat of tomato sauce.

Notes

(1) If the fish is not marinated before cooking then thoroughly dry them in a cloth or absorbent kitchen paper before battering them.

(2) The cooking temperature depends upon the size of the pieces of fish — 180 °C is regarded as standard.

(3) The fish is cooked when it floats to the surface of the fat and is evenly coloured all over. With larger cuts such as suprêmes of cod, haddock and halibut a further test is to check the weight which appears to diminish slightly in proportion to its size with cooking. However, this method of testing requires a high degree of skill and experience and a safer test is to carefully monitor the time, allowing 8 minutes for a 120 g suprême at a temperature of 180 °C.

Service and retention

As stated before ideally this type of dish should be cooked and served to order. However, if it must be held it should be placed on greaseproof paper and retained in a hot cupboard or kept in equipment specially designed for the purpose. Even so, care must still be taken when keeping deep fried fish in batter in such conditions as if the temperature is too high or the fish is kept in for too long it will become stale in appearance and lose its crispness, colour and flavour. On the other hand, if held at a moderately hot constant temperature the fish will weep and become soft.

Deep fried items in batter should not be covered with a lid once they are cooked as the steam that arises will condense against the lid and fall back on the fish causing it to become damp and soft.

Serve on an oval silver or stainless steel flat dish with a dish paper or cloth napkin.

Assessment of the completed dish

(1) The outer coating and inner layer of fish should be hot.

(2) The outer coating of batter should be a light golden colour, and the fish should be moist and white.

(3) The flavour should be a blend of the seasoned batter, the natural flavour of the fish plus that of the fat.

(4) The outer skin of the batter should be very crisp, whilst the

batter surrounding the fish should not be floury. The batter should be in correct proportion to the fish.

(5) The dish should be seasoned yet there should be no sign of seasoning on the dish paper or napkin.

(6) The garnish of lemon wedges should be neatly cut, free from excess pith, membrane and pips. The parsley sprigs should be clean and fresh in appearance.

(7) The tomato sauce should be served separately in a sauce-boat.

(8) There should be no oil or fat in evidence and when presented the dish paper should be dry.

*Possible problem**	*Possible cause and solution*
(1) Batter will not colour	— fat was not hot enough; ensure that the fat is at the correct temperature before frying the fish as this problem cannot later be rectified.
	— too many pieces of fish fried at once; this reduces the temperature of the fat and should be avoided as it cannot be rectified later.
	— fat not allowed to reheat between batches; the fat must be allowed to recover its heat before the next items are added to avoid this problem which cannot later be rectified.
	— incorrect type of flour used for the batter; care must be taken that the correct type of flour (i.e. strong) is used to make the batter to avoid this problem as it cannot be rectified later.
	— insufficient sugar used in the batter; care must be taken to prepare the batter correctly to avoid this problem which cannot be rectified later.
(2) Fish becomes soggy and breaks during cooking	— fat was not hot enough; ensure that the fat is at the correct temperature before frying the fish as this problem cannot be rectified later.
	— too many pieces of fish fried at once; this reduces the temperature of the fat and should be avoided as the problem cannot be rectified later.
	— fish handled too much during frying, e.g. stirred too often with a spider; this must be

*Any problems found with the first items to be fried may be cleared up before subsequent items are added.

Possible problem *	*Possible cause and solution*
	avoided as the problem cannot be rectified later.
	— a frying basket was used; this should be avoided as the problem cannot be rectified later.
	— outer coating of batter not allowed to set before handling with the spider; ensure that the batter has set during the initial stages before using a spider to avoid this problem which cannot later be rectified.
(3) Batter runs off fish during cooking	— batter was too thin; care must be taken when preparing the batter as this problem cannot be rectified later.
	— fish not dried before coating with flour and batter; care must be taken to follow the correct coating procedure to avoid this problem which cannot be rectified later.
	— fat was not hot enough; ensure that the fat is at the correct temperature before frying the fish as this problem cannot be rectified later.
(4) Completed item has an inner doughy layer	— batter was too thick; care must be taken when preparing the batter to avoid this as it cannot be rectified later.
	— fish not passed through flour before coating with the batter; care must be taken to follow the correct coating procedure as this problem cannot later be rectified.
(5) Batter becomes overcoloured before fish is cooked	— fat too hot; ensure that the fat is at the correct temperature before frying the fish as this problem cannot be rectified later.
	— fish pieces too thick; care must be taken when preparing the fish to avoid this as it cannot be rectified later.
(6) Completed item lacks flavour	— fish not stored correctly before or after cooking; ensure that the fish is of good quality and has been stored correctly before cooking and that the correct procedures are followed for storage after cooking.
	— batter not seasoned; care must be taken when preparing the batter as this cannot be rectified later.

Extensions

Many cuts and types of fish may be cooked in batter as in 6.41. Some examples are:

Suprême of Cod in Batter — Suprême de Cabillaud à l'Orly
Suprême of Haddock in Batter — Suprême d'Aiglefin à l'Orly
Fillet of Plaice in Batter — Filet de Plie à l'Orly

Fish deep fried in breadcrumbs

This is fish with a coating of seasoned flour, eggwash and breadcrumbs. There are a number of types of breadcrumbs in common use:

(a) fresh white breadcrumbs;
(b) dried brown breadcrumbs;
(c) purchased breadcrumbs.

6.42 COATING TECHNIQUE

Quantity	*Ingredient*
10 portions	fish
500 g	seasoned flour
6	eggs beaten with a little water (eggwash)
500 g	breadcrumbs

Method

(1) Place the flour, eggwash and breadcrumbs in shallow sided separate trays in the order of use.
(2) Pass the fish through the seasoned flour and shake off any surplus.
(3) Pass the fish through eggwash and remove surplus liquid by pulling the fish through the fingers.
(4) Pass the fish through the breadcrumbs removing any surplus crumbs.
(5) Place the breadcrumbed fish onto a table or board lightly sprinkled with breadcrumbs. Lightly bat out with the side of a large knife.
(6) Arrange on a tray and retain in a refrigerator until required.

Note

Scampi and goujons of fish need to be rolled either in the palm of the hand or on a sieve or table. This action has a twofold effect: *(a)* to reshape the fish pieces, and *(b)* to help the crumbs adhere to the fish during cooking.

6.43 FRIED FILLET OF PLAICE IN BREADCRUMBS WITH TARTARE SAUCE — FILET DE PLIE A L'ANGLAISE SAUCE TARTARE

Makes: 10 portions. Cooking time: 6 minutes.

Quantity	*Ingredient*
10 × 85 g	fillets of plaice
	flour, eggwash and breadcrumb coating (*see* 6.42)
3	lemons
	sprigs of parsley
½ l	Tartare Sauce (3.45)

Method

(1) Thoroughly dry the fish in a cloth or absorbent kitchen paper.

(2) Coat with flour eggwash and breadcrumbs.

(3) Place the fish into the hot fat away from oneself.

(4) Fry until crisp and golden turning the fillets during cooking to ensure even cooking and coloration.

(5) Drain the fillets by placing them onto absorbent kitchen paper. Season with salt.

(6) Dress on a dish paper on a flat dish. Garnish with lemon wedges and picked parsley and serve accompanied by a sauceboat of tartare sauce.

Assessment of the completed dish

Possible problem	*Possible cause and solution*
(1) Crumbs will not colour	— too many pieces of fish fried at the same time; this reduces the temperature of the fat and should be avoided as the problem cannot later be rectified. — fat not allowed to recover heat between batches; the fat must be allowed to reheat before the next items are added to avoid this problem which cannot later be rectified. — fat was not hot enough; ensure that the fat is at the correct temperature before frying the fish as this problem cannot be rectified later.
(2) Fish becomes soggy, and breaks up whilst cooking	— too many pieces of fish fried at the same time; this reduces the temperature of the fat and should be avoided as the problem cannot later be rectified. — fish was handled too much during frying;

Possible problem	*Possible cause and solution*
	this should be avoided as the problem cannot be rectified later.
	— outer coating not allowed to set before handling with the spider; ensure that the outer coating has set during the initial stages before handling to avoid this problem which cannot be rectified later.
(3) Outer coating of crumbs comes away from the fish whilst cooking	— fat was not hot enough; ensure that the fat is at the correct temperature before frying the fish to avoid this problem which cannot be rectified later.
	— fish not dried before coating with flour, eggwash and breadcrumbs; care must be taken to follow the correct coating procedure to avoid this problem which cannot be rectified later.
	— items were incorrectly stored once coated; care must be taken to follow the correct storage procedure to avoid this problem, which cannot be rectified later.

Extensions

Many types and cuts of fish may be deep fried in breadcrumbs as in 6.43. Some examples are:

Suprême of Halibut in Breadcrumbs Remoulade Sauce	— Suprême de Fletin à l'Anglaise Sauce Remoulade
Goujons of Sole Sauce Tartare	— Goujons de Sole Frits
Fillet of Sole in Breadcrumbs Remoulade Sauce	— Filet de Sole Frit à l'Anglaise Sauce Remoulade
Fried Fillets of Whiting	— Filet de Merlan Frit

Fish deep fried in flour

This is fish lightly coated with milk and seasoned flour and deep fried at a temperature of about 180 °C until lightly golden and crisp on the outside of the coating and white and moist on the inside. It is a method of cooking that is suitable for dishes for immediate consumption and is ideal for à la carte types of service.

6.44 FRIED FILLET OF SOLE FRENCH STYLE — FILET DE SOLE FRIT A LA FRANCAISE

Makes: 10 portions. Cooking time: 4 minutes.

Quantity	*Ingredient*
10 × 85 g	fillets of sole

Quantity	*Ingredient*
½ l	milk
250 g	seasoned flour
3	lemons
	sprigs of parsley

Method

(1) Dip the prepared fish in milk and drain it well, then pass through the seasoned flour and shake off any surplus flour.

(2) Place the fish into the hot fat away from oneself.

(3) Fry until crisp and lightly golden, turning the fillets during cooking to ensure even cooking and coloration.

(4) Drain the fillets by placing them onto absorbent kitchen paper. Season with salt.

(5) Dress on a dish paper on a flat dish and garnish with lemon wedges and picked parsley.

Notes

(1) This method is generally applied only to thinner and smaller cuts and types of fish such as fillets and goujons. There is the danger of damaging the structure of larger pieces of fish during cooking as there is no thick protective coating such as a yeast batter.

(2) Once the fish is cooked deterioration is very rapid. It is therefore recommended wherever possible to ensure the fish is served with the least possible delay.

(3) This method also rapidly spoils the cooking oil as the flour falls into the oil and hastens its breakdown.

6.45 DEVILLED WHITEBAIT — BLANCHAILLES DIABLEES

Makes: 10 portions. Cooking time: 5 minutes.

Quantity	*Ingredient*
1 kg	whitebait
½ l	milk
250 g	seasoned flour
3	lemons
	salt and cayenne pepper
	sprigs of parsley

Method

(1) Pass the whitebait through the milk, drain well, then pass through the seasoned flour. Place into a frying basket and shake well to remove any surplus flour.

(2) Place into a frying basket then into the hot fat.

(3) Fry until crisp and lightly golden, shaking the basket and agitating with a spider from time to time to prevent the fish from sticking together.

(4) Drain the whitebait by placing them onto absorbent kitchen paper. Season with salt and cayenne pepper.

(5) Dress on a flat dish on a dish paper or napkin. Garnish with lemon wedges and picked parsley.

6.46 FRIED WHITEBAIT — BLANCHAILLES FRITES

Prepare as in 6.45 but season with salt only.

Extensions

Other examples of fish dishes which are cooked in flour — bearing in mind *Note* (1) to 6.44 — are:

Fried Fillet of Plaice French Style — Filet de Plie à la Française
Fried Fillet of Whiting French Style — Filet de Merlan Frit à la Française

SHALLOW FRIED FISH

Shallow frying or meunière is the cooking of fish in shallow fat in a frying pan on top of the stove. The fish is served with a garnish of lemon rounds, parsley and nut brown butter (*see* 6.48). All types of fresh fish may be shallow fried, for example small whole fish such as Dover sole, lemon sole, red mullet, trout and herring, cuts of small fish such as fillets and goujons of sole and fillets and goujonettes of plaice, and cuts of large fish such as turbot steaks, suprêmes of halibut, darnes of cod and salmon steaks.

Whatever the type and cut of fish used, the application of meunière is generally always the same. Once the basic principle of shallow frying is mastered the significant aspect is the length of time required for cooking, thicker cuts such as tronçons and darnes obviously needing more time than fillets.

Fish may be shallow fried in a number of media:

(*a*) olive oil and clarified butter;

(*b*) other vegetable oils or general purpose frying oil, with or without clarified butter;

(*c*) lard.

The temperature of the fat for shallow frying can of course be measured — it should be approximately 160 °C.

The fish must be thoroughly dried and passed through seasoned flour at the last possible moment before frying. All surplus flour should be shaken from the fish before cooking.

Shallow fried fish should be cooked in a frying pan, preferably one made of iron.

The fish should always be placed into the hot cooking media presentation side first. This implies that the skin side of fillets is facing upwards, although this rule does not apply to goujons, darnes or tronçons.

6.47 FILLETS OF SOLE MEUNIERE — FILETS DE SOLE MEUNIERE

Makes: 10 portions. Cooking time: 8 minutes.

Quantity	*Ingredient*
10 × 85 g	fillets of sole
250 g	seasoned flour
3 dl	oil
3	lemons
150 g	Nut Brown Butter (6.48)
	chopped parsley

Method

(1) Heat the oil in a frying pan.

(2) Pass the fillets through the seasoned flour and shake off the surplus.

(3) Place the fish into the frying pan presentation side down (*see Note* (1) below). Fry, then turn when coloured and continue to fry until completely cooked.

(4) Test to ensure that the fish is cooked through (*see Note* (2) below).

(5) Dress on a serving dish following the shape of the dish where possible.

(6) Place a slice of peeled lemon on each portion of fish.

(7) Squeeze a little lemon juice over the fish and sprinkle with chopped parsley.

(8) Just before serving, pour the nut brown butter over the fish.

Notes

(1) The presentation side is the side of the fillet that was attached to the bone.

(2) When cooked there should be no evidence of a glassy raw appearance. The fish should be rather firm to the touch.

(3) When fish is shallow fried on the bone then the bone should be easy to remove.

Service

Serve on an oval silver or stainless steel flat, or on an oval earthenware dish on an underdish and dish paper.

Assessment of the completed dish

(1) The fish should be of an even light golden colour.

(2) The fish should be moist and not broken with no distortion to its shape.

(3) In the garnish the lemon rounds should have all traces of outer skin removed and be free from pips. The parsley should be fresh in appearance, finely chopped and evenly sprinkled over the fish. The nut brown butter should be a light nut brown in colour and in sufficient quantity to coat the fish and the base of the serving dish.

*Possible problem**	*Possible cause and solution*
(1) Fish has burnt or discoloured	— temperature of the fat was too high causing the fish to fry too quickly; ensure that the fat is at the correct temperature before frying the fish to avoid this problem which cannot be rectified later.
	— surplus flour was not shaken off when coating the fish; care must be taken to follow the correct coating procedure to avoid this problem which cannot be rectified later.
(2) Fish shows signs of breaking or flaking	— fat was not hot enough; ensure that the fat is at the correct temperature before frying the fish to avoid this problem which cannot later be rectified.
	— fish was not properly handled whilst cooking; care must be taken whilst cooking the fish to avoid breaking or flaking which cannot later be rectified.
(3) Fish surrounded by a floury outer surface	— fish was not dried before passing through the flour; care must be taken to follow the correct coating procedure to avoid this problem which cannot later be rectified.
	— fish was passed through the flour too far in advance of cooking; the fish should be prepared as close as possible to the time it is required to avoid the problems caused by lengthy storage which cannot be rectified later.

*Any problems found with the first items to be fried may be cleared up before subsequent items are added.

*Possible problem**	*Possible cause and solution*
(4) Cooked fish is distorted in shape	— incisions were not made in the skin side of the fillets; care must be taken to prepare the fish correctly before frying to avoid this problem which cannot be rectified. — fish was not properly handled whilst cooking; care must be taken when frying the fish to avoid mishandling as distortion cannot later be rectified.

6.48 NUT BROWN BUTTER — BEURRE NOISETTE

Quantity	*Ingredient*
100 g	butter
¼	juice of lemon

Method 1

(1) Heat the pan.
(2) Add knobs of butter shaking the pan continuously until the butter froths and turns a light nut brown colour.

Notes

(1) An omelette pan is ideal for making nut brown butter.
(2) It should not be made until the very last moment when the item has actually been placed on the service dish.
(3) The preparation of nut brown butter takes very little time provided the pan is hot (but not so hot that the butter melts and burns within a few seconds). It should be remembered that it is an important part of the dish and therefore requires as much care in its making as the main part of the dish.
(4) Do not attempt to produce a nut brown butter in a tin-lined or aluminium pan.

Method 2

At the point when the butter begins to colour lemon juice and chopped parsley may be added. This will result in a distinctively flavoured butter plus a lightly blanched parsley garnish.

Method 3

Knobs of butter may be added to Jus Lié (3.8). The jus lié should be of a light consistency to enable the sauce to flow easily, light brown in colour and only lightly seasoned. It may also include the appropriate garnish.

Note

Method 3 is used by some establishments to reduce significantly food costs.

Extensions

The following dishes have been selected to illustrate how a number of different types and cuts of fish may be used to give a wide choice on the menu. Additional garnishes as listed below may be placed on individual portions or sprinkled over the whole dish once it has been cooked and dished up. The basic meunière garnish of lemon slices, chopped parsley and nut brown butter may then be added.

6.49 SHALLOW FRIED TROUT WITH ALMONDS — TRUITE MEUNIERE AUX AMANDES

Allow 10 × 200 g trout. Garnish of 150 g almonds cut into strips is added to the nut brown butter at the last moment.

6.50 SHALLOW FRIED FILLET OF PLAICE BELLE MEUNIERE — FILET DE PLIE BELLE MEUNIERE

Allow 10 × 85 g fillets of plaice. A garnish of ½ small blanched, peeled and pipped tomato, a small piece of shallow fried soft herring roe and one button mushroom cooked in butter is served on top of each portion.

6.51 SHALLOW FRIED SUPREME OF COD BRETONNE — SUPREME DE CABILLAUD BRETONNE

Allow 10 × 100 g cod suprêmes. A garnish of 200 g prawns and 200 g sliced cooked button mushrooms is sprinkled over the dish.

6.52 SHALLOW FRIED SUPREME OF HALIBUT WITH CAPERS — SUPREME DE FLETIN AUX CAPRES

Allow 10 × 100 g suprêmes of halibut. A garnish of capers is sprinkled over the dish.

6.53 SHALLOW FRIED SALMON STEAK DORIA — DARNE DE SAUMON DORIA

Allow 10 × 150 g salmon steaks. A garnish of 2 cm diamond shapes of peeled and blanched cucumber is served with the dish.

6.54 SHALLOW FRIED FILLET OF SOLE GRENOBLOISE — FILET DE SOLE GRENOBLOISE

Allow 10 × 85 g fillets of sole. A garnish of segments of lemon instead of slices and 150 g capers are sprinkled over the dish.

6.55 *SHALLOW FRIED SUPREME OF TURBOT NICOISE— SUPREME DE TURBOT NICOISE*

Allow 10 × 100 g suprêmes of turbot. A garnish of Tomato Concassée (8.169), fillets of anchovy and stoned olives is added to the dish.

6.56 *SHALLOW FRIED RED MULLET GRENOBLOISE—ROUGET GRENOBLOISE*

Allow 10 × 200 g whole red mullets. A garnish of segments of lemon instead of slices and 150 g capers is sprinkled over the dish.

GRILLED FISH

Grilling is the cooking of fish under direct heat with the aid of fat or oil to prevent sticking or burning. When cooked grilled fish should be served with a garnish of lemon wedges, parsley butter and picked parsley. Examples of types and cuts of fish suitable for grilling are:

(a) small whole fish such as Dover sole, lemon sole, trout and whiting;

(b) cuts of small fish such as fillets of sole, fillets of plaice and fillets of whiting;

(c) cuts of large fish such as halibut steaks, salmon steaks, cod steaks and suprêmes of haddock.

All fish to be grilled must be thoroughly dried and are generally passed through seasoned flour at the last possible moment. All surplus flour should be shaken free from the fish before cooking. Fish may also be coated in breadcrumbs and grilled in butter to give the Saint-Germain dishes, examples of which are to be found in 6.61 and 62.

6.57 *GRILLED DOVER SOLE—SOLE GRILLEE*

Makes: 10 portions. Cooking time: 15–20 minutes.

Quantity	*Ingredient*
10 × 250 g	skinned Dover soles
250 g	seasoned flour
3 dl	oil
3	lemons
100 g	Parsley Butter (3.50)
	sprigs of parsley

Method

(1) Pass the fish through seasoned flour and shake off any surplus.

(2) Pass the fish through the oil or brush it over its surface.

(3) Place the fish on a lightly oiled grilling tray or on a hinged fish grill.

(4) Grill the fish until cooked (*see Note* (3) below).

(5) When cooked, dress on service dishes following the shape of the dish where possible.

(6) Place a slice of lemon on each portion of fish, one slice of parsley butter and some picked parsley. (Alternatively, the fish may be brushed with melted butter just before serving and garnished with lemon and picked parsley, with the parsley butter served separately in a sauceboat.)

Notes

(1) The presentation side of the fish should be placed facing downwards on the grilling tray so that when turned to cook the other side it is then the right side up for serving.

(2) For large or thick pieces of fish, after the initial colouring under the salamander, cooking may be completed in an oven. This method prevents the fish drying out during cooking and is used where large numbers are being catered for.

(3) When cooked:

(a) fillets of sole and plaice and suprêmes of larger fish should be firm to the touch;

(b) the centre bone should come away easily from tronçons and darnes;

(c) the centre bone just below the head of a whole sole should be easily felt through the flesh;

(d) the backbone of trout, herrings and other similar types of fish should be easily felt through the flesh.

(4) To simulate grill markings the fish should be passed through seasoned flour and shaken to remove any surplus and a trellis pattern marked with a red hot poker.

(5) Flat fish such as Dover sole are skinned prior to cooking, though other cuts such as suprêmes of cod or herring would not be.

Extensions

The following dishes have been selected to illustrate how a number of different types and cuts of fish may be used to give a wide choice of grilled fish on the menu.

6.58 GRILLED HERRING AND MUSTARD SAUCE — HARENG GRILLE

Allow 10 × 200 g herrings and serve accompanied by ½ l Mustard Sauce (3.18).

6.59 GRILLED SUPREME OF COD WITH PARSLEY BUTTER — CABILLAUD GRILLE

Allow 10 × 100 g suprêmes of cod and serve with slices of Parsley Butter (3.51).

6.60 GRILLED FILLET OF PLAICE WITH PARSLEY BUTTER — FILET DE PLIE GRILLE

Allow 10 × 85 g plaice fillets and serve with slices of Parsley Butter (3.51).

Grilled fish in breadcrumbs

Fish dishes which are coated in breadcrumbs and grilled in butter are generally referred to as Saint-Germain dishes. The two most popular dishes within this category are included below.

6.61 FILLET OF SOLE SAINT-GERMAIN — FILET DE SOLE SAINT-GERMAIN

Makes: 10 portions. Cooking time: 8 minutes.

Quantity	*Ingredient*
10 × 85 g	fillets of Dover sole
250 g	seasoned flour
250 g	melted butter
250 g	white breadcrumbs
40	Noisette Potatoes (9.33)
½ l	Sauce Béarnaise (3.12)
	sprigs of parsley

Method

(1) Dry the fish and pass through the seasoned flour, melted butter and breadcrumbs.

(2) Lightly flatten the fillets and mark a trellis pattern to resemble grill bars with the back edge of a large knife.

(3) Place the fish onto a liberally buttered grilling tray and sprinkle the surface of the breadcrumbed fish with melted butter. (*See Note* (1) below for an alternative method.)

(4) Grill the fillets until a light golden colour.

(5) Arrange the fillets on an oval flat dish, garnish with the noisette potatoes and sprigs of parsley. The sauce béarnaise is served separately in a sauceboat.

Notes

(1) An alternative method to stage (3) is to lay the breadcrumbed fillets in a shallow tray containing melted butter just for a few seconds, then transfer them to the grilling tray. This helps to

prevent the surface of the fish from drying whilst it is grilling under the direct heat of the salamander grill.

(2) When the fish is cooked the outer crumbed surface should be golden and moist. The fish itself should be firm to the touch.

6.62 FILLET OF SOLE CAPRICE — FILET DE SOLE CAPRICE

Prepare fillets of sole as in 6.61 but serve with a garnish of halves of banana cut lengthways and either grilled as they are or first passed through seasoned flour and butter. Serve with a sauceboat of Sauce Robert (3.32) separately.

SHELLFISH

When purchasing shellfish it is very important to ensure that they are very fresh and, in many cases, that they are alive and lively. Those with double shells must be tightly closed and those with a carapace and legs for movement must be animated.

There are two groups of shellfish.

(a) Molluscs. There are two distinct types:

(i) bivalves which have two shells joined by a hinge, the most commonly used in catering being oysters, scallops and mussels;

(ii) univalves which have just one shell and include whelks and winkles.

(b) Crustaceans. These have a single shell and legs and include crab, lobster, scampi, prawns and shrimps.

NOTE

It is worth remembering that many cases of food poisoning are caused by serving stale shellfish. A cut can quickly become infected by a scratch from live, raw or even cooked shellfish.

Crab

6.63 CRAB — CRABE

Wash the crabs in cold water and plunge them into sufficient boiling court-bouillon to cover them. Allow the crabs to simmer gently for approximately 20 minutes. When cooked leave them to cool completely in the liquid.

Lobster dishes

There are two main categories:

(a) those made from boiled lobster which are served in the shell with a variety of sauces; and

(*b*) those made from lobster cooked by a combination of boiling, shallow frying or stewing and removed from the shell at some stage before serving in a silver timbale (a silver dish with an inner lining to keep food hot).

Lobster dishes served in the shell

As outlined above, for these dishes the lobster is boiled and the flesh removed from the shell. The flesh is then cut slightly on the slant, reheated in butter and replaced in the shell with a variety of sauces. This general method is the same for all lobster dishes served in the shell; variety is achieved by the use of different sauces and garnishes as in:

Lobster Cardinal	—	Homard Cardinal
Lobster with Cheese Sauce	—	Homard Mornay
Lobster Thermidor	—	Homard Thermidor

6.64 BOILED LOBSTER

Makes: 10 portions. Cooking time: 20 minutes.

Quantity	*Ingredient*
10 × 750 g	live lobsters
	court-bouillon (*see* 6.27)

Method

(1) Plunge the live lobster into plenty of boiling court-bouillon and boil for 20 minutes.

(2) When cooked leave to cool completely in the liquid.

(3) When completely cold remove the claws by gently twisting where they join the body.

(4) Remove the claw end and the pincer. Stand the claw on its end and using a large knife enter the shell part of the claw with a light chopping action. Do not cut through the claw flesh. By twisting the knife the claw will part into two pieces leaving the flesh inside whole.

(5) Using the natural line along the length of the body as a guide, insert the point of a large knife where the head joins and with a downward movement cut through the head towards the antennae. Turn the lobster around and repeat the action from the tail end. The lobster should then fall into two equal halves.

(6) Remove the sac which is situated at the top of the head from

each half using a small knife, then remove the black trail that runs the length of each half.

(7) Remove the body flesh with the fingers, gently easing it out of the shell.

(8) Wash the shell and usable flesh under cold running water.

Notes

(1) Lobsters that are dead before cooking become waterlogged; the loss of flesh and flavour is significant.

(2) When cut open the flesh should be white, moist and full of flavour.

6.65 LOBSTER CARDINAL — HOMARD CARDINAL

Makes: 10 portions. Cooking time: 45 minutes.

Quantity	*Ingredient*
100 g	butter
5 × 750 g	lobsters { prepare the lobster as in 6.64; cut the tail into thick slices on the slant and leave the claw whole
150 g	Button Mushrooms cooked and sliced (8.91)
½ dl	brandy
½ l	Lobster Sauce (6.20–2)
2	egg yolks } liaison
½ dl	cream } liaison
50 g	grated Parmesan cheese
30 g	truffle slices
	seasoning

Method

(1) Melt the butter in a shallow sided saucepan. Add the lobster pieces and the sliced mushrooms and gently reheat.

(2) Add the brandy and flambé.

(3) Add sufficient lobster sauce to bind the lobster and mushrooms lightly together.

(4) Boil the remaining lobster sauce. Remove from the heat to prevent further boiling then add the liaison. Test for seasoning and if necessary rectify the thickness of the sauce: if too thick, thin with a little fish stock; if too thin, add more liaison.

(5) Place a little of the sauce along the length of the warmed lobster shell. Place lobster and mushrooms on top, then coat all over with the sauce. Sprinkle with grated Parmesan cheese and melted butter and lightly gratinate.

(6) Heat the slices of truffle in a little brandy and arrange them on the surface at the point of service.

Notes

(1) It is common trade practice to combine the lobster and sliced mushrooms with the sauce, add the liaison, and continue as stated.

(2) The addition of sliced truffle in this dish is traditional.

6.66 LOBSTER WITH CHEESE SAUCE — HOMARD MORNAY

Makes: 10 portions. Cooking time: 45 minutes.

Quantity	*Ingredient*
10 × 750 g	live lobsters
1 l	Mornay Sauce (6.15)
200 g	butter
50 g	grated Parmesan cheese
	sprigs of parsley

Method

(1) Prepare the lobsters as in 6.64. Cut the tail into thick slices on the slant and leave the claw whole.

(2) Warm and dry the shell.

(3) Reheat the lobster flesh and the claw in butter but do not allow it to colour or dry out.

(4) Place a line of hot mornay sauce along the length of the shell. Arrange the flesh back in the shell so as to refill it. Place the claw on the lobster flesh at the head end.

(5) Coat the lobster with the sauce, sprinkle with grated Parmesan cheese and lightly gratinate.

(6) Dress on a silver or stainless steel oval flat dish lined with a dish paper. Garnish with sprigs of parsley.

Assessment of the completed dish

(1) There should be an even light gratination over the total surface.

(2) The lobster shell should be clean, hot and with no splashes of sauce on it.

(3) The flesh should be arranged in the shape of a shallow dome. The sauce should be of a consistency to cover it yet allow the shape of the reformed flesh to be clearly seen.

(4) The dish paper should be perfectly clean with no traces of sauce. The garnish of sprigs of fresh parsley is generally placed alongside the half lobster.

Note

If the sauce is too thick it will mask the shape of the flesh rather than reveal it; if it is too thin it will run off and expose the flesh which will then become hard and dry.

6.67 LOBSTER THERMIDOR — HOMARD THERMIDOR

Prepare the lobster as in 6.64. Use a sauce made in one of the following ways:

(a) add 15 g made-up English mustard to a Cheese Sauce (6.15);
(b) add 15 g made-up English mustard to a Sauce Bercy (6.5);
(c) use Sauce Bercy in the base of the shell and bind the lobster flesh with a cheese sauce to which 15 g English mustard has been added as in *(a)*.

Lobster dishes served in a timbale

6.68 LOBSTER NEWBURG — HOMARD NEWBURG

Makes: 10 portions. Cooking time: 45 minutes.

Quantity	*Ingredient*
5 × 750 g	live lobsters
75 g	butter
½ dl	brandy
1½ dl	marsala, madeira or dry sherry
6	egg yolks } liaison
7 dl	cream } liaison
	seasoning

Method

(1) Prepare the lobsters as in 6.64. Cut the tail into thick slices on the slant and leave the claw whole.
(2) Melt the butter in a shallow sided pan. Add the lobster pieces and gently reheat.
(3) Add the brandy and flambé.
(4) Add the wine and reduce by half.
(5) Add the liaison. Allow the sauce to thicken gently by shaking the pan but do not allow it to boil.
(6) Test for seasoning.
(7) Arrange neatly in the warmed timbale.

Notes

(1) This dish may be served with Riz Pilaff (5.54) separately in a dish.
(2) Scampi may be used in place of lobster to make Scampi Newburg.

6.69 LOBSTER AMERICAINE — HOMARD AMERICAINE

Makes: 2 portions. Cooking time: 40 minutes.

Quantity	*Ingredient*
½ dl	oil
1 × 750 g	live lobster
50 g	brunoise of vegetables: carrots, shallots, celery
1 clove	crushed garlic
¼ dl	brandy
2 dl	Fish Stock (3.2)
20 g	tomato purée
100 g	Tomato Concassée (8.169)
30 g	Lobster Butter (3.50)
5 g	parsley and tarragon
	seasoning

Method — preparation of lobster

(1) Wash the lobster in cold water.

(2) With the point of a chopping knife, pierce the head so as to kill the lobster.

(3) Separate the tail end from the head.

(4) Cut the tail into sections about 2½ cm in length, retaining the end of it for decoration.

(5) Cut the head into two lengthways and discard the sac; remove the coral and creamy parts and mix with butter in a basin to make lobster butter.

(6) Remove the claws from the body and crack them so that the flesh can be removed when cooked.

Method — preparation of sauce

(1) Heat the oil in a shallow sided pan. Add the lobster and cook until it becomes red. Add the brunoise of vegetables and crushed garlic, cover with a lid and allow to sweat until the vegetables are soft.

(2) Add the brandy and flambé. Add the white wine, fish stock, tomato purée and tomato concassée. Bring to the boil, skim, cover with a lid and cook gently for approximately 20 minutes.

(3) Remove the lobster from the cooking liquid. Either remove the flesh from the shell before placing it into the service dish, or place both shell and flesh as they are directly into the dish.

(4) Reduce the cooking liquid to a sticky consistency. Remove from the heat and add knobs of butter, incorporating them using a shaking action or gently whisking them in, until the sauce is a light coating consistency. Rectify the seasoning if necessary. (The sauce may be passed through a coarse conical strainer.)

(5) Coat the lobster with the sauce and decorate it with the lobster head and the tail spread to give a butterfly effect. Sprinkle with freshly chopped parsley and tarragon.

Notes

(1) Some recipes suggest seasoning at an early stage, but care must be taken that the completed sauce does not become too salty because of the nature of the lobster flesh and the fish stock both of which contain natural salts.

(2) There are two important points that require special care and attention in the preparation of this dish.

(a) The length of time the lobster is cooked for: lobster cooked in this way shrinks considerably and becomes tough and dry if overcooked.

(b) The reduction and thickening of the sauce: if the liquid is not reduced to the correct amount the sauce either will be too thin when the butter is added or, if overreduced, may become too thick and salty and be too strong in flavour and too dark in colour.

Service

This dish is served in a timbale on a round flat dish with a dish paper.

Assessment of the completed dish

(1) The pieces of lobster should be completely coated with the sauce, and because of the dish in which it is served there should seem to be a high ratio of sauce to flesh: the sauce should cover three-quarters of the lobster.

(2) The dish should be decorated with the lobster head and tail at opposite ends. These should be clean and brushed with oil to give a good sheen before being placed in position.

(3) The flesh should be moist and in small pieces with the claw remaining whole. When cut through the flesh should be white.

(4) The sauce should be very richly flavoured and dark red in colour with a good sheen. It should be of a light coating consistency.

Mussels

The dish given in 6.70 below as an example of cooking and serving mussels has been chosen because of its lasting popularity. In it the mussels are cooked in white wine and fish stock together with chopped parsley and shallots. The liquid in which the mussels have been cooked is then slightly thickened to make the accompanying sauce.

6.70 MUSSELS IN WHITE WINE SAUCE — MOULES MARINIERE

Makes: 10 portions. Cooking time: 45 minutes.

Quantity	*Ingredient*
2½ kg	live mussels, washed and scraped
75 g	chopped shallots or onions
¼ l	dry white wine
¼ l	Fish Stock (3.2)
5 g	chopped parsley
1	juice of lemon
50 g	butter (preferably unsalted)
1 dl	cream
	seasoning of salt and cayenne pepper

Method

(1) Place the mussels into a deep sided pan with the shallots or onion, white wine, fish stock, chopped parsley and lemon juice.

(2) Cover with a lid and bring to the boil. Cook vigorously for 8–10 minutes (when cooked the shells will open).

(3) Remove the mussels from the cooking liquid.

(4) Decant the liquid into a basin and allow it to stand so that any sand will fall to the bottom of the liquid.

(5) Open the mussels and discard the top shells. Remove the mussels from the bottom shells then beard them with the finger tips.

(6) Replace each mussel into a half shell. Place the shells in an earthenware dish to keep them warm and cover with a lid to prevent them drying.

(7) Gently pour the decanted liquid into a shallow sided pan leaving the sediment in the basin.

(8) Bring the liquid to boiling point and slightly thicken with the butter. Add some chopped parsley and test for seasoning and consistency.

Notes

(1) In many instances cream is added to finish the sauce, though in classical cookery this will change the name of the dish to Moules à la Crème.

(2) As with all shellfish mussels, once cooked, are not suitable for retention in a sauce. If mussels are to be prepared in advance they should be removed from their shells once cooked, bearded and retained in the cooking liquid. All the shells should be discarded as they deteriorate rapidly.

Assessment of the completed dish

(1) The dish should consist of single layers of mussels placed in

the dish so that all are pointing in the same direction. Each mussel in its shell should be coated with the sauce.

(2) If prepared without cream the sauce should be rather transparent, garnished with finely chopped shallots or onion and chopped parsley. The addition of chopped parsley when serving is not really necessary since some has been cooked with the mussels from the initial stages. It may be added if it is considered the visual appearance of the dish will be enhanced.

(3) The sauce should have the distinct flavours of mussels and white wine and should be seasoned to the correct degree.

(4) The thickness or consistency of the sauce should be sufficiently light and flowing to cover the mussels in their shells.

(5) The mussels should be moist with the beard removed. There should be no traces of sand and they should be a little chewy when eaten.

Possible problem	*Possible cause and solution*
(1) Sand in the mussels or sauce	— shells were not washed and scraped before cooking; care must be taken to prepare the mussels correctly to avoid this problem which cannot be rectified.
	— cooking liquid not allowed to stand or was not decanted correctly; care must be taken at this stage to avoid this problem which cannot be rectified.
(2) Sauce is too thick	— cooking liquid was reduced too much; thin with a little more cooking liquid, fish stock or white wine.
(3) Sauce is too thin	— insufficient reduction of the cooking liquid; boil the sauce and whisk into it a small amount of beurre manié.
	— not enough butter used as a thickening agent; reduce the sauce further, cool and whisk onto some cream or a little velouté and cream.
(4) Mussels are dry, hard and lack flavour	— mussels have been overcooked; care must be taken to cook the mussels for the correct length of time as this cannot later be rectified.
	— once cooked the mussels were held too long before the dish was completed; the mussels should be cooked closer to the time they are required to avoid the problems caused by

Possible problem	Possible cause and solution
	prolonged retention which cannot be rectified later.
	— once cooked and completed the dish was held for too long in a hot plate; the whole dish should be prepared closer to the time it is required to avoid the problems caused by prolonged retention which cannot be rectified later.

Oysters

6.71 POACHED OYSTERS — HUITRES POCHEES

Open the oysters and remove them from their shells. Strain the oyster juice into a saucepan and bring to the boil. Add the oysters and simmer for a few seconds, then allow them to complete their cooking for a further 8 minutes without further boiling.

Note

Oysters will become rubbery and tough if permitted to overboil or overcook. They are usually used in garnishing fish dishes or as hors-d'oeuvre.

Prawns

Prawns are generally purchased in cooked and frozen form. When defrosted they may be used for hors-d'oeuvre items, e.g. Prawn Cocktail (2.38), or they may be served hot in an appropriate sauce — either one which is light and creamy such as Cream Sauce (3.16), or in a Curry Sauce (3.11) accompanied with cooked rice. These usually feature as a first course on a menu.

6.72 CURRIED PRAWNS — CURRIE DE CREVETTES

Makes: 10 portions. Cooking time: 5 minutes.

Quantity	*Ingredient*
75 g	butter
700 g	prawns
7 dl	Curry Sauce (3.11)
500 g	Boiled Rice (5.53)
	chopped parsley

Method

(1) Melt the butter in a shallow sided saucepan. Add the prawns and gently toss to heat them through.

(2) Add the curry sauce and gently incorporate the prawns.

(3) Serve the prawns and the rice in two separate entrée type dishes. Sprinkle the surface with chopped parsley.

Scallops

There are a number of ways in which scallops may be featured on the menu, but generally are served replaced in the bottom shell, surrounded with a border of Duchesse potato and coated with a sauce (*see*, for example, Scallops in Cheese Sauce (6.74)). All those sauces associated with shallow poached fish dishes may be used, either glazed or unglazed. It is common practice to add other types of shellfish or flaky fish to the scallops.

The shells are also used as a form of presentation for a wide range of dishes made with flaked fish with or without scallops. The dish then appears on the menu as Coquilles followed by the words denoting the fish and sauce used, e.g. Scallop Shells of Cod in White Wine Sauce — Coquilles de Cabillaud Sauce Vin Blanc Glacé (6.75).

6.73 SCALLOPS — COQUILLES ST JACQUES

To open place the scallops on the side of the stove or on a heated hotplate — the shells will open of their own accord. Remove the scallop from the bottom shell and cut away the frill leaving the centre red tongue attached. Wash under cold water.

The top shell is discarded, but the lower deep shell is kept for use in presenting the shellfish. It should be thoroughly washed and boiled before using.

There are different approaches to cooking scallops. Those methods in most common use are as follows.

(a) Lightly stew the scallops in butter with the addition of salt and a small bayleaf covered with a lid.

(b) Gently poach the scallops in a court-bouillon for approximately 5 minutes.

(c) Poach the scallops in milk flavoured with thyme, bayleaf, parsley stalks and shredded onion for approximately 5 minutes.

Note

When cooked scallops become firm and rather rubbery.

6.74 SCALLOPS IN CHEESE SAUCE — COQUILLES ST JACQUES MORNAY

Makes: 10 portions. Cooking time: 45 minutes.

Quantity	*Ingredient*
1 kg	Duchesse Potato Mixture (9.12)

Quantity	*Ingredient*
75 g	butter
½ l	Sauce Mornay (6.15)
10	cooked and sliced scallops (*see* 6.73)
50 g	grated Parmesan cheese
	seasoning

Method

(1) Pipe the edge of the shell with Duchesse potato, sprinkle with melted butter and dry lightly under a salamander grill without coloration.

(2) Pour a little of the mornay sauce in the bottom of the shell. Place in the cooked, sliced and drained scallops and coat with some of the mornay sauce.

(3) Sprinkle the surface of the sauce with grated Parmesan cheese and melted butter and lightly glaze under a salamander grill.

(4) Serve garnished with sprigs of parsley.

Notes

(1) Lightly butter the scallop shell where the Duchesse potato is to be piped. Place a small knob of potato under the shell to keep it level when placed onto a baking sheet for further handling.

(2) When a dish is to be glazed the potato and sauce should both be glazed to an even degree. The potato, therefore, once piped is sprinkled with melted butter and needs to be lightly dried under a salamander grill or in an oven before the fish is placed in and coated with the sauce.

(3) Always preheat the filling, either in butter or in the sauce, before placing it into the shells. Do not place the filling into the piped shells in a cold state hoping that the sauce coating will adequately heat it for serving.

Service

Serve on a silver or stainless steel flat dish on a dish paper, with sprigs of parsley placed on the dish paper.

Assessment of the completed dish

(1) The shell should be perfectly clean with no traces of sauce or potato mixture down the sides. The dish paper should be perfectly clean with no grease.

(2) The Duchesse potato should be evenly coloured a light golden brown. It should be neatly and evenly piped around the

shell and have a smooth texture. Its flavour should be a pleasant combination of nutmeg and butter.

(3) The mornay sauce should be a light creamy colour. It should also be creamy in consistency so that it evenly coats the filling, and have a cheese flavour that is not too pronounced. It should be evenly coloured following gratination and no un-melted cheese should be left on the surface.

(4) The scallops should be moist and perfectly white in colour.

6.75 SCALLOP SHELLS OF COD IN WHITE WINE SAUCE— COQUILLES DE CABILLAUD SAUCE VIN BLANC GLACEE

Makes: 10 portions. Cooking time: 45 minutes.

Quantity	*Ingredient*
1 kg	Duchesse Potato Mixture (9.12)
75 g	butter
750 g	shallow poached or boiled and flaked cod
8 dl	White Wine Sauce (6.1–3)
	picked parsley

Method

(1) Pipe the edge of the shell with Duchesse potato, sprinkle with melted butter and dry lightly under the salamander grill without coloration.

(2) Melt the butter in a shallow sided saucepan, add the flaked fish and toss to reheat.

(3) Pour a little of the white wine sauce in the bottom of the shells. Place in the reheated flaked cod and coat with the white wine sauce. Glaze under a salamander grill.

(4) Serve on a flat dish on a dish paper garnished with the sprigs of parsley.

Scampi/Dublin Bay prawns/Langoustines

These are very popular items found on most menus in all catering situations. Scampi are generally purchased in their raw frozen state and should be allowed to thaw out completely before further handling. They may be blanched in water or cooked for a few moments in a court-bouillon before being cooked in a particular dish, or they may be cooked from their raw state. The following recipes are for use with raw defrosted scampi.

6.76 FRIED SCAMPI—SCAMPI FRITS

Makes: 10 portions. Cooking time: 5 minutes.

Quantity	*Ingredient*
850 g	scampi

Quantity	Ingredient
	flour, eggwash and breadcrumb coating (6.42)
3	lemons
	sprigs of parsley
½ l	Tartare Sauce (3.45)

Method

(1) Thoroughly dry the scampi in a cloth or absorbent kitchen paper.

(2) Coat with flour, eggwash and breadcrumbs.

(3) Reshape them by rolling them in the hands.

(4) Place the scampi into a frying basket and place into hot fat. Fry until crisp and golden, shaking the frying basket from time to time to ensure even coloration.

(5) When cooked, drain the scampi by placing them onto absorbent kitchen paper. Season with salt.

(6) Dress on a dish paper on a flat dish, garnish with lemon wedges and picked parsley, and serve accompanied by a sauceboat of tartare sauce.

Note

For detailed assessment *see* p. 194.

6.77 SCAMPI MEUNIERE

Makes: 10 portions. Cooking time: 30 minutes.

Quantity	Ingredient
850 g	small scampi
250 g	seasoned flour
3 dl	oil
3	lemons
150 g	Nut Brown Butter (6.48)
	chopped parsley

Method

(1) Heat the oil in a frying pan.

(2) Pass the scampi through seasoned flour and shake off the surplus.

(3) Place the scampi in the oil and fry them to a golden brown.

(4) Dress on a service dish slightly dome shape. Place slices of lemon on top of the scampi.

(5) Squeeze a little lemon juice over the scampi and sprinkle with chopped parsley.

(6) Just before serving, pour nut brown butter over the scampi.

Note

For detailed assessment *see* p. 199.

6.78 SCAMPI PROVENCALE

Makes: 10 portions. Cooking time: 8 minutes.

Quantity	*Ingredient*
850 g	scampi
250 g	seasoned flour
75 g	butter
500 g	Tomato Concassée (8.169)
½ l	Tomato Sauce (3.10)
	chopped parsley

Method

(1) Heat the butter in a shallow pan.

(2) Pass the scampi through seasoned flour and shake off the surplus.

(3) Place in the scampi and lightly fry them without too much coloration. Drain off any surplus butter.

(4) Add the tomato concassée and tomato sauce and gently incorporate the scampi.

(5) Test for seasoning.

(6) Arrange neatly in an oval earthenware dish and sprinkle with chopped parsley.

FISH STEW

Fish stew, one example of which is bouillabaisse, may be served as two separate courses for the same meal — the cooking liquid is first served as a soup with French bread and the fish is eaten as a main course.

The "true" bouillabaisse is made using only Mediterranean fish; the recipe given below closely approximates using North Sea fish.

6.79 FISH STEW — BOUILLABAISSE

Makes: 10 portions. Cooking time: 15–20 minutes.

Quantity	*Ingredient*
3 kg	brill conger eel mackerel John Dory red mullet whiting squid
500 g	mussels
250 g	scampi
2 dl	oil
250 g	white of leek cut into julienne

Quantity	Ingredient
200 g	sliced onions
2 cloves	finely chopped garlic
pinch	fennel seed
1	bayleaf
1 sprig	thyme
pinch	saffron
5 g	chopped parsley
500 g	Tomato Concassée (8.169)
½ l	dry white wine
	seasoning

Method

(1) Clean all the fish and cut into sections approximately 5 cm long on the bone.

(2) Scrape and wash the mussels.

(3) Heat the oil in a shallow pan large enough to hold all the ingredients. Add the vegetables, herbs, garlic and fish. Cover with a lid and sweat.

(4) Add the remainder of the ingredients and allow to stew for approximately 15 minutes.

(5) When cooked rectify the seasoning and, if necessary, the balance between the fish and the liquid.

(6) Serve in a large soup tureen accompanied by slices of French bread.

Note

Any fish that is rather delicate in texture and therefore likely to disintegrate whilst cooking with the remainder of the stew, e.g. whiting, should be added at a later stage in the cooking.

Service

Bouillabaisse is usually served in a soup plate or tureen or in a deep-sided earthenware dish large enough for several portions.

Assessment of the completed dish

(1) The stew should be hot.

(2) The liquid should be unthickened, clear and have a slightly yellowish tint.

(3) The flavour should be a combination of fish and shellfish but should not have a predominantly fishy taste. The dish should be a blend of the flavours of all the ingredients but no one flavour should stand out.

(4) There should be more fish than liquid.

(5) The shellfish should not appear overcooked.
(6) The fish should be unbroken yet cooked.
(7) The French bread should be evenly cut into slices that are not too large.

FISH AU GRATIN

This is the cooking of fish in a sauce in an oven at a temperature of approximately 175 °C until the fish is cooked and the surface of the sauce coating is evenly coloured and lightly crisp. This method may be applied to whole sole, suprêmes of halibut, turbot, cod and haddock and fillets of whiting.

6.80 SOLE AU GRATIN

Makes: 10 portions. Cooking time: 30 minutes.

Quantity	*Ingredient*
10 × 250 g	whole Dover soles
250 g	butter
100 g	chopped shallots
1 l	Sauce Gratin (3.29)
250 g	sliced button mushrooms } or
30	whole button mushrooms }
3 dl	dry white wine
100 g	white breadcrumbs
100 g	melted butter
2	juice of lemons
10 g	chopped parsley

Method

(1) Remove the skin from both sides of the fish. Cut along the backbone from just below the head to the tail end and almost fillet but do not completely remove the bones. Fold back the fillets and place a small knob of butter under each. Reform the shape of the fish.

(2) Butter a shallow sided earthenware dish, season and sprinkle with chopped shallots. Add a little of the sauce barely to cover the bottom of the dish.

(3) Place the sole on the sauce and surround it with sliced mushrooms. (Alternatively, place three or four button mushrooms along the centre of each fish portion.)

(4) Add a little of the white wine and just cover the fish with the sauce.

(5) Sprinkle the surface of the sauce with white breadcrumbs and melted butter.

(6) Fully gratinate.

(7) When cooked, clean the dish and sprinkle with lemon juice and chopped parsley.

Note

To test when cooked is rather difficult — if prodded with a fork the surface will be disturbed so care must be taken. The same criteria for assessment as for poached fish apply.

Service

Serve in the shallow sided oval earthenware dish in which it has been cooked on an underdish with a dish paper.

Assessment of the completed dish

(1) There should be a light crisp surface which is unbroken to show that the dish has been completely gratinated.

(2) The fish should be cooked to the correct degree — it should be moist, white, and not have curled during cooking.

(3) The sauce should have the consistency to coat the fish lightly when it is served. The amount of sauce should be in the correct ratio to the number of portions served.

(4) There should be a slight flavour of lemon.

(5) The colour of the sauce should be a rich reddish brown.

(6) The flavour of the sauce should be rather rich with mushrooms and wine, though the wine should be rather difficult to discern amongst the stronger flavours of the other ingredients.

Possible problem	*Possible cause and solution*
(1) Fish curls during cooking breaking the surface of the sauce	— backbone of the sole not pierced in two or three places; care must be taken to prepare the fish correctly to avoid this problem which cannot be rectified later.
	— cooked at too high a temperature; care must be taken to cook the fish at the correct temperature to avoid this problem which cannot be rectified later.
(2) Surface crust has not formed	— fish cooked too slowly; care must be taken to cook the fish at the correct temperature and for the correct length of time to avoid this problem which cannot be rectified later.
	— sauce is too thin; care must be taken when preparing the sauce.

NOUVELLE CUISINE

The types and cuts of fish used and the principles and practices outlined in this chapter also apply to this style of cookery with the following exceptions.

(a) The most striking difference between traditional methods and Nouvelle Cuisine is that within the latter the fish in some instances when making hot dishes is only lightly cooked. The finished item is glassy to look at and resilient or springy to touch.

(b) Shallow fried fish is not passed through flour prior to cooking. In order to prevent sticking during cooking a non-stick frying pan is used.

(c) Roux and flour based sauces are never used. Sauces are made from fish stock, wines, vegetables and herbs using the traditional methods outlined in this chapter, namely the reduction of liquid and the addition of butter or butter and cream to the reduced liquid (*see* 6.1 and 6.2). (There are other methods of making sauces as accompaniments, of course, according to the creative ability of the chef.)

(d) Some leaders in the field of Nouvelle Cuisine do not permit any dish to be gratinated.

(e) Fish and fish sauces are never cooked until required; they are always produced to order.

6.81 *SHALLOW FRIED FILLET OF MONK FISH WITH MUSTARD AND CUCUMBER SAUCE*

Makes: 10 portions. Cooking time: 30 minutes.

Quantity	*Ingredient*	
10 × 85 g	fillets of monk fish	
3 dl	oil	
50 g	butter	
1	juice of lemon	sauce
50 g	chopped shallots	sauce
2 dl	dry white wine	sauce
3 dl	Fish Stock (3.2)	sauce
2½ dl	cream	sauce
	Dijon mustard	sauce
	seasoning of salt and cayenne pepper	sauce
1	unpeeled cucumber free from seeds and cut into strips 2½ cm × 5 mm	garnish
1 sprig	dill	garnish

Method

(1) Heat the oil in a non-stick frying pan. Place in the seasoned fish presentation side down. Fry, then turn when coloured and

continue to fry. Add the butter and lemon juice and continue to cook until the fish is just cooked.

(2) Place the chopped shallots and white wine into a shallow sided saucepan. Boil and reduce by half. Add the fish stock, boil and reduce again by half.

(3) Add the cream, boil and reduce until it reaches a light coating consistency.

(4) Whisk in the mustard, add the strips of cucumber to the sauce and gently simmer for 2 minutes. Season to taste.

Notes

(1) Take care not to overcook the cucumber in the sauce. It should be allowed to impart its flavour to the sauce but should remain crisp and green.

(2) Each brand of Dijon mustard will give a slightly different flavour. Choose one that will give a slightly fruity and not too sharp flavour.

Service

Remove the cucumber strips from the sauce with a perforated spoon, place in the centre of each plate and pour a little of the sauce around. Neatly arrange the fillets on top of the cucumber and decorate each with a small sprig of dill.

6.82 *SUPREME OF FRESH SALMON WITH HERBS AND DRY VERMOUTH IN A SAFFRON AND CREAM SAUCE*

Makes: 10 portions. Cooking time: 30 minutes.

Quantity	*Ingredient*	
10 × 100 g	suprêmes of fresh salmon	
2	lemons	marinade
	chopped tarragon, chervil and parsley	marinade
	seasoning	marinade
75 g	chopped shallots	sauce
1 dl	dry white wine	sauce
1 dl	dry vermouth	sauce
3 dl	double cream	sauce
½ g	saffron	sauce
4 dl	Fish Stock (3.2)	sauce
10	Stewed Scallops (6.73)	garnish
10	Fleurons (10.66)	garnish

Method

(1) Marinate the fish for 30 minutes.

(2) Once marinated, shallow fry the suprêmes of salmon in a non-stick pan.

(3) Place the shallots, fish stock, white wine, vermouth and saffron into a shallow sided saucepan. Boil and reduce until syrupy.

(4) Add the cream and boil. Reduce until a light coating consistency. Season to taste.

Note

The fish should be shallow fried without butter or oil and should be slightly undercooked.

Service

Place a little of the sauce in the centre of the plates. Arrange the suprêmes of salmon on the sauce and pour the sauce over the fish. Garnish with the scallops and fleurons.

6.83 VOLS-AU-VENT DE FRUITS DE MER NEPTUNE

Makes: 10 portions. Cooking time: 30 minutes.

Quantity	*Ingredient*
10	Vols-au-Vent Cases (10.71)
250 g	turbot (cut into goujons)
250 g	scampi (cut into sections)
200 g	unsalted butter
10	small lobster claws
20	Small Button Mushrooms (8.91)
1 dl	pernod
few drops	tabasco
3 dl	cream
	seasoning

Method

(1) Season and lightly fry the strips of turbot and scampi in two separate non-stick frying pans.

(2) Combine the two, add the lobster claws and button mushrooms and allow to heat through for a few moments.

(3) Transfer the fish to a receptacle and keep warm.

(4) Drain off the surplus fat. Add the pernod, tabasco and cream, boil and reduce until it forms a coating consistency.

(5) Add the turbot, scampi, lobster and mushrooms to the sauce, followed by the sliced poached scallops at the last moment. Season to taste.

(6) Place the warm pastry cases onto a suitably sized plate. Fill to overflowing, replace with the pastry cap and serve.

CONVENIENCE FISH

The range of products in this category is both broad and diverse and to attempt to deal with them all is outside the scope of this book.

Frozen fish prepared but uncooked

Fish that is purchased frozen should be stored at −18 °C. When required, time should be allowed for it to thaw out completely at a temperature of 7 °C. On no account should the process of thawing out be accelerated. Never place frozen fish in warm water in order to shorten the period of defrosting as this will result in discoloured, tasteless and undercooked fish that is completely unusable.

When defrosted fish that has been frozen may be used in any of the recipes found in this chapter with very similar results.

Pre-battered frozen fish pieces

When these items are deep fried the same principles and methods as outlined in the relevant section of this chapter apply (*see* pp. 187–97), although it will be necessary to allow the fat to recover its heat either after each item has been added or between batches.

CHAPTER SEVEN

Meat, Poultry and Game

PREPARATION OF JOINTS AND CUTS

This section gives a brief outline of the qualities to look for when purchasing items of meat, poultry and game, and includes a short description of how they may be prepared for cooking. It is important to remember that this section is directly related to every aspect of this chapter and only meats that are of the highest quality when purchased will give the best results.

In general all carcasses should be clean, free from cuts and bruises, blood stains and other blemishes. All items of meat and poultry should be stored at temperatures of 2 °C if fresh, −2 °C if chilled and −18 °C if frozen.

Beef

The flesh should be moist and firm, lightish red in colour with a fine and even grain. Marbling or flecks of fat should be visible in some of the prime joints such as sirloin and fillet. The fat should be creamy white in colour and evenly distributed over the carcass. The bones should be pink in colour and slightly porous. Table 4 gives the main joints and cuts of beef, the approximate weight, method of preparation and possible methods of cooking.

TABLE 4. JOINTS AND CUTS OF BEEF: APPROXIMATE WEIGHT, PREPARATION AND METHODS OF COOKING

Preparation of joint or cut	*Methods of cooking*
Joints from the hindquarter	
7.1 SIRLOIN ON THE BONE — ALOYAU (10 kg)	
Remove the fillet for other uses. Saw through and remove the chine bone. Lay back the outer coating of fat next to the chine bone area and remove the exposed sinew. Fold back the fat and tie the joint between each bone.	Roast Pot roast
7.2 STRIPLOIN (STRIP SIRLOIN) — CONTREFILET (7 kg)	
Remove the fillet for other uses. Bone the joint completely. Remove the chain which runs the full length at the point where the backbone was situated. Remove all excess fat and sinew. Trim along the length of the joint at the thin flank end. It may be rolled and tied or left as a full strip for cooking.	Roast Pot roast

7.3 THIN FLANK — BAVETTE D'ALOYAU (10 kg)

Remove all surplus fat and trim. It may be rolled and tied into a joint or cut into 2½ cm cubes for stewing.

Boil
Stew

7.4 RUMP — CULOTTE (9 kg)

Remove the fillet for other uses. Bone completely. Trim off all excess fat. (Mainly used for rump steaks — *see* 7.25.)

Roast
Braise

7.5 SHIN — JAMBE (7 kg)

Bone completely. Trim off all membrane, fat and sinew. Either:

(*a*) cut into 2½ cm cubes — Stew
(*b*) pass through a mincer — Use in consommé
(*c*) crack open the bone, remove the marrow and soak in cold water — For bone marrow

7.6 MIDDLE RIB — COTE DECOUVERTE (8 kg)

Bone completely. Remove surplus fat and sinew. Cut into joints, roll and tie. Also either:

Roast

(*a*) lard — Braise
(*b*) cut into steaks — Braise
(*c*) cut into 2½ cm cubes — Stew

7.7 FORE RIB — COTE PREMIERE (6 kg)

Saw through and remove the chine bone. Lay back the fat outer coating next to the chine bone area and remove the exposed sinew. Fold back the fat and tie the joint between each rib bone.

Roast

7.8 WHOLE FILLET — FILET DE BOEUF (3 kg)

Remove the fat and thin outer membrane. Cut away the chain which runs the full length of the joint. Lard or bard and tie with string to retain the shape.

Roast
Pot roast

7.9 WING RIB — COTE D'ALOYAU (4 kg)

Saw through and remove the chine bone. Lay back the outer coating of fat next to the chine bone area and remove the exposed sinew. Fold back the fat and tie the joint between each rib bone.

Roast

7.10 TOPSIDE — TRANCHE TENDRE (8 kg)

Bone completely. Trim of all membrane, fat and sinew. Cut into joints and tie. Also either:

Roast

(*a*) lard (*see* p. 281) — Braise
(*b*) cut into steaks — Braise
(*c*) cut into 2½ cm cubes — Stew

7.11 SILVERSIDE — GITE A LA NOIX (10 kg)

(*a*) Trim, cut into 2½ cm cubes. — Stew
(*b*) Trim and pickle in brine, cut into joints. — Boil

7.12 THICK FLANK — TRANCHE GRASSE (10 kg)

Trim off excess fat. Either:

(a) cut into joints, tie and lard (*see* p. 281)	Braise
(b) cut into steaks	Braise
(c) cut into 2½ cm cubes	Stew

Joints from the forequarter

7.13 SHANK — JAMBE DE DEVANT (5 kg)

Bone completely. Trim off all membrane, fat and sinew. Pass through a mincer.	Use in consommé

7.14 LEG OF MUTTON CUT — MACREUSE (8 kg)

Bone completely. Trim off all sinew. Either:

(a) cut into joints, tie and lard (*see* p. 281)	Braise
(b) cut into steaks	Braise
(c) cut into 2½ cm cubes	Stew

7.15 PLATE — PLAT DE COTE (8 kg)

Trim and remove surplus fat. Either:

(a) cut into joints and tie	Boil
(b) cut into 2½ cm cubes	Stew

7.16 BRISKET — POITRINE (12 kg)

Bone completely and remove surplus fat. Either:

(a) cut into joints, tie and pickle in brine	Boil
(b) cut into 2½ cm cubes	Stew

7.17 CLOD AND STICKING PIECE — COLLIER (10 kg)

Bone completely and remove surplus fat. Cut into 2½ cm cubes.	Stew

7.18 CHUCK RIB — COTE DE COLLIER (13 kg)

Bone completely. Either:

(a) cut into joints, tie and lard (*see* p. 281)	Braise
(b) cut into 2½ cm cubes	Stew

Prime cuts from fillet, rump and sirloin

7.19 CHATEAUBRIAND (250 g or 2–4 portions)

Cut from the thick end of the fillet and slightly flatten.	Shallow fry Grill

7.20 DOUBLE SIRLOIN STEAK — ENTRECOTE DOUBLE (400 g)

Cut from the striploin into slices 3–4 cm thick.	Shallow fry Grill

7.21 FILLET STEAK (200 g)

Cut from the prepared fillet in slices 5 cm thick.	Shallow fry Grill

7.22 *MINUTE STEAK — ENTRECOTE MINUTE (200 g)*

Cut from the striploin into slices 3 mm thick. — Shallow fry, Grill

7.23 *POINT STEAK (200 g)*

Cut from the triangular end piece of the rump approximately 2 cm thick. — Shallow fry, Grill

7.24 *PORTERHOUSE/T-BONE STEAK (650 g)*

Cut from the whole sirloin on the bone including the fillet. Cut through approximately 4 cm thick. — Shallow fry, Grill

7.25 *RUMP STEAK (200 g)*

Cut from boned rump. (The first slice across the joint is used for braising or stewing.) Cut a slice the width of the joint approximately 2 cm thick and cut into steaks across the slice. — Shallow fry, Grill

7.26 *SIRLOIN STEAK — ENTRECOTE (200 g)*

Cut from the striploin into slices 1½ cm thick. — Shallow fry, Grill

7.27 *TOURNEDOS (200 g)*

Cut from the centre of the fillet in slices 3 cm thick. Trim and tie. — Shallow fry, Grill

---

Lamb and mutton

Lamb is derived from sheep of either sex under 12 months old when slaughtered. The flesh should be "sappy" or moist, light pink in colour and have a fine grain. The fat should be creamy white in colour and be evenly distributed over the saddle. The bones should be soft and porous.

Mutton (hogget) is derived from maiden ewes or wethers (castrated male sheep or maiden ewes that have not lambed) showing not more than two permanent incisor teeth when slaughtered. The weight of the carcass should not exceed 25 kg.

Lamb and mutton may be considered jointly although the flesh of mutton is a little darker, the fat whiter and more brittle and the bones harder. Table 5 gives the main joints and cuts of both lamb and mutton, the approximate weight, method of preparation and possible methods of cooking.

TABLE 5. JOINTS AND CUTS OF LAMB AND MUTTON: APPROXIMATE WEIGHT, PREPARATION AND METHODS OF COOKING

Preparation of joint or cut	Methods of cooking
Main joints	
7.28 LEG — GIGOT (2–2½ kg)	
Remove the pelvic bone and trim off surplus fat. Saw the leg bone off at the first knuckle joint and trim off the flesh and membrane. Tie at the thick end.	Roast Pot roast White braise Boil
7.29 SHOULDER — EPAULE (1½–2 kg)	
Either:	
(*a*) remove the knuckle bone and neatly trim the flesh and membrane	Roast
(*b*) bone completely, remove surplus fat and gristle, roll and tie	Roast
(*c*) bone completely, remove surplus fat and gristle, stuff, roll and tie	Roast
(*d*) cut into even 2½ cm pieces free of excess fat and gristle	Stew
7.30 SADDLE — SELLE (Lamb 3½ kg; Mutton 5½ kg)	
Remove the outer skin. Remove the hip bones and cut away the flank in line with the joint. Tie, reforming the shape.	Roast Pot roast
Note It may be necessary to remove some of the outer coating of fat if there is an excess amount. Care must be taken not to leave the flesh bare.	
7.31 LOIN — LONGE (Lamb 1½ kg; Mutton 2½ kg)	
Split the saddle through the centre bone to make two loins. Remove the outer skin and bone completely. Cut away the flank in line with the joint. Tie, reforming shape.	Roast Pot roast
7.32 BEST END — CARRE (Lamb 1½ kg; Mutton 1¾ kg)	
Remove the outer skin. Remove the breast leaving the joint twice the length of the eye (the centre meat). Remove the sinew along the width under the fat at the chine bone end. Remove the end blade bone, the flesh and fat surrounding the cutlet bones and the skin between the cutlet bones. Lightly score the covering fat trellis fashion.	Roast Pot roast
7.33 BREAST — POITRINE (Lamb 750 g; Mutton 1¼ kg)	
Either:	
(*a*) remove the outer skin and all excess fat; cut into	Stew

5 cm squares between every other bone; trim the corners at an angle to give extra shape

(*b*) remove the outer skin and bone completely; trim excess fat, roll and tie into a joint — Roast

(*c*) prepare as for (*b*), then stuff, roll and tie into a joint — Roast

Small cuts

7.34 MIDDLE NECK — COTE DECOUVERTE (Lamb 1 kg; Mutton 1½ kg)

Split through the middle lengthways. Cut in between the cutlet bones and trim. — Stew, Grill, Shallow fry

7.35 FILLET OF NECK (Lamb ½ kg; Mutton ¾ kg)

Trim off surplus fat and sinew. Remove outer membrane. Either:

(*a*) cut into 2½ cm cubes — Stew

(*b*) open lengthways and lightly flatten — Grill, Shallow fry

7.36 SCRAG END — COU (Lamb 700 g; Mutton 1 kg)

Split through the centre lengthways and chop into 60 g pieces. Remove excess fat, sinew and bone. — Stew

7.37 LAMB/MUTTON CHOPS — CHOP D'AGNEAU/DE MOUTON (200 g)

Cut from prepared loin (7.31) unboned. Cut into chops 4 cm thick. Trim the surplus fat. — Lamb: Grill, Shallow fry; Mutton: Braise

7.38 DOUBLE LAMB CHOPS/CROWN CHOPS (400 g)

Cut from prepared saddle (7.30). Cut across the saddle to produce a double chop joined at its centre. Trim and remove excess fat. Skewer a kidney in the centre of the chop. — Grill, Shallow fry

7.39 FILLET OF SADDLE — FILET MIGNON (120 g)

Remove the fillets from inside the saddle. Trim off the outer membrane, fat and sinew. Cut open lengthways and lightly flatten. — Grill, Shallow fry

7.40 NOISETTES (2 × 75 g)

Cut from prepared loin (7.31). Bone completely and remove the chump end. Cut across the joint on a slant of 45° approximately 3 cm thick. Lightly flatten and trim away surplus fat. — Shallow fry

7.41 ROSETTES — ROSETTES/MEDAILLONS (2 × 100 g)

Cut from prepared loin (7.31). Bone completely and remove the chump end. Roll into a joint, replacing the fillet. Trim excess fat and tie at regular intervals along the — Grill, Shallow fry length. Cut in between the string to make 4 cm thick boned chops.

7.42 LAMB/MUTTON CUTLETS — COTELETTES D'AGNEAU/DE MOUTON (2 × 100 g)

Cut from prepared best end (7.32) but do not score. Cut between the bones of the joint on a slant of 45°. Trim off excess fat and reshape, leaving approximately 15 mm of bone neatly cleaned of meat, into cutlet form.	Lamb: Grill Shallow fry Stew Mutton: Stew

7.43 DOUBLE LAMB CUTLETS — COTELETTES D'AGNEAU DOUBLE (200 g)

Cut from prepared best end as in 7.32. Cut between every other bone.	Grill Shallow fry

7.44 CHUMP CHOPS (200 g)

Cut from the "chump" or leg end of the loin, cutting two chops from each loin.	Grill Shallow fry Stew

---

Pork

The flesh should be moist and light pink in colour with a fine and even grain. The skin should be shiny and very smooth. The fat should be evenly distributed over the carcass. Table 6 gives the main joints and cuts of pork, the approximate weight, method of preparation and possible methods of cooking.

TABLE 6. JOINTS AND CUTS OF PORK: APPROXIMATE WEIGHT, PREPARATION AND METHODS OF COOKING

Preparation of joint or cut	*Methods of cooking*
Main joints and small cuts	
7.45 LEG — CUISSOT (5 kg)	
Remove the pelvic bone and trotter. Saw off the leg bone and trim off the flesh and membrane leaving about 4 cm bare bone. Score the skin to a depth of 4 mm 1 cm apart. Tie with string at the thick end.	Roast
7.46 LOIN — LONGE (5½ kg)	
Either: (*a*) cut into two joints across. Score the skin to a depth of 4 mm 1 cm apart; or (*b*) cut into two joints across. Remove the bone and skin. Score the skin to a depth of 4 mm 1 cm apart. Replace the skin, roll and tie.	Roast

7.47 SPARE RIB — BASSE-COTE (3 kg)

Either:

(*a*) score the skin to a depth of 4 mm 1 cm apart; or — Roast

(*b*) remove the bone and skin. Score the skin to a depth of 4 mm 1 cm apart. Replace the skin, roll and tie.

7.48 SHOULDER/HAND — EPAULE (3 kg)

Either: — Roast

(*a*) score the skin to a depth of 4 mm 1 cm apart; or

(*b*) remove the skin and bone. Score the skin to a depth of 4 mm 1 cm apart. Replace the skin, roll and tie.

7.49 BELLY — POITRINE (3 kg)

Remove the bone and skin. Trim excess fat. Roll and tie — Roast

Cuts from loin of pork

7.50 PORK CHOPS — COTE DE PORC (200 g)

Remove the skin and excess fat from the loin and cut into even sized chops 2½ cm thick. — Grill, Shallow fry

7.51 PORK FILLET — FILET DE PORC (2 × 100 g)

Remove the fillet. Trim off excess fat and sinew. Cut lengthways and lightly flatten with a butcher's bat. — Grill, Shallow fry

7.52 PORK ESCALOPE — ESCALOPE DE PORC (120 g)

Remove the fillet. Trim off excess fat and sinew. Cut lengthways and slightly flatten with a butcher's bat until approximately 2 mm in thickness. — Shallow fry

Bacon

Bacon should be clean, have a pleasant odour and show no signs of stickiness. It should be stored fresh at a temperature of 5–7 °C. Table 7 gives the main joints and cuts, approximate weight, method of preparation and possible methods of cooking.

TABLE 7. JOINTS AND CUTS OF BACON: APPROXIMATE WEIGHT, PREPARATION AND METHODS OF COOKING

Preparation of joint or cut	*Methods of cooking*
7.53 GAMMON (5 kg)	
Saw knuckle bone through 3 mm from the end.	Boil
7.54 BACK (7 kg)	
Remove bones, tendons and skin. Slice into rashers.	Grill Shallow fry
7.55 STREAKY (3½ kg)	
Remove bones, tendons and skin. Slice into rashers.	Grill Shallow fry

7.56 COLLAR (3 kg)	
Bone, roll and tie.	Boil
7.57 HOCK (3½ kg)	
Bone, roll and tie.	Boil
7.58 GAMMON STEAK (150 g)	
Remove skin and bone from whole gammon. Cut into even sized steaks approximately 1½ cm thick. Cut nicks in the outer rim of fat to prevent curling during cooking.	Grill Shallow fry

Veal

The flesh should be whitish to very pale pink in colour and finely and evenly grained. The outer coating of fat should be thin and the configuration of bones should be large in relation to the size and amount of flesh muscle. The bones should be bluish white in colour. Table 8 gives the main joints and cuts of veal, the approximate weight, method of preparation and possible methods of cooking.

TABLE 8. JOINTS AND CUTS OF VEAL: APPROXIMATE WEIGHT, PREPARATION AND METHODS OF COOKING

Preparation of joint or cut	*Methods of cooking*
Main joints	
7.59 SADDLE — SELLE (5–8 kg)	
Remove the hip bones and cut away the flank in line with the joint. Cover the back with strips of bacon and tie into place reforming the joint.	Roast Pot roast White braise
7.60 LOIN — LONGE (2½–4 kg)	
Remove the kidneys from inside the saddle. Divide the saddle through the centre to make two loins. Remove the outer skin and bone completely. Cut away the flank in line with the joint. Reform the joint by tying it into place.	Roast Pot roast
7.61 BEST END — CARRE (3 kg)	
Remove the outer skin. Remove the breast leaving the joint twice as long as the eye (the centre meat). Remove the sinew along the width from under the back. Remove the flesh and skin from the end cutlet bones and from between the bones.	Roast
7.62 NECK — COLLET (2½ kg)	
Remove the skin and bone completely. Remove any sinew and cut into 2½ cm cubes.	Stew

7.63 BREAST — POITRINE (2½ kg)

Bone completely. Remove outer skin, sinew and fat.
Either:

(*a*) roll into a joint — Roast
(*b*) stuff, roll and tie into a joint — Roast
(*c*) cut into 2½ cm cubes — Stew

7.64 SHOULDER — EPAULE (7 kg)

Bone completely. Remove outer skin, sinew and fat.
Either:

(*a*) cut into joints and tie — Roast or white braise
(*b*) cut into 2½ cm cubes — Stew

7.65 CALF'S HEAD AND BRAIN — TETE DE VEAU

Clean and remove all traces of hair. Cut through the flesh down to the bone along the centre of the head and nostrils. Remove the flesh from the head following the shape of the head from the centre on each side. Remove the tongue, eyelids, nostrils and associated cartilage and gristle. Cut the remaining flesh into 5 cm square pieces. — Boil

Having removed the flesh from the head make an incision around the cranium using a saw. Lift the top of the cranium and gently remove the brain.

Soak the head pieces and tongue in cold water for 2–3 hours.

7.66 LEG — CUISSEAU (5–8 kg)

Remove the pelvic bone. Saw off the knuckle bone end and trim off surplus meat. — Roast, Pot roast, White braise

Joints from the leg

(12 kg)

Saw off the knuckle end at the first joint and retain. Skin the outer surface of the leg and divide into joints (7.67–71) between the membrane.

7.67 KNUCKLE/SHIN — JARRET (3 kg)

Either:

(*a*) saw across the knuckle into round small cuts leaving the centre bone and tie; or — Stew

(*b*) bone completely and trim away outer skin and sinew. Cut into 2½ cm cubes. — Stew

7.68 CUSHION — NOIX (2½ kg)

Carefully trim, cover with strips of fat bacon (*see* p. 242) and tie into shape. — Roast, Pot roast, White braise

7.69 UNDER CUSHION — SOUS NOIX (2½ kg)
Prepare as for 7.68. As for 7.68

7.70 THICK FLANK — NOIX PATISSIERE (3 kg)
Prepare as for 7.68. As for 7.68

7.71 RUMP — QUASI (2½ kg)
Prepare as for 7.68. As for 7.68

Small cuts

7.72 ESCALOPE (120 g)
Cut from under cushion, cushion or thick flank. Cut into 2 cm thick slices across the grain of the joint. Lightly beat out with a dampened cutlet bat. Shallow fry

7.73 SMALL ESCALOPE — ESCALOPINE (2 × 75 g)
Prepare as for 7.72

7.74 GRENADIN (3 × 50 g)
Cut first into 1½ cm thick slices and lightly trim into small oval pieces.

7.75 VEAL CUTLET — COTE DE VEAU (250 g)
Cut between the cutlet bones of the prepared best end. Lightly flatten and trim. Shallow fry Grill

---

Poultry

Poultry should have flexible breast bones and plump firm breasts. The skin should be white and unbroken. Table 9 gives the main types of poultry, the number of portions which may be derived from a given weight and possible ways in which they may be cooked. Further preparation is given in 7.76–79.

Preparation of poultry

The method given in 7.76 below for trussing is suitable for chicken, duck, geese and turkey for roasting, pot roasting, boiling and poaching. When pot roasting or poaching poultry the legs should be folded back onto the side of the breast and trussed; when roasting the legs should point forward. When trussing duck, geese or turkey, the legs should be removed at the first joint. In addition, guinea fowl should be barded (*see* p. 242) with bacon fat or speck when trussed.

7.76 TRUSSING POULTRY

(1) Singe the bird and remove any feather pins with the tip of a small knife. Wipe clean with a cloth.

(2) Leave the centre claw on but cut off the tip. Remove the claw on either side.

TABLE 9. TYPES OF POULTRY, WEIGHT/NUMBER OF PORTIONS AND METHODS OF COOKING

Poultry item	*Drawn weight*	*Number of portions*	*Methods of cooking*
Boiling fowl — Poule	2½–3 kg	4–6	Boil
Capon — Chapon	3–4½ kg	6–10	Roast Pot roast Boil
Chicken — Poulet	1½–2 kg	4	Roast Pot roast Poach Grill Shallow fry
Duck — Canard	2–3 kg	3–4	Roast Pot roast Braise
Duckling — Caneton	2–2½ kg	3	Roast Pot roast
Goose — Oie	4–6 kg	6–12	Roast
Guinea fowl — Pintade	1½ kg	3–4	Roast Pot roast
Spring chicken:			
Single — Poussin	300–400 g	1	Roast, Pot roast, Grill
Double — Poussin	500–750 g	2	Roast, Pot roast, Grill
Turkey:			
Young — Dindonneau	5–9 kg	250 g raw per portion	Roast
Large — Dinde	7–12 kg	250 g raw per portion	Roast
Young fattened fowl — Poularde	2–2½ kg	4–6	Roast Pot roast Poach

(3) Dip the leg as far as the scales into boiling water for a few seconds and remove all traces of the scales with a cloth. Care must be taken not to over-blanch the legs as this will cause the flesh to come away from the bone. (This is rarely practised today.)

(4) Make an incision through the tendon on the underside of the leg.

(5) Expose the wishbone by carefully scraping around the bone with a knife. Remove the wishbone completely taking care not to cut away the surrounding flesh.

(6) Cut off the winglets at the first joint end and fold them underneath.

(7) Push the trussing needle through the centre of the leg between the thigh bone and the drumstick in a straight line through the bird, entering the centre of the opposite leg and out through the other side.

(8) Pass the needle through the winglet bone in a straight line through the flap of neck skin and again through the second winglet. Tie the two ends of string together and cut off the excess.

(9) Pass the needle through the thigh flesh in a straight line through the chicken and out the opposite side, then pass the needle over the top of the drumstick through the surplus skin under the breast flesh taking care not to pierce the breast. Tie the ends of the string.

7.77 PREPARATION OF CHICKEN FOR SUPREMES

(1) Remove each leg by cutting around the skin to the ball and socket joint at the carcass bottom.

(2) Fold back the leg at the ball joint cutting between and taking off the leg.

(3) Expose the wishbone by scraping around the bone with a knife. Remove the wishbone completely taking care not to cut away the surrounding flesh.

(4) Remove the winglets taking care to leave bare about 2–3 cm of bone attached to the breast.

(5) Cut along each side of the breast bone down and between the wing joint. Cut through and remove the suprêmes by laying the carcass on its side and gently pulling the carcass free.

(6) Remove the fillet from the back of each suprême and remove the tendon from each.

(7) Make an incision along the length of the back of the suprême and place the fillet just inside. Trim off any surplus from the suprêmes and form them into a neat shape.

7.78 PREPARATION OF CHICKEN FOR SHALLOW FRYING

(1) Singe the bird and remove any feather pins with the tip of a small knife. Wipe clean with a cloth.

(2) Remove each leg by cutting around the skin to the ball and socket joint at the carcass bottom.

(3) Fold back the leg at the ball joint cutting through and taking off the leg.

(4) Cut through the centre joint of the leg where the thigh bone and the drumstick meet thus separating the leg into two pieces. Cut away the end bones on each joint.

(5) Remove the winglets taking care to leave bare about 2–3 cm of bone attached to the breast. Bare the winglet bone cutting off just before the first bone.

(6) Cut along the length of the bird just each side of the breast bone leaving ample flesh on the breast bone to form another portion. Cut downwards in a straight line until making contact

with the socket joint located close to the remaining exposed winglet bone. Cut through and remove.

(7) Chop the remaining carcass away leaving the breast which is then cut through at its centre point dividing it into two equal pieces.

(8) The carcass may be divided into three equal pieces for inclusion when serving, having been cooked with the chicken pieces.

7.79 PREPARATION OF CHICKEN AND SPRING CHICKEN FOR GRILLING

(1) Pass a large knife through the vent end of the bird just allowing the tip of the knife to show at the neck end.

(2) Cut through to one side of the backbone.

(3) Open the bird out flat and remove the backbone completely.

(4) Make an incision through the skin close to each leg and tuck the end of the drumstick through in order to hold the chicken in position.

(5) Turn the bird over onto a work-surface with the centre bones exposed and lightly nick the breast bone once or twice — this will help to retain the shape of the bird during cooking.

TABLE 10. FEATHERED GAME: SEASONS, HANGING TIMES AND METHODS OF PREPARATION

Bird	*Season*	*Hanging time*	*Methods of preparation*
Grouse — Grouse	12/8–20/12	7 days	Clean and truss as for chicken. Should be barded
Partridge — Perdreau	1/9–11/2	3–4 days	As for grouse
Pheasant — Faisan	1/10–11/2	3–8 days	As for grouse
Quail — Caille	All year	Use fresh	Do not draw. Remove gizzard and cook on its back
Snipe — Bécassine	1/8–1/3	3–4 days	As for quail
Wild duck — Canard sauvage	1/8–1/3		As for grouse
Woodcock — Bécasse	1/8–1/3	3–4 days	As for quail

Game — furred and feathered

Young game birds are suitable for roasting and may be identified by their soft, pliable bones and feet and moist appearance; older birds should be braised or stewed.

Table 10 gives the more important game birds, when they are in season, hanging times and methods of preparation.

The term furred game includes the meat from deer (venison) and hare. Rabbit, because it is very much like hare, is often classified as game though strictly speaking it is not. The quality joints are the haunch (leg) and the saddle. Preparation of furred game consists of the removal of the fine outer membrane and sinew using a flexible filleting knife followed by larding or barding of the joint. The meat is then marinated for 2–4 hours, drained and wiped prior to cooking. Furred game may be roasted, pot roasted or stewed as appropriate.

Hare — lièvre

Young hare are used in preference for roasting, pot roasting and stewing and may be identified by the ease with which the ears may be torn. They are in season between August and March. Once skinned they should be hung for a few days in a refrigerator in order to tenderise and develop a "gamy" flavour. The diaphragm containing the blood and offal used to make jugged hare should be intact.

Hare may be jointed for stewing into 16 pieces: the saddle and low neck should yield 6 pieces; each shoulder should yield 2 pieces; each leg divides into 3 pieces.

Rabbit — lapin

Young rabbit, usually about 3–4 months old, should be used in preference for cooking and may be identified by the ease with which the ears may be torn and the under-jaw broken. The flesh should be firm, moist and white.

Rabbit may be jointed for cooking into 16 pieces as for hare.

ROASTING

Roasting is the cooking of good quality joints of meat, whole poultry and game by radiated heat in the oven using fat as a basting agent. The object is to retain the juices within the meat so that the result is moist, succulent and tender. The preparation of the joint or cut of meat and poultry is of vital importance. Substandard preparation results in a poorly roasted item with excess waste when carved whilst the problems encountered are often impossible to correct. Table 11 gives the joints of meat which are suitable for roasting. *See* Table 13 for roast poultry and Table 14 for roasted game birds.

TABLE 11. ITEMS OF MEAT SUITABLE FOR ROASTING

Type of meat	*Approx. weight*	*Cooking time*	*Final internal temp.*
Beef:			
Fillet	1½ kg	45 mins	63–65 °C
Fore rib (on bone)	3 kg	2½ hours	
Middle rib (on bone)	3 kg	2½ hours	
Sirloin strip	1½ kg	45 mins	
Topside	1½ kg	1 hour	
Lamb:			
Best end	1½ kg	1¼ hours	63–65 °C
Leg	2 kg	1½ hours	
Loin	1½ kg	1½ hours	
Saddle	3 kg	2½ hours	
Shoulder	1½ kg	1½ hours	
Pork:			
Fore end	1½ kg	1½ hours	80 °C
Leg	3 kg	2½ hours	
Loin	1½ kg	1½ hours	
Shoulder	1½ kg	1½ hours	
Spare rib	1½ kg	1½ hours	
Veal:			
Cushion	1½ kg	1¾ hours	80 °C
Under cushion	1½ kg	1¾ hours	
Thick flank	1½ kg	1¾ hours	
Loin	1½ kg	1¾ hours	
Saddle	3 kg	2¾ hours	
Best end	2 kg	2 hours	
Shoulder	1½ kg	1¾ hours	

General application

All items to be roasted should first be seasoned with salt and, if desired, pepper and a range of spices and herbs before being placed in the oven. A general guide is to allow 300 g prepared raw meat per portion to be cooked on the bone, or 150 g prepared raw meat per portion to be cooked with bones removed. Allow approximately 15 minutes per 500 g plus an extra 15 minutes' cooking time for most meats but refer to individual recipes for more precise information.

All items that do not have a natural coating of fat — with the exception of chicken and turkey — should first be either larded (*see also* p. 281) or barded. (Larding means inserting the meat with strips of speck or fat bacon; barding means slices of speck or fat bacon are wrapped over the exposed surface of the meat and tied into position but removed during the last period of cooking.)

Joints of meat are placed upon bones when roasted, poultry items are not — *see* individual recipes for more precise detail.

Always select a roasting tray that is just large enough to hold the joint of meat comfortably — too large a tray will inevitably lead to the burning of the fat in the high temperatures attained during cooking.

Items of meat and poultry should be cooked at 220 °C for the first 15–20 minutes. The heat should then be reduced to 180 °C until the internal temperature of the joint reaches approximately 63–65 °C for rare, 65–70 °C and 80–85 °C for meat just cooked without traces of blood. It is usual to remove joints from the oven at 5 °C below these figures as the meat continues to cook whilst resting on the hotplate prior to carving.

Once a roasted item is cooked it should be removed from the receptacle in which it was cooked as soon as possible. Joints should be retained in a tray, preferably on a wire grid, and the juices collected for future use in making the gravy (*see* 7.80).

Notes

(1) Roasted items should never be covered with a lid during cooking. However, large joints of meat and poultry may be loosely covered with foil or damp greaseproof paper to prevent burning during long roasting periods. This should be put on once initial coloration has taken place, generally after the first 15–20 minutes of roasting, but should be placed loosely so as to avoid sealing the meat completely.

(2) Some chefs quickly shallow fry joints of meat and poultry in an effort to seal in the juices before roasting. The effectiveness of this practice is not proven.

(3) Extensions to all roast joints may be achieved by using vegetables cut into various shapes and combinations of other garnishes to form colourful dishes with contrasting flavours and textures (*see* pp. 248–9).

To test if cooked

The requirements of the customer and the recipe being prepared and, to a certain extent, the individual characteristics of the meat in question itself are factors to be taken into consideration when judging whether a particular item is cooked to the required degree. It is possible to use a variety of criteria when judging whether meat is sufficiently cooked, e.g. the general appearance, the response of the meat to pressure, by the juices that emanate, or more accurately (especially for the inexperienced) by means of a thermoneedle or thermocouple which is pushed into the centre of the joint and shows the internal temperature. The joint can then be removed from the oven cooked to the required degree thus ensuring there is no wastage from its being under- or overcooked.

Appearance
Deciding whether an item is cooked by its appearance is a method which is far from ideal as there is no degree of accuracy in comparison with other methods of testing. For the experienced, however, it does give a reasonable indication and can generally be supported by a second test by one of the following methods.

Pressure
When testing the meat by subjecting it to hand pressure a general rule is that the less resilience the meat has to pressure, the more well done it is.

Thermoneedle
When testing by thermopin or needle two methods may be adopted. The needle may be inserted into the thickest and fleshiest part of the joint to its centre to give a continuous reading whilst cooking.

Alternatively, the joint may be tested at the appropriate moment when it has been roasting for the prescribed time. The needle point should be inserted into the centre of the joint and left for a few moments until the needle stops at a constant reading. Joints that are cooked on the bone should be tested with the needle as close to the bone as possible to give an accurate reading.

Some roasting equipment have inbuilt thermocouples. The needle is inserted into the joint for the whole of the roasting process and gives a continuous temperature reading.

Juices
Piercing with a fork or trussing needle is an appropriate method for testing white meats such as lamb or veal. The fork or needle should be inserted into the centre of the thickest point and the juices that emanate should be clear when the joint is just cooked. (However, it should be remembered that lamb should be very slightly underdone therefore some traces of blood should be in evidence when tested.)

Poultry such as chicken and game items are usually tested with a fork or trussing needle. The centre of the leg joint should be pierced and the bird held in such a position that the juices can drip into a dish. If they are clear and free from all traces of blood then the bird is cooked. When testing turkey, the centre of the leg should be pierced with a fork to allow the juices to emanate; these should be clear and free from all traces of blood.

The ease with which a fork or trussing needle penetrates is also an indication as to how well the meat is cooked; the less resistance to pressure the more it is cooked.

Notes

(1) Beef should be cooked until it is firm yet pink in colour. The temperature reading at this point should be 63–65 °C.

(2) Both furred and feathered game should be kept underdone. If cooked thoroughly flavour will be lost and the flesh become stringy (*see* p. 264 for degree cooked).

(3) Lamb should be left with the flesh a slight pink colour. The term used to describe this is rosé. The temperature reading at this point should be 63–65 °C.

(4) Veal and pork should be well cooked. The juices should be clear and free from traces of blood when the meat is cooked. The temperature reading at this point should be 80 °C.

Assessment of items roasted

(1) The meat should be cooked to the correct degree. It should be moist and succulent, surrounded with a little clear roast gravy sufficient to cover the bottom of the dish. (This does not apply to roast joints of veal or turkey in which case the gravy should be slightly thickened.)

(2) The gravy should be clear, fairly brown in colour, free from fat or grease and seasoned. It should have the flavour of the meat it is served with.

(3) The garnish of picked watercress should be clean and fresh looking.

Gravy

As a general rule all roast items require a clear unthickened gravy as given in 7.80 below, with the exception of turkey and veal which require a slightly thickened gravy (*see* 7.99 for veal gravy and *Note* (7) to 7.101 for turkey gravy). Brown veal stock is considered ideal as a basis for most roast gravies because its rather delicate flavour will blend with other flavours without predominating. However, brown stock made from turkey giblets and carcass bones is used as a basis for roast turkey gravy.

The flavour of the meat that the gravy is to be served with is derived mainly from the sediment of the roasting pan in which the item has been cooked. One litre of brown stock should yield sufficient roast gravy for 10 portions. Some loss is experienced when making the stock into gravy because it is boiled and skimmed during the preparation and gives 6 dl of completed gravy. If served in a separate dish, however, then probably a little more will be required.

7.80 ROAST GRAVY

Method

(1) Once the item roasted is cooked to the required degree remove it from the roasting tray and retain it in a warm place — *see* p. 243.

(2) Put the roasting tray on the stove and gently heat, allowing the sediment to settle.

(3) Drain off all the surplus fat allowing any sediment to remain in the tray.

(4) Add the brown stock and allow to simmer gently for a few minutes.

(5) Strain through a fine conical strainer into a deep pan. Reboil, skim off all traces of fat and other impurities that may come to the surface and season to taste.

(6) If necessary retain in a hot bain-marie for use as required.

Notes

(1) Some chefs insist on using either brown game or veal stock as a basis for roast gravy to be served with game.

(2) Roast gravy should be slightly brown in colour, free from all traces of fat or grease and seasoned to taste.

(3) If the gravy is not brown enough then the colour may be adjusted with a little gravy browning.

Carving

All joints of meat, poultry and game which are to be carved immediately once they are cooked should be allowed to stand for at least 10–20 minutes after removal from the oven. This allows the muscle to relax to make carving easier and so yield the maximum number of portions.

Roasted items that are to be carved and served cold should be allowed to cool completely before carving. For best results allow the item to cool in a cold larder at a temperature of 10 °C and then carve. When cool they must be stored in a refrigerator at a temperature of 8 °C on a tray standing on a wire grid to allow any juices to drain away. (If meat is refrigerated the muscle and fat will stiffen and the quality may suffer somewhat.)

NOTE

Any string should be completely removed from the cooked meat before carving.

General rules for carving meats are as follows.

Beef
Beef is carved across the grain. Joints such as *sirloin*, *ribs* and *topside* are sliced thinly, and *fillet* slightly thicker. However, it is acceptable to carve sirloin of beef thickly and give each customer one thick slice rather than two thin ones.

Lamb
The *legs* are carved to a thickness of approximately 3–4 mm starting at the knuckle end and working backwards to the thicker end of the joint at a 45° angle. As the slices increase in size due to the shape of the joint change direction of carving — slice from alternate sides of the joint thus yielding two smaller slices and continue by turning the joint to remove all meat from both sides.

Shoulder roasted on the bone should be carved to a thickness of 3–4 mm starting at the thickest part of the joint at an angle of 45°. Continue carving following the shape of the bones.

Shoulder boned and stuffed should be carved into slices 5 mm thick across the joint.

Saddle should be carved:

(a) lengthways either side of the backbone into slices approximately 5 mm in thickness or at an angle of 45° across the joint commencing carving at the neck end; or
(b) lengthways either side of the backbone releasing the joint from the saddle bone by cutting lengthways along the side of the joint just above the bone. Remove and carve into 5 mm slices across the meat at an angle of 45°, then replace and reform onto the saddle carcass.

The meat underneath the saddle can be removed and sliced and served with the slices from the top of the joint.

Loin boned and rolled should be carved across the joint at an angle of 45° to a thickness of 5 mm.

Best ends should be carved into cutlets between each rib bone. The end rib bone is usually unusable due to its smallness, therefore remove and discard before carving.

Pork
Remove the crackling from the joint and chop into 2 cm pieces.

Leg, shoulder and loins are carved in exactly the same way as for lamb into slices approximately 3–4 mm thick.

Veal

Carve *legs*, *leg joints*, *saddle*, *loin*, *breast* and *best ends* in exactly the same way as for lamb into slices approximately 2–3 mm thick.

Poultry

When carving chicken, duck, pheasants and guinea fowl:

(1) Remove the legs, cut into two, remove the bone from the drumstick and chop away the joint at the top of the thigh piece.

(2) Remove the winglets. Carve halfway up the side of the bird each side of the breast bone down to the wing joint, cutting through the wing joint to release the wing portions. Remove and discard any bone from underneath the portion and trim neatly.

(3) Remove the remaining breast from the carcass and cut in two lengthways. Remove any breast bone that may remain and neatly trim.

Turkey

Turkey may be carved whole or the legs and breast may be removed from the carcass and carved on a cutting board.

If to be carved on the bone remove the legs and divide into drumstick and thigh. Remove bones and tendons and carve into slices on a slant 3–4 mm thick. Commence carving slices from the wing end towards the breast bone 3–4 mm thick — slices will inevitably become larger as one progresses.

If to be boned first and then carved remove the legs and divide into drumstick and thigh. Remove bones and tendons and carve into slices on a slant 3–4 mm thick. Remove the winglets. Remove the breast completely by cutting each side of the breast bone down towards the wing joint, cut through the joint by following the ball and socket joint and remove. Bone out the end wing bone and trim. Commence carving from the thick end towards the pointed thinner end on a slant of 45° 3–4 mm thick.

Capon

Capon may be carved into portions as for chicken but may make six or more portions. Capon may also be carved as for turkey either whole or removed from its carcass.

Garnishes and accompaniments

The following list details the most widely used garnishes and accompaniments served with roast meats. The list is by no means exhaustive.

Beef — Yorkshire pudding, horseradish sauce, clear roast unthickened gravy, watercress

Chicken —	Clear roast unthickened gravy, bread sauce, game chips, watercress, grilled bacon (optional)
Duck —	Sage and onion stuffing, apple sauce, watercress, clear roast unthickened gravy, game chips (optional)
Game birds —	Fried bread croûtons cooked in butter and spread with a game farce au gratin, clear roast unthickened gravy, bread sauce, golden fried breadcrumbs, game chips, watercress
Goose —	As for roast duck
Lamb —	Mint sauce or mint jelly, clear roast unthickened gravy, watercress
Mutton —	White onion sauce or redcurrant jelly, clear roast unthickened gravy
Pork —	Sage and onion stuffing, clear roast unthickened gravy, watercress, apple sauce
Turkey —	Generally stuffed with chestnut or thyme and parsley stuffing, lightly thickened roast gravy, watercress, bread sauce or cranberry sauce, grilled chipolata sausages, grilled bacon or slices of ham, game chips (optional).
Veal —	Thyme, parsley and lemon stuffing, grilled bacon rashers, lightly thickened roast gravy, watercress

Stuffings are used to stuff the item before it is roasted and in most instances the fat of the meat it is to be served with is used to bind it. Alternatively, the stuffing may be prepared and cooked separately, in which case beaten eggs are added to the basic recipe as the binding agent. The stuffing may then be rolled into a cylindrical shape in buttered greaseproof paper and cooked in steamer for about 20 minutes. When cooked the paper is removed and the stuffing cut into round slices and served as a garnish. A further method of cooking stuffings separately is to place them in a saucepan covered with greaseproof paper and a lid and put into an oven at 150 °C for about 20 minutes.

Table 12 gives an indication of the type of stuffing associated with a particular meat, though the list is by no means exhaustive.

TABLE 12. STUFFINGS

Stuffing	*Roast meat/poultry*
Chestnut (7.81)	Turkey
Sage and onion (7.82)	Duck, geese, pork, turkey
Sage, thyme and onion (7.83)	All meat and poultry
Sausage meat (7.84)	Turkey
Thyme, parsley and lemon (7.85)	Veal, lamb

7.81 CHESTNUT STUFFING

Gently mix together 750 g pork sausage meat and 250 g Braised Chestnuts (8.139).

7.82 SAGE AND ONION STUFFING

Makes: 500 g. Cooking time: 30 minutes.

Quantity	*Ingredient*
150 g	pork or duck dripping
100 g	chopped onion
10 g	finely rubbed sage
5 g	chopped parsley
250 g	white breadcrumbs
	seasoning of salt and pepper

Method

(1) Heat the dripping in a shallow saucepan. Add the onions and cook without allowing them to colour.

(2) Add the sage and allow to cook for a few minutes.

(3) Add and incorporate the breadcrumbs and chopped parsley. Season to taste.

Note

Where stuffing is prepared as a separate item, two options are available: *(a)* moisten the ingredients with extra dripping to bind them lightly; or *(b)* add a quantity of the accompanying clear roast gravy to bind the ingredients.

7.83 SAGE, THYME AND ONION STUFFING

Proceed as in 7.82 using 5 g sage and 5 g thyme finely rubbed.

7.84 SAUSAGE MEAT STUFFING

Makes: 1 kg.

Mix 1 kg pork sausage meat with 20 g chopped parsley. Stuff the turkey before roasting.

Alternative method for cooking separately

Place cylindrically shaped pork sausage meat into gently simmering white stock with salt and a bayleaf and cook for 30 minutes. Remove from the liquid, cool and cut into neat round slices.

Note

When cooked the sausage meat may be retained in the liquid until cold to use as a garnish for cold roast turkey. This method lends itself to catering for large numbers as it is clean, neat and the amount required can be gauged exactly, thereby avoiding wastage.

7.85 THYME, PARSLEY AND LEMON STUFFING

Makes: 500 g. Cooking time: 20 minutes.

Quantity	Ingredient
250 g	white breadcrumbs
150 g	chopped suet
5 g	chopped parsley
10 g	finely rubbed thyme
1	grated rind and juice of lemon
2	eggs
¼ dl	milk
	salt, pepper, nutmeg

Method

(1) Place all the dry ingredients into a mixing bowl. Add the beaten eggs and milk and season to taste.

(2) Roll into a cylindrical shape approximately 5 cm in diameter and wrap in buttered greaseproof paper.

(3) Cook in a steamer for about 20 minutes.

7.86 YORKSHIRE PUDDING

Makes: 10 portions. Oven temperature: 220 °C. Cooking time: 30 minutes.

Quantity	Ingredient
225 g	soft flour
5 g	salt
2	eggs
4 dl	milk
½ dl	water
2 dl	beef dripping

Method

(1) Sieve the flour and salt into a basin.

(2) Whisk together the eggs and milk.

(3) Add the beaten eggs and milk to the flour and whisk to a smooth texture. Add the water to bring the consistency of the batter to that of single cream.

(4) Strain through a conical strainer into a clean basin and allow the batter mixture to stand for one hour in a cool area in order to permit the mixture to relax.

(5) Heat the dripping in 10 individual moulds or two 15 cm frying pans.

(6) Pour in the batter mixture in equal amounts into the moulds. As the dripping begins to smoke, place into the oven to bake until it has risen, is crisp and golden.

Note

Although this batter is a little thicker than pancake batter it is similar in every other way. *See* 10.1 for an analysis of the problems that may be encountered.

Roast beef

7.87 ROAST FILLET OF BEEF WITH VEGETABLES — FILET DE BOEUF ROTI BOUQUETIERE

Proceed as for Roast Sirloin of Beef (7.88). Garnish with 200 g Glazed Carrots (8.64), 200 g Glazed Turnips (8.118), 100 g Minted Peas (8.99), 50 g Buttered French Beans (8.76), 10 Chateau Potatoes (9.50) and 10 × 30 g pieces of cauliflower coated with Hollandaise Sauce (3.12).

7.88 ROAST RIB OF BEEF WITH YORKSHIRE PUDDING

Using 3 kg Prepared Rib of Beef (7.7) proceed as for Roast Sirloin of Beef (7.89), roasting for approximately 2½ hours. Serve an extra garnish of Yorkshire Pudding (7.86).

Notes

(1) There is no need to cook ribs of beef on a base of bones. The joint should be placed into the roasting tray fat side uppermost.

(2) After the initial 20 minutes of cooking, reduce the temperature and lightly cover with a piece of foil or damp greaseproof paper.

7.89 ROAST SIRLOIN OF BEEF — CONTREFILET DE BOEUF ROTI

Makes: 10 portions. Cooking time: 45 minutes. Oven temperature: 220 °C reducing to 180 °C. Temperature at centre of joint: 63–65 °C.

Quantity	*Ingredient*
1½ kg	Prepared Sirloin (7.2)
2 dl	melted dripping or oil
	salt
1 l	Brown Stock (3.1)
2	bunches picked watercress
1 dl	horseradish sauce

Method

(1) Season the joint and place onto the bones in a roasting tray fat side uppermost. Coat with dripping and place into the oven reducing the temperature after approximately 20 minutes. Baste at regular intervals.

(2) When cooked, remove from the roasting tray and retain in a tray, preferably standing on a wire grid. Any juices collected may be used in making the gravy.

(3) Place the roasting tray on the stove and gently heat allowing the sediment to settle.

(4) Drain off all surplus fat allowing any sediment to remain in the tray.

(5) Add the brown stock and allow to simmer gently for a few minutes.

(6) Strain through a fine conical strainer into a deep sided saucepan. Reboil, skim all traces of fat and other impurities that may come to the surface and season to taste.

(7) Neatly arrange the slices of meat slightly overlapping on an oval flat dish. Coat with some of the roast gravy and garnish with watercress.

(8) Serve the remainder of the roast gravy and the horseradish sauce in sauceboats.

Possible problem	*Possible cause and solution*
(1) Meat is dry, lacks flavour and has shrunk excessively	— meat was of poor quality; only good quality meat should be used as these problems cannot be rectified. — meat was cooked at too high a temperature; care must be taken to roast the meat at the correct temperature to avoid these problems which cannot be rectified. — item was not basted during the roasting process; care must be taken to follow the correct roasting procedure basting regularly to avoid these problems which cannot be rectified. — meat without a natural fat coating was not larded or barded; care must be taken when preparing the meat as once cooked these problems cannot be rectified.
(2) Item yields less meat than expected	— meat was of poor quality; only good quality meat should be used to avoid the problem of shrinkage as the quality of the item cannot be rectified.

Possible problem	*Possible cause and solution*
	— meat was cooked at too high a temperature; care must be taken to roast the meat at the correct temperature to avoid this problem which cannot be rectified.
	— item was not allowed to rest once cooked before it is carved; it is important to allow the meat to rest before carving to avoid a low yield which cannot be rectified.
	— item was not properly carved; care must be taken to carve the meat correctly to achieve the maximum yield from the item.
(3) Gravy is dark in colour and has a burnt or bitter flavour	— item was cooked in too large a roasting tray; the meat should be roasted in a suitably sized tray to prevent the fat and sediment in the bottom from burning and passing the flavour and colour onto the gravy — this cannot be rectified.
	— basic stock was of poor quality; care must be taken when preparing the basic stock as if it is overcooked, dark and bitter these characteristics will be passed on to the gravy and cannot be rectified.

Roast lamb

7.90 ROAST BEST END OF LAMB PERSILLE—CARRE D'AGNEAU PERSILLE

Makes: 10 portions. Cooking time: 1½ hours. Oven temperature: 220 °C reducing to 180 °C. Temperature at centre of joint: 63–65 °C.

Quantity	*Ingredient*
4	Prepared Best Ends of Lamb
200 g	butter
50 g	chopped shallots
250 g	white breadcrumbs
10 g	chopped parsley
	seasoning
6 dl	Roast Gravy (7.80)

Method

(1) Roast the best ends as in 7.89 and transfer them to a clean roasting tray fat side uppermost.

(2) Melt the butter in a shallow sided saucepan, add the shallots

and cook without colouring. Add the breadcrumbs and parsley and combine. Season to taste.

(3) Cover the fat side of the joints with the mixture, press gently and mark trellis fashion.

(4) Return to the oven to allow the surface of the covering mixture to colour a light brown.

(5) Arrange the joints on a flat oval dish. Garnish with watercress and serve the gravy in a sauceboat.

Note

The best ends may also be carved into portions and served with the cutlets arranged criss-cross fashion on the dish, with cutlet frills.

7.91 ROAST BEST END OF LAMB WITH SAVOURY POTATOES — CARRE D'AGNEAU BOULANGERE

Makes: 10 portions. Cooking time: 1¼ hours. Oven temperature: 220 °C reducing to 180 °C. Temperature at centre of joint: 63–65 °C.

Quantity	*Ingredient*
4	Prepared Best Ends of Lamb (7.32)
10	portions Savoury Potatoes (9.35)
1 l	brown stock for gravy

Method

(1) Roast the best ends of lamb as in 7.89.

(2) During the last 10 minutes of cooking, place the meat on top of the almost cooked savoury potatoes.

(3) Serve the best ends of lamb on top of the savoury potatoes previously cooked in earthenware dishes. Serve on an underdish accompanied by a sauceboat of roast gravy.

Notes

(1) In trade practice the lamb and savoury potatoes are sometimes cooked separately. The best ends are carved and served arranged criss-cross fashion on top of the potatoes.

(2) Dripping from the roast lamb is sometimes used in place of butter when cooking the savoury potatoes.

(3) Whilst roasting the best ends need to be turned during cooking.

(4) If the best ends curl during roasting, it is generally because the sinew that runs along the back of the eye of the joint has not been removed.

7.92 ROAST LEG OF LAMB WITH MINT SAUCE — GIGOT D'AGNEAU ROTI SAUCE MENTHE

Makes: 10 portions. Cooking time: 1½ hours. Oven temperature: 220 °C reducing to 180 °C. Temperature at centre of joint: 63–65 °C.

Quantity	*Ingredient*
2 kg	Prepared Legs of Lamb (7.28)
2 dl	melted dripping or oil
	salt
2	bunches picked watercress
1 dl	Mint Sauce (3.49)

Method

Proceed as for Roast Sirloin of Beef (7.89). Serve the mint sauce separately.

Note

In trade practice legs of lamb are generally roasted without standing them on bones. The legs are turned whilst cooking to ensure roasting on all sides.

7.93 ROAST LOIN OF LAMB WITH MINT SAUCE — LONGE D'AGNEAU ROTIE SAUCE MENTHE

Using 1½ kg Prepared Loin of Lamb (7.31) roast for approximately 1½ hours as in 7.89. Serve the Mint Sauce (3.49) separately.

7.94 ROAST SADDLE OF LAMB — SELLE D'AGNEAU ROTIE

Using 3 kg Prepared Saddle of Lamb (7.30) roast for approximately 2½ hours as in 7.89.

7.95 ROAST STUFFED SHOULDER OF LAMB — EPAULE D'AGNEAU ROTIE FARCIE

Using 1½ kg Prepared Shoulder of Lamb (7.29) stuffed with 500 g Thyme, Parsley and Lemon Stuffing (7.85) roast for approximately 1½ hours as in 7.89.

Roast pork

Pork should never be undercooked. When cooked the juices should be free from all traces of blood.

7.96 ROAST LEG OF PORK — CUISSOT DE PORC ROTIE

Using 3 kg Prepared Leg of Pork (7.45) roast for approximately 2½ hours as in 7.89.

7.97 ROAST LOIN OF PORK WITH APPLE SAUCE — LONGE DE PORC ROTIE

Makes: 10 portions. Cooking time: 1½ hours. Oven temperature: 220 °C reducing to 180 °C. Temperature at centre of joint: 80 °C.

Quantity	*Ingredient*
1½ kg	Prepared Loin of Pork (7.46)
2 dl	melted dripping or oil
	salt
1 l	Brown Stock (3.1)
2	bunches of picked watercress
1 dl	Apple Sauce (3.46)

Method

Proceed as for 7.89. When serving place a piece of the crackling on each portion of pork. Serve the apple sauce in a sauceboat.

7.98 ROAST STUFFED SHOULDER OF PORK WITH APPLE SAUCE — EPAULE DE PORC ROTIE FARCIE

Using 1½ kg Prepared Shoulder of Pork (7.48) stuffed with 500 g Sage and Onion Stuffing (7.82) roast as for 7.89.

Roast veal

Joints of veal should be covered with slices of speck or fat bacon tied into position. These should be removed during the final moments of cooking. Thyme, parsley and lemon stuffing is generally served as an accompaniment together with a roast gravy lightly thickened with arrowroot.

Examples of roast veal as they appear on the menu are as follows:

Roast Shoulder of Veal — Epaule de Veau Rôtie
Roast Loin of Veal — Longe de Veau Rôtie
Roast Best End of Veal — Carré de Veau Rôti

7.99 ROAST CUSHION OF VEAL — NOIX DE VEAU ROTIE

Makes: 10 portions. Cooking time: 1¾ hours. Oven temperature: 220 °C reducing to 180 °C. Temperature at centre of joint: 80 °C.

Quantity	*Ingredient*
1½ kg	Prepared Cushion of Veal (barded) (7.68)
2 dl	melted dripping or oil
	salt
1 l	Brown Stock (3.1)
50 g	arrowroot
500 g	Thyme, Parsley and Lemon Stuffing (7.85)
2	bunches of picked watercress

Method

(1) Season the joint and place onto some veal bones. Coat with the dripping and place into the oven. Reduce the temperature after approximately 20 minutes. Baste at regular intervals during cooking.

(2) Cut the string and remove the fat covering during the last 15 minutes of roasting to permit the joint to colour lightly.

(3) When cooked, remove the joint from the roasting tray and retain in a tray, preferably standing on a wire grid. Any juices collected may be used in the making of the gravy.

(4) Place the roasting tray on the stove and gently heat, allowing the sediment to settle.

(5) Add the brown stock and allow to simmer gently for a few minutes.

(6) Strain through a fine conical strainer into a deep sided saucepan. Reboil and skim off all traces of fat and other impurities that may come to the surface. Thicken with the diluted arrowroot and allow to simmer. Skim, season to taste and strain into a clean saucepan. If necessary retain in a bain-marie for use as required.

(7) Carve the joint on a slant of about 45° to a thickness of 3 mm.

(8) Neatly arrange the slices of meat, slightly overlapping on an oval flat dish. Coat with some of the slightly thickened roast gravy. Garnish each portion with a slice of the stuffing and the dish with the watercress.

(9) Serve the remainder of the roast gravy in a sauceboat.

Roast poultry

Table 13 gives a cooking chart for roast poultry providing information on cooking times, approximate weights and numbers of portions and the final internal temperature when cooked for each bird.

TABLE 13. COOKING CHART FOR ROAST POULTRY

Bird	*Approx. weight*	*Serves*	*Cooking time*	*Final internal temp.*
Capon — Chapon	2½–3½ kg	6–8	2 hours	80 °C
Chicken — Poulet	1¼–1¾ kg	3–4	1 hour	80 °C
Duck — Canard	2¼–3 kg	4	1 hour	80 °C
Duckling — Caneton	2–2½ kg	3–4	1 hour	80 °C
Goose — Oie	4–6 kg	8–10	2 hours	80 °C
Guinea fowl — Pintade	1½ kg	3–4	1 hour	80 °C
Spring chicken:				
Single — Poussin	300–500 g	1	20 minutes	80 °C

Bird	Approx. weight	Serves	Cooking time	Final internal temp.
Double — Poussin	500–750 g	2	25 minutes	80 °C
Turkey:				
Young — Dindonneau	5–7 kg	15–20	2½ hours	80 °C
Large — Dinde	12 kg	40–50	2½ hours (legs removed)	80 °C
Young fowl	2–2¼ kg	4–6	1½ hours	80 °C

7.100 ROAST CHICKEN — POULET ROTI

Makes: 12 portions. Cooking time: 1 hour. Oven temperature: 200 °C. Temperature at centre of legs: 80 °C.

Quantity	Ingredient
3 × 1½ kg	chicken, trussed for roasting (*see* 7.76)
	salt
2 dl	melted dripping or oil
½ l	brown stock
3	bunches of picked watercress
150 g	Game Chips (*see* p. 475)
2 dl	Bread Sauce (3.47)

Method

(1) Season the chicken inside and outside with salt.

(2) Select a roasting tray large enough to enable the birds to be moved during cooking. Lay in the chickens on their sides on one leg, cover with the melted dripping and place in the oven to roast.

(3) After approximately 20 minutes turn the birds over onto the other leg for a similar period, basting from time to time.

(4) Lay the birds on their backs with the breasts uppermost. Continue to roast for a further 20 minutes.

(5) During the last 10 minutes of roasting, stack the birds on their ends with the neck ends against the bottom of the roasting tray and the breasts downwards to allow the juices to lubricate the flesh.

(6) When cooked, remove the chickens from the roasting tray and retain in a tray stacked as in (5). Any juices collected may be used in making the gravy.

(7) Drain off all the surplus fat allowing any sediment to remain in the tray.

(8) Add the brown stock and allow to simmer gently for a few minutes.

(9) Strain through a fine conical strainer into a deep sided saucepan. Reboil, skim off all traces of fat and other impurities

that may come to the surface and season to taste. If necessary retain in a bain-marie for use as required.

(10) Remove the string from the chickens and serve on an oval flat dish with a little of the roast gravy. Garnish with picked watercress and game chips accompanied by sauceboats of roast gravy and bread sauce.

Notes

(1) To test if cooked, pierce the centre of the legs with a fork, hold the chicken over a dish and allow the juices to escape onto the dish. The clarity of these juices gives an indication of how well the bird is cooked; when the juices are quite clear with no traces of blood the bird is cooked.

(2) Chicken may also be carved into portions when served.

(3) Chicken may be roasted with their legs and under-side of the carcass removed. In such cases they are roasted with the breasts uppermost during cooking, allowing ¾ hour roasting time.

7.101 ROAST TURKEY

Roast turkey is cooked in exactly the same way as Roast Chicken (7.100).

Notes

(1) Allow 250 g raw turkey weight to each portion to be served.

(2) Allow approximately 2½ hours roasting time per 12 kg bird.

(3) Turkey may be stuffed with various stuffings at the neck end.

(4) Braised Chestnuts (8.139) may also be incorporated into the stuffings, either mixed with sage, thyme and onion stuffing or sausage meat stuffing.

(5) Turkey is trussed in exactly the same way as chicken.

(6) Turkey may be garnished with watercress, Bread Sauce (3.47), Cranberry Sauce (3.48), Braised Chestnuts (8.139), Grilled Chipolata Sausages (7.232), Grilled Bacon (7.218) or slices of ham, and Game Chips (*see* p. 475).

(7) Turkey gravy is made from brown stock if derived from the giblets and carcass bones. It is possible to thicken it slightly if desired with diluted arrowroot and should be cooked for at least 30 minutes, including the sediment from the roasting tray in which the turkey has been cooked.

To test when cooked

Exert light pressure on the breast. If it is rather firm to the touch then the bird is cooked. Alternatively, drive the point of a trussing needle into the thickest and fleshiest part of the bird. Remove the needle and with the flat side of the fork press gently against the point of entry. If the juices which emerge are clear then the bird is cooked.

However, if whilst cooking the breast bone projects through the breast this is a sign that the turkey as a whole is overcooked, although the legs may still not be quite cooked. Where the legs rest against the breast is the last and most difficult part of the turkey to be cooked. Continuous basting, however, will help to lessen the problem.

When testing if cooked pay close attention to the innermost part of the leg and breast. If it is considered that the breast is cooked but not the legs remove the turkey from the oven and open up the legs by removing the trussing string. Cut the skin around the top of the leg, force them apart and return the bird to the oven to continue cooking. Alternatively remove the legs completely and cook them separately.

Some establishments prefer to remove the legs from the turkey, bone and stuff them and roast quite separate from the trunk to give a higher portion yield when carved. This approach is most favoured where large numbers are involved but there is no reason why this method cannot be adopted when catering for smaller quantities. The following procedure for preparation and cooking is in line with current trade practice, as will be noted cooking time is greatly reduced.

7.102 ROAST STUFFED TURKEY — DINDONNEAU ROTI A L'ANGLAISE

Makes: 40 portions. Cooking time: Breast: 2½ hours.
Legs: 1 hour.

Oven temperature: 220 °C reducing to 180 °C.

Quantity	*Ingredient*
1 × 12 kg	Prepared Turkey (7.76)
	salt
3 dl	melted dripping or oil
500 g	Thyme and Parsley Stuffing (7.85, but *see Notes* (3) and (4) to 7.101)
5 l	thickened brown turkey stock (*see Note* (7) to 7.101)
8	bunches picked watercress
4 dl	Cranberry Sauce (3.48)

Method

(1) Remove each leg by cutting around the skin to the ball and

socket joint at the bottom of the carcass. Fold back the leg at the joint. Cut through and take off the leg.

(2) Bone the legs removing all sinew and gristle.

(3) Lay the legs on a piece of foil with the skin side down. Overlap the flesh where necessary to form a continuous length of turkey meat.

(4) Season with salt and place a roll of stuffing about 10 cm in diameter along the length of the legs. Roll the stuffing into the legs with the foil and twist the foil at each end of the roll to prevent the stuffing seeping out during cooking. (It is unnecessary to tie the roll with string.)

(5) Place into a shallow sided dish making sure that the rolls of foil do not touch one another. Add sufficient water to ¼ cover the legs and put the dish in the oven to cook.

(6) Place the turkey trunk into a separate roasting tray standing on the carcass base. Season with salt both inside and outside, cover with melted dripping and place in the oven to roast. After approximately 20 minutes when the outer skin has lightly coloured, place a piece of foil or damp greaseproof paper over the surface. Baste occasionally during cooking.

(7) When cooked remove from the roasting tray and retain in a tray, preferably standing on a wire grid. Any juices collected may be used in making the gravy.

(8) Place the roasting tray on the stove and gently heat, allowing the sediment to settle.

(9) Drain off all surplus fat allowing any sediment to remain in the tray.

(10) Add the slightly thickened brown turkey stock and allow to simmer for a few minutes.

(11) Strain through a fine conical strainer into a deep sided saucepan. Reboil, skim all traces of fat and other impurities that may come to the surface and season to taste.

(12) Neatly arrange the slices of meat, leg and breast slightly overlapping on an oval flat dish, coat with some of the roast gravy. Garnish with the watercress and any other items as desired (*see* p. 249).

(13) Serve the remainder of the roast gravy and cranberry sauce in sauceboats.

Notes

(1) There is no need to truss the turkey if the legs are cooked separately.

(2) The trunk may be stuffed if desired but this is not necessary if the legs are stuffed instead. The trunk should be stuffed at the

neck end and sealed by folding under the skin and holding it in position with a skewer or sewing it with a trussing needle and string. Sage and Onion Stuffing (7.82), Sage, Thyme and Onion Stuffing (7.83) or Sausage Meat and Chestnut Stuffing (7.81) may be used.

(3) For best results the legs and trunk should be cooked in separate dishes.

(4) To prevent burning or scorching the foil around the legs a little water may be added.

(5) If using a thermoneedle or meat thermometer to test if the meat is cooked the needle should be inserted as deeply as possible — almost to the bone — at the fleshiest part of the bird about 2½ cm up from the wing. (*See* also p. 260.)

(6) It should be remembered when testing to see if the legs are cooked that the centre of the roll consists of stuffing. It is the flesh that needs to be tested, not the filling which will be cooked simultaneously. Test the point where the flesh and stuffing meet.

The following dishes are prepared by roasting the bird as for Roast Chicken (7.100) with appropriate stuffings, accompaniments and garnishes:

Roast Chicken with Bacon — Poulet Rôti au Lard
Roast Chicken with Thyme and Parsley Stuffing — Poulet Rôti à l'Anglaise
Roast Spring Chicken — Poussin Rôti
Roast Spring Chicken with Thyme and Parsley Stuffing — Poussin Rôti à l'Anglaise
Roast Duckling — Caneton Rôti
Roast Stuffed Duck — Canard Rôti à l'Anglaise
Roast Duckling with Orange Salad — Caneton Rôti, Salade d'Orange
Roast Stuffed Goose — Oie Rôtie à l'Anglaise
Roast Guinea Fowl — Pintade Rôtie

Notes

(1) Ducks may also be roasted with their leg and under-carcass removed. In such cases they are roasted with their breasts uppermost during cooking, allowing ¾ hour roasting time.

(2) To test if duck is cooked, prick the breast several times with a fork. The juices should be quite clear with no traces of blood when cooked. Alternatively, test in the same manner as for chicken (*see Note* (1) to (7.100)).

(3) Sometimes the drumstick of duck remains tough when cooked, in such instances do not serve them.

(4) Single and double spring chicken may be served whole or, in the case of a double poussin, may be cut through into two equal halves lengthways to form two portions.

Roast feathered game

The following points should be borne in mind when roasting game birds.

(a) Some game birds require hanging in order to improve their flavour and texture when cooked — *see* Table 10.

(b) Large game birds should be barded to protect the breasts from drying during roasting — *see* Table 10.

(c) All game birds are cooked in a hot oven at a temperature of 220 °C.

(d) Roast game should not be too well cooked. It should be slightly underdone.

(e) Once roasted the bird should be served on a croûton of bread covered with Game Liver Farce (7.106).

(f) Whenever possible game birds should be cooked to order as the meat deteriorates rapidly if retained in a hot cupboard for any length of time.

(g) Where possible all garnishes and accompaniments should be prepared before cooking the bird, with the exception of the roast gravy which is prepared with juices from the roast. This will ensure that the bird is held for the shortest possible time before serving.

(h) When serving game birds picked watercress should be placed at the tail end and game chips at the neck of the bird. Bread Sauce (3.47) and clear Roast Gravy (7.80) should be served in sauceboats together with white breadcrumbs shallow fried in melted butter until they are golden.

Table 14 gives a cooking chart for roasting certain feathered game — cooking times, degree each should be cooked to and the number of portions to be gained from each bird.

TABLE 14. COOKING CHART FOR ROAST FEATHERED GAME

Bird	*Cooking time (approx.)*	*Degree cooked (final internal temp.)*	*Serves*
Grouse	20 mins	Rare or medium (65 °C)	1 (serve whole)
Partridge — Perdreau	20–25 mins	Just cooked (78 °C)	1 (serve whole)

Bird	*Cooking time (approx.)*	*Degree cooked (final internal temp.)*	*Serves*
Pheasant — Faisan	45 mins	Just cooked (78 °C)	3–4
Quail — Caille	10 mins	Just cooked (76 °C)	Serve 2 birds per portion
Snipe — Bécassine	10 mins	Just cooked (80 °C)	1 (serve whole)
Wild duck — Canard sauvage	25 mins	Rare or medium (65 °C)	2 (serve whole)
Woodcock — Bécasse	10 mins	Just cooked (80 °C)	1 (serve whole)

The following birds may be roasted following the general method outlined in 7.103:

Roast Grouse
Roast Partridge — Perdreau Rôti
Roast Pheasant — Faisan Rôti
Roast Quail — Caille Rôtie
Roast Snipe — Bécassine Rôtie
Roast Woodcock — Bécasse Rôtie
Roast Wild Duck — Canard Sauvage Rôti

7.103 ROAST GAME BIRD

Makes: 10 portions. Cooking time: 10–25 minutes. Oven temperature: 220 °C.

Quantity	*Ingredient*	
10	prepared bird (trussed, barded, and seasoned as necessary)	
3 dl	melted dripping or oil	
3 dl	Brown Stock (3.1)	
10	Croûtons 5 cm in diameter (*see* 7.105)	garnish and accompaniments
150 g	Game Liver Farce (7.106)	garnish and accompaniments
100 g	white breadcrumbs (*see* 7.104)	garnish and accompaniments
2 dl	melted butter (*see* 7.104)	garnish and accompaniments
2 dl	Bread Sauce (3.47)	garnish and accompaniments
3	bunches picked watercress	garnish and accompaniments

Method

(1) Heat the fat in a roasting tray, the size of which is in keeping

with the size of the birds to be roasted, on top of the stove.

(2) Place the prepared birds into the hot fat and lightly colour them on both sides. Lay them on their sides on one leg and place in the oven to roast.

(3) After approximately 5 minutes turn the birds over onto the other leg for a similar period, basting from time to time.

(4) Lay the birds on their backs with the breasts uppermost. Continue to roast for a further 5–8 minutes.

(5) When almost cooked remove the barding. Baste and allow the breasts to colour slightly.

(6) When cooked, remove the birds from the roasting pan and retain in a warm place. Stack the birds with the neck ends against the bottom of the roasting tray and breasts downwards to allow the juices to lubricate the flesh.

(7) Drain off all the surplus fat allowing any sediment to remain in the tray.

(8) Add the brown stock and allow to simmer gently for a few minutes.

(9) Strain through a fine conical strainer into a deep sided saucepan. Reboil, skim off all traces of fat and other impurities that may come to the surface and season to taste. If necessary retain in a bain-marie for use as required.

(10) Shallow fry the croûtons in the fat in which the grouse were roasted until they are golden. Drain them and spread with the game farce.

(11) Remove the trussing string. Neatly arrange the birds on the croûtons on an oval flat dish with a little of the gravy. Garnish with picked watercress and game chips. Serve accompanied by sauce-boats of roast gravy, breadcrumbs tossed in butter until golden and bread sauce.

Notes

(1) Remember that *(a)* grouse, partridge and pheasant must be cooked on each leg first before being turned on their backs and removing the barding bacon; and *(b)* woodcock, quail and snipe are small birds which do not require turning and so should be roasted on their backs throughout.

(2) It is essential to use a sharp knife to remove the string holding the barding to avoid damaging the delicate breast.

(3) Where possible retain some of the fat in which the birds have been roasted for making game farce and frying the bread croûtons.

(4) The quality of pheasant is at times unpredictable. In such instances the legs may be rather tough so avoid using them, discard

them and use for alternative preparations such as Pâté Maison (2.36).

To test if cooked

Birds that should be left underdone should be tested by pressing on the breast and legs. A light firmness of the flesh is an indication that they are cooked to the correct degree.

For birds that should be medium-cooked pierce the centre of the legs with a fork and allow the juices to escape into a clean dish. The clarity of these juices is an indication of how well the bird is cooked — red indicates underdone; pink indicates medium or slightly undercooked; quite clear indicates that the bird is fully cooked. Such birds may also be tested by pressing the breast, in which case the less resistance to pressure the more cooked the bird.

Accompaniments for roast game

7.104 BROWNED WHITE BREADCRUMBS

Shallow fry 100 g white breadcrumbs in 2 dl melted butter until light golden in colour, continually turning and tossing to prevent them from burning. Constant attention is required.

7.105 CROUTONS

Croûtons to be placed under the cooked bird should be cut oblong in shape with the corners removed. The overall size should be in relation to the size of the bird which will be placed on it. Cut a groove the length of the croûton to prevent the bird, once set on it, from rolling off.

Croûtons to be placed at the side of a dish, e.g. when serving carved portions of pheasant, should be oval or round in shape no bigger than 2½ cm across. They should be shallow fried in melted butter or, if possible, the fat from the roasted bird if it is clean and clear. They should be cooked until a golden colour on the outside but still soft within.

Large numbers of croûtons — including heart shaped ones that are served with a number of other preparations such as Fricassée of Chicken (*see* 7.161) — should be either shallow fried in melted butter or lightly soaked in melted butter, placed onto a baking sheet and toasted under a salamander grill until golden on each side.

7.106 GAME LIVER FARCE — FARCE A GRATIN

Makes: 800 g. Cooking time: 5–8 minutes.

Quantity	Ingredient
1 dl	fat in which game has been roasted or melted butter or oil
200 g	fatty bacon cut into small pieces
100 g	sliced onion
500 g	game liver with the gall bladders removed
1 sprig	thyme
1	bayleaf
	salt and pepper

Method

(1) Heat the fat, butter or oil in a frying pan. Add the onions followed by the bacon and fry until both onion and bacon are cooked and light brown in colour.

(2) Add the seasoned liver, thyme and bayleaf. Increase the heat and shallow fry very quickly, tossing frequently.

(3) Place onto a stainless steel tray or into a bowl and allow to cool. Do not drain off the surplus fat.

(4) Pass through a fine sieve or mincer. Season to taste and place into a clean basin covered with cling foil. Retain in a refrigerator if not required for immediate use.

Notes

(1) If large quantities of game liver are required the total amount may be made up with chicken liver.

(2) Do not overcook the liver.

(3) Remember that the garnish is as important as the bird itself and requires similar careful preparation.

Service

Spread the game farce on the croûtons very slightly dome shaped. To reheat them the croûtons may be gently fried in the same fat as the game was cooked in but care must be taken not to scrape off the farce as they are turned. Alternatively, sprinkle the croûtons with game cooking fat or melted butter and gently heat at the bottom of a salamander grill or in an oven.

Roast furred game

Furred game such as joints of hare, rabbit and venison may be roasted as in 7.107, e.g.

Roast Venison — Chevreuil Rôti

7.107 ROAST SADDLE OF HARE — RABLE DE LIEVRE ROTIE

Makes: 10 portions. Cooking time: 20 minutes. Oven temperature: 220 °C. Temperature at centre of joint: 63–65 °C.

Quantity	*Ingredient*
1½ kg	Prepared Saddle of Hare (larded — *see* p. 281)
	Marinade Preparation (7.125)
	salt
2 dl	melted dripping or oil
1 l	brown stock
2	bunches of picked watercress
2 dl	redcurrant jelly
	seasoning

Method

(1) Select a roasting tray just large enough to hold the joints comfortably — too large a tray will inevitably lead to the burning of the fat in the high temperature attained during cooking.

(2) Remove the hare from the marinade. Drain and dry then season with salt and place in the roasting tray. Coat the items with dripping and place in the oven to cook. Baste at regular intervals.

(3) When cooked, remove the saddles from the roasting tray. Retain in a tray, preferably standing on a wire grid, and use any juices collected in making the gravy.

(4) Prepare the roast gravy as in 7.80.

(5) Bone the saddles lengthways then carve it into very thin slices along the length. Place the slices directly onto a serving dish, neatly arranged slightly overlapping.

(6) Lightly cover with a little of the roast gravy but do not reheat.

(7) Garnish with the watercress and serve the remainder of the gravy and redcurrant jelly in sauceboats.

Note

If the saddle is to be carved in the kitchen allow it to rest for at least 5 minutes before carving.

POT ROASTING

This is the cooking of good quality joints of meat, poultry or game in butter on a layer of vegetables and herbs in a deep sided receptacle with a close fitting lid. Cooking takes place in an oven at a temperature of 175–80 °C without coloration. During the latter stages of cooking the lid is removed in order to allow the surface of the meat to colour slightly. Joints of beef (*see* Table 15), on the other hand, are quickly shallow fried to colour on the outside *before* cooking.

Pot roasting is a moist method of cooking and the meat used

must be of high quality. The loss through shrinkage is significantly less than with traditional roasting — on average 20 per cent compared with approximately 30 per cent for traditionally roasted meats. Table 15 gives the main items of meat, poultry and game suitable for pot roasting.

TABLE 15. ITEMS OF MEAT, POULTRY AND GAME SUITABLE FOR POT ROASTING

Beef	*Lamb*	*Veal*	*Pork*	*Poultry*	*Game*
Fillet*	Best end	Nut*	Loin	Spring chicken	Pheasant
Sirloin	Loin	Cushion*		Chicken (up to 2 kg)	
	Saddle	Thick flank*		Duck	
		Loin*		Guinea fowl	
		Rump*			

*These items should first be either larded or barded.

General application

All items that do not have a natural layer of fat — with the exception of chicken — should first be either larded or barded (*see* Table 15 and p. 281.

The garnishes served with traditional roasts may also be served with pot roasted items (*see* pp. 248–9) unless they are part of a particular regional speciality, e.g. Roast Beef and Yorkshire Pudding. All items that have been pot roasted are served with a slightly thickened gravy.

Examples of pot roasted dishes include:

Pot Roasted Sirloin of Beef — Contrefilet de Boeuf Poêlé
Pot Roasted Loin of Lamb — Longe d'Agneau Poêlée
Pot Roasted Loin of Pork — Longe de Porc Poêlée
Pot Roasted Nut of Veal — Noix de Veau Poêlée
Pot Roasted Chicken — Poulet en Casserole
Pot Roasted Duckling — Caneton Poêlé
Pot Roasted Pheasant — Faisan Poêlé

7.108 POT ROASTED MEAT

Makes: 10 portions. Oven temperature: 180 °C.

Quantity	*Ingredient*	
1½ kg	prepared meat	
150 g	melted butter	
200 g	sliced carrot	bed of root vegetables
200 g	sliced onion	bed of root vegetables
150 g	sliced celery	bed of root vegetables
1	bayleaf	bed of root vegetables

Quantity	*Ingredient*	
1 sprig	thyme	bed of root vegetables
1	parsley stalk	
1	crushed clove garlic	
1 l	Jus Lié (3.8)	
	seasoning	

Method

(1) Butter and season the bottom of a deep sided receptacle which is sufficiently large to afford room for basting and covering with a lid without touching the meat. (A braising pan is ideal for this purpose.)

(2) Place in the bottom of the pan the bed of root vegetables.

(3) Season the prepared meat and place on the vegetables. Coat with the melted butter.

(4) Cover with a lid and pot roast in the oven at the required temperature, basting the meat from time to time.

(5) When the meat is nearly cooked, remove the lid and allow the meat to colour slightly for the last 10–20 minutes.

(6) When cooked remove the meat and keep it warm. Place the pan on top of the stove but do not allow the vegetables to colour. Add the jus lié and allow to simmer until the flavour from the juices and butter has been absorbed into the sauce.

(7) Pass the sauce through a very fine conical strainer without using pressure. Reboil and skim all traces of fat and other impurities. Season to taste and correct the consistency of the gravy so that it just coats the meat.

Assessment of the completed dish

(1) The meat should be moist, succulent and full of flavour.

(2) The top surface should be an even light golden colour.

(3) The sauce should be brown in colour but not too dark and should have a slight tinge of tomato colour. It should be light in consistency sufficient to coat the meat; mellow in flavour with the influence of the meat, vegetables and herbs; smooth in texture and slightly transparent so that the meat is clearly visible.

(4) Garnishes should be in the correct ratio for the number of portions and should be neatly and evenly prepared.

Possible problem	*Possible cause and solution*
(1) Meat is rather dry and lacks flavour	— meat was not sufficiently basted during cooking; care must be taken to follow the correct pot roasting procedure basting from time to time to avoid these problems which cannot later be rectified.

Possible problem	*Possible cause and solution*
	— meat without a natural fat coating was not larded or barded; care must be taken when preparing the meat as once cooked these problems cannot be rectified.
(2) Gravy is dark and bitter	— dish has been cooked at too high a temper ature overcolouring the vegetables, especially the onions, which are susceptible to burning; care must be taken to cook the dish at the prescribed temperature to avoid burning the vegetables which will affect the gravy and cannot be rectified.
	— poor quality jus lié was used; care must be taken when preparing the basic sauce as if it is overcooked, dark and bitter these characteristics will be passed on to the gravy and cannot be rectified.

Extensions

NOTE

For chicken the term *en casserole* and *en cocotte* imply that the chicken has been pot roasted in an earthenware dish and served in the dish in which it was cooked. Current trade practice, however, is to pot roast the chickens separately in a deep-sided receptacle with a tight fitting lid (e.g. a braising pan or deep-sided saucepan) then transfer them to earthenware dishes at the point of service.

Chickens to be pot roasted are traditionally trussed with their legs folded back along the breast, but this is only necessary if they are to be served whole to the customer; there is little point in following this procedure if the birds are to be carved into portions. Very few establishments follow this special method of trussing as it has no effect on the flavour or texture, but is needlessly time-consuming.

7.109 POT ROASTED CHICKEN BONNE FEMME — POULET EN CASSEROLE BONNE FEMME

Pot roast the chicken as outlined in 7.108. Garnish with Olivette Potatoes (9.32), Brown Glazed Button Onions (8.94) and lardons of lightly fried bacon.

7.110 POT ROASTED CHICKEN CHAMPEAUX — POULET EN COCOTTE CHAMPEAUX

Pot roast the chicken as outlined in 7.108. When making the gravy swill the pan in which the chicken have been cooked with 2 dl dry white wine, reduce by two-thirds and then add the jus lié. Garnish with Olivette Potatoes (9.32) and Brown Glazed Button Onions (8.94).

7.111 POT ROASTED CHICKEN GRAND-MERE — POULET POELE GRAND-MERE

Pot roast the chicken as outlined in 7.108. Garnish with quartered button Mushrooms (8.91) and diced fried bread Croûtons (*see* p. 267).

7.112 CASSEROLE OF CHICKEN WITH VEGETABLES — POULET EN CASSEROLE PAYSANNE

Pot roast the chicken as outlined in 7.108. Garnish with Mixed Vegetables (8.88) cut into paysanne shapes.

7.113 POT ROASTED DUCKLING WITH CHERRIES — CANETON POELE AUX CERISES

Pot roast the duckling as outlined in 7.108. When making the gravy swill the pan in which the duck has been cooked with 2 dl madeira, reduce by two-thirds and then add the jus lié. Garnish the sauce with stoned cherries before coating the duck.

7.114 POT ROASTED DUCKLING WITH ORANGE SAUCE — CANETON POELE A L'ORANGE

Makes: 12 portions. Cooking time: 2 hours including sauce. Oven temperature: 220 °C. Temperature at centre of legs: 80 °C.

Quantity	*Ingredient*
4 × 2 kg	Pot Roasted Duckling (*see* 7.108)
½ dl	vinegar
50 g	sugar
3	juice of oranges
3	orange peel cut into fine strips and blanched for 5 minutes, flesh cut into segments (*see* 2.40)
30 g	butter

Method

(1) Place the sugar and sufficient water to dissolve it into a saucepan. Boil and reduce until a light caramel (i.e. resembles a toffee-like mixture).

(2) Add vinegar to stop the caramel darkening further. Reduce by half and then add the orange juice.

(3) Add the strained sauce made from the jus lié and pot roasted vegetables and sediment. Gently simmer for 5 minutes and skim any impurities that may surface. Strain the sauce into a clean

saucepan, season to taste and add the blanched strips of orange. Complete with knobs of butter.

(4) Carve the duck into portions. Serve neatly arranged on a flat oval dish, coated with the orange sauce. Garnish each portion with segments of orange.

Note

If the sauce is bitter in flavour, this can be rectified by adding a further reduction of vinegar and sugar.

Assessment of the completed dish

(1) The portions of duckling should be arranged to follow the shape of the dish and should be coated with the sauce. Three segments of orange as a garnish should be neatly placed on each portion in a pattern to improve the appearance.

(2) The duckling should be moist and trimmed of all excess skin, bone and sinew. If the legs are to be served as part of the portion then the bone should be removed; no splintered bones should be served. If the breast is to be served it should be trimmed, leaving only a small bone at the wing end; all excess bone and gristle to be found on the underside should be removed.

(3) If the sauce is removed from the surface of the duckling the skin underneath should be soft and moist and lightly coloured.

(4) The sauce should be a rich dark brown in colour with a definite sheen and should have sufficient consistency to cover the pieces of duckling. There should be no trace of bitterness yet it should not be oversweet. There should be a definite taste of orange and the strips of orange peel should be soft but unbroken, without pith and of an even length.

(5) The garnish of orange segments should be cleanly cut and free of pips and all traces of pith.

7.115 POT ROASTED LOIN OF LAMB DUBARRY — LONGE D'AGNEAU DUBARRY

Pot roast boned and rolled loin of lamb as outlined in 7.108. Garnish with cauliflower coated with Cheese Sauce (3.15) and then glazed and Château Potatoes (9.50).

7.116 POT ROASTED LOIN OF PORK WITH VEGETABLES — LONGE DE PORC POELEE PAYSANNE

Pot roast the prepared loin of pork as outlined in 7.108. Garnish with Mixed Vegetables (8.88) cut into paysanne shapes.

7.117 POT ROASTED NUT OF VEAL CLAMART — NOIX DE VEAU POELEE CLAMART

Pot roast the prepared cushion of veal as outlined in 7.108. Garnish with Artichoke Bottoms (8.120) filled with Minted Peas (8.99) together with Château Potatoes (9.50).

Note

Peas French Style (8.153) or Purée of Peas (8.102) may be used in place of minted peas.

7.118 POT ROASTED PHEASANT WITH CELERY — FAISAN AUX CELERIS OR FAISAN CAREME

Makes: 12 portions. Cooking time: 2 hours including sauce. Oven temperature: 180 °C. Temperature at centre of legs: 80 °C.

Quantity	*Ingredient*
4 × 1½ kg	Pot Roasted Pheasant (*see* 7.108)
6 dl	Veal Velouté (3.5)
2 dl	cream
12 × 50 g	garnish portions of Braised Celery (8.136)
10 g	Meat Glaze (p. 38)
	seasoning

Method

(1) Once cooked, remove the pheasant and retain in a warm place.

(2) Remove the vegetables and fat from the pan in which the pheasants were cooked. Add the veal velouté, cream and meat glaze. Gently simmer for about 5 minutes.

(3) Strain the sauce through a fine conical strainer into a clean saucepan. Reboil, season to taste and if necessary adjust the consistency which should be sufficient to coat the pheasants.

(4) Carve the pheasant into portions. Serve neatly arranged on a flat oval dish and place in between the garnish of braised celery. Coat completely with the sauce and serve.

Notes

(1) When straining the sauce a muslin cloth is preferable to a conical strainer.

(2) The colour of the sauce should be light coffee.

7.119 POT ROASTED SIRLOIN OF BEEF RICHELIEU — CONTREFILET DE BOEUF RICHELIEU

Pot roast the prepared sirloin of beef as outlined in 7.108. Garnish with Stuffed Tomatoes (8.176), Stuffed Mushrooms (8.175), Braised Lettuce (8.154) and Château Potatoes (9.50).

7.120 POUSSIN POLONAISE

Pot roast the poussin as outlined in 7.108 stuffed with a mixture of 100 g white breadcrumbs soaked in 2 dl milk and 500 g Game Liver Farce (7.106). When serving heat 250 g butter in a small frying pan, add 150 g white breadcrumbs and fry until golden. Pour the mixture over the chicken. Finish with the juice of ½ lemon and chopped parsley.

7.121 SLICED POT ROASTED DUCK WITH ORANGE SAUCE — AIGUILLETTES DE CANETON BIGARRADE

Proceed as for 7.114. Remove the legs and reserve for other uses. Remove the breasts from the carcass. Remove and discard the skin. Carve the breasts into very thin slices. Neatly arrange on a flat oval dish and coat with Orange Sauce (*see* 7.114). Garnish with segments of orange.

BRAISING

Braising is the application of moist cookery to small cuts and joints of meat, poultry, game and offal. The main commodity is two-thirds covered with liquid, vegetables and herbs are added, the receptacle is tightly covered and the dish is cooked in an oven at a temperature of 180 °C. Braising, in simple terms, is stewing in an oven.

There are two methods of braising:

(*a*) *white braising* — this may be applied to white meats such as veal and poultry and offal such as sweetbreads;
(*b*) *brown braising* — this may be applied to meats such as beef, veal, mutton, and duck and offals such as heart, tongue and oxtail.

Table 16 gives the main items of meat suitable for this method of cooking.

TABLE 16. ITEMS OF MEAT SUITABLE FOR BRAISING

Beef	*Lamb/Mutton*	*Veal*	*Poultry*	*Offal*
Chuck rib	Leg	Cushion	Chicken	Heart
Leg of mutton cut	Chops	Leg joints	Duck	Sweetbread
Middle rib		Loin		Tail
Rump		Nut or under cushion		Tongue
Steaks cut from these joints		Rump		
Thick flank		Saddle		
Topside		Thick flank		

White braising

Methods of white braising are traditional in their approach and are rarely used today for cooking joints of meat or whole poultry items. More acceptable results are achieved by pot roasting (*see* pp. 269–76).

Examples of white braised meat dishes as they appear on the menu are as follows:

Braised Chicken with Paysanne of Vegetables — Poularde Braisée Paysanne

Braised Nut of Veal with Celery — Noix de Veau Braisée aux Céleris

Braised Leg of Lamb with Glazed Carrots — Gigot d'Agneau Braisé aux Carottes

7.122 WHITE BRAISED MEAT

Makes: 10 portions. Cooking time: 1½ hours. Oven temperature: 180 °C.

Quantity	*Ingredient*	
1½ kg	prepared meat	
250 g	sliced carrots	bed of roots
250 g	sliced onions	bed of roots
200 g	sliced celery	bed of roots
80 g	bacon trimmings	bed of roots
1 sprig	thyme	bed of roots
1	bayleaf	bed of roots
	parsley stalks	bed of roots
1	crushed clove of garlic	bed of roots
150 g	butter	
1 l	white veal stock	
1	juice of lemon	
	salt and pepper	

Method

(1) Melt the butter in a braising type of pan. Add the bed of roots and lightly cook without colouring for a few minutes.

(2) Place in the seasoned meat, coat the meat with butter, cover with a lid and cook in the oven for approximately 20 minutes.

(3) Remove the lid, and add the stock. Bring to the boil and skim as necessary.

(4) Re-cover with a lid and return it to the oven to braise, basting from time to time until cooked.

(5) Remove the meat from the cooking liquid and retain in a covered dish to keep warm.

(6) Strain the cooking liquid into a clean saucepan. Boil and skim off any traces of fat or grease that surface. Slightly thicken with the diluted arrowroot, add the lemon juice and season to taste. Strain the liquid through a fine conical strainer.

(7) Remove the string from the joint. Carve into 3 mm thick slices across the grain of the joint.

(8) Neatly arrange the slices of meat on an oval dish, coat with the sauce and serve.

Notes

(1) The sauce should be transparent and of a consistency that will enable it to flow lightly over the surface of the meat.

(2) Lemon is associated with many veal recipes, partly to add a little sharpness to the flavour and partly to compliment the delicate flavour of the veal.

To test if cooked

The joint may be tested with a trussing needle. When cooked the needle should penetrate to the centre of the joint without undue pressure and the juices released should be clear. The reading of a thermoneedle should be 80 °C.

White braised offal

Braised sweetbreads as given in 7.123 are fundamental to several other dishes. Once cooked they should be transferred to a shallow dish, covered completely with the strained cooking liquid and buttered greaseproof paper. If not required for immediate use they should be permitted to cool as quickly as possible for use as necessary and covered with cling foil. Store in a refrigerator at a temperature of 8 °C.

7.123 BRAISED VEAL SWEETBREADS — RIS DE VEAU BRAISE

Makes: 10 portions. Cooking time: 1 hour. Oven temperature: 180 °C.

Quantity	*Ingredient*	
1½ kg	veal sweetbreads	
150 g	butter	
250 g	sliced carrots	bed of roots
250 g	sliced onions	bed of roots
200 g	sliced celery	bed of roots
80 g	bacon trimmings	bed of roots
1 sprig	thyme	bed of roots
1	bayleaf	bed of roots

Quantity	*Ingredient*	
	parsley stalks	bed of roots
1	crushed clove of garlic	
1 l	white veal stock	
	salt and pepper	

Method

(1) Soak the sweetbreads for about 1 hour under gently running cold water or in a basin of cold water.

(2) Place the sweetbreads into a saucepan, cover with cold water and bring to the boil for approximately 5 minutes. Place the saucepan under hot running water to remove scum and grease, then refresh under cold running water and drain in a colander. This is referred to as blanching.

(3) Remove any nerves or gristle and membrane that covers the outer area.

(4) Place the sweetbreads in between a damp cloth and place a heavy chopping board on top in order to slightly flatten them. Leave for approximately 15 minutes.

(5) Butter a shallow sided saucepan and place in the bed of roots. Put the sweetbreads on top, season with salt and pepper, cover with a sheet of buttered greaseproof paper, and cover with a lid. Allow to cook gently in the oven for about 10 minutes without allowing it to colour.

(6) Remove from the oven, take off the greaseproof paper and add the stock. Bring to the boil, re-cover with greaseproof paper and cover with a lid. Return it to the oven to braise, basting from time to time until cooked.

(7) Remove the sweetbreads from the cooking liquid and place them in a shallow dish. Strain the liquid over the sweetbreads and retain for serving.

Note

When sweetbreads are required for extension dishes they should be sliced to a thickness of 1 cm on a slant of about 45°.

To test if cooked

Remove a sweetbread from the liquid with a fork or perforated spoon and gently press between the fingers. It should feel firm, so if it is springy it means it is not cooked. If uncertain, increase the finger pressure until the bread begins to break at the inter-membrane sections. The inside should be off white in colour. There should be no pinkness in the centre when cut in half.

Service

Serve sweetbreads in an entrée type dish.

Possible problem	*Possible cause and solution*
(1) The sweetbreads are dry and dark in colour	— sweetbreads were not soaked before cooking; care must be taken when preparing the sweetbreads as this cannot be rectified.
	— sweetbreads were not blanched correctly; care must be taken to follow the correct blanching procedure as this cannot be rectified later.
	— sweetbreads were cooked too quickly at too high a temperature; care must be taken to braise the sweetbreads for the prescribed length of time at the correct temperature as this cannot be rectified later.
	— sweetbreads were not covered with a lid during cooking; care must be taken to follow the correct procedure for cooking the sweetbreads to avoid this problem which cannot be rectified.
	— greaseproof paper was not buttered so that it sticks and may burn onto the surface of the sweetbreads; care must be taken over this aspect to avoid this problem which cannot be rectified.
	— during retention in the refrigerator the sweetbreads were not submerged in the liquid or covered with cling film; care must be taken to follow the correct procedure for retention to avoid problems which cannot be rectified.
	— stock in which the sweetbreads were braised was of poor quality; care must be taken when preparing the basic ingredients as problems arising at a later stage cannot be rectified.

7.124 BRAISED VEAL SWEETBREADS WITH VEGETABLES — RIS DE VEAU BONNE MAMAN

Prepare the sweetbreads as in 7.123. Cut 150 g carrots, 150 g leeks and 150 g celery into julienne strips approximately 4 cm × 2 mm × 2 mm and cook by boiling gently in some of the braising liquid.

Reduce the remainder of the braising liquid by half and skim off any impurities that may surface. Season to taste. Serve the sliced sweetbreads neatly arranged in an entrée type dish. Place the cooked vegetables over the sweetbreads and coat with the reduced braising liquid.

Brown braising

The meat, when jointed, should be freed from excess fat and sinew. Large joints should be tied with string to help retain their shape during cooking. Avoid rolled joints of meat for braising. They will become distorted and may fall to pieces because this type of joint is usually made up of several pieces of meat held together by string.

Larding

Because joints used for braising are lacking in natural fat content, strips of ice-cooled speck or fat bacon are inserted into the flesh by means of a larding or daubing needle during the initial preparation in order to improve the texture and flavour of the product. Small joints have small strips of fat approximately 6 cm in length threaded through the top of the flesh using a larding needle, whilst a daubing needle is used to insert long strips of fat horizontally through the length of larger joints. It is sometimes the custom to marinate large strips of fat in brandy, herbs such as thyme, bayleaf and parsley stalks and seasoning before inserting them into the meat.

NOTE

It is advisable to stiffen the strips of fat in ice water to make them easier to handle.

Marinating

The marinade is an acid solution consisting of red wine, oil, herbs, vegetables and seasonings into which the prepared meat is placed prior to cooking. The aim of this procedure is to tenderise the meat and enhance its colour and flavour.

NOTE

Veal is not usually marinated (*see* p. 294).

7.125 MARINADE

Makes: For 1½ kg meat (10 portions).

Quantity	*Ingredient*
1 l	red wine

Quantity	*Ingredient*	
1 dl	oil	
200 g	carrots	roughly cut
200 g	onion	roughly cut
150 g	celery	roughly cut
1	crushed clove of garlic	
1	bayleaf	
1 sprig	thyme	
15 g	parsley stalks	
2	cloves	
20	peppercorns	

Method

(1) Place all the prepared ingredients into a non-aluminium basin.

(2) Place in the prepared meat, cover with greaseproof paper and allow to soak at a temperature of about 4 °C for the prescribed time.

Notes

(1) It is advisable to turn the meat from time to time whilst it is marinating.

(2) The liquid and the vegetables and herbs are cooked with the meat and therefore replace those items listed in the following recipes.

(3) Once marinated the meat is removed and dried, the vegetables and herbs drained and the liquid added to the braised item at the same time as the stock.

Retention

Braised meats do not lend themselves to retention and reheating under traditional methods. Whenever possible they should be cooked for immediate use. If joints are carved in advance of requirements the meat may become dry very quickly, unless coated with either brown stock or the accompanying sauce.

7.126 BROWN BRAISED MEAT

Makes: 10 portions. Cooking time: 2 hours. Oven temperature: 180 °C.

Quantity	*Ingredient*	
1½ kg	joint meat previously larded and marinated as necessary	
2 dl	dripping or oil	
200 g	carrots	roughly cut
200 g	onion	roughly cut

Quantity	*Ingredient*
150 g	celery, roughly cut
1 clove	crushed garlic
1 l	brown stock
1 l	Jus Lié (3.8) or Sauce Espagnole (3.6)
1	bouquet garni
	seasoning

Method

(1) Heat the dripping in a shallow sided saucepan, preferably a frying pan.

(2) Add the seasoned meat and fry until light golden brown on all sides.

(3) Transfer the meat to a braising pan.

(4) Fry the vegetables in the same pan as the meat was fried in, drain, and add to the meat.

(5) Add the stock and brown sauce and seasoning. Bring to the boil and skim. Add the bouquet garni.

(6) Cover with a lid and braise in the oven until cooked.

(7) Remove the meat from the cooking liquid and retain in a covered dish to keep warm.

(8) Remove and discard the bouquet garni. Boil the sauce and skim off any traces of fat or grease that surfaces.

(9) Season to taste. Correct the consistency and colour of the sauce if necessary.

(10) Pass the sauce through a fine strainer and reboil. Skim if necessary.

(11) Remove the string from the joint, carve into slices 3 mm thick across the grain of the joint.

(12) Neatly arrange the slices of meat on an oval dish, coat with the sauce and serve.

Notes

(1) Butter may be placed on the surface of the completed sauce to prevent a skin forming but this should be done very sparingly as fat may reappear when served.

(2) Vegetable garnishes are cooked separately and added at the point of service. Buttered noodles may also be served as a garnish once the meat has been sliced and coated with the sauce.

(3) If necessary the sauce may be thickened with diluted arrowroot which should be added to the boiling sauce. It should then be strained.

(4) Once cooked the meat may be removed from the cooking liquid and placed on a shallow sided dish. It should then be coated

with sufficient cooking liquid to enable basting to take place, put into the oven at approximately 200 °C and basted frequently until the surface juices caramelise. This can be identified by the light sheen that appears on the surface of the joint and is referred to as glazing. (Glazing is not often carried out in trade practice unless, perhaps, the joint is to be presented whole to the customer and carved before him.)

(5) Braised joints may be served whole with the sauce as an accompaniment or sliced coated with the sauce with an appropriate garnish.

To test if cooked

The joint may be tested with a trussing needle. When cooked the needle should penetrate to the centre of the joint without undue pressure. The meat should be free from all traces of blood.

Note

Taking temperature readings with a thermoneedle is not an accurate guide as the temperature reading may suggest that the meat is cooked yet it may still be tough and undercooked.

Assessment of the completed dish

The meat should be:

(1) carved into slices across the grain about 5 mm thick;
(2) if larded the speck set at regular intervals;
(3) moist in appearance, no traces of blood and cooked to the correct degree;
(4) evenly coated with sauce with no exposed areas;
(5) soft in texture (unless cut with the grain in which case it should be rather stringy).

The sauce should be:

(1) a rich red brown in colour and should have a definite sheen;
(2) free of all traces of fat and any impurities or pieces of cooked meat;
(3) of such a consistency that it flows easily and evenly over the meat.

The vegetable garnish should be:

(1) evenly shaped and cooked to the correct degree;
(2) sized in proportion to the meat it is to accompany and of a suitable quantity for the number of portions.

Possible problem	*Possible cause and solution*
(1) The sauce does not have a rich appearance,	— poor quality stock, jus lié or espagnole was used; boil the sauce and add tomato purée and gravy browning, then skim off any fat,

Possible problem	*Possible cause and solution*
is dull and only light brown in colour	grease or other impurities that may surface and strain through a fine conical strainer. — the meat and vegetables were not browned to the correct degree; care should be taken in the initial stages to fry the meat sufficiently but the problem can be rectified by adjusting the colour with tomato purée and gravy browning.
(2) Completed sauce is too thick	— braising has taken place at too high a temperature; boil the sauce and thin with brown stock as necessary, then strain through a fine conical strainer. — product has been overcooked; boil the sauce and thin with brown stock as necessary, then strain through a fine conical strainer. — braising was not carried out with a lid; boil the sauce and thin with brown stock as necessary, then strain through a fine conical strainer.
(3) Excess fat in the completed sauce	— fat was not drained off the meat and vegetables after coloration; boil the sauce and skim until all traces of fat and grease have been removed then strain through a fine conical strainer. — braising has taken place at too high a temperature; boil the sauce and skim until all traces of fat and grease have been removed then strain through a fine conical strainer.
(4) The meat is stringy and dry	— the meat has been overcooked; care must be taken to cook the meat for the correct length of time as the problems caused by overcooking cannot be rectified. — the meat has been carved incorrectly, e.g. with the grain; care must be taken to carve the meat correctly as this cannot be rectified.
(5) Little meat is obtained from size of joint cooked	— the meat was incorrectly prepared at the butchery stage; care must be taken to prepare the meat correctly as failure to do so cannot later be rectified. — the meat has been overcooked causing

Possible problem	*Possible cause and solution*
	shrinkage; care must be taken to cook the meat for the correct length of time as the problems caused by overcooking cannot be rectified.
	— the meat was incorrectly carved, e.g. with the grain; care must be taken to carve the meat correctly as this cannot be rectified.
(6) Completed sauce is too thin	— incorrect ratio of stock to brown sauce; either *(a)* boil the sauce, thicken as necessary with diluted arrowroot, skim and strain through a fine conical strainer; or *(b)* reduce the quantity of sauce by boiling, add a quantity of sauce espagnole to bring it back to the original volume, skim and strain through a fine conical strainer.

Braised beef
See Table 16 for joints of beef and steaks suitable for braising. Vegetables cut into various shapes, e.g. jardinière, paysanne or barrel-shaped, and noodles are used as garnishes.

7.127 BRAISED BEEF BOURGUIGNONNE — PIECE DE BOEUF BRAISEE BOURGUIGNONNE

Marinate the meat as in 7.125 and proceed as for 7.126. Just before serving add the following garnish to the sauce: 250 g lardons of lightly fried bacon, 20 glazed Button Onions (8.94) and 30 cooked Button Mushrooms (8.91).

7.128 BRAISED BEEF WITH NOODLES — PIECE DE BOEUF BRAISEE AUX NOUILLES

Proceed as for 7.126. When serving garnish the sauced meat with 300 g Buttered Noodles (*see* 5.40).

7.129 BRAISED BEEF WITH VEGETABLES — PIECE DE BOEUF BRAISEE JARDINIERE

Proceed as for 7.126. When serving garnish with 250 g Mixed Vegetables (8.88) cut into baton shapes.

Steaks
Steaks cut from suitable joints such as topside and thick flank, leg of mutton cut, chuck rib and middle rib should be cut into 1 cm thick slices. Excess fat, sinew and gristle should be removed.

7.130 BRAISED STEAKS

Makes: 10 portions. Cooking time: 1½ hours. Oven temperature: 180 °C.

Quantity	*Ingredient*
10 × 150 g	steaks for braising (approximately 1 cm thick)
2 dl	dripping or oil
250 g	seasoned flour
200 g	carrots } roughly cut
200 g	onion } roughly cut
150 g	celery } roughly cut
75 g	flour
50 g	tomato purée
2 l	Brown Stock (3.1)
1	bouquet garni
	seasoning

Method

(1) Heat the dripping in a shallow sided saucepan, preferably a frying pan.

(2) Pass the steaks through seasoned flour and fry until a light golden brown on both sides.

(3) Drain off any fat and transfer the steaks into a shallow sided saucepan or special braising pan.

(4) Fry the vegetables in oil until a light golden colour. Drain in a colander and add to the meat.

(5) Add the tomato purée and stock. Bring to the boil, skim and season.

(6) Add the bouquet garni, cover with a lid and braise in the oven until cooked.

(7) Remove the meat and place into a clean saucepan. Remove and discard the roughly cut vegetables and bouquet garni. (This is termed decanting.)

(8) Place the steaks into a clean saucepan.

(9) Strain the sauce into another clean pan, bring to the boil and skim as necessary to remove all traces of fat and grease.

(10) Correct the consistency of the sauce so that it just coats the meat and, if necessary, adjust the colour. Season to taste.

(11) Add the sauce to the steaks.

(12) Serve the steaks neatly arranged in an entrée type dish coated with the sauce.

Notes

(1) The assessment for the completed dish is similar to that for brown meat stews. *See* 7.145.

(2) Problems which may be encountered are also similar to those for brown meat stews.

(3) When cooked the steaks should yield under finger pressure.

7.131 BRAISED STEAK WITH BEER AND ONIONS — CARBONADE DE BOEUF FLAMANDE

Makes: 10 portions. Cooking time: 1½ hours. Oven temperature: 180 °C.

Quantity	*Ingredient*
10 × 150 g	steaks for braising (approximately 1 cm thick)
2 dl	dripping or oil
250 g	seasoned flour
750 g	sliced onions } shallow fried (*see* 8.158)
100 g	butter } shallow fried (*see* 8.158)
½ l	beer
1½ l	Brown Stock (3.1)
	seasoning

Method

(1) Heat the dripping in a shallow sided saucepan, preferably a frying pan.

(2) Pass the steaks through seasoned flour and fry until a light golden brown on both sides.

(3) Drain off any fat and transfer the steaks to a shallow sided saucepan or a special braising pan.

(4) Add the cooked onions and pour in sufficient stock and beer just to cover them.

(5) Bring to the boil and skim. Season, cover with a lid and braise in the oven until cooked.

(6) Place the steaks into a clean saucepan.

(7) Boil the sauce and skim as necessary to remove all traces of fat and grease.

(8) Correct the consistency of the sauce so that it just coats the meat and, if necessary, adjust the colour. Season to taste.

(9) Add the sauce to the steaks.

(10) Serve the steaks neatly arranged in an entrée type dish coated with the sauce and onions.

Braised duck

Due to its very high fat content duck first requires roasting until it is a quarter cooked. Once all the fat is drained off the duck can be braised.

7.132 BRAISED DUCKLING WITH GREEN PEAS — CANETON BRAISE AUX PETITS POIS

Makes: 8 portions. Cooking time: 1½ hours. Oven temperature: 180 °C.

Quantity	*Ingredient*
2 × 2½ kg	prepared duck, quarter roasted (*see* 7.100).
½ l	brown stock
½ l	Demi-glace Sauce (3.7) or Jus Lié (3.8)
200 g	blanched lardons of streaky bacon
16	button onions, shallow fried in butter until light golden (*see* 8.158)
400 g	small peas
	seasoning

Method

(1) Drain the part roasted duck and place in a deep sided saucepan.

(2) Add the brown stock and sauce to two-thirds cover the duck. Bring to the boil, skim and cover with a lid.

(3) Braise until three-quarters cooked.

(4) Add the rest of the ingredients and continue to cook in the oven covered with a lid until cooked.

(5) Remove the duck from the liquid and retain in a warm place.

(6) Boil the sauce and skim until all traces of fat have been removed. Season to taste and, if necessary, correct the consistency of the sauce.

(7) Cut the duck into portions and place in an entrée type dish. Coat with the cooking liquid and the peas.

Notes

(1) To test if cooked prick the top of the bird with a fine pointed fork. When the juices that are produced show no traces of blood the duck should be cooked. Pay particular attention to the legs when testing — they should yield to finger pressure.

(2) The duck may also be served in a shallow earthenware dish or cocotte/casserole, set on an underdish with a dish paper.

Assessment of the completed dish

The duck should be:

(1) moist with plenty of flesh and no trace of stringiness in the meat;

(2) without pieces of splintered bone;

(3) without a crisp outer skin because of the method of cooking;

(4) in the correct quantity, a suitable portion being a piece of boned leg and a piece of breast or a piece of breast only. The leg alone should not be served as a portion as there is generally very little flesh on the drumstick.

The sauce should be:

(1) flavoured by the duck with a hint of sweetness from the peas;

(2) a rich dark brown in colour and free from all traces of fat;

(3) of a light consistency so that it flows over the meat without clinging to the flesh.

The peas should be fairly green in colour, sweet and moist. The bacon lardons should be evenly cut, moist and not salty.

Braised ham

7.133 BRAISED HAM WITH MADEIRA SAUCE — JAMBON BRAISE AU MADERE

Makes: 10 portions. Cooking time: 1½ hours. Oven temperature: 180 °C.

Quantity	*Ingredient*
1½ kg	boiled ham with skin removed and trimmed of surplus fat (*see* 7.243).
1 l	Demi-glace Sauce (3.7) or Jus Lié (3.8)
2 dl	madeira
100 g	sugar
	seasoning

Method

(1) Place the ham in a deep sided saucepan just large enough to hold it.

(2) Add the madeira, cover with a lid and place in the oven for approximately 1 hour, basting frequently.

(3) Remove the ham and place on a shallow sided dish. Sprinkle the surface of the ham with the sugar and place it back in the oven until the outer surface caramelises. (This is termed glazing.)

(4) Add the sauce to the cooking liquid, bring to the boil and skim.

(5) Pass the sauce through a conical strainer without using pressure.

(6) Re-boil the sauce, skim and season to taste.

(7) Carve into thin slices and neatly arrange them overlapping on a flat dish. Coat with the sauce and serve.

7.134 BRAISED HAM WITH MADEIRA WINE AND SPINACH — JAMBON BRAISE AUX EPINARDS

Proceed as for 7.133. When serving, coat the ham with the sauce and garnish with 250 g Purée of Spinach (8.107).

Braised lamb and mutton

See Table 16 for cuts of lamb and mutton suitable for braising. Vegetables cut into various shapes, e.g. jardinière, paysanne and barrel-shaped, are used as garnishes for chops which should be trimmed of all excess fat, gristle and sinew.

7.135 BRAISED LAMB CHOPS — CHOPS D'AGNEAU BRAISES

Makes: 10 portions. Cooking time: 1½ hours (*see Notes* below). Oven temperature: 180 °C.

Quantity	*Ingredient*
10 × 200 g	Prepared Lamb Chops (7.37)

Method

Proceed as for 7.143.

Notes

(1) When cooked the meat should begin to come away from the bone under finger pressure.

(2) Mutton chops may take considerably longer to cook, up to approximately 2 hours.

(3) The assessment for the completed dish is similar to that for Brown Meat Stews. (*See* 7.145.)

(4) Problems which may be encountered are also similar to those for brown meat stews.

7.136 BRAISED LAMB CHOPS WITH VEGETABLES — CHOPS D'AGNEAU BRAISES AUX LEGUMES

Proceed as in 7.135. Garnish with 250 g Mixed Vegetables (8.88) cut into dice, jardinière, paysanne or barrel-shaped.

Braised offal

See Table 16 for items of offal suitable for braising. Vegetables cut into various shapes, e.g. jardinière, paysanne and barrel-shaped, are used as garnishes for braised lambs' hearts which should be prepared for cooking by removing excess fat and tubes.

7.137 BRAISED LAMBS' HEARTS — COEURS D'AGNEAU BRAISES

Makes: 10 portions. Cooking time: 2–2½ hours. Oven temperature: 180 °C.

Quantity	*Ingredient*
10 × 150 g	prepared lambs' hearts

Method

Proceed as for Braised Steaks (7.130).

Notes

(1) To test if cooked pierce with a trussing needle or fork. When cooked the point should penetrate to the centre of the heart without undue pressure.

(2) The assessment for the completed dish is similar to that for Brown Meat Stews. (*See* 7.145.)

(3) Problems which may be encountered are also similar to those for brown meat stews.

7.138 BRAISED LAMBS' HEARTS WITH VEGETABLES — COEURS D'AGNEAU BRAISEES AUX LEGUMES

Proceed as in 7.137. Garnish with 250 g Mixed Vegetables (8.88) cut into dice, jardinière, paysanne or barrel-shaped.

Vegetables cut into various shapes, e.g. jardinière, paysanne and barrel-shaped, are used as garnishes for oxtail which should be prepared for cooking by cutting into sections along the natural joints.

7.139 BRAISED LAMBS TONGUES—LANGUES D'AGNEAU BRAISEES

Makes: 10 portions. Cooking time: 1½ hours. Oven temperature: 180 °C.

Quantity	*Ingredient*
6	lambs' tongues
1 l	Brown Stock (3.1)
1 l	Sauce Espagnole (3.6) or Jus Lié (3.8)

Method

(1) Place the tongues into a saucepan, cover with cold water and bring to the boil for approximately 5 minutes. Place the saucepan under hot running water to remove the scum and grease and then refresh under cold running water. Drain in a colander. Remove any sinew from the tongues.

(2) Cover the tongues with the brown stock, bring to the boil and gently simmer for approximately 1 hour.

(3) Remove the tongues from the stock, allow to cool and then remove the skins using a small knife. The skin should peel away from the tongues with ease.

(4) Place the tongues in a shallow sided saucepan, add the brown sauce and bring to the boil. Cover with a lid and braise in the oven until cooked.

(5) Remove the tongues from the cooking liquid and retain in a covered dish to keep warm.

(6) Strain the cooking liquid into a clean saucepan, boil, skim

and remove all traces of fat and other impurities that may surface. Strain the sauce once again through a conical strainer without using pressure and reboil.

(7) Season to taste and if necessary correct the consistency and colour.

(8) Slice the tongues approximately 3 mm thick and neatly arrange the slices on a flat oval dish. Coat with the sauce and serve.

Notes

(1) To test if the tongue is cooked insert a trussing needle. When cooked the needle will penetrate to the centre without undue pressure and the juices released should be clear.

(2) The dish may be assessed as for Braised Joint of Beef (7.126).

(3) For retention, remove the tongues from the braising liquid, rinse in warm brown stock to remove the cooking liquid and retain in cold stock with the cooking liquid quite separate. Store in a refrigerator at a temperature of 8 °C.

(4) To reheat, arrange the slices of tongue 2–3 mm thick on the serving dish, coat with a little white stock and gently heat. Do not allow the tongues to boil as this will cause them to distort. Drain off the stock, coat with the sauce and serve. (It is general trade practice to make the sauce separately from the tongues which are reheated in this way when required.)

(5) To carve the tongue, commence across the thick end of the tongue. When the length of the slice becomes impractical begin to cut across the tongue lengthways towards the tip.

7.140 BRAISED LAMBS' TONGUES WITH MADEIRA WINE AND SPINACH—LANGUES D'AGNEAU BRAISEES AUX EPINARDS

Proceed as in 7.139 following *Notes* (3–4). When serving lightly sprinkle the tongues with madeira wine, coat with Madeira Sauce (3.30) and garnish with 250 g Purée of Spinach (8.107).

7.141 BRAISED OXTAIL — QUEUE DE BOEUF BRAISEE

Makes: 10 portions. Cooking time: 4 hours. Oven temperature: 180 °C.

Quantity	*Ingredient*
2½ kg	prepared oxtail

Method

Proceed as for 7.145.

Notes

(1) When cooked the meat should begin to come away from the centre bone under finger pressure.

(2) The assessment for the completed dish is similar to that for Brown Meat Stews. (*See* 7.145.)

(3) Problems which may be encountered are also similar to those for brown meat stews.

7.142 BRAISED OXTAIL WITH VEGETABLES — QUEUE DE BOEUF BRAISEE AUX LEGUMES

Proceed as for 7.145. When serving garnish with 250 g Mixed Vegetables (8.88) cut into baton shapes.

Braised veal

See Table 16 for joints of veal suitable for brown braising. Joints of veal are larded when braised (*see* p. 281). They are not, however, marinated as the process is unnecessary for this rather tender type of meat with its own delicate flavour. All veal joints may be brown braised as in 7.126. Vegetables cut into various shapes, e.g. jardinière, paysanne and barrel-shaped, and noodles may be used as garnishes.

7.143 BRAISED CUSHION OF VEAL WITH NOODLES — NOIX DE VEAU BRAISEE AUX NOUILLES

Proceed as for 7.126. When serving garnish with 300 g Buttered Noodles (*see* 5.40).

7.144 BRAISED NUT OF VEAL WITH VEGETABLES — NOIX DE VEAU BRAISEE AUX LEGUMES

Proceed as for 7.126. Garnish with 250 g Mixed Vegetables (8.88) cut into paysanne shapes.

STEWING

Stewing is the application of moist cookery to small pieces and cuts of meat, joints of poultry and game. Stews may be subdivided into the following three categories.

(*a*) Brown and special stews such as curries and goulash. Brown stews in particular are closely related to braised items and the procedure followed is similar. They may be cooked in an oven in a receptacle with a tight fitting lid at a temperature of 180 °C or they may be cooked by gentle simmering on top of the stove.

(*b*) White velouté based stews such as blanquettes and fricassées. Both are cooked on top of the stove, although a fricassée may also be cooked in an oven.

(c) Those that contain no flour but incorporate potatoes. Irish stew, Lancashire hot pot and chops champvallon are the three main dishes of this type. Hot pot type dishes are cooked in an oven without a lid so that the top layer of potatoes may be cooked until they are golden.

Brown and special stews

Brown stews such as ragoût of beef and navarin of lamb and special stews such as curries and goulashes are all cooked in the same basic way. A variety of vegetable garnishes form a wide range of extensions to the basic recipe.

Table 17 lists those cuts and joints of meat, game and offal suitable for brown and special stews.

TABLE 17. ITEMS OF MEAT SUITABLE FOR BROWN AND SPECIAL STEWS

Beef	*Lamb/Mutton*	*Veal*	*Game*	*Offal*
Chuck steak	Breast	Knuckle	Game birds	Oxtail
Clod or sticking piece	Chops	Neck end	Hare	Ox liver
Leg of mutton cut	Fillet from neck end	Scrag	Rabbit	
Shin	Middle neck	Shoulder	Venison	
Thick flank	Shoulder			
Thin flank				
Topside				

7.145 BROWN STEWED MEAT

Makes: 10 portions. Cooking time: 1½ hours. Oven temperature: 180 °C.

Quantity	*Ingredient*
1½ kg	prepared meat (*see* Table 17)
2 dl	dripping or oil
200 g	carrots } roughly cut
200 g	onions } roughly cut
150 g	celery } roughly cut
75 g	flour
50 g	tomato purée
2 l	Brown Stock (3.1)
1	bouquet garni
	seasoning

Method

(1) Season the meat and fry in the oil or dripping until a light golden colour on all sides. Drain the meat in a colander and transfer to a suitable receptacle for stewing.

(2) Fry the vegetables until golden, drain in a colander and add to the meat.

(3) Singe the meat and vegetables — sprinkle with flour and place in a hot oven until the flour takes on a brown colour (approximately 10 minutes).

(4) Add the tomato purée and gently add the stock. Bring to the boil, skim and season and add the bouquet garni.

(5) Cook either in an oven with a tight fitting lid or gently simmer on top of the stove.

(6) When cooked transfer the meat to another saucepan and remove and discard the roughly cut vegetables and bouquet garni. Strain the sauce through a conical strainer onto the meat.

(7) Bring to the boil and skim as necessary to remove all traces of fat and grease. Correct the consistency of the sauce so that it just coats the meat and if necessary adjust the colour. Season to taste.

Notes

(1) It is preferable to cook stews in an oven because of the evenness of temperature which it is possible to achieve.

(2) If the sauce requires considerable adjustments then it may be easier to do so in a separate saucepan before adding the sauce to the meat. Once completed all sauces should be re-strained through a conical strainer and reboiled with the meat.

Service

Serve stews in an entrée dish with the meat arranged slightly dome shaped with the sauce on an underdish with a dish paper.

Possible problem	*Possible cause and solution*
(1) The sauce is pale in colour	— the meat was fried too slowly; care must be taken when frying the meat in the initial stages, although the colour of the sauce may be carefully adjusted with gravy browning. — attempting to fry too much meat at one time (if the pan used for frying is overfilled with meat then it will not fry quickly; instead juices are extracted from the meat and it boils in the juices); drain the meat im-

Possible problem	*Possible cause and solution*
	mediately into a colander and begin the process again.
	— the meat was not singed with flour correctly; carefully adjust the colour with gravy browning.
	— brown stock was of poor quality and colour; carefully adjust the colour with gravy browning.
	— the vegetables were not fried and coloured; carefully adjust the colour with gravy browning.
(2) The sauce is dark brown and bitter	— meat was over-coloured when fried; care must be taken when frying the meat in the initial stages as this cannot be rectified later.
	— the stew was either cooked at a high temperature or for too long; care must be taken to cook the stew for the correct length of time and at the correct temperature as this cannot be rectified later.
	— prolonged holding in a hot cupboard; the stew should be prepared as close to the time it is required as possible to avoid the problems caused by prolonged retention.
(3) The sauce is too thin	— insufficient flour used when singed; adjust the consistency by adding a quantity of diluted arrowroot to the simmering stew.
	— too much stock was added; adjust the consistency by adding a quantity of diluted arrowroot to the simmering stew.
(4) The sauce is too thick	— dish has been cooked at too high a temperature for too long; thin the sauce with brown stock.
	— dish has been held in a hot cupboard for too long at a high temperature; thin the sauce with brown stock.
(5) The sauce has excess grease on the surface	— dish has been cooked for too long at too high a temperature; boil the sauce and skim until all the fat and grease have been removed.
	— dish has been held in a hot cupboard for too long at a high temperature; may be rectified as above.

Possible problem	*Possible cause and solution*
(6) Meat is overcooked, stringy and low in flavour	— dish has been cooked at too high a temperature for too long; care must be taken to cook the dish for the prescribed length of time at the correct temperature to avoid this problem which cannot be rectified.
	— dish has been held in a hot cupboard for too long at a high temperature; the dish should be prepared as close as possible to the time it is required to avoid this problem which cannot be rectified.
	— dish has been held and reheated; stews do not lend themselves to retention and reheating and should be prepared as close as possible to the time they are required to avoid this problem which cannot be rectified.

Beef stews

The terms ragoût and sauté are used on the menu to indicate a brown beef stew. The term sauté in this instance, however, should not be confused with either shallow fried or quick sautéed beef (*see* 7.165–72 and 7.210).

Table 17 gives the joints and cuts of beef suitable for stewing. The meat should be trimmed of excess fat, sinew and gristle and cut into 2½ cm cubes. Vegetables cut into various shapes, e.g. jardinière, paysanne, barrel-shaped, may be used as garnishes.

7.146 BEEF STEW BOURGUIGNONNE — SAUTE DE BOEUF BOURGUIGNONNE

Stew the beef as in 7.145. Just before serving add 250 g lardons of lightly fried bacon, 20 Glazed Button Onions (8.94) and 30 cooked Button Mushrooms (8.91).

7.147 BEEF STEW WITH VEGETABLES — RAGOUT DE BOEUF JARDINIERE/PAYSANNE

Stew the beef as for 7.145. When serving garnish with 250 g Mixed Vegetables (8.88) cut into baton shapes for jardinière or paysanne shapes as required.

Lamb/mutton stews

The term navarin is used on the menu to indicate that a stew is made from lamb or mutton. Table 17 gives the cuts and joints most suitable for stewing. The meat should be trimmed of excess fat, sinew and gristle and cut into 2½ cm cubes. As with beef stews various cuts of vegetables are used as garnishes.

NOTE
Some chefs add a little more tomato purée to lamb and mutton stews to give the sauce a more distinctive colour.

7.148 *LAMB STEW WITH HARICOT BEANS — HARICOT DE MOUTON*

Stew the mutton as in 7.145. Just before serving add 500 g cooked Haricot Beans (8.179), 250 g lardons of lightly fried bacon and 20 Glazed Button Onions (8.93).

7.149 *LAMB STEW WITH VEGETABLES — NAVARIN D'AGNEAU JARDINIERE/PAYSANNE*

Stew the lamb as in 7.145. When serving garnish with 250 g Mixed Vegetables (8.88) cut into baton shapes for jardinière or paysanne shapes as required.

Veal stews

The term sauté is used on the menu to denote a veal stew. As with beef stews, it must not be confused with shallow fried or quick sautéed veal dealt with later in this chapter.

Table 17 gives the cuts and joints of veal suitable for stewing. The meat should be trimmed of skin, fat, gristle and sinew and cut into 2½ cm cubes. As with other stews various cuts of vegetables are used as garnishes.

7.150 *SAUTE OF VEAL WITH MUSHROOMS — SAUTE DE VEAU AUX CHAMPIGNONS*

Stew the veal as in 7.145. When serving garnish with 500 g Button Mushrooms (8.91).

7.151 *SAUTE OF VEAL WITH VEGETABLES — SAUTE DE VEAU JARDINIERE/PAYSANNE*

Stew the veal as in 7.145. When serving garnish with 250 g Mixed Vegetables (8.88) cut into baton shapes for jardinière or paysanne shapes as required.

Venison stews

The term braised is used on the menu to indicate that venison has been stewed and it is usual to use lower quality cuts and joints of venison. These include the shoulder, neck and breast, but in practice the meat from the leg is used as it is less wasteful. The meat should be trimmed of membrane, fat, gristle and sinew and cut into 2½ cm cubes. It is usually marinated before being stewed and the marinating vegetables and liquid (*see* 7.125) are used in place of those given in 7.145. As with other various cuts vegetables are used as garnishes.

7.152 BRAISED VENISON BOURGUIGNONNE — CIVET DE CHEVREUIL BOURGUIGNONNE

Stew the marinated venison as in 7.145 using the marinating liquid and vegetables in place of the listed ingredients. Just before serving add 250 g lardons of lightly fried bacon, 20 Glazed Button Onions (8.94) and 30 Button Mushrooms (8.91).

7.153 BRAISED VENISON WITH VEGETABLES — CIVET DE CHEVREUIL JARDINIERE/PAYSANNE

Stew the marinated venison as in 7.145 using the marinating liquid and vegetables in place of the listed ingredients. When serving garnish with 250 g Mixed Vegetables (8.88) cut into baton shapes for jardinière or paysanne shapes as required.

Special stews

The basic method for preparing the following group of dishes is the same as for Brown Stews (7.145). Any problems that will be encountered will be similar to those found on pp. 296–8.

7.154 COTTAGE PIE/SHEPHERD'S PIE

Makes: 10 portions. Cooking time: 1½ hours. Oven temperature: 180 °C.

Quantity	*Ingredient*
1½ kg	minced meat (*see* Note (1) below)
2 dl	dripping or oil
250 g	chopped onion
1	bouquet garni
20 g	tomato purée
2 l	Demi-glace (3.7) or Jus Lié (3.8)
1 kg	Mashed Potato (9.6) or Duchesse Mixture (9.12)
100 g	melted butter
	seasoning

Method

(1) Heat the dripping or oil in a deep sided saucepan, add the minced meat and allow to fry until it is slightly coloured. Add the chopped onion and allow to cook until it becomes rather soft, but do not brown.

(2) Drain off any surplus fat. Add the tomato purée and brown sauce and bring to the boil. Season. Gently simmer until the meat

is cooked. Skim as necessary removing all traces of fat and grease that may surface. Season to taste.

(3) Transfer the cooked meat and sauce into shallow sided earthenware dishes to a depth of about 5 cm.

(4) Spread the surface with mashed potato or duchesse mixture and mark with a palate knife. Alternatively pipe the potato to form a scroll design with a star tube.

(5) Sprinkle the surface of the potato with melted butter.

(6) Place in the oven until the surface is crisp and golden.

(7) When cooked, clean the sides of the earthenware dish, brush the surface with melted butter and serve on a dish paper on a flat underdish.

Notes

(1) Cottage pie is made with minced beef; shepherd's pie is made with minced lamb or mutton.

(2) When cooked the meat should be soft and tender but not chewy.

7.155 CURRIED LAMB — CURRIE D'AGNEAU

Makes: 10 portions. Cooking time: 1½ hours.

Quantity	*Ingredient*
1½ kg	prepared lamb
2 dl	dripping or oil
50 g	butter
2	crushed and chopped cloves of garlic
500 g	chopped onion
75 g	curry powder
25 g	flour
50 g	tomato purée
2 l	white stock
50 g	peeled, pipped and diced tomatoes
75 g	chutney
100 g	apple cut into small dice
10 g	desiccated coconut
	seasoning
500 g	Boiled Rice (5.53)
	accompaniments (*see* below)

Method

(1) Heat the dripping or oil in a frying pan.

(2) Add the seasoned meat and fry until a light golden brown on all sides. Drain in a colander and retain.

(3) Place the butter, garlic and onions in a suitable receptacle for stewing and gently cook for a few moments. Add the meat,

curry powder and flour, stir in with a wooden spatule and place in the oven for approximately 10 minutes.

(4) Remove from the oven, stir in the tomato purée and add the stock.

(5) Bring to the boil and skim. Add the remainder of the ingredients, season and simmer until cooked.

Notes

(1) Beef may also be used to make a curry.

(2) The amount of curry powder suggested should be used as a guide and should be adjusted according to the requirements of the customer. The curry should not be so hot that it burns the mouth but should rather have a distinctive yet pleasant taste of curry spice.

(3) The sauce is not passed once cooked.

(4) When cooked, the meat should show signs of breaking under slight finger pressure.

(5) Not all the suggested accompaniments need be served, except perhaps poppadums and Bombay ducks.

Service

Serve the curried lamb in an entrée dish accompanied with the boiled rice in a vegetable dish. The following are suggestions for accompaniments to be served separately in individual dishes:

5 poppadums grilled or deep fried in oil
5 grilled Bombay ducks
50 g mango chutney
50 g lime pickle
50 g grated coconut
50 g chopped onion
50 g chopped apple with a little lemon juice
50 g sliced banana
50 g peeled and sliced cucumber } combined with 2 dl natural
25 g peeled, pipped and diced tomato } yogurt

The following dish is not strictly a stew but consists of a previously cooked and reheated game bird. Any type of game bird may be used and the description on the menu should specify which is used, e.g. salmis of partridge. As the dish makes use of left-over cooked game birds it is essential to ensure that the meat is thoroughly reheated. As with any reheated dish it should on no account be reheated for a second time, but should be discarded.

7.156 GAME STEW or SALMIS OF PHEASANT — SALMIS DE FAISAN

Makes: 10 portions. Cooking time: 40 minutes. Oven temperature: 180 °C.

Quantity	*Ingredient*	
10	portions of breast of cooked pheasant (*see* 7.103)	
75 g	butter	
2 dl	dry red wine	
6 dl	Demi-glace (3.7) or Jus Lié (3.8)	
¼ dl	brandy	
250 g	lardons of lightly fried bacon	garnish
20	Brown Glazed Button Onions (8.94)	garnish
30	cooked Button Mushrooms (8.91)	garnish
10	fried heart shaped Croûtons (7.105)	garnish
10 g	chopped parsley	garnish
50 g	butter	

Method

(1) Place the butter in a shallow sided saucepan and add the portions of cooked pheasant. Cover with buttered greaseproof paper and a lid and heat in the oven.

(2) In a second pan, add the red wine, boil and reduce by half. Add the brown sauce and allow to simmer gently. Skim all impurities from the surface. Pass through a fine conical strainer without pressure and retain hot until required.

(3) Remove the game from the oven and drain off any surplus fat.

(4) Add the brandy and set it alight.

(5) Add the prepared sauce, lardons, button onions and mushrooms.

(6) Season to taste. If necessary adjust the consistency so that the sauce just coats the game pieces.

(7) Serve in an entrée type dish with the portions of game neatly arranged and coated with the sauce and garnish.

(8) Dip the tips of the heart shaped croûtons in some of the sauce and then into chopped parsley. Garnish the dish and serve.

Note

If the sauce tastes too strong because of the game then mellow it with a few knobs of butter at the last moment.

7.157 JUGGED HARE — CIVET DE LIEVRE

Makes: 8 portions. Cooking time: 2 hours.

Quantity	*Ingredient*	
1	jointed hare (*see* p. 241)	
	blood and liver	mixed to complete sauce
½ dl	vinegar	
	Marinade (7.125)	
2 dl	dripping or oil	
75 g	flour	
50 g	tomato purée	
2 l	Brown Stock (3.1)	
	seasoning	
200 g	lardons of lightly fried bacon	garnish
16	Glazed Button Onions (8.94)	
24	cooked Button Mushrooms (8.91)	
8	heart shaped Croûtons (7.105)	

Method

(1) Marinade the pieces of hare for approximately 24 hours.

(2) Remove the hare, drain the vegetables and retain the liquid.

(3) Proceed as in 7.145 adding the marinating liquid with the stock.

(4) Strain the sauce through a conical strainer into a clean pan, bring to the boil and skim as necessary to remove all traces of fat and grease.

(5) Whisk in the mixture of blood, liver and vinegar but do not allow to boil. Season to taste and pass through a conical strainer onto the cooked hare.

Service

Neatly arrange the hare in an entrée type dish. Garnish with the lardons of bacon, button onions and mushrooms. Dip the tips of the heart shaped croûtons in some of the sauce and then into chopped parsley. Garnish the dish and serve.

The following is an Italian veal and vegetable stew made from a knuckle of veal. The knuckle should be cut into sections across the bone approximately 3–4 cm thick and tied with string to retain the shape during cooking.

7.158 OSSO BUCCO or OSSI BUCCHI

Makes: 10 portions. Cooking time: 2 hours.

Quantity	*Ingredient*
2 kg	prepared knuckle of veal (7.67)
3 dl	dripping or oil
100 g	flour
50 g	tomato purée

Quantity	*Ingredient*
2½ l	White Stock (preferably veal) (3.1)
1	bouquet garni
50 g	peeled, pipped and diced tomatoes
75 g	carrots } cut into very small dice (brunoise)
75 g	turnips } cut into very small dice (brunoise)
50 g	celery } cut into very small dice (brunoise)
75 g	leek } cut into very small dice (brunoise)
2	crushed and chopped cloves of garlic
1	juice and grated peel of lemon
	chopped parsley
	seasoning

Method

(1) Heat the dripping or oil in a frying pan.

(2) Add the seasoned meat and fry until golden brown on all sides.

(3) Drain in a colander and transfer to a suitable receptacle for stewing.

(4) Add the flour, stir with a wooden spatule and place in the oven for approximately 10 minutes.

(5) Remove from the oven, stir in the tomato purée and gently add the stock.

(6) Bring to the boil, skim and season. Add the tomatoes, carrots, turnips, celery, leek and bouquet garni. Gently simmer, continuously skimming, until cooked.

(7) When cooked, remove the veal, cut off the string and dress in an earthenware type dish. Remove and discard the bouquet garni.

(8) Boil the cooking liquid, if necessary slightly thicken with diluted arrowroot, until it lightly coats the meat.

(9) Complete the liquid with the lemon juice and grated peel and crushed garlic. Season to taste and add the chopped parsley.

(10) Coat the veal with the cooking liquid and serve.

Notes

(1) Polenta (5.52) or Braised Rice (5.54) may be served as an accompaniment to this dish.

(2) When cooked the meat should come away from the centre bone under slight finger pressure.

(3) This stew is not passed once cooked.

Assessment of the completed dish

(1) The meat should be cut into slices on the bone free from excess fat, sinew and gristle.

(2) The meat should break with little effort under finger pressure. It should not be stringy but should be moist and tender.

(3) The sauce should be brown with a reddish tint and glossy in appearance.

(4) The consistency of the sauce should enable it to coat lightly the meat.

(5) The garnish should be of even size and in the correct proportions.

7.159 VEAL GOULASH — GOULASH DE VEAU HONGROISE

Makes: 10 portions. Cooking time: 1–1½ hours. Oven temperature: 180 °C.

Quantity	*Ingredient*
1½ kg	prepared veal cut into 2½ cm cubes
2 dl	dripping or oil
500 g	chopped onions
75 g	paprika
50 g	flour
50 g	tomato purée
2 l	White Stock (preferably veal) (3.1)
75 g	peeled, pipped and diced tomatoes
1	bouquet garni
20	small Plain Boiled Potatoes (9.1)
2	crushed and chopped cloves of garlic
	seasoning

Method

(1) Heat the dripping or oil in a shallow sided saucepan, add the seasoned veal and lightly fry until a light golden brown on all sides.

(2) Add the onions and gently cook for a few minutes.

(3) Add the paprika and flour, stir with a wooden spatule and place into the oven for approximately 10 minutes until the flour and paprika has coloured.

(4) Remove from the oven, stir in the tomato purée and gently add the stock.

(5) Bring to the boil, skim and season. Add the tomatoes, bouquet garni and garlic and gently simmer until cooked.

(6) Remove from the oven. Remove and discard the bouquet garni.

(7) Skim off any surplus fat or grease. Season to taste.

(8) Serve in an entrée dish with the meat arranged slightly dome shaped. Garnish with the boiled potatoes.

Notes

(1) A little caraway seed may be added to this stew during cooking for a more distinctive flavour.

(2) Gnocchi Parisienne (5.50) finished in butter may be served as an additional garnish.
(3) When cooked the meat should show signs of breaking under slight finger pressure.
(4) The sauce is not passed once cooked.

White velouté based stews

White velouté based stews may be divided into two categories:

(a) blanquettes — generally associated with lamb, mutton and rabbit;
(b) fricassées — generally associated with veal, chicken and rabbit.

For a blanquette small pieces of meat are blanched in water and then cooked in white stock with vegetables and herbs. The accompanying sauce is then made from the liquid in which the meat has been cooked. For a fricassée the meat is first sealed in butter to which flour is added, then white stock is added to make a sauce in which the meat is cooked.

NOTES
(1) Some chefs suggest that these dishes may be improved by finishing a blanquette with cream and a fricassée with a liaison of cream and egg yolks.
(2) The same garnishes may be used for both blanquettes and fricassées.

Table 18 lists the main types and cuts of meat suitable for both blanquettes and fricassées. All fat, gristle and sinew should be cut from items of meat which should then be cut into 2½ cm cubes. Chicken and rabbit should be jointed.

TABLE 18. ITEMS OF MEAT, POULTRY AND GAME SUITABLE FOR BLANQUETTES AND FRICASSEES

Blanquettes		*Fricassées*		
Lamb/mutton	*Veal*	*Veal*	*Poultry*	*Game*
Fillet from neck end	Neck end	Neck end	Chicken	Rabbit
Middle neck	Shoulder	Shoulder		
Scrag end				
Shoulder				

Blanquettes
Some examples of blanquettes as they appear on the menu are:

Blanquette of Lamb with Button Mushrooms — Blanquette d'Agneau aux Champignons

Blanquette of Veal with Button Mushrooms and Button Onions — Blanquette de Veau à l'Ancienne

Blanquette of Rabbit with Mushrooms — Blanquette de Lapin aux Champignons

7.160 BLANQUETTE

Makes: 10 portions. Cooking time: 1½ hours.

Quantity	*Ingredient*
1½ kg	prepared meat (*see* Table 18)
2 l	White Stock (3.1)
1	whole carrot
1	onion } studded onion
	bayleaf } studded onion
	clove } studded onion
1	bouquet garni
75 g	butter
75 g	flour
2 dl	cream (optional)
¼	juice of lemon
	salt and cayenne pepper

Method

(1) Place the meat into a saucepan, cover with cold water and bring to the boil for approximately 5 minutes. Place the saucepan under hot running water to remove scum and grease and then refresh under cold running water. Drain in a colander. (The meat is now blanched.)

(2) Place the blanched meat into a shallow sided saucepan, add the stock, bring to the boil and skim.

(3) Add the onion, carrot and bouquet garni and season. Allow to simmer gently until cooked.

(4) Remove and discard the onion, carrot and bouquet garni.

(5) Make a second stage roux with the butter and flour whilst the stew is cooking and allow to cool.

(6) Make a velouté sauce from most of the cooking liquid which should first be strained but keep the meat submerged and moist in the remainder.

(7) Allow the velouté to cook for approximately 1 hour. Strain through a fine strainer or muslin and reboil.

(8) Remove the meat from the retention liquid and add to the strained velouté. Allow to simmer for a few minutes.

(9) Correct the consistency of the sauce if necessary, thinning it with some of the spare cooking liquid.

(10) Add the cream and lemon juice at the last moment, season to taste.

(11) Serve the meat in a slight dome shape coated with the sauce in an entrée dish.

Notes

(1) As stated previously adding the cream is optional but it does improve the dish as regards the taste and colour.

(2) Any problems that may be encountered will be similar to those for Fricassée (*see* 7.161).

Fricassées

Some examples of fricassées as they appear on the menu are as follows:

Fricassée of Chicken with Button Onions and Button Mushrooms — Fricassée de Volaille à l'Ancienne

Fricassée of Rabbit — Fricassée de Lapin

Fricassée of Veal with Mushrooms — Fricassée de Veau aux Champignons

7.161 FRICASSEE

Makes: 10 portions. Cooking time: 1 hour. Oven temperature: 180 °C.

Quantity	*Ingredient*
1½ kg	prepared meat (*see* Table 18)
120 g	butter
100 g	flour
2½ l	White Stock (3.1)
1	bouquet garni
2½ dl	cream } liaison (optional)
3	egg yolks } liaison (optional)
10	heart shaped Croûtons (7.105)
10 g	chopped parsley
	salt and cayenne pepper

Method

(1) Melt the butter in a shallow sided saucepan but do not allow it to get too hot or colour.

(2) Season the meat, add to the melted butter and cover with a lid. Allow to set without coloration, although a slight degree of colour is acceptable.

(3) Sprinkle in the flour and stir it in gently with a wooden spatule to form a roux. Cook to a second stage roux and allow to cool.

(4) Add the hot stock a little at a time until it reaches a light sauce consistency.

(5) Bring to the boil, skim, add the bouquet garni, cover with a lid and place in the oven for approximately ¾ hour until cooked.

(6) Remove and discard the bouquet garni. Place the meat in a clean saucepan.

(7) Whisk the liaison into the sauce until the sauce thickens but do not allow it to boil.

(8) Season the sauce to taste.

(9) Serve the meat in an entrée dish neatly arranged and coated with the sauce.

(10) Dip the tips of the heart shaped croûtons in some of the sauce and then into chopped parsley. Garnish the dish and serve.

Notes

(1) This dish may also be cooked on top of the stove.

(2) The liquid in which mushrooms have been cooked if used to garnish the sauce may be reduced and added to the sauce before completing with the liaison.

(3) It may be advantageous to cook the leg joints of chicken in one saucepan and the breasts and wings in a second saucepan. This makes serving the correct combination of legs and breast or wing per portion easier.

(4) A reduction of white stock, celery stalks and mushroom trimmings may be strained into the sauce before completing with the liaison to enhance the flavour of the dish.

Possible problem	*Possible cause and solution*
(1) Sauce is dark in colour	— poor quality stock used; the colour may be improved by the addition of extra cream.
	— the roux has been overcoloured; the colour may be improved by the addition of extra cream.
	— type or quality of mushrooms, if used, was incorrect; the colour may be improved by the addition of extra cream.
(2) Sauce contains flecks of meat	— stew was overcooked; strain the sauce through a fine muslin cloth.
	— once cooked the stew was held for too long in a hot cupboard or bain-marie; strain the sauce through a fine muslin cloth.
(3) Sauce has curdled	— stew was allowed to boil once the liaison had been added; whisk the sauce onto a

Possible problem	*Possible cause and solution*
	small amount of velouté and cream and then pass it through a fine strainer or muslin cloth.
(4) Meat is stringy	— stew was overcooked; care must be taken to avoid this as once the stew is overcooked the meat cannot be rectified. — once cooked the stew was held for too long in a hot cupboard or bain-marie; prolonged retention must be avoided as the result cannot be rectified.

Assessment of the completed dish

(1) The meat should be neatly cut. Jointed chicken should have no splintered bones. The flesh should be moist.

(2) The sauce should be creamy yellow in colour with no sign of curdling.

(3) The consistency of the sauce should enable it to lightly mask the meat and any garnish.

(4) The sauce should have a sheen to it with a delicate flavour of the type of meat it is cooked with.

(5) There should be no flecks of meat in the sauce.

(6) If used as garnishes, mushrooms should be firm and white in colour, and button onions should be white and remain whole with the root end neatly trimmed.

(7) If garnished with heart shaped croûtons, they should be of a suitable size, crisp and golden on the outside with no dry or curled ends.

Stews thickened with potato

There are three main stews which are thickened with potatoes rather than flour. These are Irish stew, Lancashire hot pot and chump chop Champvallon which is a French regional dish similar to an English hot pot. All may be cooked in an oven but some chefs prefer to cook Irish stew on top of the stove so that it can be skimmed continuously whilst cooking.

The joints and cuts of meat most suitable for these stews are:

(a) for Irish stew and Lancashire hot pot use the shoulder, middle neck or fillet from the neck end of lamb or mutton, trimmed of excess fat, gristle and sinew and cut into cubes approximately 2½ cm thick; or cutlets from the middle neck for Irish stew;

(b) for chump chops Champvallon use chump chops of lamb or mutton, trimmed of skin, excess fat and gristle.

NOTE

Trimmed lamb cutlets may also be used for an Irish stew.

7.162 IRISH STEW

Makes: 10 portions. Cooking time: 1½ hours.

Quantity	*Ingredient*	
1½ kg	prepared lamb	
200 g	celery	cut into paysanne shape
200 g	white of leek	cut into paysanne shape
150 g	white cabbage (optional)	cut into paysanne shape
150 g	onion	cut into paysanne shape
1 kg	potatoes	cut into paysanne shape
1	bouquet garni	
10 g	chopped parsley	
	seasoning	
(to taste)	Worcester sauce	
20	small plain Boiled Potatoes (9.1)	garnish
20	White Glazed Button Onions (8.93)	garnish

Method

(1) Place the meat into a saucepan, cover with cold water and bring to the boil for approximately 5 minutes. Place the saucepan under hot running water to remove scum and grease and then refresh under cold running water. Drain in a colander.

(2) Place the blanched meat into a shallow sided saucepan, cover with cold water and bring to the boil. Skim.

(3) Add the vegetables, reboil and skim. Add the bouquet garni and season. Allow to cook gently for 45 minutes, continuously skimming as necessary.

(4) Add the paysanne of potatoes and continue to cook.

(5) When cooked, remove and discard the bouquet garni. Remove any traces of fat or grease from the surface of the stew.

(6) Season to taste and complete with a few drops of Worcester sauce and coarsely chopped parsley.

(7) Serve in an entrée type dish with the meat neatly dome shaped in the centre. Garnish with the plain boiled potatoes and glazed button onions.

Notes

(1) This stew may be finished in two ways. The vegetables may be cut paysanne as above, or cut into small rough pieces and puréed once cooked.

(2) Raw button onions may be added to the stew at the

commencement of cooking and blanched small potatoes about 15 minutes before completion.

(3) The garnish of onions and potatoes may also be cooked separately, as above, as there is perhaps less likelihood of them breaking up either during cooking or due to haste when serving.

Assessment of the completed dish

(1) The meat should be tender and moist, whitish in colour and full of flavour. It should be free from excess fat, sinew and gristle. It should not be stringy.

(2) The cooking liquid should be slightly clear (although some consider that the potatoes should thicken the stew). It should have a distinctive flavour of lamb, and when eaten it should not leave a trace of fat around the lips.

(3) The flavours of the vegetables should be evenly balanced with no one flavour predominating. They should be evenly and neatly cut into shapes, and should not be mashed due to overcooking.

(4) The garnish should not be overcooked. It should be of an even shape and size. The button onions should be whole with no visible sign of root ends and have a light glazed appearance.

(5) The parsley should be coarsely chopped without a raw green colour.

Possible problem	*Possible cause and solution*
(1) Stew is rather grey in colour and has particles floating in it	— either meat was not blanched or if it was blanched the scum and grease was not skimmed off; care must be taken to follow the correct blanching procedure to avoid this problem which cannot be rectified at a later stage.
	— stew was not skimmed continuously throughout the cooking process; care must be taken to carry out this procedure as the problem cannot be rectified later.
(2) Stew is greasy	— meat was incorrectly trimmed; reboil the sauce and skim off the excess fat.
	— stew was not skimmed continuously throughout the cooking process; reboil the sauce and skim off the excess fat.
	— stew has been held in a hot cupboard or bain-marie for too long once cooked; reboil the sauce and skim off the excess grease.

Possible problem	*Possible cause and solution*
(3) Stew appears mushy	— stew has been overcooked; care must be taken to not overcook the stew as it cannot be rectified later. — cooking liquid reduced whilst cooking and was not replaced with additional water; care must be taken over this aspect as once the stew is cooked it cannot be rectified. — stew has been held in a hot cupboard or bain-marie for too long once cooked; the stew should be prepared as close as possible to the time it is required to avoid the problems caused by prolonged retention. — stew has been served incorrectly; care must be taken when serving the stew to avoid stirring the stew or mixing the ingredients further with a spoon as this cannot be rectified.

7.163 LANCASHIRE HOT POT

Makes: 10 portions. Cooking time: 1½ hours. Oven temperature: 180 °C.

Quantity	*Ingredient*
1½ kg	prepared lamb cut into 2½ cm cubes
2 dl	dripping or oil
500 g	sliced onion } shallow fried (*see* 8.158)
100 g	butter } shallow fried (*see* 8.158)
1½ kg	sliced potatoes (about 2 mm thick)
2 l	White Stock (3.1)
75 g	melted butter
	seasoning

Method

(1) Heat the dripping or oil in a shallow sided saucepan, preferably a frying pan.

(2) Add the seasoned meat and fry until light golden on all sides. Drain in a colander and retain.

(3) Place the sliced potatoes in another colander and season with salt and pepper.

(4) Butter a deep sided earthenware dish, place in a layer of sliced potatoes and cooked sliced onion followed by the meat. Continue to alternate the layers until all the meat has been included and complete with a layer of sliced potatoes, neatly overlapping and following the shape of the dish.

(5) Add the hot white stock to fill the dish just below the top layer. Bring gently to the boil.

(6) Sprinkle the top layer of potatoes with melted butter. Place the dish on a baking sheet and transfer to the oven.

Notes

(1) During cooking it is important to press down the surface layer of potato with a palette knife or flat utensil to prevent them from curling and burning.

(2) To test if cooked, carefully remove part of the top layer of potato, take out a piece of meat and test between the fingers. If cooked it should yield to slight pressure. Replace the layer of potato.

(3) When cooked the contents of the dish should be moist. Most of the stock should have been soaked up by the potatoes during cooking but some should remain.

(4) This dish may be served in the dish in which it was cooked or transferred to smaller dishes when serving.

(5) It is trade practice to forecast demand and make a number of multi-portion dishes accordingly.

Service

Clean the sides of the earthenware dish, brush the surface with melted butter and serve on a dish paper on a flat underdish.

7.164 CHUMP CHOP CHAMPVALLON

Makes: 10 portions. Cooking time: 1½ hours. Oven temperature: 180 °C.

Quantity	*Ingredient*
10 × 200 g	prepared chump chops
200 g	peeled, pipped and diced tomatoes

Method

Substituting lamb chops for cubed lamb and adding diced tomatoes, proceed as for 7.163 with the same ingredients and using the same method.

Note

This item should be cooked in a shallow sided earthenware dish. Smaller amounts may also be cooked in individual dishes.

SHALLOW FRYING

This is the cooking of small items of tender meat in shallow fat on top of the stove. Shallow fried items may be served quite plainly or in breadcrumbs and coated with nut brown butter, with a range of garnishes or in a number of different types of sauces. The term sauté implies that foods are shallow fried, though this should not be confused with the same term indicating a stew (*see* p. 298).

The cooking medium is melted butter or oil or a mixture of equal quantities of both. Once cooked shallow fried items should not be dried on a cloth or piece of kitchen paper before serving unless they have become very greasy through faulty cooking.

All shallow fried items not coated with a sauce should be completed with nut brown butter — unless otherwise requested — after being placed on the serving dish. It is also often the custom to pour a thread of jus lié around before completing with the butter, particularly with such items as shallow fried liver. Items served in a sauce are, once cooked, removed from the frying pan and kept warm whilst the sauce is prepared in the same pan, although it is trade practice in many instances to prepare the sauce quite separately and coat the item once on the serving dish.

Although a fat temperature guide is not given it should be remembered that small items such as very thin steaks will take only 2–3 minutes and are therefore cooked considerably faster than items that are thicker or have an outer coating of breadcrumbs. The aim is to present an item that is evenly coloured, moist, and cooked to the required degree, bearing in mind that cooking continues even after the item has been removed from the pan.

NOTE

Once a batch of shallow fried items has been cooked always clean out the pan to remove all impurities that may be left, or use a clean pan for each batch. This rule applies to all items whether a sauce is made in the pan after the article has been cooked or not.

Shallow fried and grilled meats are generally rather thin and so are not easily tested by thermoneedle. Suggested cooking times are given on p. 344, but should be used only as a guide. The most favoured method for testing these shallow fried items is by subjecting the food to hand pressure. A general rule is that the less resilience the meat has to pressure, the more well done it is. *See* individual recipes for alternative or more appropriate methods and terms used to describe the degree to which they should be cooked.

Plain shallow frying

All kinds of steak, small cuts of other meats, certain types of offal and cuts of chicken may be shallow fried uncoated. Table 19 gives the cuts of meat, poultry and offal suitable for shallow frying uncoated, though escalopes of veal and suprêmes of chicken may

TABLE 19. ITEMS OF MEAT, POULTRY AND OFFAL SUITABLE FOR PLAIN SHALLOW FRYING

Beef steaks	*Lamb/mutton*	*Pork*	*Veal*	*Poultry*	*Offal*
Chateaubriand	Chops	Chops	Cutlet	Chicken:	Liver (calf's, lamb's, pig's)
Fillet	Chump chops	Escalope	Escalope	Suprême	Sweetbreads (white braised — 7.124)
Minute	Crown chops	Fillet		Leg (boned)	
Point	Cutlets, single and double				
Porterhouse/T-bone	Fillet of neck				
Rump	Fillet of saddle (fillet mignons)				
Sirloin, single and double	Noisettes				
Tournedos	Rosettes				

first be passed through seasoned flour before being fried. (This is not strictly necessary as these are usually finished with a flour based sauce.) Liver, however, must be passed through seasoned flour as it is very moist.

Some examples of shallow fried items as they appear on the menu are as follows:

Shallow Fried Sirloin Steaks — Entrecôtes sautées
Shallow Fried Lamb Cutlets — Côtelettes d'Agneau Sautées
Shallow Fried Pork Chops — Chops de Porc Sautés
Shallow Fried Veal Cutlets — Côtes de Veau Sautées

7.165 SHALLOW FRIED MEAT

Cooking time: 5–8 minutes.

Quantity	*Ingredient*
	prepared pieces of meat (*see* Table 19)
2 dl	melted butter or oil
	seasoning
150 g	Nut Brown Butter (6.48)

Method

(1) Heat a thick bottomed frying pan and add the oil or butter to a depth of not more than 5 mm. When hot a light haze will appear.

(2) Season the meat, place in the pan and shallow fry. When sufficiently coloured turn the item over and continue cooking until the required degree is reached.

(3) Place onto a warm serving dish neatly arranged to follow the shape of the dish.

(4) Cover with nut brown butter. Clean the sides of the dish and serve.

Notes

(1) If the item is thick, e.g. fillet steak, or where there is a coating of fat, e.g. on lamb or pork chops, the item should be stood on its edge during the last moments of cooking to ensure that it is thoroughly cooked and evenly coloured.

(2) If not for immediate use, once cooked the items should be placed in a tray on a drainer and retained in a hotplate for service. They should not be covered with a lid as this will trap the steam arising from the hot item causing them to become soft.

Extensions

7.166 CALF'S LIVER AND BACON — FOIE DE VEAU AU LARD

Pass the prepared liver sliced ½ cm thick through seasoned flour and shake off any surplus. Shallow fry quickly as outlined in 7.165. Neatly arrange the cooked liver on an oval flat dish and place rashers of Grilled Bacon (7.218) in a criss-cross fashion on top. Surround the liver with a thread of Jus Lié (3.8) and pour over Nut Brown Butter (6.48).

Note

Liver should be slightly undercooked and be left pink inside. When traces of blood appear on the surface of the liver during cooking it is ready to be turned. When blood shows on the coloured surface it should be almost cooked.

7.167 CALF'S LIVER AND ONIONS — FOIE DE VEAU LYONNAISE

Proceed as in 7.165 omitting the bacon. Serve in an earthenware dish coated with Lyonnaise Sauce (3.26).

7.168 VEAL CUTLETS BONNE FEMME — COTES DE VEAU BONNE FEMME

Shallow fry veal cutlets as outlined in 7.165. Neatly arrange in an earthenware dish adding lardons of lightly fried bacon, Cocotte Potatoes (9.32) and Brown Glazed Button Onions (8.94). Add Jus Lié (3.8), cover with a lid and place in an oven for approximately 5 minutes. Serve in the earthenware dish on an oval flat dish lined with a dish paper.

Shallow fried items coated with demi-glace or jus lié based sauces

Basic demi-glace or jus lié or any of their extensions (*see* pp. 60–3) may be served with shallow fried items. All of these sauces may be finished with a few knobs of butter at the last moment if it is desired to mellow the flavour. A range of vegetable garnishes may also be used to extend the basic shallow fried and coated item further, and in many instances the same garnish can be added to a number of cuts.

Beef

Shallow fried beef steaks may be served neatly arranged on an oval flat dish coated with a number of demi-glace and jus lié based sauces and appropriately named, e.g. using Chasseur Sauce (3.27):

Entrecôte Chasseur

Tournedos Chasseur

NOTE
Tournedos steaks are always served on a fried bread Croûton (7.105) and then coated with the sauce. The string should be removed before serving.

7.169 ENTRECOTE BORDELAISE

Shallow fry the sirloin steaks as outlined in 7.165 and neatly arrange on an oval flat dish. Coat with Bordelaise Sauce (3.25) to which has been added the juice of half a lemon and diced bone marrow previously poached in White Stock (3.1).

7.170 ENTRECOTE MINUTE MARCHAND DE VINS

Shallow fry the minute steaks as outlined in 7.165 and neatly arrange on an oval flat dish. Coat with Bordelaise Sauce (3.25) to which has been added finely chopped cooked shallots and diced bone marrow previously poached in white stock.

7.171 ENTRECOTE AU POIVRE

Season the sirloin steaks with salt and crushed peppercorns (these should be pressed slightly into the meat). Shallow fry as outlined in 7.165 and neatly arrange on an oval flat dish. Drain the fat from the pan, add 2 dl brown stock, boil and reduce by half and add 100 g butter. Coat the steaks with the sauce and sprinkle with a little chopped parsley.

7.172 TOURNEDOS ROSSINI

Shallow fry the tournedos as outlined in 7.165 and neatly arrange on a fried bread Croûton (7.105). Garnish each steak with a slice of Pâté de Foie Gras (2.35) and coat with Madeira Sauce (3.30). Garnish each portion with a slice of truffle.

Lamb
The following dishes (7.173–177) may all be prepared using noisettes, rosettes or filets mignons, coated with a variety of sauces, appropriately named and served with a number of garnishes. For example, using a coating of Chasseur Sauce (3.27):

Noisettes d'Agneau Chasseur
Rosettes d'Agneau Chasseur
Filets Mignons d'Agneau Chasseur

NOTE
Items of lamb are served on heart shaped Croûtons (7.105).

7.173 FILETS MIGNONS D'AGNEAU FLEURISTE

Shallow fry the filets mignons as outlined in 7.165 and neatly arrange on the heart shaped Croûtons (7.105). Coat with Madeira Sauce (3.30) and garnish with halves of tomatoes filled with batons of Glazed Mixed Vegetables (8.88).

7.174 FILETS MIGNONS D'AGNEAU MASCOTTE

Shallow fry the filets mignons as outlined in 7.165 and neatly arrange on the heart shaped Croûtons (7.105). Coat with Jus Lié (3.8) and garnish with Cocotte Potatoes (9.32) and quarters of Artichoke Bottoms (8.120).

7.175 NOISETTES D'AGNEAU DUBARRY

Shallow fry the noisettes as outlined in 7.165 and neatly arrange on the heart shaped Croûtons (7.105). Garnish with small pieces of Cauliflower Mornay (8.71) and Château Potatoes (9.50).

7.176 ROSETTES D'AGNEAU CLAMART

Shallow fry the rosettes as outlined in 7.165 and neatly arrange on the heart shaped Croûtons (7.105). Coat with Madeira Sauce (3.30) and garnish with Artichoke Bottoms (8.120) filled with Minted Peas (8.99) and Château Potatoes (9.50).

7.177 ROSETTES D'AGNEAU CRECY

Shallow fry the rosettes as outlined in 7.165 and neatly arrange on the heart shaped Croûtons (7.105). Coat with Madeira Sauce (3.30) and garnish with Glazed Carrots (8.64) cut barrel shaped.

Pork

7.178 PORK CHOPS FLAMANDE — COTES DE PORC FLAMANDE

Shallow fry the pork chops as outlined in 7.165 and neatly arrange in an earthenware dish. Place quarters of peeled apple around the chops and brush them with melted butter. Place into the oven for approximately 5–8 minutes until the apples and pork chops are cooked. Serve in the earthenware dish on a flat dish with a dish paper. Serve a little Jus Lié (3.8) separately.

7.179 PORK CUTLETS CHARCUTIERE — COTELETTES DE PORC CHARCUTIERE

Makes: 10 portions. Cooking time: 30 minutes.

Quantity	*Ingredient*
10 × 200 g	shallow fried pork chops (*see* 7.165)
2 dl	dry white wine
6 dl	Demi-glace (3.7) or Jus Lié (3.8)

Quantity	*Ingredient*
5 g	English mustard (diluted with a little water)
75 g	strips of gherkins
50 g	butter

Method

(1) Neatly arrange the pork chops on an oval flat dish.

(2) Drain the fat from the pan. Add the white wine, boil and reduce by two-thirds.

(3) Add the demi-glace or jus lié, gently simmer and reduce until it has a consistency that will enable it to lightly coat the chops.

(4) Add the diluted mustard and garnish with the strips of gherkin. Season to taste and finish with knobs of butter.

(5) Coat the chops with the sauce and serve.

Note

Once the mustard has been added to the sauce it should not be allowed to boil.

Veal

Items of shallow fried veal such as escalopes may be neatly arranged in an earthenware dish, coated with a sauce and named accordingly, e.g.

Escalope of Veal with Madeira Sauce — Escalope de Veau au Madère

Escalope of Veal with Marsala Sauce — Escalope de Veau au Marsala

Shallow fried items coated with a white sauce

Shallow fried items such as escalopes of veal, breast and suprême of chicken and previously white braised sweetbreads may be coated with a white or coffee coloured cream sauce made from a basic chicken or veal velouté as appropriate.

7.180 SHALLOW FRIED MEAT IN A CREAM SAUCE — VIANDE SAUTEE A LA CREME

Cooking time: 30 minutes.

Quantity	*Ingredient*
	shallow fried items of meat (7.165)
1 dl	sherry
5 dl	Veal or Chicken Velouté as appropriate (3.5)
3 dl	cream
	seasoning

Method

(1) Drain off all the fat from the pan in which the meat has been fried. Add the sherry, boil and reduce by half, then add the velouté and cream. Reduce to a consistency that will enable the sauce to coat the meat lightly.

(2) Season to taste and pass the sauce through a fine conical strainer into a clean saucepan. Reheat, pour over the meat and serve.

Notes

(1) Escalopes of veal may be coated with a sauce made in advance of the main meat item.

(2) If the items are covered with a lid when shallow fried, they should not be allowed to boil.

(3) Chicken produced in this manner may be served in a glass dome dish. It is then known as *sous cloche.*

Extensions

The basic cream sauce may be extended with a number of vegetables such as mushrooms and garnished, for example with asparagus tips, to form a range of other dishes.

7.181 BREAST OF CHICKEN IN WHITE WINE SAUCE WITH MUSHROOMS — SUPREME DE VOLAILLE SAUTEE A LA CREME ET CHAMPIGNONS

Proceed as for 7.165 using 10 × 120 g Suprêmes of Chicken (7.77) and 500 g sliced cooked Button Mushrooms (8.91).

7.182 ESCALOPE OF VEAL IN CREAM SAUCE WITH MUSHROOMS — ESCALOPE DE VEAU A LA CREME ET CHAMPIGNONS

Proceed as in 7.165 with the addition of 500 g sliced cooked Button Mushrooms (8.91).

7.183 SWEETBREADS IN SHERRY CREAM SAUCE — RIS DE VEAU A LA CREME

White braise the sweetbreads (7.123), slice and then heat them in 50 g butter. Drain off the fat and add 1 dl sherry. Boil until it has reduced by half. Add 5 dl veal velouté and 2 dl cream and boil and reduce until it is a light coating consistency. Season to taste. Serve the sweetbreads neatly arranged in an entrée type dish coated with the sauce.

7.184 *SWEETBREADS IN SHERRY CREAM SAUCE WITH MUSHROOMS — RIS DE VEAU A LA CREME ET CHAMPIGNONS*

Proceed as for Sweetbreads in Sherry Cream Sauce (7.183) adding 500 g sliced Button Mushrooms (8.91) to the sauce.

7.185 *SWEETBREADS IN WHITE SAUCE GARNISHED WITH ASPARAGUS TIPS — ESCALOPE DE RIS DE VEAU PRINCESSE*

Proceed as for Sweetbreads in Sherry Cream Sauce (7.183) and garnish with small Asparagus Tips (8.41).

Items shallow fried in breadcrumbs

Items suitable for shallow frying in breadcrumbs include escalopes of veal, suprêmes and boned legs of chicken, escalopes of pork loin, lamb cutlets, previously white braised sweetbreads and bitocks and mock escalopes.

The main problem encountered when shallow frying some of the thicker items in breadcrumbs such as suprêmes of chicken and, in particular, lamb cutlets is that the breadcrumbs colour much faster than the item itself will cook. That the outer surface is golden is no indication that the item is cooked inside — *see (e)* below.

The following notes should be borne in mind when shallow frying items coated with breadcrumbs.

(a) Arrange uncooked breaded items on a tray sprinkled with breadcrumbs. If stacked in layers place a sheet of greaseproof paper between each layer but avoid too many layers as those underneath will begin to sweat making the breadcrumbs damp. For freshness and quality, breadcrumb the meat as close as possible to cooking.

(b) Use the minimum amount of fat for cooking but ensure that it is hot before commencing to fry.

(c) Always cook the items presentation side down first and use a palate knife for turning, although a fork may be used with care.

(d) Most items shallow fried in breadcrumbs are surrounded with a thread of jus lié then completed with some nut brown butter at the moment of serving.

(e) Once coloured on the presentation side lamb cutlets or suprêmes of chicken which are slightly thicker than other items may be placed in a moderate oven to complete cooking.

(f) When cooked the items should be retained in a dish with a drainer. They should not be allowed to dry out. Do not cover them with a lid at this stage as this will cause the outer coating to lose its crispness.

7.186 BREADED MEAT FOR SHALLOW FRYING

Quantity	*Ingredient*
10	standard portions of prepared meat or poultry
500 g	seasoned flour
6	beaten eggs (eggwash)
500 g	White Breadcrumbs (7.187)

Method

(1) Place the flour, eggwash and breadcrumbs in shallow sided separate trays in the order of use.

(2) Pass the meat through the seasoned flour and shake off any surplus.

(3) Pass the meat through the eggwash and remove surplus liquid by pulling the meat through the fingers.

(4) Pass the meat through the breadcrumbs removing any surplus crumbs.

(5) Place the breadcrumbed meat onto a table or board lightly sprinkled with breadcrumbs. Lightly bat out with the side of a large knife, then mark trellis fashion with the back edge of the knife on the presentation side.

(6) Arrange on a tray and retain in a refrigerator until required (*see* p. 324 under *(a)*).

7.187 WHITE BREADCRUMBS

Remove the crust from a stale loaf, cut into rough pieces and place into the mixing bowl of an electric mixer with the spade attachment. Turn the machine on at a slow gear to begin then move through to the second. When crumbed, remove from the machine and pass through a sieve.

Note

If the bread is not stale enough to make crumbs a small amount of flour with the bread will help.

7.188 BROWN BREADCRUMBS

Dry the crusts of bread in a hotplate without allowing them to colour. Pass through a mincing machine, then through a sieve.

7.189 SHALLOW FRIED BREADED MEAT — VIANDE PANEE

Quantity	*Ingredient*
	item of meat breaded as in 7.186
2 dl	melted butter or oil
4 dl	Jus Lié (3.8)
150 g	Nut Brown Butter (6.48)

Method

(1) Heat a thick bottomed shallow sided pan and add the butter or oil to a depth of not more than 5 mm.

(2) Place in the breaded item presentation side downwards and gently shallow fry until golden.

(3) Turn and fry the other side.

(4) Neatly arrange the items on a flat oval dish and surround them with a thread of the jus lié. Finish with the nut brown butter. Serve the remainder of the jus lié separately.

Assessment of the completed dish

(1) Each portion piece should be even in size and thickness.

(2) The outer coating of breadcrumbs should be firm but not too crisp, light golden in colour over the total surface and the trellis markings should be clearly visible.

(3) The meat should be moist, cooked to the correct degree and neatly arranged on the dish.

(4) The sauce should be light in colour, very smooth and a little on the thin side to allow it to flow. There should be just enough to cover the bottom of the dish.

(5) The butter should be nut brown in colour, hot and bubbling and coat each meat item.

Bitocks and mock escalopes

A bitock is made of finely minced raw meat free of all fat, sinew and gristle, seasoned, mixed with white breadcrumbs soaked in milk and shaped like a scone. It should be shallow fried until golden and cooked. Bitocks generally weigh 100–120 g and are about 7 cm in diameter. They can be made with beef, pork or veal and may be served with devilled sauce, tomato sauce or chasseur sauce. Suitable garnishes include tyrolienne for beef bitocks and milanaise and napolitaine for pork or veal bitocks. Some examples are:

Bitock of Pork Devilled Sauce — Bitock de Porc Sauce Diable

Bitock of Veal Chasseur Sauce — Bitock de Veau Sauce Chasseur

Mock escalopes are made of finely minced veal or pork, generally weigh 100 g and are about 12 cm in diameter. They may be cooked and served with the same sauces and garnishes as genuine escalopes of veal, for example:

Mock Veal Escalopes Holstein — Mock Pork Escalopes Holstein
Mock Veal Escalopes Milanaise — Mock Pork Escalopes Milanaise
Mock Veal Escalopes Napolitaine — Mock Pork Escalopes Napolitaine
Mock Veal Escalopes Viennoise — Mock Pork Escalopes Viennoise

7.190 BITOCKS AND MOCK ESCALOPES

Makes: 10 portions.

Quantity	*Ingredient*	
1 kg	finely minced meat as appropriate	
30 g	butter	
250 g	White Breadcrumbs (7.187)	soaked and squeezed to remove excess milk
2 dl	milk	
	seasoning of salt, pepper and nutmeg	
	flour, egg and breadcrumbs (*see* 7.186)	

Method

(1) Place all the bitock ingredients in a basin and thoroughly mix until fine and smooth.

(2) Divide into standard portions (approximately 100 g).

(3) Mould into the required shape by dipping the hands occasionally into a basin of water to increase efficiency and prevent sticking.

(4) Coat with the flour, egg and breadcrumbs as in 7.186 and arrange on a tray and retain in a refrigerator until required for cooking.

Note

Bowl choppers (either of the vertical or horizontal type) are ideal machines for making these products because the meat can then be minced very finely.

To test if cooked

Bitocks and mock escalopes should be cooked until medium to well done. This can be tested by finger pressure — when firm to the touch they are done. They may also be tested by inserting a trussing needle or skewer into the centre. If the juices are clear and free from traces of blood then the item is cooked.

As escalopes are made rather thin they should be cooked by the time they are coloured to the correct degree. Test the resilience to finger pressure to make absolutely certain that the item is fully cooked.

Service

Bitocks should be served as any other steak with a sauce. Similarly escalopes should be served as veal escalopes.

Assessment of the completed dish

Bitocks may be assessed as if they were steaks. Similarly, mock escalopes may be assessed as if they were veal escalopes.

Possible problem	*Possible cause and solution*
(1) The item has distorted during cooking	— not all the gristle and sinew was removed during preparation; care must be taken when preparing the meat as subsequent problems cannot be rectified. — meat was too coarsely minced; care must be taken when preparing the ingredients as later problems cannot be rectified. — not enough binding agent was used; care must be taken to use the correct amount of binding agent to achieve the correct consistency as once cooked the problem cannot be rectified.
(2) The items fall to pieces when cooked	— mixture was too dry; care must be taken to achieve the correct consistency when binding the mixture as once the item is cooked the problem cannot be rectified. — mixture was too wet; care must be taken to achieve the correct consistency when binding the mixture as once the item is cooked the problem cannot be rectified. — meat was too coarsely minced; care must be taken when preparing the ingredients as later problems cannot be rectified. — not all the sinew and gristle was removed during preparation; care must be taken when preparing the meat as subsequent problems cannot be rectified.

Chicken

Suprêmes and boned legs of chicken may be breaded and shallow fried in the same ways as follows:

Shallow Fried Breaded Suprême of Chicken — Suprême de Volaille Panée Sautée

Shallow Fried Breaded Leg of Chicken — Cuisse de Volaille Panée Sautée

Leg of Chicken Doria — Cuisse de Volaille Doria

Leg of Chicken Maréchale — Cuisse de Volaille Maréchale

Leg of Chicken Maryland — Cuisse de Volaille Maryland

NOTE

When cooked suprêmes will be firm to the touch at their thickest point. If uncertain gently lift the fillet from the back of a sample. As this is generally the last area to cook it will be white and firm if the whole suprême is cooked and any indication of raw flesh will easily be seen. A further point to check is around the winglet bone — any sign of rawness here is also an indication that the suprême is not fully cooked.

7.191 *SUPREME OF CHICKEN DORIA — SUPREME DE VOLAILLE DORIA*

Shallow fry breaded suprêmes of chicken as in 7.189 and garnish with 150 g cucumber cut into small diamond shaped pieces gently cooked for a few moments in butter.

7.192 *SUPREME OF CHICKEN MARECHALE — SUPREME DE VOLAILLE MARECHALE*

Shallow fry breaded suprêmes of chicken as in 7.189 and garnish each portion with three Asparagus Sprue (*see* 8.41).

7.193 *SUPREME OF CHICKEN MARYLAND — SUPREME DE VOLAILLE MARYLAND*

Shallow fry breaded suprêmes of chicken as in 7.189 and garnish with 10 small Grilled Tomatoes (8.171), 10 rashers of Grilled Bacon (7.218), 10 halves of banana breadcrumbed and deep fried and 10 small Sweetcorn Cakes (8.159). Serve horseradish sauce separately.

Lamb

7.194 *SHALLOW FRIED BREADED LAMB CUTLETS — COTELETTES D'AGNEAU PANEES*

Proceed as in 7.189 using breaded lamb cutlets.

Note

When cooked the cutlets will be firm to the touch. If uncertain gently fold back a sample at the point where the fat and the nut of meat join. The meat should be pinkish in colour.

7.195 *LAMB CUTLETS MILANAISE — COTELETTES D'AGNEAU MILANAISE*

Proceed as in 7.189 using breaded lamb cutlets and garnish with 500 g Spaghetti Milanaise (*see* 5.45).

7.196 LAMB CUTLETS NAPOLITAINE — COTELETTES D'AGNEAU NAPOLITAINE

Proceed as in 7.189 using breaded lamb cutlets and garnish with 500 g Spaghetti Napolitaine (*see* 5.46).

7.197 LAMB CUTLETS WITH REFORME SAUCE — COTELETTES D'AGNEAU SAUCE REFORME

Proceed as in 7.189 using breaded lamb cutlets and serve with a sauceboat of Reforme Sauce (3.33).

Pork

Escalopes of loin or fillet of pork may be prepared, cooked and served in the same ways as escalopes of veal. They would therefore appear as follows:

Shallow Fried Escalopes of Pork — Escalopes de Porc Panées

Shallow Fried Escalopes of Pork Holstein — Escalopes de Porc Holstein

Shallow Fried Escalopes of Pork Milanaise — Escalopes de Porc Milanaise

Shallow Fried Escalopes of Pork Napolitaine — Escalopes de Porc Napolitaine

Shallow Fried Escalopes of Pork Viennoise — Escalopes de Porc Viennoise

Sweetbreads

Sweetbreads should first be white braised (*see* 7.123), allowed to cool completely and drained. They should then be sliced on a slant of 45° before breadcrumbing.

7.198 SHALLOW FRIED BREADED SWEETBREADS — RIS DE VEAU PANES

Proceed as in 7.189 using breaded sweetbreads.

Notes

(1) As they are rather moist sweetbreads should be dried slightly with a cloth before breadcrumbing.

(2) Wherever possible they should be shallow fried to order. As they have already been braised they are quite moist and if held for any length of time before frying the flour coating may thicken and become rather like a batter.

7.199 SWEETBREADS MARECHALE — ESCALOPE DE RIS DE VEAU MARECHALE

Proceed as in 7.189 using breaded sweetbreads and garnish each portion with three Asparagus Tips (8.41).

Note

Traditionally this dish is also garnished with slices of truffle.

Veal

Escalopes and cutlets of veal may be prepared, cooked and served in the same way. Veal escalopes are rather thin and should be cooked as soon as the coating is coloured. The flesh should be moist and white — pinkness is a sign that it is undercooked. In many instances the garnishes are the same as for lamb cutlets:

Shallow Fried Breaded Escalopes of Veal — Escalopes de Veau Panées
Shallow Fried Breaded Veal Cutlets — Côtes de Veau Panées
Veal Cutlets Holstein — Côtes de Veau Holstein
Escalopes of Veal Milanaise — Escalopes de Veau Milanaise
Veal Cutlets Milanaise — Côtes de Veau Milanaise
Escalopes of Veal Napolitaine — Escalopes de Veau Napolitaine
Veal Cutlets Napolitaine — Côtes de Veau Napolitaine
Veal Cutlets Viennoise — Côtes de Veau Viennoise

7.200 ESCALOPES OF VEAL HOLSTEIN — ESCALOPES DE VEAU HOLSTEIN

Proceed as in 7.189 using breaded escalopes of veal. Garnish each escalope with a Shallow Fried Egg (5.15) decorated with anchovy fillets placed criss-cross fashion on top of each egg and a slice of lemon.

7.201 ESCALOPES OF VEAL VIENNOISE — ESCALOPES DE VEAU VIENNOISE

Proceed as in 7.189 using breaded escalopes of veal. Before arranging the escalopes decorate the dish at one end (or both ends if desired) with alternate semi-circles of chopped parsley, sieved hard boiled white of egg, sieved hard boiled yolk of egg and strips of anchovy. Arrange the escalopes neatly on the dish and decorate each with a slice of lemon with a ring of anchovy fillet placed in its centre and a stoned olive. Around the anchovy arrange chopped parsley and sieved white and yolk of hard boiled egg.

Sautéed chicken

This method of sautéing chicken is quite different from that outlined in the section on stewing (*see* pp. 294–315). The joints of chicken are not cooked in the sauce in which they are served but, once cooked, are removed from the receptacle and kept warm whilst the sauce is being prepared in the same pan.

7.202 POULET SAUTE CHAMPEAUX

Makes: 10 portions. Cooking time: 1 hour.

Quantity	*Ingredient*	
3 × 1½ kg	jointed chicken (7.78)	
2 dl	melted butter or oil	
150 g	chopped shallots	
2 dl	dry white wine	
6 dl	Jus Lié (3.8)	
5 g	chopped parsley	
50 g	butter	
	seasoning	
20	Brown Glazed Button Onions (8.94)	garnish
30 pieces	Cocotte Potatoes (9.32)	garnish

Method

(1) Heat a thick bottomed shallow sided pan and add the oil or melted butter to a depth of not more than 5 mm.

(2) Season and add the chicken pieces and shallow fry until golden on all sides. Cover with a lid and allow to cook rather slowly.

(3) When cooked, remove the chicken and place them neatly in an earthenware dish and keep warm.

(4) Add the shallots to the pan and gently cook for a few moments, then drain off the surplus fat.

(5) Add the white wine, boil and reduce by half. Add the jus lié and gently simmer until the sauce is of a light coating consistency.

(6) Finish the sauce with the chopped parsley and knobs of butter and season to taste. Garnish with the glazed button onions and cocotte potatoes. Pour the sauce over the chicken and serve.

Notes

(1) When cooking the chicken it is inevitable that the breast and wings will cook first. They should therefore be removed and the legs permitted to cook a little longer.

(2) Where larger numbers of portions are cooked it will be advantageous to cook the legs and thighs in one saucepan and the wings, winglets and breasts in another. Apart from the point highlighted in (1) above, keeping the white and dark flesh together

helps during the service as each portion consists of one joint of white flesh and one of dark.

(3) Once the chicken has been shallow fried and covered with a lid it may be transferred to an oven at a moderate temperature to complete cooking.

(4) It is general trade practice to make the sauce separately from the chicken. The two are then brought together at the time of service.

(5) Sautéed chicken dishes may be held in a bain-marie with a lid or in a hot cupboard provided the temperature is not too high. Too high a temperature invariably leads to the top sauce drying out and the extraction of fat from the dish. This may also make the chicken stringy and thicken the sauce.

(6) Some chefs pass the raw chicken through seasoned flour before being fried to give a better colour to the chicken. This will of course thicken the finished sauce and must be taken into consideration. Add a thinner jus lié or reduce the wine less.

(7) If the sauce is too thick it may be thinned with a little stock. If it is too thin some diluted arrowroot may be added to the boiling sauce.

(8) Tomato purée may be added to give a deeper and richer colour if so desired, but not to the finished sauce; this aspect should be considered when adding the brown sauce. If a mistake is made then the purée may be diluted with some hot stock before it is added.

(9) Chicken carcasses left after jointing should be used for making the jus lié sauce which forms the basis for many of these types of dishes. (*See* 3.8 for recipe.)

To test if cooked

Remove a sample of both leg and breast with a fork. Test with finger pressure — the thigh and drumstick should yield until the bone is easily felt and the breast should be firm and resilient. Alternatively, if the juices that run from the fork marks are clear then the joint is cooked.

Assessment of the completed dish

(1) The portions should be arranged to resemble as closely as possible the general shape of a chicken with the legs and thighs at the side. The sauce should lightly coat all parts and leave no area exposed.

(2) The chicken should be light golden brown on the outside with the flesh moist and breast parts white. The sauce should not have discoloured the flesh — a sign that it has been boiled in the sauce. When jointing the chicken the bones should have been

removed without splintering. The ends of the winglets should also be removed.

(3) The sauce should be a rich brown colour; in extensions where mushrooms have been added they should be neatly sliced and without stalks, and tomatoes should be free from pips, neatly diced and soft with no hard centre pieces.

Extensions

7.203 POULET SAUTE BERCY

Proceed as in 7.202. Garnish with 20 small Grilled Chipolata Sausages (7.232) and 30 button mushrooms cooked in lemon juice.

7.204 POULET SAUCE BONNE FEMME

Proceed as in 7.202. Garnish with 20 Brown Glazed Button Onions (8.94), 250 g lardons of lightly fried bacon, and 30 pieces of Cocotte Potatoes (9.32).

7.205 POULET SAUTE BOURGUIGNONNE

Proceed as 7.202 substituting red wine for white. Garnish with 24 Brown Glazed Button Onions (8.94), 250 g lardons of lightly fried bacon, 36 button mushrooms cooked in lemon juice and 12 heart shaped Croûtons (7.105).

7.206 POULET SAUTE AUX CHAMPIGNONS

Proceed as in 7.202, at Stage (4) adding 500 g sliced button mushrooms just before adding the shallots.

7.207 POULET SAUTE CHASSEUR

Proceed as for 7.202 adding sliced button mushrooms, Tomato Concassée (8.169) and chopped tarragon to the sauce.

7.208 POULET SAUTE HONGROISE

Makes: 12 portions. Cooking time: 1 hour.

Quantity	*Ingredient*
3 × 1½ kg	jointed chicken sautéed as in 7.202
2 dl	melted butter or oil
500 g	chopped onions
50 g	paprika
50 g	flour
20 g	tomato purée
2 l	White Stock (3.1)
200 g	peeled, pipped and diced tomato

Quantity	*Ingredient*	
2 dl	cream	
500 g	Savoury Rice (5.54)	mixed together
150 g	Tomato Concassée (8.169)	
	seasoning	

Method

(1) Add the chopped onions to the pan in which the chicken was sautéed and gently cook for a few moments without colouring.

(2) Add the paprika, flour and tomato purée and stir in with a wooden spatule. Add the stock and allow to simmer for approximately 10 minutes. Add the tomato concassée, boil and gently simmer until the sauce is of a light coating consistency.

(3) Add the cream to the sauce, season to taste, and replace the chicken.

(4) Serve the chicken in an earthenware dish with a border of savoury rice mixed with tomato concassée.

7.209 POULET SAUTE MADRAS

Sauté jointed chicken as outlined in 7.202 and when cooked neatly arrange in an earthenware dish. Pour Curry Sauce (3.11) over and serve with Boiled Rice (5.53) in a vegetable dish and a selection of the accompaniments given in 7.155 in separate individual dishes.

Ballotines

A ballotine of chicken (7.78, stages 1–4) is a chicken leg with the thigh bone removed leaving the drumstick in place stuffed with Chicken Forcemeat (*see* 7.255) and tied. They may be cooked in the same way as any of the sautéed chicken dishes above. For example:

Ballotine de Volaille Bonne Femme
Ballotine de Volaille Chasseur

Quick sautés

As implied the meat is shallow fried very quickly in hot fat. It is important to bear in mind the following points.

(a) Once the meat has been shallow fried on no account should it be allowed to boil in the accompanying sauce as this makes it tough, dry and tasteless. It should be tender, moist and full of flavour.

(b) Once cooked quick sautéed dishes must be consumed as soon as possible.

(c) Because the sauce is made in the same pan as the meat has been cooked use a shallow tin lined copper pan and not a frying pan. It is prudent to produce several small batches rather than one large one.

(d) The meat should be shallow fried quickly in either melted butter or oil or a mixture of equal quantities of oil and butter.

(e) When quick sautéing make certain the fat is hot and do not overfill the pan as this will immediately bring down the temperature of the fat. In these circumstances the fat takes a long time to reheat which results in the extraction of water and juices from the meat so that it boils rather than fries. If this should happen, drain the commodities into a colander and begin again in a clean hot pan.

(f) After the initial coloration and cooking of the item drain off all excess fat and place the meat in a dish to keep warm before returning the pan to the stove in order to make the sauce.

(g) Items should always be slightly underdone when served so an allowance must be made for finishing off in the sauce even though it does not boil. The period between the completion of the dish and service to the customer must also be borne in mind.

(h) Care, however, must be taken that the meat is evenly coloured.

7.210 BEEF STROGONOFF — SAUTE DE BOEUF STROGONOFF

Makes: 10 portions. Cooking time: 10 minutes.

Quantity	*Ingredient*
1 kg	strips of tail end of fillet of beef (5 cm long × 1 cm)
2 dl	melted butter or oil
50 g	chopped shallots
6 dl	cream
1	juice of lemon
	seasoning

Method

(1) Heat a thick bottomed shallow sided pan and add the oil or melted butter to a depth of not more than 5 mm.

(2) Season and add the strips of fillet. Quickly shallow fry, keeping them on the underdone side. Remove the beef and retain in a warm place.

(3) Return the pan to the stove, add the shallots and cook without colouring them. Drain off any excess fat.

(4) Add the cream, boil and reduce by half. Add the previously cooked and drained meat and incorporate the two by gently tossing. Do not boil.

(5) Add the lemon juice, season to taste. Neatly arrange in an earthenware dish and serve.

Notes

(1) This dish is Russian in style and may be finished in the typical Russian way with sour cream.

(2) There are several different ways of dealing with the meat and these have a direct effect on the thickness of the sauce and certainly the colour and flavour of the dish.

(a) the strips of beef may be shallow fried without any coating;
(b) the strips of beef may be passed through seasoned flour before shallow frying;
(c) the strips of beef may be passed through a mixture of flour and paprika before shallow frying.

(3) Sliced mushrooms are sometimes included in the recipes. It is usual to finish the dish with chopped tarragon.

(4) If the sauce is a little too thick it may be thinned with a little dry white wine or white stock but care must be taken not to unbalance the flavour.

Assessment of the completed dish

(1) The sauce should be off white or slightly coffee coloured; if made with paprika it will be pinkish.

(2) The sauce should have a creamy consistency so that it lightly coats the meat.

(3) The flavour should have a slight hint of lemon juice.

(4) The meat should be moist, tender, slightly undercooked and full flavoured.

Possible problem	*Possible cause and solution*	
(1) During frying the strips of beef begin to boil in their own juices	— fat was not permitted to reach a high enough temperature before adding the meat — pan was overfilled with strips of beef — once the beef was added the fat did not reheat quickly enough.	drain the pan immediately, reheat a clean pan, add a little oil and continue to fry quickly for a very short period.
	— too much oil or butter was used in the	

Possible problem	*Possible cause and solution*
	bottom of the pan; care must be taken to avoid this as it cannot be rectified.
(2) The meat is tough and dry and lacks flavour	— meat was fried slowly; care must be taken to sauté the beef quickly as this problem cannot be rectified (*see* (1) above for solution).
	— meat was boiled in the sauce; care must be taken to avoid this happening as it cannot be rectified.
	— dish was held for too long before being served; the dish should be prepared as close as possible to the time it is required to avoid the problems caused by prolonged retention which cannot be rectified.

7.211 SAUTEED CHICKEN LIVERS WITH SAVOURY RICE — PILAFF DE FOIES DE VOLAILLE

Makes: 10 portions. Cooking time: 10 minutes.

Quantity	*Ingredient*
1 kg	chicken livers (gall bladder removed, cut in half and trimmed)
½ dl	melted butter or oil
	seasoning
6 dl	Madeira Sauce (3.30)
500 g	Savoury Rice (5.54)

Method

(1) Heat a thick bottomed shallow sided pan and add the oil or melted butter to a depth of not more than 5 mm.

(2) Season and add the liver pieces. Quickly shallow fry, keeping them on the underdone side. Drain in a colander and return to the saucepan.

(3) Add sufficient of the sauce to moisten the livers and season to taste. Do not boil.

(4) Place the savoury rice in an earthenware dish, slightly dome shape, making an indentation in its centre. Fill with the livers and its sauce. Pour a thread of sauce around the outer edges of the rice, and serve with the remainder of the sauce separately.

Notes

(1) A savarin mould can be filled with the savoury rice, turned out onto a service dish and the centre filled with the livers and some of the sauce. Alternatively, a basin may be used for

moulding the rice: the basin is lined with the savoury rice, filled with the livers and some of the sauce, sealed with more rice and turned out onto the service dish surrounded with a thread of madeira sauce.

(2) Any problems that may be encountered are similar to those for Sautéed Kidneys (*see* 7.212).

7.212 SAUTEED KIDNEY—ROGNONS SAUTES

Makes: 10 portions. Cooking time: 10 minutes.

Quantity	*Ingredient*
20	prepared lambs' kidneys cut in halves (*see* p. 345, stage 5)
2 dl	melted butter or oil
6 dl	Demi-glace (3.7) or Jus Lié (3.8)
	seasoning

Method

(1) Heat a thick bottomed shallow sided pan and add the oil or melted butter to a depth of not more than 5 mm.

(2) Season and add the kidney pieces. Quickly shallow fry, keeping them on the underdone side. Drain in a colander and retain in a warm place.

(3) Return the pan to the stove, add the brown sauce and allow to boil for a few moments. Take off the boil, add the drained kidneys and season to taste.

(4) Neatly arrange in an earthenware dish and serve.

Assessment of the completed dish

(1) The sauce should be a rich brown colour.
(2) The kidneys should be undercooked but not raw.
(3) The centre core of the kidneys should have been removed.

Possible problem	*Possible cause and solution*	
(1) Kidneys weep a fluid (protein) which solidifies and causes brown specks	— fat was not hot enough before the kidneys were added — pan was overfilled — fat not allowed to recover heat once the kidneys have been added.	Drain the kidneys at once. Heat some fat in a clean pan and begin to fry again but at a higher temperature as some of the water will have been retained by the kidneys.

Possible problem	*Possible cause and solution*
(2) Sauce contains small specks of coagulated protein from the kidneys	— kidneys have been cooked at too low a temperature; ensure that the fat is hot enough to cook the kidneys quickly to avoid this problem which cannot be rectified later. — kidneys have been held too long; this should be avoided as the kidneys will continue to cook in the sauce and the result cannot be rectified.
(3) Kidneys are tough and leathery	— kidneys have been overcooked; care must be taken to avoid overcooking as this cannot be rectified. — kidneys have been allowed to boil in the sauce; this should be avoided as the kidneys will overcook which cannot be rectified.

7.213 SAUTEED KIDNEY WITH MADEIRA SAUCE — ROGNONS SAUTES AU MADERE

Proceed as in 7.212 using Madeira Sauce (3.30) in place of the demi-glace or jus lié.

7.214 SAUTEED KIDNEY TURBIGO — ROGNONS SAUTES TURBIGO

Proceed as in 7.212 using Madeira Sauce (3.30). Garnish with 10 small Grilled Chipolata Sausages (7.232) and 450 g button mushrooms cut into quarters and cooked in butter. When serving place the kidneys onto small oblong fried bread Croûtons (7.105) approximately 6 cm × 4 cm.

DEEP FRYING

All meats which are to be deep fried need to be coated as a protection against the high temperature of the fat. The coating may be of breadcrumbs or batter and the types of coating and thickness of the meat will determine the temperature of the fat. The aim is to seal the coating to prevent the fat from penetrating the food, but remember that the item must stay in the deep fat fryer long enough to cook thoroughly before the coating becomes too dry and brown.

Further details on methods of deep frying will be found in Chapter Six.

7.215 CHICKEN A LA KIEV — SUPREME DE VOLAILLE A LA KIEV

Makes: 10 portions. Cooking time: 5 minutes. Cooking temperature: 170 °C.

Quantity	Ingredient
10 × 120 g	Prepared Suprêmes of Chicken (7.77)
200 g	Parsley Butter (3.51)
	flour, egg and breadcrumb coating (7.186)
	seasoning
	sprigs of picked parsley } garnish
250 g	straw potatoes } garnish

Method

(1) Lay the skinned suprême on the work surface with the side that was covered with the skin downwards. Remove the small fillet.

(2) Remove the light silver sinew from the fillet and slightly flatten the fillet.

(3) Make an incision from the wing bone down the length of the suprême, then make lateral cuts each side to form a pocket.

(4) Insert the butter into this pocket and then insert the flattened fillet over the butter but under the flesh of the suprême.

(5) Coat with the flour, eggwash and breadcrumbs (*see* 7.186); reform into an oval shape.

(6) Place the chicken pieces into a frying basket and immerse them in the hot fat. Fry for the prescribed time until crisp and golden, turning the suprêmes during cooking to ensure even cooking and coloration.

(7) Drain the suprêmes by placing them onto absorbent kitchen paper. Season with salt.

(8) Serve on an oval flat dish, garnish with the straw potatoes and deep fried sprigs of parsley.

Notes

(1) The parsley butter may be slightly flavoured with garlic.

(2) Pâté may also be used as a filling in place of the butter.

(3) Watercress is sometimes used in place of fried parsley to form the garnish.

7.216 FRIED CHICKEN

Makes: 10 portions. Cooking time: 20 minutes. Oven temperature: 170 °C.

Quantity	Ingredient
10 × 120 g	prepared jointed chicken (7.78) in flour, egg and breadcrumbs (*see* 7.186)
2	lemons cut into wedges
10	sprigs of picked parsley
	seasoning
1 dl	melted butter

Method

(1) Place the chicken into the hot fat away from oneself.

(2) Fry until crisp and golden turning them during cooking to ensure even cooking and coloration.

(3) Drain the escalopes by placing them onto absorbent kitchen paper. Season to taste with salt.

(4) Arrange the chicken neatly on an oval flat dish. Pour over the melted butter and garnish with segments of lemon and deep fried sprigs of parsley.

Note

Chicken wings and breast are likely to curl during deep frying. To prevent this cook them lying in single layers in a frying basket with a smaller basket standing on top, although this must be removed to allow even cooking. Even so, it is doubtful if curling can be prevented entirely and should be accepted as a characteristic of the dish.

GRILLING

This is the application of direct heat to high quality seasoned items of meat which are normally no thicker than 7–8 cm first brushed with oil. The outer surfaces should caramelise with the natural juices, be evenly and lightly coloured and have seared cross marks from the grill bars. Inside the food should be succulent and cooked to the desired degree.

Grilling equipment

There is a wide range of equipment and fuel available for grilling:

(a) a charcoal grill provides under-heat;

(b) a char-grill provides under-heat and uses gas or electricity;

(c) a salamander grill provides overhead heat and uses gas or electricity;

(d) an infra-red grill provides over or under-heat and uses electricity;

(e) a griddle plate stands on top of the stove and uses gas or electricity.

All grills and grill bars should be cleaned frequently before, during and after use. If attention is not given to cleaning during prolonged use burnt particles stick to the food affecting flavour and appearance.

Garnishes

The basic garnish for all grilled meats and poultry consists of Straw Potatoes (*see* p. 476), Parsley Butter (3.51) and watercress. The French term to denote this on the menu is *vert-pré.*

Another French term commonly used for a general garnish is *garni.* This allows flexibility and generally includes the same items as vert-pré plus Grilled Tomatoes and Mushrooms (8.171 and 170).

Sauces may be featured as an accompaniment, those most commonly used are buttered based sauces such as Béarnaise (3.12) or piquante flavoured sauces such as Diable (3.28). They are served separately in sauceboats.

Some examples of these garnishes and sauces are as follows:

Grilled Tournedos Steak with Sauce Béarnaise — Tournedos Grillé Béarnaise

Grilled Chicken with Sauce Diable — Poulet Grillé Diablé

Grilled Entrecote Steak Vert-Pré — Entrecôte Grillée Vert-Pré

Grilled Pork Chop with Tomatoes and Mushrooms — Chop de Porc Grillé aux Tomates et Champignons

General application

Table 20 gives items of meat, poultry and offal suitable for grilling, their approximate weight per portion and length of time they should be grilled for. Items to be grilled should first be trimmed of all sinew, gristle and excess fat. They should then be seasoned (with the exception of bacon and gammon) and brushed with oil.

7.217 GRILLED MEAT

Method (using under-heat)

(1) Heat the grill — it must be hot *before* grilling commences.

(2) Brush all over with oil and season the raw food.

(3) Place the food on the previously oiled grill bars.

(4) If there are different heat zones in the grill then place the item onto the hottest part to give the searing marks of the grill bars. Turn the meat sideways so that a criss-cross effect is marked on both sides of the food and when marked move it away from this point to enable the food to cook to the desired degree without burning.

(5) Brush the bars of the grill continuously with oil to prevent sticking.

TABLE 20. COOKING CHART FOR GRILLING SUITABLE ITEMS OF MEAT, POULTRY AND OFFAL

Cut of meat	*Approx. weight per portion*	*Time (mins)*[1] *(medium cooked)*
Beef		
Chateaubriand[2]	250 g	15–18
Double sirloin steak	400 g	15–18
Fillet steak	200 g	10–15
Minute steak	200 g	3–4
Point steak	200 g	10–12
Porterhouse steak (T-bone)	650 g	15–18
Rib steak	650 g	15–18
Rump steak	200 g	8–10
Single entrecôte steak	200 g	8–10
Tournedos	200 g	8–10
Lamb		
Chop	200 g	15–18
Chump chop	250 g	15–18
Crown chop	400 g	15–18
Cutlet	100 g	8–10
Double cutlet	200 g	15–18
Noisette	100 g	3–5
Rosette	100 g	5–8
Liver	200 g	5–6
Kidney	75 g	3–8
Pork		
Bacon	100 g	3–8
Chop	200 g	15–18
Gammon steak	150 g	8–10
Poultry		
Chicken (1½–2 kg)	—	45
Spring chicken	400 g	20–25
Veal		
Cutlets	250 g	8–10
Liver	200 g	5–6
Escalopes[3]	150 g	8–10

1. The cooking times indicated are intended as a guide for cooking an individual item and do not always correspond with those indicated in recipes where allowances have been made for other associated work to be carried out.
2. Chateaubriand is usually grilled first then transferred to an oven for roasting. This prevents it drying out during the long time it would take to grill until cooked right through.
3. It is very unusual to grill veal escalopes due to their lack of natural fat content.

Method (using overhead heat — a salamander grill)

(1) Light the salamander grill — it must be hot *before* grilling commences. If using a grill of this type with a specially designed grilling plate proceed as above but remember the heat is from above.

(2) If using a grilling tray place the seasoned and oiled meat onto a lightly greased tray.

(3) Grill the items as quickly as possible until evenly coloured, turn them over and cook until coloured. Reduce the heat by lowering the grill rack and continue cooking until the item is cooked to the desired degree.

Notes

(1) A tray containing oil may be used to pass the raw meat through. Ensure that all excess oil is drained off as drips will easily catch fire on an open type of grill.

(2) In trade practice where an authentic grill is not installed, a salamander grill is used. It is common practice to sear the food on both sides in a criss-cross pattern using a red hot poker before placing it under the salamander.

(3) If grilling chicken coated with breadcrumbs the chicken is grilled first, sprinkled with breadcrumbs and melted butter and placed under a salamander grill or put in a hot oven to colour.

(4) Skewered items such as Kebabs (7.229) are usually marinated in oil and seasoning before being grilled. They must be turned continuously to ensure even cooking and prevent burning as they are generally small in diameter.

(5) Kidneys need to be skinned, cut through lengthways and opened. A small incision should then be made in the centre part with a knife and a skewer passed through both sides to keep the kidney open.

(6) Meat, once grilled, should be served at once as it dries out very quickly and so is not suitable for holding for any length of time.

(7) It is general practice to brush the surface of the main grilled item with melted butter when it is served to enhance its flavour and to give a shine to the product.

(8) It is usual practice to place a slice of Parsley Butter (3.51) on the surface of the main item to enhance its appearance and improve flavour. This must be done at the last possible moment or the butter will melt. Some chefs serve parsley butter separately in a sauceboat with a little ice to prevent melting.

Possible problem	*Possible cause and solution*
(1) Meat is dry and lacks flavour	— during cooking the meat was not brushed with melted fat; care must be taken to follow the correct procedure whilst grilling to avoid this problem which cannot be rectified.
	— meat was overcooked; care must be taken to cook the meat for the correct length of time to avoid this problem which cannot be rectified.
	— meat was held for too long before service; care must be taken to grill the meat as close to the time it is required as possible to avoid this problem which cannot be rectified.
	— a previously grilled item was reheated; grilled meat is not suitable for retention and reheating — the meat should be prepared and cooked as close as possible to the time it is required to avoid this problem.
(2) Meat has distorted during cooking	— poor quality meat was used; care must be taken to purchase the best quality items for grilling as low quality meat gives rise to problems which cannot be rectified.
	— meat was not properly butchered; care must be taken when preparing the meat as problems arising at this stage cannot be rectified.
	— meat was overcooked; care must be taken to cook the meat for the correct length of time to avoid this problem which cannot be rectified.
	— meat was held for too long before service; care must be taken to grill the meat as close to the time it is required as possible to avoid this problem which cannot be rectified.

Bacon

7.218 GRILLED BACON

Bacon may be grilled on an open grill but care must be taken over fat falling into the fire and catching alight. The usual procedure is to remove the rind from the bacon and arrange the rashers slightly overlapping on a tray. They are then grilled under a salamander grill, the rashers all being turned together as they become lightly crisp on one side.

7.219 GRILLED GAMMON

Proceed as for Grilled Sirloin Steak with Parsley Butter (7.220).

Beef

Terms used to denote or describe the degree to which steaks are cooked are as follows:

Au bleu — underdone or rare
Saignant — underdone
A point — medium
Bien cuit — well done

7.220 GRILLED SIRLOIN STEAK WITH PARSLEY BUTTER — ENTRECOTE VERT-PRE

Makes: 10 portions. Cooking time: 8–10 minutes.

Quantity	*Ingredient*	
10 × 200 g	Prepared Sirloin Steaks (7.26)	
2 dl	oil	
	seasoning	
250 g	Straw Potatoes (*see* p.476)	garnish
100 g	Parsley Butter (3.51)	garnish
2 bunches	picked watercress	garnish

Method

(1) Grill the steaks as in 7.217.

(2) Serve neatly arranged on an oval flat dish. Garnish with the straw potatoes and watercress and serve the parsley butter separately in a sauceboat on a little crushed ice.

7.221 ENTRECOTES TYROLIENNE

Grill the steaks as in 7.217. Place a garnish around the steaks of 200 g Shallow Fried Onions (8.158) and 200 g cooked Tomato Concassée (8.169).

Chicken

7.222 GRILLED SPRING CHICKEN — POUSSIN GRILLE

Makes: 10 portions. Cooking time: 20–25 minutes.

Quantity	*Ingredient*	
10 × 400 g	spring chicken prepared for grilling (7.79)	
2 dl	oil	
	seasoning	
250 g	Straw Potatoes (*see* p.476)	garnish
100 g	Parsley Butter (3.51)	garnish
2 bunches	picked watercress	garnish

Method

(1) Grill the spring chicken as in 7.217. When almost cooked remove the rib bones and breast bone from the inside of the chicken.

(2) Serve neatly arranged on a flat oval dish. Garnish with the straw potatoes and watercress and serve the parsley butter separately in a sauceboat on a little crushed ice.

7.223 GRILLED CHICKEN WITH DEVILLED SAUCE — POULET GRILLE SAUCE DIABLE

Cooking time: 45 minutes.

Proceed as for Grilled Spring Chicken (7.222). Serve a sauceboat of Devilled Sauce (3.28) separately.

7.224 GRILLED CHICKEN AMERICAN STYLE — POULET GRILLE AMERICAINE

Proceed as for Grilled Spring Chicken (7.222). Garnish with Grilled Tomatoes (8.171) and Grilled Mushrooms (8.170) in addition to the straw potatoes, parsley butter, and picked watercress. Serve a sauceboat of Devilled Sauce (3.28) separately.

7.225 GRILLED DEVILLED SPRING CHICKEN — POUSSIN GRILLE DIABLE

Proceed as for Grilled Spring Chicken (7.222). When cooked and the rib and breast bones have been removed, brush the inside of the chicken with diluted English mustard. Sprinkle with 150 g white breadcrumbs and 100 g melted butter and place under a salamander grill until golden. Serve a sauceboat of Devilled Sauce (3.28) separately, in addition to the garnish of straw potatoes and watercress.

7.226 BROCHETTE DE FOIES DE VOLAILLE

Makes: 10 portions. Cooking time: 10 minutes.

Quantity	*Ingredient*
1 kg	chicken livers (gall bladder removed, cut in halves and trimmed)
	seasoning
½ dl	oil
250 g	streaky bacon ½ cm thick cut into 3 cm squares
40	grilling mushrooms shallow fried until almost cooked
75 g	white breadcrumbs
½ dl	melted butter
2 bunches	picked watercress

Method

(1) Heat a thick bottomed pan and add the oil to a depth of not more than 5 mm.

(2) Season and add the liver pieces. Quickly shallow fry them, keeping them on the underdone side. Drain in a colander.

(3) Arrange the pieces of chicken livers, bacon and mushrooms on a skewer in that order, each skewer containing sufficient for one portion.

(4) Grill the skewered items until light golden in colour.

(5) Arrange on a shallow grilling tray, sprinkle with breadcrumbs and melted butter and place under a salamander grill until the breadcrumbs are golden.

(6) Serve on a flat oval dish garnished with watercress.

Lamb

7.227 *GRILLED LAMB CUTLET WITH PARSLEY BUTTER — COTELETTE D'AGNEAU GRILLEE VERT-PRE*

Makes: 10 portions. Cooking time: 8–10 minutes.

Quantity	*Ingredient*
20 × 100 g	Prepared Lamb Cutlets (7.42)
2 dl	oil
	seasoning
250 g	Straw Potatoes (*see* p. 476)
100 g	Parsley Butter (3.51)
2 bunches	picked watercress

Method

(1) Grill the cutlets as in 7.217.

(2) Serve the cutlets neatly arranged in criss-cross fashion with the eyes of the cutlets pointing in the same direction. Garnish with the straw potatoes and watercress. Serve the parsley butter separately in a sauceboat on a little crushed ice.

Note

Some establishments prefer cutlets to be served on round flat dishes since the shape of the cutlets lend themselves more easily to a round dish for presentation. Cutlet frills may also form part of the presentation.

Assessment of the completed dish

The cutlets should be evenly coloured light golden with clear sear marks criss-crossed on the eye. They should be correctly trimmed, moist on the outside and moist and pink inside.

7.228 MIXED GRILL

Makes: 10 portions. Cooking time: *See* Table 20.

Quantity	Ingredient
10 × 100 g	Grilled Lamb Cutlets (7.227)
10	Grilled Lambs' Kidneys (7.230)
10	Grilled Chipolata Sausages (7.232)
10	Grilled Mushrooms (8.170)
10	Grilled Tomatoes (8.171)
10	Grilled Rashers of Bacon (7.218)
250 g	Straw Potatoes (*see* p. 476)
100 g	Parsley Butter (3.51)
2 bunches	picked watercress

Method

Neatly arrange all the grilled items on an oval flat dish with a small piece of parsley butter in the centre of each kidney. Garnish with the straw potatoes and watercress.

Notes

(1) Items listed under ingredients are intended as an indication of the types of meats used when serving mixed grills. Small pieces of grilled steak may also feature as may small pieces of liver.

(2) As each item to be grilled requires a different cooking time care must be taken when planning the cooking in order to avoid deterioration of any one item.

7.229 KEBABS — KEBABS D'AGNEAU

Makes: 10 portions. Cooking time: 5–8 minutes.

Quantity	Ingredient
1½ kg	Prepared Fillets of Lamb (7.35) cut into 1 cm thick slices on a slant
2	juice of lemons
	seasoning
1 dl	oil
pinch	powdered thyme
30	bayleaves
250 g	onions cut into 2 cm square pieces
500 g	Savoury Rice (5.54)
5 dl	Jus Lié (3.8)

Method

(1) Place the pieces of lamb in a tray. Add the lemon juice, seasoning, oil, thyme, bayleaves and onions and allow to marinade for 2–3 hours.

(2) Arrange the pieces of lamb, bayleaves and onion on a

skewer in that order, each skewer containing sufficient for one portion.

(3) Grill the kebabs as in 7.217.

(4) Neatly arrange the kebabs on a bed of savoury rice on an entrée type dish, leaving the skewers in place.

(5) Serve the sauce separately.

7.230 GRILLED LAMBS' KIDNEYS — ROGNONS GRILLES

Makes: 10 portions. Cooking time: 5–8 minutes.

Quantity	*Ingredient*	
20	Prepared and Skewered Kidneys (*see* p. 345 stage 5)	
2 dl	oil	
	seasoning	
250 g	Straw Potatoes (*see* p. 476)	garnish
100 g	Parsley Butter (3.51)	garnish
2 bunches	picked watercress	garnish

Method

(1) Grill the skewered kidneys as in 7.217 keeping them slightly underdone.

(2) Remove the skewers and neatly arrange the kidneys on a flat oval dish. Place a piece of parsley butter in the centre of each kidney. Garnish with the straw potatoes and watercress and serve the remainder of the parsley butter in a sauceboat with a little crushed ice.

Pork

7.231 GRILLED PORK CHOPS WITH PARSLEY BUTTER — COTES DE PORC GRILLEES VERT-PRE

Proceed as for Grilled Lamb Cutlets with Parsley Butter (7.227).

Sausages

7.232 SAUSAGES AND CHIPOLATA SAUSAGES

Method

(1) Prick the sausages with a fork and arrange them on a slightly greased tray which will not buckle when placed under the grill. Do not place the sausages too closely together.

(2) Place them under the salamander grill at a moderate heat. Turn them with a palate knife as they begin to colour to ensure even coloration on all sides until cooked.

(3) When cooked drain off immediately all excess fat in a colander and place them on a warm tray. Retain in a hot cupboard or bain-marie.

Notes

(1) Sausages to be grilled on an open grill may be blanched first in water, drained and dried and then grilled.

(2) Once slightly coloured on all sides under the salamander grill they may be transferred to a moderately hot oven to complete their cooking.

(3) Sausages may also be shallow fried very gently in a little fat. They should be pricked first and turned as they colour with a palette knife.

Veal

7.233 GRILLED VEAL CUTLETS WITH PARSLEY BUTTER — COTES DE VEAU GRILLEES VERT-PRE

Proceed as for Grilled Lamb Cutlets with Parsley Butter (7.227).

BAKING

Baking is in general terms the application of dry heat in an oven, moisture coming only from the item being cooked. Meat itself is rarely baked but is encased in pastry to make a pie as in steak and kidney pie and chicken pie.

Meat pies

There are two main methods of making pies — with raw filling or with a cooked filling. The simplest type of pie is made by placing the pre-cooked filling in a pie dish and covering with short or puff paste. Savoury meat pies made from raw meat require puff pastry as this stands up better to prolonged cooking than other pastes.

Pies may also be made with pre-cooked meat enclosed between two layers of pastry, the bottom one being made of short paste and the top either of puff or short paste. The filling for pies made in this way must be rather thick and not contain too much sauce or else the bottom crust will become soggy. Gravy may be served with this kind of pie, but not with single crust pies as the filling will contain sufficient gravy itself.

Simple fillings may be made by plain boiling diced meat with onions and seasoning and thickening it with either a mixture of flour and water (known as a jazey) or diluted cornflour or arrowroot. An alternative method is to cook the meat as for Brown Stewed Meat (Ragoût of Beef) (*see* 7.145) before turning it into a pie dish.

NOTE

In order to distinguish a savoury pie from a fruit pie it is general practice to eggwash and decorate the former and to leave the latter plain. (Sometimes fruit pies are also sprinkled with sugar before cooking which caramelises when cooked.) The decoration of a meat pie is usually in the form of leaves and a small hole is made in the centre of the pie to allow the steam to escape thus preventing the pastry topping from becoming soggy.

7.234 MEAT PIES

Quantity	*Ingredient*
	prepared filling (*see* 7.235–236)
650 g	Puff Paste (10.43)
2	eggs (eggwash)

Method

(1) Divide the cold filling into the required number of pie dishes.

(2) Line the edge of the pie dish with a strip of puff paste 3 mm in thickness and lightly eggwash.

(3) Cover with a sheet of puff paste 3 mm thick. Seal firmly and crimp the edges.

(4) Trim around the edges to remove excess paste holding the knife at an angle of 45° from underneath the dish. Decorate with leaves of paste. Make a small hole in the centre to allow steam to escape.

(5) Allow to rest for as long as possible (approximately 1 hour).

(6) Lightly eggwash the surface.

(7) Place in the oven standing on a baking sheet until lightly brown in colour. Reduce the temperature of the oven and cover the pie paste with foil to prevent burning. Cook until ready.

(8) Remove from the oven, clean round the edges of the dish, place on an underdish lined with a dish paper and place a pie collar around the pie.

Note

See individual recipes for appropriate cooking times.

7.235 STEAK PIE (FILLING COOKED FROM RAW)

Makes: 10 portions. Cooking time: 3 hours. Oven temperature: 200 °C to seal then reduce to 150 °C.

Quantity	*Ingredient*
1 kg	stewing steak cut into cubes about 2½ cm
400 g	ox kidney cut into small cubes
250 g	sliced or quartered button mushrooms
250 g	sliced or chopped onion
½ l	brown stock or water

Quantity	*Ingredient*	
5 g	chopped parsley	
few drops	Worcester sauce	
	seasoning	
650 g	Puff Paste (10.43)	pie covering
2	eggs (eggwash)	pie covering

Method

(1) Combine all the ingredients in a basin and mix together.
(2) Divide into pie dishes of the required size.
(3) Proceed as in 7.234.

Note

The most effective way to test if this type of filling is cooked is to gently release the pastry from the dish with a small knife, carefully lift it and remove a sample piece of meat. This can then be squeezed between the fingers or eaten to see if it is cooked.

7.236 STEAK PIE (PRE-COOKED FILLING)

Makes: 10 portions. Cooking time: Filling: 1½ hours.
Pie: ¾ hour.
Oven temperature: 200 °C to seal then reduce to 150 °C.

Quantity	*Ingredient*	
1 kg	stewing steak cut into cubes about 2½ cm	
400 g	ox kidney cut into small cubes	
250 g	sliced or quartered button mushrooms	
250 g	sliced or chopped onion	
2 l	water	
	seasoning	
100 g	flour or arrowroot diluted in 3 dl cold water	
5 g	chopped parsley	
few drops	Worcester sauce	
650 g	Puff Paste (10.43)	pie covering
2	eggs (eggwash)	pie covering

Method

(1) Place the meat and kidney into a deep sided pan and cover with cold water. Bring to the boil and skim.

(2) Add the mushrooms, onions and seasoning. Reboil and skim.

(3) Lightly thicken with either flour or arrowroot diluted in cold water.

(4) Continue to simmer and skim throughout until cooked; add chopped parsley.

(5) Finish with a few drops of Worcester sauce and season to taste. The thickness of the liquid should enable it to just coat the meats.

(6) Turn into a tray, preferably not too deep, so that any fat that comes to the surface and solidifies can be removed before the filling is divided up into suitable dishes.

(7) Cover with puff paste and bake as described in 7.234.

Notes

(1) The filling should always be cold when covered with the paste.

(2) It is not necessary to colour the liquid with gravy browning as it should resemble as much as possible that of a pie cooked with a raw meat filling rather than a brown stew.

(3) It should not be too thick in consistency when compared with a brown stew.

(4) The pie dishes should be placed on a baking sheet for easier handling as some seepage of the liquid is unavoidable.

Service

All cooking stains should be removed from the pie dish which should be presented with a pie frill around the dish and standing on a dish paper on an oval underdish.

Assessment of the completed pie

(1) The pastry should be an even golden colour and the decoration should be clearly visible. Before serving, however, the pie crust may be divided into portions.

(2) When the pastry is lifted it should be light, flaky and moist underneath but not soggy. When eaten it should not leave a greasy taste in the mouth but have a flavour influenced by the meat filling.

(3) The filling should be hot and all the ingredients tender and moist. The kidney and mushrooms should be firm yet soft when eaten.

(4) The liquid should be clear with the full flavour of all the ingredients. No single flavour should predominate.

(5) The liquid should not be fatty, but a little fat on the meat is acceptable.

(6) The seasoning should be quite prominent and enhanced by the addition of a few drops of Worcester sauce.

7.237 CHICKEN PIE

Makes: 12 portions. Cooking time: 1½ hours. Oven temperature: 200 °C to seal then reduce to 150 °C.

Quantity	*Ingredient*
3 × 1½ kg	jointed Chicken (7.78) or boned and cut into 2 cm dice
12	rashers of bacon

Quantity	*Ingredient*	
250 g	sliced button mushrooms	
150 g	chopped onion	
½ l	white stock	
5 g	chopped parsley	
few drops	Worcester sauce	
	seasoning	
650 g	Puff Paste (10.43)	pie covering
2	eggs (eggwash)	pie covering

Method

(1) Wrap the chicken pieces in bacon and place into pie dishes of the required size.

(2) Add the remainder of the ingredients.

(3) Proceed as in 7.234.

Note

Cold chicken pie is made as described above with the addition of 25 g (10) soaked leaves of leaf gelatine.

Other baked meat dishes

7.238 BREAST OF CHICKEN IN PUFF PASTRY

Makes: 10 portions. Cooking time: 40 minutes. Oven temperature: 200 °C to seal then reduce to 150 °C.

Quantity	*Ingredient*
10 × 120 g	Suprêmes of Chickens (7.77)
200 g	Duxelle of Mushrooms (8.167)
1½ kg	Puff Paste (10.43)
2	eggs (eggwash)
	seasoning
	sprigs of parsley

Method

(1) Stuff the suprême of chicken with the filling from the underside and season (*see* 7.215).

(2) Reform into an oval shape.

(3) Roll out the pastry 3 mm thick and cut into strips 15 mm wide and 30 cm in length.

(4) Wrap the suprêmes in the strips of paste, spiralling and just overlapping the paste from the pointed end to the bone.

(5) Eggwash then allow to rest for as long as possible (approximately 1 hour).

(6) Bake in the oven until cooked.

(7) Serve on a flat oval dish with a dish paper garnished with the sprigs of parsley.

Notes

(1) To test if cooked insert a trussing needle. When cooked the needle should penetrate without undue pressure and the juices released should be clear.

(2) 50 g Pâté Maison (2.36) may be added to the duxelle of mushroom.

7.239 FILLET OF BEEF WELLINGTON — FILET DE BOEUF WELLINGTON

Makes: 10 portions. Cooking time: 30 minutes. Oven temperature: 200 °C to seal during first 10 minutes then reduced to 150 °C.

Quantity	*Ingredient*
1 kg	Prepared Fillet of Beef (7.8)
2 dl	oil
	seasoning
500 g	Duxelle of Mushrooms (8.167)
1½ kg	Puff Paste (10.43)
2	eggs (eggwash)

Method

(1) Heat the oil in a shallow sided saucepan, preferably a frying pan.

(2) Add the seasoned fillet and fry until a light golden brown on all sides. Remove from the pan and allow to cool and drain by standing on a wire grid. (Allow to cool completely before further handling.)

(3) Roll out the paste 3 mm thick, a little longer than the fillet to allow for sealing the ends and wide enough to surround the fillet with a little overlap for sealing.

(4) Place some of the mushroom duxelle in the centre of the paste. Place the fillet on the filling and cover the surface area of the beef with the remainder of the filling.

(5) Surround the meat with the paste, overlapping the top at least 1 cm. Eggwash and seal. Seal the ends in a similar fashion. (Generally the end pieces are discarded when serving.)

(6) Place on a baking sheet which has been greased or sprinkled with water.

(7) The presentation surface may be decorated with leaves of pastry but this is unnecessary if the dish is to be cut up into portions for serving.

(8) Allow the paste to rest for as long as possible (approximately 1 hour).

(9) Bake in the oven until cooked.

(10) Remove from the oven, allow to settle for a few moments

before cutting and serving. Serve on a shallow sided earthenware or silver or stainless steel dish accompanied with an appropriate sauce.

Notes

(1) This dish may be served with a Madeira Sauce (3.30) or any similar sauce.

(2) The dish may be presented whole or cut into portions. The portioning must be left to the last moment.

(3) This dish is generally produced in multiples of two to six portions.

(4) Pâté may also be added to the duxelle of mushrooms. Ideally foie gras would be used in place of pâté but costs prevent this in all but the most expensive establishments.

(5) The meat should be medium cooked, that is pink in the centre. However, it is impossible to see or feel the meat so a meat thermometer should be used (the temperature at the centre of the meat should be 65 °C). Only the very experienced should rely on the length of time the dish has cooked.

Assessment of the completed dish

(1) The pastry should be an even golden colour as for pies (*see* p. 355).

(2) The meat should be medium cooked, moist, tender and fresh looking when sliced and evenly surrounded with the filling.

(3) Where the pastry has come into contact with the filling and meat it should not be wet and soggy.

7.240 TOAD-IN-THE-HOLE

Makes: 10 portions. Cooking time: 45 minutes. Oven temperature: 220 °C.

Quantity	*Ingredient*
1 kg (20)	beef sausages
2 dl	dripping
8 dl	Yorkshire Pudding Batter (7.86)
6 dl	Jus Lié (3.8)

Method

(1) Heat the dripping in a shallow roasting dish or tray. Add the sausages and shallow fry until lightly golden on all sides.

(2) Arrange the sausages in the tray and pour in the batter mixture.

(3) Place in the oven to bake until the sausages are cooked and the batter is crisp and golden.

(4) Cut into portion sizes. Neatly arrange on an entrée type dish and serve accompanied by the sauce.

BOILING

This method of cooking should be carried out by simmering rather than boiling. It is a method generally applied to joints of meat and whole chicken. Cold savoury mousses are made from previously boiled meats, ham and chicken. Hot savoury mousses, mousselines and quenelles are made from the raw flesh of chicken poached in a white stock and are therefore also included in this section.

Table 21 gives an indication of the joints of meat, poultry and offal which may be boiled. It might be thought that only a limited range of dishes may be made by boiling meat but it should be remembered that all listed items may be served both hot and cold and that they form the basis of many other dishes. The whole range is in fact extensive.

TABLE 21. ITEMS OF MEAT, POULTRY AND OFFAL SUITABLE FOR BOILING

Beef	*Chicken*	*Lamb and mutton*	*Pork*	*Veal*
Brisket* Flat rib Ox tongue* Silverside* Thin flank	Young fattened fowl Boiling fowl	Leg	Leg Gammon	Calf's head, cheek, tongue and brain

*These may be used either fresh or pickled.

Points to remember

(a) Where the item is cooked with the specific intention of serving it cold the quality, flavour and moistness will be greatly enhanced if the meat is allowed to cool in the liquid in which it has been cooked.

(b) If there is a high humidity in the kitchen area where they are cooled there may be a danger of the liquid in which the item is kept becoming sour. Adding a small quantity of cold water will help to reduce the temperature of the liquid thereby keeping it sound.

(c) Pickled items such as ox tongue and silverside should be soaked in cold water for a period of 12 hours before cooking. They should not be cooked in the water in which they have been soaked.

(d) All items should be brought to the boil in cold liquid. Calf's head and tongue are exceptions which should be cooked in a boiling blanc preparation.

(e) Where fresh root vegetables form part of the main garnish, they should be boiled in the cooking liquid with the meat they are to accompany. For large quantities they may be cooked quite separate in some of the liquid from the boiled meat.

(f) All hot cooked meats once carved should be brought back to the temperature they are to be served at in the liquid in which they were cooked, but should not be allowed to boil as the slices may become distorted in shape.

(g) Skin from tongue and ham is more easily removed while it is still warm and moist. This avoids the possibility of its tearing.

(h) Stock that accompanies the meat should be passed through a cloth after sediment has been allowed to sink to the bottom of the pan.

Boiled meat and offal

7.241 BOILED BEEF FRENCH STYLE — BOEUF BOUILLI A LA FRANCAISE

Makes: 10 portions. Cooking time: 2½–3 hours.

Quantity	*Ingredient*	
1½ kg	Prepared Thick Flank (7.12) or Brisket (7.16)	
12	peppercorns	tied in a muslin
1	bayleaf	tied in a muslin
1 sprig	thyme	tied in a muslin
4	cloves	tied in a muslin
4	juniper berries	tied in a muslin
250 g	carrots (barrel shaped)	
200 g	turnips (barrel shaped)	
250 g	button onions	
5	leeks	tied in bundles
2	celery	tied in bundles
½ kg	cabbage, tied	
	salt	
	gherkins	accompaniments
	sea salt or coarse salt	accompaniments
	French mustard	accompaniments

Method

(1) Place the meat into a deep sided saucepan and cover with cold water. Bring to the boil and skim thoroughly.

(2) Add the bag of herbs and salt and gently simmer for approximately 2 hours.

(3) Add the vegetables in the order that they take to be cooked: first the celery, button onions, leeks, cabbage and turnips.

(4) When cooked transfer the meat to one saucepan and the

vegetables to another with some of the cooking liquid. Discard the muslin bag of herbs.

(5) Carve the meat into slices 3–4 mm thick across the grain at an angle of 45°.

(6) Neatly arrange the slices on a flat oval type dish and garnish with the vegetables. Moisten with some of the strained cooking liquor.

(7) Serve with the accompaniments of gherkins, coarse salt and French mustard.

Note

To test if cooked *see* 7.244.

7.242 BOILED LEG OF MUTTON — GIGOT DE MOUTON BOUILLI

Makes: 10 portions. Cooking time: 2½–3 hours.

Quantity	*Ingredient*
1½ kg	Prepared Leg of Mutton (7.28)
250 g	small whole carrots
1	onion studded with a bayleaf and clove
1	bouquet garni
	seasoning
6 dl	Caper Sauce (3.22)

Method

(1) Place the meat into a deep sided saucepan and cover with cold water. Bring to the boil and skim thoroughly.

(2) Add the studded onion, whole carrots and bouquet garni. Add the seasoning and gently simmer for the prescribed time.

(3) Carve the meat into slices and neatly arrange on a flat oval type dish moistened with some of the strained cooking liquid. Serve the caper sauce separately.

Note

To test if cooked *see* 7.244.

7.243 BOILED GAMMON

Makes: 6 kg. Cooking time: 3 hours

Quantity	*Ingredient*
6 kg	Prepared Gammon (7.53)

Method

(1) Soak the gammon in cold water for 12 hours. Pour off the liquid it has been soaked in and wash the gammon in fresh cold water.

(2) Place the gammon into a deep sided saucepan and cover with cold water. Bring to the boil and skim thoroughly. Gently simmer for the prescribed time.

(3) When cooked, retain the gammon in the liquid until the liquid is cold and leave for 12 hours (*see* p. 359). However, if the gammon is to be served hot it may be used immediately.

To test if cooked

If the gammon has been simmered continuously for the correct length of time it should be cooked. When the joint is cooked the mustard bone can be easily and cleanly removed and the meat can be pierced with a needle at its thickest point without using pressure.

Notes

(1) Examples of dishes using gammon are given in the braised meat section on p. 290.

(2) It may be served boiled with Pease Pudding (8.182), in which case it is sliced and served with some of the cooking liquid and garnished with the pease pudding.

7.244 BOILED SILVERSIDE WITH VEGETABLES AND DUMPLINGS

Makes: 10 portions. Cooking time: 3 hours.

Quantity	*Ingredient*
1½ kg	salted silverside of beef
1	onion studded with a bayleaf and clove
1	bouquet garni
400 g	carrots (barrel shaped)
300 g	button onions
300 g	turnips (barrel shaped)
500 g	Suet Paste (10.44) for dumplings

Method

(1) Soak the pickled meat by standing it under cold running water for 2–3 hours.

(2) Place the meat into a deep sided saucepan and cover with cold water. Bring to the boil and skim thoroughly.

(3) Add the studded onion and bouquet garni and gently simmer for approximately 2 hours.

(4) Add the vegetables in the order they take to be cooked: first the button onions followed by the carrots and then the turnips.

(5) When cooked transfer the meat to one saucepan and the vegetables to another with some of the cooking liquid. Discard the bouquet garni and studded onion. Retain and keep them warm.

(6) Divide the suet paste into 20 small pieces and mould them into round balls. Place into a shallow sided saucepan with some of the cooking liquor whilst it is gently simmering. Allow to cook for approximately 15–20 minutes.

(7) Carve the meat into slices 3–4 mm thick across the grain at an angle of 45°.

(8) Neatly arrange the slices on a flat oval type dish and garnish with the vegetables and dumplings. Moisten with some of the strained cooking liquid.

Note

To test if cooked pierce the meat with a trussing needle or skewer. If it penetrates the meat without having to use pressure the meat is cooked.

Assessment of the completed dish

(1) The meat should be evenly carved both in thickness and size. It should be pickled right through to the centre and have a characteristic reddish colour. The slices should just overlap and be surrounded with alternating bouquets of vegetables and dumplings. Some of the clear cooking liquid should be put in the dish to fill it just below the level of the meat.

(2) The meat should be moist and tender and full of flavour. It should be carved across the grain.

(3) The vegetables should be a suitable size in relation to the other commodities. They should be just cooked, of an even size and neat shape.

(4) The dumplings should be a suitable size in relation to the other commodities. They should be soft on the outside, slightly fluffy yet have a firm texture on the inside.

(5) The liquid should be clear and free from fat or other impurities.

7.245 CALF'S HEAD ENGLISH STYLE — TETE DE VEAU A L'ANGLAISE

Makes: 4 portions. Cooking time: 1½ hours.

Quantity	*Ingredient*
1	Prepared Calf's Head (7.65)
5 l	Blanc Preparation (8.119)
1	whole carrot
1	small whole onion
1	bouquet garni
1 l	Court-bouillon (6.27)
	sprigs of parsley

Method

(1) Bring the blanc to the boil with the carrot, onion and bouquet garni. Place in the head pieces and tongue, cover with a damp cloth and gently simmer for the prescribed time until cooked.

(2) Place the brain into the court-bouillon. Bring to the boil and gently simmer for 5 minutes.

(3) Neatly arrange in an earthenware dish with an underdish and dish paper. Garnish with sprigs of parsley.

To test if cooked

(1) Remove a sample from the liquid and squeeze it gently between the fingers. When cooked it will feel soft and yield easily.

(2) Pierce the tongue with a needle. When cooked it will penetrate very easily and the juices extracted will be clear.

(3) The brain will feel rather firm to the touch as it stiffens when cooked.

Assessment of the completed dish

(1) The tongue should be sliced and the slices arranged lengthways slightly overlapping in the shape of a fan at one end of the dish. In the centre of the dish the pieces of cheek should be placed in a small neat pile with the skin side showing.

(2) The slices of brain should be placed so as to balance the visual appearance of the dish and the whole dish should be lightly coated with some of the cooking liquid.

(3) The brain should be soft yet firmly set.

(4) The cheek flesh should be very white, soft textured and rather gluey and moist.

(5) The tongue should be reddish brown in colour, moist and tender.

Boiled chicken

When chicken is cooked by boiling it is generally referred to as being poached. This is a more acceptable term as it implies cooking by gentle boiling.

Poached chicken may be served as a chicken dish in its own right (*see* below), as a cold item or used in the preparation of many other dishes, e.g. pancakes, vols-au-vent and cold chicken mousse.

7.246 POACHED CHICKEN — POULET POCHE

Makes: 12 portions. Cooking time: 1 hour.

Quantity	*Ingredient*
3 × 1½ kg	prepared young fowl (*see* Table 9)
1 kg	small whole carrots
½ kg	whole small onions
1	celery
2	leeks
1	bayleaf
	salt

Method

(1) Place the chicken in a deep sided saucepan and cover with cold water. Bring to the boil and skim thoroughly.

(2) Add the remainder of the ingredients and gently simmer for the prescribed time, skimming continuously throughout.

(3) When cooked, if required for cold dishes retain in the strained liquid until cold (*see* p. 359).

7.247 POACHED CHICKEN WITH SUPREME SAUCE — POULET POCHE AU RIZ SAUCE SUPREME

Makes: 12 portions. Cooking time: 1½ hours.

Quantity	*Ingredient*
3 × 1½ kg	Poached Young Fowl (*see* 7.246)
6 dl	Sauce Suprême (3.23)
600 g	Savoury Rice (5.54)

Method

(1) Remove the string and skin from the chickens and carve into portions.

(2) Neatly arrange the chicken in an entrée type dish and coat with the sauce. Serve accompanied by a dish of savoury rice.

Notes

(1) Once carved the chicken may be held in a shallow sided receptacle covered with some of the strained cooking liquid and retained in a hotplate or bain-marie.

(2) The chicken may be served whole in which case the string and skin is removed and the chicken coated with the sauce. The rice is served separately.

(3) The chicken may be carved and served neatly arranged on the rice and before being coated with the sauce.

(4) A reduction of some of the cooking liquid together with button mushroom trimmings and a piece of celery added to the sauce will enhance its flavour.

(5) *See* pp. 45–6 for an analysis of the problems associated with veloutés.

Assessment of the completed dish

(1) The leg and thigh portions should be neatly concealed under the wing and the breast portions should follow the general shape of the dish.

(2) Each piece of chicken should be coated with some of the sauce with only the outline discernible.

(3) No part of the meat should be exposed. It should be covered with the sauce.

(4) The skin of the chicken should always be removed when serving.

(5) The chicken wings should be free from bone with the exception of the wing bone joint and extending bone which should be cut off at an angle. All excess pieces of chicken should be removed leaving a full shaped wing with all the gristle removed from underneath.

(6) The breast should be carved into two identically shaped pieces.

(7) The thigh and drumstick should have the bone and tendons removed and be reshaped.

(8) The sauce should be a rich ivory colour with an apparent sheen. It should be thick enough to coat the chicken without masking its shape. It should be smooth and velvety in texture and seasoned to bring out the full but delicate flavour of the chicken.

Note

See 5.54 for an analysis of savoury rice.

7.248 CHICKEN A LA KING

Makes: 10 portions. Cooking time: ½ hour.

Quantity	*Ingredient*
1 kg	Poached White of Chicken free from skin and bone (7.246)
75 g	butter
250 g	Sliced Button Mushrooms cooked in lemon juice and water (8.91)
150 g	red pimento, skinned, pipped and cut into dice
6 dl	Sauce Suprême (3.23)
600 g	Savoury Rice (5.54)

Method

(1) Cut the chicken into small pieces on the slant 3–4 mm thick.

Place into a shallow sided saucepan with the heated butter and gently reheat.

(2) Add the sliced mushrooms and diced pimento and bind with the sauce. Heat but do not boil.

(3) Serve in an entrée type dish with a border of savoury rice.

7.249 CHICKEN PANCAKES WITH MORNAY SAUCE — CREPES DE VOLAILLE MORNAY

Makes: 10 portions. Cooking time: ½ hour.

Quantity	*Ingredient*
750 g	Poached Chicken free from skin and bone (7.246)
4 dl	Sauce Suprême (3.23)
20	Savoury Pancakes (10.1)
6 dl	Mornay Sauce (3.15)
50 g	grated Parmesan cheese
50 g	melted butter

Method

(1) Cut the chicken into small dice and combine with the sauce suprême. Heat but do not boil and season to taste.

(2) Lay out the pancakes on a work surface. Evenly divide the chicken mixture onto the pancakes and roll them up, folding the ends underneath.

(3) Place a little of the sauce on the bottom of an earthenware dish and neatly arrange the pancakes with the folded ends down.

(4) Coat with the mornay sauce, sprinkle with grated cheese and melted butter and glaze in a hot oven until hot and golden.

7.250 CHICKEN VOLS-AU-VENT — VOLS-AU-VENT DE VOLAILLE

Makes: 10 portions. Cooking time: 20 minutes.

Quantity	*Ingredient*
10	cooked Vol-au-Vent Cases (10.71)
1 l	Sauce Suprême (3.23)
800 g	Poached Chicken (7.246) free from skin and bone and cut into 1 cm dice or cut into small pieces on the slant
	sprigs of picked parsley

Method

(1) Place the chicken into a shallow pan.

(2) Add sufficient sauce to combine, then gently heat to boiling point.

(3) Ensure that the ratio of sauce to chicken is correct. The

consistency should be reasonably light but sufficient to coat the chicken. Season to taste.

(4) Serve on a flat oval dish garnished with sprigs of parsley.

Assessment of the completed dish

(1) The vol-au-vent pastry case should be straight-sided, about 8 cm in diameter with an even rise and golden coloration, and overflow with the filling. The lid of pastry taken from the centre should be replaced at a slanting angle with a little sprig of picked parsley projecting.

(2) The chicken in the filling should be cut into even sized pieces and consist mainly of white meat from the breast with a smaller amount from the legs.

(3) The sauce should be smooth, ivory white in colour with a sheen, and have a chicken flavour.

(4) The vol-au-vent cases should be full, crisp, flaky and shiny, and have a pleasant flavour of the fat used. They should not leave a film of grease around the mouth and lips.

7.251 CHICKEN AND MUSHROOM VOLS-AU-VENT — VOLS-AU-VENT DE VOLAILLE ET CHAMPIGNONS

Proceed as for 7.250 with the addition of cooked White Button Mushrooms (8.91).

7.252 VOLS-AU-VENT TOULOUSAINE

Proceed as for 7.250 with the addition of White Braised Sweetbreads (7.123).

Hot and cold savoury mousses, mousselines and quenelles (forcemeats)

Cold savoury mousses are made from a finely minced preparation of pre-cooked meat — usually ham or chicken — bound with a velouté sauce. Lightly whipped cream is added to give the texture lightness and aspic jelly is included to enable it to set in a mould. The surface is decorated with a pattern of previously cooked vegetables cut into neat shapes. For example:

Cold Chicken Mousse — Mousse de Volaille
Cold Ham Mousse — Mousse de Jambon

Hot savoury mousses are made from a finely minced preparation of poultry or game bound together with a panada. Egg whites and cream are added to give the texture lightness. Mousses are cooked in a mould in the oven, turned out when cooked and served with an appropriate garnish and sauce. For example:

Hot Chicken Mousse with Suprême Sauce — Mousse de Volaille Sauce Suprême

Mousselines and quenelles are made from the same finely minced preparation as hot savoury mousses. Mousselines are spoon moulded and poached in chicken stock in the oven. They may be served as a starter or as a main course. Quenelles are similar to mousselines but are moulded into smaller shapes using either spoons or a piping tube. Those that are piped are generally used for garnishing soups or as part of a garnish for a main course. Those that are spoon moulded may be used as a garnish or as a dish in their own right. They may be served as a starter or as a main course. For example:

Chicken Mousselines with Suprême Sauce — Mousselines de Volaille Sauce Suprême

Veal Quenelles with Suprême Sauce — Quenelles de Veau Sauce Suprême

NOTE

Forcemeats may also be made using fish such as pike or sole (*see* p. 178). Fish forcemeats may be used to stuff fillets before they are poached.

7.253 FRANGIPANE PANADA

Cooking time: 10 minutes.

Quantity	*Ingredient*
5 dl	milk
150 g	butter
8	egg yolks
250 g	flour
	seasoning of salt, pepper and nutmeg

Method

(1) Heat the milk and butter and add the seasoning.

(2) Mix the egg yolks in a basin and add the flour.

(3) Pour the hot milk onto the mixture of eggs and flour, return to the saucepan and gently cook until the preparation loosens from the bottom of the pan.

(4) Turn out onto a lightly greased tray and cool slightly before use.

Note

This preparation is used primarily to give sufficient binding power to all forcemeats (mousses, mousselines and quenelles), though it must be borne in mind that it does also lighten the colour and texture of the mixture.

7.254 COLD SAVOURY MOUSSE

Makes: 10 portions. Preparation time: 1 hour.

Quantity	*Ingredient*
500 g	cooked meat
2 dl	cool Chicken or Veal Velouté (3.5)
2 dl	melted aspic jelly
3 dl	lightly whipped cream
	salt, pepper and nutmeg
1 dl	melted aspic jelly (coating)

Method

(1) Finely mince the meat and pass through a sieve.

(2) Place the mixture in a basin and add the cool velouté and melted aspic jelly, stirring with a wooden spatule.

(3) Place the mixture on ice and continue to stir until it shows signs of beginning to set. Fold in the lightly beaten whipped cream and season to taste.

(4) Pour the setting mixture into a suitable earthenware or glass dish and place into a refrigerator to set.

(5) Decorate as desired with cooked vegetables cut into neat shapes to form a pattern. Cover with a coating of melted aspic jelly and allow to set in a refrigerator.

Note

Cold ham mousse and cold chicken mousse are made in this way. A little vegetable colouring may be added to cold ham mousse to give it more colour.

Assessment of the completed dish

(1) The mousse should be of an even fine texture and just firm enough to allow it to set.

(2) It should be of a delicate flavour; the flavour of the aspic jelly should not be allowed to predominate.

(3) Decoration should be simple and neat.

Possible problem	*Possible cause and solution*
(1) Mixture lacks flavour and is dry	— cream has been overwhipped; care must be taken to avoid this as it cannot be rectified.

Possible problem	*Possible cause and solution*
(2) Mixture curdles when the cream is added to the purée, appears broken or curdled or becomes lumpy	— cream has been overwhipped; care must be taken to avoid this as it cannot be rectified. — aspic jelly was too cold when added; ensure that the aspic jelly is warm when added or else it will set when it comes in contact with mixture giving rise to these problems which cannot be rectified.
(3) Mixture lacks volume	— aspic was too hot when added; care must be taken to avoid this as it will soften the mixture and remove the air — this cannot be rectified.

NOTE

Curdled mixture may be rectified by slowly beating it on to a little velouté or velouté and cream, but this is not always entirely successful.

7.255 HOT SAVOURY MOUSSES

Makes: 10 portions. Cooking time: 30–40 minutes. Oven temperature: 200 °C.

Quantity	*Ingredient*
500 g	raw meat with any sinew and tendons removed
200 g	Frangipane Panada (7.253)
2	egg whites
3 dl	cream
	salt, pepper and nutmeg

Method

(1) Finely mince the flesh and pass through a sieve.

(2) Mix the puréed flesh with the warm panada and egg whites in a basin, using a wooden spatule and working it hard.

(3) Allow the mixture to rest by either standing the basin containing the mixture in a refrigerator or a basin containing ice and a little water for about 30 minutes.

(4) Gradually add the cream, working it well with a spatule and season to taste.

(5) Place the mixture into buttered dariole moulds and cook, standing in a tray of hot water in the oven. When the surface begins to colour cover with a piece of kitchen foil or greaseproof paper.

(6) When cooked, allow to cool for a few moments, turn out of the moulds into a porcelain or earthenware dish.

(7) Serve on an underdish with a dish paper.

Notes

(1) When cooked the mousse should be firm to touch. Insert a trussing needle or a skewer into the centre of the mousse; if cooked, when removed it should be clean and free from any traces of soft, uncooked mixture.

(2) If the raw mixture will not absorb the cream it is because the mixture is not fine enough.

(3) If the item disintegrates during cooking it is because the mixture is not fine enough.

(4) Chicken mousse is usually served with a sauceboat of Suprême Sauce (3.23).

Extensions

7.256 HOT CHICKEN SOUFFLE SAUCE SUPREME — SOUFFLE DE VOLAILLE SAUCE SUPREME

This is made from the same preparation as Hot Mousse (7.255) made with chicken but is cooked in a porcelain mould in which it is served, accompanied by the sauce.

7.257 MOUSSELINES

Makes: 10 portions. Cooking time: 10–15 minutes. Oven temperature: 200 °C.

Quantity	*Ingredient*
	Hot Mousse Mixture (7.255)
1 l	hot white Chicken Stock (3.1)

Method

(1) Mould the mixture into 20 cigar shapes approximately 8 cm in length using two large spoons.

(2) Lightly butter a deep sided tray and place in the moulded pieces.

(3) Pour the hot stock around the mousselines, bring gently to the boil, cover with buttered greaseproof paper and poach in the oven for the prescribed time.

(4) Carefully remove the mousselines from the liquid and neatly arrange on a porcelain or earthenware dish.

(5) Serve on an underdish with a dish paper coated with a suitable sauce.

Notes

(1) Mousselines may be made from chicken, veal or fish.

(2) When cooked they should be rather firm to touch.
(3) When cooked they should be off white or ivory in colour and have a delicate flavour. The texture should be fine, firm and smooth. They should have a characteristic cigar shape.

7.258 QUENELLES

Proceed in exactly the same way as for Mousselines (7.257). Mould the mixture into small cigar shapes approximately 2 cm in length.

Notes

(1) Quenelles may be made from chicken, veal or fish.
(2) If required for a soup garnish, pipe the mixture through a small plain tube and poach in the oven as described in 7.257. When cooked they may be retained in a basin covered with the liquid in which they were cooked.
(3) When cooked they should be rather firm to the touch.

STEAMING

Although steaming may appear to be limited to such items as steamed puddings, boiled meats may also be cooked by this method. However, in many instances it must be remembered that there will be little cooking liquid to make an accompanying sauce.

NOTE
It is advisable to refer to the cookery guides supplied by the manufacturers of the equipment used for cooking times for meat dishes. Times given in this section are intended only as a general guide. Refer to Chapter 8, pp. 429–30, for further notes on steaming.

Steak and kidney pudding and variations of it may also be cooked in a pressure cooker. The ingredients are the same as for Steak Pie (7.235 or 236) except that suet paste is used instead of puff paste. The fillings may be placed raw into basins lined with the suet paste or may be pre-cooked. If the filling is pre-cooked the pudding need only be steamed for 1 hour, whereas a raw filling requires to be steamed for 3–4 hours.

7.259 STEAK AND KIDNEY PUDDING (RAW FILLING)

Makes: 10 portions. Cooking time: 3–4 hours.

Quantity	*Ingredient*
1½ kg	Steak Pie Filling (7.235 or 236)
1 kg	Suet Paste (10.44)

Method

(1) Line 3 greased medium sized pudding basins with suet paste rolled out 3 mm thick.

(2) Add the raw filling. Dampen the rim of the paste with water, place on a top layer of paste and seal it.

(3) Cover the top of the pudding with greaseproof paper and a cloth and tie with string, or cover with kitchen foil folded under the rim of the basin.

(4) Steam the pudding in the pressure steamer for the required length of time.

Note

Steamed items made with suet paste are not suitable for prolonged retention or holding before or after cooking, nor should they be reheated. Such handling has an adverse effect on the quality of the pastry.

Service

The pudding may be served whole in the basin in which it has been cooked providing it is cleaned of all cooking stains and surrounded with a clean napkin. It should be placed on a round flat dish with a dish paper.

Assessment of the completed dish

(1) The surface of the suet pastry should be white and fresh looking with no wetness caused through undercooking or incorrect sealing of the pudding. A dark pastry is an indication of prolonged cooking or holding once cooked. It should be a light aerated pastry that is tender and soft to eat.

(2) The filling should be similar to that for Baked Pie (7.235 or 236) but the different method of cooking does give a quite different result.

NOUVELLE CUISINE

The cuts of meat and types of poultry and game may all be used in this style of cooking. Most of the procedures and principles outlined in this chapter may also be used except that items are never brown braised or singed and stews are never thickened with flour. It must also be remembered that any sauce added to or accompanying any dish in the Nouvelle Cuisine style should not be roux or flour based.

7.260 *BLANQUETTE OF VEAL WITH VEGETABLES AND CREAM*

Makes: 10 portions. Cooking time: 1 hour.

Quantity	*Ingredient*
1½ kg	prepared veal (*see* Table 18) cut into 2½ cm squares
2 l	white stock (preferably veal)
100 g	carrots (leave whole)
75 g	onions (leave whole)
100 g	turnips (leave whole)
100 g	celery (leave whole)
100 g	leek (leave whole)
1	bouquet garni
2½ dl	cream (liaison)
3	egg yolks (liaison)
10	heart shaped Croûtons (7.105)
5 g	chopped chervil
	seasoning

Method

(1) Proceed as for Blanquette of Lamb (*see* 7.160) cooking with all the vegetables listed above.

(2) Remove and discard the bouquet garni, place the meat into a receptacle and keep warm.

(3) Remove the vegetables, coarsely purée them and return to the cooking liquid.

(4) Reheat, whisking the liaison into the liquid and vegetable purée, until the sauce thickens but do not allow it to boil, then add the meat. Season to taste. Serve the meat neatly arranged on appropriately sized plates with a sauce.

(5) Dip the tips of the heart shaped croûtons in some of the sauce then into the chopped chervil. Garnish the dish and serve.

7.261 *ESCALOPETTES OF BEEF AURORA*

Makes: 10 portions.

Quantity	*Ingredient*
2 kg	prepared middle cut of fillet of beef
2 dl	melted unsalted butter
150 g	sliced button mushrooms
1 dl	whisky
3 dl	chicken stock (reduced by two-thirds)
4 dl	cream
10 g	chopped chervil and parsley
	seasoning

Method

(1) Cut the prepared fillet into 20 × 75 g slices.

(2) Heat the butter in a shallow sided pan. Season the pieces of meat, place into the pan and shallow fry without colouring, keeping them undercooked.

(3) Transfer the meat to a receptacle and keep warm.

(4) Add the sliced mushrooms to the pan and cook for a few moments (do not overcook them).

(5) Drain off the surplus fat, add the whisky and flambé. Add the stock and cream. Boil and reduce to a light coating consistency.

(6) Add the herbs to the sauce and season to taste. Serve the pieces of meat on appropriately sized plates, masked with the sauce.

7.262 ESCALOPES OF VEAL ADRIENNE — ESCALOPINES DE VEAU ADRIENNE

Makes: 10 portions.

Quantity	*Ingredient*	
20 × 75 g	Prepared Small Escalopes (7.73)	
100 g	butter	
200 g	prepared red pimento (8.27)	cut into small strips
100 g	prepared green pimento (8.27)	
1 dl	whisky	
3 dl	chicken stock (reduced by two-thirds)	
4 dl	cream	
12	green peppercorns	
	seasoning	

Method

(1) Heat the butter in a shallow sided pan. Season the escalopes, place into the pan and shallow fry without colouring.

(2) When cooked, transfer them to a receptacle and keep warm.

(3) Add the strips of red and green pimento and gently cook for 2–3 minutes (do not overcook them).

(4) Drain off the fat, add the whisky and flambé. Add the chicken stock, cream and green peppercorns. Boil and reduce to a light coating consistency.

(5) Season to taste. Serve the escalopes on appropriately sized plates, masked with the sauce.

7.263 SAUTEED CHICKEN HOLLYWOOD — POULET SAUTE HOLLYWOOD

Makes: 12 portions. Cooking time: 1 hour.

Quantity	*Ingredient*
3 × 1½ kg	jointed chicken (7.78)
50 g	curry powder
	crushed sage
2 dl	melted butter
6 dl	orange juice
3	avocado pears (scooped into balls)
200 g	chicken livers
½ dl	butter
	seasoning

Method

(1) Heat the butter in a shallow sided pan.

(2) Season the chicken pieces with curry powder and crushed sage and shallow fry until golden on all sides. Cover with a lid and allow to cook rather slowly.

(3) When half cooked moisten with the orange juice, cover with a lid and continue to cook in the oven.

(4) When fully cooked season to taste. Remove the chicken pieces and neatly arrange in an earthenware dish. Pour the liquid over the chicken.

(5) Garnish with the avocado pear balls and chicken livers lightly fried in butter.

7.264 SAUTEED CHICKEN WITH SHERRY WINE VINEGAR

Makes: 10 portions. Cooking time: 1 hour. Oven temperature: 180 °C.

Quantity	*Ingredient*	
3 × 1½ kg	jointed chicken (7.78)	
2 dl	oil	
2 dl	sherry wine vinegar	
	salt and freshly ground pepper	
5 cloves	garlic	
½ l	Chicken Stock (3.1)	
½ l	double cream	
150 g	carrots	barrel shaped tossed in butter
100 g	cucumber or courgette	barrel shaped tossed in butter
20 g	butter	
	seasoning	

Method

(1) Heat the oil in a shallow sided pan.

(2) Season the chicken pieces and shallow fry until golden on all sides.

(3) Pour off the excess oil and sprinkle about half the vinegar over the chicken. Add the cloves of garlic, cover with a lid and

allow to cook rather slowly either over a very low heat or in the oven.

(4) Check the chicken every 5 to 10 minutes and sprinkle with a little more vinegar.

(5) When cooked, remove the chicken and keep them warm. Remove and discard the garlic.

(6) Add the chicken stock to the pan in which the chicken has been cooked. Boil and reduce by half.

(7) Add the cream, boil and reduce until a light coating consistency.

(8) Strain the sauce into a clean pan. Reboil and season to taste.

(9) Pour the sauce onto the centre of each plate, neatly arrange the chicken portions and garnish with the vegetables previously tossed in butter.

Notes

(1) Additional sherry wine vinegar may be added to the completed sauce if so desired.

(2) The completed sauce may be enriched by adding 50 g firm butter at the last moment.

(3) If desired the chicken may be served on a bed of savoury Braised Rice (5.54).

7.265 SAUTEED NOISETTES OF LAMB ON A BED OF LEEK PUREE WITH A SHALLOT AND ROSEMARY SAUCE

Makes: 10 portions. Cooking time: 30 minutes.

Quantity	*Ingredient*	
20 × 75 g	Noisettes of Lamb (7.40)	shallow fried
3	crushed cloves of garlic	
2 dl	oil	
	seasoning	
450 g	Prepared Leeks (8.20) thinly sliced	leek purée
200 g	unsalted butter	
1 dl	chicken stock	
	seasoning	
150 g	chopped shallots	sauce
3	crushed cloves of garlic	
1 dl	dry vermouth	
¾ l	Jus Lié (3.8) made from Veal Stock (3.1)	
25 g	rosemary leaves	
	seasoning	

Method

Leek purée

(1) Heat the butter in a shallow sided pan, add the freshly

sliced, washed and drained leek. Add the chicken stock and season. Gently cook until most of the liquid has reduced and the leeks are soft.

(2) Purée the leeks in a food processor. Remove, reheat in a clean pan and season to taste.

Sauce

(1) Place the shallots, crushed garlic and vermouth in a shallow sided saucepan. Boil and reduce by three-quarters. Add the jus lié, boil and reduce by one-third.

(2) Add the rosemary leaves and gently simmer for approximately 5 minutes. Season to taste.

Noisettes

Rub the crushed garlic into the noisettes, season and shallow fry, keeping the meat underdone.

Note

Do not overcook the leeks as they will discolour.

Service

Place a bed of leek purée in the centre of each plate and surround it with the sauce. Carve the noisettes into slices at an angle of 45° and place on top of the purée to form the shape of a flower.

7.266 SAUTEED SIRLOIN STEAK WITH CREAMED ENDIVE WITH RED WINE AND PORT SAUCE

Makes: 10 portions. Cooking time: 30 minutes.

Quantity	Ingredient	
10 × 200 g	sirloin steaks trimmed of all fat	shallow fried
2 dl	melted butter	
	seasoning	
75 g	chopped shallots	Sauce 1
1 sprig	thyme	
½ l	dry red wine	
2 dl	port	
¾ l	Jus Lié (3.8) made from veal	
25 g	arrowroot (diluted in cold water)	
	seasoning	
¼ l	double cream	Sauce 2 and garnish
150 g	Belgium endive thinly sliced across to form strands	
pinch	castor sugar	

Method

Sauce 1

Place the chopped shallots, thyme, red wine, port and jus lié into a shallow sided saucepan. Boil and reduce by half. Lightly thicken with the diluted arrowroot and simmer for a few minutes. Pass the sauce through a muslin cloth into a clean pan, reboil and season to taste. Retain in a bain-marie.

Sauce 2 and garnish

Place the cream into a shallow sided saucepan, boil and reduce until it thickens slightly. Add the sliced endive and cook for a few moments, keeping them slightly crisp. Add the castor sugar to relieve the bitterness and season to taste.

Service

Place the creamed endive in the centre of the plates and pour the red wine and port sauce around. Carve the cooked steaks into slices at an angle of 45° and neatly arrange crescent fashion around the endive.

CONVENIENCE PRODUCTS

The range of products available to the caterer in pre-packed, pre-cooked and/or frozen form is most comprehensive and to deal with even a fraction would require a separate volume. This section can only cover the very basic principles of this very important area.

Meat may be obtained either frozen, chilled, canned or dehydrated. If packaged with Cryovac it should be removed from the wrapper at least one hour before actual use so that air can circulate around the item and remove any traces of fustiness.

Frozen items

Items of meat which have been deep frozen should be allowed ample time to defrost completely before use unless they may be cooked from frozen in accordance with the manufacturers' instructions on the packaging. Once thawed, however, such items should not be re-frozen for use at later date.

A microwave oven may be used to reheat small amounts unless packaged in a foil or metal container. A forced air convection oven is ideal, especially for large numbers of frozen meals.

Once thawed, frozen items may be used in exactly the same way as fresh items for any of the dishes outlined in this chapter. In addition, extra garnishes of fresh vegetables, for example, may be used to improve the general appearance, taste and quality of many products such as tinned and boil-in-the-bag stews bought in convenience form.

Frozen uncooked poultry

Great care should be taken to avoid contamination when handling frozen poultry. Items should be stored in a deep freeze at a temperature of −18 °C and without exception should be thawed completely before cooking. Frozen poultry items should be allowed to thaw at their own rate and under no circumstances should attempts be made to accelerate the process by placing the item in cold water or under a cold running tap. Table 22 gives a guide to the length of time poultry items need for thawing.

Once thawed poultry items should not be washed. By doing so — or by trying to speed up the thawing process under water — can spread food poisoning bacteria (salmonella) over the sink, draining board and other work surfaces ready to contaminate other food.

TABLE 22. THAWING GUIDE FOR FROZEN POULTRY

Approx. weight	*Room temperature (below 12 °C)*	*Refrigerator (4–5 °C)*
2½–4 kg	20 hours	30 hours
6–7 kg	30 hours	75 hours
10–12 kg	48 hours	96 hours

Chilled foods

These are items that have been cooked in the usual way and then blast-quick chilled. They should be kept at a temperature of 3 °C and may only be stored for a maximum of five days. Reheating should be carried out in an infra-red oven rather than in a microwave, or as recommended by the manufacturers.

Canned meat

Meats such as ham, tongue, corned beef and luncheon meat are familiar to most people in canned form. Pie fillings such as stewed steak and chicken suprême are also commonly bought in cans as are foie gras and pâtés. They may be used directly from the can as recommended by the manufacturers.

AFD

Stews are generally available in accelerated freeze dried form and are reconstituted by adding water and boiling. The quality may be enhanced by adding a further garnish of appropriate fresh vegetables.

CHAPTER EIGHT

Vegetables

INTRODUCTION

Vegetables are served with or incorporated into a wide range of dishes to add interest, variety, nutritional value, colour, flavour and texture, and so contribute much to an enjoyable meal. They have a large part to play in many courses, and make good hors-d'oeuvres, are widely used in making soups, and form garnishes for fish, meat, poultry and game as well as being featured in salads. Used as a garnish for main items they may be cooked either with the dish or separately and arranged around the dish when serving. Some are used solely to add flavour to stocks, soups, sauces and stews and are discarded when they have given up their flavour and nutritional value. Several expensive vegetables such as asparagus and globe artichokes may be served as dishes in their own right, partly because they do not combine well with other items but also because they are excellent as a separate course either hot or cold.

This chapter deals first with the preparation of vegetables for cooking, including a detailed list of the shapes into which they may be cut for various culinary uses, and then proceeds through the various methods of cooking which may be applied — boiling, steaming, braising, and so on. At the beginning of each recipe there is a guide to the number of portions the quantities given will yield and the time taken to cook the vegetable. The number of portions and the cooking times indicated are intended solely as a guide and experience will yield the best results. (Where vegetables require cooking by two different methods, e.g. boiling then deep frying, then cooking time is given for the second method only.) Throughout the chapter methods of retaining the vegetables once they are cooked and how best to reheat them are also indicated. Although it is realised that specialised equipment is available to deal with these aspects, this chapter covers the traditional approaches practised in many catering establishments in the industry.

PREPARATION

The correct preparation of all vegetables cannot be overstressed. If this aspect is badly carried out food costs will rise considerably due to wastage. Further problems may be encountered at subsequent stages of cooking, for example some vegetables may fall to pieces when they are to be served whole whilst others may be completely inedible because the outer woodiness had not been removed when peeled, and invariably the visual effect of the final result will be adversely affected. A controlled and systematic approach to this aspect of cooking is essential in order that high standards of quality are maintained.

8.1 ARTICHOKE BOTTOMS — FONDS D'ARTICHAUTS

Remove the hard stem with a knife or, holding the artichoke in one hand, grasp the stem with the other and break it off (this latter method removes the fibres in the base of the artichoke). Using a sharp knife cut away all the leaves to within 1½ cm from the bottom of the vegetable. Turn the bottom upside down in the hand and remove all traces of any leaves and green, at the same time smoothing the surface with a peeler. Immediately rub all over with lemon to prevent discoloration. Remove the choke (the fibrous inside of the artichoke bottom) using a spoon. Wash in cold water and immediately place into a basin of cold water and lemon juice to prevent discoloration.

8.2 ASPARAGUS/SPRUE — ASPERGES/POINTS D'ASPERGES

Remove the small hard leaves or spurs at the head of the vegetable just below the point using the back of a small knife. Remove the outer hard skin of the stem with a peeler, peeling in a downward motion away from the point. Break off the stem at the bottom at its hardest and woodiest point. Wash in plenty of cold water. Firmly tie into portion sized bundles with string. Trim off the stems so that they are of an even length.

Note

As sprue are young shoots of asparagus there is generally no need to remove the small spurs or to peel the stems.

8.3 BABY MARROW — COURGETTE

Remove the stalk. With the aid of a peeler remove strips of the outer skin along the length of the vegetable leaving alternate strips of skin and exposed flesh. Trim each end of the vegetable to give a rounded effect. (An alternative method is to completely remove all the outer skin with a peeler, but care should be taken not to peel too deeply to expose the underlayer of light green flesh.) Wash in cold water.

8.4 BROAD BEANS — FEVES DE MARAIS

Shell the beans retaining the inner bean within its skin. Wash in cold water.

8.5 BROCCOLI SPEARS — BROCOLIS

Cut away any discoloured outer leaves and trim any excess and hard stems. Wash in cold salt water.

8.6 BRUSSELS SPROUTS — CHOUX DE BRUXELLES

Trim away any discoloured or coarse outer leaves. Cut an incision approximately 1 mm into the stem. Wash in cold salt water.

8.7 CABBAGE — CHOU

For boiling

Remove any discoloured or coarse outer leaves. Cut the cabbage into quarters and remove the centre stalks. Wash in cold salt water.

For braising

Remove any discoloured or coarse outer leaves. Cut the cabbage in half, remove the centre stalks and wash in cold salt water.

8.8 CARROTS — CAROTTES

Peel lengthwise with a peeler then cut off top and tail.

8.9 CAULIFLOWER — CHOU-FLEUR

Trim away the coarse outer leaves retaining some of the inner tender leaves surrounding the flower. With a small knife hollow out the stem in the shape of a cone to a depth of about 2 cm. Wash in cold salt water.

8.10 CELERIAC — CELERI-RAVE

Trim the end of the vegetable. Peel in a circular motion with a small knife making certain to remove the skin below the line of fibrous flesh which can be seen inside. Wash in cold water and place immediately into a basin of cold water and lemon juice to prevent discoloration.

8.11 CELERY — CELERI

Remove any outside discoloured stems. Trim and cut away leaves at the head of the vegetable. Carefully trim the root end taking care not to cut away so much of the root that the celery falls apart. Wash under cold running water.

8.12 CHESTNUTS — MARRONS

(1) Slit the shells of the nuts with the point of a small knife and place them into a frying basket.

(2) Either *(a)* dip the basket into boiling water; or *(b)* dip the basket into deep fat at a temperature of 160 °C; or *(c)* place them onto a tray under a salamander grill until the shells split open.

(3) Remove the outer shells and inner skin with the point of a small knife and retain in a basin covered with a damp cloth until required.

Note

Whilst it is appreciated that chestnuts are not vegetables they fit into this section because of the method of preparation.

8.13 CORN ON THE COB — EPIS DE MAIS

Using a small knife trim away any excess stalk, coarse outer leaves and silky fibres. Wash in cold water.

8.14 EGGPLANT — AUBERGINE

For deep frying

Remove the stalk and green part attached to it. With the aid of a peeler remove strips of the outer skin along the length of the vegetable leaving alternate strips of skin and exposed flesh. Cut into slices on the slant about ½ cm thick. Place into a colander and sprinkle with salt which draws out any excess moisture and/or bitterness.

Note

This vegetable should be prepared as close to the time of cooking as possible to prevent discoloration.

For stuffing

Remove the stalk and green part attached to it. Cut in half lengthwise. With the point of a small knife make a slight incision around the inside edge to within ½ cm from the edge. Cut trellis fashion across the exposed part of the plant to a depth of approximately ½ cm.

8.15 ENDIVE (BELGIAN CHICORY)—ENDIVE BELGE

Trim away any discoloured outer leaves. Wash in cold water.

8.16 FENNEL—FENOUIL

Trim away the leaves at the head of the vegetable and carefully trim the root end. If rather large in size then cut through the length into two equal parts. Wash in cold water.

8.17 FRENCH BEANS—HARICOTS VERTS

For the small variety top and tail. For the larger variety, top and tail the beans, cut in half lengthwise then in half crosswise. Wash in cold water.

8.18 GLOBE ARTICHOKES—ARTICHAUTS

Remove the hard stems with a small knife or, holding the artichoke in one hand, grasp the stem with the other and break it off (this latter method removes the fibres in the base of the artichoke). Using a sharp knife remove the top of the vegetable cutting off approximately 2 cm. Trim away any discoloured outer leaves using a pair of scissors. Lightly trim the bottom of the artichoke (known as the fond) using a small knife or peeler. Rub the bottom of the artichoke with lemon and tie a piece of string around the vegetable so that it retains its shape whilst cooking. Also tie a piece of lemon against the base.

8.19 JERUSALEM ARTICHOKES—TOPINAMBOURS

Wash the vegetables to remove the dirt. Peel with a peeler.

Note

Once peeled Jerusalem artichokes should be placed immediately into cold water and lemon juice to prevent discoloration.

8.20 LEEKS—POIREAUX

Remove any discoloured or coarse outer leaves. Remove the coarse green leaves at the top of the vegetable with a large knife taking care not to cut back too far as this will cause unnecessary waste. Trim the root end taking care not to remove the root completely as this holds the vegetable together. Cut in half lengthwise commencing approximately 2 cm from the root end and going through to the top. Wash under cold running water gently opening the two halves to allow the water to penetrate into the centre of the vegetable to remove any dirt. Tie in manageable bundles of about 4–6 leeks with the root ends together.

8.21 *LETTUCE — LAITUE (round leaf type)*

Remove any discoloured or coarse outer leaves and neatly trim the root end. Wash in cold water.

8.22 *MARROW — COURGE*

Peel the vegetable lengthwise with a peeler. Cut into half lengthwise and with a spoon remove the seeds. Cut across into servable sizes about 5 cm square. Trim the corners of each piece of marrow with a small knife to give each a rounded effect. Wash in cold water.

For braised stuffed marrow
Peel the vegetable lengthwise with a peeler. Cut a slice from the tail end and remove the seeds with a long handled spoon, leaving the vegetable whole. Wash in cold water.

8.23 *MUSHROOMS — CHAMPIGNONS*

For grilling

Trim the stalks back to about 1 mm from the mushroom head.

Turned mushrooms — champignons tournés

Shape the top of firm white button mushrooms in a whirl fashion with a small knife. Once turned rub with lemon to help retain the whiteness. Place in a basin of cold water and lemon juice to prevent discoloration.

8.24 *ONIONS — OIGNONS*

Remove the outer skin with a small knife taking care not to remove the root end as this holds the vegetable together. Carefully trim the root.

8.25 *PARSLEY — PERSIL*

Picked parsley

Wash the parsley in cold water. Remove small sprigs from the stem about 2 cm in length.

Chopped parsley

Wash the parsley in cold water. Remove the parsley from the stalks and chop with a large knife until finely chopped. Place the parsley into a cloth and squeeze out the liquid and place into a suitable basin.

8.26 PARSNIPS — PANAIS

Peel lengthwise with a peeler. Cut into quarters lengthwise and remove the inner hard core with a small knife. Wash in cold water.

8.27 PIMENTO — PIMENT

For braised stuffed pimentoes

To remove the skin place onto a baking tray and either pass through an oven at a temperature of approximately 175 °C or under a salamander grill for a few minutes until the outer skin is easily removable with a small knife. Cut and remove the stem end. Remove the seeds from the inside taking care not to pierce the outer flesh.

Note

If pimentoes are for use other than stuffing the above method is still applicable. However, it is easier to cut the pimento in half, remove the stem and seeds and then proceed by placing in an oven or under a salamander grill in order to remove the skin.

8.28 RED CABBAGE — CHOU-ROUGE

Remove any discoloured or coarse outer leaves. Cut the cabbage into quarters and remove the centre stalks. Finely shred the cabbage and wash in cold water.

8.29 RUNNER BEANS — HARICOTS D'ESPAGNE

Top and tail. Remove the coarse fibrous parts on the leading edges using a peeler. Cut into strips at an angle across the bean about 1 mm thick. Wash in cold water.

8.30 SALSIFY — SALSFIS

Method 1

Wash the vegetables to remove the dirt. Peel lengthways with a peeler and cut into lengths of about 5 cm.

Method 2

Wash the vegetables thoroughly, removing all traces of dirt. Boil in salt water for 5 minutes then refresh under cold water. Remove the outer skin with the point of a small knife running the length of the vegetable through the fingers. Cut the salsify into lengths of about 5 cm.

Note

Once peeled and cut into lengths salsify should be placed

immediately into cold water and lemon juice to prevent discoloration.

8.31 SEAKALE — CHOUX DE MER

Remove any discoloured leaf stems. Trim the root end taking care not to remove the root completely as this holds the vegetable together. Wash in cold water. Tie into manageable bundles of about 4–6 seakale with the root ends together.

8.32 SHALLOTS — ECHALOTES

Remove the outer skin with a small knife taking care not to remove the root end as this holds the vegetable together. Carefully trim the root.

8.33 SPINACH — EPINARDS

Tear off the coarse stems. Wash several times in changes of clean cold water in a deep receptacle or sink.

8.34 SPRING CABBAGE — CHOU DE PRINTEMPS

Trim any discoloured or coarse outer leaves. Trim the stalk and cut an incision approximately 1 mm into the stem. Wash in cold salt water. Tie into manageable bundles of about 4–6 cabbages with the root end together.

8.35 SUGAR PEA — MANGE-TOUT

Top and tail the pods. Wash in cold water.

Note

This is a pea pod containing immature peas. The whole pod is eaten.

8.36 SWEDE — RUTABAGA

Proceed as for Turnips (8.37).

8.37 TURNIPS — NAVETS

Trim the ends of the vegetable. Peel in a circular motion with a small knife making certain to remove the skin below the line of fibrous flesh which can be seen inside. Wash in cold water.

8.38 TOMATOES — TOMATES

For salads and other dishes

Remove the stalk end using the point of a small knife. Place the tomatoes into a dipper or frying basket and plunge into boiling water for a period of about 14 seconds. Drain well and remove the skins with the point of a small knife.

For concassée

Peel as above then cut into halves across the tomato and remove the pips and centre core with a small spoon. Cut the flesh into 1 cm dice.

For stuffing (whole)

Wash the tomatoes and remove the stem. Cut a slice across the end to a depth of about 2 cm and retain. Remove the inner pips and centre core with a small spoon.

For stuffing (halves)

Wash the tomatoes and remove the stem. Cut through the centre of the tomato dividing it into two halves. Remove the inner pips and centre core with a small spoon.

Note

Tomatoes to be prepared for grilling or stuffed and served as a vegetable dish are not usually skinned.

8.39 WATERCRESS — CRESSON DE FONTAINE

Picked watercress

Remove and discard the stalks by cutting through with a knife, leaving approximately 5 cm of stalk. Thoroughly wash the cress in cold water, changing the water several times if necessary to remove any small insects or small snails. To retain for future use neatly arrange with stalks together in a receptacle with a little ice water.

Vegetable cuts and shapes

Table 23 provides a list of the traditional shapes of cut vegetables. They are prepared so as to enhance the appearance and add variety in terms of flavour and texture to a wide range of dishes including hors-d'oeuvre, soups, stews, meat, game and poultry items, vegetables and potato dishes, farinaceous and egg items. One important aspect of these cuts is their neatness and uniformity of size; mechanical aids are used to produce most shapes, with the exception of barrel-shaped vegetables.

Some of these are used as an integral part of a dish and to a certain extent become indistinguishable whereas others remain a recognisable part of the dish in question.

TABLE 23. VEGETABLE CUTS AND SHAPES

Cut of vegetable	*Shape and size*	*Uses*
Bed of roots	Sliced carrots, onions, celery, thyme, bayleaf, parsley stalks, garlic and bacon pieces	Used for braising and pot roasting
Brunoise	Very small dice, 4 mm × 1 mm	Garnish for soups, broths, stews (e.g. Osso Bucco)
Grooved	Grooved vegetable slices	Generally applied to carrots, lemon and cucumber and cut with a special grooving knife
Jardinière	Baton shape, 2 mm × 2 mm in length	In hors-d'oeuvre and vegetable dishes
Julienne	Thin strips, 1 mm × 4 cm in length	Garnish for soups, potato dishes, poached fish, entrées, hors-d'oeuvre
Macédoine	Dice, ½ cm × ½ cm	Garnish for soups, hors-d'oeuvre, vegetable and potato dishes
Paysanne	(1) Triangles 6 mm across (2) Squares 1 cm × 1 cm (3) Hexagon 1 cm across (4) Rounds 1 cm across	Garnish for soups, stews, entrée dishes and pot roasts
Rondelles	Thin slices of vegetables 1 cm in diameter	Potatoes and, in particular, carrots are cut in this way
Turned barrel shape (tourné)*	The size of this item is dependent upon its use, e.g. as a vegetable dish 1 cm long × ½ cm	In potato dishes and as garnish for entrée dishes, pot roasts and roasts

*The term tourné or turned when applied to mushrooms is quite different (*see* 8.23).

BOILED VEGETABLES

Most vegetables may be cooked by boiling, although different techniques are used to enhance the flavour and texture of various kinds. Green vegetables such as asparagus, Brussels sprouts, cauliflower, French beans, marrow and peas are plunged into sufficient boiling salted water to enable them to float freely whilst cooking. When cooking such vegetables it is advisable to cover the pan with a lid and bring them back to the boil as quickly as possible, then remove the lid immediately to allow any volatile acids to escape. This helps to retain the chlorophyll and so gives a good colour. To prevent some vegetables from discolouring when cooked in this manner a small amount of lemon juice is added to the boiling salted water. Globe artichokes, cauliflower and seakale are such examples.

Root vegetables may also be boiled by barely covering them with cold water, adding salt and bringing them to the boil, boiling them steadily until they are cooked. It appears that this method is fast losing favour in the industry, the preference being for the conservative method described above.

Cabbage type vegetables and spinach are cooked by placing them into a small amount of boiling salted water, covering them with a lid and boiling them steadily until they are cooked. Root vegetables such as carrots and turnips are cooked in a relatively small quantity of cold salted water to the volume of vegetables, covering them with a lid and boiling steadily until they are cooked. This method is sometimes referred to as the conservative method of cooking vegetables.

Some vegetables, e.g. Jerusalem artichokes and salsify, are cooked in a preparation termed a blanc to prevent them from discolouring (*see* pp. 424–9). This consists of water, a small amount of flour, lemon juice and salt.

Root vegetables such as carrots, turnips, swedes and button onions may also be boiled by a method termed glacé (*see* p. 398). The vegetables are barely covered with cold water to which salt, sugar and butter is added. The liquid is allowed to evaporate completely during the cooking of the vegetables.

To test if cooked

Stated cooking times can only act as a guide as to when vegetables are cooked. In the final analysis experience will help to make the decision. Factors influencing the length of time the vegetables should be cooked for include quality, size and prior storage conditions as well as ensuring that the vegetables are actually boiling for the prescribed time.

The appearance of the vegetable may be used to gauge when it is cooked and can be used for certain types of vegetable with a fair degree of accuracy, e.g. turnips become glassy looking or transparent when cooked as does marrow, seakale, salsify, celeriac and swede. However, it is not an accurate method for testing, especially when the aim is to cook vegetables to the exact degree, and can be misleading.

The method most favoured by those with experience is to *feel* whether the vegetable is cooked. (Persons who have yet to gain this experience find it difficult to make decisions in this way and prefer to taste them to gauge if sufficiently cooked.) Gently remove a sample of the vegetables from the cooking liquid using either a perforated spoon or a spider to allow the hot liquid to drain off. Test between the fingers by exerting an even gentle pressure. The vegetables are cooked when there is no apparent resistance or hardness. (*See* also, however, individual recipes for alternative or more appropriate ways of testing to see if particular vegetables are cooked.)

It is important to bear in mind that most types of vegetable need to be undercooked, the word "undercooked" being used advisedly. (Alternatively the terms "nutty" or "al dente" can be used meaning just undercooked but by no means hard.)

Retention of boiled vegetables

It is trade practice to cook some types of vegetables in salt water in advance of customer demand for the following reasons:

(a) the vegetables are to be served cold, e.g. asparagus and globe artichokes;

(b) the vegetables, once boiled, are to be subjected to a second method of cookery, e.g. cauliflower and salsify subsequently deep fried in a yeast batter;

(c) the vegetables are to appear as boiled vegetables on a menu.

Once the vegetables are cooked they should be "refreshed". This means reducing the temperature of the cooked vegetables as quickly as possible to prevent further cooking by either replacing the hot liquid with cold water or by transferring the vegetables to a container of cold water. The choice as to which method to use depends on the nature of the vegetables themselves, some are more delicate than others, and whether they have been slightly overcooked by accident, in which case they need to be cooled with extreme care and speed. Transferring them to a container of cold water is perhaps the best method to use.

Appropriate ways to refresh particular vegetables are outlined as follows.

(a) Less delicate types of vegetables such as Brussels sprouts, corn on the cob, French beans, spinach and peas. Place the saucepan containing the cooked items in a sink and allow cold water to run gently and steadily onto the vegetables until they are cold.

(b) Broccoli, cauliflower, marrow and vegetables of a rather delicate nature. Place the saucepan containing the cooked items in a sink. Tie a cloth around the tap to prevent the force of the

running water concentrating on one particular area and breaking the vegetables before proceeding as in *(a)*.

(c) Asparagus, broccoli, cauliflower (alternative method to *(b)*). Transfer the cooked vegetables gently to a container of really cold water.

NOTES

(1) Cabbage, curly kale, spring cabbage and the like do not lend themselves readily to this method of cooling in cold water as they become watery and inedible.

(2) *See* also individual recipes for alternative or more appropriate ways of refreshing particular vegetables.

Once the vegetables have been refreshed they should be stored on a tray, preferably stainless steel or plastic (aluminium is far from ideal as cooked vegetables discolour when they come into contact with the metal), in a refrigerator at a temperature of 8 °C. It is important to allow air to circulate between the vegetables, therefore do not pile the items on top of each other, especially when storing delicate items such as asparagus, cauliflower and broccoli. For best results these vegetables should be layed on a damp cloth and covered with another damp cloth or cling film.

Reheating of vegetables boiled in salt water

Vegetables boiled in salt water should be reheated in a chaudfont — a saucepan of salted water (using approximately 15 g salt to 1 l water) just below boiling point. The vegetables should be placed in a vegetable strainer or basket and put into the hot salt water chaudfont. After a few moments the vegetables should be hot through to the centre. Drain completely of water before transferring to the service dishes.

NOTES

(1) Vegetables best suited to this method of reheating include asparagus and sprue, broccoli, cauliflower, marrow, French and runner beans, peas and corn on the cob. *See* also, however, individual recipes for alternative or more appropriate ways of reheating particular vegetables.

(2) If the chaudfont is used continuously for any length of time without changing the water, or is used to reheat several different types of vegetables, then the flavour and general appearance of the vegetables will be damaged beyond repair. The flavour of each vegetable will become contaminated by those of the others with a strong or distinctive flavour smothering the flavour of the more delicate. In addition, there is

a likelihood that pieces of different vegetables will find their way into the service dish of another vegetable.

(3) All boiled vegetables when served should be free from all traces of cooking liquid. They should be a natural fresh colour and well seasoned. They should be cooked to the nutty stage, a point that needs to be considered when reheating vegetables because they continue to cook when subjected to this process.

General summary

The following is a summary of particular points which require special attention when cooking vegetables by boiling.

(a) The vegetables should be of the finest quality when purchased and in top class condition.

(b) The length of time between delivery and use, storage conditions and stock turnover are also vital factors which must be taken into consideration.

(c) Correct preparation of the vegetables is just as important as correctly cooking them, therefore due consideration should be given to this aspect.

(d) The correct type and size of saucepan used is very important, as is the use of cold or boiling water to commence cooking and the addition of sufficient salt.

(e) The vegetables must be cooked for the correct length of time, and should not be allowed to go off the boil during cooking.

(f) Once cooked, those vegetables cooked in salt water should not be retained for any length of time in the liquid in which they have been cooked.

(g) If the vegetables are to be retained for future use they should be quickly cooled, once cooked, to prevent further cooking. Those cooked in salt water should be refreshed in cold water, drained and stored in a refrigerator at 8 °C for as short a period as possible.

(h) If the vegetables are reheated in a chaudfont the correct procedure must be followed.

(i) The length of time the vegetables are held and the temperature they are held at either in a hot cupboard or bain-marie are all factors that will have an effect on the quality of the vegetable when served to the customer.

Extensions of boiled vegetables

Buttered vegetables

Boiled (or steamed) vegetables when cooked may be completed using melted butter and are known as *au beurre.*

8.40 BUTTERED VEGETABLES — LEGUMES AU BEURRE

Method

Three methods may be used to butter vegetables.

(a) Most boiled and steamed vegetables when served may be brushed with melted butter.

(b) Vegetables such as French beans, turnips and celeriac may be quickly tossed in melted butter without permitting them to colour.

(c) Vegetables of a delicate nature such as cauliflower and baby marrow may be gently cooked in melted butter without coloration. They should be turned whilst cooking with a palette knife or a vegetable slice.

Note

Buttered vegetables must not be confused with vegetables coated with butter carefully melted to avoid separating the constituent fats and sediments known as Beurre Fondu (3.53).

Service

Serve in a stainless steel or silver vegetable dish. The size of the dish should be in proportion to the number of portions contained in it. The serving dish should be hot or cold accordingly.

Assessment of the completed dish

(1) The vegetables should appear fresh. They should be of an even size and, where appropriate, neatly cut.
(2) They should be a fresh colour depending upon type.
(3) They should be nutty in texture and not overcooked.
(4) They should have a full flavour with a hint of seasoning.
(5) There should be no water in which the vegetables have been cooked in the bottom of the dish.
(6) Those vegetables that have been either tossed in butter or lightly cooked in butter should not appear as though they have been fried.

Possible problem	*Possible cause and solution*
(1) Vegetables have discoloured and broken up	— too many vegetables were tossed in the butter at the same time — vegetables were tossed too slowly

Possible problem	*Possible cause and solution*	
	— once completed the vegetables were retained in a hot cupboard or bain-marie for too long	Once vegetables have been badly handled or improperly cooked there is little that can be done to rectify the problems that arise. Careful preparation and cooking as close to the time they are required are the safest ways to avoid problems.
(2) Flavour of the vegetables has deteriorated	— generally the vegetables have been retained in a hot cupboard or bain-marie for too long	

Gratinated vegetables

Light gratination may be applied to boiled vegetables. They are coated with a Cheese Sauce (3.15), sprinkled with grated cheese and melted butter and placed under a salamander grill to colour (gratinate). They then appear on the menu as Légumes Mornay or Légumes au Gratin.

Certain boiled and steamed vegetables may be sprinkled with grated cheese and melted butter then placed under a salamander grill until the cheese has melted and golden. The vegetables then appear on the menu as Légumes Milanaise and is generally applied to asparagus, broccoli, cauliflower, marrow and seakale.

NOTES

(1) Broccoli flowers and the tips of asparagus presented in this manner are not coated with the sauce but are brushed with melted butter and covered with kitchen foil as an added protection to prevent them from drying out under the salamander grill.

(2) The flavour of cauliflower and marrow is enhanced by heating the vegetable very gently in butter in a pan on top of the stove before coating with the sauce. The vegetables should be seasoned to taste with salt and pepper from the mill but not allowed to colour.

Creamed vegetables

Boiled vegetables may be bound either with cream or Cream Sauce (3.16) and appear on the menu as Légumes à la Crème. Once cooked the boiled vegetables (generally shaped for this practice) should be drained of all surplus liquid. They should then be gently simmered in the cream until the cream has slightly reduced, or be carefully incorporated into the cream sauce. They are then seasoned to taste.

Glazed vegetables

Glazed vegetables are cooked in a minimum of liquid together with salt and butter. During cooking the liquid evaporates leaving the vegetables with a distinct sheen and a glazed appearance.

There are two methods of glazing.

(a) White glazing is known as glacé à blanc and is applied to carrots, turnips, swedes and button onions. The vegetables are generally shaped for this method of glazing (with the exception of the onions) — diced, paysanne, barrel-shaped, or in batons or rondels — and may be used as a garnish to accompany a range of meat and poultry dishes. They may also appear as dishes in their own right.

(b) Brown glazing is known as glacé à brun and is applied to button onions usually as part of a garnish, as in Braised Beef Bourguignonne (7.127).

NOTES

(1) Salt should be added with caution because the reduction of the liquid will inevitably make the vegetables salty.

(2) When cooking root vegetables such as carrots, turnips and peas in this manner a little sugar may be added during cooking in order to complement their natural sweetness.

(3) Turnips when glazed may be completed during the last few moments of cooking by adding some brown sugar and allowing it to caramelise.

(4) When cooking several vegetables in this manner which are to be mixed once cooked (e.g. carrots, turnips and swede) they may also be cooked together. First begin cooking the swede and the carrots and when these are practically cooked add the turnips. The aim is to bring all the vegetables to the point of glazing at the same time.

(5) When cooked the vegetables should have a sheen, be cooked to the correct degree and have a natural colour. They should not be over-salty or over-sweet.

Vegetable purées

Boiled vegetables such as carrots, turnips, Jerusalem artichokes and spinach can be passed through a sieve or a machine to make a purée. Vegetables which have been puréed in this way are termed Légumes en Purée.

NOTES

(1) It is more effective to use a machine first, followed by a sieve in order to achieve a very fine purée.

(2) Once prepared, vegetable purées may be refrigerated for future use in earthenware or plastic containers.

(3) To reheat vegetable purées place a little butter in a shallow sided saucepan and allow it to melt. Add the purée and heat, stirring with a wooden spatule.

(4) For service season the purée and serve in a vegetable dish in the shape of a dome. Decorate with a scroll effect over the surface using a palette knife.

(5) Turnips and swedes have a high water content and need the addition of dry mashed potato to give them the correct texture. The amount of potato added should not be allowed to distort the flavour of the vegetable to which it is added.

Vegetable purées bound with cream or cream sauce

Certain vegetables may be bound with cream or Cream Sauce (3.16). This method is generally associated with spinach and carrots and is known as en Purée à la Crème. They are served in exactly the same way as vegetable purées with a band of cream on the surface.

Vegetables Polonaise style

Some boiled vegetables, e.g. cauliflower, broccoli, may be served with a coating of a mixture of white breadcrumbs shallow fried until golden, sieved yolk and white of hard boiled egg and chopped parsley. Once cooked the hot drained vegetables are placed in a serving dish, seasoned with salt and pepper from the mill. They are then covered with the combination of golden fried breadcrumbs, sieved egg white and yolk and chopped parsley.

VEGETABLES BOILED IN SALT WATER

Asparagus

Asparagus boiled in plenty of salt water forms the basis of all other extensions of the vegetable. They are often used as a garnish for a variety of dishes both hot and cold, as well as being served as a special dish in its own right (*see* 8.42–44). Sprue, which are the young shoots, are also often used as a garnish. The following French menu terms denote that asparagus appears in some form in the completed dish: Argenteuil, Princess, Grand-Duc, Maréchale and Petit-Duc. For example:

Suprême of Chicken Princess — Suprême de Volaille Princesse
(suprême of chicken in a cream type sauce garnished with asparagus tips)

Suprême of Chicken Maréchale — Suprême de Volaille Maréchale
(suprême of chicken breaded, shallow fried and garnished with asparagus tips)

8.41 BOILED ASPARAGUS — ASPERGES A L'ANGLAISE (NATURE)

Makes: 10 portions. Cooking time: 15–20 minutes.

Quantity	*Ingredient*
60–80	sticks of prepared asparagus tied into portion sized bundles (8.2)
70 g	salt
6 l	boiling water

Method

(1) Place the bundles of asparagus into gently simmering water using a shallow sided saucepan so that they may easily be removed once cooked.

(2) When cooked remove them carefully from the water, lifting each bundle by the string with the point of a knife.

(3) Serve on a special asparagus dish with an inset drainer.

(4) Remove the string with a sharp knife, cutting away from the direction of the tips.

To test if cooked

Gently remove a sample bundle by lifting it out of the water with the point of a knife under the string taking care not to damage the delicate points. Test by pressing between the fingers just below the tip or point — they should be firm yet yield to finger pressure.

Retention

Place the cooked bundles in a receptacle of ice cold water to bring down the temperature immediately and prevent further cooking. When cold remove from the water and place on a stainless steel, plastic or earthenware container that has been lined with a damp cloth. Cover with a damp cloth or cling film and store in a refrigerator at 8 °C.

Reheating

(1) Place the tied bundles in a chaudfont (*see* p. 394) until the asparagus is hot.

(2) Gently remove from the water, lifting each bundle by the string with the point of a knife.

(3) Serve on a special asparagus dish with an inset drainer.

(4) Remove the string with a sharp knife, cutting away from the direction of the tips.

Note

Asparagus may also be served on a silver flat dish lined with a dish paper with a folded napkin on top of the dish paper. The end of the napkin is folded over the stems of the vegetables to just below the tips. If served in this way they should be placed onto a cloth to dry before they are served on the napkin.

Assessment of the completed dish

(1) The asparagus tips should be hot.

(2) The asparagus should be a pleasant green colour unless it is the French type (Argenteuil) which is rather white.

(3) The asparagus should be cooked until nutty. The correct seasoning should be apparent.

(4) All the tips or points should be pointing in the same direction and the vegetables should be of an even length. None should be broken or damaged.

(5) If served on a cloth napkin there should be no traces of water on the cloth.

(6) The correct size of standard portion should be served. (Generally 2–3 sprue are suitable as a garnish and 6–8 tips are suitable depending on their thickness when serving asparagus as a separate dish.)

Possible problem	*Possible cause and solution*
(1) Sand in the tips of the asparagus	— asparagus not properly washed before cooking; care must be taken to wash the asparagus thoroughly during preparation as this is difficult to rectify except by continuously changing the refreshing water — this is not always effective as the sand can penetrate to the tips.
(2) Asparagus is poor in colour	— asparagus was not stored correctly; care must be taken to store asparagus correctly as it is an expensive vegetable needing careful treatment to avoid problems at a later stage which cannot be rectified.
	— asparagus was overcooked; care must be taken to cook the vegetable for the correct length of time as this problem cannot be rectified.

Possible problem	*Possible cause and solution*
	— asparagus left in the cooking liquid after cooking or reheating; care must be taken to avoid this as the problem cannot be rectified.
	— asparagus held too long once cooked; the vegetable should be prepared as close as possible to the time it is required to avoid the problems caused by prolonged retention.
	— asparagus retained under poor refrigeration; care must be taken to follow the correct procedure for retention as this problem cannot be rectified.
	— water used for cooking or reheating has been used before; care must be taken to avoid this as the problem cannot be rectified.
	— asparagus held too long once served; care must be taken to avoid this as the problem cannot be rectified.
(3) Asparagus tips have broken	— asparagus has been overcooked; care must be taken to cook the vegetable for the correct length of time as this problem cannot be rectified.
	— asparagus has been poorly handled during storage, preparation or cooking; careful treatment is required at all times as asparagus is an expensive and delicate vegetable.
(4) Flavour of the asparagus is impaired	— insufficient salt in the water used for cooking or reheating; care must be taken over this aspect as the problem cannot be rectified.
	— asparagus has been under or overcooked; care must be taken to cook the asparagus for the correct length of time as this problem cannot be rectified.
	— asparagus has been left in the cooking water for too long once cooked; care must be taken to avoid this as the problem cannot be rectified.
	— asparagus retained for too long once cooked or after being served; care must be taken to avoid this as the problem cannot be rectified.

Extensions

Asparagus served as a dish in its own right may be prepared as follows.

8.42 ASPARAGUS WITH HOLLANDAISE SAUCE — ASPERGES SAUCE HOLLANDAISE

Serve as in 8.41 accompanied with a sauceboat of Sauce Hollandaise (3.12).

8.43 ASPARAGUS MILANAISE — ASPERGES MILANAISE

Dress the cooked asparagus on a silver, stainless steel or earthenware dish previously brushed with melted butter. Season, sprinkle finely grated Parmesan cheese and melted butter over the entire surface and rapidly gratinate under a salamander grill. When lightly coloured, remove from the grill and complete the dish with Nut Brown Butter (6.48).

8.44 ASPARAGUS WITH MELTED BUTTER — ASPERGES AU BEURRE FONDU

Serve as in 8.41 accompanied with a sauceboat of Beurre Fondu (3.53).

Broad beans

8.45 BOILED BROAD BEANS — FEVES A L'ANGLAISE (NATURE)

Makes: 10 portions. Cooking time: 10–15 minutes.

Quantity	*Ingredient*
1 kg	Prepared Broad Beans (8.4)
20 g	salt
1½ l	boiling water

Method

(1) Place the beans into the boiling salted water and simmer gently until cooked.

(2) Drain the vegetables in a colander.

(3) Serve slightly dome shape in a vegetable dish.

Extensions

8.46 BROAD BEANS WITH BUTTER — FEVES AU BEURRE

Proceed as for 8.45. When serving brush the surface with 50 g melted butter.

8.47 BROAD BEANS WITH CREAM — FEVES A LA CREME

Proceed as for 8.45. Gently simmer the cooked and drained beans in 3 dl cream until the cream has slightly reduced. Season to taste with salt and cayenne pepper.

Notes

(1) The outer skins of the beans may be removed before serving. Therefore, once cooked, refresh under cold running water. Remove the outer shell by gently squeezing between the fingers. If this practice is followed it should be remembered that they become far more delicate to handle and prone to breaking and should be handled with care. Portion yield is reduced by approximately 40 per cent.

(2) When serving beans in a cream sauce without their outer shells there is a greater likelihood of them breaking. The beans should be just lightly bound with cream.

(3) Instead of the cream 3 dl Cream Sauce (3.16) may be substituted.

Broccoli spears

Fresh broccoli may be cooked in exactly the same way as cauliflower — *see* 8.65. The following recipe is for frozen broccoli spears.

8.48 BOILED BROCCOLI SPEARS — BROCOLI A L'ANGLAISE (NATURE)

Makes: 10 portions. Cooking time: 5 minutes.

Quantity	*Ingredient*
1 kg	frozen broccoli
35 g	salt
2½ l	boiling water

Method

(1) Place the broccoli into the boiling salted water and simmer gently until cooked.

(2) Gently remove the spears from the water with a spider, placing them into a colander to drain.

(3) Place them into a vegetable dish with the points or spears pointing in the same direction.

Extensions

Notes

(1) The flower ends of the broccoli are not coated with a sauce but are brushed with melted butter when served.

(2) In those dishes that require the broccoli to be placed under a

salamander grill, e.g. milanaise and mornay, the flowers of the broccoli are protected from drying by brushing with melted butter and covering with kitchen foil. The foil must be removed before serving.

8.49 *BUTTERED BROCCOLI SPEARS — BROCOLI AU BEURRE*

Proceed as in 8.48. When serving brush the surface with 50 g melted butter.

8.50 *BROCCOLI SPEARS WITH CREAM SAUCE — BROCOLI SAUCE CREME*

Proceed as in 8.48. When serving coat the vegetables with Cream Sauce (3.16), or serve the sauce separately in a sauceboat as an accompaniment.

8.51 *BROCCOLI SPEARS WITH HOLLANDAISE SAUCE — BROCOLI HOLLANDAISE*

Proceed as in 8.48. When serving accompany with a sauceboat of Hollandaise Sauce (3.12).

8.52 *BROCCOLI SPEARS MILANAISE — BROCOLI MILANAISE*

Proceed as in 8.48. When serving sprinkle the surface of the vegetables with 50 g grated Parmesan cheese and 50 g melted butter and glaze under a salamander grill. Complete with 100 g Nut Brown Butter (6.48).

8.53 *BROCCOLI SPEARS MORNAY/AU GRATIN — BROCOLI MORNAY/AU GRATIN*

Proceed as in 8.48. When serving coat the vegetables with 6 dl Mornay Sauce (3.15), sprinkle the surface with 75 g grated Parmesan cheese and 50 g melted butter and glaze under a salamander grill.

8.54 *BROCCOLI SPEARS POLONAISE — BROCOLI POLONAISE*

Proceed as in 8.48. When serving coat the surface of the vegetables with Polonaise mixture (*see* p. 399).

Brussels sprouts

8.55 *BOILED BRUSSELS SPROUTS — CHOUX DE BRUXELLES (NATURE)*

Makes: 10 portions. Cooking time: 15–20 minutes.

Quantity	*Ingredient*
1 kg	Prepared Brussels Sprouts (8.6)
70 g	salt
6 l	boiling water

Method

(1) Place the sprouts into the boiling salted water and boil steadily until cooked.

(2) Gently remove the sprouts from the water with a spider, placing them into a colander to drain.

(3) Serve slightly dome shape in a vegetable dish.

Notes

(1) When cooked the sprouts should be nutty in texture and of a pleasant green colour.

(2) Refresh them either under gently running cold water or transfer them to a container of very cold water using a spider.

(3) To retain them carefully drain them in a colander and store on a tray as described on pp. 393–4.

Extensions

8.56 BUTTERED BRUSSELS SPROUTS — CHOUX DE BRUXELLES AU BEURRE

Proceed as in 8.55. When serving brush the surface with 50 g melted butter.

8.57 SAUTEED BRUSSELS SPROUTS — CHOUX DE BRUXELLES SAUTES

Proceed as in 8.55. When serving toss the drained vegetables in 75 g butter until they are slightly golden. Season to taste with salt and pepper from the mill.

Cabbage

Cabbage may be cooked either in plenty of boiling salted water, or placed into a saucepan with a minimum amount of water — the conservative method as described on p. 392 and outlined below. The former method is fast losing favour as the vegetable becomes watery and rather tasteless and loses much of its vitamins during cooking.

8.58 BOILED CABBAGE — CHOU A L'ANGLAISE (NATURE)

Makes: 10 portions. Cooking time: 8–12 minutes.

Quantity	*Ingredient*
2 kg	Prepared Cabbage (8.7)
20 g	salt
¾ l	boiling water

Method

(1) Place the prepared cabbage into the boiling salted water, cover with a lid and boil steadily until cooked.
(2) Drain the cabbage in a colander.
(3) Serve in a vegetable dish neatly arranged.

Extension

8.59 BUTTERED CABBAGE — CHOU AU BEURRE

Proceed as in 8.58. When serving brush the surface with 50 g melted butter.

Carrots

When prepared for serving as a vegetable dish carrots may be cooked in the following shapes and sizes:

Small new carrots: whole, leaving approximately 1 cm of the stem
Barrel shaped: approximately 3 cm in length
Diced: ½ cm × ½ cm
Baton shaped: 2 mm × 2 mm in length
Rondelles: approximately 1 cm in diameter × 2 mm thick using either a mandolin or machine

When cooked for purée they are cut into rough pieces approximately 5 cm in size.

Carrots may be cooked by barely covering them with cold water with the addition of salt using 20 g salt and 1 l water to 1 kg carrots. The following method is called the conservative method and only a small amount of water is used.

8.60 BOILED CARROTS — CAROTTES A L'ANGLAISE (NATURE)

Makes: 10 portions. Cooking time: 10–15 minutes.

Quantity	*Ingredient*
1 kg	Prepared Carrots (8.8)
6 g	salt
¾ l	water

Method

(1) Place the water and salt into a shallow sided saucepan. Add

the prepared carrots, cover with a lid and boil steadily until cooked.

(2) Drain the carrots in a colander.

(3) Serve slightly dome shape in a vegetable dish.

Extensions

8.61 BUTTERED CARROTS — CAROTTES AU BEURRE

Proceed as in 8.60. When serving brush the surface of the vegetables with 50 g melted butter.

8.62 CARROTS IN CREAM SAUCE — CAROTTES A LA CREME

Proceed as in 8.60. Gently simmer the cooked drained carrots in 3 dl cream until the cream has slightly reduced. Season to taste with salt and cayenne pepper.

8.63 PUREE OF CARROTS — CAROTTES EN PUREE

Proceed as in 8.60 and continue as for vegetable purées outlined on p. 398

8.64 GLAZED CARROTS — CAROTTES GLACEES
VICHY CARROTS—CAROTTES VICHY

Makes: 10 portions. Cooking time: 15–20 minutes. (Glaced Carrots). 30 minutes (Vichy Carrots).

Quantity	*Ingredient*		
1 kg	carrots,	Cut into dice, baton or barrel shapes	Glazed Carrots
		sliced into rondelles approx. 1 cm in diameter and 2 mm thick	Vichy Carrots
6 g	salt		
20 g	sugar		
50 g	butter		
¾ l	water		

Method

(1) Place the carrots into a shallow sided saucepan and barely cover with cold water. Add the salt, sugar and place knobs of butter on top.

(2) Cover with a lid and allow to boil until almost cooked.

(3) Remove the lid, continue to boil until the liquid has evaporated leaving a syrupy glaze over the carrots.

(4) Lightly toss the carrots to ensure that the vegetables are coated with the glazing liquid.

(5) Serve slightly dome shape in a vegetable dish.

Cauliflower

8.65 BOILED CAULIFLOWER — CHOU-FLEUR A L'ANGLAISE (NATURE)

Makes: 10 portions. Cooking time: 15–20 minutes.

Quantity	*Ingredient*
1½ kg	Prepared Cauliflower (8.9)
150 g	salt
10 l	boiling water
2	juice of lemons

Method

(1) Place the cauliflower into the boiling salted water and simmer until cooked.

(2) Gently remove the cauliflower with a spider and drain well.

(3) Serve in a vegetable dish either whole, leaving the outer tender green leaves, or cut into portion sizes, removing any excess stem but not to the extent that the vegetable falls to pieces. Do not place one portion on top of another.

Notes

(1) When cooked, cauliflower should be white in colour, the flower part of the vegetable well formed and rather compact and without blemish, and nutty in texture.

(2) Cauliflower that turns yellow during cooking may be due to the hardness of the water in which it was boiled. Hard water has an alkali reaction on a colourless substance in the vegetable known as flavone which turns yellow. In conditions of hard water lemon juice should be added to the salt water when cooking the vegetable.

(3) Place the vegetable into the boiling salt water root end uppermost.

(4) Some cooks cover cauliflower with either a cloth or greaseproof paper during cooking to help keep it submerged in the boiling water.

Extensions

8.66 BUTTERED CAULIFLOWER — CHOU-FLEUR AU BEURRE

Proceed as in 8.65. When serving brush the surface with 50 g melted butter.

8.67 CAULIFLOWER SAUTEED IN BUTTER — CHOU-FLEUR SAUTE AU BEURRE

Proceed as in 8.65. Shallow fry in butter (*see* also p. 440 on shallow fried vegetables).

8.68 CAULIFLOWER WITH CREAM SAUCE — CHOU-FLEUR SAUCE CREME

Proceed as in 8.65. When serving either coat the vegetable with Cream Sauce (3.16) or serve the sauce separately in a sauceboat as an accompaniment.

8.69 CAULIFLOWER HOLLANDAISE — CHOU-FLEUR HOLLANDAISE

Proceed as in 8.65. When serving accompany with a sauceboat of Hollandaise Sauce (3.12).

8.70 CAULIFLOWER MILANAISE — CHOU-FLEUR MILANAISE

Proceed as in 8.65. When serving sprinkle the surface of the cauliflower with 50 g grated Parmesan cheese and 50 g melted butter and glaze under a salamander grill. Complete with 100 g Nut Brown Butter (6.48).

8.71 CAULIFLOWER MORNAY/AU GRATIN — CHOU-FLEUR MORNAY/AU GRATIN

Proceed as in 8.65. When serving coat the vegetable with 6 dl Mornay Sauce (3.15), sprinkle the surface with 75 g grated Parmesan cheese and 50 g melted butter and glaze under a salamander grill.

8.72 CAULIFLOWER POLONAISE — CHOU-FLEUR POLONAISE

Proceed as in 8.65. When serving coat the surface of the vegetable with Polonaise mixture (*see* p. 399).

Corn on the cob

8.73 CORN ON THE COB — EPIS DE MAIS

Makes: 10 portions. Cooking time: 15–20 minutes.

Quantity	*Ingredient*
10	Prepared Corn on the Cob (8.13)
6 l	boiling water
200 g	melted butter — Beurre Fondue (3.53)

Method

(1) Place the corn into the boiling water and boil steadily until cooked.

(2) Remove the corn from the water with a spider and placing them into a colander allow them to drain well.

(3) Remove the outer leaves and silky fibre and fold back the remaining outer leaves.

(4) Serve the corn on a folded napkin accompanied by a sauceboat of melted butter.

Note

Cooking corn on the cob in salted water may harden the grains, therefore season them just before serving on the napkin.

Extensions

8.74 CREAMED SWEETCORN — MAIS A LA CREME

Using fresh corn on the cob

Proceed as in 8.73. When cooked, refresh under cold running water and drain. Scrape off the grains of corn into a basin and reheat with the addition of 3 dl cream or light Cream Sauce (3.16). Season to taste with a little salt and sugar. Serve in a vegetable dish.

Using frozen sweetcorn grains

Makes: 10 portions. Cooking time: 5–8 minutes.

Quantity	*Ingredient*
1 kg	sweetcorn grains
1½ l	water
15 g	salt (*see Note* to 8.73)
50 g	melted butter

Method

(1) Place the grains of corn into boiling water and boil steadily until cooked.

(2) Drain in a colander and season with the salt.

(3) Serve slightly dome shape in a vegetable dish and brush the surface with melted butter.

French beans

8.75 BOILED FRENCH BEANS — HARICOTS VERTS A L'ANGLAISE (NATURE)

Makes: 10 portions. Cooking time: 10–15 minutes.

Quantity	*Ingredient*
1 kg	Prepared French Beans (8.17)
45 g	salt
3 l	boiling water

Method

(1) Place the beans into the boiling salted water and boil them fairly rapidly until cooked.

(2) Gently remove the beans from the water with a spider, placing them into a colander to drain.

(3) Serve slightly dome shape in a vegetable dish.

Notes

(1) When cooked the beans should be nutty in texture and of a pleasant green colour.

(2) Refresh them either under gently running cold water or transfer them to a container of very cold water using a spider.

(3) To retain them carefully drain them in a colander and store them on a tray as described on p. 394.

Extensions

8.76 BUTTERED FRENCH BEANS — HARICOTS VERTS AU BEURRE

Proceed as in 8.75. When serving brush the surface with 50 g melted butter.

8.77 SAUTEED FRENCH BEANS — HARICOTS VERTS SAUTE AU BEURRE

Proceed as in 8.75. When serving toss the drained vegetables in 75 g butter and season with salt and pepper from the mill.

Globe artichokes

8.78 BOILED GLOBE ARTICHOKES — ARTICHAUTS (NATURE)

Makes: 10 portions. Cooking time: 25–30 minutes.

Quantity	*Ingredient*
10	Prepared Globe Artichokes (8.18)
70 g	salt
6 l	water
2	juice of lemons

Method

(1) Place the artichokes into gently simmering water until they are cooked.

(2) Carefully remove the artichokes with a spider, drain them on a cloth and remove the string and lemon.

(3) Remove the central inner leaves using the fingers, if possible taking them out in one piece.

(4) Remove the choke which is to be found deep inside the

vegetable at its base using either a small spoon or the end of a vegetable peeler. Take care when removing the choke not to damage or cut away part of the fond. (The choke may be identified by its fibrous nature.)

(5) Replace the centre leaves previously removed. Select those leaves which have the most pleasant appearance and replace them upside down.

Notes

(1) To test if cooked remove one of the artichokes by using a spider and pierce the base with the point of a knife. If the knife enters without undue pressure the artichoke is cooked.

(2) *See* 8.1 for artichoke bottoms.

Service

Serve on a silver or stainless steel dish on a folded napkin and with a sprig of parsley set into the top of the inserted inner leaf.

Assessment of the completed dish

(1) The vegetable should be hot and cooked to the right degree which is firm.

(2) The outer leaves should be a pleasant green colour and should be easily removed using the finger tips when eaten.

(3) The fond should be whitish in colour, not brown or black.

(4) The napkin upon which it is served should be clean and the parsley should be clean and a fresh green colour.

Extensions

Globe artichokes may be served either hot or cold as a first course in their own right. Some examples follow.

8.79 HOT GLOBE ARTICHOKES WITH HOLLANDAISE SAUCE — ARTICHAUTS EN BRANCHES SAUCE HOLLANDAISE

Prepare the artichokes as in 8.78 and serve hot accompanied by a sauceboat of Sauce Hollandaise (3.12).

Leeks

8.80 BOILED LEEKS — POIREAUX A L'ANGLAISE (NATURE)

Makes: 10 portions. Cooking time: 15–20 minutes.

Quantity	*Ingredient*
10 × 125 g	Prepared Leeks (8.20)
70 g	salt
6 l	boiling water

Method

(1) Place the leeks into the boiling salted water and simmer gently until cooked.

(2) Gently remove the leeks from the water with a spider, placing them into a colander to drain.

(3) Place onto a cutting board and remove the string.

(4) Taking each leek separately, cut in two lengthways, fold in halves by folding the tops under to form a triangle shape.

(5) Serve in a vegetable dish. Do not pile one portion on top of another.

Extension

See pp. 436–7 on braised vegetables for other leek dishes.

8.81 BUTTERED LEEKS — POIREAUX AU BEURRE

Proceed as in 8.80. When serving brush the surface with 50 g melted butter.

Marrow

8.82 BOILED MARROW — COURGE A L'ANGLAISE (NATURE)

Makes: 10 portions. Cooking time: 15 minutes.

Quantity	*Ingredient*
1 kg	Prepared Marrow (8.22)
70 g	salt
6 l	boiling water

Method

(1) Place the marrow into the boiling salted water and simmer gently until cooked.

(2) Gently remove from the water with a spider and drain on a cloth.

(3) Serve neatly arranged in a vegetable dish but do not place one portion on top of another.

Extensions

8.83 BUTTERED MARROW — COURGE AU BEURRE

Proceed as in 8.82. When serving brush the surface with 50 g melted butter. (*See* p. 395–7 on buttered vegetables for an alternative method.)

8.84 MARROW SAUTEED IN BUTTER — COURGE SAUTEE AU BEURRE

Proceed as in 8.82. Lightly shallow fry the marrow in 75 g butter until they are slightly golden. Season to taste with salt and pepper from the mill.

8.85 *MARROW MILANAISE — COURGE MILANAISE*

Proceed as for Cauliflower Milanaise (8.70).

8.86 *MARROW MORNAY AU GRATIN — COURGE MORNAY AU GRATIN*

Proceed as for Cauliflower Mornay (8.71).

8.87 *MARROW POLONAISE — COURGE POLONAISE*

Proceed as for Cauliflower Polonaise (8.72).

Mixed vegetables

8.88 *BOILED MIXED VEGETABLES — MACEDOINE DE LEGUMES*

This dish consists generally of a mixture of carrots, turnips, peas and French beans in a ratio of one-third carrots to two-thirds of the other vegetables. It may be served as a complete vegetable dish in its own right or it may form part of a garnish for a variety of meat and poultry dishes. It also serves as a basis for an hors d'oeuvre.

When cooking several vegetables which are to be mixed as in this dish they may be cooked together.

Notes

(1) The root vegetables may be cut into small dice or macédoine ½ cm × ½ cm, baton shape or jardinière 2 mm × ½ mm in length, triangles or paysanne 6 mm across; they may also be turned barrel shape 1 cm long × ½ cm, depending upon their use. When served as a vegetable dish they are generally cut into either dice or baton shapes. The French beans are cut into diamond shapes and the peas remain in their natural form.

(2) When served as a separate dish, the vegetables are drained when cooked and served slightly dome shape in a vegetable dish.

8.89 *BUTTERED MIXED VEGETABLES — MACEDOINE DE LEGUMES AU BEURRE*

Proceed as in 8.88. When serving brush the surface of the vegetables with 50 g melted butter.

8.90 *GLAZED MIXED VEGETABLES — MACEDOINE DE LEGUMES GLACEE*

The root vegetables, carrots and turnips are cooked glacé (*see* p. 398 on glazed vegetables). The French beans and peas are boiled separately and, when cooked, are drained and mixed with the glazed vegetables at the last moment.

Mushrooms

8.91 SLICED BUTTON MUSHROOMS — CHAMPIGNONS EMINCES

Makes: 10 portions as a garnish. Cooking time: 5–8 minutes.

Quantity	*Ingredient*
250 g	sliced button mushrooms
1 dl	water
½	juice of lemon
25 g	butter
3 g	salt

Method

Place the mushrooms, water, lemon juice, butter and salt into a saucepan. Cover with a lid and gently simmer until cooked.

8.92 TURNED BUTTON MUSHROOMS — CHAMPIGNONS TOURNES

Proceed as in 8.91, allowing one or two mushrooms per portion of garnish.

Notes to 8.91 and 8.92

(1) Mushrooms cooked in this manner are generally used for garnishing such items as omelettes and fish dishes and also as part of other garnishes.

(2) For future use transfer the mushrooms to a porcelain or plastic basin and allow to cool. Cover with cling film and keep in a refrigerator at 8 °C.

(3) Reheat in the liquid in which they were previously cooked (this rule generally applies to the turned mushrooms).

(4) Some chefs prefer to boil turned mushrooms in a blanc (*see* p. 424).

(5) Once cooked mushrooms become rather rubbery in texture and prolonged cooking will not alter this characteristic. Indeed, it is not the intention to alter this quality by cooking them for long periods.

Onions

Onions are not normally boiled except when glazing. *See* 8.93 and 8.94 for braising and shallow frying.

Extensions

8.93 SMALL WHITE GLAZED ONIONS — PETITS OIGNONS GLACES A BLANC

Makes: 10 portions. Cooking time: 40 minutes.

Quantity	*Ingredient*
750 g	Prepared Button Onions (8.24)
6 g	salt
½ l	water
50 g	butter

Method

(1) Place the onions in a shallow pan. Barely cover with water and add the salt and knobs of butter. Cover with a lid and allow to boil gently until cooked.

(2) Remove the lid and continue cooking until the liquid has evaporated leaving a syrupy glaze over the onions.

(3) Lightly toss the onions to ensure that all the onions are coated with the glazing liquid.

8.94 SMALL BROWN GLAZED ONIONS — PETITS OIGNONS GLACES A BRUN

Makes: 10 portions. Cooking time: 40 minutes.

Quantity	*Ingredient*
750 g	Prepared Button Onions (8.24)
½ l	Brown Stock (3.1)
6 g	salt
50 g	butter

Method

(1) Melt the butter in a shallow pan, add the onions and lightly colour the onions golden.

(2) Barely cover with the brown stock and add the salt. Cover with a lid and allow to boil gently until cooked.

(3) Remove the lid and continue cooking until the liquid has evaporated leaving a syrupy glaze over the onions.

(4) Lightly toss the onions to ensure that all the onions are coated with the glazing liquid.

Parsnips

When being served as a vegetable dish parsnips may be cooked in the following shapes and sizes:

Barrel shaped approximately 3 cm in length
Diced ½ cm × ½ cm

Baton shaped 2 mm × 2 mm in length

When cooked for a purée they are cut into rough pieces approximately 5 cm in size.

Parsnips may be cooked by barely covering them with cold salted water using 20 g salt, and 1 l water to 1 kg parsnips. The following method is called the conservative method of cookery in which only a small amount of water is used.

8.95 BOILED PARSNIPS — PANAIS A L'ANGLAISE (NATURE)

Makes: 10 portions. Cooking time: 10–15 minutes.

Quantity	*Ingredient*
1 kg	Prepared Parsnips (8.26)
6 g	salt
½ l	water

Method

(1) Place the water and salt into a shallow sided saucepan, add the prepared parsnips, cover with a lid and boil steadily until cooked.

(2) Drain the parsnips in a colander.

(3) Serve slightly dome shape in a vegetable dish.

Extensions

8.96 BUTTERED PARSNIPS — PANAIS AU BEURRE

Proceed as in 8.95. When serving brush the surface of the vegetables with 50 g melted butter.

8.97 BUTTERED PARSNIPS WITH PARSLEY — PANAIS PERSILLES

Proceed as in 8.95. When serving sprinkle with approximately 5 g freshly chopped parsley.

8.98 PUREE OF PARSNIPS — PANAIS EN PUREE

Proceed as in 8.95 and continue as on p. 398 on vegetable purées.

Peas

The following recipe is based upon the use of frozen peas to reflect current trade practice. Where fresh peas are cooked then the cooking time is longer, approximately 15 minutes.

8.99 BOILED PEAS ENGLISH STYLE — PETITS POIS A L'ANGLAISE/A LA MENTHE

Makes: 10 portions. Cooking time: 5–8 minutes.

Quantity	*Ingredient*
1 kg	frozen peas
15 g	salt
1½ l	boiling water
50 g	mint

Method

(1) Remove the mint leaves from the stalks and blanch them. Retain them in a basin of cold water for use when serving. Tie the stalks with string to add flavour to the peas whilst cooking.

(2) Place the peas into the boiling salted water whilst still frozen, add the tied mint stalks and boil steadily until cooked.

(3) Gently remove the peas from the water with a spider, placing them into a colander to drain. Discard the mint stalks.

(4) Serve slightly dome shape in a vegetable dish. Place the blanched mint leaves on top of the peas, each leaf denoting one portion.

Notes

(1) If the peas are to be retained refresh them under gently running cold water or transfer them to a container of very cold water using a spider.

(2) To retain them carefully drain them in a colander and store them either on a tray or in a basin covered with a damp cloth. Store in a refrigerator at 8 °C.

(3) Boiled peas may be reheated in a chaudfont (*see* p. 394) which may be flavoured with mint by placing a small bunch of mint or mint stalks tied with string into the water. However the chaudfont water needs to be changed frequently as it becomes rather dark in colour from the continuous cooking of the mint.

(4) Buttered Peas (8.100) may be quickly reheated with a little sugar and butter in a shallow sided saucepan. Mint leaves may be included but should be removed when the peas are served and used as a garnish.

8.100 BUTTERED PEAS — PETITS POIS AU BEURRE

Proceed as for 8.99. When cooked and drained, toss the peas in 50 g butter with a pinch of sugar.

8.101 PEAS FLEMISH STYLE — PETITS POIS A LA FLAMANDE

This consists of equal quantities of Glazed Carrots (8.64) and Boiled Peas English Style (8.99).

8.102 PUREE OF PEAS — PUREE DE PETITS POIS

Proceed as for Purée of Spinach (8.107) (*see* also p. 398 on puréed vegetables).

Runner beans

8.103 BOILED RUNNER BEANS — HARICOTS D'ESPAGNE A L'ANGLAISE (NATURE)

Runner beans are cooked, refreshed, reheated and served in any of the ways applicable to French beans (8.75–77).

Seakale

8.104 BOILED SEAKALE — CHOU DE MER A L'ANGLAISE (NATURE)

Makes: 10 portions. Cooking time: 15–20 minutes.

Quantity	*Ingredient*
1 kg	Prepared Seakale (8.31)
70 g	salt
6 l	boiling water
2	juice of lemon

Method

(1) Place the bundles of prepared seakale into gently simmering salted water with the addition of lemon juice, using a shallow sided saucepan so that the vegetable is easily removed when cooked.

(2) When cooked lift carefully from the water and drain in a colander.

(3) Serve on an asparagus dish with a drainer or on a silver flat dish lined with a dish paper and a folded napkin on top of the dish paper. Remove the string.

Notes

(1) When cooked the vegetable should be white in colour and rather glassy in appearance.

(2) To test if cooked — *see* Asparagus (8.41).

(3) Retention and reheating is as for Asparagus (*see* 8.41).

Extensions

Seakale may be served in any of the ways applicable to Asparagus (8.42–44).

Spinach

Spinach may be boiled in plenty of boiling salted water or placed into a saucepan with a minimum amount as described below. The former approach is fast losing favour as the spinach becomes rather watery and tasteless and loses many of its vitamins during cooking. With the advent of high pressure steamers the spinach can be cooked and served without having to squeeze out the water gained when cooked in the traditional manner.

8.105 BOILED SPINACH — EPINARDS A L'ANGLAISE (NATURE)

Makes: 10 portions. Cooking time: 10–15 minutes.

Quantity	*Ingredient*
2 kg	Prepared Spinach (8.33)
20 g	salt
¾ l	boiling water

Method

(1) Place the spinach into the boiling salted water, cover with a lid and boil steadily until cooked.

(2) Drain in a colander.

(3) Serve slightly dome shape in a vegetable dish.

Notes

(1) When serving boiled or buttered spinach do not pat it down with a palette knife; it should appear as loose as possible.

(2) Refresh spinach by placing the saucepan in which it has been cooked under gently running cold water. Drain in a colander and make into 100 g balls; do not attempt to squeeze the balls of spinach so that they become dry. Store on a tray covered with cling film in a refrigerator at a temperature of 8 °C.

Extensions

8.106 LEAF SPINACH IN BUTTER — EPINARDS EN BRANCHES

Makes: 10 portions. Cooking time: 5 minutes.

Quantity	*Ingredient*
1 kg	Boiled Spinach (8.105) cooked and refreshed
75 g	butter
	seasoning of salt and pepper

Method

(1) Heat the butter in a shallow sided saucepan or frying pan.

(2) Loosen the balls of spinach, cut through once or twice with a large knife and add to the butter, gently separating and incorporating the vegetable with the butter.

(3) Season to taste with salt and pepper from the mill. Toss the spinach until it is reheated and serve slightly dome shape in a vegetable dish.

8.107 PUREE OF SPINACH — PUREE D'EPINARDS

Makes: 10 portions. Cooking time: 5–10 minutes.

Quantity	Ingredient
500 g	Boiled Spinach (8.105) cooked, refreshed and squeezed into balls
50 g	butter
	seasoning of salt, pepper and nutmeg

Method

(1) Pass the spinach through a fine sieve (*see* also p. 398 on puréed vegetables).

(2) Heat butter in a shallow sided saucepan and add the purée, stirring with a wooden spatule until the purée is hot enough to serve. Season to taste with salt, pepper and nutmeg.

(3) Serve in a vegetable dish in the shape of a slight dome. Decorate with a scroll effect over the surface using a palette knife.

8.108 CREAMED PUREE OF SPINACH — PUREE D'EPINARDS A LA CREME (EPINARDS A LA CREME)

Makes: 10 portions. Cooking time: 5–10 minutes.

Proceed as in 8.107. Reheat with the addition of 2 dl cream or a light Cream Sauce (3.16). Serve exactly the same as for purée of spinach surrounding the vegetable with a band of cream.

Assessment of the completed dish

(1) The colour should be a light natural green.

(2) The texture should be fine and light, even and smooth, the cream sauce or cream having completely integrated with the spinach.

(3) The flavour should be of cream and spinach with a hint of nutmeg.

(4) It should be in the shape of a slight dome with a scroll effect marked across the surface, and surrounded by a light band of cream.

8.109 PUREE OF SPINACH WITH CROUTONS — PUREE D'EPINARDS AUX CROUTONS

Proceed as in 8.107. Garnish the completed dish with small triangular shaped bread croûtons lightly fried in butter until golden.

Spring cabbage

8.110 BOILED SPRING CABBAGE — CHOU DE PRINTEMPS

Makes: 10 portions. Cooking time: 10–15 minutes.

Quantity	*Ingredient*
5 × 350 g	Prepared Spring Cabbage tied into portion sizes (8.34)
70 g	salt
6 l	boiling water

Method

(1) Place the prepared cabbage into the boiling salted water and boil steadily until cooked.

(2) Remove from the liquid, place onto a cutting board and remove the string.

(3) Taking each cabbage separately, cut in two lengthways and fold in halves by folding the tops under. Lightly squeeze out any excess liquid but not to the extent that the vegetables become dry. Reform into wedge shapes.

(4) Serve in a vegetable dish. Do not pile one portion on top of another.

Note

Spring cabbage may also be boiled in the same way as Cabbage (8.58) in which case they are not tied into portion bundles.

8.111 BUTTERED SPRING CABBAGE — CHOU DE PRINTEMPS AU BEURRE

Proceed as in 8.110. When serving brush the surface with 50 g melted butter.

Sugar peas

8.112 BOILED SUGAR PEAS — MANGE-TOUT

They are prepared and served in exactly the same way as French beans (8.75–77).

Swedes

8.113 BOILED SWEDES — RUTABAGAS A L'ANGLAISE (NATURE)

Swedes are cooked and presented in the same way as Turnip (8.114–118).

Turnips

When prepared for serving as a vegetable dish turnips may be cut into the following shapes and sizes:

Barrel shaped approximately 3 cm in length
Diced ½ cm × ½ cm
Baton shaped 2 mm × 2 mm in length

When cooked for making into purée they are cut into rough pieces approximately 5 cm in size.

Turnips may be cooked by barely covering them with cold salted water using 20 g salt and 1 l water to 1 kg turnips. The following method is called the conservative method of cookery in which only a small amount of water is used.

8.114 BOILED TURNIPS — NAVETS A L'ANGLAISE (NATURE)

Makes: 10 portions. Cooking time: 8–10 minutes.

Quantity	*Ingredient*
1 kg	Prepared Turnips (8.37)
6 g	salt
¾ l	water

Method

(1) Place the water and salt into a shallow sided saucepan, add the prepared turnips, cover with a lid and boil steadily until cooked.

(2) Drain the turnips in a colander.

(3) Serve slightly dome shape in a vegetable dish.

Extensions

8.115 BUTTERED TURNIPS — NAVETS AU BEURRE

Proceed as in 8.114. When serving brush the surface of the vegetables with 50 g melted butter.

8.116 TURNIPS IN A CREAM SAUCE — NAVETS A LA CREME

Proceed as in 8.114. Gently simmer the cooked drained turnips in 3 dl cream until the cream has slightly reduced. Season to taste with salt and cayenne pepper.

8.117 PUREE OF TURNIPS — NAVETS EN PUREE

Proceed as in 8.114 and continue as on p. 398 on vegetable purées.

8.118 GLAZED TURNIPS — NAVETS GLACES

Cut the turnips into shapes and proceed as for Glazed Carrots (8.64).

VEGETABLES BOILED IN A BLANC

Vegetables cooked in a blanc include artichoke bottoms, celeriac, Jerusalem artichokes and salsify. A blanc consists of water and lemon juice which is lightly thickened with flour.

8.119 *PREPARATION OF A BLANC*

Quantity	*Ingredient*
50 g	flour
2½ l	cold water
2	juice of lemons
20 g	salt

Method

(1) Place the flour into a receptacle and whisk in the water.
(2) Strain through a conical strainer.
(3) Add the lemon juice and salt.
(4) Bring to the boil.

Notes

(1) This preparation is now ready to receive the vegetables. Items cooked in this preparation should be covered with a muslin cloth during cooking and retention.

(2) A blanc preparation needs to be very light and the ratio of flour to water should be approximately 100 g of flour to 5 litres of water.

Retention

Vegetables that have been cooked in a blanc should be retained for future use in the blanc in which they have been cooked, not in an aluminium container as this will cause the vegetables to discolour but preferably in a receptacle made of plastic, stainless steel or china. Vegetables cooked in this way must be covered with a damp cloth when cold and stored in a refrigerator at approximately 8 °C. (*See* also individual recipes for variations to this general method.)

Reheating

To reheat vegetables cooked in a blanc, reboil the blanc in which they were originally cooked. This will bring them back to their original state. If the vegetables are to be used in a dish which is to be cooked by a process in addition to boiling then this rule does not apply.

Artichoke bottoms

8.120 *BOILED ARTICHOKE BOTTOMS — FONDS D'ARTICHAUT*

Makes: 10 portion garnish. Cooking time: 15 minutes.

Quantity	*Ingredient*
10	Prepared Artichoke Bottoms (8.1)
1 l	Blanc Preparation (8.119)

Method

(1) Place the artichoke bottoms into the gently simmering blanc and cover with a muslin cloth until they are cooked.

(2) Remove the saucepan from the stove and allow the artichokes to remain in the blanc until required.

Reheating

If required whole reheat the artichokes in the liquid in which they were originally cooked or in hot water with the addition of lemon juice and salt.

Quartered artichoke bottoms however are generally reheated in butter with the addition of a little lemon juice.

Assessment of the completed dish

(1) The bottoms should be cooked but firm and undamaged.
(2) They should not be fibrous.
(3) They should be whitish in colour, not grey or brown.
(4) They should be well shaped and cleanly cut with the choke completely removed.

Extensions

Artichoke bottoms may be served as part of an hors-d'oeuvre, as a garnish to accompany meat and poultry items, as a garnish to or an integral part of potato and fish dishes, and also as a vegetable in its own right. For example:

(a) as an hors-d'oeuvre dish:

8.121 ARTICHOKE BOTTOMS GREEK STYLE — FONDS D'ARTICHAUT A LA GREQUE

Cook in water with lemon juice and a little oil with the addition of herbs *(see* 2.9).

(b) as a garnish:

8.122 GARNISH CHORON

Fill cooked artichoke bottoms with peas and serve with Noisette Potatoes (9.33).

(c) as part of a dish; e.g. Fillet of Sole Murat—Filet de Sole Murat in which shallow fried goujons of fillets of sole are served with artichoke bottoms cut into quarters together with Pommes Olivette (9.32).

Celeriac

8.123 BOILED CELERIAC — CELERI-RAVE NATURE

Makes: 10 portions. Cooking time: 15–20 minutes.

Quantity	*Ingredient*
1 kg	Prepared Celeriac (8.10)
2½ l	Blanc Preparation (8.119)

Method

(1) Place the prepared celeriac into the gently simmering blanc and cover with a muslin cloth until cooked.

(2) Remove the saucepan from the stove and allow the vegetables to remain in the blanc until required.

Notes

(1) When cooked they will be rather glassy in appearance and easily pierced with a knife.

(2) Celeriac may also be stewed rather than cooked as above. *See* 8.165.

Extensions

8.124 BUTTERED CELERIAC — CELERI-RAVE AU BEURRE

Proceed as in 8.123. Lightly toss the drained celeriac in 75 g butter and season to taste with salt and pepper from the mill.

8.125 BUTTERED CELERIAC WITH FRESH HERBS — CELERI-RAVE AUX FINES HERBES

Proceed as in 8.123 with the addition of freshly chopped tarragon, parsley, chives and chervil.

Jerusalem artichokes

8.126 BOILED JERUSALEM ARTICHOKES — TOPINAMBOURS NATURE

Makes: 10 portions. Cooking time: 10–15 minutes.

Quantity	*Ingredient*
1 kg	Prepared Jerusalem Artichokes (8.19)
2½ l	Blanc Preparation (8.119)

Method

(1) Place the prepared Jerusalem artichokes into the gently simmering blanc, cover with a muslin cloth until they are cooked.

(2) Remove the saucepan from the stove and allow the artichokes to remain in the blanc until required.

Note

When cooked the artichokes should be firm to the touch and rather transparent in appearance.

Assessment of the completed dish

(1) The artichokes should be cooked yet relatively firm to the touch.

(2) They should not be fibrous or stringy.

(3) They should be a pleasant off-white colour.

(4) There should be no flavour of lemon apparent.

Possible problem	*Possible cause and solution*
(1) Artichokes are of poor colour	— vegetable of poor quality when purchased; care must be taken to purchase only the best quality products to avoid problems at later stages which cannot be rectified.
	— kept under poor storage conditions before cooking; care must be taken to store vegetables correctly to avoid problems at a later stage which cannot be rectified.
	— once peeled the vegetable was not immediately put into water and lemon juice; care must be taken not to leave the peeled vegetable exposed even for a short time to avoid this problem at a later stage which cannot be rectified.
	— insufficient lemon juice used in the blanc; care must be taken to prepare the blanc correctly as this problem cannot be rectified later.
	— once cooked the vegetable was removed from the liquid and retained dry; care must be taken to follow the correct procedure for retention to avoid this problem which cannot be rectified.

Extensions

8.127 BUTTERED JERUSALEM ARTICHOKES — TOPINAMBOURS AU BEURRE

Proceed as in 8.126. When serving brush the surface of the artichokes with 50 g melted butter.

8.128 BUTTERED JERUSALEM ARTICHOKES WITH PARSLEY — TOPINAMBOURS PERSILLES

Proceed as in 8.126. Lightly toss the drained artichokes in 75 g butter and a little chopped parsley. Season with salt and pepper to taste.

Salsify

8.129 BOILED SALSIFY — SALSIFIS

Makes: 10 portions. Cooking time: 10–15 minutes.

Quantity	*Ingredient*
1 kg	Prepared Salsify (8.30)
2½ l	Blanc Preparation (8.119)

Method

(1) Place the pieces of salsify into the gently simmering blanc and cover with a muslin cloth until cooked.

(2) Remove the saucepan from the stove and allow the salsify to remain in the blanc until required.

Note

When cooked salsify are firm to the touch, rather glassy in appearance and easily pierced with a knife.

Extensions

8.130 BUTTERED SALSIFY — SALSIFIS SAUTES AU BEURRE

Proceed as in 8.129. Lightly toss the drained salsify in 75 g melted butter and season to taste with salt and pepper from the mill.

8.131 SALSIFY WITH FRESH HERBS — SALSIFIS AUX FINES HERBES

Proceed as in 8.129 with the addition of freshly chopped tarragon, parsley, chives and chervil.

STEAMED VEGETABLES

All vegetables which may be boiled in salt water may also be steamed. In all other respects — preparation, retention, reheating and production of other dishes from the basic vegetable — procedures are exactly the same as for boiling.

NOTE

A pressure steamer may also be used to reheat vegetables. In this case they should be seasoned to taste before reheating.

To discuss the scientific, technical and design feature of the wide range of pressure steamers commercially available is outside the scope of this book. However, cooking times for vegetables cooked in pressure steamers are greatly reduced when compared with traditional methods. It is advisable always to refer to the cookery guides supplied by the manufacturers of the equipment.

NOTE

Certain safety procedures must be followed when using pressure steamers. In the interest of personal safety reference should be made to such information supplied by the manufacturers before using such equipment.

BRAISED VEGETABLES

Vegetables may be braised in a liquid in a saucepan covered with a lid in an oven at a temperature of 175 °C. The process may be applied to Belgian chicory or endives, cabbage, celery, fennel, leek, lettuce, marrow, onions, peas and pimentoes.

General method for braising vegetables

Celery, fennel, cabbage, leeks, lettuce and onions may all be braised in the following manner. *See* also individual recipes on pp. 431–40 for further details on particular vegetables.

8.132 BRAISED VEGETABLES — LEGUMES BRAISEES

Makes: 10 portions. Cooking temperature: 175 °C.

Quantity	*Ingredient*	
	prepared vegetables	
50 g	butter	
100 g	sliced carrots	bed of roots
100 g	sliced onion	bed of roots
50 g	sliced celery	bed of roots
1 sprig	thyme	bed of roots
1	bayleaf	bed of roots
1 clove	crushed garlic	bed of roots
75 g	bacon pieces	
1½ l	white stock	
10	grooved slices of carrot (*see* Table 23)	
20 g	salt	
	pepper	

Method

(1) Blanch the vegetables by placing them into the boiling salt water, boiling them for 10 minutes then refreshing them under cold water.

(2) Drain the vegetables.

(3) Butter and season the saucepan and place in the bed of roots.

(4) Place in the vegetables and three-quarters cover with the white stock. Add the grooved sliced carrot.

(5) Cover the vegetables with buttered greaseproof paper, cover with a lid and bring to the boil.

(6) Braise the vegetables for the appropriate time until cooked (*see Note* (2) below).

(7) Remove the vegetables and set aside the grooved carrot for garnish.

(8) Strain the cooking liquid into a saucepan, skim, remove any grease and season to taste.

(9) Arrange the vegetables in a vegetable dish with a little of the cooking liquid. Garnish each portion with the slices of grooved carrot.

Notes

(1) When braising lettuce omit the grooved carrot (*see* 8.154).

(2) When cooked the vegetables should have a glossy appearance. The point of a small knife should also penetrate the root ends of the vegetables with ease, or if gently squeezed between the fingers the vegetables should not resist pressure.(*See* also individual recipes below for alternative or more appropriate methods for testing if cooked.)

8.133 BRAISED VEGETABLES IN SAUCE — LEGUMES BRAISEES AU JUS

Makes: 10 portions. Cooking time: 10 minutes.

Quantity	*Ingredient*
	Braised Vegetables (8.132)
1 l	cooking liquid from vegetables
3 dl	Jus Lié (3.8) or Demi-glace (3.7)
25 g	butter

Method

(1) Strain the cooking liquid into a shallow sided saucepan, boil and reduce until it is of a sticky consistency.

(2) Add the jus lié or sauce demi-glace and boil and skim. Adjust the consistency and season to taste. Strain and re-boil.

(3) Complete the sauce by adding small knobs of butter and shaking the pan to incorporate.

(4) Serve the vegetables in a vegetable dish, lightly coat with the sauce and garnish each vegetable portion with the slices of grooved carrot.

Retention

(a) Celery, endives, fennel, cabbage, leeks, lettuce, marrow,

pimento: Once braised these vegetables should be placed in a stainless steel or earthenware dish and the cooking liquid strained over them. When cold they should then be covered with cling foil and stored in a refrigerator at 8 °C.

NOTES

(1) Stuffed vegetables do not lend themselves readily to retention as they tend to take on a shrivelled appearance when reheated using traditional methods.

(2) If the vegetables have been coated with a sauce they do not lend themselves to retention. When reheated the sauce adversely affects the colour, taste and texture of the food.

(b) Peas: Once braised the vegetables should be placed in a stainless steel or earthenware dish with the cooking liquid. When cold they should be covered with cling film and stored in a refrigerator at 8 °C.

(c) Red cabbage: Once braised, remove and discard the muslin bag containing the herbs and the bacon fat. The cabbage should be placed in a stainless steel or earthenware dish with the cooking liquid. When cold the vegetables should be covered with cling film and stored in a refrigerator at 8 °C.

Reheating

Reheat the vegetable gently in an oven in the liquid in which it was braised, covered with buttered greaseproof paper and a lid. If necessary a little white stock may be added.

Cabbage

8.134 BRAISED SMALL CABBAGES — PETITS CHOUX BRAISES

Makes: 10 portions. Cooking time: 1 hour. Oven temperature: 175 °C.

Quantity	*Ingredient*
2½ kg	Prepared Cabbage (8.7)
	seasoning of salt and pepper

Method

(1) Blanch the cabbage for 10 minutes and drain in a colander.

(2) Select the largest and greenest leaves and spread them on a cloth.

(3) Divide the remainder of the cabbage into ten equal parts and place in the centre of the leaves. Season with salt and pepper.

(4) Enclose the cabbage in the outer leaves to form a ball shaped vegetable and extract some of the excess water by squeezing the balls in a cloth.

(5) Proceed as in 8.132. When serving coat with the strained cooking liquid.

Extension

8.135 BRAISED SMALL CABBAGES IN SAUCE — PETITS CHOUX BRAISES AU JUS

Proceed as in 8.134. When serving coat with Braised Vegetable Sauce (*see* 8.133).

Celery

8.136 BRAISED CELERY — CELERIS BRAISES

Makes: 10 portions. Cooking time: 2 hours. Oven temperature: 175 °C.

Quantity	*Ingredient*
5 sticks (1 kg)	Prepared Celery (8.11)

Method

Proceed as in 8.132.

Note

When serving cut the celery into lengths of approximately 5 cm.

Extensions

8.137 BRAISED CELERY IN SAUCE AU JUS — CELERIS BRAISES AU JUS

Proceed as in 8.132. When serving coat with Braised Vegetable Sauce (8.133).

8.138 CELERY MILANAISE — CELERIS MILANAISE

Proceed as in 8.132. When serving sprinkle the surface of the celery with 50 g grated Parmesan cheese and 50 g melted butter and glaze under a salamander grill. Complete with 100 g Nut Brown Butter (6.48).

Chestnuts

8.139 BRAISED CHESTNUTS — MARRONS BRAISES

Makes: 10 portions of garnish. Cooking time: 30 minutes. Oven temperature: 175 °C.

Quantity	*Ingredient*
1½ kg	Prepared Chestnuts (8.12)
50 g	butter
½ l	white stock
1 stick	celery
	salt and pepper

Method

(1) Butter a shallow sided saucepan and add the chestnuts. Barely cover with the stock and add the stick of celery and seasoning. Bring to the boil and cover with buttered greaseproof paper and a lid.

(2) Braise the chestnuts for the prescribed time until the nuts are soft yet remain whole.

(3) Remove the chestnuts from the liquor and place them in a basin to one side.

(4) Boil and reduce the liquor until it forms a syrupy glaze. Replace the chestnuts and carefully incorporate them into the glaze.

Notes

(1) Once cooked and retained in the glaze they will disintegrate, especially if retained in a bain-marie for any length of time.

(2) It is prudent to retain the chestnuts in the stock in a refrigerator for further use rather than in the glazed stock. Reheating in the glaze may be difficult and cause them to fall to pieces.

(3) Reheating should be slow and carefully carried out to avoid breaking or puréeing the chestnuts.

Endives

8.140 BRAISED ENDIVES — ENDIVES BRAISEES

Makes: 10 portions. Cooking time: 30 minutes. Oven temperature: 175 °C.

Quantity	*Ingredient*
10 × 100 g	Prepared Endives (8.15)
2	juice of lemons
50 g	butter
	salt and pepper

Method

(1) Butter and season a shallow sided saucepan.

(2) Place in the endives and sprinkle with lemon juice.

(3) Cover the endives with buttered greaseproof paper and then cover with a lid.

(4) Place into the oven and braise for the prescribed time until cooked.

(5) Remove from the liquid and place onto a chopping board. Cut in two lengthways and fold the top half underneath to form a triangular shape.

(6) Arrange in a vegetable dish and coat with the cooking liquid.

Notes

(1) Do not add water to the endives when braising them as it may make them bitter.

(2) When cooked the endives should be perfectly white in colour.

Extensions

When serving 8.141–144 below omit the cooking liquor.

8.141 BRAISED ENDIVES IN SAUCE AU JUS — ENDIVES BRAISEES AU JUS

Proceed as in 8.140. When serving coat with Braised Vegetable Sauce (8.133).

8.142 ENDIVES MILANAISE

Proceed as in 8.140. When serving sprinkle the surface of the endives with 25 g grated Parmesan cheese and 25 g melted butter and glaze under a salamander grill. Complete with 50 g Nut Brown Butter (6.48).

8.143 ENDIVES MORNAY

Proceed as in 8.140. Coat with 2 dl Mornay Sauce (3.15), sprinkle with grated cheese and melted butter and gratinate under a salamander grill.

8.144 SAUTEED ENDIVES — ENDIVES SAUTEES AU BEURRE (or ENDIVES MEUNIERE)

Proceed as in 8.140. Drain and shallow fry the endives in butter. Arrange the endives in a vegetable dish, squeeze a little lemon juice over them and sprinkle with chopped parsley. Complete with 100 g Nut Brown Butter (6.48).

Fennel

8.145 BRAISED FENNEL — FENOUILS BRAISES

Makes: 10 portions. Cooking time: 1½ hours. Oven temperature: 175 °C.

Quantity	*Ingredient*
5 × 200 g	Prepared Fennel (8.16)

Method

Proceed as in 8.132. When serving coat with the strained cooking liquid.

Extensions

8.146 BRAISED FENNEL IN SAUCE AU JUS — FENOUILS BRAISES AU JUS

Proceed as in 8.132. When serving coat with Braised Vegetable Sauce (8.133).

8.147 BRAISED FENNEL MILANAISE — FENOUILS BRAISES MILANAISE

Proceed as in 8.132. When serving sprinkle the surface of the fennel with 50 g grated Parmesan cheese and 50 g melted butter and glaze under a salamander grill. Complete with 100 g Nut Brown Butter (6.48).

Leeks

8.148 BRAISED LEEKS — POIREAUX BRAISES

Makes: 10 portions. Cooking time: 1 hour. Oven temperature: 175 °C.

Quantity	*Ingredient*
5 × 125 g	Prepared Leeks (8.20)

Method

Proceed as in 8.132. When serving coat with the strained liquid.

Note

When serving cut the leeks lengthways and fold the top half underneath to form a triangular shape.

Extensions

8.149 BRAISED LEEKS IN SAUCE AU JUS — POIREAUX BRAISES AU JUS

Proceed as in 8.132. When serving coat with Braised Vegetable Sauce (8.133).

8.150 BRAISED LEEKS MILANAISE — POIREAUX BRAISES MILANAISE

Proceed as in 8.132. When serving sprinkle the surface of the leeks with 50 g grated Parmesan cheese and 50 g melted butter and glaze under a salamander grill. Complete with 100 g Nut Brown Butter (6.48).

Onions

8.151 *BRAISED ONIONS — OIGNONS BRAISES*

Makes: 10 portions. Cooking time: 1 hour. Oven temperature: 175 °C.

Quantity	*Ingredient*
10 × 120 g	Prepared Onions (8.24)

Method

Proceed as in 8.132. When serving coat with the strained cooking liquid.

Extension

8.152 *BRAISED ONIONS IN SAUCE AU JUS — OIGNONS BRAISES AU JUS*

Proceed as in 8.132. When serving coat with Braised Vegetable Sauce (8.133).

Marrow

See 8.172 for Braised Stuffed Marrow.

Peas

8.153 *BRAISED PEAS (or PEAS IN THE FRENCH STYLE) — PETITS POIS A LA FRANCAISE*

Makes: 10 portions. Cooking time: 1 hour. Oven temperature: 175 °C.

Quantity	*Ingredient*
1 kg	peas
20	button onions
1 × 150 g	shredded lettuce
10 g	sugar
1 l	white stock
50 g	butter (for thickening when cooked)
	salt

Method

(1) Place all the ingredients into a shallow sided saucepan and bring to the boil.
(2) Cover with buttered greaseproof paper and a lid.
(3) Braise in the oven for the prescribed time until cooked.

(4) When cooked lightly thicken the vegetable liquid by adding knobs of butter, incorporating them by shaking the pan with the peas.

(5) Season to taste with salt and pepper.

Note

A mixture of even amounts of flour and butter (Beurre Manié (3.54)) may be used as the thickening agent.

Pimentoes

Pimentoes may be stuffed and braised in the same way as marrow. *See* 8.172.

Lettuce

8.154 BRAISED LETTUCE — LAITUES BRAISEES

Makes: 10 portions. Cooking time: 45 minutes. Oven temperature: 175 °C.

Quantity	*Ingredient*
5 × 150 g	Prepared round leaf Lettuce (8.21)
10	heart shaped Croûtons (7.105)
	finely chopped parsley

Method

(1) Blanch the lettuce for 5 minutes.

(2) Remove from the water and place onto a chopping board. Cut in two lengthways and fold the top half underneath to form a triangular shape.

(3) Proceed as in 8.132.

(4) When cooked reform into triangular shapes, squeezing out a little of the cooking liquid.

(5) Arrange in a dish but do not overlap. Coat with the strained cooking liquid.

(6) Dip the end of each croûton into the liquid then into the chopped parsley and place between each portion.

Extension

8.155 BRAISED LETTUCE IN SAUCE — LAITUES BRAISEES AU JUS

Proceed as in 8.154. When serving coat with Braised Vegetable Sauce (8.133).

Red cabbage

8.156 BRAISED RED CABBAGE — CHOU ROUGE BRAISE

Makes: 10 portions. Cooking time: 2 hours. Oven temperature: 175 °C.

Quantity	Ingredient
50 g	butter
100 g	sliced onions
1½ kg	Prepared Red Cabbage (8.28) coarsely shredded
1 dl	vinegar
1	bouquet garni
1	muslin bag containing peppercorns, juniper berries, coriander seeds, cinnamon stick and cloves
450 g	bacon fat
250 g	cooking apples, peeled and diced
10 g	sugar
20 g	salt

Method

(1) Place the butter into the saucepan in which the cabbage is to be braised. Add the sliced onions and allow to gently cook but do not colour.

(2) Season the prepared cabbage and place in the pan. Add the vinegar, bouquet garni and the bag of herbs.

(3) Cover the surface with the bacon fat, buttered greaseproof paper and a lid.

(4) Braise for about 1¼ hours.

(5) Remove from the oven and add the apples and sugar.

(6) Continue to braise for a further 30–45 minutes until cooked.

(7) Remove and discard the bacon fat and the bag of herbs. Season to taste with salt and pepper.

(8) Serve slightly dome shaped in a vegetable dish.

8.157 BRAISED SAUERKRAUT WITH GARLIC SAUSAGE — CHOUCROUTE BRAISEE

Makes: 10 portions. Cooking time: 2 hours. Oven temperature: 175 °C.

Quantity	Ingredient
1½ kg	sauerkraut
3	whole carrots
2	whole onions
1	bouquet garni
1	muslin bag containing peppercorns, juniper berries, coriander seeds and cloves
½ l	dry white wine
500 g	streaky bacon
450 g	bacon fat (slices)
500 g	thickly sliced garlic sausage
10	Boiled Potatoes (9.1)

Method

(1) Place half the cabbage into the saucepan in which the

cabbage is to be braised. Place in the whole vegetables, bouquet garni, muslin bag and streaky bacon. Add the remainder of the cabbage and white wine.

(2) Place the slices of bacon fat on top, buttered greaseproof paper and lid.

(3) Braise for about 1 hour.

(4) Remove the streaky bacon and place in the garlic sausage. Continue to braise until the cabbage is cooked.

(5) Serve in an earthenware dish; garnish with slices of sausage, bacon, carrot and boiled potato.

SHALLOW FRIED VEGETABLES

Certain raw vegetables, e.g. sliced onions and sliced baby marrow, may be shallow fried in butter in a pan on top of the stove. Vegetables that have previously been boiled or steamed and refreshed may be reheated in a chaudfont, well drained and then also shallow fried. Alternatively they may be drained immediately they are cooked and then shallow fried in butter until they are lightly coloured, e.g. cauliflower, marrow, Brussels sprouts. Shallow fried vegetables appear on the menu as Légumes Sautés or Légumes Sautés au Beurre.

Service

Serve in a stainless steel or silver vegetable dish. The size of the dish should be in proportion to the number of portions contained in it. The serving dish should be hot.

Assessment of the completed dish

(1) The vegetables should appear fresh. They should be of an even size and, where appropriate, neatly cut.

(2) They should be a fresh colour depending upon type.

(3) They should be nutty in texture and not overcooked.

(4) There should be no water or fat in which the vegetables have been cooked in the bottom of the dish.

(5) They should be lightly and evenly coloured on all sides.

Possible problem	*Possible cause and solution*
(1) Vegetables have discoloured and broken up	— too many vegetables shallow fried at the same time — vegetables were shallow fried too slowly

Possible problem	*Possible cause and solution*	
	— vegetables were badly handled when being fried — once cooked the vegetables were held too long in the pan in which they were fried — vegetables were fried too quickly	Once vegetables have been badly handled or improperly cooked there is little that can be done to rectify the problems that arise. Careful preparation and cooking as close to the time they are required are the safest ways to avoid any problems.
(2) Flavour of the vegetables has deteriorated	— once cooked the vegetables were held too long in the pan in which they were fried — generally the vegetables have been retained in a hot cupboard or bain-marie for too long	

8.158 SHALLOW FRIED ONIONS — OIGNONS SAUTES (OIGNONS LYONNAISE)

Makes: 10 portions. Cooking time: 15 minutes.

Quantity	*Ingredient*
750 g	sliced onions prepared for shallow frying
100 g	butter
	salt

Method

(1) Melt the butter in a shallow sided saucepan. Add the sliced onions and season with salt.

(2) Cook gently on top of the stove tossing frequently until lightly golden and cooked. Season to taste.

(3) Drain off any excess fat and serve in a vegetable dish.

8.159 SWEETCORN CAKES

Makes: 10 portions. Cooking time: 5 minutes.

Quantity	*Ingredient*
250 g	nibs of sweetcorn (canned or boiled and drained)
2	eggs
100 g	flour
	seasoning of salt and pepper
1 dl	oil

Method

(1) Mix the sweetcorn and eggs together. Add the flour and mix to a rather stiff mixture. Season to taste.

(2) Heat the oil in a shallow sided pan and place in 10 spoonfuls of the mixture to form a small pancake. Fry until golden on each side and drain.

DEEP FRIED VEGETABLES

Vegetables to be deep fried fall into two categories

(a) Items that have to be boiled or steamed before being deep fried may be coated in batter, e.g. cauliflower and salsify.

(b) Items which are deep fried without prior cooking, e.g. eggplant, baby marrow and onions, are generally fried in the French style (à la Française) by passing them first through milk and then seasoned flour. The vegetables are usually cut into slices before frying.

Vegetables deep fried in batter

Retention

Ideally, this type of product should be cooked and served to order. If it must be held and where there is no specialised equipment available, it should be placed on absorbent kitchen paper and kept in a hot cupboard at a temperature of 26 °C.

If the vegetables are held at too high a temperature, this will adversely affect their crispness, colour and flavour and they will become stale looking. If held at a moderately hot constant temperature, the items will weep and become soft.

Do not cover deep fried vegetables with a lid once they are cooked as the steam will condense against the lid and fall back upon the food causing it to become damp and soggy.

8.160 DEEP FRIED SALSIFY — BEIGNETS DE SALSIFIS (or SALSIFIS FRITS)

Makes: 10 portions. Cooking time: 5–8 minutes. Cooking temperature: 175 °C

Quantity	*Ingredient*	
1½ kg	Boiled Salsify (8.129)	
1 dl	oil	marinade
1	juice of lemon	marinade
5 g	chopped parsley	marinade
	salt and pepper	marinade
250 g	seasoned flour	
	Yeast Batter (6.40)	
	salt	

Method

(1) Marinade the cooked and drained salsify for approximately 30 minutes.

(2) Pass through seasoned flour and shake off all the surplus.

(3) Pass the vegetables through the batter, drain off all the excess and deep fry.

(4) Once cooked, drain thoroughly on absorbent kitchen paper and season with salt.

(5) Serve on a dish paper in a vegetable dish.

Service

Serve in a vegetable dish lined with a dish paper, or serve on an oval silver or stainless steel flat dish with a dish paper or a cloth napkin. This item should not be served covered with a lid.

Assessment of the completed dish

(1) Outer coating of batter should be light golden in colour, crisp and firm.

(2) The outer skin of the batter should be crisp with no floury batter inside surrounding the vegetable pieces.

(3) The vegetable should be seasoned but with no sign of salt on the dish paper or napkin.

(4) There should be no sign of oil on the dish paper or napkin.

(5) The vegetables should be loosely but neatly arranged in a heap in the centre of the dish.

*Possible problem**	*Possible cause and solution**
(1) Batter will not colour	— fat was not hot enough; ensure that the fat is at the correct temperature before frying as this problem cannot later be rectified.
	— too many vegetable pieces fried at once; this reduces the temperature of the fat and should be avoided as it cannot be rectified later.
	— fat not allowed to reheat between batches; the fat must be allowed to recover its heat before the next items are added to avoid this problem which cannot later be rectified.
	— incorrect type of flour used for the batter; care must be taken that the correct type of flour (i.e. soft or ordinary) is used to make

*These problems, causes and solutions are similar to those found for deep fried fish — *see* p. 191–2. A small sample should be tested first and any problems rectified before frying the main quantity.

Possible problem	*Possible cause and solution*
	the batter to avoid this problem as it cannot be rectified later.
	— insufficient sugar used in the batter; care must be taken to prepare the batter correctly to avoid this problem which cannot be rectified later.
(2) Vegetable pieces become soggy and break during cooking	— fat was not hot enough; ensure that the fat is at the correct temperature before frying as this problem cannot be rectified later.
	— too many vegetable pieces fried at once; this reduces the temperature of the fat and should be avoided as the problem cannot be rectified later.
	— items were handled too much during frying, e.g. stirred too often with a spider; this must be avoided as the problem cannot be rectified later.
	— a frying basket was used; this should be avoided as the problem cannot be rectified later.
	— outer coating of batter not allowed to set before handling with the spider; ensure that the batter has set during the initial stages before using a spider to avoid this problem which cannot later be rectified.
(3) Batter runs off the vegetable pieces during cooking	— batter was too thin; care must be taken when preparing the batter as this problem cannot be rectified later.
	— fat was not hot enough; ensure that the fat is at the correct temperature before frying as this problem cannot be rectified later.
(4) Completed item has an inner doughy layer	— batter was too thick; care must be taken when preparing the batter to avoid this as it cannot be rectified later.
	— vegetables were not passed through flour before coating with the batter; care must be taken to follow the correct coating procedure as this problem cannot later be rectified.
(5) Completed items lack flavour	— items were not held correctly after cooking; ensure that the correct procedures are followed for storage after cooking.
	— batter not seasoned; care must be taken

Possible problem	*Possible cause and solution*
	when preparing the batter as this cannot be rectified later.

8.161 DEEP FRIED CAULIFLOWER IN BATTER — CHOU-FLEUR FRIT

Proceed as in 8.160 using 1½ kg cauliflower pieces, approximately 10 g each in weight, boiled as in 8.65.

Vegetables deep fried in milk and flour

8.162 FRENCH FRIED ONIONS — OIGNONS FRITS A LA FRANCAISE (or OIGNONS FRITS)

Makes: 10 portions. Cooking time: 5 minutes. Cooking temperature: 180 °C.

Quantity	*Ingredient*
1 kg	onions, peeled and cut into rings approximately 3 mm thick
½ l	milk
250 g	seasoned flour
5 g	salt

Method

(1) Dip the onion rings in milk, drain well and pass through seasoned flour. Place the floured rings of onion into a frying basket, shake off surplus flour and deep fry.

(2) Once cooked, drain thoroughly on absorbent kitchen paper and lightly season with salt. Serve on a dish paper in a vegetable dish.

To test when cooked

As these vegetables are rather thin they should be cooked when they are a light golden colour. However, a more accurate test is to remove the vegetables when coloured, drain and test with finger pressure. If the inside yields then they are cooked.

8.163 DEEP FRIED EGGPLANT — AUBERGINE FRITE

Cut the eggplant into slices ½ cm thick and proceed as in 8.162.

8.164 DEEP FRIED BABY MARROW — COURGETTE FRITE

Cut the baby marrow into slices ½ cm thick and proceed as in 8.162.

STEWED VEGETABLES

Vegetables may be stewed on top of the stove either in their own juices or a little water, covered with a lid.

8.165 CELERIAC — CELERI-RAVE ETUVE

Makes: 10 portions. Cooking time: 5 minutes.

Quantity	*Ingredient*
1 kg	Prepared Celeriac (8.10)
100 g	butter
1	juice of lemon
5 g	salt

Method

(1) Cut the celeriac into half moon shapes approximately 3 cm in length and immediately place them into a saucepan containing water and half the quantity of lemon juice. Blanch for 5 minutes.

(2) Drain the vegetables, place them into a shallow sided saucepan with the butter, the remainder of the lemon juice and seasoning, cover with a lid and stew them until cooked.

(3) Drain the vegetables and serve them slightly dome shape in a vegetable dish.

8.166 SUGAR PEAS — MANGE-TOUT

Makes: 10 portions. Cooking time: 5–8 minutes.

Quantity	*Ingredient*
1 kg	Prepared Sugar Peas (8.35)
100 g	butter
1 dl	water
5 g	salt

Method

(1) Melt the butter in a saucepan, add the prepared peas, salt and water. Cover with a lid and stew them until cooked.

(2) Drain the vegetables and serve slightly dome shape in a vegetable dish.

8.167 MUSHROOM PUREE — DUXELLES

Makes: Preparation for a variety of uses. Cooking time: 15 minutes.

Quantity	*Ingredient*
750 g	finely chopped mushrooms (or mushroom stalks and trimmings)
50 g	butter
75 g	finely chopped shallots or onion
5 g	finely chopped parsley
	salt and pepper

Method

(1) Melt the butter in a saucepan, add the chopped shallots or onion and cook without colouring.

(2) Add the chopped mushrooms, cover with a lid and stew for the prescribed time, allowing the liquid from the mushroom to reduce in quantity until the mushrooms are fairly dry.

(3) Add the chopped parsley and season to taste with salt and pepper.

Notes

(1) Duxelles is a mushroom preparation which is used in the production of many other dishes such as Delice of Plaice Cubat (6.17), Stuffed Tomatoes (8.176) and Stuffed Eggplant (8.174).

(2) The addition of white breadcrumbs will produce a firm mushroom stuffing.

(3) For future use, transfer the duxelles mixture to a porcelain, stainless steel or plastic basin and allow to cool. Cover with cling film and keep in a refrigerator at 8 °C.

8.168 RATATOUILLE NICOISE

Makes: 10 portions. Cooking time: 40 minutes.

Quantity	*Ingredient*
2 dl	olive oil
750 g	sliced onions
750 g	eggplant cut into 1 cm dice
500 g	red pimento, pips removed, cut into thin slices
500 g	courgette cut into 1 cm dice
3 cloves	crushed and chopped garlic
500 g	peeled, pipped and diced tomatoes
6	coriander seeds
5 g	chopped parsley
	basil
20 g	salt

Method

(1) Heat the oil in a shallow sided saucepan. Add the onions and cook but do not allow them to colour.

(2) Add the eggplant, red pimento, courgette and garlic. Cover with a lid and allow to gently stew for approximately 30 minutes.

(3) Add the tomatoes and coriander seeds and season to taste.

(4) Allow to gently stew for a further 10 minutes until all the vegetables are soft but on no account mushy.

(5) Complete by adding the chopped parsley and basil.

(6) Serve slightly dome shape in a vegetable dish.

Note

This dish may also be served cold as part of an hors-d'oeuvre.

8.169 *TOMATO CONCASSEE — TOMATES CONCASSEES*

Makes: Preparation for a variety of uses. Cooking time: 10 minutes.

Quantity	*Ingredient*
50 g	chopped shallots or onion
50 g	butter
500 g	blanched, peeled and pipped tomatoes cut into dice (*see* 8.38)
1 sprig	thyme
1	bayleaf
1 clove	crushed garlic (optional)
	salt and pepper

Method

(1) Melt the butter in a saucepan, add the chopped shallots or onion and cook without colouring.

(2) Add the diced tomato, cover with a lid and stew for a few moments. Add the remainder of the ingredients and complete cooking for the prescribed time.

Notes

(1) Tomato concassée preparation is used in the production of many other dishes such as Tomato Omelette (5.20), Spaghetti Napolitaine (5.46) and Suprême of Cod Dugléré (6.12).

(2) For future use, transfer the tomato concassée preparation to a porcelain, stainless steel or plastic basin and allow to cool. Cover with cling film and keep in a refrigerator at 8 °C.

GRILLED VEGETABLES

Certain vegetables such as mushrooms and tomatoes may be brushed or sprinkled with oil or melted butter and grilled. Grilled vegetables do not lend themselves to retention — mushrooms become dry and rubbery whilst tomatoes appear shrivelled.

8.170 *GRILLED MUSHROOMS — CHAMPIGNONS GRILLES*

Makes: 10 portions of garnish. Cooking time: 5–8 minutes.

Quantity	*Ingredient*
10–20	Prepared Cup Mushrooms (8.23)
1 dl	oil
	salt

Method

(1) Place the mushrooms on an oiled grilling tray, sprinkle with oil and season with salt.
(2) Grill until cooked.

Note

Mushrooms may be stuffed after they have been grilled — *see* 8.175.

8.171 GRILLED TOMATOES — TOMATES GRILLEES

Makes: 10 portions of garnish. Cooking time: 5–8 minutes.

Quantity	*Ingredient*
10	medium sized tomatoes
1 dl	oil
	salt

Method

(1) Wash the tomatoes, remove the stalk and the eye.
(2) Place on an oiled grilling tray eye side down and make a criss-cross incision on the top.
(3) Season and brush with oil.
(4) Grill until cooked

Notes

(1) Tomatoes may be blanched and skinned before being grilled whole, or may be cut in half without being peeled and then grilled.
(2) When cooked they will yield to slight finger pressure; lightly squeeze between the fingers.

STUFFED VEGETABLES

Some vegetables may be stuffed with an appropriate filling before being cooked either under a salamander grill or in a hot oven.

8.172 BRAISED STUFFED MARROW — COURGE FARCIE BRAISEE

Makes: 10 portions. Cooking time: 45 minutes. Oven temperature: 175°C.

Quantity	*Ingredient*
2 kg	Prepared Marrow (8.22)
250 g	Rice Pilaff (5.54)
2 dl	oil
4 dl	thin Jus Lié (3.8) or Demi-glace (3.7)
	seasoning

Method

(1) Stuff the marrow with the rice pilaff.

(2) Shallow fry the marrow in oil very quickly until light golden over the outer surface of the vegetable.

(3) Place into a saucepan, season and add the jus lié or demi-glace.

(4) Cover the marrow with buttered greaseproof paper then with a lid and bring to the boil.

(5) Braise for the prescribed time until cooked.

(6) Remove the marrow from the liquid and allow to stand for approximately 5 minutes before slicing; it will be easier to handle with less likelihood of it breaking into pieces when sliced.

(7) Boil, skim and strain the cooking liquid. Season to taste with salt and pepper.

(8) Cut the marrow into 1 cm slices and serve in a vegetable dish slightly overlapping surrounded with the sauce.

Notes

(1) Some chefs suggest cutting the marrow into two lengthways to remove the pips before stuffing (*see* 8.22).

(2) Baste the marrow at regular intervals during cooking to prevent dryness on the surface of the vegetable.

(3) The finished sauce may be completed with 25 g butter.

(4) Additional ingredients may be added to the rice stuffing such as sliced cooked mushrooms, tomato concassée, diced cooked chicken, and so on.

8.173 BRAISED STUFFED PIMENTOES — PIMENTS FARCIS BRAISES

Stuffed pimentoes are prepared and braised as for marrow using 10 × 100 g pimentoes. *See* 8.172.

8.174 STUFFED EGGPLANT — AUBERGINES FARCIES

Makes: 10 portions. Cooking time: 30 minutes. Oven temperature: 180 °C.

Quantity	*Ingredient*
5 × 150 g	Prepared Eggplants (8.14)
1 dl	oil
250 g	Duxelles Mixture (8.167) (garlic optional)
150 g	Tomato Concassée (8.169)
5 g	finely chopped parsley
	salt and pepper
50 g	white breadcrumbs
25 g	melted butter
3 dl	Jus Lié (3.8) or Demi-glace (3.7)

Method

(1) Place the prepared eggplant onto a previously oiled baking tray, sprinkle with oil and cook in the oven until the centre of the vegetable is soft.

(2) Remove the centre pulp from the egg plant with a spoon, place onto a cutting board and chop with a large knife.

(3) Add the pulp to the hot duxelles mixture followed by the tomato concassée and parsley. Season to taste.

(4) Fill the halves of the eggplant with the filling slightly dome shape and mark trellis fashion with the edge of a palette knife.

(5) Replace onto the baking tray, sprinkle the surface of the vegetables with breadcrumbs and melted butter and place into the oven to gratinate.

(6) Serve in a vegetable dish surrounded with either jus lié or demi-glace.

8.175 STUFFED MUSHROOMS — CHAMPIGNONS FARCIS

Makes: 10 portions. Cooking time: 5 minutes. Oven temperature: 200 °C.

Quantity	*Ingredient*
20	Grilled Flat Mushrooms (8.170)
500 g	Duxelles Mixture (8.167)
50 g	white breadcrumbs
50 g	melted butter

Method

(1) Place the duxelles mixture into a piping bag with a star tube. Pipe whirl-shape into the centre of the grilled mushrooms.

(2) Sprinkle with breadcrumbs and melted butter. Reheat and gratinate the surface either in an oven or under a salamander grill on a low shelf.

8.176 STUFFED TOMATOES — TOMATES FARCIES

Makes: 10 portions. Cooking time: 5 minutes. Oven temperature: 180 °C.

Quantity	*Ingredient*	
10 × 100 g	Prepared Tomatoes (8.38)	
250 g	Duxelles Mixture (8.167) (garlic optional)	filling
20 g	white breadcrumbs	filling
1 dl	Jus Lié (3.8) or Demi-glace (3.7)	filling
2 g	finely chopped parsley	filling
25 g	melted butter	
	salt	
	sprigs of parsley	

Method

(1) To the duxelles mixture add the breadcrumbs, jus lié or demi-glace and chopped parsley, and season to taste.

(2) Fill the tomatoes with the mixture slightly dome shape; mark trellis fashion with the edge of a palette knife, sprinkle with breadcrumbs and melted butter, and replace the tomato lids.

(3) Place the tomatoes onto a previously buttered baking tray, season with salt, brush with melted butter and place in the oven to gratinate.

(4) Serve in a vegetable dish garnished with sprigs of parsley.

Notes

(1) The filling should be moist, therefore adjust accordingly with either breadcrumbs if too soft and sauce if too firm.

(2) Use a piping bag with plain 2 cm tube for filling the tomatoes.

(3) The filling outlined in Tomatoes Provençale (8.177) may be substituted for the duxelles mixture filling.

8.177 TOMATOES PROVENCALE — TOMATES FARCIES PROVENCALE

Makes: 10 portions. Cooking time: 5 minutes. Oven temperature: 180 °C.

Quantity	*Ingredient*	
10 × 100 g	Prepared Tomatoes (8.38)	
100 g	melted butter	filling
100 g	finely chopped onion	filling
1 clove	crushed and chopped garlic	filling
500 g	white breadcrumbs	filling
2 g	finely chopped parsley	filling
50 g	melted butter	
	salt and pepper	
	sprigs of parsley	

Method

(1) Heat the oil in a shallow sided saucepan, add the chopped onion and garlic and allow to cook gently but do not colour.

(2) Add the breadcrumbs and chopped parsley and season to taste.

(3) Fill the tomatoes with the filling slightly dome shape and mark trellis fashion with the edge of a palette knife.

(4) Place the tomatoes onto a previously buttered tray. Sprinkle the surface with melted butter.

(5) Place the tomatoes in the oven to gratinate the filling and cook the tomatoes.

(6) Serve in a vegetable dish garnished with sprigs of parsley.

Notes

(1) To test if cooked, gently press the tomato between the fingers, it will yield to the slightest pressure when cooked.

(2) Remember the filling is already cooked and so requires no further cooking but should be heated throughout.

BAKED VEGETABLES

Vegetables may also be baked in the form of soufflés and are generally served as a savoury item towards the end of a meal. They are cooked in special porcelain dishes, usually for a set number of portions. They are cooked in a bain-marie in the oven and are served in the same dish that they are cooked in.

8.178 SPINACH SOUFFLE — SOUFFLE FLORENTINE

Makes: 4 portions. Cooking time: 30 minutes. Oven temperature: 200 °C.

Quantity	*Ingredient*
2 dl	Béchamel (3.4)
2	egg yolks
50 g	Spinach Purée (*see* 8.107)
3	egg whites (stiffly beaten)
	salt, pepper and nutmeg
25 g	melted butter (for the mould)

Method

(1) Whisk the egg yolks into the warm béchamel.

(2) Incorporate the purée using a wooden spatule, season to taste and allow to cool.

(3) Stiffly beat the egg whites and fold into the mixture in two stages until all is incorporated.

(4) Butter a 15 cm soufflé mould. Pour in the mixture until the mould is approximately two-thirds full.

(5) Cook in the oven in a bain-marie for the prescribed time.

(6) When cooked serve at once.

Note

To test if cooked, assessment of the completed dish, possible problems and causes are similar to those outlined under sweet soufflés — *see* pp. 572–3.

PULSE VEGETABLES

Haricot beans, small kidney beans and yellow and green split peas are perhaps the most common varieties in use in catering, although the range is much wider. Whatever type is used the same principles discussed below hold true.

Chefs do not agree whether pulse vegetables should be soaked before cooking or not, and if so whether they should be soaked in cold water or covered with hot water before soaking them. In this respect the same guide is given for cooking pulse vegetables as outlined under purée soups based on pulse vegetables (*see* pp. 94–7). Pulse vegetables with an outer shell, e.g. haricot and kidney beans, require soaking in cold water for approximately 12 hours before cooking; they are then washed in cold water in preparation for cooking. Pulse vegetables such as yellow and green split peas with no outer shell do not require soaking before cooking as it may make them difficult to cook through.

Some difficulty may be experienced when cooking some pulse vegetables. They remain tough or hard at the centre of the vegetable when cooked for the prescribed time. Adding 10 g of baking soda to every 1 kg of pulse vegetable and 2 l of water when soaking or cooking will help to alleviate the problem.

Retention

Once cooked, remove and discard any whole vegetables, bouquet garni and bacon trimmings or ham bone. The vegetables should be placed in a stainless steel or earthenware dish with the cooking liquid. When cold the vegetables should be covered with cling film and stored in a refrigerator at 8 °C.

Reheating

Reheat the vegetables gently in an oven in the liquid in which they were cooked covered with a lid.

8.179 HARICOT BEANS — HARICOTS BLANC

Proceed as in 8.180. When cooked, drain the vegetables and gently incorporate 3 dl Tomato Sauce (3.10), and 250 g Tomato Concassée (8.169).

8.180 KIDNEY BEANS — FLAGEOLETS

Makes: 10 portions. Cooking time: 2½–3 hours. Oven temperature: 150 °C.

Quantity	*Ingredient*
750 g	kidney beans (soaked for 12 hours)

Quantity	*Ingredient*
75 g	whole carrots
1	whole onion
150 g	bacon trimmings or ham bone
1	bouquet garni
	seasoning

Method

(1) Wash the soaked beans, place them into a saucepan and cover with cold water. Bring to the boil and skim.

(2) Add the remainder of the ingredients and allow to simmer for 1 hour.

(3) Cover with a lid and transfer to an oven until cooked.

(4) When cooked, remove and discard the whole vegetables, bacon trimmings or ham bone and the bouquet garni. Season to taste.

(5) Serve in a vegetable dish with a little of the liquid.

Notes

(1) Do not season the vegetables until they are nearly cooked. To do so may make them oversalted due to the salt in the bacon or ham bone.

(2) To test if cooked remove some of the vegetables with a perforated spoon and test them between the fingers. When cooked they are soft and yield to finger pressure.

8.181 KIDNEY BEANS IN BUTTER — FLAGEOLETS AU BEURRE

Proceed as in 8.180. When cooked, drain the vegetables and gently toss them in 50 g melted butter.

8.182 PEASE PUDDING

Makes: 10 portions of garnish. Cooking time: 2 hours. Oven temperature: 150 °C.

Quantity	*Ingredient*
400 g	yellow split peas
1 l	water (approximately)
50 g	whole carrots
1	whole onion
75 g	bacon trimmings
75 g	butter
	seasoning

Method

(1) Wash the split peas, place them into a saucepan and cover with cold water. Bring to the boil and skim.

(2) Add the remainder of the ingredients, cover with a lid and cook in the oven for the prescribed time.

(3) When cooked, remove and discard the whole vegetables and bacon trimmings.

(4) Pass the peas through a sieve or liquidiser, return to a clean saucepan and mix in the butter with a wooden spatule. Season to taste.

(5) Serve as a garnish to the main item in the shape of a slight dome decorated scroll fashion with a palette knife.

Notes

(1) Pease pudding may be retained in a basin covered with cling film in a refrigerator.

(2) The mixture may be reheated with a little butter in a saucepan on top of the stove and stirred with a wooden spatule to prevent burning.

NOUVELLE CUISINE

The preparation of vegetables and methods of cooking outlined in this chapter are also in accord with the Nouvelle Cuisine. There are, however, a number of points to bear in mind.

(a) All vegetables are cooked to order. They are never refreshed and subsequently reheated.

(b) Vegetables are never cooked beyond the crisp or nutty stage.

(c) Any sauce added to or accompanying any vegetables should not be roux or flour based.

(d) Some leaders in the field of Nouvelle Cuisine do not allow gratination to be applied to any dish.

CONVENIENCE VEGETABLES

Vegetables are available in a variety of frozen, dehydrated, canned and other pre-prepared forms, either whole or cut into the required shapes. Frozen and dehydrated vegetables are without doubt the most commonly used convenience forms.

Frozen vegetables

Boiling is the fundamental method of cooking vegetables, whether fresh or frozen. The main difference is that frozen vegetables need to be boiled for less time.

Frozen vegetables should always be placed into boiling salted water in their frozen state. To defrost them before cooking will have an adverse effect in terms of colour, texture and flavour. Cooking time depends upon the type of vegetable and the manufacturers' instructions should always be referred to.

The principles and practices covering testing when cooked, refreshing, retention and re-heating as well as problems encountered during cooking and assessment are exactly the same for frozen as for fresh vegetables. However, it should be borne in mind that, although the two products are similar in many respects, they are not exactly the same because of the processes through which vegetables pass during freezing.

Dehydrated vegetables (Accelerated Freeze Dried (AFD))

The same principles apply to boiling dehydrated vegetables as to frozen and fresh vegetables. One common error is to soak all dehydrated vegetables before boiling. Before cooking always refer to the manufacturers' instructions.

Dehydrated vegetables should be plunged into boiling salted water. Cooking times are different to those for similar fresh and frozen vegetables and once again the manufacturers' instructions should always be noted before cooking.

(*See* 8.179–182 for the preparation and cooking of pulse vegetables.)

CHAPTER 9

Potatoes

VARIETIES

There are many different varieties of potatoes grown in this country and around the world, and a knowledge of their names and optimum uses will help in selecting those most suitable for a particular potato dish, or range of dishes. Table 24 provides a simple guide to the more popular varieties and their uses.

British potatoes are available all the year round. The early varieties become available in late May and carry on into August; the main crop varieties take over in September through to May.

The early new potatoes are Jersey Royals, Home Guard, Maris Peer, Pentland, Javelin, Ulster, Sceptre and Wilja, and these are generally available nationally. Others such as Epicure, Maris Bard, Estima, Ulster Prince, Craig Alliance and Red Craig Royals may not be available everywhere.

The main crop varieties are Desiree, King Edwards and Maris Piper; Pentland Crown, Pentland Dell, Pentland Hawk, Pentland Ivory and Pentland Squire are not nationally available.

Some potatoes have a tendency to turn black after cooking, e.g. Pentland Ivory.

Most new potatoes are waxy in texture, but none of the main crop are and it is necessary to purchase Dutch Bintjes potatoes if waxy ones are required for use when making, for example, Pommes Macaire (9.46).

New potatoes are imported from Spain, the Canary Islands, Cyprus, Egypt and elsewhere before the British early varieties come to market. These foreign varieties are good replacements when the old main crop is coming to an end and are reasonably good when fried. However, in comparison with the early season Jersey Royals these imports do not have anywhere near their exquisite flavour nor approach them in smallness of size.

STORAGE

New potatoes should be purchased for immediate use and should not be kept in store for longer than forty-eight hours because, being freshly dug, they dry out quickly and will not scrape easily.

Main crop potatoes are waxy in the autumn but go floury during storage.

TABLE 24. TYPES AND OPTIMUM USES OF POTATOES

Uses	Early			Main crop		
	Excellent	*Very good*	*Good*	*Excellent*	*Very good*	*Good*
Boiled	Home Guard	Rutland Javelin Ulster Sceptre Wilja	Rutland Javelin Ulster Sceptre Wilja	King Edwards	Desiree Maris Piper Pentland Hawk	Pentland Crown Pentland Dell
Mashed	None	None	None	King Edwards	Desiree Maris Piper Pentland Hawk	Pentland Crown Pentland Dell
Roasted	None	Maris Peer Ulster Sceptre	Home Guard Ulster Sceptre Wilja	Desiree	King Edwards Maris Piper	Pentland Crown Pentland Dell Pentland Hawk
Chips	None	Ulster Sceptre	Home Guard Wilja	Desire Maris Piper King Edwards	None	Pentland Crown Pentland Dell Pentland Hawk
Baked/ Jacket	None	None	None	King Edwards	Desiree	None

Potatoes should be kept in a cool dark dry store in bags and on wooden slats. If they become warm they will begin to sprout and if kept in the light they go green and should not then be used.

Potatoes pick up other smells easily so should be kept away from strong smelling materials or commodities. Potatoes also bruise easily, even in their bags, therefore they should be handled with care.

BASIC METHODS OF COOKING POTATOES

Whilst there are hundreds of recipes for the preparation of potatoes to accompany a main dish, there are only ten basic ways of cooking them. All potato dishes are based on one or more of these basic methods of cooking. This makes it easier to understand the vast range of potato dishes and to help choose an appropriate potato dish to complement the main dish.

NOTE

As some potato recipes involve more than one method of cooking, for convenience these have been placed in the most important section. For example, boiling applies not merely to dishes that are based on the whole boiled potatoes but also to those that are boiled, then cut into slices and given further treatment.

Classification of potato dishes

(a) Boiled and steamed: steamed, plain boiled, parsley, minted, new.

(b) Mashed potatoes (some may be completed with milk): snow, purée, mousseline, biarritz, à la crème, maître d'hôtel.

(c) Duchesse potatoes: duchesse, marquise, galette, croquette, St. Florentine.

(d) Duchesse potatoes with chou paste: dauphine, elizabeth, lorette.

(e) Deep fried potatoes: pailles, allumettes, game chips, chips, mignonette, gaufrette, pont-neuf, bataille.

(f) Shallow fried potatoes:

(i) half cooked in their skins: sautées, provençale, lyonnaise;

(ii) cooked from raw: à cru, columbine, parmentier, sablées, noisette, parisienne, rissolées, en cocotte or olivette.

(g) Etuvé potatoes: boulangère, savoyarde, fondantes, cretin.

(h) Anna potatoes: anna, voisin, mireille, darphin.

(i) Potatoes cooked in their skins:

(i) served in their skins: jacket;

(ii) pulped variety: macaire, arlie, byron.

(j) Roast potatoes: roast, château.

PREPARATION OF POTATOES

Loss or wastage due to peeling may vary significantly between 15–30 per cent depending upon the type of potato used. Loss may become even higher through poor planning and adverse handling.

Grade the potatoes according to size before peeling. For example, where they are to be turned barrel shape to a certain size, then select those that are of an approximate size. Once peeled and shaped it is inevitable that there will be some potato trimmings — these may be used for soups or a small quantity may be incorporated into the Boulangère type of potato dish (*see* 9.35). In no circumstances should trimmings be used for the mashed or purée type of potato dishes, as they will become dark in colour, gluey in texture and almost inedible.

Hand-peeled main crop variety

Where necessary wash the potatoes to remove any dirt. Peel using a potato peeler. Remove and discard any blemishes or green parts (these give a bitter taste when eaten) with a small knife. Rewash the potatoes and place them into a non-aluminium type container covered with cold water.

Machine-peeled main crop variety

Avoid overfilling the machine to allow the correct peeling action. The time it takes to peel potatoes by machine will depend upon the abrasive material incorporated into the design of the equipment. A general guide is not to leave them in the machine too long, just long enough to remove the peel without undue wastage. Remove and discard any blemishes and green parts with a small knife. Rewash and place them into a non-aluminium type container covered with cold water.

Storage of main crop varieties once peeled

Some practitioners avoid overnight storage due to loss of nutrients. However, if they are to be stored they should be retained in a receptacle covered with cold water in a refrigerator at a temperature of 8 °C for as short a time as possible.

New potatoes

There are two methods of preparing new potatoes for boiling or steaming.

(a) Wash the potatoes and cook them in their skins. As soon as they are cooked, peel them. (The overriding factor in favour of this method is enhanced flavour but it is rather time consuming.)

(*b*) Wash and peel the potatoes before they are cooked. (The advantage with this method is that time and labour costs are greatly reduced.)

If (*a*) is followed the potatoes should be washed to remove the dirt and then boiled. As soon as they are cooked they should be peeled and placed into very hot salt water and held in a bain-marie until required.

New potatoes may be scraped in their raw state but must be well washed to remove the dirt before scraping. Once they are prepared they should be retained in cold water until required.

BOILED AND STEAMED POTATOES

Boiled old potatoes

The potatoes are first covered with cold water, brought to the boil and then gently simmered until cooked. Allow approximately 18 g salt to every 1½ kg potatoes and 1½ litres of water which should barely cover them. Approximate cooking times for potatoes will depend on the type of potato and the size into which it is cut for cooking. For example, potatoes cut into small dice will need only 10 minutes, whereas whole medium sized potatoes will require 20–25 minutes.

The following recipes apply to main crop varieties of potatoes which should be prepared either barrel shaped 4–5 cm long or neatly trimmed and evenly cut to the size and approximate shape of a new potato. Unless they require further attention (as in 9.2), boiled — or steamed — potatoes should be served quite plainly.

9.1 BOILED POTATOES — POMMES NATURE

Makes: 10 portions. Cooking time: 20–25 minutes.

Quantity	*Ingredient*
1½ kg	Prepared Potatoes (*see* pp. 461–2)
18 g	salt
1½ l	water

Method

(1) Cover the prepared potatoes with cold water, add the correct proportion of salt and bring gently to the boil.

(2) When boiling remove any impurities that may surface during cooking.

(3) Simmer gently until cooked (*see* below).

Notes

(1) Potatoes do not cook any faster by boiling them rapidly; in fact this may make them break up.

(2) It is not trade practice to cover potatoes with a lid whilst boiling.

To test if cooked (boiled or steamed)

Remove a potato with a perforated spoon and pierce it with a knife. If cooked the point will enter without resistance. It is also possible to apply gentle pressure to the potato with the hand — the potato will yield if cooked.

Possible problem	*Possible cause and solution*
(1) The potatoes have discoloured between peeling and cooking	— potatoes have become bruised during storage due to careless handling; care must be taken when storing potatoes as bruising cannot be rectified.
	— prolonged period in potato machine; care must be taken to avoid this although the potatoes may be re-peeled using a potato peeler.
	— once peeled the potatoes were not completely submerged in cold water; always store peeled potatoes in cold water in a refrigerator at 8 °C, although if discoloured for this reason they may be re-peeled using a potato peeler.
	— retained in warm atmosphere even though covered with cold water; always store peeled potatoes in cold water in a refrigerator at 8 °C, although if discoloured for this reason they may be re-peeled using a potato peeler.
	— retained in an aluminium container; utensils made from aluminium should always be avoided, although if discoloured for this reason they may be re-peeled using a potato peeler.
(2) The potatoes have discoloured during or after cooking	— *see* causes and solutions to (1) above.
	— some potatoes tend to discolour during cooking because of the way they were grown; add the juice of half a lemon to every litre of water to prevent this problem which cannot otherwise be rectified.
(3) The potatoes break up once cooked	— pan has been overfilled; always select shallow sided saucepans to boil potatoes in for ease of serving and, where possible, produce several smaller batches.

Possible problem	*Possible cause and solution*
	— potatoes were cooked too far in advance of demand; where possible always boil potatoes as close as possible to the time they are required to avoid the problems caused by retention.
	— potatoes were incorrectly handled when being served; always select shallow sided saucepans to boil potatoes in for ease of serving and, where possible, produce several smaller batches.
	— incorrect type of potato used; always select a variety of potato that is suitable for the method of cooking to be applied.

9.2 MINTED POTATOES — POMMES A LA MENTHE

Makes: 10 portions. Cooking time: 20–25 minutes.

Quantity	*Ingredient*
1½ kg	shaped potatoes
100 g	butter
	mint

Method

(1) Pick off the mint leaves allowing one leaf for each portion to be served. Blanch and completely refresh them and reserve the leaves in cold water until required.

(2) Boil the potatoes together with the mint stalks tied with a piece of string as in 9.1.

Service

Either:

(a) carefully remove the potatoes from the liquid with a perforated spoon and place in a vegetable dish. Brush the surface of the potatoes with melted butter and place one blanched mint leaf on each portion; or

(b) melt the butter in a shallow sided saucepan. Add the cooked and drained potatoes and roll them carefully until coated. Serve in a vegetable dish and place one blanched mint leaf on each portion.

Possible problem	*Possible cause and solution*
(1) The potatoes discolour during or after cooking	— too much mint cooked with the potatoes. — mint left in with the potatoes once cooked; always remove the mint from the water

Possible problem	*Possible cause and solution*
	once the potatoes are cooked to avoid discoloration which cannot be rectified.

Steamed old potatoes

There are a number of different types of pressure steamer available; some cook by moist heat, others by dry heat. Different steam pressures, whether cooking by moist or dry heat, the size and type of potato to be cooked, all have a bearing on the time it takes to cook the potatoes which may take from 5–30 minutes accordingly. It is therefore advisable to refer to the cookery manual supplied by the manufacturer with the equipment. For example, one manufacturer recommends 6–8 minutes at a steam pressure of 7 kg for an average sized potato.

Some steamer trays are made of stainless steel whilst others are made of non-stainless steel metals. For the latter type it is advisable to place the potatoes on a damp cloth and cover them with another to prevent discoloration during cooking.

Season the potatoes before cooking either by carefully distributing the salt over the food using approximately 18 g salt to every 1½ kg potatoes, or by using a solution of 18 g salt to 1 l water for the same quantity.

9.3 STEAMED POTATOES — POMMES VAPEUR

Makes: 10 portions.

Quantity	*Ingredient*
1½ kg	prepared potatoes
18 g	salt (or salt solution of 18 g salt : 1 l water)

Method

(1) Place the potatoes into a steamer tray. Carefully distribute the salt or salt solution.

(2) Steam until cooked.

(3) Serve neatly arranged in a vegetable dish.

Possible problem	*Possible cause and solution*
(1) The potatoes have discoloured once peeled before cooking	— *see* problems, causes and solutions to 9.1.
(2) The potatoes have discoloured during or after cooking	— *see* causes and solutions to 9.1 above. — some potatoes tend to discolour during cooking because of the way they were grown; use 18 g salt, 1 l water and the

Possible problem	*Possible cause and solution*
	juice of half a lemon to every 1½ kg potatoes to prevent discoloration.
	— steamer tray is made of a metal other than stainless steel; place the potatoes on a damp cloth and cover them with another damp cloth during and after cooking to help minimise the problem of discoloration which cannot be rectified.

9.4 PARSLEY POTATOES — POMMES PERSILLEES

Makes: 10 portions. Cooking time: 20 minutes.

Quantity	*Ingredient*
1½ kg	shaped potatoes
100 g	butter
	finely chopped parsley

Method

Cook the potatoes as in 9.1 or 3 then finish in either of the following ways.

(*a*) Drain off all excess water and place in a vegetable dish. Brush the surface of the potatoes with melted butter and sprinkle with chopped parsley as they are served.

(*b*) Melt some butter in a shallow sided pan. Add the chopped parsley and gently place in the drained potatoes. Roll them carefully in the butter and parsley until they are evenly coated.

Service

Place the coated potatoes into a vegetable dish, neatly arranged in a slight dome shaped pile. Care must be taken that they do not become broken when served due to overfilling the dish.

Assessment of the completed dish

(1) The potatoes should be of an even size, either barrel shape or simply trimmed. The complete outer surface of each potato should be coated in butter and finely chopped parsley.

(2) The texture of the potato will differ with the type used.

(3) The potatoes should be seasoned and cooked to the correct degree; none should be broken.

New potatoes

New potatoes may be boiled or steamed in exactly the same way as old ones. In no circumstances should new potatoes be used for mashed or purée types of potato dishes as they become dark in colour, lumpy, gluey in texture and almost inedible.

New potatoes should always be named as such on the menu. For example:

New Minted Potatoes — Pommes Nouvelles à la Menthe

Parsley New Season Potatoes — Pommes Nouvelles Persillées

9.5 STEAMED NEW JACKET POTATOES — POMMES NOUVELLES EN ROBES DE CHAMBRE

Wash the potatoes well and cut a line all round just piercing the outer skin. Steam as in 9.3 until cooked.

Serve in their skins either in a vegetable dish or place on a napkin on an underdish.

MASHED POTATOES

Basic method

9.6 MASHED POTATOES — POMMES PUREE

Makes: 10 portions. Cooking time: 30 minutes.

Quantity	*Ingredient*
1½ kg	prepared and peeled potatoes
100 g	butter
1 dl	milk
18 g	salt
	pepper
	nutmeg

Method

(1) Boil the potatoes as in 9.1.

(2) Once cooked, drain off all the liquid. Return the potatoes to the pan in which they have been cooked and place them on the stove in order to dry off all the surplus water.

(3) Pass the potatoes through a sieve, returning them to a clean saucepan on the stove to keep warm.

(4) Add the knobs of butter, hot milk and seasoning and stir with a wooden spatule until the mixture is of a creamy consistency.

Service

Serve heaped in a vegetable dish into the shape of a slight dome decorated scroll fashion with a palette knife.

Assessment of the completed dish

The potatoes should be white, light and creamy textured with a very slight flavour of nutmeg.

Possible problem	*Possible cause and solution*
(1) Mixture is dark in colour and gluey in texture	— incorrect type of potato used; always select a variety of potato that is suitable for the method of cooking to be applied.
	— the potatoes were not dried out thoroughly once cooked; care must be taken over this critical phase in the preparation to avoid this problem which cannot be rectified.
	— too many potatoes were passed through the sieve at the same time; care must be taken to avoid this as it makes the potatoes cold and difficult to pound and the result cannot be rectified.
	— potatoes were rubbed through the sieve rather than pounded vigorously; care must be taken to follow the correct procedure for passing the potatoes to avoid this problem which cannot be rectified.
	— once prepared the mixture was held too long in a bain-marie; prepare the mixture as close as possible to the time it is required to avoid the problems caused by prolonged retention.
(2) Mixture has a watery texture	— potatoes have been overcooked; add some potato powder mix until the correct consistency is achieved provided the mixture is very hot, or add the watery mixture to a dry potato powder mix.
	— potatoes were not drained and dried correctly; add some potato powder mix until the correct consistency is achieved provided the mixture is very hot, or add the watery mixture to a dry potato powder mix.

9.7 CREAMED POTATOES — POMMES MOUSSELINE

Proceed as in 9.6 but substitute cream for milk.

9.8 POMMES BIARRITZ

Proceed as in 9.6 but add finely chopped ham, diced, skinned and cooked red pimento and chopped parsley.

9.9 POMMES PUREE AU GRATIN

Proceed as in 9.6 but when serving the surface is sprinkled with grated cheese and melted butter and placed under a salamander grill until evenly coloured a golden brown.

Boiled or steamed potatoes completed in milk

9.10 POMMES A LA CREME

Makes: 10 portions. Cooking time: 40 minutes.

Quantity	*Ingredient*
1½ kg	potatoes boiled or steamed in their skins (⅔ cooked)
1 dl	milk
2 dl	cream
	salt
	pepper
	nutmeg

Method

(1) Remove the skins and cut the potatoes into slices 3–4 mm thick.

(2) Place the sliced potatoes into a saucepan and barely cover them with milk. Season to taste and cook on top of the stove until tender.

(3) Complete by adding the cream at the point of service.

9.11 POMMES MAITRE D'HOTEL

Proceed as in 9.10 but add chopped parsley.

DUCHESSE POTATO

Duchesse potato may either be served as a potato dish in its own right or prepared as the basis of a variety of garnishes and other potato dishes.

Basic duchesse potato mixture

The basic mixture is a combination of dry mashed potato, butter, egg yolks and seasoning. The texture of the mixture depends upon its ultimate use either:

(a) piped through a star tube; or
(b) hand moulded and fried.

If the mixture is to be piped through a tube the texture needs to be a little softer than for other uses; to soften it a little more butter should be used. Hand moulded duchesse mixture needs to be a little on the firm side as there is a tendency for the moulded potato to disintegrate when it is fried. To adjust the mixture, a little potato flour or powder mix may be added if necessary.

NOTE

The mixture should on no account be sticky or gluey, whatever its use.

9.12 BASIC DUCHESSE MIXTURE

Makes: 10 portions. Cooking time: 35 minutes.

Quantity	*Ingredient*
1½ kg	prepared and peeled potatoes
75 g	butter
3	egg yolks
18 g	salt
	pepper
	grated nutmeg

Method

(1) Boil the potatoes until cooked.

(2) Once cooked drain off all the liquid and return the potatoes to the pan in which they were cooked. Place it on the stove in order to dry off all the surplus water.

(3) Pass the potatoes through a sieve, returning them to a clean saucepan on the stove to keep warm.

(4) Add the knobs of butter, egg yolks and seasoning to bind the mixture and stir on the stove with a wooden spatule until the desired texture and flavour is achieved.

Piped duchesse potatoes

Duchesse potato mixture is used for decorating and complementing the texture and flavour of certain shell fish dishes, e.g. Scallops in Cheese Sauce (6.74). It is also used extensively to complement certain fish dishes that require a sauce coating, particularly where large numbers of the dish are to be served simultaneously, e.g. at a banquet, where each service dish generally contains ten portions. Although serving a dish such as Suprême of Turbot Bonne Femme (6.14) with a border of duchesse potato is not classically correct, the border of potato gives the dish extra depth enabling additional sauce to be served to ensure that there is sufficient for the number of portions of fish.

The piping and decoration of the serving dish for a fish dish with a sauce is carried out on the inner rim, never the lip, of the dish. The inner rim of the dish is first brushed with melted butter, then a line of duchesse potato is piped following the shape of the dish — this line of potato is to give height. This is followed by piping a decorative line of the same mixture on top. The surface of the mixture is sprinkled with melted butter.

When the fish sauce is to be glazed then the dish with the piped duchesse mixture is first passed through an oven or under a salamander grill to dry the surface without coloration before any other item is placed onto it. The fish and the sauce is then placed onto the dish and returned to the salamander grill in order to colour and glaze the potato and sauce at the same time.

When using a fish sauce that does not require glazing then the duchesse potato mixture may be coloured under a salamander grill before dressing the fish and coating with the sauce.

9.13 DUCHESSE POTATOES — POMMES DUCHESSE

Makes: 10 portions. Cooking time: 1 hour. Oven temperature: 200 °C.

Quantity	*Ingredient*
1½ kg	Duchesse Potato Mixture (9.12)
50 g	melted butter

Method

(1) Pipe the mixture onto a greased baking sheet through a star tube in a spiral shape with a base approximately 2 cm and to a height of 2½ cm.

(2) Sprinkle the surface of the potatoes with melted butter.

(3) Place in the oven until the outer surface becomes a light golden colour and the inside of the item is hot.

(4) Serve neatly arranged in a vegetable dish.

9.14 MARQUISE POTATO — POMMES MARQUISE

Proceed as in 9.13 but pipe into a nest shape and fill the centre with Tomato Concassée (8.169). Complete by sprinkling with melted butter and reheat as for 9.13.

Hand moulded duchesse potatoes

9.15 GALETTE POTATOES — POMMES GALETTE

These are made with basic Duchesse Potato Mixture (9.12) moulded into the shape of small cakes approximately 4 cm in diameter by 1½ cm in depth. They are marked with a trellis pattern on the presentation side and then shallow fried. When moulding, a little potato flour helps to prevent them from sticking. The aim is to produce a potato dish the outer surface of which is very lightly and evenly coloured a golden brown.

Notes

(1) Difficulty may be experienced in handling these potatoes during cooking as they are of a delicate nature.

(2) The minimum amount of oil or melted butter should be used for frying and it should be carried out in a thick bottomed pan preferably made of iron.

(3) Place in the fat, heat gently until a light haze arises, drain off most of the fat, and then shallow fry.

(4) If the temperature of the fat is too low there is a danger that the potatoes will disintegrate during cooking or stick to the pan so handle as little as possible during cooking.

Service

Serve on a vegetable dish very lightly brushed with melted butter with the trellis markings clearly visible.

9.16 CROQUETTE POTATOES — POMMES CROQUETTES

Makes: 10 portions. Cooking time: 1 hour. Fat temperature: 190 °C.

Quantity	*Ingredient*
1½ kg	Basic Duchesse Mixture (9.12)
	seasoned flour
	eggwash
	breadcrumbs
5 g	salt
	picked parsley

Method

(1) Mould the mixture into 30 g pieces cylindrical in shape about 4 cm in length by 1½ cm in diameter.

(2) Pass the pieces of potato through the flour, eggwash and breadcrumbs; remould and place on a tray sprinkled with a few crumbs.

(3) Deep fry at 190 °C using a frying basket until crisp and an even golden brown.

(4) Once cooked, drain on kitchen paper and season with salt.

(5) Serve in a vegetable dish with a dish paper, neatly arranged in a pile.

(6) Garnish with deep fried or freshly picked parsley.

Note

There are two ways of presenting this dish: either in a deep-sided vegetable dish or on an oval flat; in both instances a dish paper is used.

Assessment of the completed dish

(1) The croquettes should be of an even size and golden in colour with no sign of the outer coating splitting or cracking.

(2) The texture should be crisp on the outside and smooth on the inside.

(3) The flavour should have a pleasant hint of nutmeg combined with butter and potato.

(4) There should be no sign of either salt or fat on the dish paper on which they are served.

(5) The parsley should, if fried, be crisp and of a deep green colour.

Possible problem	*Possible cause and solution*
(1) Potatoes split open during frying	— mixture was too soft; care must be taken to heat the eggs sufficiently to bind the mixture to avoid this problem, or add some potato flour or dry potato mix to make the mixture firmer (potato flour or arrowroot may also help when moulding the potatoes before coating and a small batch should be tested before proceeding with the main quantity).
	— fat is either too cool or too hot; ensure that the fat is at the correct temperature before frying the potatoes.
	— fryer has been overfilled; care must be taken to avoid this as the problems it causes cannot be rectified.
	— fat not given sufficient time to reheat between batches; care must be taken to ensure that the fat is allowed to reach the correct temperature after each batch before frying the next.
	— potatoes were not coated correctly; care must be taken to follow the correct coating procedure to avoid this problem which cannot be rectified.
(2) Potatoes are greasy	— fat was not hot enough; ensure that the fat is at the correct temperature before frying the potatoes.
	— once cooked the potatoes have been held on a tray that does not allow them to dry; care must be taken to follow the correct retention procedure to avoid this problem.
	— potatoes have been covered with a lid once cooked; care must be taken to follow the correct retention procedure to avoid this problem.

9.17 POMMES AMANDINES

Proceed as for 9.16 but substitute finely chopped almonds for white breadcrumbs.

Note

It is trade practice to mix chopped almonds with the breadcrumbs in a ratio of about two-thirds breadcrumbs to one-third chopped almonds.

9.18 POMMES ST FLORENTINE

Proceed as for 9.16 adding some finely chopped ham to the mixture and substituting very small pieces of vermicelli for the white breadcrumbs.

Note

It is trade practice to mix the vermicelli with breadcrumbs using a ratio of about two-thirds breadcrumbs to one-third vermicelli.

DUCHESSE POTATO WITH CHOU PASTE

This is a mixture consisting of two-thirds basic duchesse potato and one-third unsweetened chou paste and is known as pommes dauphine mixture. The addition of the chou paste gives the mixture extra lightness which can make handling a little difficult particularly when moulding.

9.19 DAUPHINE POTATOES — POMMES DAUPHINE

Makes: 10 portions. Cooking time: 1 hour. Fat temperature: 190 °C.

Quantity	*Ingredient*
1 kg	Basic Duchesse Mixture (9.12)
500 g	unsweetened Chou Paste (10.45)
	flour or arrowroot
5 g	salt
	picked parsley

Method

(1) Thoroughly mix the duchesse mixture and chou paste together with a wooden spatule whilst both are still warm.

(2) Mould the mixture into 30 g pieces ball, cork or egg shaped using flour to prevent sticking.

(3) Place the moulded potatoes onto small pieces of greaseproof paper just large enough to take one or two portions.

(4) Place the paper containing the potato portions into the fryer in a frying basket. During cooking the paper will separate and float to the surface making it easy to remove with a spider. Carefully turn the potatoes whilst cooking to ensure even coloration.

(5) Once cooked, drain on kitchen paper and season with salt.

(6) Serve in a vegetable dish with a dish paper, neatly arranged in a pile.

(7) Garnish with deep fried or freshly picked parsley.

Note

Egg shaped potatoes are moulded with two tablespoons which have been dipped into hot water or warm oil to prevent sticking.

9.20 ELIZABETH POTATOES — POMMES ELIZABETH

Proceed as for 9.19 but add a little chopped cooked spinach to the mixture.

9.21 LORETTE POTATOES — POMMES LORETTE

The Basic Dauphine Mixture (9.19) should be formed into cigar shapes. If desired, once moulded the potatoes may be passed through a mixture of flour, eggwash and white breadcrumbs before deep frying.

DEEP FRIED POTATOES

This is cooking raw, shaped potatoes in deep fat or oil at a fairly high temperature (160–190 °C) until golden and crisp. The size and shape of the dish to be prepared and cooked, and whether the potatoes are cut by hand or machine (the latter being more accurate and producing less waste), will both affect the number of portions to be derived from a given weight of potato. However, 2–3 kg of unpeeled potatoes should yield ten standard portions.

The following list shows the possible shapes and cuts of potato which may be deep fried:

Pailles — thin strips 3 cm × ¼ cm
Allumettes — strips 4 cm × ¼ cm
Mignonette — strips 2 cm × ½ cm
Frites — 4 cm long × 1 cm
Pont-neuf — 4 cm long × 2 cm
Bataille — 1½ cm wedges
Pommes chips or game chips — thin slices
Pommes gaufrette or wafer potatoes — thin slices cut trellis shape

Some of these cuts should first be blanched (which in this context means that the potatoes are initially deep fried or steamed without coloration, drained and retained for further use on demand). Once blanched in fat — which is the general practice — then they should not be stored in a refrigerator as they tend to go soggy, but should be retained on a tray covered with absorbent paper permitting air to circulate freely between the items. Such cuts are pommes mignonette, frites, pont-neuf and bataille.

Other cuts such as pailles, allumettes, game chips and gaufrette are cooked until golden crisp in one operation.

9.22 DEEP FRIED POTATOES

Method

(1) Once the potatoes have been cut to the required shape, they should be washed free of starch in cold water and dried. Those of a very fine nature such as straw potatoes and game chips should be dried in a cloth or absorbent kitchen paper before being fried.

(2) Once golden all deep fried potatoes must be well drained of all traces of oil using absorbent paper, then seasoned with salt and served on a dish paper.

Notes

(1) Do not attempt to deep fry too many potatoes in one batch as there is a tendency for these to stick together during the initial stages of cooking. This results in parts of the potatoes being undercooked and unevenly coloured.

(2) Deep fried potatoes must not be covered with a lid as this will cause them to lose their crispness.

To test if cooked

Those items that are not blanched initially are cooked when they float to the surface of the oil and are golden in colour and crisp.

Blanched items are cooked when they are soft to the touch; during subsequent deep frying, they are cooked when they are golden and crisp.

9.23 CHIPS — POMMES FRITES

Makes: 10 portions. Blanching temperature: 170 °C. Colouring temperature: 190 °C.

Quantity	*Ingredient*
2 kg	peeled potatoes
5 g	salt

Method

(1) Cut the potatoes into even sized pieces approximately 4 cm long × 1 cm. Wash in cold water to remove excess starch and either dry in a cloth or allow to drain in a frying basket.

(2) Plunge into deep fat until cooked but without colour.

(3) Drain them well and retain them on a tray covered with absorbent paper until required.

(4) When required place the blanched chips into a frying basket and plunge into hot fat until crisp and golden.

(5) Remove the chips from the frying basket, place onto absorbent paper and season with salt.

(6) Serve on a dish paper on a flat silver or stainless steel dish.

Assessment of the completed dish

(1) The chips should be of an even size.

(2) They should be light golden in colour, crisp on the outside and white and fluffy inside.

(3) They should be presented on a dish paper with no trace of salt or fat on it.

(4) A standard portion consists of approximately 100 g.

Possible problem	*Possible cause and solution*
(1) The chips are soggy	— potatoes were not washed after cutting into chips to remove starch; care must be taken to follow this procedure as once the chips are fried the problem cannot be rectified. — the chips were blanched at too low a temperature; this problem may be rectified in some instances by finishing the potatoes at a higher temperature than recommended. — the frying basket or fryer was overfilled; attempting to fry too many chips at once should be avoided as the problem cannot be rectified. — the fat has been overused; the fat should be drained and replaced at regular intervals to avoid this problem which cannot be rectified. — the fat was not allowed to reheat between batches; care must be taken not to allow the temperature of the fat to fall before frying another batch to avoid this problem which cannot be rectified. — once cooked and ready to serve the chips have been covered with a lid; care must be taken to follow the correct retention procedure as this problem cannot be rectified.

SHALLOW FRIED POTATOES

This is cooking raw or partially boiled or steamed potatoes — cut into either slices, dice, barrel or ball shapes with a special cutter — in a small quantity of fat in a frying pan on top of the stove until they are golden brown. The term used for cooking potatoes in this way is *sauter*, which means tossing the potatoes to obtain even cooking and coloration.

9.24 SAUTE POTATOES — POMMES SAUTEES

Makes: 10 portions. Cooking time: 45 minutes.

Quantity	*Ingredient*
2 kg	potatoes, boiled or steamed in their skins (9.2 or 9.3)
¼ l	oil
75 g	butter
5 g	salt
	chopped parsley

Method

(1) Peel, cool and cut the potatoes into ½ cm slices.

(2) Heat the oil in a frying pan. Place in the sliced potatoes and gently toss or sauteé until an even golden colour.

(3) Drain the cooked potatoes in a colander, then replace them in a frying pan with the melted butter.

(4) Toss gently and season with salt.

(5) Arrange in a vegetable dish in the shape of a dome and serve finished with chopped parsley.

Notes

(1) It is trade practice in some kitchens to peel the potatoes before boiling or steaming, but there is a distinct loss of flavour in doing so.

(2) The flavour of the potatoes will also be influenced by the type of fat or oil used.

(3) Always thoroughly clean the frying pan with a cloth between batches.

Assessment of the completed dish

(1) The potatoes should glisten and be of an even light golden colour.

(2) They should be rather crisp on the outside and fluffy inside.

(3) They should be evenly sliced but slightly broken.

(4) They should have the distinctive flavour associated with potatoes cooked in their skins.

Possible problem	*Possible cause and solution*
(1) Completed potatoes are broken into very small pieces, undercoloured and soft with black specks	— potatoes were overcooked when boiled or steamed and so fall to pieces when sliced and sautéd; care must be taken when preparing the potatoes to be sautéd as problems in the initial stages cannot be rectified.
	— the frying pan has been overfilled and the potatoes have been cooked at too fast a rate in insufficient fat; care must be taken to avoid overfilling the pan, overheating the fat and cooking too fast as the resulting problem cannot be rectified.
	— the potatoes have been sautéd at too low a temperature; care must be taken to heat the fat to the correct temperature before cooking to avoid this problem which cannot be rectified.
(2) Completed potatoes are soggy	— potatoes overcooked at the boiling or steaming stage; care must be taken when preparing the potatoes to be sautéd as problems in the initial stages cannot be rectified later.
	— wrong type of potato used; always select the most suitable variety of potato for the method of cooking to be applied.
	— the potatoes have been sautéd at too low a temperature; care must be taken to heat the fat to the correct temperature before cooking to avoid this problem which cannot be rectified.
(3) Completed potatoes are overcoloured with black burnt specks	— too few potatoes have been sautéd in each batch, and have been cooked too fast; ensure that the pan is about one-third full when sautéing the potatoes and monitor the temperature of the fat.
	— frying pan was not cleaned with a cloth between each batch; care must be taken over this aspect as the resulting problem cannot be rectified.

Extensions

9.25 LYONNAISE POTATOES — POMMES LYONNAISE

Proceed as for 9.24 and add Shallow Fried Sliced Onions (8.158).

9.26 PROVENCALE POTATOES — POMMES PROVENCALE

Proceed as for 9.24 and add finely crushed garlic.

Sauté potatoes cooked from raw

9.27 POMMES COLUMBINE

Proceed as for 9.31 and add strips of cooked pimento.

9.28 POMMES NOUVELLES RISSOLEES

Peel new potatoes and shallow fry. Complete with butter and parsley. In trade practice the potatoes are first peeled and boiled before being sautéd.

9.29 POMMES PARMENTIER

Proceed as for 9.31 but cut into ½ cm dice.

9.30 POMMES SABLEES

Proceed as for 9.29 and add white breadcrumbs during the last few moments of cooking, tossing them over with the potatoes.

9.31 POMMES SAUTEES A CRU

This is ½ cm slices of new potatoes shallow fried until cooked and coloured. These potatoes must be shallow fried at a slower rate than sautéd potatoes previously described.

Noisette, Parisienne and Cocotte potatoes

It is trade practice to blanch but not to refresh the potatoes for these dishes by bringing them just to the boil in cold water then draining them completely. They are then lightly coloured in oil or melted butter, seasoned with salt and placed to complete cooking in an oven at 175 °C.

This method requires less attention than the traditional method of cooking from the unblanched state and the finished dish may be held for a longer period without deterioration.

Noisette and cocotte potatoes are used extensively as part of a garnish for a wide range of dishes.

9.32 POMMES COCOTTES (or OLIVETTES)

Shallow fry small barrel shaped potatoes 1–1½ cm in length.

9.33 POMMES NOISETTE

This is shallow fried potatoes which have been cut into small balls with a special cutter.

9.34 POMMES PARISIENNE

Cut the potatoes into balls slightly larger than for Pommes Noisette (9.33). Shallow fry them and when cooked complete by rolling them in melted meat glaze (*see* p. 38).

ETUVE POTATOES

This is a method of cooking which combines baking and stewing, the potatoes being cooked in a dry heat with moisture coming from the potatoes themselves plus added white stock. When cooked most of this liquid should be absorbed into the potatoes making them quite moist and leaving a little surplus.

There are two ways of preparing these dishes:

(a) the potatoes are cut into pieces of various shapes and sizes before being cooked, e.g. sliced or diced;

(b) they are left whole or slightly shaped by trimming, e.g. as in 9.37.

9.35 BOULANGERE POTATOES — POMMES BOULANGERE

Makes: 10 portions. Cooking time: 1 hour. Cooking temperature: 200 °C for 20 minutes, then 175 °C for 40 minutes.

Quantity	*Ingredient*
1½ kg	peeled potatoes sliced 3 mm thick
250 g	sliced onions
50 g	chopped parsley
¾ l	White Stock (3.1)
75 g	melted butter
18 g	salt
	pepper

Note

The sliced onions may be lightly cooked in fat before being combined with the other ingredients.

Method

(1) Put to one side enough neatly sliced potatoes to cover the surface of the potatoes in the dish in which they are to be cooked.

(2) Place the remainder of the sliced potatoes, the onions, and parsley into a colander, season and mix together.

(3) Place the potatoes to a depth of 5 cm into an earthenware dish that has been previously buttered.

(4) Arrange the potatoes that have been put to one side neatly overlapping and covering the entire surface.

(5) Add the white stock to moisten the potatoes so that it comes three-quarters of the way up the dish.

(6) Brush the surface with melted butter.
(7) Bring to the boil on top of the stove.
(8) Place into the oven to cook, pressing down from time to time to protect the top surface from becoming dry.

To test if cooked

Pierce the potatoes with the point of a knife; if the point penetrates with ease the potatoes are cooked. If under slight finger pressure the potatoes feel firm rather than soft on the surface they are not cooked.

Notes

(1) Boulangère potatoes are sometimes served as the potato garnish with joints of lamb and may be served as a potato dish with any other main course items.
(2) During cooking it is important to press the surface potatoes down with either a palate knife or a flat utensil to avoid them curling and burning; it also helps to keep the top surface moist.
(3) It is also important to brush the surface with melted butter during cooking to prevent it drying.
(4) When cooked the surface area should be an even light golden brown colour.
(5) This kind of potato may be served in the dish in which it was cooked as this helps to control the size of portions and at the same time gives the impression that the dish was cooked especially for the customer.
(6) When cooked the dish should still be moist but most of the stock should have evaporated.
(7) The dish must be cleaned around the edges before serving.

Extension

9.36 SAVOYARDE POTATOES — POMMES SAVOYARDE

These are prepared as for 9.35 but small pieces of bacon lardons are added which have been previously blanched and tossed in butter. The surface of the potatoes is sprinkled with grated cheese and melted butter and then placed to cook in the oven.

9.37 FONDANT POTATOES — POMMES FONDANTES

Makes: 10 portions. Cooking time: 45 minutes. Oven temperature: 200 °C.

Quantity	*Ingredient*
1½ kg	waxy potatoes, barrel shaped approximately 5 cm in length

Quantity	Ingredient
1 l	white stock
50 g	melted butter
18 g	salt

Method

(1) Place the shaped potatoes into a shallow sided oven dish about 5 cm in depth. They should be placed in a single layer only.

(2) Moisten with enough white stock to come three-quarters of the way up the potatoes, season and bring them gently to the boil on top of the stove.

(3) Brush the surfaçe of the potatoes liberally with melted butter and place into the oven to bake.

Notes

(1) It is important to brush these potatoes with melted butter during cooking to prevent them drying.

(2) When cooked the potatoes should be moist, almost all of the stock having evaporated; the potatoes should be white except for the top surface which should be a very light golden colour.

To test if cooked

The potatoes should be soft to the touch. If pierced with the point of a knife it should enter without any pressure being applied.

Service

Serve neatly arranged in a vegetable dish. Do not stack them one on top of another.

Assessment of the completed dish

(1) The potatoes should be evenly sized and shaped, moist and with a very light golden surface colour.

(2) Allow approximately three potatoes per portion.

Extension

9.38 POMMES CRETIN

Proceed as for 9.37 but add finely powdered or rubbed thyme to the stock whilst cooking.

Possible problem	Possible cause and solution
(1) When cooked the potatoes are broken, cooked on all sides and dry	— incorrect type of potato used; always select a variety of potato that is suitable for the method of cooking that is to be applied. — potatoes were baked at too high a temperature; ensure that oven is at the correct

Possible problem	*Possible cause and solution*
	temperature for cooking the potatoes.
	— potatoes were overcooked; care must be taken to cook the potatoes for the correct length of time to avoid this problem which cannot be rectified.
	— potatoes were not brushed at frequent periods during baking; care must be taken to follow the correct procedure during cooking to avoid this problem which cannot be rectified.
(2) The potatoes are colourless and there is too much stock left in the dish after cooking	— incorrect type of potato used; always select a variety of potato that is suitable for the method of cooking that is to be applied.
	— too much stock was added; care must be taken to measure the ingredients accurately to avoid this problem; drain off surplus stock, brush with melted butter, return to a very hot oven to colour the surface of the potatoes.
	— oven was not hot enough; ensure that the oven is at the correct temperature for cooking the potatoes.

ANNA POTATOES

These are potatoes either sliced or, in the case of extensions, cut into thin julienne strips baked in a special anna mould. This is a deep sided mould approximately 12 cm in diameter made of either copper lined with tin or black iron and wrought steel.

9.39 ANNA POTATOES — POMMES ANNA

Makes: 10 portions. Cooking time: 45 minutes. Oven temperature: 220 °C.

Quantity	*Ingredient*
1½ kg	peeled potatoes sliced ½ mm thick
2 dl	oil
75 g	melted butter
18 g	salt
	pepper

Method

(1) Retain enough of the neatly sliced potatoes for lining the bottoms of the moulds.

(2) Place the remainder of the potatoes in a colander. Season with salt and pepper.

(3) Heat the oil in the moulds on top of the stove, using just enough to grease the bottom and sides.

(4) Place those potatoes retained neatly overlapping around the bottom of the mould. Wait until gently frying.

(5) Fill the moulds to the top with the remainder of the seasoned potatoes.

(6) Brush the surface with melted butter and allow the moulds to become very hot and the potatoes begin to fry.

(7) Place the moulds onto baking trays and bake in the oven.

(8) Whilst cooking the potatoes should be firmly pressed down and brushed with melted butter at frequent intervals.

(9) When cooked, remove the moulds from the oven and place them on the top of the stove for a few moments away from any direct heat. Make sure that the potatoes are not stuck to the sides of the mould; if so, release them from the edges with a palette knife by running it around the inner rim.

(10) To turn the potatoes out of their moulds, give them a final press down, place a lid over the top of the mould and turn it upside down so releasing the moulded potatoes onto the lid. Slide the whole item either onto a flat serving dish if they are to be served whole, or onto a cutting board in order to cut into wedges. Cut the potatoes with a sharp knife or they may break up.

(11) Neatly arrange either in a vegetable dish or on a flat silver dish and brush the surface with melted butter just before serving.

Note

To prevent sticking clean the moulds thoroughly by heating them with a little salt in them, then wiping out with a cloth. Some establishments refrain from washing the moulds so as to avoid sticking during cooking.

Service

These may be served whole or cut into portions and reformed.

Assessment of the completed dish

(1) The outer surface of the potatoes should be of an even golden colour, the top layer (that cooked at the base of the mould) presenting a neatly overlapping pattern of golden, almost crisp, potatoes.

(2) The potatoes should be evenly cut into portions and neatly reformed.

(3) The surface should glisten from the melted butter brushed on at the last moment.

(4) The potato inside should be soft but should not separate and fall out of the surrounding crust.

(5) The potatoes should be well seasoned.

Possible problem	*Possible cause and solution*
(1) Although well formed and coloured when cut into portions the potato falls to pieces	— potatoes were sliced too thickly; care must be taken over this aspect during the preparation of the potatoes as once they are cooked the problem cannot be rectified.
	— potatoes were not pressed down firmly either during or at the end of cooking; care must be taken over this aspect as once the potatoes are cooked the problem cannot be rectified.
(2) The potatoes stick to the mould	— moulds were dirty; ensure that all utensils are clean before use — in particular anna moulds should be cleaned with salt.
	— potatoes were not fried correctly; care must be taken to fry the potatoes gently at the prescribed time to avoid this problem which cannot be rectified once the potatoes are cooked.

9.40 POMMES DAUPHIN

Proceed as for 9.39 but cut the raw potatoes into julienne strips. Omit Stage (4).

9.41 POMMES MIREILLE

Proceed as for 9.39 but add quarters of cooked artichoke bottoms and small pieces of truffle.

Note

Pommes Mireille may also be made by adding artichoke bottoms and small pieces of truffle to Pommes Sautées à Cru (9.31). A third method is to cook them as for Anna Potatoes but in individual dariole moulds.

9.42 POMMES VOISIN

Proceed as for 9.39 but add 50 g Parmesan cheese at the seasoning stage.

POTATOES BAKED IN THEIR SKINS

There are three methods of dealing with baked potatoes.

(*a*) They may be served plainly in their skins (9.43).

(*b*) The pulp may be removed, other ingredients added, then the mixture replaced in the skin and further cooked (9.44).

(*c*) The pulp may be removed, mixed with other ingredients and either moulded into potato cakes and shallow fried or baked in moulds (9.48).

Plain baked potatoes

9.43 BAKED POTATOES IN THEIR JACKETS — POMMES AU FOUR

Makes: 10 portions. Cooking time: 1–1½ hours. Oven temperature: 200–220 °C.

Quantity	*Ingredient*
10 × 200 g	evenly sized potatoes

Method

(1) Wash the potatoes free from all traces of dirt.

(2) Make a slight incision around the sides with the point of a small knife to a depth of not more than ¾ cm.

(3) Either wrap them in foil or leave unwrapped as desired then place on a baking sheet (unwrapped potatoes should be placed on a bed of preferably coarse salt).

(4) Bake in the oven until cooked.

Notes

(1) Wrapping the potatoes prevents them from drying out during cooking. Potatoes cooked in this way remain warm and moist for longer periods than those left unwrapped, but not wrapping them in foil results in a traditional flavoured and textured baked potato.

(2) Unwrapped potatoes placed on a tray without salt will dry out where they come into contact with the tray unless they are turned from time to time.

(3) To test if cooked, hold the potato in a cloth and apply gentle pressure. The potato will yield if it is cooked.

Service

When cooked, remove the foil and make a cross cut in the centre of the potato and lay back the skin to expose the inner pulp. Gently squeeze the potato permitting the pulp to rise above the level of the skin. Serve on a flat dish in a folded napkin or in a vegetable dish, garnished with a small piece of sprig parsley. If desired a small knob of butter may be placed in the centre of the potato.

Pulped baked potatoes

Once baked the centre pulp is removed, mashed with a fork whilst still hot, butter and seasoning added. This is then referred to as a basic macaire mixture and may be used as it is, moulded into shapes and cooked once again, or placed back into the skins with the addition of other ingredients.

9.44 POMMES ARLIE

Makes: 10 portions. Cooking time: ½ hour.

Quantity	*Ingredient*
10 × 200 g	even sized potatoes baked in their skins (9.43)
100 g	butter
20 g	chopped chives
1 dl	cream
18 g	salt
	pepper and grated nutmeg
75 g	grated Parmesan cheese
50 g	melted butter

Method

(1) Cut a slice from the top of the potato lengthways. Carefully remove the pulp from the skins using a tablespoon and place in a basin.

(2) Crush the potato with a fork and add the butter, chopped chives, cream and seasoning, mixing lightly with a wooden spatule.

(3) Fill the empty skins with the mixture slightly dome shaped. Sprinkle with grated cheese and melted butter and allow to colour either in an oven or under a salamander grill.

(4) Serve neatly arranged in a vegetable dish.

9.45 BASIC MACAIRE MIXTURE

Makes: 10 portions. Cooking time: 1–1½ hours.

Quantity	*Ingredient*
2½ kg	Baked Potatoes in their Skins (9.43)
100 g	butter
18 g	salt
	pepper and grated nutmeg

Method

(1) Cut the potatoes in two lengthways, remove the pulp from the skins using a tablespoon and place in a basin.

(2) Crush the potato with a fork and add the butter and seasoning, mixing lightly with a wooden spatule.

Notes

(1) Do not attempt to pass the potato pulp through a sieve as it will become gluey and dark in colour.

(2) Do not allow the potatoes or pulp to become cool before crushing with a fork or it will become sticky and dark through overworking.

(3) Avoid using aluminium receptacles as these may also have an adverse effect on the colour of the completed mixture.

(4) The mixture should be creamy in colour with a firm texture which is not sticky.

Pulped and moulded baked potatoes

The following potato dishes derived from a basic macaire mixture may be either moulded into small potato cakes or cooked in an anna mould or an omelette pan. The name of the dish remains the same irrespective of the manner in which they are completed.

9.46 POMMES MACAIRE

Makes: 10 portions. Cooking time: ¾ hour. Oven temperature: 220 °C.

Quantity	*Ingredient*
1½ kg	Basic Macaire Mixture (9.45)
200 g	melted butter

Method

(1) Heat a heavy omelette pan and cover the base with melted butter to a depth of 3 mm.

(2) Add the macaire mixture 3 cm deep; press it down and smooth the surface flat. Sprinkle with melted butter.

(3) Cook in the oven for 30–35 minutes until it becomes golden brown on all sides.

(4) Turn out onto a hot round flat dish, cut into segments and brush with melted butter before serving.

9.47 POMMES BYRON

Makes: 10 portions. Cooking time: ¾ hour. Oven temperature: 220 °C.

Quantity	*Ingredient*
1½ kg	Basic Macaire Mixture (9.45)
1 dl	cream
100 g	grated Parmesan and Gruyère cheese
50 g	melted butter

Method 1

Proceed as for Pommes Macaire (9.46). When turned out of the pan:

(*a*) make a small identation in the centre of the potato, fill with cream and sprinkle with grated cheese and melted butter;

(*b*) put into the oven or place under a salamander grill until the surface is evenly gratinated.

Assessment of the completed dish

(1) The outer surface of the potatoes should be of an even golden colour.

(2) The top or presentation side should be evenly gratinated with a little of the cream in evidence.

(3) The potato inside should be soft and buttery in flavour but should not separate and fall out of the surrounding crust.

(4) The potatoes should be well seasoned.

Method 2

Proceed as for Pommes Galette (9.15). When cooked:

(*a*) make a small indentation in the centre of each potato cake, fill with cream and sprinkle with grated cheese and melted butter;

(*b*) put under a salamander grill until the surface is evenly gratinated.

Assessment of the completed dish

(1) The potato inside should be soft and buttery in flavour, well seasoned with a hint of nutmeg.

(2) The outer surface should be very lightly and evenly coloured brown golden.

(3 The trellis markings on the presentation side should be evenly and clearly marked.

9.48 POMMES PINSON

Makes: 10 portions. Cooking time: 1¾ hours. Oven temperature: 220 °C.

Quantity	*Ingredient*	
1½ kg	Basic Macaire Mixture (9.45)	mixed together in a basin
100 g	finely chopped ham	
30 g	chopped parsley	

Method 1

Place the mixture in an anna mould and proceed as for Pommes Macaire (9.46).

Method 2

Mould the mixture into small cakes and proceed as for Pommes Galette (9.15).

ROAST POTATOES

This is cooking potatoes in an oven in dry heat with the addition of fat which is used to baste the potatoes from time to time.

9.49 ROAST POTATOES — POMMES ROTIES

Makes: 10 portions. Cooking time: 30–40 minutes. Oven temperature: 220 °C.

Quantity	*Ingredient*
1½ kg	evenly-sized and trimmed potatoes, lightly dried
1½ dl	dripping or oil
50 g	melted butter
10 g	salt

Method

(1) Heat the fat in a thick bottomed baking tray.

(2) Add the potatoes. Roll and turn them until they are very lightly coloured. Season with salt and roast until cooked (*see Note* below).

(3) When cooked, drain well, lightly season with salt and when serving brush with melted butter.

Note

To test if cooked, press gently with the fingers. If the potatoes yield to the pressure they are cooked.

Possible problem	*Possible cause and solution*
(1) Potatoes break up during cooking as a result of sticking	— incorrect type of potato used; always select a variety of potato that is suitable for the method of cooking that is to be applied. — potatoes were placed into cold fat in a cold tray and then into an oven that is not hot enough; care must be taken over these aspects of preparation as once the potatoes are cooked the problem cannot be rectified.

Possible problem	*Possible cause and solution*
	— potatoes were overhandled during cooking, especially at the latter stages when they are soft and almost cooked; care must be taken to avoid overhandling as the problems caused cannot be rectified.
(2) Potatoes have a thick outer skin	— potatoes were overcooked; care must be taken to cook the potatoes for the prescribed length of time to avoid this problem which cannot be rectified.
	— potatoes were cooked at too high a temperature; care must be taken to ensure that the oven is at the correct temperature for roasting the potatoes to avoid this problem which cannot be rectified.
	— potatoes were held once cooked for too long in a warm or hot cupboard; care must be taken to follow the correct retention procedure and if possible the potatoes should be cooked as close to the time they are required as possible to avoid the problems caused by prolonged retention.

9.50 CHATEAU POTATOES — POMMES CHATEAU

Makes: 10 portions. Cooking time: 30–40 minutes. Oven temperature: 220 °C.

Quantity	*Ingredient*
1½ kg	barrel shaped potatoes approximately 5 cm in length
1½ dl	dripping or oil
50 g	melted butter
10 g	salt

Method

Blanch the potatoes by just bringing to the boil. Do not refresh but drain them well, then proceed as for roast potatoes.

Assessment of the completed dish

(1) The potatoes should be even in shape and size, the outer surface firm and evenly coloured to a golden brown.

(2) The inside of the potato should be fluffy and white depending upon the variety of potato used.

NOUVELLE CUISINE

The potato dishes, principles and practices outlined in this chapter may also be used in the Nouvelle Cuisine style of cooking.

CONVENIENCE POTATOES

Potatoes are available to the caterer in a variety of forms: powdered, dehydrated, canned, frozen, pre-peeled, and in their skins, washed and graded according to type and size.

Powdered and dehydrated potato

From these products a basic mashed potato is made that may require the addition of butter and seasoning depending upon the type purchased. This basic mashed potato may be served as it is, or additional ingredients may be added to produce extension dishes such as Mousseline, Purée au Gratin and Biarritz in exactly the same way as when using fresh produce.

To this mashed potato, the correct quantity of egg yolks and butter may be added to produce a basic duchesse mixture (the instant potato mix needs to be kept on the firm side before the yolks and butter are added or else the mixture will be too soft to handle). Nutmeg will also add to the flavour of this mixture just as it does to fresh produce. This may then be used to make Pommes Duchesse and Pommes Marquise.

Hand moulded and croquette potatoes made from a duchesse base, however, cannot be made successfully using instant mix, nor can dishes made from a duchesse base with chou paste. They invariably disintegrate during frying due to the high proportion of water with which the instant mashed potato is made up.

Canned potatoes

Once the liquid in which the potatoes have been processed and canned has been drained away the potatoes may be heated in salt water, drained and blended with butter and mint or parsley as in 9.2 and 9.4. They may also be used for Rissolé Potatoes (9.28).

Convenience potatoes for deep frying

These include chips and croquette products and are cooked in the same way as fresh potatoes. When frying frozen products the fat must be allowed to reheat between batches and too many must not be cooked at once.

CHAPTER TEN

Sweets and Confectionery Items

The repertoire covered in this chapter is by no means exhaustive, but all the basic procedures for the production of a full range of biscuits, pastries, sponges, cakes, bread, rolls, buns and hot and cold sweets are included.

PANCAKES, FRITTERS AND SPONGES

Items such as pancakes and sponges are made from batter mixes which consist of equal amounts of flour and a liquid which can be made up of milk, milk and water or eggs, or a mixture of these.

Pancakes

Pancakes are made from a batter mixture of thin cream consistency and are cooked in a special pancake pan approximately 15 cm in diameter. They should be as thin and as delicate as possible and evenly cooked to a light golden colour on each side. They feature mainly as a sweet item on a menu but may also be served with savoury fillings. (*see Notes* to 10.1).

10.1 PANCAKES — CREPES

Makes: 30 pancakes. Cooking time: 30 minutes.

Quantity	*Ingredient*
350 g	strong flour
pinch	salt
20 g	sugar
3	eggs
7 dl	milk
60 g	butter
200 g	lard

Method

(1) Sieve the flour and salt into a basin.

(2) Whisk together the eggs and half the quantity of milk; add the sugar.

(3) Add the beaten eggs, milk and sugar to the flour and whisk to a smooth texture. Add the remainder of the milk and continue to whisk until smooth. Strain through a conical strainer into a clean basin.

(4) Heat the butter and incorporate it into the batter with a whisk.

(5) Allow the batter mixture to stand for one hour in a cool place in order to permit the mixture to relax.

(6) Heat some of the melted lard in the pancake pan until it reaches a temperature of about 200 °C or until a light haze rises from it.

(7) Pour off all the surplus fat from the pan. Add ⅓ dl of the pancake mixture to the heated and greased pan and evenly distribute the mixture until it coats the pan.

(8) Cook rather quickly until lightly golden on one side. Either turn the pancake with a palate knife or toss and continue to cook until golden on both sides.

(9) Remove the pancake to a plate and keep warm (*see* below) whilst continuing to make more.

Notes

(1) For a savoury pancake mixture omit the sugar.

(2) For the pancakes accompanying Consommé Celestine (4.7) add a mixture of finely chopped herbs, parsley, tarragon and chervil.

Retention

If not for immediate service, once cooked the pancakes should be turned out onto a plate and allowed to cool completely. They should then be stacked on a plate, covered with cling film and retained in a cool area.

Reheating

Since pancakes are never served plain they should be filled with the required filling, folded or rolled up with the ends folded underneath or trimmed, and then placed in the serving dish. They should then be covered with foil or greaseproof paper and placed in an oven to reheat without drying up, or placed under a salamander grill for a few moments. Alternatively unfilled pancakes, or those such as pear pancakes (*see* 10.7), may be reheated on a griddle top. When warm those that require a filling are filled and folded or rolled and are then ready to serve.

Service

Where appropriate, fill the pancakes with the garnish and either fold in half then half again, or roll up and either fold the ends under or trim the ends neatly. Arrange on a dish, sprinkle with castor sugar and reheat quickly.

Assessment of the completed dish

(1) The pancakes should be an even light golden colour on each side.

(2) They should be tender and soft in texture.

(3) The ends or edges of the pancakes should not be dry as this is a sign of reheating under direct heat.

*Possible problem**	*Possible cause and solution*
(1) Batter mixture is lumpy and will not flow when poured into the pan	— batter mixture not well whisked or given time to relax; care must be taken to prepare the batter correctly. Pass through a conical strainer.
	— too much flour was added to the liquid; care must be taken to use the correct quantities of ingredients. Pass through a conical strainer.
(2) Pancakes stick to the pan	— pan is dirty; ensure all utensils are clean before beginning any cookery work.
	— too little or too much lard was used for frying; care must be taken at this stage of the preparation.
	— pancake mixture was too light and thin; care must be taken when preparing the batter mixture to avoid this problem. Adjust by whisking mixture on to sufficient flour to thicken; pass through a conical strainer.
(3) Pancakes will not turn out of the pan	— incorrect size or shape of pan used; ensure that a special pancake pan approximately 15 cm in diameter is used to avoid this problem.
	— either the pan or the lard was not hot enough when the mixture was added; take care to heat the pan and the lard to the correct temperature before adding the mixture. Dirty pan used; ensure that pan is always clean.
(4) Pancakes are rubbery	— batter mixture too thick; care must be taken when preparing the batter mixture to achieve the correct consistency — add more milk.

*If any of these problems are encountered the batter mixture should be rectified before proceeding with more pancakes and particular procedures should be followed.

Possible problem	*Possible cause and solution*
	— too much batter mixture used; care must be taken not to add too much batter mixture to the pan as this will make the pancake thick and difficult to cook through.
	— cooked pancakes have been retained too long; pancakes should be made as close as possible to the time they are required to avoid the problems caused by prolonged retention.
(5) Pancakes are dry	— batter mixture not allowed to relax; care must be taken at this stage to avoid this problem later.
	— pancakes were held incorrectly between cooking and filling; ensure that the correct storage procedure is carried out to avoid this problem.
	— pancakes not reheated correctly; ensure that the correct procedure is followed for reheating the pancakes once filled.
(6) Pancakes smell a little rancid	— once cooked the pancakes were not allowed to cool before stacking for retention; ensure that the correct storage procedure is followed.

Extensions

10.2 APPLE PANCAKES — CREPES A LA MARMALADE DE POMMES

Equally divide 500 g Apple Purée (*see* 10.175) into the centre of the pancakes. Roll the pancakes to encase the filling and fold the ends of each pancake underneath. Neatly arrange on a dish, sprinkle with castor sugar and reheat in the oven for a few moments; may be served with Apricot Sauce (10.177).

10.3 CREPES SUZETTE

Makes: 4 portions. Cooking time: 5–6 minutes.
Melt 75 g butter in a gueridon pan (a special pan used in the service area). Add 75 g castor sugar and cook until it begins to caramelise. Add ½ dl curaçao and ½ dl brandy and mix together with a spoon. Dip each pancake into the mixture, fold into four and push to the side of the pan. Continue until all the pancakes have been coated. Add 1 dl curaçao or brandy and tip the pan to one side so that the liqueur flambées. Sprinkle with sugar and serve whilst still flaming.

10.4 CREPES NORMANDE

Lightly cook 250 g peeled apple cut into very small dice in butter with a little cinnamon. Add the diced apple to the mixture whilst making the pancakes. Serve flat sprinkled with castor sugar.

10.5 JAMAICAN PANCAKES

Makes: 10 portions. Cooking time: 25 minutes.

Quantity	*Ingredient*
20	Pancakes (10.1)
5	bananas (cut into 1½ cm lengths)
75 g	unsalted butter
100 g	demerara sugar
1 dl	rum
3	juice of oranges
1	juice of lemon

Method

(1) Heat the butter in a shallow sided saucepan, add the pieces of banana and cook gently for 3 minutes on all sides. Remove and keep them warm.

(2) Add the sugar and continue to cook until lightly caramelised.

(3) Return the bananas to the pan, add the rum and flambé. Add the fruit juice and incorporate into the caramel mixture.

(4) Remove the banana pieces, roll into the pancakes and trim the ends.

(5) Place the filled pancakes onto a suitably sized plate. Coat with the sauce which should be of a light syrupy consistency and serve.

10.6 LEMON PANCAKES — CREPES AU CITRON

Makes: 10 portions. Cooking time: 25 minutes.

Quantity	*Ingredient*
20	Pancakes (10.1)
5	lemons
150 g	castor sugar

Method

(1) Fold the pancakes into quarters to form a triangular shape. Lightly sprinkle with lemon juice and castor sugar. Garnish with lemon wedges neatly trimmed, free from pips and pith on the leading edge.

(2) Neatly arrange on a dish and serve.

10.7 PEAR PANCAKES — CREPES DU COUVENT

Add 250 g Poached Pears (*see* 10.144) cut into very small dice to the mixture whilst making the pancakes. Serve flat sprinkled with castor sugar.

10.8 SCOTCH PANCAKES

Sift 350 g soft flour with 10 g baking powder, 20 g sugar and a pinch of salt. Whisk 3 eggs with 5 dl sour milk and gradually mix into the flour to form a stiffer batter than for ordinary pancakes. Drop spoonfuls onto a moderately hot well greased griddle plate and cook until golden on both sides. Serve with jam, honey, cream, etc., for breakfast or tea.

10.9 BLINIS

These are a type of pancake made with buckwheat flour and yeast batter and are cooked in special pans. They are served with caviar.

Fritters

Fritters are items coated with batter or with egg and breadcrumbs and then deep fried. (There are others that do not need a protective coating.) The most common fritters are:

(*a*) fruit fritters using apples, bananas and pineapple;
(*b*) rice and semolina fritters;
(*c*) soufflé fritters made with chou paste.

Sweet fritters may be served with Apricot or Custard Sauce (10.177 or 179).

Fruit fritters

10.10 APPLE FRITTERS — BEIGNETS DE POMMES

Makes: 10 portions. Cooking time: 5 minutes. Cooking temperature: 180 °C.

Quantity	*Ingredient*
1 kg	peeled and cored cooking apples
50 g	castor sugar
6 g	cinnamon
1	juice of lemon
	Yeast Batter (6.40)
15 g	icing sugar
4 dl	Apricot Sauce (10.177)

Method

(1) Cut the prepared apples into 5 mm thick rings. Place onto a

tray, sprinkle with castor sugar and cinnamon and allow to stand for approximately 30 minutes.

(2) Pass the apple slices through the batter. Drain off all excess batter by gently pulling through the fingers.

(3) Place into the hot fat away from oneself (*see* p. 189).

(4) Fry until crisp and golden, turning the apple rings with a spider during cooking to ensure even cooking and coloration.

(5) Drain the apple rings by placing them onto absorbent kitchen paper.

(6) Place the fritters onto a tray, dust with icing sugar and place under a salamander grill to glaze.

(7) Neatly arrange the fritters on a dish lined with a dish paper. Serve the hot apricot sauce separately.

Notes

(1) The apple rings may also be sprinkled with rum in addition to castor sugar and cinnamon before cooking.

(2) *See* Chapter 6, pp. 191–2, for any problems, causes and solutions.

10.11 BANANA FRITTERS — BEIGNETS DE BANANES

Proceed as for Apple Fritters (10.10) using 10 bananas peeled and cut in two lengthways. Serve with hot Apricot Sauce (10.177).

10.12 PINEAPPLE FRITTERS — BEIGNETS D'ANANAS

Proceed as for Apple Fritters (10.10) using 20 pineapple rings dipped into hot Pastry Cream (10.187) and then batter and allowed to cool on an oiled baking sheet. Serve accompanied by hot Apricot Sauce (10.177).

Notes

(1) The pineapple rings may be divided into segments if desired.

(2) The rings or segments may be macerated with kirsch for approximately 1 hour before proceeding as above.

Rice and semolina fritters

10.13 RICE FRITTERS

Makes: 10 portions. Cooking time: 5 minutes. Cooking temperature: 180 °C.

Quantity	*Ingredient*
1 l	rice for condé (*see* 10.127) used cold
250 g	flour
	Yeast Batter (6.40)

Quantity	*Ingredient*
15 g	icing sugar
4 dl	Apricot Sauce (10.177)

Method

(1) When the rice is cooked turn out onto a buttered tray to a depth of 1½ cm.

(2) When cold cut into 5 cm squares, pass through the flour and then the batter. Drain off all excess batter by gently pulling through the fingers.

(3) Place into the hot fat away from oneself (*see* p. 198).

(4) Fry until crisp and golden turning the pieces during cooking to ensure even cooking and coloration.

(5) Drain the fritters by placing them onto absorbent kitchen paper.

(6) Place the fritters onto a tray, dust with icing sugar and place under a salamander grill to glaze.

(7) Neatly arrange on a dish lined with a dish paper. Serve the hot apricot sauce separately.

10.14 SEMOLINA FRITTERS

Prepare the condé as in 10.127 using semolina in place of rice. Proceed then as in 10.13.

Soufflé fritters

These are made with chou paste which can withstand the high temperature required for deep frying without a protective coating. The heat of the fat seals the outside of the paste allowing a build up of steam which causes splitting and expansion. This process repeats itself until the beignet is hollow.

10.15 BEIGNETS SOUFFLES

Makes: 10 portions. Cooking time: 5–6 minutes. Cooking temperature: 180 °C.

Quantity	*Ingredient*
750 g	Chou Paste (10.45)
50 g	icing sugar
4 dl	Apricot Sauce (10.177)

Method

(1) Take desertspoons of chou paste, mould with another spoon and drop into the deep fat, allowing approximately 40–50 pieces for 10 portions.

(2) Fry until crisp and golden, turning the pieces during cooking to ensure even coloration.

(3) Drain the beignets by placing them onto absorbent kitchen paper.

(4) Roll the beignets in icing sugar on a tray.

(5) Neatly arrange on a dish lined with a dish paper. Serve the hot apricot sauce separately.

10.16 BEIGNETS SOUFFLES GEORGETTE

Proceed as in 10.15. When cooked and drained fill with Pastry Cream (10.187) with chopped pineapple and kirsch. Serve accompanied by a sauceboat of Apricot Sauce (10.177) flavoured with kirsch.

10.17 CHEESE FRITTERS — BEIGNETS SOUFFLE AU PARMESAN

Add 100 g grated Parmesan cheese to the prepared chou paste at the final stage. Proceed as in 10.15. When cooked and drained sprinkle with grated Parmesan cheese and serve neatly arranged on a dish lined with a dish paper. Garnish with sprigs of parsley.

Sponges

Genoese sponge

This is a low fat all-purpose sponge that is widely used to make a range of gateaux and individual sponge-based items. It is extremely light and well aerated and should not be confused with a Victoria sponge which is made quite differently (*see* 10.25).

The aeration of a Genoese sponge comes only from the beaten eggs. Other sponges are aerated by using a smaller number of eggs and adding raising agents such as baking powder.

10.18 GENOESE SPONGE

Makes: 1 × 22 cm gateau. Cooking time: 25–30 minutes. Oven temperature: 195 °C.

Quantity	*Ingredient*
5	eggs
150 g	castor sugar
150 g	soft flour
75 g	melted butter

Method

(1) Prepare the mould by lightly greasing with clarified margarine or softened white fat and coat with flour.

(2) Place the eggs and sugar into the clean and warmed mixing bowl of an electric mixer.

(3) Whisk at high speed until the mixture is thick and creamy. It is ready when the drops falling from the raised whisk leave a mark on the surface. Whisk until the mixture is cold.

(4) Carefully fold in the flour using a metal spoon or a scraper, turning the mixing bowl at the same time.

(5) Pour in the cooled melted butter down the side of the bowl, mixing gently. Do not overmix.

(6) Pour into the prepared mould and cook immediately for the prescribed time.

(7) When cooked remove from the mould at once onto a wire cooling tray.

Note

If whisking by hand, stand the bowl in a pan of hot water but do not allow the water to boil.

To test if cooked

Lightly press the surface of the baked sponge with the flat or back of the hand. When the pressure is released no marks should be left.

Alternatively, a thin needle may be used — it should be inserted into the centre of the sponge and if the needle is hot and clean when removed the sponge is cooked.

The sponge should be golden brown all over and, if the tin has been properly prepared, it should come out whole.

Assessment of the completed sponge

(1) The volume of the sponge should increase at least three-fold during baking but should be light in weight in relation to its size. It should shrink away from the side of the tin only slightly.

(2) In texture it should be highly aerated with tiny holes and be able, when cold, to accept soaking with stock syrup or liqueur yet still hold its fineness of grain.

(3) It should cut easily and hold fillings and coatings without losing shape so that it can be used for a variety of individual sponge cakes. There should be no large air pockets.

(4) The sponge should be light brown in colour on the outside, and light yellow on the inside.

(5) It should be extremely light and soft yet rich and sweet; it should be easily digestible.

(6) The general appearance of the sponge should be smooth with a light top and bottom crust that does not come away from the cake. It should not break easily or crumble.

Possible problem	*Possible cause and solution*
(1) Sponge does not rise during cooking	— incorrect type of flour used; ensure that only soft flour is used in preparing the mixture to avoid this problem which cannot be rectified.
	— mixture of eggs and sugar was not sufficiently aerated; care must be taken to beat the mixture thoroughly to avoid this problem which cannot be rectified.
	— the eggs and sugar were over-extended during whisking; care must be taken, on the other hand, not to *over*beat the mixture as this cannot be rectified later.
	— the eggs and sugar were overheated during whisking; care must be taken not to warm the bowl too much before whisking or during whisking as this problem cannot be rectified later.
	— air was forced out of the mixture when adding the flour and/or butter; care must be taken when folding in the flour and adding the butter as overworking the mixture at this stage cannot be rectified later.
	— oven was not hot enough or the sponge was baked in the cool part of the oven; ensure that the oven is at the correct temperature and that the sponge is put into the hottest part at the top.
(2) Sponge dips in the centre when cooked	— sponge put into an oven that had not reached the correct baking temperature; ensure that the oven is at the correct temperature before putting in the sponge.
	— oven door was opened before the sponge had baked sufficiently; do not open the oven door until the sponge has baked for the prescribed time as this lowers the temperature interrupting the baking process and cannot be rectified later.

Possible problem	*Possible cause and solution*
(3) Cooked sponge is dry	— insufficient butter used in the mixture; take care to use correct quantities of the ingredients to avoid this problem which cannot be rectified.
	— aeration was lost through overmixing; care must be taken when beating the eggs and sugar and when adding the flour and butter as this cannot be rectified later.
	— incorrect type of flour used; ensure that only soft flour is used in preparing the mixture as this cannot be rectified.

Extensions

10.19 CHOCOLATE GENOESE SPONGE

Proceed as for Genoese Sponge (10.18), replacing 30 g of the flour with 30 g of cocoa. The flour and cocoa should be sieved together.

10.20 JAM SWISS ROLL

Makes: 1 25 cm roll. Cooking time: 6–8 minutes. Oven temperature: 200 °C.

Quantity	*Ingredient*
4	eggs
120 g	castor sugar
120 g	soft flour
60 g	semolina
200 g	raspberry jam

Method

(1) Prepare as for Genoese Sponge (10.18) to Stage (4).

(2) Pour the mixture into a swiss roll tin lined with greaseproof paper and brushed with clarified margarine. Spread the mixture evenly with a palette knife and cook immediately for the prescribed time.

(3) When cooked, turn over onto greaseproof paper sprinkled with semolina and remove the lining paper on which it was baked. Spread with the warmed jam.

(4) Roll up immediately fairly tightly and allow to cool.

(5) Remove the paper, trim the ends neatly and it is ready for use.

Notes

(1) A few drops of glycerine may be added to the Genoese sponge mixture at Stage (5). This will soften the sponge so that it may be kept longer without deterioration.

(2) Lemon curd, Butter Cream (10.186) or Whipped Cream (10.188) may be used in place of jam. Where butter cream or whipped cream are to be used as a filling, roll the swiss roll in sugared paper as described above and allow to cool. Carefully unroll, spread with the filling and re-roll.

10.21 CHOCOLATE SWISS ROLL

Proceed as for Jam Swiss Roll (10.20), replacing 25 g of the flour with 25 g cocoa. The flour and cocoa should be sieved together.

Gateaux

The following outline is intended as a guide for preparing Genoese sponge when using butter cream as a filling and for decoration. It should be remembered that the range of fillings for such items is very extensive.

10.22 GENOESE SPONGE FOR GATEAUX

Method

(1) When cooked, remove the sponge from the mould at once and cool face down on a cloth on a wire cooling tray.

(2) Slice through the sponge making small incisions around to act as a guide before slicing. The sponge may be divided into two or three sections depending upon size (making certain that it is flat side uppermost and level).

(3) Lay out the sections of sponge and sprinkle with a small amount of Stock Syrup (10.173) to moisten and flavour.

(4) Spread with the desired filling and re-assemble.

(5) Spread the top and sides with Butter Cream (10.186) making certain the top is absolutely level by smoothing over the surface with a palette knife dipped in warm water.

(6) Cover the sides with either toasted nib or flaked almonds or chocolate vermicelli.

(7) Decorate the top with Butter Cream (10.186).

Note

The Genoese sponge should be cooked 12–24 hours before use in gateaux.

Extensions

10.23 CHOCOLATE GATEAU — GATEAU AU CHOCOLAT

This consists of a Chocolate Genoese Sponge (10.19 and 22) filled and decorated with chocolate Butter Cream (10.186). The sides are coated with chocolate vermicelli.

10.24 COFFEE GATEAU — GATEAU MOKA

This consists of Genoese Sponge (10.22) filled and decorated with coffee flavoured Butter Cream (10.186). The sides are coated with toasted nib or flaked almonds and the word "Moka" is piped in the centre of the gateau.

Note

Approximately 500 g of butter cream is required for a 22 cm gateau.

Victoria sponge

This is a high fat sponge cake made by what is called a sugar-batter method. Compared with a Genoese sponge a Victoria sponge is rather sturdier and closer textured. The aeration of this kind of sponge is brought about by:

(a) the creaming of the fat and sugar to incorporate air;
(b) the action of the eggs (not enough in itself to aerate such a weight of flour);
(c) the baking powder which becomes moist and gives off carbon dioxide gas.

10.25 VICTORIA SPONGE

Makes: 2 × 18 cm or 1 × 22 cm. Cooking time: 25 minutes. Oven temperature: 180 °C.

Quantity	*Ingredient*
160 g	butter or margarine
160 g	castor sugar
3	eggs (slightly beaten)
160 g	soft flour } sieved together
10 g	baking powder } sieved together

Method

(1) Prepare the mould(s) by lightly greasing with clarified margarine or softened white fat and coat with flour.
(2) Cream the fat and sugar until light, white and fluffy.
(3) Gradually add the beaten eggs to the creamed butter and sugar.
(4) Beat in the flour and baking powder using a metal spoon or a scraper, but do not overmix.
(5) Transfer the mixture to the prepared mould(s) and cook for the prescribed time.
(6) When cooked remove from the mould(s) at once onto a cooling tray.

Notes

(1) Care must be taken not to let the mixture curdle when adding the eggs as this will lead to loss of aeration. To avoid this have the butter and eggs at room temperature at least one hour beforehand.

(2) Margarine may be substituted for butter.

(3) It is usual to sandwich two small sponges together with jam and whipped cream and to dust the top with icing sugar. Large single sponges are cut through in half and spread with jam and cream and the top replaced and dusted with icing sugar.

To test if cooked

See the relevant section of Genoese Sponge (10.18).

Assessment of the completed dish

(1) The volume of the sponge should increase at least three-fold during baking and shrink away from the sides of the tin only slightly.

(2) The sponge should be rather firm in texture, although rather crumby, with small aerated holes.

(3) It should be light brown in colour on the outside, and light yellow on the inside.

(4) It should be rather firm and moist yet sweet and crumby.

(5) The general appearance of the sponge should be smooth with a light top and bottom crust that does not come away from the cake.

SCONES AND CAKES

Items made from a soft mixture consisting of two parts of flour to one of liquid include scones, rock cakes, madeira and fruit cake.

Scones

Scones can be individual items or part of a round cake made to be split and filled and have a characteristic dryish taste. Scones are very popular at teatime because the dry texture and somewhat neutral flavour easily complement sweet fillings such as butter and jam, and jam and cream.

10.26 SCONES

Makes: 8 scones. Cooking time: 15 minutes. Oven temperature: 210 °C.

Quantity	*Ingredient*
120 g	strong flour
120 g	soft flour
10 g	baking powder
60 g	margarine or butter
60 g	castor sugar
1 dl	milk

Method

(1) Pass the two kinds of flour and the baking powder through a sieve twice into a basin.

(2) Add the fat and rub in until it forms a texture like fine breadcrumbs.

(3) Add the sugar and milk and mix quickly to a dough.

(4) Dust with flour, roll out 2 cm thick and cut out with a 5 cm round plain cutter.

(5) Place on a greased baking sheet and brush with milk.

(6) Bake in the oven for the prescribed time.

Note

The scone mixture can be divided into two, moulded round and flat approximately 15 cm in diameter, placed on the baking tray and then almost cut through into six wedges.

Extension

10.27 FRUIT SCONES

Proceed as in 10.26 adding 60 g sultanas to the mixture.

Small cakes

A number of small cakes are made in a similar manner using either of the following two methods:

(a) rubbing the sieved flour and baking powder and fat together to form a sandy type texture, then adding the remainder of the ingredients; or

(b) mixing the fat and sugar together, then adding first the eggs to form a creamy texture followed by the sieved flour and baking powder and then the liquid.

10.28 ROCK CAKES

Makes: 8–10. Cooking time: 15 minutes. Oven temperature: 210 °C.

Quantity	*Ingredient*
120 g	strong flour

Quantity	*Ingredient*
120 g	soft flour
10 g	baking powder
120 g	margarine or butter
120 g	castor sugar
1	egg
1 dl	milk
few drops	lemon essence
60 g	mixed fruit
1	egg (eggwash)
25 g	granulated sugar

Method 1 (rubbing in)

(1) Sift the flours and baking powder into a bowl.
(2) Add the fat and mix to a sandy texture.
(3) Add the sugar, the beaten egg and milk, the fruit and flavouring, and mix to a soft dough.
(4) Divide into roughly shaped pieces and place onto a baking sheet. Brush with eggwash and sprinkle with granulated sugar.
(5) Bake in the oven for the prescribed time.

Method 2 (creaming)

(1) Sieve the two kinds of flour and baking powder together twice.
(2) Cream the fat and sugar together.
(3) Add the beaten egg a little at a time, mixing well to form a creamy texture.
(4) Add the sifted flours, the baking powder, the milk, flavouring and fruit.
(5) Divide into roughly shaped pieces and place onto a baking sheet. Brush with eggwash and sprinkle with granulated sugar.
(6) Bake in the oven for the prescribed time.

Extensions

10.29 CHERRY CAKES

Prepare as for Rock Cakes (10.28) but add 75 g of chopped, washed and dried glacé cherries and a few drops of vanilla essence in place of the dried mixed fruit and lemon essence.

10.30 COCONUT CAKES

Prepare as for Rock Cakes (10.28) but add 25 g desiccated coconut and a few drops of vanilla essence in place of the dried mixed fruit and lemon essence.

10.31 RASPBERRY BUNS

Prepare as for Rock Cakes (10.28) without the dried mixed fruit and a few drops of vanilla essence in place of the lemon essence. Mould each piece into a ball and flatten with a palette knife retaining a round shape. Eggwash the tops and sides and dip the tops into granulated sugar. Place onto a greased baking sheet. Make a small hollow in the centre of each and fill with a little raspberry jam.

10.32 RICE BUNS

Prepare as for Raspberry Buns (10.31) dipping them into sugar nibs and placing half a glacé cherry in the centre of each.

10.33 SULTANA SCONES

Prepare as for Rock Cakes (10.28) but add 120 g sultanas and a few drops of vanilla essence in place of the dried mixed fruit and lemon essence. Mould each piece into small rounds or triangles.

10.34 JAM SCONES

Prepare as for Sultana Scones (10.33) omitting the sultanas. When cooked they are split and filled with jam.

Cake mixture

All large cakes to be cut into slices or wedges ranging from plain madeira cake to ordinary fruit cakes and rich fruit cakes are made by creaming the ingredients together. For the best results it is advisable to use margarine or shortening rather than butter as these fats will cream much quicker, and to use general purpose or medium flour with baking powder.

10.35 CAKE MIXTURE

Makes: 1 × 20 cm. Cooking time: 2–2½ hours. Oven temperature: 165 °C.

Quantity	*Ingredient*
250 g	compound fat or cake margarine
250 g	castor sugar
5	eggs
250 g	flour (*see* above)
10 g	baking powder

Method

(1) Beat the fat and the sugar in an electric mixer on second speed until the mixture is very creamy.

(2) Add the eggs one at a time beating each well into the mixture.

(3) Mix in the sieved flour and baking powder by hand, being careful not to overmix.

(4) Fill the prepared cake tin and bake for the prescribed time (*see* below).

Note

If necessary a little milk may be added with the flour to soften the mixture.

Baking of cakes

Baking the cake is the most difficult part of cake making and the temperature of the oven is vitally important if the result is to be a success. The cake must be protected against the heat of the oven by several layers of paper at the bottom, around the side and also on top.

The larger the cake the lower the oven temperature should be, but also the greater the protection, with several thicknesses of paper especially at the bottom as a cake bakes from the bottom upwards. By having a high sideband a top covering can be supported.

The more cakes baked together at one time, the better as the humidity in the oven is an important factor in achieving a thin top crust. The normal domestic oven produces a lot of heat at the top so it is advisable to put a metal sheet at the top and the cakes on a shelf 20 cm below. A tin of water at the bottom of the oven will supply moisture throughout the baking process thereby keeping the top crust flat and giving a good colour.

To test if cooked

The surest way to determine if the cake is cooked is to check that it has been cooked for the prescribed time at the correct temperature. Insert a skewer into the centre of the cake and leave it for a few moments. When removed it should be clean. If the skewer has some cake mixture stuck to it the cake needs further baking.

Possible problem	*Possible cause and solution*
(1) Cake has sunk in the centre	— fat, sugar and eggs have been overmixed; care must be taken when preparing the mixture to avoid this as it cannot be rectified once the cake is baked.
	— too much baking powder has been used;

Possible problem	*Possible cause and solution*
	care must be taken not to add too much baking powder as this will over-aerate the mixture and cannot be rectified later.
	— cake has been undercooked (this applies mainly to fruit cakes); continue to cook for the prescribed time until the cake is baked thoroughly.
	— too much liquid used in proportion to the flour; care must be taken to get this balance right as the result cannot be rectified once the cake is baked.
	— oven door was opened too soon; allow the cake to bake at the prescribed temperature for the prescribed length of time as opening the door lowers the temperature interrupting the baking process and the result cannot be rectified.
(2) Fruit has sunk to the bottom	— cake mixture was too weak; care must be taken when preparing the mixture as this cannot be rectified later.
	— cake mixture was too light due to overbeating; care must be taken to avoid this as it cannot be rectified later.
	— too much sugar used in the mixture; care must be taken to avoid this when preparing the mixture as it cannot be rectified later.
	— too much baking powder used in the mixture; care must be taken at this point as the result cannot be rectified later.
	— wet fruit was used in the mixture; care must be taken to ensure that any fruit added is dry to avoid adding to the moisture in the mixture.
	— incorrect type of flour used in the mixture; care must be taken not to use the wrong type of flour as it cannot be rectified later.
(3) Cake has a thick crust all round	— oven was too hot; care must be taken to bake the cake at the correct temperature, making sure that it does not exceed 165 °C, to avoid this problem as it cannot be rectified.
	— insufficient paper used to protect the outside of the cake; ensure that the cake is well

Possible problem	*Possible cause and solution*
	protected with several layers of paper — particularly if the cake is large — to avoid this problem which cannot be rectified.
	— tins were overfilled and needed baking for too long; care must be taken to fill the tins to a maximum depth of 7 cm to avoid this problem which cannot be rectified.
	— too much sugar used in the mixture; care must be taken to measure the ingredients accurately when preparing the mixture to avoid this problem which cannot be rectified.
(4) Cake is small in volume and light in texture	— insufficient baking powder used; care must be taken to weigh the ingredients accurately when preparing the mixture to avoid this problem which cannot be rectified.
	— insufficient sugar used in the mixture; care must be taken to weigh the ingredients accurately to avoid this problem which cannot be rectified.
	— batter not beaten sufficiently; care must be taken to cream the batter well at a temperature of 21 °C to give proper aeration to avoid this problem which cannot be rectified.
	— oven temperature too low; ensure that the oven is at the correct temperature before putting in the cake.
	— fat was too hot or too cold when preparing the mixture; the ideal temperature to cream the mixture is 21 °C — below this the mixture will not aerate well, above it will become oily.
	— eggs were too fresh; use eggs that are at least two weeks old as they will help to strengthen the mixture.
(5) Top of the cake is cracked or peaked	— mixture has been overmixed causing it to toughen; the flour should be folded in carefully by hand, not machine, using a spoon with a shaking action.
	— incorrect type of flour used; ensure that the correct type of flour is used and avoid strong flour.
	— insufficient liquid used in the mixture; care

Possible problem	*Possible cause and solution*
	must be taken when preparing the mixture that it achieves the correct dropping consistency.
	— oven temperature too high causing a skin to form quickly which later cracks; care must be taken to bake the cake at the correct temperature, making sure that it does not exceed 165 °C.
	— the atmosphere in the oven was too dry; if possible fill the oven and if necessary place a tray of water at the bottom of the oven to ensure constant humidity.
	— cake was baked too slowly so that it dries out; ensure that the cake is baked as quickly as possible at the correct temperature.
(6) White spots appear on the top crust	— mixture was not beaten sufficiently; care must be taken to beat the mixture thoroughly — the fat and sugar mixture may be creamed in an electric mixer for 7 minutes at second speed before adding the eggs.
(7) Cake has not baked all the way through	— oven temperature and cooking time not adhered to; care must be taken to bake the cake at the correct temperature for the prescribed length of time.
	— faulty oven; check the efficiency of the oven.

Extensions

The following are variations that may be made from the cake mixture given in 10.35 and includes approximate times and oven temperatures for cooking.

10.36 CHERRY CAKE

Add 150 g whole glacé cherries to the mixture. Bake for approximately 1¼ hours at a temperature of 165 °C.

10.37 DUNDEE CAKE

Use brown sugar in place of castor sugar and add 300 g dried mixed fruit. Bake for approximately 1¾ hours at a temperature of 150 °C.

10.38 FRUIT CAKE

Add 150 g dried mixed fruit to the mixture. Bake for approximately 1 hour at a temperature of 160 °C.

10.39 MADEIRA CAKE

Prepare the basic cake mixture in 10.35. Place a slice of candied citron peel on top. Bake for approximately 1¼ hours at a temperature of 165 °C.

10.40 RICH FRUIT CAKE

Use brown sugar in place of castor sugar and butter in place of the compound fat or cake margarine. Add 500 g dried mixed fruit, 5 g mixed spice and 50 g glacé cherries. Bake for approximately 3–3½ hours at a temperature of 150 °C.

BASIC PASTES

Stiff mixtures made with approximately four times as much flour as liquid include all the different kinds of paste such as short paste, sweet paste, puff paste, suet paste and chou paste. Apart from biscuit paste dealt with later in the chapter (*see* pp. 543–6), most of these are merely the vehicle for conveying a filling, therefore they should be sufficiently robust to carry even quite soft fillings whilst at the same time short and crisp in texture and pleasant to taste. The type of fat used has an effect upon the taste and texture of the paste and it is possible to purchase margarines and shortenings that are purpose made for particular kinds of paste. Butter gives a good flavour but is expensive and not necessarily better than margarine.

For short and sweet pastes, soft flour gives the best results; for puff paste strong flour must be used. Self-raising flour is good for suet paste and can be used for short paste but the result is soft rather than short. General purpose flour gives very good results in all pastes except puff paste.

Care must be exercised when working paste by machine as it quickly becomes overmixed which gives a tough result.

Short and sweet paste

The difference between short and sweet paste is that sugar is used in the latter. As it is used for fruit flans and the like it is advisable to use egg as the mixing liquid rather than water as this will give a special firmness when baked.

Short paste is usually made by rubbing the fat into the flour, sweet paste by creaming the fat with the sugar and egg and then incorporating the flour.

10.41 SHORT PASTE — PATE A FONCER

Makes: 1 kg. Time: 15 minutes.

Quantity	*Ingredient*
600 g	soft flour
4 g	salt
300 g	margarine
1½ dl	water

Method

(1) Sieve the flour and salt into a basin or mixer bowl.

(2) Add the fat and rub together until the consistency of breadcrumbs.

(3) Make a bay in the centre, pour in the cold water and mix lightly until it binds to form the paste.

(4) Wrap the paste in greaseproof paper and place it in the refrigerator for at least 30 minutes before proceeding to roll it out.

Note

This paste may also be used for making fruit pies and the like, in which case 120 g castor sugar may be added.

10.42 SWEET PASTE — PATE SUCREE

Makes: 1 kg. Time: 25 minutes.

Quantity	*Ingredient*
500 g	soft flour
2 g	salt
300 g	margarine
125 g	castor sugar
2	eggs

Method 1

(1) Sieve the flour and salt onto a working surface and make a bay in the centre.

(2) Place the softened fat and sugar into the bay and cream them together.

(3) Add the eggs one by one and mix in well.

(4) Incorporate the flour to form a cohesive paste.

(5) Scrape the paste twice with the blade of a palette knife and knead it well together.

(6) Wrap the paste in greaseproof paper and place in the refrigerator for at least 30 minutes before proceeding to roll it out.

Method 2

(1) Cream together the margarine and sugar and add the eggs one by one in an electric mixer.

(2) Blend in the sifted flour and salt and knead together to form a cohesive paste.

(3) Wrap the paste in greaseproof paper and place it in the refrigerator for at least 30 minutes before proceeding to roll it out.

Puff paste

Puff paste is finely interleaved but separate layers of dough and fat baked to a light, crisp, flaky structure of good volume and appearance. The volume is produced by steam generated by the moisture in the dough forcing apart the layers of dough and fat which has melted because of the heat to form a liquid insulation between the layers.

To ensure the best quality products are produced it is important that the *Notes* to 10.43 are studied and the correct baking temperatures are used. As a general rule filled puff pastry items require a medium hot oven (215–220 °C), whilst unfilled varieties require a hotter oven (225–230 °C).

In order to make the pastry rise successfully it is important that a fairly high temperature is applied to puff paste goods during the initial stages of cooking so that the moisture in the dough turns to steam as quickly as possible. The steam then rises and comes into contact with the insulating films of fat and pressure forces the layers upwards, thus giving volume and lightness to the pastry.

There are several methods of producing puff pastry but the one given below is that most commonly used. However, all the information given in this section is relevant to puff pastry produced by most other methods. Strong flour should be used together with a firm fat such as butter or pastry margarine.

10.43 PUFF PASTE — FEUILLETAGE

Makes: 1 kg.

Quantity	*Ingredient*
400 g	flour
4 g	salt
400 g	fat
½	juice of lemon
2¼ dl	cold water

Method

(1) Rub a quarter of the fat into the sifted flour and salt.

(2) Make a bay in the centre of the mixture and add the water and lemon juice.

(3) Knead all the ingredients to form a smooth dough.

(4) Allow the dough to relax in a cool place for about 30 minutes.

(5) Cut a cross halfway through the ball of dough, then pull it open from the centre to form a star shape. Lightly roll out the corners allowing the centre part to remain rather thicker than the four sides.

(6) Place the remainder of the fat (if it is too hard knead it until soft and the same consistency as the dough) into the centre of the paste. Fold over the four flaps to seal the fat in.

(7) Roll out the paste into a rectangular shape about 7 mm thick, then give it four double turns as follows. Fold the two ends to the centre then fold the paste over in half again. Repeat this procedure three more times allowing 30 minutes between each turn for the paste to relax. The paste must have four turns exactly.

Notes

(1) Strong flour must be used. If soft flour is used the dough will be softer and easier to handle but the final volume will be low and the flake will be dull.

(2) The use of special puff pastry fat is recommended. It is important that the fat used can be rolled out to an extremely fine layer without breaking. A poor quality fat or pastry margarine which is not waxy enough will lessen the quality of the finished pastry.

(3) The pastry margarine or fat should also be pliable. If it is not it should be worked to make it plastic or until it is of the same consistency as the dough. Working a soft fat would not render it pliable.

(4) The consistency of the dough should match that of the fat. If the dough is too soft the harder fat layers may rupture the dough layers thus resulting in uneven lift during cooking. If the dough is too firm it will be more difficult to roll out and tend to shrink during rolling and cooking and the fat layers may be squeezed out or damaged.

(5) The water must be as cool as possible, particularly during warm weather. It should be between 3 and 7 °C.

(6) The addition of salt improves the flavour of the pastry and also has an effect on the gluten in the flour, but it should be remembered that pastry margarine also contains 2 per cent salt on average.

(7) An acid may be used either in the form of lemon juice or cream of tartar. It is claimed that the addition of one of these ingredients helps to strengthen the protein thereby improving the gluten and resulting in better volume. There is a danger, however, that the dough may become sour if too much acid is used.

(8) Allowing the paste to rest between turns is important as it allows it to recover from the tension brought about by the folding

and rolling out. The time allowed may vary between 20 minutes and 1 hour.

(9) The paste must be moved through 90° either to the right or left between every turn.

(10) Irrespective of the time the paste is allowed to rest between turns, the most important point to allow it to rest is after the goods have been cut out and placed on trays. If insufficient time is allowed at this stage shrinkage during baking is inevitable.

(11) It is common practice to allow puff paste to rest overnight to prevent distortion and shrinkage during cooking as much as possible. The paste should be wrapped either in a damp cloth, in polythene or in some other moisture-proof material to avoid loss of moisture and then stored in a refrigerator at approximately 5 °C.

(12) The layers of fat and paste in puff paste are built up by the turns as follows:

Turn:	1st	2nd	3rd	4th
Number of layers:	12	48	192	768 (in pastry terms)

(13) There are bound to be trimmings and surplus pieces of paste left after cutting out the required shapes. It is essential that these are allowed to rest before they are used again. Some goods may be produced entirely from such trimmings, e.g. cream horns, cream slices and cheese straws. Trimmings may also be successfully incorporated into fresh paste before giving it the final turn. They should not, however, make up more than 15 per cent of the total amount of paste. They should be stored flat and not rolled into a ball.

Assessment of the completed pastry

(1) The pastry should have increased considerably in height from the raw state.

(2) It should have risen evenly and not have toppled to one side during baking.

(3) It should be crisp and flaky, have a pleasant flavour of the fat used and should not leave an after-taste or film of grease on the tongue.

(4) The unfilled pastry should be extremely light in weight and well puffed out in size.

(5) It should be an even brown colour; if eggwashed it should appear shiny and golden.

(6) The finished size should be appropriate for its use and the number of portions involved. It should not have shrunk unduly during baking.

Possible problem	*Possible cause and solution*
(1) Pastry lacks volume	— oven was not hot enough; care must be taken to ensure that the oven is at the correct temperature for baking the paste.
	— paste was poorly laminated, i.e. the fat came out whilst it was being rolled; care must be taken when preparing the paste to avoid this problem.
	— incorrect type of flour used; care must be taken to use the correct type of flour as this cannot be rectified later.
	— the fat used was too soft; ensure that good quality waxy fat is used — special puff pastry fat is available and ideal for the purpose.
	— too high a proportion of trimmings used in the paste; ensure that not more than 15 per cent of the paste is made up of the trimmings.
	— paste was given too many turns; ensure that the paste is given only four turns to avoid this problem.
(2) Pastry has shrunk or distorted	— paste was too stiff because insufficient water was added; care must be taken to achieve the correct consistency when preparing the paste as this cannot be rectified later.
	— paste was not allowed sufficient rest between turns or before baking; care must be taken to follow the correct procedure for resting the paste between turns and before baking to avoid this problem.
	— too high a proportion of trimmings used in the paste; ensure that not more than 15 per cent of the paste is made up of trimmings.
(3) Pastry topples over during cooking	— paste was given too few turns; ensure that the paste is given the correct number of turns to avoid this problem.
	— paste not allowed sufficient rest between turns or before baking; care must be taken to follow the correct procedure for resting the paste between turns and before baking.
	— paste was rolled too thick; care must be taken to avoid this as it cannot be rectified later.

Possible problem	*Possible cause and solution*
(4) Pastry turns out tough	— too little fat used in the paste; care must be taken to measure the ingredients accurately to avoid problems later.
	— paste was cut too thick; care must be taken to avoid this as it cannot be rectified later.
	— the fat used was too soft; ensure that good quality waxy fat is used — special puff pastry fat is available and ideal for the purpose.
	— too much pressure was used when rolling out the paste; care must be taken to avoid this as it cannot be rectified later.
	— paste was not given enough turns; ensure that the paste is given the correct number of turns to avoid problems later.
	— oven was not hot enough; care must be taken to ensure that the oven is at the correct temperature for baking the paste.
(5) Pastry bubbles or comes apart during cooking	— paste was poorly laminated, i.e. the fat was pressed out when being rolled; care must be taken to avoid this and prevent problems later.
	— too high a proportion of trimmings used in the paste; ensure that not more than 15 per cent of the paste is made up of trimmings.
(6) Folds or layers of pastry comes apart during cooking	— excess dusting flour not brushed away during folding; care must be taken over this aspect when preparing the paste to avoid problems later.
(7) Layers have ruptured	— fat used was too hard; care must be taken to use the correct type of good quality waxy fat — special puff pastry fat is available and ideal for the purpose.
	— paste rolled out whilst still very cold after resting in the refrigerator; the paste should be allowed to warm through to room temperature before rolling to avoid unevenly stretching it and causing problems later which cannot be rectified.
(8) Cooked pastry leaves an after-taste	— incorrect type of pastry margarine or fat used; care must be taken to use the correct type of good quality waxy fat — special puff

Possible problem	*Possible cause and solution*
	pastry fat is available and ideal for the purpose.

Suet paste

Suet paste is similar to the other pastes in that it contains flour, fat and water. The suet gives the short texture a subtle firmness whilst the use of self-raising flour gives the paste lightness. The shredded suet, when mixed with other ingredients, is held in pieces in the dough. When cooked the light paste absorbs the melted suet leaving pockets of air whilst the absorbed fat imparts its richness to the paste.

Care must be taken not to undermix the paste as this will not develop the strength of the flour and, although the paste may be light, it will not be suitable for making puddings that are turned out of the basin when served, i.e. they will not stand up after turning out. On the other hand, overmixing will break down the pieces of suet smoothing out the paste. It would then be similar to a short paste and when cooked would be heavy with a yellowish finish and lacking in texture and lightness.

10.44 SUET PASTE

Makes: 1 kg. Time: 15 minutes.

Quantity	*Ingredient*
500 g	self-raising flour
4 g	salt
250 g	suet
2½ dl	water

Method

(1) Sieve the flour and salt into a basin.
(2) Add the suet, mix together and make a bay in the centre.
(3) Mix in the water to form a fairly stiff paste.

Note

If soft flour is used, add 12 g baking powder to the flour and salt and sift them together. Then proceed to make the paste.

Chou paste

Chou paste is a liquid mixture which produces steam causing the product to rise during baking, and solids which give it strength and structure. When placed in the oven a skin forms over the surface while the moisture inside boils to form steam. Pressure builds up and splits the skin bringing raw paste to the surface which again forms a skin. This process is repeated until there is no paste left with moisture to produce steam leaving a hollow solid shell which has a very aerated appearance, is yellow in colour and crisp on the outside. It has very little flavour of its own.

10.45 CHOU PASTE — PATE A CHOU

Makes: 16 éclairs, or 16 chou buns, or 32 profiteroles.

Quantity	*Ingredient*
2 dl	water
pinch	salt
pinch	sugar
100 g	butter
125 g	strong flour
4–5	eggs

Method

(1) Place the water, salt, sugar and butter in a pan to boil.

(2) When the butter has melted, remove from the heat and add all the flour, stirring vigorously with a wooden spatule.

(3) Return to the heat and mix until the mixture leaves the sides of the pan clean. Remove from the stove.

(4) Allow to cool. Beat in the eggs one at a time until the mixture just drops from the spoon. (*See* 10.61–63.)

Assessment of the completed item

(1) The articles should be of good volume and a light golden colour.

(2) The outer skin should be rather firm and crisp to the touch.

(3) When removed from the oven they should not go soft or deflate.

(4) The items should be completely aerated inside, hollow and slightly soft.

(5) They should be slightly sweet to taste and chewy in texture with the heavy egg content noticeable.

Possible problem	*Possible cause and solution*
(1) Paste does not rise or hold its shape whilst cooking	— eggs were added to the paste whilst it was still warm; ensure the paste is cold before adding the eggs or else they will cook prematurely.
(2) Paste does not rise, leaving a pale, heavy, solid product	— the oven was not hot enough to form a skin on the surface of the paste so that the moisture evaporates into the oven and the paste does not rise; ensure that the oven is at the correct temperature to bake the paste.

Possible problem	*Possible cause and solution*
	— incorrect type of flour used to make the paste; ensure that the correct type of strong flour is used to make the paste.
(3) The baked item lacks volume	— ingredients were not properly beaten together; care must be taken to mix the ingredients thoroughly during the preparation of the paste.
	— incorrect type of flour used; ensure that the correct type of flour is used to make the paste to avoid problems later.
	— oven was too hot; care must be taken to bake the paste at the correct temperature to avoid ruining the product.
	— paste was made with too few eggs so that when baked a thick skin forms which cannot be ruptured by the steam which causes the product to rise; care must be taken to use the correct amounts of the ingredients to avoid problems later.

SWEET PASTRIES

Flans, tartlets and barquettes

Flans, tartlets and boat-shaped tartlets known as barquettes are used for sweets and afternoon tea pastries and are made with either sweet paste or sweetened short paste. It must be remembered that the paste will have to hold the filling without going soggy or breaking up but care must be taken to avoid wasteful making of paste that is so short it takes a considerable time to line a flan ring or so fragile that the items crumble as they are taken out of the baking tins.

Lining a flan ring

(1) Grease the ring and place it on a greased baking tray.

(2) Mould the paste into a round flat shape on a floured work surface.

(3) Dust the paste with a little flour and roll it out lightly, turning the paste so that it retains a round shape to fit the flan ring. It should be approximately 2 mm thick and a little larger than the ring to allow for lining the sides.

(4) Roll the paste around the rolling pin and unroll it over the ring.

(5) Press the paste into the ring on the tray using a spare piece of paste dipped in flour to prevent sticking.

(6) Bring up the edges on the inside of the ring and roll off any surplus paste.

(7) Use the fingers to form a rim of paste above the rim and decorate with a pair of pastry tweezers or the back of a small knife dipped in flour to prevent sticking.

Lining tartlet moulds

(1) Grease the moulds.

(2) Cut the paste out with a fancy cutter that is slightly larger than the moulds.

(3) Turn the paste cuttings over and lay them in the moulds, pressing them down.

(4) Bring the fancy edges of the paste up over the edge of the mould, bearing inwards.

Lining barquette moulds

(1) Lay the moulds closely together and place the rolled out paste across on top of them.

(2) Press the paste into each mould using a spare piece of paste dipped in flour to prevent sticking.

(3) Remove the surplus by rolling the pin across the top of the moulds.

(4) Decorate the edges of the barquettes as required.

NOTE

The items described in 10.47–58 should be allowed to rest for 30 minutes after moulding and before baking to prevent shrinkage.

Baking blind

Some items should first be cooked without the filling, e.g. soft fruit flans, tartlets and barquettes containing strawberries, freshly poached fruit or tinned fruit such as pear, peach or pineapple. In order to prevent the paste cases from distorting whilst cooking because they contain no filling to help them retain their shape they should be filled with baking beans or, in the case of smaller items, rice. This is termed to cook or to bake blind.

10.46 BAKING BLIND

To cook an empty flan, prick the bottom with a fork and fill it with baking beans resting on a round piece of greaseproof paper. Tartlets and barquettes should be pricked with a fork and filled with baking beans or, if very small, rice, but there is no need to use paper.

10.47 APPLE FLAN — FLAN AUX POMMES

Makes: 1 × 20 cm flan. Cooking time: 30 minutes. Oven temperature: 215 °C.

Quantity	*Ingredient*
120 g	Sweet Paste (10.42)
750 g	cooking apples
120 g	castor sugar
1	juice of lemon
1½ dl	Apricot Glaze (10.176)

Method

(1) Stand the greased flan ring on a greased baking sheet and line with the paste.

(2) Make three-quarters of the apple into an apple marmalade — cook the peeled, cored and quartered apples with very little water, sugar and lemon juice covered with a lid on top of the stove. When soft lightly whisk and turn out onto a tray to cool before use.

(3) Fill the flan with the apple marmalade.

(4) Arrange slices of the remaining apple neatly overlapping on top following the round shape of the flan.

(5) Bake in the oven for the prescribed time removing the flan ring when about three-quarters cooked in order to colour and further cook the paler areas previously covered by the ring.

(6) Remove from the oven. Coat the surface of the flan with hot apricot glaze. Serve on a board on a round flat dish lined with a doily.

Assessment of the completed dish

(1) The flan should have a neat decorative border of pastry of an even light golden colour. The centre should be filled with a firm lightly sweetened apple marmalade which is light in colour topped with overlapping symmetrical slices of apple.

(2) The glaze should be a light apricot colour, fairly clear, not too thick and have a natural shine. It should not be runny but should show signs of being absorbed into the fruit.

(3) The pastry should hold the filling without collapsing.

Extensions

Flans may also be filled with apple purée (*see* 10.175), baked and covered with meringue and cooked at 230 °C for a few minutes until lightly coloured. They may also be made with canned or freshly poached soft fruit such as pears and peaches. Banana, raspberry and strawberry flans are cooked blind and generally filled with pastry cream and completed with the fruit and a jam glaze — either apricot for most fruits or raspberry glaze for the red variety such as cherry and strawberry.

Fruits that can actually be cooked in the flan include fresh cherries, gooseberries, plums and apricots.

Almond Cream (10.174) and Pastry Cream (10.187) are sometimes used in conjunction with a fruit. An appropriately flavoured and coloured glaze is brushed over the flan and its contents once cooked.

10.48 BANANA FLAN —FLAN AUX BANANES

Makes: 1 × 20 cm flan. Cooking time: 30 minutes. Oven temperature: 215 °C.

Quantity	*Ingredient*
120 g	Sweet Paste (10.42)
	Pastry Cream (10.187)
400 g (3)	bananas
1½ dl	Apricot Glaze (10.176)

Method

(1) Stand the greased flan ring on a greased baking sheet and line with the pastry. Bake blind (*see* p. 526).

(2) When cooked fill three-quarters full with pastry cream.

(3) Arrange slices of banana neatly overlapping on top following the round shape of the flan.

(4) Coat the surface of the flan with the hot apricot glaze.

Extensions

10.49 APRICOT FLAN — FLAN AUX ABRICOTS

Proceed as for Banana Flan (10.48) using 400 g drained apricots either poached or canned.

10.50 CHERRY FLAN — FLAN AUX CERISES

Proceed as for Banana Flan (10.48) using 400 g drained stoned cherries either poached or canned. Coat with Raspberry Glaze (*see Note* to 10.176) in place of the apricot glaze.

10.51 CHERRY MERINGUE FLAN — FLAN AUX CERISES MERINGUEE

Bake the washed stoned cherries in the flan. When cooked decorate with meringue and complete in the oven as described under Lemon Meringue Pie (10.56), Stage (3).

10.52 PEAR FLAN — FLAN AUX POIRES

Proceed as for Banana Flan (10.48) using 400 g drained sliced pears either poached or canned.

10.53 PINEAPPLE FLAN — FLAN AUX ANANAS

Proceed as for Banana Flan (10.48) using 400 g segments of either fresh or canned drained pineapple.

10.54 RASPBERRY TARTLETS — TARTELETTES AUX FRAMBOISES

Proceed as for Banana Flan (10.48) using 200 g of previously washed and drained raspberries. Coat with Raspberry Glaze (*see Note* to 10.176) in place of the apricot glaze.

10.55 STRAWBERRY BARQUETTES — BARQUETTES AUX FRAISES

Proceed as for Banana Flan (10.48) using 200 g of previously picked and washed strawberries. Coat with Raspberry Glaze (*see Note* to 10.176) in place of the apricot glaze.

10.56 LEMON MERINGUE PIE

Makes: 1 × 20 cm flan. Cooking time: 40 minutes. Oven temperature: 215 °C.

Quantity	*Ingredient*	
120 g	Sweet Paste (10.42)	
4 dl	water	filling
85 g	sugar	filling
2	lemons (zest and juice)	filling
45 g	cornflour diluted with cold water	filling
30 g	butter	filling
3	egg yolks	filling
3	egg whites	meringue (*see* 10.101)
55 g	castor sugar	meringue (*see* 10.101)
5 g	icing sugar	meringue (*see* 10.101)

Method

(1) Stand the greased flan ring on a greased baking sheet and line with the paste. Bake blind (*see* 10.46).

(2) Boil the water, sugar, lemon zest and juice and thicken with diluted cornflour. Allow to cool for a few moments and add the butter and egg yolks.

(3) Fill the flan with the mixture. Decorate with the meringue. Sprinkle the surface with icing sugar and place in the oven to lightly colour at a temperature of 230 °C.

10.57 BAKEWELL TART

Makes: 1 × 20 cm flan. Cooking time: 30 minutes. Oven temperature: 215 °C.

Quantity	*Ingredient*
120 g	Sweet Paste (10.42)
75 g	raspberry jam
500 g	Almond Cream (10.174)
1½ dl	Apricot Glaze (10.176)
50 g	melted fondant

Method

(1) Stand the greased flan ring on a greased baking sheet and line with the paste.

(2) Prick the bottom and spread with jam. Three-quarters fill with the almond cream.

(3) Bake in the oven for the prescribed time. When cooked, brush the surface with apricot glaze then with fondant.

Notes

(1) Bakewell tart may be decorated with glacé cherries and diamonds of angelica.

(2) When cooked it may be sprinkled with icing sugar in place of apricot glaze and fondant.

10.58 MINCE PIES

Makes: 24. Cooking time: 15 minutes. Oven temperature: 215–220 °C.

Quantity	*Ingredient*
1 kg	Puff Paste (10.43)
300 g	mincemeat
1	egg (eggwash)
15 g	icing sugar

Method

(1) Roll out the paste 2½ mm thick and fold in two. Cut out into 7 cm round pieces.

(2) Place the small rounds on a dampened baking sheet and place a little mincemeat in the centre of each.

(3) Brush the edges with eggwash, cover with the larger rounds and press well together; allow to rest for at least 45 minutes.
(4) Brush with eggwash and bake for the prescribed time.
(5) When cooked remove from the oven, place onto a wire cooling tray and dust liberally with icing sugar.

Fruit pies

These may be made with a number of different fruits or a combination of fruit, e.g.

Apples — peeled, cored and sliced
Apple and picked blackberry
Damsons, greengages and plums — remove the stalks
Gooseberries — top and tail

The prepared and washed fruit is placed in a pie dish with sugar to sweeten, a little water and any other flavouring that may be associated with that particular fruit. The pie dish is covered with short or sweet pastry, brushed with eggwash and sprinkled with castor sugar. It is then baked in the oven at 180 °C until the fruit inside and the pastry is cooked.

NOTE

Some chefs do not use eggwash when making fresh fruit pies. Once cooked the surface of the pastry is brushed with milk and sprinkled with castor sugar and returned to the oven to caramelise the sugar on top.

10.59 APPLE PIE

Makes: 10 portions. Cooking time: 35–40 minutes. Oven temperature: 180 °C.

Quantity	*Ingredient*
1 kg	peeled, cored and sliced apples
145 g	castor sugar
1	juice of lemon
6	cloves
1 dl	water
750 g	Short Paste (10.41)
1	egg (eggwash)

Method

(1) Well fill 3 × 20 cm pie dishes with the sliced apple. Add 120 g sugar, the lemon juice, cloves and a little water.
(2) Line the edges of the pie dish with a strip of pastry 3 cm in thickness and lightly eggwash.

(3) Cover the pie with a sheet of pastry 3 cm thick. Seal firmly and crimp the edges.

(4) Trim around the edges to remove excess paste holding the knife at an angle of 45° from underneath the dish. Make a small hole in the centre of the pie.

(5) Brush the surface with eggwash, sprinkle with castor sugar and place on a baking sheet. Bake for the prescribed time.

Dumplings

10.60 APPLE DUMPLINGS — POMMES EN CAGE

Makes: 10 portions. Cooking time: 25–30 minutes. Oven temperature: 180 °C.

Quantity	*Ingredient*
1½ kg	Short Paste (10.41)
10 × 100 g	peeled and cored apples
150 g	currants
150 g	demerara sugar
10	cloves
2	eggs (eggwash)
25 g	castor sugar

Method

(1) Roll out the pastry 5 mm thick. Cut into 12 cm squares and wet the edges with water.

(2) Place the prepared apple in the centre of the pastry. Fill the centre with currants, demerara sugar and a clove.

(3) Bring the edges of the pastry together and seal them.

(4) Eggwash the entire surface. Place a small piece of pastry cut out with a pastry cutter on top, make a hole in the centre and eggwash.

(5) Place onto a lightly greased baking sheet and bake for the prescribed time.

(6) When cooked sprinkle with castor sugar and serve hot with Custard Sauce (10.179) or cream.

Note

Puff Paste (10.43) may be used in place of short paste.

Eclairs and profiteroles

10.61 CHOCOLATE ECLAIRS — ECLAIRS AU CHOCOLAT

Makes: 16. Cooking time: 25 minutes. Oven temperature: 220 °C reducing to 130 °C

Quantity	*Ingredient*
	Chou Paste (10.45)
1	egg (eggwash)
500 g	fondant icing
60 g	plain chocolate
7 dl	Whipped Cream (10.188)

Method

(1) Using a 1 cm plain tube pipe the paste onto a greased baking sheet in 10 cm lengths. Lightly eggwash.

(2) Bake for the prescribed time, reducing the temperature of the oven after 15 minutes.

(3) When cooked, allow to cool on a wire cooling tray.

(4) Cut the éclairs along one side, open them up and fill with cream using a piping bag and plain tube. Ensure that none comes out when the éclairs are closed up.

(5) Melt the fondant and chocolate in a shallow sided pan to not more than 37 °C, mix together and if desired darken with a little colouring.

(6) Dip the top surface of each éclair into the fondant and smooth off any surplus. Keep the fondant well mixed, adding some lukewarm Stock Syrup (10.173) as necessary to keep the fondant from becoming too stiff.

(7) Allow the fondant to set then arrange the éclairs on a doily on a silver dish.

Note

Pastry Cream (10.187) may be used in place of whipped cream.

Assessment of the completed dish

(1) The chou case should be of an even light brown colour and regular shape with no excessive cracks.

(2) The case should be thin, delicate and have a crisp, short texture which melts in the mouth.

(3) There should be no apparent hole where the filling was inserted.

(4) The fondant should be of a colour corresponding to the filling; it should have a definite shine, be smooth and not runny. It should cover about one-third of the surface area with a clean clear cut edge.

(5) The fondant should not be overcoloured and should enhance the flavour of the éclair.

(6) The filling should be slightly sweetened, have a smooth texture and not be too heavy.

10.62 CHOU BUNS — CHOUX A LA CREME

Makes: 16. Cooking time: 15–20 minutes. Oven temperature: 220 °C reducing to 130 °C.

Quantity	*Ingredient*
	Chou Paste (10.45)
1	egg (eggwash)
7 dl	Whipped Cream (10.188)
15 g	icing sugar

Method

(1) Using a 1 cm plain tube pipe the paste into rounds 3 cm in diameter on a greased baking sheet. Lightly eggwash.

(2) Bake for the prescribed time, reducing the temperature of the oven after about 10 minutes.

(3) When cooked, allow to cool on a wire cooling tray.

(4) Either cut halfway round the centre of each chou bun and fill with cream using a piping bag and plain tube, or press the end of the piping tube into the base of the bun and fill it full of cream.

(5) Dust with icing sugar then arrange the buns on a doily on a silver dish.

10.63 PROFITEROLES AU CHOCOLAT

Makes: 30. Cooking time: 15 minutes. Oven temperature: 220 °C reducing to 130 °C.

Quantity	*Ingredient*
	Chou Paste (10.45)
1	egg (eggwash)
5 dl	Whipped Cream (10.188)
5 dl	Chocolate Sauce (10.178)

Method

(1) Using a 1 cm plain tube pipe the paste into rounds 1½ cm in diameter on a greased baking sheet. Lightly eggwash.

(2) Bake for the prescribed time, reducing the temperature of the oven after about 10 minutes.

(3) When cooked, allow to cool on a wire cooling tray.

(4) Fill the profiteroles with cream using a piping bag and plain tube by inserting the point of the tube into the base.

(5) Neatly arrange dome shape in glass bowls, dust with icing sugar and serve the sauce cold separately in a sauceboat.

Bandes, gateaux and miscellaneous puff pastry items

Bandes may be made with any of the fruits and other combinations of fruit and pastry cream associated with fruit flans, tartlets and barquettes (*see* pp. 525–31).

10.64 APRICOT SLICE — BANDE AUX ABRICOTS

Makes: 1 × 10 portions. Cooking time: 30–35 minutes. Oven temperature: 215–220 °C.

Quantity	*Ingredient*
350 g	Puff Paste (10.43)
5 dl	Pastry Cream (10.187)
1	egg (eggwash)
400 g	apricot halves
1 dl	Apricot Glaze (10.176)

Method

(1) Roll out the pastry 20 cm in length and 11 cm in width. Cut two strips the length of the pastry 1 cm wide.

(2) Place the large strip onto a dampened baking sheet. Brush the edges with eggwash and lay the thin strips one each side, pressing well to the base strip.

(3) Notch the edges with the back of a floured small knife to seal. Eggwash and prick the centre paste with a fork and allow to rest for at least 45 minutes.

(4) Bake for the prescribed time. Place onto a wire cooling tray and allow to cool.

(5) Spread the pastry cream along the centre, neatly arrange the halves of apricots and coat with hot apricot glaze.

(6) Cut across the bande into 10 even portions.

10.65 BANBURY CAKES

Makes: 24. Cooking time: 15 minutes. Oven temperature: 215–220 °C.

Quantity	*Ingredient*	
1 kg	Puff Paste (10.43)	
350 g	currants	filling
100 g	brown sugar	filling
1	lemon (juice and grated zest)	filling
100 g	butter	filling
little	mixed spice	filling
2	egg whites	
50 g	castor sugar	

Method

(1) Roll out the pastry 2½ mm thick and fold in two. Cut out 24 × 10 cm rounds, turn over and eggwash the bottom half.

(2) Place a little of the filling in each. Fold over the edges, sealing in the filling.

(3) Roll out slightly oval shape, place onto a dampened baking sheet, brush with slightly beaten egg white and dip the top into castor sugar.

(4) Make three incisions in the centre. Allow to rest for at least 45 minutes.

(5) Bake in the oven for the prescribed time.

10.66 FLEURONS

Roll out Puff Paste (10.43) 3 mm thick and cut into crescent shapes with a 5 cm fluted round cutter. Turn over, place onto a dampened baking sheet, eggwash and allow to rest for at least 45 minutes. Bake in the oven until golden at a temperature of 225–230 °C for approximately 8–10 minutes.

10.67 GATEAU PITHIVIER

Makes: 1 × 10 portions. Cooking time: 30–35 minutes. Oven temperature: 215–220 °C.

Quantity	*Ingredient*
500 g	Puff Paste (10.43)
50 g	raspberry jam
200 g	Almond Cream (10.174)
1	egg (eggwash)
25 g	icing sugar

Method

(1) Roll out the pastry 2½ mm thick and fold in two. Cut out two circles, one 23 cm and the other 24 cm in diameter.

(2) Lay the small round on a dampened baking sheet. Spread with jam and then with almond cream to within 1½ cm of the edge. Eggwash the edges.

(3) Cover with the other round of pastry, seal well together and notch the edge all round.

(4) Eggwash and cut slits scroll fashion starting at the centre with the point of a small knife without penetrating the pastry. Allow to rest for at least 45 minutes.

(5) Bake for the prescribed time. Dust with icing sugar and glaze either in the oven or under a salamander grill for a few moments.

10.68 PALMIERS

Makes: 24. Cooking time: 10 minutes. Oven temperature: 225–230 °C.

Quantity	*Ingredient*
1 kg	Puff Paste (10.43)
100 g	castor sugar
100 g	raspberry jam
2 dl	Whipped Cream (10.188)

Method

(1) Roll out the pastry 2½ mm thick using castor sugar instead of flour and fold in two forming a strip 48 cm × 30 cm.

(2) Brush with water and sprinkle with sugar. Lightly mark the centre line and fold each side three times towards the line. Fold together to give a 6 cm strip.

(3) Cut into 1 cm strips across and place wide apart on a greased baking sheet. Open the folded ends outwards and allow to rest for at least 45 minutes. Bake for the prescribed time until caramelised to a light golden brown. Place onto a wire cooling tray and allow to cool.

(4) Spread one piece with jam and cream and place another palmier on top to form a sandwich.

SAVOURY PASTRIES

Savoury flans, tartlets and barquettes are made with ordinary short paste and generally consist of savoury egg custard combined with pre-cooked fillings such as mushrooms, bacon, onion and cheese. The filling is placed into the pastry case once it has been baked blind (*see* p. 526), and returned to the oven to complete cooking with the filling.

Other savoury items such as sausage rolls and vols-au-vent are made with puff paste.

10.69 QUICHE LORRAINE

Makes: 1 × 20 cm flan. Cooking time: 30 minutes. Oven temperature: 215 °C.

Quantity	*Ingredient*
120 g	Short Paste (10.41)
75 g	lardons of bacon (blanched and lightly fried)
50 g	grated Gruyère cheese
3 dl	savoury Raw Egg Custard (10.117)

Method

(1) Stand the greased flan ring on a greased baking sheet and line with the paste. Bake blind (*see* p. 526) for approximately 10 minutes.

(2) Remove the beans, layer the bottom with the lardons of bacon and cheese and fill the flan with the raw egg custard.

(3) Replace into the oven for approximately 20 minutes until the custard is cooked, set and lightly coloured.

(4) Serve hot on a flat dish.

10.70 SAUSAGE ROLLS

Makes: 24 × 6 cm. Cooking time: 15–20 minutes. Oven temperature: 215–220 °C.

Quantity	*Ingredient*
650 g	Puff Paste (10.43)
2	eggs (eggwash)
450 g	sausage meat

Method

(1) Roll out the pastry 75 cm × 16 cm and cut in half lengthways.

(2) Roll the sausage meat into two 75 cm lengths, using a little flour to prevent sticking.

(3) Place one sausage meat roll onto each piece of pastry.

(4) Brush the edges with eggwash, fold the pastry over the sausage meat and seal together with a fork. Brush the top with eggwash.

(5) Cut into 6 cm lengths at an angle of 45°. Place onto a dampened baking sheet and allow to rest for at least 45 minutes.

(6) Bake in the oven for the prescribed time.

10.71 VOL-AU-VENT CASES

Makes: 10. Cooking time: 25 minutes. Oven temperature: 225–230 °C.

Quantity	*Ingredient*
650 g	Puff Paste (10.43)
1	egg (eggwash)

Method

(1) Roll out the pastry 2½ mm thick and fold in two. Using a 7 cm round pastry cutter cut out rounds of pastry, turn over and place onto a damp baking sheet. Cut halfway through each piece with a second cutter 5 cm in diameter and allow to rest for at least 45 minutes.

(2) Carefully eggwash and bake for the prescribed time. Place onto a wire cooling tray and allow to cool.

(3) Carefully remove and retain the centre pieces to replace

when filled. Remove and discard any soft dough remaining inside the pastry cases and reserve the cases for use.

10.72 BOUCHEES

These are similar to vol-au-vent but are much smaller measuring approximately 3 cm in diameter. They are generally filled with savoury items and served either hot or cold as desired.

STEAMED PUDDINGS

Steamed puddings are made either from suet paste or a sponge mixture prepared like a Victoria sponge. Breadcrumbs may be added to the suet paste as in 10.75 and 76 to give a much lighter textured pudding.

NOTE

The times indicated for cooking all steamed puddings should be checked in the equipment manual supplied by the manufacturer of the pressure cooker being used.

Steamed suet puddings

10.73 STEAMED APPLE PUDDING

Makes: 10 portions (2 × 1 litre basins). Cooking time: 2 hours.

Quantity	*Ingredient*
850 g	Suet Paste (10.44)
2 kg	peeled and cored cooking apples
350 g	castor sugar
1	juice of lemon
1 dl	water
4	cloves

Method

(1) Take three-quarters of the paste and divide it into three. Roll two pieces into pocket shapes that will fit the basins and place into the greased basins.

(2) Fill with the sliced apple and add the sugar, lemon juice, water and cloves.

(3) Roll out the remainder of the paste into two circular pieces to fit the top of the basin.

(4) Dampen the edges of the paste, place on the tops and seal. Cover with buttered greaseproof paper and a cloth. Tie with string. Alternatively, cover with foil.

(5) Steam for the prescribed time. Allow to stand for 5 minutes then turn out of the basin onto a dish and serve.

Notes

(1) Fruit suet puddings such as this may be served in the basins in which they have been cooked. The basin is covered with a napkin and placed on a dish lined with a doily.

(2) These puddings are generally served with Custard Sauce (10.179).

(3) Other fruits that may be used are rhubarb, plums, damsons and a combination of blackberry and apple.

10.74 STEAMED JAM ROLL

Makes: 10 portions. Cooking time: 1½ hours.

Quantity	*Ingredient*
1 kg	Suet Paste (10.44)
300 g	jam

Method

(1) Roll out the pastry 30 cm × 35 cm and evenly spread with jam to within 1 cm of the edges.

(2) Dampen the edges with water and roll up fairly loosely.

(3) Cover with greaseproof paper and either place into a pudding sleeve which is specially designed to cook such items or tie in a pudding cloth.

(4) Steam for 1½ hours and serve cut into slices accompanied with Custard Sauce (10.179).

10.75 REINA PUDDING

Makes: 10 portions (2 × 1 litre basins). Cooking time: 4 hours.

Quantity	*Ingredient*
250 g	soft flour
10 g	baking powder
250 g	shredded suet
250 g	white breadcrumbs
250 g	demerara sugar
250 g	stoned raisins
4 dl	milk
12 g	bicarbonate of soda

Method

(1) Sieve the flour and baking powder together in a basin, mix all the dry ingredients together.

(2) Dissolve the bicarbonate of soda in a little hot water and add to the milk.

(3) Add the liquid to the dry ingredients and mix together.

(4) Pour into the previously buttered basins. Cover with

buttered greaseproof paper and a cloth and tie with string, or cover with foil.

(5) Steam for the prescribed time. Allow to stand for 5 minutes then turn onto a dish and serve.

Notes

(1) This pudding is generally served with Custard Sauce (10.179).

(2) Extensions may be made with the addition of glacé cherries, walnuts, currants and sultanas to a total quantity of 250 g.

(3) Unlike most puddings of a similar type, the uncooked mixture is rather wet and loose.

(4) When cooked it should be a rich brown colour and very light in texture.

10.76 STEAMED SUET PUDDING

Makes: 10 portions. Cooking time: 1¼ hours.

Quantity	*Ingredient*
350 g	soft flour
10 g	baking powder
pinch	salt
250 g	shredded suet
250 g	white breadcrumbs
150 g	castor sugar
3	eggs
1 dl	milk

Method

(1) Sieve the flour, baking powder and salt into a basin. Add the breadcrumbs, sugar and suet and mix together.

(2) Mix the eggs and milk together and add to the dry ingredients. Mix to a soft paste.

(3) Divide into individual greased moulds. Cover with buttered greaseproof papers and foil and steam for the prescribed time.

(4) Turn out of the moulds and serve with Custard Sauce (10.179).

Note

Extensions to this pudding may be made by putting a jam, marmalade, syrup or fruit such as apple marmalade in the bottom of the moulds before the pudding mixture.

Steamed sponge puddings

These may be made with a number of different flavourings, e.g.

chocolate, various types of jams and marmalade, lemon, orange and syrup. The sponge mixture is made by the sugar-batter method in exactly the same way as Victoria Sponge (*see* 10.25). When cooked the sponge should be moist and light in texture similar to that of a sponge cake.

Steamed sponge puddings may be cooked in individual moulds, multi-portioned pudding basins, or pudding sleeves. The basins are prepared by brushing them with melted butter and sprinkling with castor sugar.

Sponge puddings may be served with a number of different sauces, e.g. custard sauce, jam sauce, and so on. It is usual to serve a sauce reflecting the flavour of the pudding, e.g. lemon sauce with lemon sponge pudding.

10.77 SPONGE PUDDING MIXTURE (BASIC)

Makes: 10 portions (2 × 1 litre basins). Cooking time: 1½ hours.

Quantity	*Ingredient*	
150 g	butter or margarine	
150 g	castor sugar	
3	lightly beaten eggs	
225 g	soft flour	sieved together
10 g	baking powder	sieved together
½ dl	milk	

Method

(1) Butter and sugar the pudding basins.

(2) Cream the fat and sugar until light, white and fluffy.

(3) Gradually add the beaten eggs to the creamed butter and sugar.

(4) Fold in the flour and baking powder using a metal spoon or a scraper, but do not overmix. Add milk if necessary.

(5) Transfer the mixture to the prepared basins. Cover with buttered greaseproof paper and a cloth and tie with string or use foil.

(6) Steam for the prescribed time. Allow to stand for 5 minutes, then turn out of the basin onto a dish and serve.

Extensions

10.78 CHOCOLATE SPONGE PUDDING

Proceed as for Sponge Pudding (10.77) reducing the flour content by 50 g and replacing with sifted chocolate powder. Serve accompanied with hot Chocolate Sauce (10.178)

10.79 LEMON SPONGE PUDDING

Proceed as for Sponge Pudding (10.77) with the addition of the grated zest and juice of 3 lemons. Serve accompanied with hot Lemon Sauce (10.181).

10.80 ORANGE SPONGE PUDDING

Proceed as for Sponge Pudding (10.77) with the addition of the grated zest and juice of 3 oranges. Serve accompanied with hot Orange Sauce (10.183).

10.81 SYRUP SPONGE PUDDING (GOLDEN SPONGE PUDDING)

Proceed as for Sponge Pudding (10.77). Place 100 g warm syrup in the bottom of the basin followed by the sponge pudding mixture. Serve accompanied with hot Syrup Sauce (10.184).

BISCUITS

There are several kinds of biscuits used as an accompaniment to sweets, as part of a sweet dish or served with ice cream instead of wafers. Perhaps the most widely used biscuits are brandy snaps, biscuits à la cuillère, langues de chat, ratafias, shortbread and viennese biscuits.

10.82 BRANDY SNAPS

Makes: 10. Cooking time: 10 minutes. Oven temperature: 175 °C.

Quantity	*Ingredient*
120 g	butter
120 g	castor sugar
120 g	golden syrup
½	juice of lemon
120 g	soft flour
2 g	ground ginger

Method

(1) Melt the butter, sugar and syrup and add the lemon juice. Remove from the heat and beat in the sieved flour and ground ginger.

(2) Deposit spoonfuls of the mixture onto a well greased baking sheet keeping them at least 7 cm apart.

(3) Bake for the prescribed time. When cooked, allow to rest for just a few seconds.

(4) Mould each piece around the greased handle of a wooden spoon. Place onto a wire cooling tray and allow to cool and become crisp before use.

10.83 CAT'S TONGUE BISCUITS — LANGUES DE CHAT

Makes: 20–25. Cooking time: 7–8 minutes. Oven temperature: 215 °C.

Quantity	*Ingredient*
120 g	butter
120 g	castor sugar
3	egg whites
1 g	soft flour
	vanilla essence

Method

(1) Prepare a baking sheet by brushing with melted butter and sprinkling with flour.

(2) Cream the butter and sugar together until light and fluffy.

(3) Add the egg whites one at a time beating thoroughly.

(4) Mix in the sifted flour and vanilla essence.

(5) Pipe the mixture onto the baking sheet in 7 cm lengths using a 5 mm plain tube.

(6) Bake in the oven for the prescribed time until brown around the edges.

(7) Remove from the baking sheet and place onto a wire cooling tray to cool.

10.84 FINGER BISCUITS — BISCUITS A LA CUILLERE

Makes: 20 biscuits. Cooking time: 15 minutes. Oven temperature: 165 °C.

Quantity	*Ingredient*
4	eggs
100 g	castor sugar
100 g	soft flour
15 g	icing sugar

Method

(1) Prepare a baking sheet by brushing with melted butter and sprinkling with flour.

(2) Place the egg yolks and sugar in a basin and whisk until stiff, firm and white.

(3) Whisk the egg whites in a separate bowl until firm.

(4) Fold in half the quantity of egg whites into the yolks, then carefully fold in the sifted flour and the remainder of the whites.

(5) Pipe the mixture onto the baking sheet in 10 cm lengths using a 2 cm plain tube.

(6) Sprinkle the items with icing sugar twice, removing any excess.

(7) Bake in the oven for the prescribed time. Allow to cool for approximately 5 minutes then remove from the baking sheet and place on a wire cooling tray to cool completely.

10.85 CHAMPAGNE BISCUITS

These are prepared as for Finger Biscuits (10.84) except that they should be sprinkled with castor sugar instead of icing sugar, causing them to sparkle when baked.

10.86 RATAFIA BISCUITS

Makes: 25. Cooking time: 7–8 minutes. Oven temperature: 175 °C.

Quantity	*Ingredient*
2	egg whites
125 g	castor sugar
30 g	ground rice
125 g	ground almonds

Method

(1) Place all the ingredients into a bowl and mix well until thoroughly blended together.

(2) Pipe onto a baking sheet brushed with melted butter and sprinkled with flour or onto rice paper into 2½ cm rounds using a 1 cm plain tube.

(3) Bake for the prescribed time. When cooked they should be slightly coloured.

10.87 SHORTBREAD

Makes: 20. Cooking time: 20 minutes. Oven temperature: 200 °C.

Quantity	*Ingredient*
175 g	soft flour
25 g	ground rice
225 g	butter
110 g	castor sugar

Method

(1) Sieve the flour and ground rice together into a basin and retain.

(2) Cream the butter and sugar together in a bowl.

(3) Add the flour and ground rice and press together to form a stiff paste.

(4) Roll out 4 mm thick dusting with ground rice or castor sugar. Cut into desired shapes, e.g. rounds, triangles, oblongs, etc.

(5) Place onto a greased baking sheet and prick all over with a fork.

(6) Bake for the prescribed time without letting them colour.

Notes

(1) When baked shortbreads may be sprinkled with castor sugar.

(2) They should be baked until crisp but not too coloured.

(3) To obtain the short texture required it is important to use soft flour.

10.88 VIENNESE BISCUITS

Makes: 20. Cooking time: 15 minutes. Oven temperature: 170 °C.

Quantity	*Ingredient*
300 g	butter
100 g	icing sugar
2	eggs
375 g	soft flour
15 g	icing sugar

Method

(1) Cream the butter and sugar together until light and fluffy. Add the eggs and continue beating.

(2) Add the sifted flour and mix until smooth.

(3) Pipe the mixture onto a baking sheet brushed with melted butter and sprinkled with flour using a large star tube into shapes such as shells or rosettes.

(4) Bake for the prescribed time until lightly coloured. Place onto a wire cooling tray and sprinkle with icing sugar.

BREAD DOUGHS

A wide range of goods can be produced using yeast as a raising agent together with flour, water and other ingredients. Many kinds of bread, rolls, buns, baps, savarins, babas and some frying batters are based on yeast dough.

To make a dough the essential ingredients of yeast, flour, salt and water are thoroughly mixed. This wets the protein in the flour and forms a gluten. It is how this gluten develops and is worked and moulded that determines the final shape of the item and the structure of the crumb inside.

There are many different types of dough. Plain doughs are used for bread and rolls; sweet doughs are used for buns such as Chelsea buns; rich doughs made with extra butter, eggs and sugar are used for savarins.

The following is a short list of terms frequently used in the baking of these products.

Elasticity. This is the ability of the dough to return to its original shape after it has been moulded.

Green dough. This refers to a dough which is under-proved.

Over-proving. This occurs when the dough has been fermented for too long at too high a temperature. The bread, when cooked, is a pale yellow colour and may collapse during baking.

Proving. This refers to the resting period during the making of bread items where the dough is allowed to ferment (prove) in a warm area or proving cabinet. Carelessness during proving will result in an uneven production of carbon dioxide and adversely affect the final crumb texture.

Proving is carried out during the making of the dough at several stages at a temperature of 30 °C. (The ideal working temperature for making dough is usually considered to be 3 °C lower than that for proving.) Once moulded the dough is proved and then baked at a high temperature to give a golden brown crust and an even crumb texture.

Baking

A 400 g small loaf will take about 35 minutes baking at 200 °C whilst a 1 kg loaf will take about 40 minutes at 225 °C. The dough will continue to rise in the oven until the yeast is killed as the temperature inside the loaf reaches 57 °C. The temperature inside the loaf will only rise to 100 °C maximum, even though the air temperature in the oven is twice that.

Assessment of the completed bread product

(1) The baked item should have a good volume in relation to the amount of dough put in the tin.

(2) The top crust should be evenly coloured to a light golden brown and be fairly crisp.

(3) The item should have a good shape.

(4) When tapped the bottom of a loaf should sound hollow to indicate that it has lost a lot of its moisture during baking.

(5) The crumb should be soft.

(6) The smell of fresh bread is most pleasant and should remain with the item even after it has gone stale.

Possible problem	*Possible cause and solution*
(1) The bread lacks volume	— wrong type of flour used to make the dough; care must be taken to use the correct

Possible problem	*Possible cause and solution*
	ingredients as once the bread is baked the problem cannot be rectified.
	— dough was too soft; care must be taken when preparing the dough to achieve the correct consistency as once the bread is baked the problem cannot be rectified.
	— dough was under or over proven; care must be taken to follow the correct proving procedure as once the item is baked the problem cannot be rectified.
(2) The bread has an irregular shape	— dough was too tough; care must be taken to avoid this as once the item is baked the problem cannot be rectified.
	— dough was underproven; care must be taken to follow the correct proving procedure as once the item is baked the problem cannot be rectified.
	— oven was too hot; care must be taken to bake the item at the correct temperature as once the item is baked the problem cannot be rectified.
	— dough was not moulded correctly; care must be taken over this aspect as once the item is baked the problem cannot be rectified.
(3) The bread has a very dark crust	— too much salt or sugar added to the dough mixture; care must be taken to use the correct quantities in the dough as once the item is baked the problem cannot be rectified.
	— oven was too hot; care must be taken to bake the item at the correct temperature as the problem cannot be rectified.
(4) Crust lacks colour	— oven not hot enough; care must be taken to bake the item at the correct temperature to avoid this problem which cannot be rectified once the item is baked.
	— dough was overproven; care must be taken to follow the correct proving procedure as once the item is baked the problem cannot be rectified.
	— temperature of the dough was too high; care must be taken to mix the dough at the

Possible problem	*Possible cause and solution*
	correct temperature to avoid problems that cannot be rectified later.
(5) The bread has a loose crumb texture	— dough was overproven; care must be taken to follow the correct proving procedure as once the item is baked the problem cannot be rectified.
	— dough was soft; care must be taken when preparing the dough to achieve the correct consistency as once the bread is baked the problem cannot be rectified.
	— wrong type of flour used to make the dough; care must be taken to use the correct ingredients as once the bread is baked the problem cannot be rectified.

Plain dough items

10.89 BRIDGE ROLLS

Makes: 30. Cooking time: 10–15 minutes. Oven temperature: 240 °C.

Quantity	*Ingredient*
	White Bread dough (10.91)
1	egg

Method

(1) Proceed as for White Bread (10.91), mixing the egg with the liquid.
(2) Divide the dough into 30 equal pieces. Mould oval shape and place onto a greased baking sheet.
(3) Allow to prove until double their size.
(4) Bake for the prescribed time.

10.90 DINNER ROLLS

Makes: 20. Cooking time: 15 minutes. Oven temperature: 230 °C.

Ingredient
White Bread dough (10.91)

Method

(1) Divide the dough into 20 equal pieces. Mould round shape and place onto a greased baking sheet.
(2) Allow to prove until double their size.
(3) Bake for the prescribed time.

10.91 WHITE BREAD

Makes: 2 × 400 g loaves. Cooking time: 35–40 minutes. Oven temperature: 200 °C.

Quantity	*Ingredient*
500 g	strong flour
10 g	salt
10 g	milk powder
10 g	lard
30 g	yeast
3 dl	water (at 45 °C)
10 g	sugar

Method

(1) Sieve the flour, salt and milk powder into a warmed bowl. Rub in the fat.

(2) Dissolve the yeast and sugar in the water and mix into the flour to form a medium soft dough.

(3) Knead the dough thoroughly. Replace in the bowl, cover with a cloth and allow to prove in a warm place for approximately 1 hour.

(4) Knead the dough and divide into two equal pieces. Mould and place into greased bread tins.

(5) Allow to prove until double its size.

(6) Bake for the prescribed time.

10.92 WHOLEMEAL BREAD

Proceed as for White Bread (10.91), using 450 g wholemeal flour and 50 g white strong flour.

Sweet dough items

10.93 CHELSEA BUNS

Makes: 25. Cooking time: 15 minutes. Oven temperature: 230 °C.

Quantity	*Ingredient*
1 kg	bun dough (as for Fruit Buns (10.94) omitting the fruit)
50 g	melted butter
40 g	castor sugar
10 g	cinnamon
100 g	mixed dry fruit
25 g	mixed peel (diced)
	Bun Wash (10.172)
25 g	castor sugar

Method

(1) Roll out the dough to 65 cm × 35 cm.

(2) Brush with melted butter, sprinkle with sugar, cinnamon, fruit and peel.

(3) Roll up like a Swiss roll, keeping the length to 65 cm. Seal the edges.

(4) Divide by cutting into 25×2½ cm pieces. Arrange the circles of dough fairly close together in a greased baking tray with fairly deep sides so that they become square in shape as they expand with proving.

(5) Allow to prove until double their size.

(6) Bake for the prescribed time.

(7) Remove from the oven and brush immediately with bun wash and sprinkle with castor sugar.

10.94 FRUIT BUNS

Makes: 25. Cooking time: 10–15 minutes. Oven temperature: 230 °C.

Quantity	*Ingredient*
550 g	strong flour
4 g	salt
60 g	butter
40 g	yeast
1¾ dl	water } (at 45 °C)
1¾ dl	milk } (at 45 °C)
1	egg
100 g	sugar
100 g	mixed dried fruit
25 g	mixed peel
	Bun Wash (10.172)

Method

(1) Sieve the flour and salt into a warmed bowl and rub in the butter.

(2) Dissolve the yeast and sugar in the water and milk and add the beaten egg. Mix into the flour to form a medium dough.

(3) Knead thoroughly. Replace in the bowl, cover with a cloth and allow to prove in a warm place for approximately 1 hour.

(4) Knead the dough. Add the fruit, divide into 25 equal pieces and mould into round shapes. Place onto a greased baking sheet.

(5) Allow to prove until double their size.

(6) Bake for the prescribed time.

(7) Remove from the oven and brush immediately with bun wash.

10.95 HOT CROSS BUNS

Makes: 25. Cooking time: 10–15 minutes. Oven temperature: 230 °C.

Quantity	*Ingredient*	
	Fruit Bun Dough (10.94)	
3 g	mixed spice	
100 g	soft flour	mixed to a batter
25 g	lard	mixed to a batter
pinch	baking powder	mixed to a batter
9 cl	cold water	
	Bun Wash (10.172)	

Method

(1) Add 3 g mixed spice to the dough.

(2) Divide the dough into 25 equal pieces and mould into round shapes.

(3) Place onto a greased baking sheet and pipe a cross on each with the batter. Allow to prove until double their size.

(4) Bake for the prescribed time.

(5) Remove from the oven and brush immediately with bun wash.

Rich dough items

10.96 SAVARIN PASTE — PATE A SAVARIN

Makes: 2 × 15 cm diameter. Cooking time: 25–30 minutes. Oven temperature: 230–240 °C.

Quantity	*Ingredient*
225 g	strong flour
20 g	yeast
¾ dl	water
3	eggs
80 g	melted butter
12 g	sugar
pinch	salt

Method

(1) Sift the flour into a warm bowl and warm.

(2) Dissolve the yeast in the water which has been heated to 35 °C.

(3) Make a well in the centre of the flour and add the dissolved yeast. Mix in enough flour to make a light batter and dust a little of the flour over the top.

(4) Cover with a cloth and place to prove in a warm area until the ferment breaks through the flour.

(5) Break in the eggs and mix to a smooth dough. Add the salt, sugar and butter, then mix until it is smooth and elastic.

(6) Allow to prove covered with a cloth in a warm area until double its size.

(7) Half fill the prepared greased and floured moulds and allow to prove further until it reaches the top of the moulds.
(8) Bake the mixture in the oven at the required temperature until cooked.

Assessment of the completed item

(1) The baked savarin should be a deep golden brown colour all over, well cooked and dry and easy to remove from the mould.
(2) It should be light in weight and the inside should be full of small evenly shaped air holes.

Extensions

10.97 SAVARIN WITH FRUIT — SAVARIN AUX FRUITS

Makes: 6 portions. Time: 30 minutes.

Quantity	*Ingredient*
1	Savarin (10.96)
2 l	Stock Syrup (10.173)
½ dl	Apricot Glaze (10.176)
300 g	Fruit Salad (10.148) (with kirsch)
1 dl	Whipped Cream (10.188)

Method

(1) Soak the savarin in the hot syrup. Remove carefully and allow to drain on a wire tray.
(2) Brush over the entire surface with hot apricot glaze and place on a round flat dish.
(3) Drain the fruit salad and place in the centre.
(4) Pipe rosettes of cream on top of the savarin.

Notes

(1) A little rum may be sprinkled over the savarin once soaked.
(2) Savarins can be filled with stoned cherries mixed with raspberry or cherry sauce, with halves of apricots mixed with apricot sauce, or with whipped cream only.

10.98 MARIGNANS

Marignans are made from Savarin Paste (10.96) baked in boat-shaped moulds and finished by soaking in Stock Syrup (10.173) and glazing with Apricot Glaze (10.176). The recipe for Savarin Paste in 10.96 will make 14–18 Marignans.

10.99 POMPONETTES

These are similar to marignans and made from savarin paste

except that they are baked in queen cake tins (fluted moulds). The recipe for savarin paste given in 10.96 will make 10–12 × 40 g pomponettes. These too are soaked in hot Stock Syrup (10.173), drained and brushed over with hot Apricot Glaze (10.176).

10.100 RUM BABAS

These are made from Savarin Paste (10.96) to which 50 g of currants have been added. They are baked in individual dariole moulds and allowed to dry out before being immersed in hot rum-flavoured stock syrup. Neat rum may be sprinkled on before the babas are glazed with Apricot Glaze (10.176).

MERINGUES

Meringues are light confectionery items made from egg whites and castor sugar which are piped into various shapes. They are usually filled with whipped cream or ice cream and decorated in some way.

10.101 MERINGUE SHELLS

Makes: 30 shells. Cooking time: 8 hours (until shells are dry). Oven temperature: 38 °C.

Quantity	*Ingredient*
10	egg whites
few grains	salt
600 g	castor sugar

Method

(1) Place the egg whites into a basin, copper bowl or the mixing bowl of an electric mixer.
(2) Add a pinch of salt.
(3) Whisk to a stiff peak with either a balloon whisk or the whisk attachment of an electric mixer.
(4) Whisk in half the sugar, then remove the bowl from the machine (if used).
(5) Fold in the remainder of the sugar.
(6) Place the meringue into a piping bag fitted with a 1 cm plain tube.
(7) Pipe onto silicone paper (waxed paper) on a baking sheet.
(8) Bake without colouring until the shells are dry throughout.

Notes

(1) The addition of an acid or alkali such as cream of tartar, lemon juice or vinegar will help the egg whites to peak. They give

greater body and strength to the albumen and give greater volume. Only one, however, should be used.

(2) Meringue used for topping dishes such as lemon meringue pie must be lighter than that used for meringue shells. Less sugar must be used for the same number of eggs, though the method is the same; approximately 50 g sugar per egg white is sufficient.

(3) When baked the shells should be firm and white and come easily away from the paper they were baked on. Shells that are baked thoroughly dry before storage will keep well and remain firm and crisp.

Assessment of the completed item

(1) If piped correctly they will have a nice smooth appearance, be round or oval in shape and be even in size.

(2) They should be white in colour and shiny.

(3) They should be dry, and crisp and fragile so that they disintegrate in the mouth. They should not be chewy.

Possible problem	*Possible cause and solution*
(1) Egg whites will not peak	— eggs were too fresh; the whites of eggs which are approximately two weeks old should be used (but *see* also *Note* (1)).
	— egg yolk has contaminated the whites; care must be taken when separating the yolks from the whites to avoid this as it cannot be rectified.
	— grease may have contaminated the whites from, for example, the whisk, the bowl or the spoon; ensure that all utensils are clean before use.
	— whites were too cold before whisking; ensure that the whites have warmed to room temperature before whisking to avoid this problem.
(2) Egg whites peak but become syrupy when the sugar is added	— sugar added too fast; care must be taken when adding the sugar as this problem cannot be rectified.
	— second half of sugar was whisked in instead of folded; care must be taken when adding the sugar to follow the correct procedure as the problem cannot be rectified.
	— mixture was allowed to stand too long before use after it had been made; the

Possible problem	*Possible cause and solution*
	mixture should be prepared as close as possible to the time it is required to avoid the problems caused by prolonged retention.
(3) Meringues are cracked and discoloured	— meringues were baked too fast; care must be taken to follow the correct procedure for baking the meringues as the problem cannot be rectified.
(4) Meringues weep whilst baking	— meringues were baked too slowly; care must be taken to follow the correct procedure for baking as the problem cannot be rectified; care must be taken to bake the meringues for the correct length of time at the correct temperature.
	— meringues were left in the oven for too long; care must be taken to bake the meringues for the correct length of time as the problem cannot be rectified.
	— oven not hot enough; care must be taken to ensure that the oven is at the correct temperature for baking the meringues as the problem cannot be rectified.

Extensions

This kind of meringue has many other uses and can be piped into a wide variety of shapes such as small nests to hold cherries, strawberries and other fruit, or large circles or squares to fit together, e.g. a vacherin, or as a pavlova. It can, of course, be used to cover flans, fruit and omelettes.

10.102 ITALIAN MERINGUE

Cook the sugar with 2½ dl water to 140 °C until it reaches the soft crack stage and pour onto the beaten whites. Meringue made in this way is often used instead of meringue made in the ordinary way for any of the uses outlined in this section.

10.103 MERINGUE CHANTILLY

Sandwich two Meringue Shells (10.101) with whipped cream. Place it on its side, decorate with a rosette of whipped cream and sprinkle with grated chocolate or decorate with glacé cherries or angelica.

10.104 OEUFS A LA NEIGE

Take scoops of ordinary Meringue (10.101) and poach in milk at

180 °C, turning them over carefully as they poach. Arrange in a dish on a bed of cold Egg Custard Sauce (10.107) and decorate with flaked almonds.

10.105 PAVLOVA

Makes: 2.

Quantity	*Ingredient*	
10	egg whites	meringue mixture
600 g	castor sugar	
40 g	cornflour	
2½ cl	vinegar	
½ kg	various fresh fruits, e.g. sliced kiwi fruit, sliced bananas, raspberries and strawberries	
4 dl	Whipped Cream (10.188)	

Method

(1) Make the meringue mixture as for Meringue Shells (10.101) to Stage (5), then fold in the sieved cornflour and vinegar.

(2) Pipe into two 25 cm rings to form the bottom or base, and smaller rings to build up from the base to form a nest shape.

(3) Bake without colouring as in 10.101.

(4) Build up the rings on the bases, one on top of the other, with a little uncooked meringue between to hold them in place.

(5) Fill with the prepared fruit and decorate with the cream.

10.106 VACHARIN AUX FRAISES

Makes: 10 portions.

Quantity	*Ingredient*
	Meringue Shells (10.101)
10	scoops of vanilla ice cream
250 g	fresh strawberries (picked and washed)
2 dl	Melba Sauce (10.182)
2 dl	Whipped Cream (10.188)

Method

(1) Pipe 10 meringue nests approximately 8 cm in diameter. Proceed as described in 10.101.

(2) When serving, fill with a scoop of ice cream and strawberries, coat with melba sauce and decorate with whipped cream.

EGG CUSTARDS

Egg custard made with milk, eggs and sugar has a number of different applications as a basis for hot and cold sweets. It is also used to make a sauce and if sugar is omitted forms the basis for a variety of savoury dishes. It is therefore a very versatile preparation, but because of its rather delicate nature needs careful handling in order to produce top quality results.

The applications for egg custard are as follows:

(a) egg custard sauce base:
(i) as a sauce in its own right known as Sauce Anglaise;
(ii) as a basis for various bavarois and cold charlottes;
(iii) as the custard used to make ice cream (*see* pp. 583–4).

(b) raw egg custard base baked in pie dishes and moulds:
(i) as a sweet baked custard on its own or with other ingredients, e.g. bread and butter pudding, cream caramels, diplomat pudding and cabinet pudding;
(ii) as a savoury custard used in making Royale for garnishing consommé, quiches and various tartlettes used as hot hors-d'oeuvre.

Items based on egg custard sauce

10.107 EGG CUSTARD SAUCE — SAUCE ANGLAISE

Makes: ¾ litre. Cooking time: 15–20 minutes.

Quantity	*Ingredient*
4	eggs
125 g	castor sugar
½ l	milk
few drops	vanilla essence

Method

(1) Mix the eggs and sugar in a basin.

(2) Heat the milk with the vanilla essence to just below boiling point.

(3) Add the heated milk to the eggs and sugar and mix well but without making it frothy. Strain through a conical strainer into a clean pan.

(4) Place the heated mixture in a bain-marie of water on top of the stove. Stir occasionally with a wooden spatule until the mixture coats the back of the spatule. When cooked, strain the mixture through a fine strainer.

Notes

(1) Egg custard sauce is sufficiently cooked when it coats the back of a wooden spatule.

(2) The mixture should not be allowed during cooking to reach a temperature in excess of 90 °C, or the custard will curdle.

(3) If required as a sauce to accompany other sweet dishes, retain in a bain-marie of hot water which should not be permitted to boil.

(4) Be careful not to cook the sauce to the limit as the heat from the saucepan will cause the sauce to continue to cook once removed from the stove and result in the sauce curdling.

Bavarois

This is a cold custard cream usually made from Egg Custard Sauce (10.107) with Whipped Cream (10.188) to give lightness and smoothness and leaf gelatine to make it set. It can be made in various flavours such as coffee and chocolate, using soft fruits and liqueurs to enhance them.

Nowadays bavarois are very close to mousses, although the traditional recipes were very different. A mousse used to be made from a fruit purée base containing gelatine and aeration was obtained by the addition of whipped egg whites, until changing tastes dictated that various amounts of whipped cream should be added. On the other hand, although the traditional recipe for bavarois does not include any whisked egg whites, they are sometimes added to give an even lighter texture and, of course, an increase in volume.

Bavarois can also be made with fruit purée in place of egg custard, the purée being mixed with an equal quantity of stock syrup, stiffened with gelatine and finished with whipped cream. In practice, fruit bavarois are made with egg custard sauce and equal amounts of sieved fruit and cream.

10.108 BAVAROIS

Makes: 10 portions. Cooking time: 30 minutes.

Quantity	*Ingredient*	
4	egg yolks	Sauce Anglaise (10.107)
125 g	castor sugar	
½ l	milk	
25 g	leaf gelatine (soaked in cold water)	
5 dl	lightly whipped cream	

Method

(1) Add the soaked and drained gelatine to the hot custard and stir until it dissolves. Strain the mixture through a conical strainer into a clean bowl.

(2) Continue to stir until the mixture is on the point of setting and fold in the lightly whipped cream.

(3) Pour into medium size moulds and place in a refrigerator until set.

(4) Shake the moulds to loosen the bavarois and turn out onto a dish. Serve decorated with whipped cream.

Assessment of the completed dish

(1) The bavarois should be well formed to the lines of the mould in which it has been set. It should be extremely smooth in appearance and texture and have a creamy white colour all through.

(2) It should be smooth on the tongue and have a rich creamy taste. It easily dissolves in the mouth and is not chewy in texture.

(3) It should be served cold but not chilled or frozen.

Possible problem	*Possible cause and solution*
(1) The bavarois will not set properly	— gelatine was soaked in hot instead of cold water; care must be taken to follow the correct procedures as this cannot be rectified later.
	— insufficient gelatine used in the mixture; care must be taken to use the correct quantities as this cannot be rectified later.
	— bavarois not kept in the refrigerator for a long enough period; keep the bavarois in the refrigerator for the prescribed length of time unless it will not set for one of the reasons above.
(2) The bavarois is too firm in texture	— too much gelatine was used in the mixture; care must be taken to use the correct quantities as this cannot be rectified later.
	— mixture was warm when the cream was added; care must be taken to avoid this as once the bavarois is set the problem cannot be rectified.
(3) There are streaks of gelatine in the bavarois	— when the soaked gelatine was added the mixture was not warm enough so the gelatine did not melt completely; care must be taken at this stage as once the bavarois is set it cannot be rectified.
(4) The texture is very fluffy, over-aerated and has large air holes	— too much cream added to the mixture; care must be taken to use the correct amounts as once the bavarois is set the problem cannot be rectified.
	— cream was beaten until too firm; care must be taken not to overbeat the cream as once

Possible problem	*Possible cause and solution*
	the bavarois is set the problem cannot be rectified.
	— cream was whisked vigorously when added to the mixture; care must be taken not to overwhisk at this stage as once the bavarois is set the problem cannot be rectified.
(5) The bavarois does not have sufficient flavour	— too much cream used; care must be taken to use the correct amounts as once the bavarois is set the problem cannot be rectified.
	— cream was beaten until it was too firm; care must be taken to avoid this as once the bavarois is set the problem cannot be rectified.

Extensions

10.109 CHARLOTTE MONTREUIL

Place 1 dl orange jelly in the bottom of a charlotte mould and allow to set. Line the sides of the mould with Finger Biscuits (10.84). Fill the mould with Vanilla Bavarois (10.108) mixed with 50 g peach purée and 75 g diced peaches soaked in kirsch. Allow to set. Turn out of the mould onto a flat silver dish and serve.

10.110 CHARLOTTE MOSCOVITE

Place 1 dl raspberry jelly in the bottom of a charlotte mould and allow to set. Line the sides of the mould with Finger Biscuits (10.84). Fill the mould with Vanilla Bavarois (10.108), and allow to set. Turn out of the mould onto a flat silver dish and serve.

10.111 CHARLOTTE ROYALE

Place 1 dl raspberry jelly in the bottom of a charlotte mould and allow to set. Line the sides of the mould with slices of Swiss Roll (10.20). Fill the mould with Vanilla Bavarois (10.108), and allow to set. Turn out of the mould onto a flat silver dish and serve.

10.112 CHOCOLATE BAVAROIS — BAVAROIS AU CHOCOLAT

Proceed as for 10.108. Add a few drops of vanilla essence and 175 g grated chocolate to the sauce anglaise mixture whilst it is hot so that the chocolate melts.

10.113 COFFEE BAVAROIS — BAVAROIS AU CAFE

Proceed as for 10.108. Add sufficient coffee extract to flavour and colour.

10.114 RASPBERRY BAVAROIS — BAVAROIS AUX FRAMBOISES

Proceed as for 10.108. Add 450 g raspberry purée to the cold mixture just before folding in the cream.

10.115 STRAWBERRY BAVAROIS — BAVAROIS AUX FRAISES

Proceed as for 10.108. Add 450 g strawberry purée to the cold mixture just before folding in the cream.

10.116 VANILLA BAVAROIS — BAVAROIS VANILLE

Proceed as for 10.108. Add a few drops of vanilla essence to the milk.

Items based on raw egg custard

10.117 RAW EGG CUSTARD

Makes: 1½ litres. Cooking time: 3 minutes.

Quantity	*Ingredient*
8	eggs
100 g	castor sugar
1 l	milk
few drops	vanilla essence

Method

(1) Mix the eggs and sugar in a basin.

(2) Warm the milk with the vanilla essence, add to the eggs and sugar and mix well without making it frothy.

(3) Strain through a conical strainer into a clean receptacle.

Note

For savoury egg custard omit the sugar and season with salt and cayenne pepper.

To test if cooked

Items cooked in moulds should be firm and slightly resistant to pressure so that they will not collapse when turned out. If a needle or the point of a very small knife inserted into the item comes out clean and free from traces of custard then the egg custard is cooked. If the needle or knife is fully inserted and then moved slightly to one side and no trace of liquid custard fills the hole, then the custard can be seen to be cooked.

Assessment of the completed dish

(1) There should be an evenly and lightly coloured skin over the surface of the dish.

(2) When cut open the inside should be a pleasant pale yellow.

(3) The texture should be perfectly smooth and free from air holes.

(4) It should have a rather delicate flavour of eggs.

Possible problem	*Possible cause and solution*
(1) Moulded items curdle or contain large air holes	— custard has been overheated during cooking; care must be taken when preparing the custard as once it is baked the problem cannot be rectified.
(2) Moulded custard will not set when cold	— insufficient eggs were used; care must be taken to use the correct quantities as once the pudding is baked the problem cannot be rectified.
	— mixture was not cooked sufficiently; care must be taken to prepare the mixture correctly as once the pudding is baked the problem cannot be rectified.
	— pudding not allowed to cool thoroughly in a refrigerator before being turned out of the mould; allow the pudding to cool completely before turning it out of the mould.

10.118 BAKED EGG CUSTARD

Makes: 10 portions. Cooking time: 45 minutes. Oven temperature: 175 °C.

Quantity	*Ingredient*
1½ l	Raw Egg Custard (10.117)
	grated nutmeg

Method

(1) Pour the raw egg custard into a pie dish and sprinkle the surface with grated nutmeg.

(2) Bake in the oven in a bain-marie for the prescribed time.

(3) When cooked, clean the pie dish and serve on a flat dish with a pie collar around it.

10.119 BREAD AND BUTTER PUDDING

Makes: 10 portions. Cooking time: 45 minutes. Oven temperature: 175 °C.

Quantity	*Ingredient*
100 g	sultanas (washed in cold water)
5	slices bread and butter, crusts removed

Quantity	*Ingredient*
1½ l	Raw Egg Custard (10.117)
25 g	castor sugar
	cinnamon or nutmeg

Method

(1) Sprinkle the sultanas into the bottom of a pie dish.

(2) Cut the bread into 4 neat triangles and arrange overlapping in the dish.

(3) Pour over the raw egg custard and sprinkle the surface with castor sugar.

(4) Bake in the oven au bain-marie for the prescribed time.

(5) When cooked, clean the pie dish and serve on a flat dish with a pie collar around it.

10.120 CABINET PUDDING

Makes: 10 portions. Cooking time: 45 minutes. Oven temperature: 175 °C.

Quantity	*Ingredient*
150 g	sponge cut into ½ cm dice
50 g	glacé cherries (small dice)
50 g	currants } washed in cold water and dried
50 g	sultanas } washed in cold water and dried
25 g	melted butter } for moulds
25 g	castor sugar } for moulds
1½ l	Raw Egg Custard (10.117)
4 dl	Apricot Sauce (10.177)

Method

(1) Lightly mix the sponge, glacé cherries, currants and sultanas together and place into previously buttered and sugared charlotte moulds.

(2) Pour in the raw egg custard to fill the moulds and allow to stand for a few moments.

(3) Bake in the oven in a bain-marie for the prescribed time.

(4) When cooked allow to set for a few minutes and turn out of the moulds onto a flat dish accompanied with hot apricot sauce.

10.121 CREME BEAU-RIVAGE

Proceed as for Cream Caramels (10.123) but cook in a savarin mould. Serve cold garnished with cornet shaped Langues de Chat (10.83), filled with Whipped Cream (10.188).

10.122 CREME BRULEE

Using half cream and half milk make a Raw Egg Custard (10.117).

Pour the mixture into individual portioned pie dishes and cook au bain-marie in the oven at a temperature of 175 °C for 30 minutes until set. Sprinkle the surface of each with icing sugar and place under a salamander grill to glaze. Serve on an underdish on a doily.

Note

A richer, smoother cooked cream may be produced by using 4 whole eggs and 4 yolks when making the raw custard.

10.123 CREAM CARAMEL — CREME CARAMEL

Makes: 10 portions. Cooking time: 45 minutes. Oven temperature: 170 °C.

Quantity	*Ingredient*
200 g	castor sugar } caramel
1½ dl	water } caramel
1½ l	Raw Egg Custard (10.117)

Method

(1) Place the sugar and 1 dl water into a copper sugar boiler. Bring to the boil and continue boiling until the mixture turns a golden brown. Carefully add ½ dl cold water.

(2) Pour the caramel mixture into 10 dariole moulds. Fill each mould with raw egg custard.

(3) Bake in the oven in a bain-marie for the prescribed time.

(4) When cooked remove from the bain-marie and allow to thoroughly cool and set in a refrigerator.

(5) Turn out onto a flat dish with the caramel liquid and serve.

10.124 DIPLOMAT PUDDING

Proceed as for Cabinet Pudding (10.120) but serve when cold.

10.125 QUEEN OF PUDDINGS

Place 180 g fresh white breadcrumbs in a buttered pie dish. Cover with Raw Egg Custard (10.117) and cook in a bain-marie in the oven at a temperature of 175 °C for 30 minutes until set. Pipe the top trellis-fashion with Meringue (10.101) using 3 egg whites and 150 g sugar. Place into the oven for a few seconds to colour. Fill the spaces between the lines of meringue with red and yellow jams.

MILK PUDDINGS

These are hot sweets made with milk and a cereal or pasta and are sweetened and flavoured. Some are baked entirely in the oven and are so described. An alternative method is to cook the cereal in the milk on top of the stove, then transfer the mixture into pie dishes, sprinkle with castor sugar, then brown the surface either in the oven or under a salamander grill. The description "baked" should not be used if the pudding is cooked in this way.

Milk puddings with rice

Rice is one of the few cereals which can be baked entirely in the oven. Others such as sago, tapioca and semolina must first be simmered in milk on top of the stove or mixed with boiling milk until they form a light pudding. When completely cooked and sweetened they can be transferred to dishes, sprinkled with castor sugar and coloured in the oven or under a salamander grill.

10.126 BAKED RICE PUDDING

Makes: 10 portions. Cooking time: 2 hours. Oven temperature: 150 °C.

Quantity	*Ingredient*
180 g	short grain rice
1½ l	milk
180 g	castor sugar
	grated nutmeg
75 g	butter

Method

(1) Wash the rice, place into pie dishes and add the sugar and milk. Sprinkle the surface with grated nutmeg and distribute knobs of butter.

(2) Place onto a baking sheet and bake in the oven at the prescribed temperature until cooked.

(3) Remove the puddings from the oven and clean the edges of the dishes with a damp cloth.

(4) Serve on a flat dish lined with a dish paper, placing a pie collar around each dish.

10.127 BOILED RICE PUDDING (WITH A LIAISON)

Makes: 10 portions. Cooking time: 1 hour. Oven temperature: 150 °C.

Quantity	*Ingredient*	
180 g	short grain rice	
1½ l	milk	
180 g	castor sugar	
3	egg yolks	liaison
1 dl	cream	liaison
few drops	vanilla essence	

Quantity	*Ingredient*
	grated nutmeg
75 g	butter

Method

(1) Place the milk in a saucepan and bring to the boil. Rain in the washed rice, reboil and simmer gently until cooked, stirring occasionally; remove from the heat.

(2) Mix in the sugar, egg yolks, cream and essence.

(3) Pour into pie dishes and sprinkle the surface with a little nutmeg and knobs of butter.

(4) Place into the oven or under a salamander grill to colour the surface.

10.128 RICE PUDDING FRENCH STYLE — POUDING AU RIZ A LA FRANCAISE

The French version of rice pudding is made as in 10.127 using a liaison consisting of 3 egg yolks followed by 3 whisked egg whites added to the cooked rice pudding during the last stages of cooking.

Assessment of the completed dish

(1) The pudding should have a light golden skin evenly covering the whole surface.

(2) Most of the milk should have been absorbed and there should be no stodgy parts.

(3) If made with a liaison of egg yolks and cream or beaten whites it should be a light yellow in colour; if not, it should be a creamy white.

(4) It should be hot, light and creamy, not too sweet and with a slight flavour of nutmeg. The rice should be thoroughly cooked.

Possible problem	*Possible cause and solution*
(1) Pudding is too thick	— too much rice or not enough milk used; check during the cooking process and dilute with more milk as necessary.
	— pudding cooked for too long; care must be taken to cook the pudding for the correct length of time as once overcooked the pudding cannot be rectified.
(2) Rice will not soften, becomes sticky and contains broken grains	— incorrect type of rice used; ensure that short grain rice is used to make the pudding as this cannot be rectified.

Possible problem	*Possible cause and solution*
(3) If completed with a liaison the pudding appears curdled	— liaison allowed to boil in the mixture; care must be taken to avoid this as once it has occurred it cannot be rectified.

10.129 EMPRESS RICE

Prepare the rice as for Pineapple Créole (10.130) but fold into the mixture an equal amount of cool but not set Vanilla Bavarois mixture (10.116) in place of the gelatine and whipped cream.

10.130 PINEAPPLE CREOLE

Makes: 10 portions. Cooking time: 40 minutes.

Quantity	*Ingredient*
120 g	short grain rice
1 l	milk
120 g	castor sugar
few drops	vanilla essence
25 g	leaf gelatine (soaked in cold water)
2 dl	Whipped Cream (10.188)
20	pineapple slices
1 dl	Apricot Glaze (10.176)
75 g	angelica
10 g	currants

Method

(1) Place the milk in a pan to boil and add the vanilla essence. Rain in the washed rice, reboil, cover with a lid and cook in the oven for the prescribed time, stirring occasionally.

(2) Mix in the sugar and add the soaked leaves of gelatine. Stir and allow the gelatine to dissolve. Cool the mixture and fold in the whipped cream.

(3) Mould the rice on an oval silver dish in the shape of a halved pineapple.

(4) Sprinkle the surface with a little castor sugar and mark trellis fashion with a red hot poker.

(5) Neatly arrange the slices of pineapple around the rice, brush all with hot apricot glaze.

(6) Arrange the angelica at one end to resemble the leaves of the fruit (alternatively use the leaves of the fresh fruit). Dot with currants to give a realistic effect.

Note

With this rice dish and Empress Rice (10.129) great care must be taken when incorporating the lightly whipped cream or bavarois mixture. The two preparations must be of exactly the same consistency to produce a homogenous result and form a light and delicate sweet.

Milk puddings with pasta

10.131 MACARONI PUDDING

Makes: 10 portions. Cooking time: 40 minutes. Oven temperature: 150°C.

Quantity	*Ingredient*
250 g	short cut macaroni
1 l	milk
180 g	castor sugar
90 g	butter
	grated nutmeg

Method

(1) Boil the milk and rain in the macaroni. Cover with a lid and allow to simmer gently, stirring occasionally, for approximately 30 minutes.

(2) Add the sugar and butter. Pour into buttered pie dishes, dot the surface with knobs of butter, sprinkle with grated nutmeg and sugar and place in the top of the oven to colour.

Notes

(1) If required a liaison of 2 dl cream and 3 egg yolks may be added once the macaroni is cooked.

(2) Other Italian pastas can be used to make this type of pudding, e.g. spaghetti or vermicelli.

SOUFFLES AND MOUSSES

Soufflés

There are several different types of soufflé. The only thing they have in common, however, is their lightness which is achieved by incorporating stiffly beaten egg whites.

(a) Cold soufflés. These are made from egg yolks and sugar whisked until thick and creamy as when making a genoese sponge, stiffened with gelatine, enriched with whipped cream and lightened with stiffly beaten egg whites. A wide range of flavours is possible using, for example, freshly squeezed fruit juice, essences, liqueurs and spirits. This type is called a soufflé because the soufflé dish in which it is set is filled beyond the brim to give the effect that it has risen. In fact, apart from the cooked egg yolks and sugar,

this type of soufflé is not cooked at all and must be kept in a refrigerator until set.

(b) *Souffléed puddings*. These are small individual hot puddings made from a base of milk, sugar and flour boiled to a stiff consistency and contain butter to give richness. The egg yolks are added raw, stiffly beaten whites are folded in and the mixture is poured into previously buttered and sugared moulds, allowing room to rise. They are then cooked in the oven au bain-marie and served with an appropriate sauce.

(c) Soufflés proper are cooked in special porcelain dishes usually for a set number of people, and can be either sweet or savoury. They are served in the same dish they are cooked in and do not usually have anything served with them.

(d) There are a number of dishes which are also called soufflés such as Soufflé en Surprise (*see* 10.139).

Cold soufflé puddings

10.132 COLD ORANGE SOUFFLE

Makes: 10 portions.

Quantity	*Ingredient*	
9	egg yolks	
360 g	castor sugar	
4	oranges — juice and grated zest	
25 g	leaf gelatine (soaked in cold water)	
4 dl	lightly whipped cream	
5	stiffly beaten egg whites	
100 g	toasted nib almonds	decoration
2 dl	Whipped Cream (10.188)	decoration
25 g	angelica	decoration
25 g	glacé cherries	decoration

Method

(1) Place the egg yolks, sugar, orange juice and grated zest into a clean, warmed mixing bowl standing in a bain-marie of hot water. Whisk until the mixture is thick and creamy. (It is ready when the drops falling from the raised whisk leave a mark on the surface.)

(2) Remove from the bain-marie and add the soaked and drained gelatine dissolved in a little warm water. Continue beating until the mixture is cold.

(3) When the mixture is on the point of setting fold in the lightly beaten cream followed by the stiffly beaten whites, adding it in two or more stages.

(4) Pour the mixture into the prepared moulds (*see Note* below). Place in a refrigerator until chilled and set.

(5) To serve remove the paper from the outside of the soufflé moulds and cover the exposed sides with nib almonds. Decorate the top surface with whipped cream, glacé cherries and angelica.

Note

To prepare the moulds line the outside with a ring of greaseproof paper to a height of 10 cm above the level of the mould.

10.133 COLD LEMON SOUFFLE — SOUFFLE FROID MILANAISE

Proceed as in 10.132 substituting lemons for oranges.

Assessment of the completed dish

(1) The dish should not be over-decorated and the sides of the soufflé above the edges of the mould should be straight so as to give the impression that it has risen during cooking.
(2) It should be a delicate shade reflecting type of fruit used.
(3) The top should be level with no signs of cracking.
(4) The soufflé should be smooth and light with a delicate taste of the citrus fruit used. It should not be over-sweet.
(5) It should be cold but not chilled.

Hot soufflé puddings

These are very light hot sweets that may be flavoured with essences such as vanilla, with the grated zest and juice of oranges or lemons, or with coffee or chocolate. These soufflés are turned out of their moulds when cooked and may be served with an appropriate sauce.

The moulds used are individual dariole moulds which should be lightly brushed on the inside with melted butter, then coated with castor sugar. Shake off any surplus.

10.134 HOT VANILLA SOUFFLE PUDDINGS

Makes: 10 portions. Cooking time: 35 minutes. Oven temperature: 200 °C.

Quantity	*Ingredient*
150 g	butter
150 g	castor sugar
75 g	flour } sifted together
75 g	cornflour } sifted together
5 dl	milk
few drops	vanilla essence
5	yolks of egg
6	stiffly beaten egg whites
10 g	icing sugar

Method

(1) Mix the butter, sugar, flour and cornflour together in a basin.

(2) Heat the milk and vanilla essence and whisk onto the butter, sugar and flour mixture until smooth and thick. Allow to cool.

(3) Mix in the egg yolks one at a time with a wooden spatule.

(4) Fold the stiffly beaten egg whites into the mixture in two stages until all is incorporated.

(5) Pour the mixture into the prepared moulds, filling them two-thirds full.

(6) Cook in the oven au bain-marie for the prescribed time.

(7) Allow to settle for a few moments. Turn out of the moulds onto a flat serving dish and serve.

Note

Soufflé puddings do not need to be dusted with icing sugar when turned out of their moulds.

To test if cooked

Insert a fine needle into the centre of the pudding and leave it for a few moments before withdrawing it. If it comes out quite clean with no trace of the mixture on the needle then the pudding is cooked.

Assessment of the completed dish

(1) The soufflé should appear to be extremely light in texture and should have risen straight up in the moulds without toppling over to one side.

(2) It should be easy to remove it from the mould, and should not deflate once it has been turned out onto the serving dish.

(3) A vanilla soufflé should be a pale yellow in colour.

(4) It should be smooth in texture and have a delicate flavour of vanilla and egg. It should be slightly sweet and dissolve in the mouth almost immediately.

Possible problem	*Possible cause and solution*
(1) Pudding topples over during cooking	— base mixture was too soft; care must be taken when preparing the mixture as once baked it cannot be rectified.
	— too much egg white was used; care must be taken to use the correct amounts when preparing the mixture as once baked it cannot be rectified.

Possible problem	*Possible cause and solution*
	— edge of the mould not wiped clean before being put in the oven to bake; care must be taken over this aspect as once baked it cannot be rectified.
	— pudding was baked at too high a temperature; ensure that the oven is at the correct temperature before baking the pudding as once baked it cannot be rectified.
(2) Soufflé is hard in texture	— base mixture too stiff; care must be taken when preparing mixture as once baked it cannot be rectified.
	— egg whites were not beaten stiffly; ensure that the egg whites are beaten sufficiently as once baked it cannot be rectified.
	— egg whites were not folded in correctly; care must be taken at this stage to avoid any problems as once baked it cannot be rectified.

Sweet or savoury soufflés

These are very light hot soufflés that are cooked and served in multi-portioned soufflé dishes. They may be savoury, e.g. Cheese Soufflé (10.135), Chicken Soufflé (7.256) or Spinach Soufflé (8.178), or sweet such as chocolate, lemon or orange.

10.135 CHEESE SOUFFLE — SOUFFLE AU PARMESAN

Proceed as for Spinach Soufflé (8.178) substituting 50 g grated Parmesan cheese for the spinach and omitting the nutmeg from the seasoning. The soufflé dish in this instance should be buttered and dusted with Parmesan cheese before the mixture is added.

10.136 VANILLA SOUFFLE

Makes: 10 portions. Cooking time: 35 minutes. Oven temperature: 210 °C.

Quantity	*Ingredient*
100 g	butter
150 g	castor sugar
30 g	flour } sifted together
45 g	cornflour } sifted together
2½ dl	milk
few drops	vanilla essence
9	yolks of egg
10	stiffly beaten egg whites

Method

Proceed as for Hot Vanilla Soufflé Pudding (10.134), putting the mixture into two 15 cm buttered and sugared soufflé dishes.

Notes

(1) This type of soufflé is not usually cooked in a bain-marie as it needs the intense heat of an oven to rise properly..

(2) Other flavourings may be used in place of vanilla — *see* below.

(3) Egg Custard Sauce (Sauce Anglaise) (10.107) may be served with a vanilla soufflé.

Extensions

10.137 CHOCOLATE SOUFFLE — SOUFFLE AU CHOCOLAT

Proceed as for Vanilla Soufflé (10.136) adding 50 g grated chocolate to the milk.

10.138 LEMON SOUFFLE — SOUFFLE AU CITRON

Proceed as for Vanilla Soufflé (10.136) using the juice and grated zest of two lemons in place of the vanilla essence.

Soufflé omelettes

These consist of a sponge base with ice cream and fruit covered with meringue lightly baked in an oven for a few moments until lightly coloured. The correct name is Omelette Soufflé en Surprise.

10.139 OMELETTE SOUFFLE EN SURPRISE

Makes: 10 portions. Cooking time: 3 minutes. Oven temperature: 200 °C.

Quantity	*Ingredient*	
250 g	Genoese Sponge (10.18)	
2 dl	Stock Syrup (10.173)	
½ l	Vanilla Ice Cream (10.155)	
10	egg whites	Meringue (*see* 10.101)
600 g	castor sugar	

Method

(1) Trim the sponge to the shape of the dish the sweet is to be served in.

(2) Sprinkle with warm stock syrup and allow to cool.

(3) Place 10 scoops of ice cream on the sponge base in the shape of a dome.

(4) Cover with meringue and shape with a palette knife dipped in warm water. Decorate the omelette with some of the meringue in a piping bag using a star tube.

(5) Place in the oven to set and lightly colour a pale golden. Serve immediately.

Extensions

10.140 BAKED ALASKA — OMELETTE SOUFFLE PAQUITA

Proceed as for Soufflé en Surprise (10.139), using two or three flavours of Ice Cream (10.151–155) and Fresh Fruit Salad (10.148).

10.141 OMELETTE SOUFFLE MILORD

Proceed as for Soufflé en Surprise (10.139), using Vanilla Ice Cream (10.155) and halves of Poached Pears (*see* 10.144). Serve hot Chocolate Sauce (10.178) separately.

10.142 OMELETTE SOUFFLE MILADY

Proceed as for Soufflé en Surprise (10.139), using Vanilla Ice Cream (10.155) and halves of Poached Peaches (*see* 10.144). Serve Melba Sauce (10.182) separately.

Mousses

These may be made with a variety of soft fruits such as loganberries, raspberries, strawberries, etc. The fruit is first made into a purée by passing the raw soft fruit through a fine sieve. Tinned and frozen fruits of a similar type may also be used in exactly the same way.

10.143 MOUSSE

Makes: 10 portions. Cooking time: 30 minutes.

Quantity	*Ingredient*
2½ dl	water
250 g	castor sugar
1	juice of lemon
25 g	leaf gelatine (soaked in cold water)
2½ dl	fruit purée (*see* 10.144)
5 dl	lightly whipped cream
2 dl	Whipped Cream (10.188) for decoration

Method

(1) Place the water, sugar and lemon juice into a saucepan and apply gentle heat until the sugar has melted.

(2) Add the soaked and drained gelatine and stir until it dissolves.

(3) Allow to cool slightly.

(4) Add the fruit purée and thoroughly incorporate.

(5) Transfer the mixture to a basin and continue to stir until the mixture is on the point of setting. Fold in the lightly whipped cream.

(6) Pour into moulds and place in a refrigerator until set.

(7) Shake the moulds to loosen the mousse and turn out onto a dish. Serve decorated with whipped cream.

FRUIT DISHES

Compotes of fruits

This is fresh fruit cooked in Stock Syrup (10.173), either on top of the stove or in an oven at a temperature of 150 °C. The liquid is not permitted to boil. Soft fruits are not poached — it is sufficient to cover them with hot stock syrup and allow to cool.

There are a number of extra ingredients that can be added to poached fruits if desired in order to enhance the flavour but there are no hard and fast rules. For example, lemon and clove may be added to apples, and cinnamon stick and juniper berries or cinnamon, red wine and a bayleaf may be added to pears.

The ratio of sugar to water which gives the density of the syrup varies according to the type and group of fruits being poached. A very light syrup is more suitable for soft fruits such as raspberries and strawberries whilst a heavy one is best for firmer fruits such as cherries and gooseberries. An even heavier syrup is required for such fruits as apples and pears.

10.144 POACHED FRUIT — COMPOTE DE FRUITS

Apples and pears:

(1) Using a peeler remove the outer skin. Cut the fruit into quarters and remove the core. Alternatively, leave the peeled fruit whole but remove the centre core of the apples with a corer.

(2) Retain the fruit as soon as it is peeled in either stock syrup and lemon juice or in a basin of cold water with lemon juice to prevent it from discolouring.

(3) Poach the fruit in a shallow sided saucepan covered with wet greaseproof paper and a lid.

Note

The pear stalks may be left on for a better appearance when being served.

To test if cooked

Remove a piece of fruit with a perforated spoon and squeeze very gently between the fingers. The fruit will yield if cooked.

Loganberries, raspberries and strawberries:

(1) Wash the fruit and, in the case of strawberries, remove the tops.

(2) Place into a glass bowl and pour a warm light syrup over them. Allow to cool. Because of the delicate nature of these fruits it is not necessary to cook them.

Apricots and peaches:

(1) Blanch the fruit in water for a few seconds, then refresh them and remove the skin.

(2) Poach in a medium syrup.

Gooseberries:

(1) Remove the tops and tails of the fruit and wash in cold water.

(2) Poach in a medium syrup.

Greengages and plums:

(1) Remove the stalks and wash in cold water.

(2) Poach in a medium syrup.

Rhubarb:

(1) Remove the leaves. If outer skin is tough, peel the stems and cut into 3 cm lengths.

(2) Poach in a medium syrup.

Blackcurrants, cranberries, redcurrants and blackberries:

(1) Remove the stalks and hulls.

(2) Poach in a medium syrup.

Note

Cranberries are poached for approximately 30 minutes and may be served whole or puréed either hot or cold as an accompaniment with roast turkey.

Service

Poached fruits are generally served chilled in glass bowls set on an underdish with a doily.

Assessment of the completed fruit

(1) When cooked poached fruits should be of a similar shape to that before cooking.

(2) Apples and pears should be whitish in colour.

(3) Peaches, where the skin has been removed, should have slightly yellowish to white flesh depending on the variety used.

Fruit fools

These consist of equal quantities of purée of poached fruit and whipped cream. The mixture is placed into glass coupes (Paris goblets) for serving and chilled to allow the dish to set. Fools are decorated with whipped cream and served with biscuits. They should be light and smooth in texture, the flavour should reflect the characteristics of the fruit used, e.g. gooseberries and raspberries should be a little "tart" when compared with strawberries which should be rather sweet. It may be desirable to add a little colouring to the mixture.

10.145 GOOSEBERRY FOOL

Makes: 10 portions.

Quantity	*Ingredient*
500 g	gooseberry purée (*see* 10.144)
½ l	Whipped Cream (10.188)
½ l	Whipped Cream (10.188) for decorating
10	Biscuits (10.83–8)

Method

(1) Place the whipped cream into a basin, fold in the fruit purée and adjust the colour if desired.

(2) Place into the glass coupes, smooth off the surface and place into the refrigerator to set.

(3) Decorate the top of each with a whirl of whipped cream. Serve accompanied with the biscuits.

Stewed dried fruit

This is previously soaked dried fruit cooked in stock syrup with lemon peel and a vanilla pod. Examples are:

Poached (Stewed) Apples — Compote de Pommes
Poached (Stewed) Pears — Compote de Poires
Poached Peaches — Compote de Peches
Poached (stewed) prunes — Compote de Prunes

10.146 STEWED FRUIT

Dried apricots, apple rings, pears and prunes are washed in cold water and allowed to soak in cold water for about 12 hours. The water in which they have been soaked is drained and the fruit gently simmered in Stock Syrup (10.173) covered with wet greaseproof paper. When cooked the fruit will yield to gentle pressure between the fingers.

Service

Stewed dried fruits are generally served in glass bowls set on an underdish with a doily.

Assessment of the completed fruit

The flavour of stewed fruit will be modified by any flavourings added to the stock syrup. Where such flavourings are used they should complement the flavour of the fruit, not mask it.

Possible problem	*Possible cause and solution*
(1) The fruit is broken or becomes mashed	— fruit has been overcooked; care must be taken to cook the fruit for the correct length of time to avoid this problem. — fruit has been allowed to boil; care must be taken to avoid this as it cannot be rectified later.
(2) Apples or pears are dark in colour	— syrup lacks lemon juice; care must be taken to use the correct ingredients when preparing the syrup as this cannot be rectified later. — the fruit was not placed immediately into either cold stock syrup or cold water and lemon juice to prevent discoloration; care must be taken in the preparation of the items before cooking as once discoloured they cannot be rectified.

Baked fruit

10.147 BAKED APPLES — POMMES BONNE FEMME

Makes: 10 portions. Cooking time: 30 minutes. Oven temperature: 200 °C.

Quantity	*Ingredient*
10 × 200 g	cooking apples
100 g	castor sugar
100 g	sultanas
100 g	butter
10	cloves

Method

(1) Wash and core the apples and make a small incision around the centre of each with the point of a small knife.

(2) Place the apples into a shallow baking tray, fill the centres with sugar, fruit and a clove, and top with a knob of butter.

(3) Cover the bottom of the tray with water and bake in the oven for the prescribed time.

(4) Serve on a silver or earthenware dish with an appropriate sauce.

Note

When cooked the apples should be rather soft to the touch and lightly browned on top.

Fruit salad

Fresh fruit salad is made from roughly equal quantities of a whole range of fresh fruits. It is often, however, trade practice to incorporate some tinned fruit with the fresh fruits in different amounts depending upon budgets. In instances where preserved or tinned fruits are used then the term fresh should not be used in the name on the menu.

Stock syrup forms the basic liquid in which the fruit, once prepared, is kept and served. Liqueurs such as kirsch and curaçao are suitable for complementing the flavour of the salad but it should be remembered that the flavour of the stock syrup with or without a liqueur should not be allowed to mask the delicate flavours of the fruit. The density or ratio of sugar to water ranges from about 250–350 g sugar to 6 dl of water depending upon the type of fruit used.

10.148 FRESH FRUIT SALAD — SALADE DE FRUITS or MACEDOINE DE FRUITS

Ingredients: apples, pears, apricots, bananas, cherries, grapes, oranges, pineapple, raspberries, strawberries, peaches, stock syrup

Method

Apples and pears are peeled, quartered, cored and cut into thin slices.

Apricots and peaches are cut into halves, the stones removed and the fruit cut into wedge shaped pieces.

Bananas are peeled and cut into slices on the slant. It is advisable to add bananas to the salad at the last possible moment to avoid discoloration.

For cherries remove the stones leaving the fruit whole.

Grapes may be skinned, cut into halves and the pips removed.

For oranges remove the outer skin and pith and cut into segments.

For the pineapple remove the skin and cut into halves lengthways; remove the centre core and cut the fruit into wedge shaped pieces.

Raspberries are added at the last moment, as are strawberries from which the hulls have been removed.

Once prepared the fruit should be placed immediately into cold stock syrup. It is served chilled and flavoured with a suitable liqueur in glass bowls.

Notes

(1) Store in a refrigerator in a glass receptacle covered with either a damp cloth or cling film.

(2) Avoid putting the hands in the stock syrup. Fruit salad is prone to fermentation if natural yeast is introduced into the preparation, even when stored in a refrigerator.

Assessment of the completed dish

(1) There should be a suitable balance of fruits with a ratio of not more than two parts apple to other fruits.

(2) There should be suitable colour contrast between the fruits.

(3) There should be suitable mixture of flavours and textures between the fruits.

(4) The shape of the individual pieces of fruit should be even and neatly cut.

(5) The stock syrup should be clear, its flavour complementing the different fruits.

(6) The fruit should be chilled and have a fresh appearance.

Fruit trifle

English trifle consists of diced genoese sponge soaked with a stock syrup, fruit salad and coated with custard finished with a little cream and allowed to set. It is then decorated with whipped cream, glacé cherries and angelica. Sherry may be added either by soaking the sponge with it or adding to the custard with the cream. Trifles are generally made and served in glass bowls.

10.149 SHERRY TRIFLE

Makes: 10 portions.

Quantity	*Ingredient*
250 g	Genoese Sponge (10.18)
75 g	raspberry jam
1 dl	stock syrup
250 g	diced Fruit Salad (10.148)
½ l	Custard Sauce (10.179)
1 dl	cream
1 dl	sherry
4 dl	Whipped Cream (10.188)
25 g	glacé cherries
25 g	angelica

Method

(1) Cut the sponge through and spread with jam. Reform and cut into 1 cm cubes and place into a glass bowl.

(2) Moisten with the stock syrup and evenly distribute the fruit salad.

(3) Cover with the cold custard combined with cream and sherry and allow to set.

(4) Decorate with whipped cream, glacé cherries and diamonds of angelica.

(5) Serve on a flat dish with a doily.

Other fruit dishes

10.150 KIWI CUPS

Makes: 10 portions. Cooking time: 2 minutes.

Quantity	*Ingredient*
20	kiwi fruit
1 dl	raspberry purée
1 dl	Pastry Cream (10.187)
1 dl	Whipped Cream (10.188)
2 cl	kirsch
50 g	demerara sugar

Method

(1) Cut the hard end off the fruit and discard.

(2) Hollow out the centre of the fruit using a small scoop or spoon. Cut into small dice and retain.

(3) Place the fruit shells into egg cups and evenly distribute the raspberry purée into each. Half fill with the diced fruit.

(4) Mix together the pastry cream, whipped cream and kirsch and fill the fruit with the cream mixture level with the tops.

(5) Sprinkle the surface with the sugar and place under the salamander grill until the top is crisp.

Notes

(1) The fruit should be medium to large and just ripe.

(2) This dish may be prepared and filled in advance of requirements but should be coloured under the salamander grill at the last possible moment before being served.

Service

Serve as boiled eggs in egg cups with Finger Biscuits (10.84).

ICE CREAM, WATER ICES AND ICE CREAM SWEETS

Ice cream

Ice cream may be served on its own accompanied by a suitable wafer or biscuit or may be served with fruit such as fruit salad or fresh strawberries, etc. It is served in well chilled coupes or silver timbales packed with crushed ice using a scoop to produce balls of ice cream known as "rochers". If served alone it is usual to allow two rochers per portion; if served with fruit or other sweets one rocher per portion is sufficient.

10.151 CHOCOLATE ICE CREAM — GLACE AU CHOCOLAT

Proceed as for Vanilla Ice Cream (10.155) adding 250 g of grated chocolate to the milk and vanilla essence when heating.

10.152 COFFEE ICE CREAM — GLACE AU CAFE

Proceed as for Vanilla Ice Cream (10.155) using sufficient coffee extract to colour and flavour instead of the vanilla essence.

10.153 RASPBERRY ICE CREAM — GLACE AUX FRAMBOISES

Proceed as for Strawberry Ice Cream (10.154) using raspberries instead of strawberries.

10.154 STRAWBERRY ICE CREAM — GLACE AUX FRAISES

Makes: 1 litre. Cooking time: 1 hour.

Quantity	*Ingredient*
1 l	milk
600 g	castor sugar
10	egg yolks
1 kg	strawberries
few drops	red colouring
6 dl	cream

Method

(1) Place the milk in a pan and bring to the boil.

(2) Whisk the castor sugar and egg yolks together in a basin. Add the milk whisking continuously.

(3) Return the mixture to the pan and cook gently, stirring with a wooden spoon until the mixture thickens sufficiently to coat the back of the spoon.

(4) Pass the custard through a fine strainer into a bowl and cool quickly, stirring occasionally.

(5) Clean and wash the strawberries and pass through a fine sieve. Add to the mixture with a few drops of red colouring if necessary.

(6) Whisk in the cream thoroughly. Pour the mixture into the container of an ice cream machine and freeze. Once frozen store in an ice cream conservator.

Note

Take care not to overheat the custard mixture in the early stages.

10.155 VANILLA ICE CREAM — GLACE VANILLE

Makes: 3½ litres. Cooking time: 1 hour.

Quantity	*Ingredient*
2 l	milk
few drops	vanilla essence
600 g	castor sugar
20	egg yolks
6 dl	cream

Method

(1) Place the milk and vanilla essence in a pan and bring to the boil.

(2) Whisk together the castor sugar and egg yolks in a basin. Add the milk, whisking continuously.

(3) Return the mixture to the pan and cook gently, stirring with a wooden spoon until the mixture thickens sufficiently to coat the back of the spoon.

(4) Pass the custard through a fine strainer into a bowl and cool quickly, stirring occasionally.

(5) Add the cream to the mixture and whisk in thoroughly. Pour the mixture into the container of an ice cream machine and freeze. Once frozen store in an ice cream conservator.

Note

Take care not to overheat the custard mixture in the early stages.

Fruit water ices

10.156 APRICOT WATER ICE — GLACE A L'ABRICOT

Makes: 2½ litres. Cooking time: 1 hour.

Quantity	*Ingredient*
1 l	water
600 g	sugar
1½ kg	ripe apricots

Method

(1) Place the sugar and water into a pan. Reduce to form a syrup which registers 32° on a saccharometer. Allow to cool completely.

(2) Wash and remove the stones from the apricots. Pass the flesh through a sieve and add to the syrup. Mix together and adjust the colour if necessary.

(3) Put the mixture into the container of an ice cream machine and freeze. Once frozen store in an ice cream conservator.

10.157 LEMON WATER ICE — GLACE AU CITRON

Makes: 2½ litres. Cooking time: 1 hour.

Quantity	*Ingredient*
2 l	water
1 kg	sugar
10	juice of lemons
4	grated zest of lemons

Method

(1) Boil the water, sugar, lemon juice and grated zest in a pan and reduce until the syrup registers 22° on a saccharometer.

(2) Pass through a fine strainer and allow to cool completely.

(3) Pour the mixture into the container of an ice cream machine and freeze. Once frozen store in an ice cream conservator.

10.158 ORANGE WATER ICE — GLACE A L'ORANGE

Proceed as for Lemon Water Ice (10.157) using oranges instead of lemons. Colour the syrup a light orange.

10.159 PEACH WATER ICE — GLACE AUX PECHES

Proceed as for Apricot Water Ice (10.156) using skinned peaches instead of apricots.

Sorbets

Sorbets are very light water ices with Italian meringue served usually as refreshers between main meat courses in extended dinner menus. It is best to make sorbets at the time they are required as the fluffy texture quickly deteriorates.

10.160 LEMON SORBET — SORBET AU CITRON

Makes: 2 litres. Cooking time: 1 hour.

Quantity	*Ingredient*
1 l	water
500 g	sugar
6	juice of lemons
2	grated zest of lemons
½ l	Italian Meringue (10.102)

Method

(1) Place the water, sugar, lemon juice and grated zest in a pan and bring to the boil. Reduce until the syrup registers 17° on a saccharometer. Pass through a fine strainer and allow to cool completely.

(2) Pour the mixture into the container of an ice cream machine and begin to freeze. As the mixture begins to thicken add the meringue and continue to freeze until light and fluffy.

Service

Serve in frosted glass coupes or goblets on doilies on silver dishes.

10.161 ORANGE SORBET — SORBET A L'ORANGE

Proceed as for Lemon Sorbet (10.160) using oranges instead of lemons and colouring the syrup a light orange.

Miscellaneous ice cream sweets

10.162 FRAISES CARDINAL

Place fresh whole strawberries in a glass bowl or a timbale and coat with Melba Sauce (10.182). Sprinkle the surface with toasted flaked almonds. Serve accompanied by balls of Vanilla Ice Cream (10.155) decorated with Whipped Cream (10.188).

10.163 MERINGUE GLACEE VANILLE

Sandwich two Meringue Shells (10.101) together using Vanilla Ice Cream (10.155). Serve decorated with Whipped Cream (10.188) on a doily on a silver dish.

Note

Any appropriate flavour of ice cream may be used, e.g. strawberry ice cream giving meringue glacée aux fraises.

10.164 PEACH MELBA

Place a bed of Vanilla Ice Cream (10.155) in a timbale or glass bowl and cover with whole or halves of skinned peaches. Coat with Melba Sauce (10.182) and decorate with Whipped Cream (10.188).

10.165 PECHES CARDINAL

Proceed as for Fraises Cardinal (10.162) using whole skinned peaches instead of strawberries.

10.166 POIRES BELLE HELENE

Place a bed of Vanilla Ice Cream (10.155) in a timbale or glass bowl and cover with whole or halves of skinned poached peaches. Coat with Melba Sauce (10.182) and decorate with Whipped Cream (10.188).

10.167 RASPBERRY MELBA

Proceed as for Peach Melba (10.164) using raspberries instead of peaches.

10.168 STRAWBERRY MELBA

Proceed as for Peach Melba (10.164) using strawberries instead of peaches.

Coupes

These consist of combinations of different flavoured ice creams, fruits and sauces served in chilled cups known as coupes accompanied by a suitable wafer or biscuit. The whole range is extensive and the following are examples of those in most common use.

10.169 COUPE ALEXANDRA

Place a little Fruit Salad (10.148) flavoured with kirsch in the coupe with a scoop of Strawberry Ice Cream (10.154) on top. Decorate with Whipped Cream (10.188) and a strawberry.

10.170 COUPE EDNA MAY

Place some stoned cherries in the coupe and a scoop of Vanilla Ice Cream (10.155) on top. Coat with Melba Sauce (10.182) and decorate with Whipped Cream (10.188).

10.171 COUPE JACQUES

Place a little Fruit Salad (10.148) flavoured with maraschino in the coupe, and a scoop of ice cream consisting of half Lemon Water

Ice (10.157) and half Strawberry Ice Cream (10.154). Decorate with Whipped Cream (10.188).

Note

It is important to chill the coupes before filling because the ice cream is likely to melt before it reaches the customer.

STOCK SYRUP, SWEET SAUCES AND CREAMS

Stock syrup

Stock syrup is a preparation of sugar and water that is boiled for a few moments. (The word "stock" indicates that it is a pre-prepared item that is kept in reserve.) It may be used as a base for thinning fondant icing and for soaking gateaux and poaching fruit.

The basic recipe can be varied, however, to produce a syrup which reflects and complements the flavour of a wide range of confectionery items. For example, when used for poaching various fruits additional water may be added to the sugar to give a lighter syrup; cloves and lemon may be used to complement the flavour of apples; cinnamon may be used similarly with pears; cloves, juniper berries, a cinnamon stick, a bayleaf, lemon or coriander seeds may be added to the stock syrup for soaking certain yeast goods such as savarins; rum is added to that used for soaking rum babas.

10.172 BUN WASH

Boil 1 dl water with 100 g sugar until dissolved; use whilst still hot immediately the buns are removed from the oven.

10.173 STOCK SYRUP

Boil 1 l water with 750 g sugar for a few moments until the sugar is dissolved.

Sweet sauces and glazes

Sweet sauces are served with a range of hot and cold dishes that include puddings, pies, and chilled coupes. They are also served as an accompaniment to items of meat and poultry dishes such as roast duck with apple sauce.

NOTE

Sauces and accompaniments such as Cranberry Sauce (*see* p. 577) will be found with the dish with which they are most frequently associated.

10.174 ALMOND CREAM — CREME D'AMANDE

Makes: 500 g.

Quantity	*Ingredient*
125 g	butter
125 g	castor sugar
2	eggs (slightly beaten)
30 g	soft flour } sieved together
125 g	ground almonds } sieved together

Method

(1) Cream the butter and sugar until light and fluffy.

(2) Gradually add the beaten eggs to the creamed butter and sugar.

(3) Fold in the flour and almonds using a metal spoon or a scraper, but do not overmix.

10.175 APPLE SAUCE — SAUCE POMMES (APPLE PUREE)

Makes: ½ litre. Cooking time: 10 minutes.

Quantity	*Ingredient*
750 g	peeled, cored and quartered cooking apples
100 g	castor sugar
1	juice of lemon
1 dl	water
25 g	butter

Method

(1) Place the prepared apples, sugar, lemon juice and water into a saucepan. Cover with a lid and boil until the apples purée.

(2) Pass through a sieve, replace into a clean pan and complete by mixing in the butter.

10.176 APRICOT/RASPBERRY GLAZE

Makes: 1 litre. Cooking time: 10 minutes.

Quantity	*Ingredient*
500 g	apricot or raspberry jam as appropriate
250 g	castor sugar
1 dl	water

Method

Place all of the ingredients into a thick bottomed pan. Bring to the boil stirring. Skim, boil to 103 °C (the thread stage) and pass through a conical strainer. Use hot.

Assessment of the completed glaze

The glaze is a light coloured, fruit flavoured syrup which will jell when cold because of the pectin in the jam. The balance of ingredients is extremely important in producing a good quality glaze and can be affected in a number of ways.

(1) If undercooked, although the glaze will contain the right amount of pectin, the syrup will be too light and therefore soak into the goods leaving no indication of a glazed surface, merely a residue of the jam used as a base.

(2) If overcooked the glaze will begin to take on a deep toffee colour and become thick and viscous thus making it difficult to handle, unsightly and extremely sweet.

(3) If too much sugar is used the pectin content will increase proportionately, and even if cooked to the thread stage it will form a heavy syrup incapable of jelling, lack flavour and have an insipid colour.

(4) If too much jam is used this will produce a heavy glaze that is difficult to handle as there will be insufficient sugar to lighten it. It will colour easily and will not readily flow to produce a high quality even finish.

10.177 APRICOT SAUCE — SAUCE ABRICOT

Makes: 1 litre. Cooking time: 10 minutes.

Quantity	*Ingredient*
500 g	apricot jam
100 g	castor sugar
½ l	water
50 g	cornflour (diluted in cold water)
1	juice of lemon

Method

(1) Boil the jam, sugar and water. Whisk in the diluted cornflour, reboil and simmer for 5 minutes.

(2) Strain through a conical strainer, add the lemon juice and, if necessary, adjust the colour.

10.178 CHOCOLATE SAUCE — SAUCE AU CHOCOLAT

Makes: ½ litre. Cooking time: 10 minutes.

Quantity	*Ingredient*
2 dl	water
250 g	castor sugar
few drops	vanilla essence
250 g	chocolate
250 g	couverture

Method

(1) Boil the water, sugar and vanilla essence in a saucepan.

Remove from the stove.

(2) Add the block cocoa and couverture and stir until it has completely melted. If necessary adjust the colour.

(3) Strain through a conical strainer.

Note

If required cold add an additional 1 dl Stock Syrup (10.173).

10.179 CUSTARD SAUCE

Makes: ¾ litre. Cooking time: 5 minutes.

Quantity	*Ingredient*
7 dl	milk
75 g	custard powder
100 g	castor sugar

Method

(1) Place the custard powder and sugar in a basin and add sufficient cold milk to mix into a smooth paste.

(2) Boil the remainder of the milk and whisk into the basin of diluted custard powder.

(3) Return to the saucepan and bring back to the boil stirring continuously until the mixture reboils.

Notes

(1) Retain in a bain-marie of hot water until required. Sprinkle the surface with a little sugar to help prevent a skin from forming.

(2) This sauce may also be flavoured with lemon, orange, coffee or chocolate.

(3) Add an additional 10 g custard powder to the mixture for Sherry Trifle (10.149).

10.180 JAM SAUCE

Proceed as for Apricot Sauce (10.177) using any type of jam suitable for a sweet item.

10.181 LEMON SAUCE — SAUCE CITRON

Makes: 1 litre. Cooking time: 5 minutes.

Quantity	*Ingredient*
1 l	water
4	lemons, juice and grated zest
250 g	castor sugar
50 g	cornflour (diluted in cold water)

Method

(1) Boil the water, lemon juice, grated zest and sugar.

(2) Whisk in the diluted cornflour and simmer for 5 minutes.

Note

This sauce may be strained if desired to remove the grated zest.

10.182 MELBA SAUCE

Makes: ½ litre. Cooking time: 20 minutes.

Quantity	*Ingredient*
500 g	raspberries
500 g	castor sugar
1 dl	water

Method

(1) Place all the ingredients into a saucepan, bring to the boil, cover with a lid and simmer for the prescribed time.

(2) Strain through a conical strainer and if necessary adjust the colour.

10.183 ORANGE SAUCE — SAUCE ORANGE

Proceed as for Lemon Sauce (10.181) using oranges instead of lemons.

10.184 SYRUP SAUCE

Makes: 1 litre. Cooking time: 10 minutes.

Quantity	*Ingredient*
500 g	golden syrup
100 g	castor sugar
2 dl	water
25 g	cornflour (diluted in cold water)
1	juice of lemon

Method

(1) Boil the syrup, sugar and water. Whisk in the diluted cornflour, reboil and simmer for 5 minutes.

(2) Strain through a conical strainer. Add the lemon juice and if necessary adjust the colour.

Creams and butters

10.185 BRANDY BUTTER

Makes: 250 g.

Cream together 125 g unsalted butter with 125 g castor sugar and slowly incorporate ½ dl brandy.

10.186 BUTTER CREAM

Makes: 2 kg. Cooking time: 2 minutes.

Quantity	*Ingredient*
2 dl	milk
350 g	castor sugar
4	eggs
850 g	unsalted butter

Method 1

(1) Place the milk, sugar, eggs and 100 g of the butter in a thick bottomed pan. Bring to the boil for 2 minutes.

(2) Place into the bowl of a mixing machine with the spade attachment on low speed until the mixture is cold.

(3) Add the remainder of the butter, increasing speed as the mixture becomes creamy and light.

Note

This mixture may be flavoured and coloured as desired, e.g. chocolate with the addition of 150 g melted couverture, or coffee with the addition of coffee extract.

Method 2

Mix together equal quantities of sieved icing sugar and unsalted butter until almost white, soft and creamy.

Note

This mixture may be flavoured and coloured as with Method 1.

10.187 PASTRY CREAM—CREME PATISSIERE

Makes: 1½ litres. Cooking time: 20 minutes.

Quantity	*Ingredient*
1 l	milk
few drops	vanilla essence
3	eggs
5	egg yolks
250 g	castor sugar
125 g	flour

Method

(1) Mix the eggs, sugar and flour in a basin.

(2) Heat the milk with the vanilla essence to just below boiling point.

(3) Pour the heated milk onto the egg, sugar and flour mixture, whisking vigorously.

(4) Return to the saucepan, and return the pan to the stove for a few minutes, stirring all the time, whilst it boils.

Notes

(1) Pastry cream may be used immediately or retained in a basin with the surface sprinkled with sugar and a buttered greaseproof paper to prevent a skin forming.

(2) Pastry cream is similar to egg custard but the extra flour gives added stiffness. It is used as a filling for éclairs and other pastry items.

10.188 WHIPPED CREAM — CREME CHANTILLY

Makes: 1 litre.

Quantity	*Ingredient*
1 l	cream
100 g	castor sugar
few drops	vanilla essence

Method

Place the cooled cream into a cold basin with the sugar and essence. Whisk until the cream stands in peaks.

Notes

(1) Allow fresh cream to "mature" for approximately 12 hours before whisking. The cream can then be whisked stiffly.

(2) Be careful not to overwhisk as this causes the fat globules which are in suspension in the milk liquid to combine. These larger particles then begin to separate out (this is the process by which butter is made). Slight overwhisking is not always apparent but when such cream is piped the pressure causes separation to take place and the cream weeps thus reducing its shelf life and that of the item it is used in.

CONVENIENCE PRODUCTS

As with other convenience products, confectionery items may be obtained in many forms. It may well be true to say that items in this chapter are obtainable in more convenience forms than any other, from the pastry mix requiring the addition of water to the sponge and gateau mixtures needing eggs and milk or water and a decoration of jam or whipped cream and the innumerable number of tinned and pre-packaged goods from rice puddings to biscuits and cakes. The range of products available is so wide that it is virtually impossible to itemise them in the short space of this text. With the exercise of a little imagination the student will be able to produce top quality sweets and confectionery items of almost infinite variety.

APPENDIX I

Glossary

NOTE

The following list of brief definitions is intended simply to act as a guide to some of the more frequently found terms in this and other cookery manuals.

à cru: sliced raw potatoes shallow fried
à la broche: roasted on a spit
à la crème: lightly bound with cream
acidulated water: water, lemon juice and salt
aiguillette: long thin slice of cooked meat cut usually from the breast
aileron: winglet of poultry
al dente: degree to which pasta should be cooked
aloyau: whole unboned sirloin of beef
amuse-bouches: cocktail canapés
appareil: prepared mixture of food ready for further processing
aromates: mixture of vegetables and herbs used to impart flavour
aspic: originally an entrée moulded in aspic but now used to refer to savoury jelly
assiette anglaise: selection of sliced cold meats
au beurre: cooked in butter; finished with knobs of butter
au bleu: a method of preparing and cooking trout in a court-bouillon
au four: baked in the oven

bain-marie: container of hot water used for keeping food hot or slowing down a cooking process
ballotine: boned and stuffed leg of poultry
barder: cover with thin slices of fat bacon
baron: double sirloin and rumps of beef or the saddle and two legs of lamb, in both cases as one whole joint
barquette: boat shaped pastry case
barrel shape: shape for vegetables
beard: the frilly part of shellfish such as oysters or mussels; to remove this part
Béarnaise sauce: basic butter sauce
béchamel: basic white sauce
beignets: fritters
beurre fondu: melted butter with a little lemon juice to prevent the constituent fats and sediment separating
beurre manié: thickening agent made from equal amounts of butter and flour
beurre noir: black butter
beurre noisette: nut brown butter
blanc: water and lemon juice lightly thickened with flour used to boil certain vegetables
blanch: cover with cold water, bring to the boil and immediately refresh under cold water to remove bitterness or preserve colour; deep frying potatoes until cooked and soft but not coloured
blanchaille: whitebait
blinis: type of small pancake made

from buckwheat served with caviar

bombay duck: dried fillets of fish served as an accompaniment to curries

boulangerie: bakery department

bouquet garni: herbs tied into a bundle — usually parsley stalks, thyme, bayleaf, leek and celery

braisière: a braising pan

brider: truss

brine: salted liquid used for preserving meat

brochette: skewer

broil: alternative term for grill

brunoise: items cut into very small dice

calvados: spirit distilled from cider

canapé: small piece of fried or toasted bread covered with another item

caramelise: cook sugar until it begins to colour and become sticky and like toffee

carapace: the shell of any kind of shellfish after removing the flesh

casserole: earthenware dish with a lid; cook in such a dish

caviar: salted sturgeon roe

chapelure: brown breadcrumbs

charcuterie: items of pork butchery

chaudfont: pan of just boiling salted water used to reheat food

chemiser: line a mould or coat an item with jelly

chinois: conical strainer

chipolata: type of long thin sausage, usually pork

choke: fibrous centre of an artichoke

Choron: garnish of artichoke bottoms filled with peas together with noisette potatoes

chou paste: light paste used for éclairs, fritters, etc.

ciseler: shred finely; cut incisions

Clamart: garnish of peas and artichoke bottoms

clarify: clear of impurities and sediment

cocotte: shallow earthenware or porcelain dish with a lid

cocotte à oeuf: individual porcelain egg dish

cohere: lightly bind ingredients into a sauce

compote: fruit cooked and served in stock syrup

concassée: (usually) peeled, pipped and diced tomatoes

concasser: roughly dice or chop

contrefilet: boned sirloin of beef

corbeille de fruits: basket of fruit

cordon: line of sauce or gravy poured around an item of food once placed on the serving dish

coulis: essence made from shellfish used as basis for a sauce

court-bouillon: cooking liquid used for poaching and boiling fish

crêpes: pancakes

croûtons: bread cut into various shapes and sizes and fried in butter generally for use as a garnish

cru: raw

crushed garlic: cloves or sections of garlic made into a fine paste by removing the outer skin, chopping with a knife and crushing with the flat side using a little salt as an abrasive

cuisine: kitchen

cuisson: cooking liquid

cuissot: large leg, e.g. of pork or venison

cuit: cooked

curaçao: liqueur made from the rinds of bitter oranges

dariole: deep, round mould with sloping sides

darne: fish steak cut across and through the bone of a large whole round fish
decant: pour off a liquid after allowing any sediment in it to settle
deglaze: add a liquid such as wine or stock to the sediment left in a pan after cooking
dégraisser: remove the fat from a sauce or stock
déjeuner: lunch
délice: shaped fillet of fish
demi-glace: basic brown sauce
dessert: last course of a meal, generally the sweet course
diablé: devilled
dorer: make golden brown
duxelles: basic mushroom preparation

egg and breadcrumb: coat with flour, eggwash and either white or brown breadcrumbs
émincé: cut into thin slices or shredded
en buisson: items dressed on top of each other in a pile
en cocotte: eggs poached in a special dish; poached chicken
en entrée: a method of trussing suitable for cooking en cocotte or pot roasting in which the legs are folded back at the drumstick joint and inserted into an incision made in the skin
en papillote: a method of cooking food in a paper case
entrée: main dish of meat or poultry, properly served before the roast and consisting of a lightly sauced item with a garnish
entremets: sweet dishes
entremettier: vegetable chef
escalope: thin round slice cut from fish, meat or poultry usually flattened
estouffade: brown stock; brown beef stew
extension dishes: dishes produced from a basic recipe with added ingredients, sauces and garnishes

farce: stuffing or forcemeat
fécule: starch such as cornflour, arrowroot or potato flour
fines herbes: mixture of chopped fresh herbs usually comprising chives, chervil, tarragon and parsley
flambé: set alight (using brandy or a suitable liqueur) during the cooking process
fleurons: crescent shaped pieces of puff pastry
foie gras: fattened goose liver
fondue: vegetable such as tomato cooked until reduced to a pulp; cheese preparation
frangipane: almond cream
frappé: chilled
friandises: alternative name for petits fours
friture: frying kettle
full gratination: cooking or heating an item in the oven in order to give the surface even coloration

game farce: stuffing made from game liver
gaufrettes: wafers
givré: frosted
glacer: make ice cold; ice, i.e. a cake, *see* glaze
glaze: colour under a salamander grill; cook vegetables in water and butter to give a sheen
gnocchi: type of small dumpling made from semolina, potato or chou paste
gratinate: sprinkle with breadcrumbs or cheese and colour under a salamander grill or in an oven

goujons: small strips of fillets of fish
Greek style: method of cooking vegetables in water, lemon juice, oil, thyme, bayleaf and coriander seed
grooved lemon: lemon cut with a special cutter to give a design
gros sel: coarse salt
hacher: chop
hachis: finely chopped cooked meat reheated in a suitable sauce
hâtelet: ornamental silver skewer
haute cuisine: finest type of high-class cookery
holding period: the length of time that elapses between completion of a dish and its actual service to the customer
Hollandaise sauce: basic butter sauce
infuse: allow an ingredient to stand in boiled water to extract the flavour and aroma
jardinière: mixture of vegetables used as a garnish or as a vegetable in its own right comprising equal amounts of carrots and turnips baton shaped, french beans cut diamond shaped and peas
julienne: items cut into thin strips
jus: gravy, e.g. jus lié; juice, e.g. lemon juice
jus lié: thickened gravy; basic brown sauce
kebab: meat, onion, bayleaf, etc. skewered and grilled
kirsch: cherry flavoured spirit used to flavour sweet dishes
kohlrabi: turnip-like vegetable
larder: insert strips of salt fat pork or fat bacon into pieces of meat
lardons: small strips of fat bacon
liaison: thickening agent such as a mixture of egg yolks and cream
light gratination: coating of sauce and sprinkling of grated cheese or breadcrumbs and melted butter placed under a salamander grill to brown the surface slightly
luter: seal a cocotte with paste
macédoine: mixture of various fruits or vegetables cut into dice
macérer: steep in wine or liqueur
madeleine mould: large or small scallop shaped mould with a hinge
mandolin: hand tool for slicing vegetables
maraschino: cherry flavoured liqueur used to flavour sweet dishes
marinate: tenderise and add flavour by soaking in a liquid such as wine with added herbs etc.
matelote: fish stew
médaillon: round, flat shaped piece of fish or meat
meunière: shallow frying
mie de pain: white breadcrumbs
mignardises: alternative term for petits fours
Milanaise: garnish for cooked vegetables sprinkled with grated cheese and melted butter and gratinated under a salamander grill
mijoter: simmer slowly
mirepoix: roughly cut vegetables
monter au beurre: add butter to thicken and enrich a sauce
Murat: garnish of olive shaped potatoes, artichoke bottoms and strips of fish
napkin: serviette made from cloth
napper: coat with sauce

natives: name given to English oysters
nature: cooked plainly
Navarin: brown mutton stew
nut brown butter: butter cooked in an omelette pan until golden brown
nutty: term used to describe when vegetables are cooked to the correct degree, i.e. firm

panada: preparation used to bind forcemeats of fish and meat
pané à l'anglaise: coated with flour, eggwash and breadcrumbs
partie: section of the kitchen responsible for a course on the menu
pass: strain
pâté de foie gras: pâté made from goose liver and truffle
paupiette: rolled and stuffed fillets of fish
paysanne: vegetables cut into small square, round or triangular shapes
persillé: sprinkled with chopped parsley
petits fours: assortment of sweetmeats served at the end of dinner
piquante: sharp or spicy in flavour
plat à sauter: shallow pan for frying
plier: fold over
pluches: sprays of chervil or other fresh herbs used as a garnish
poêle: frying pan
poêler: pot roast
Polonaise: vegetables cooked and sprinkled with browned breadcrumbs, chopped parsley and chopped hard boiled yolk and white of eggs
primeurs: spring vegetables
Printanier: garnish of new season's vegetables cut into various shapes
profiteroles: small balls made from chou paste
prosciutto: Parma ham
prove: place a dough or paste made with yeast in the warm to increase in size
purée: smooth thick pulp made from food passed through a sieve

quenelles: farce made from chicken or fish moulded with spoons or piped, used as a garnish

rafraîchir: chill; cool rapidly under running water
ragoût: stew
rapé: grated
ravier: a hors-d'oeuvre dish
réchauffer: reheat
réduire: reduce
reduction: boiling a liquid so that it reduces in volume
relax: allowing a raw paste to stand without handling
relevé: a braised, roasted or pot roasted joint with a garnish, properly served as the second meat course of a formal dinner
rennet: secretion from a calf's stomach used to set milk for junket
rissoler: fry brown on all sides
rocher: scoop of ice cream
rondeau: large shallow pan
roux: thickening agent made from flour and fat

sabayon: cooked egg yolks
saccharometer: instrument used to measure the density of a syrup
saffron: dried stamens of a species of crocus used for flavouring and colouring
saignant: underdone
saisir: seal over heat without colouring
salamander grill: type of grill with an overhead source of heat
salmis: game stew

salpicon: mixture of diced meat, vegetables or fruit used as a filling
sauerkraut: choucroute; salted shredded white cabbage
sauter: shallow fry; toss whilst frying
sauteuse: shallow pan with sloping sides
score: cut shallow incisions
savarin: sweet item made from a light yeast sponge
smorgasbord: open Scandinavian sandwich
soft flour: flour low in gluten
soy sauce: sauce made from soya beans used extensively in Chinese cooking
speck: bacon fat
spit: rod on which an item of food is impaled for roasting over an open fire
spatule/spatula: wooden spoon
sweat: cook in butter without colouring
suprême of chicken: fillet of chicken breast and wing

Tabasco: proprietary brand of pepper sauce
tamis: unbleached calico cloth used for straining thick sauces
terrine: earthenware fireproof dish with a lid
timbale: deep round silver dish
tourte: round covered pie or tart
tomato concassée: *see* concassée
tourner: trim vegetables or potatoes barrel shaped
tranche: slice or cut
trellis fashion: markings in a criss-cross pattern
tronçon: section of fish cut on the bone from a large flat fish

vandyked lemon: lemon halves with a decorated edge
vert-pré: basic garnish for grilled meat and poultry comprising straw potatoes, parsley butter and watercress
vésiga: dried spinal cord of the sturgeon
vinaigrette: basic sauce made from oil and vinegar
velouté: basic white sauce
vol-au-vent: shaped puff pastry case

zabaglione: sweet made from whisked eggs, sugar and wine or liqueur
zest: the thin outer rind of fruit such as oranges or lemons

APPENDIX II

Abbreviations and Conversion Tables

ABBREVIATIONS

g = gram
kg = kilogram
dl = decilitre
l = litre
mm = millimetre
cm = centimetre
°C = Centigrade (Celsius)

LIQUID MEASUREMENTS

10 decilitres = litre = 1000 millilitres = 1.76 pints

Metric capacity		*Imperial equivalent* (actual)	*Imperial equivalent* (approx.)
¼ dl	=	0.88 fl oz	1 fl oz
½ dl	=	1.76 fl oz	1¾ fl oz
1 dl	=	3.52 fl oz	3½ fl oz
¼ l	=	8.81 fl oz	9 fl oz
½ l	=	17.63 fl oz	18 fl oz
1 l	=	35.27 fl oz	1¾ pt
5 l	=	176.35 fl oz	8¾ pt

LENGTH

1 metre = 100 centimetres = 1000 millimetres = 39.37 inches

Metric length		*Imperial equivalent* (actual)	*Imperial equivalent* (approx.)
1 mm	=	0.039 inch	1/25 inch
5 mm	=	0.197 inch	⅕ inch
1 cm	=	0.39 inch	⅖ inch
5 cm	=	1.97 inches	2 inches
10 cm	=	3.93 inches	4 inches
20 cm	=	7.86 inches	8 inches
50 cm	=	19.68 inches	20 inches
1 metre	=	39.37 inches	3¼ ft

WEIGHT

1 kg = 1000 grams = 2 lb 3.27 oz

Metric weight		*Imperial equivalent (actual)*	*(approx.)*
1 g	=	0.035 oz	
5 g	=	0.17 oz	
10 g	=	0.35 oz	⅓ oz
20 g	=	0.70 oz	¾ oz
50 g	=	1.76 oz	1¾ oz
100 g	=	3.52 oz	3½ oz
250 g (¼ kg)	=	8.81 oz	9 oz
500 g (½ kg)	=	17.63 oz	1 lb 2 oz
750 g (¾ kg)	=	26.44 oz	1 lb 10 oz
1000 g (1 kg)	=	35.27 oz	4 lb 4 oz

OVEN TEMPERATURES

Regulo	*Centigrade*	*Fahrenheit*	*Definition*
½	130	250	very cool
1	140	275	cool
2	150	300	warm
3	170	325	moderate
4	180	350	moderate
5	190	375	moderate
6	200	400	hot
7	220	425	hot
8	230	450	very hot
9	240	475	very hot

TEMPERATURE

°C	°F	°C	°F	°C	°F	°C	°F
−20	−4	60	140	130	266	200	392
−18	0	65	149	135	275	205	401
0	32	70	158	140	284	210	410
5	41	75	167	145	293	215	419
10	50	80	176	150	302	220	428
15	59	85	185	155	311	225	437
20	68	90	194	160	320	230	446
25	77	95	203	165	329	235	455
30	86	100	212	170	338	240	464
35	95	105	221	175	347	245	473
40	104	110	230	180	356	250	482
45	113	115	239	185	365	255	491
50	122	120	248	190	374	260	500
55	131	125	257	195	383	300	575

APPENDIX III

Storage Information

Type of food	Refrigerator (2–8 °C)	Deep freeze (−18 °C)
Cooked meat	2 days	1–2 months
offal	1–2 days	3–4 months
Fish:		
fresh	2 days	3–4 months
smoked	2 days	6–12 months
Joints of raw meat:		
beef	3–4 days	6–8 months
chicken	3–4 days	6–8 months
game	3–7 days according to type	6–8 months
goose	7 days	6–8 months
lamb	3–4 days	6–8 months
pork	3–4 days	6–8 months
turkey	7 days	12 months
veal	3–4 days	6–8 months
Salads	2 days	—
Sauces	2 days	6–12 months } without liaisons
Soups	2 days	6–12 months } without liaisons
Vegetables:		
fresh	2 days according to type	—
retained once cooked	2 days	6–12 months

Index of Recipes

NOTE: Recipes marked with an asterisk include full assessment sections together with an analysis of possible problems, causes and solutions.